National Atlas

Road Maps & Town Plans - Great Britain

George Philip & Son Limited

Contents

Key Map   1

Sectional Maps of Great Britain   2-64
General Scale 5 miles = 1 inch

Sectional Maps of Approaches to London   65-72
Scale $\frac{3}{4}$ inch = 1 mile

Sectional Maps of Central London   73-80
Scale 5 inches = 1 mile

Conversion Tables   81

Motorway Map   82

Motorway Service Areas   83

Distance Tables   84-85

Addresses for Tourist Information   86

Inland Ferries and Tolls   87

Local Radio Stations   88

Town Plans   89-120
See Contents List on page 89

Index to Sectional Maps of Great Britain   1-48

Index to Sectional Maps of London   49

ISBN 0 540 05324 4

©1977 George Philip & Son Ltd.

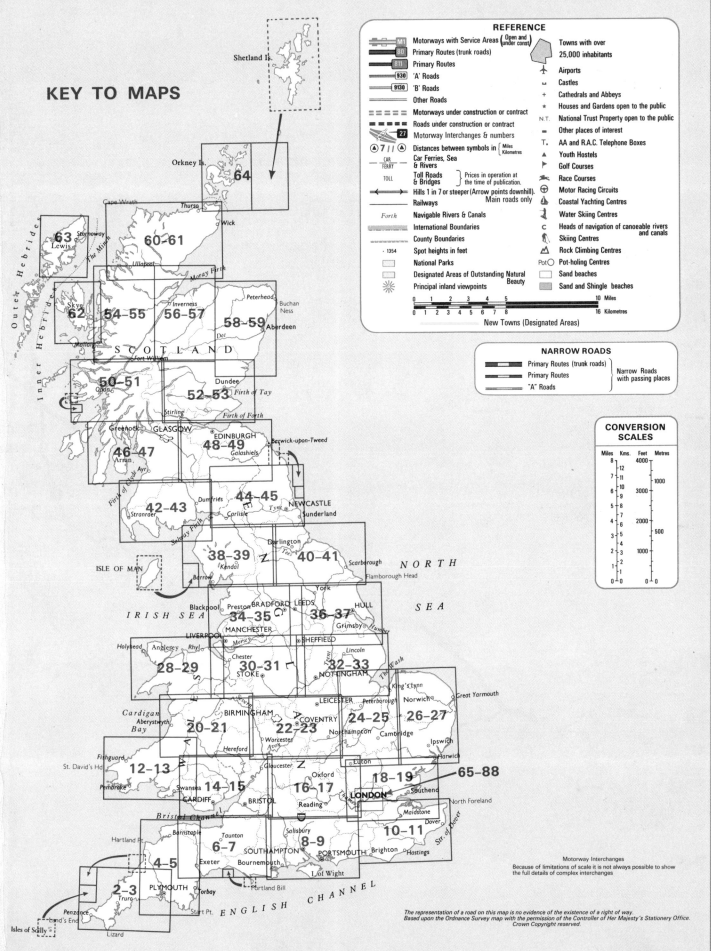

KEY TO MAPS

REFERENCE

Motorways with Service Areas (Open and under const)
Primary Routes (trunk roads) **80**
Primary Routes **811**
'A' Roads **930**
'B' Roads **9130**
Other Roads
Motorways under construction or contract
Roads under construction or contract
Motorway Interchanges & numbers **27**
Distances between symbols in { Miles Kilometres }
Car Ferries, Sea & Rivers **CAR FERRY**
Toll Roads & Bridges **TOLL** } Prices in operation at the time of publication.
Hills 1 in 7 or steeper (Arrow points downhill). Main roads only
Railways
Forth Navigable Rivers & Canals
International Boundaries
County Boundaries
· 1354 Spot heights in feet
National Parks
Designated Areas of Outstanding Natural Beauty
✳ Principal inland viewpoints

Towns with over 25,000 inhabitants
✈ Airports
☗ Castles
+ Cathedrals and Abbeys
⚹ Houses and Gardens open to the public
N.T. National Trust Property open to the public
━ Other places of interest
T. AA and R.A.C. Telephone Boxes
▲ Youth Hostels
▸ Golf Courses
⚘ Race Courses
⊕ Motor Racing Circuits
⚓ Coastal Yachting Centres
⚐ Water Skiing Centres
C Heads of navigation of canoeable rivers and canals
⚞ Skiing Centres
⚠ Rock Climbing Centres
Pot○ Pot-holing Centres
☐ Sand beaches
▨ Sand and Shingle beaches

0 1 2 3 4 5 10 Miles
0 1 2 3 4 5 6 7 8 16 Kilometres

New Towns (Designated Areas)

NARROW ROADS

Primary Routes (trunk roads)
Primary Routes
"A" Roads
} Narrow Roads with passing places

CONVERSION SCALES

Miles	Kms.	Feet	Metres
8	12	4000	
7	11		1000
6	10 9	3000	
5	8 7	2000	
4	6		500
3	5 4	1000	
2	3		
1	2 1		
0	0	0	0

Motorway Interchanges
Because of limitations of scale it is not always possible to show the full details of complex interchanges

The representation of a road on this map is no evidence of the existence of a right of way.
Based upon the Ordnance Survey map with the permission of the Controller of Her Majesty's Stationery Office.
Crown Copyright reserved.

COPYRIGHT, GEORGE PHILIP & SON, LTD.

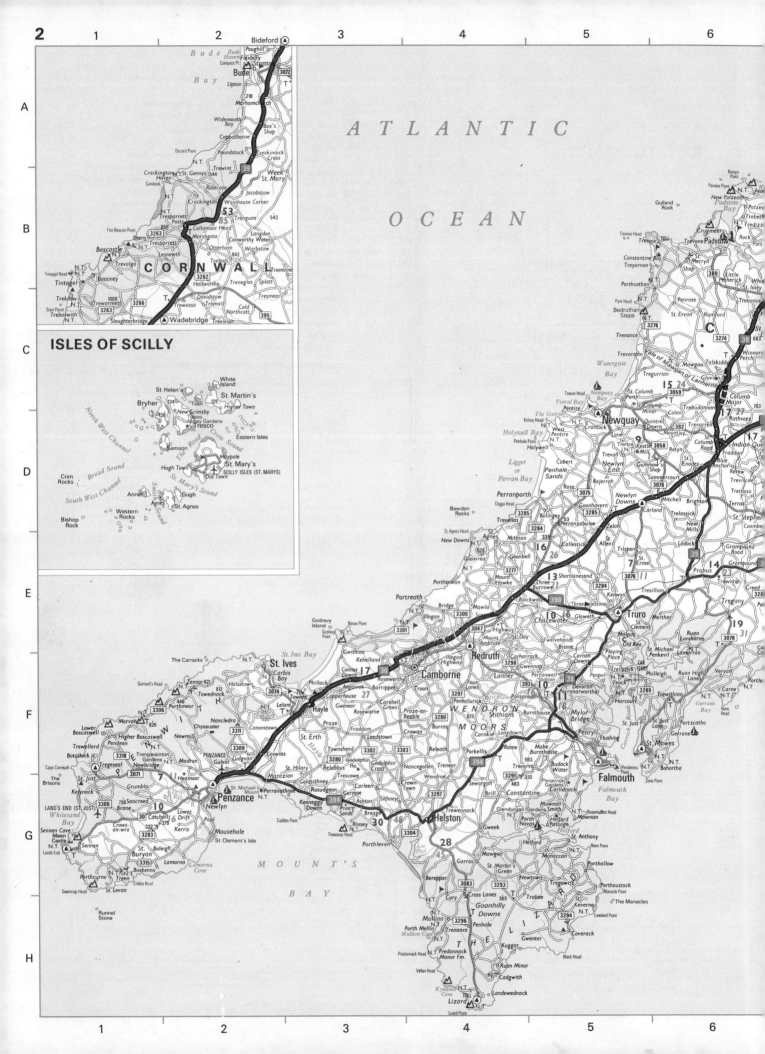

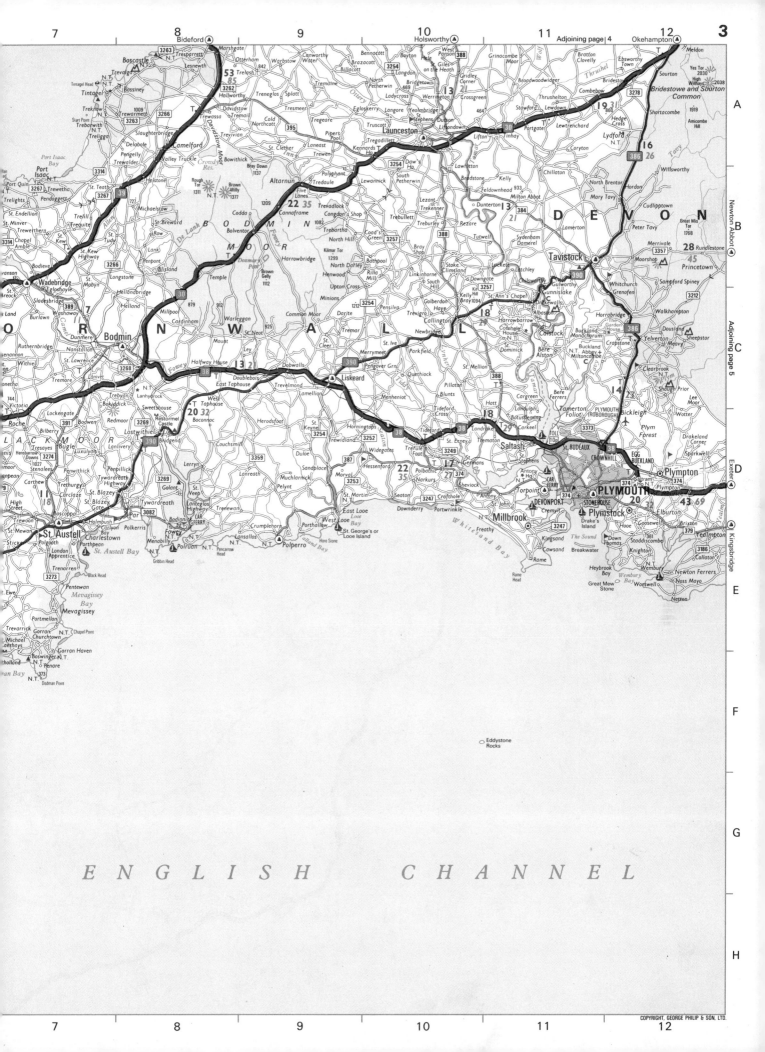

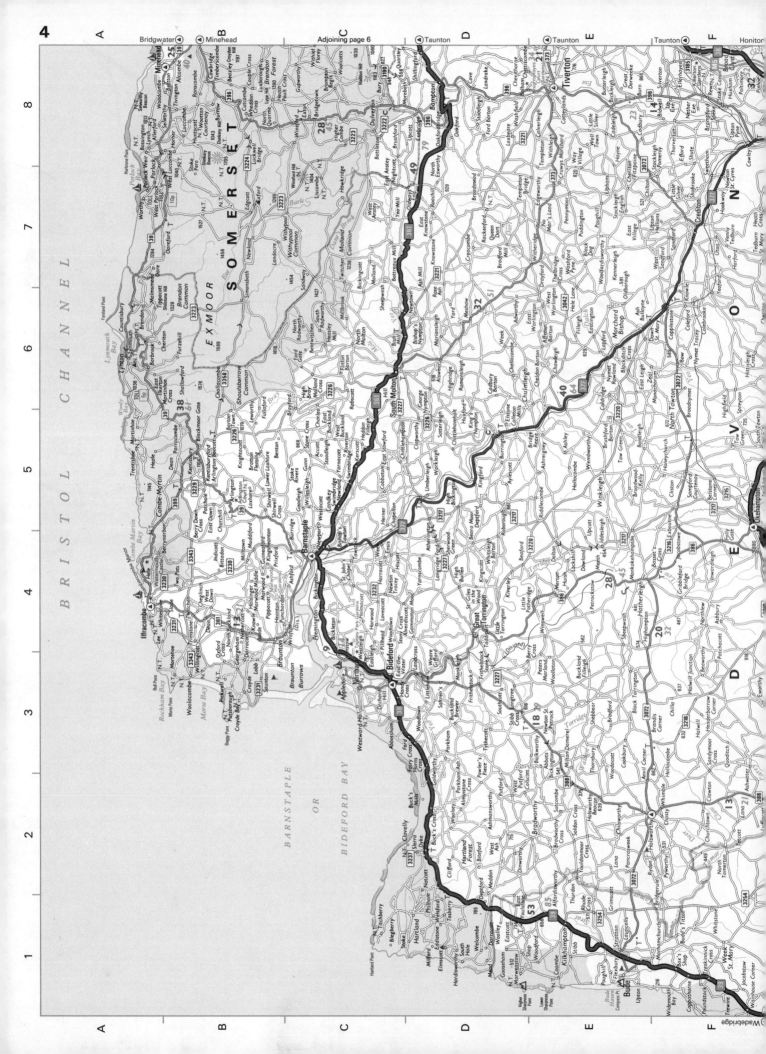

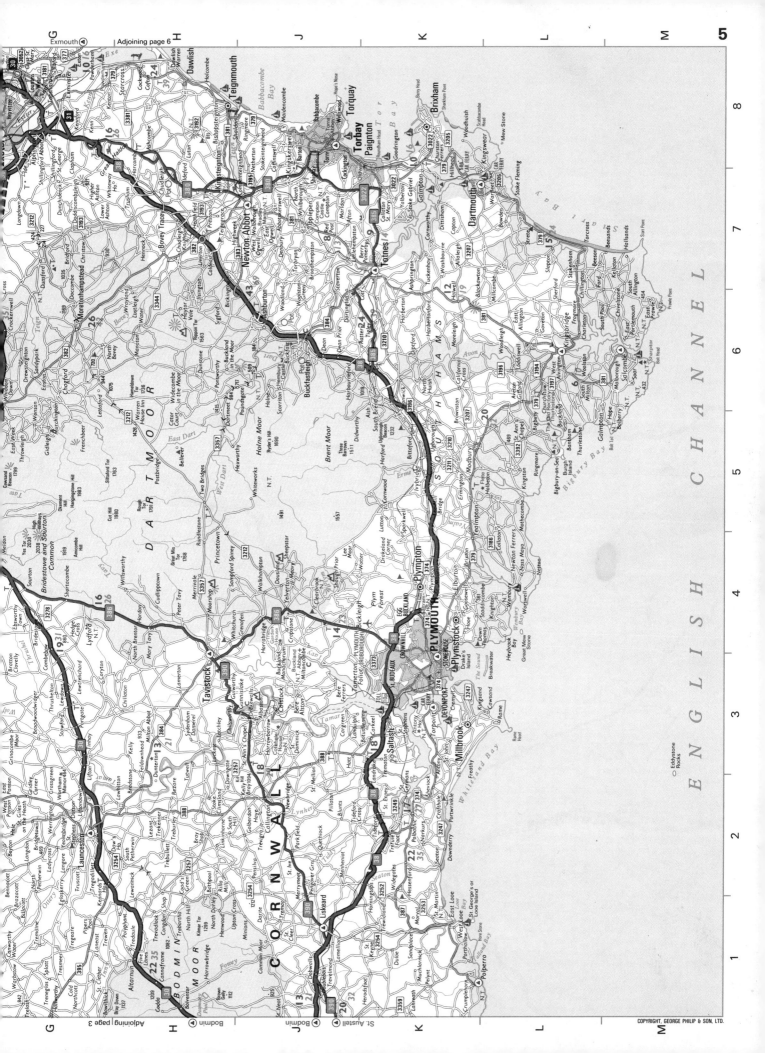

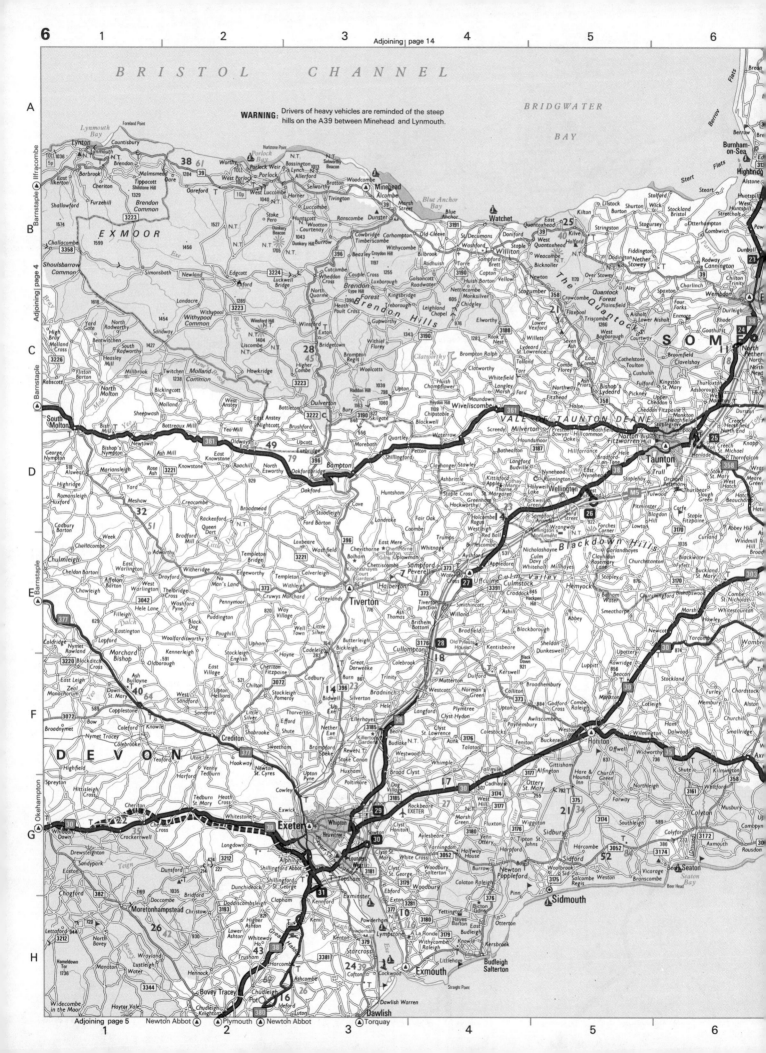

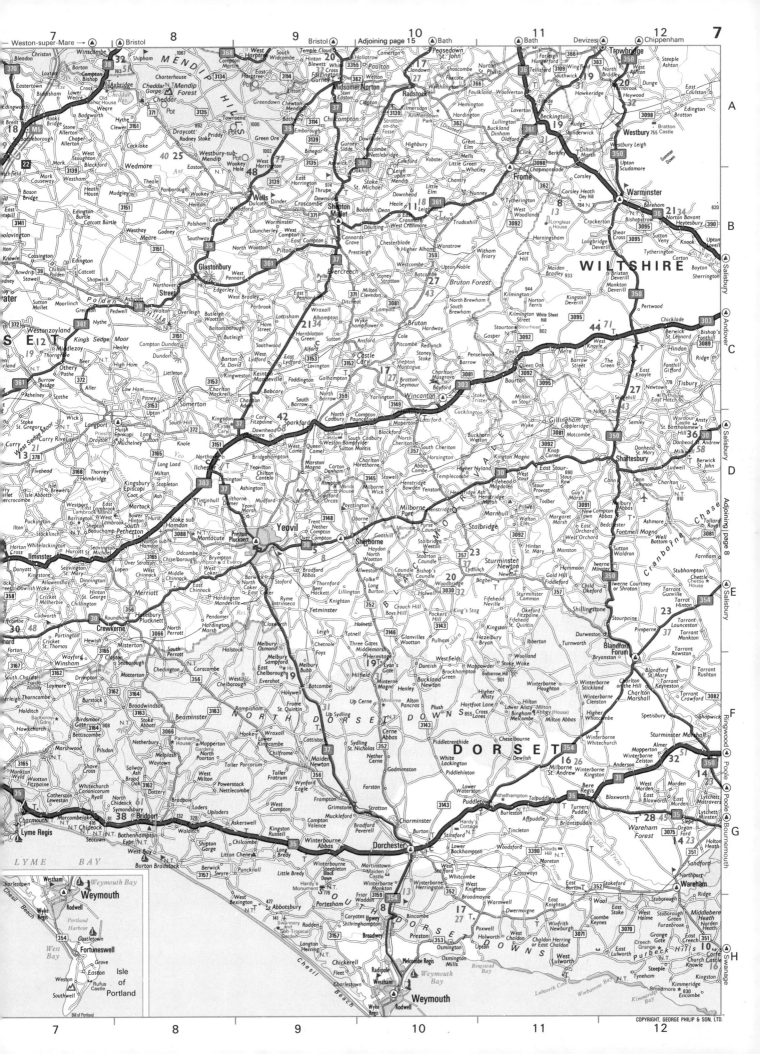

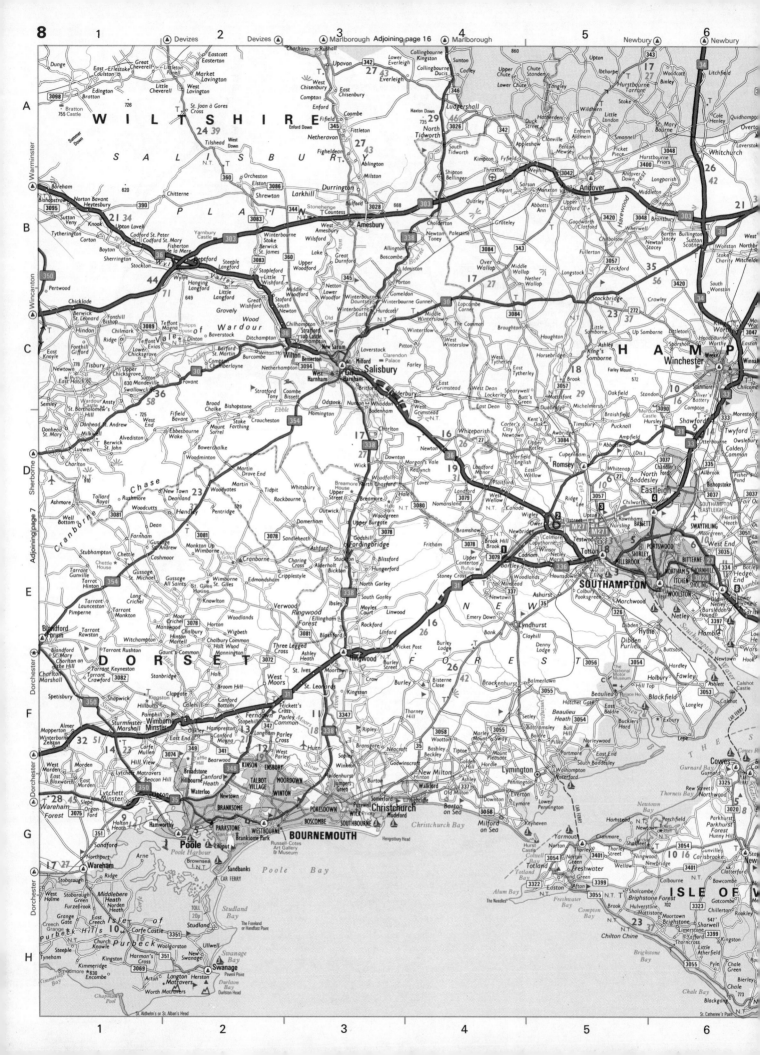

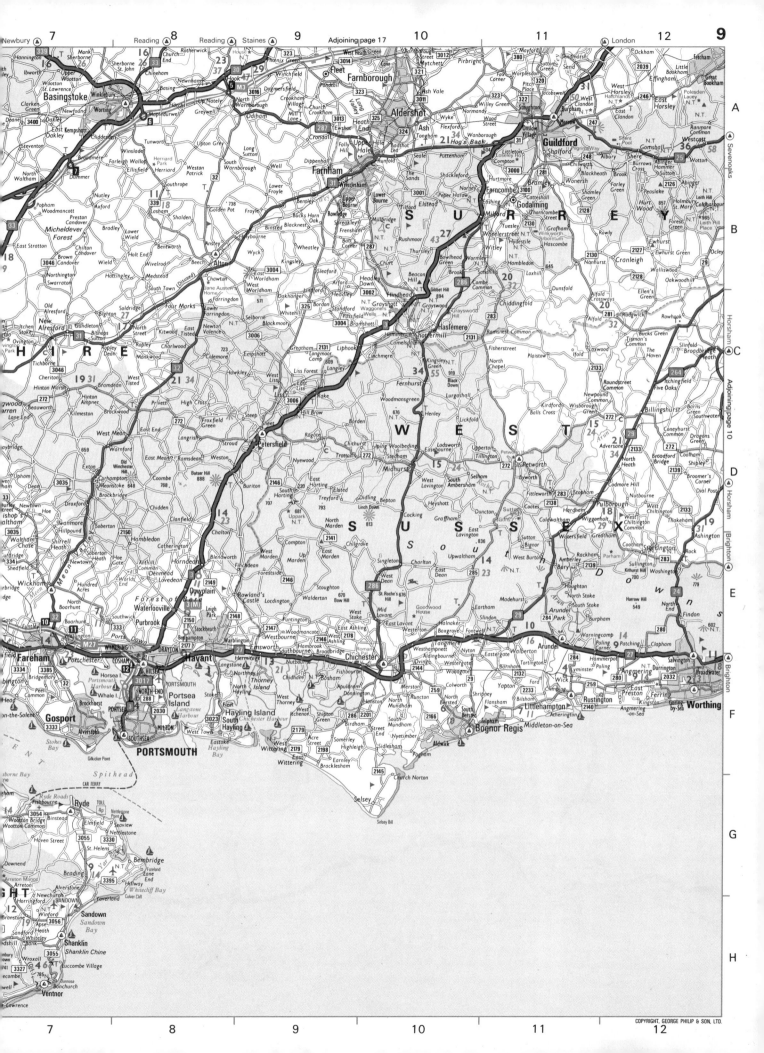

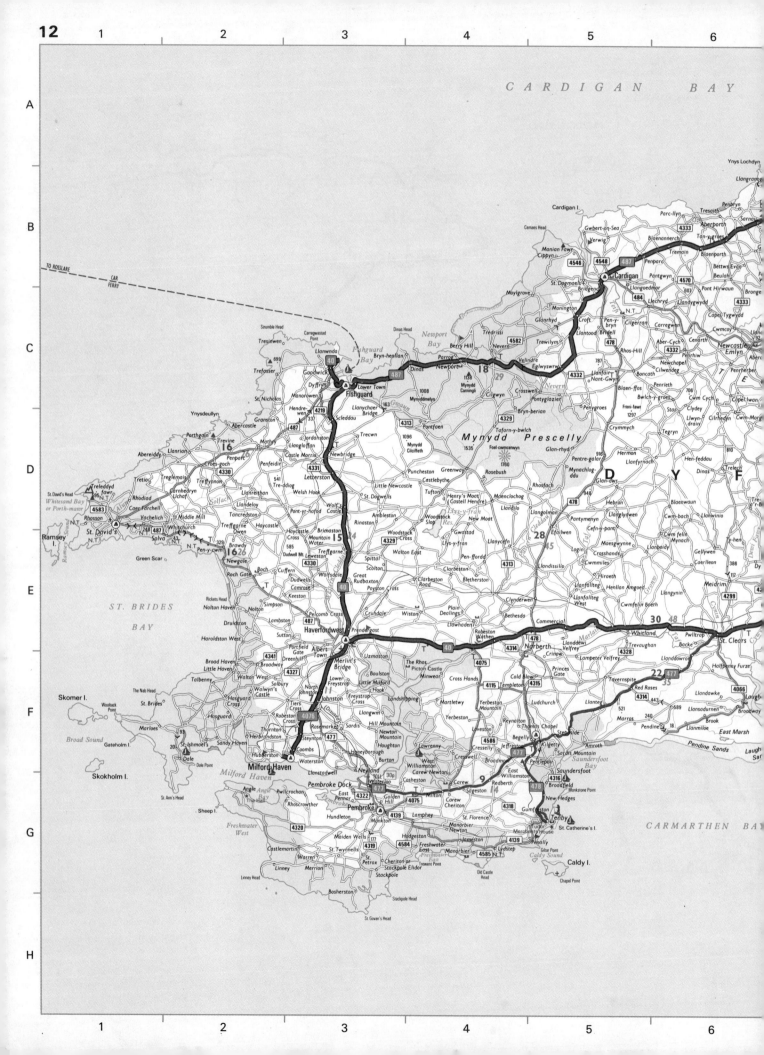

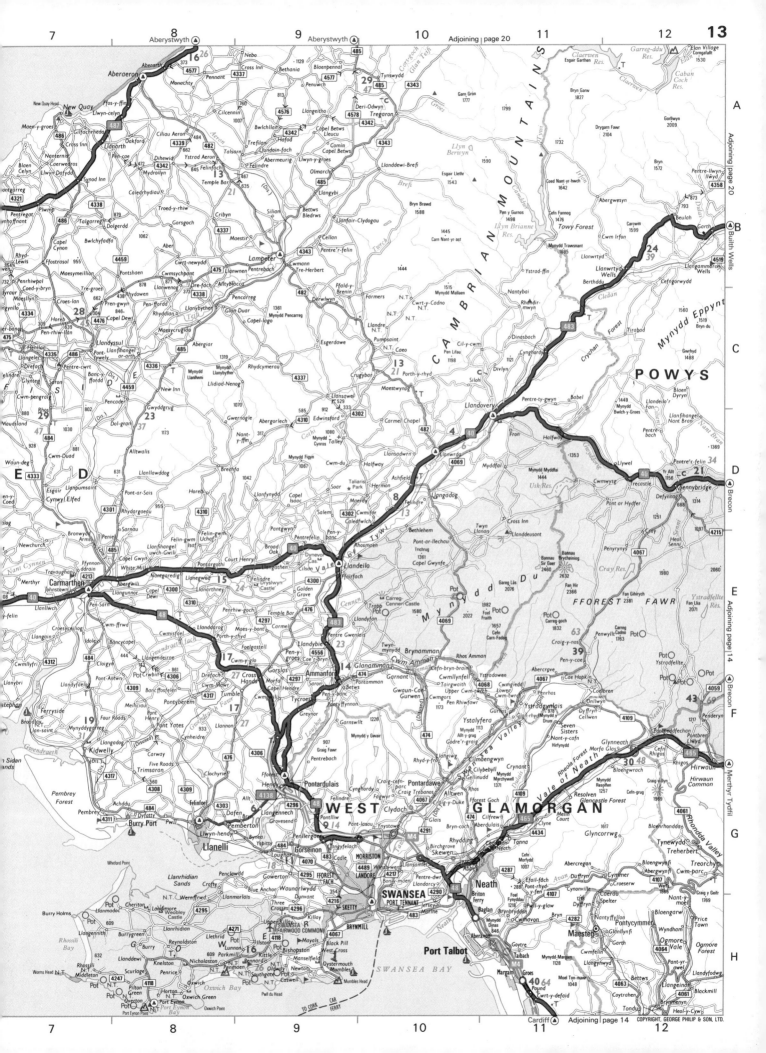

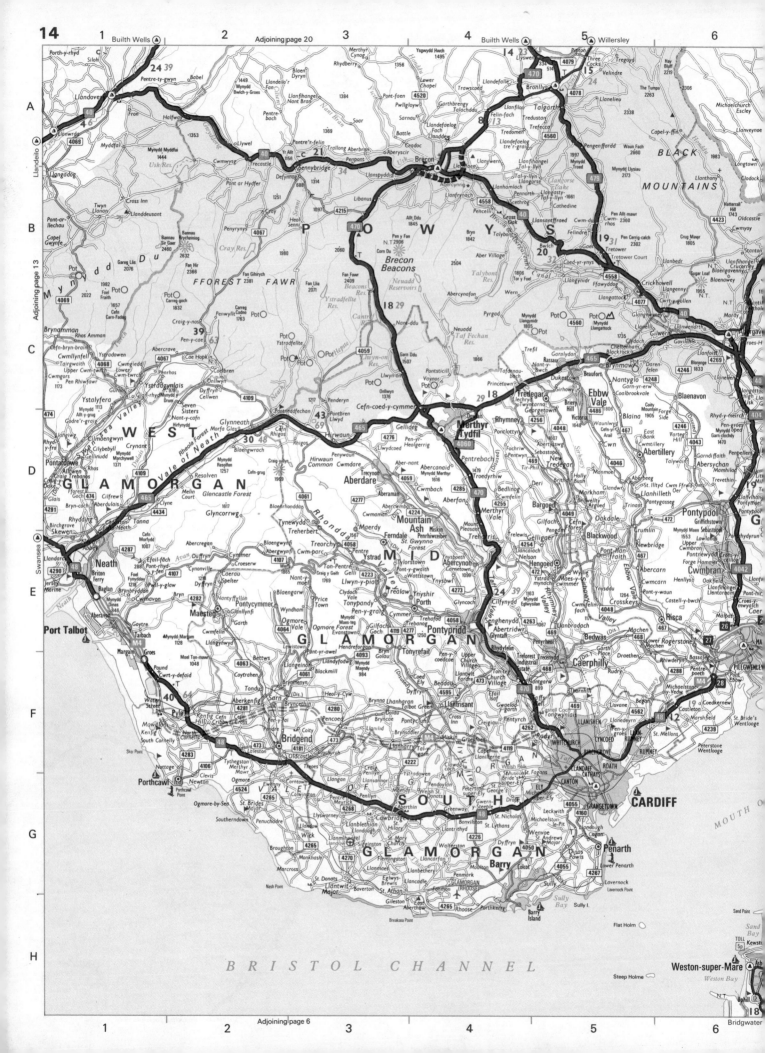

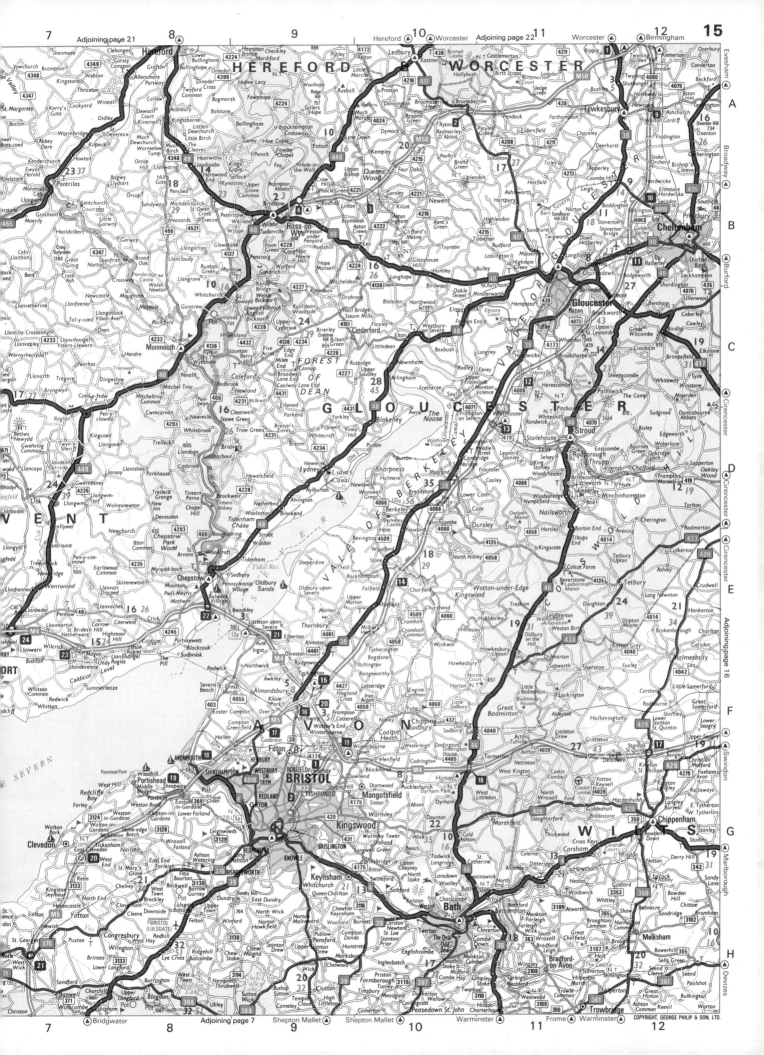

Evesham · Stratford upon Avon · Evesham · Adjoining page 22 · Warwick · Stratford-upon-Avon · Banbury

1 2 3 4 5 6

A B C D E F G H

GLOUCESTER · **OXFORD** · **WILTSHIRE** · **BERKSHIRE** · **HAMPSHIRE** · **VALE OF WHITE HORSE** · **MARLBOROUGH DOWNS** · **LAMBOURN DOWNS** · **BERKSHIRE DOWNS**

Cheltenham · Prestbury · Charlton Kings · Leckhampton · Cleeve Hill · Cleeve Common · Winchcombe · Sudeley Castle · Dumbleton · Beckford · Teddington · Oxenton Hill · Alstone · Dixton · Gretton · Greet · Hailes N.T. · Stanway · Stanton · Snowshill · Broadway Hill · Buckland · Laverton · Childswickham · Broadway · Willersey · Saintbury · Weston-sub-Edge

Moreton-in-Marsh · Bourton-on-the-Hill · Batsford · Blockley · Aston Magna · Todenham · Great Wolford · Little Wolford · Cherington · Stourton · Whichford · Long Compton · Hook Norton · Wigginton · Milcombe · Bloxham · Adderbury · King's Sutton · Charlton · Croughton · Aynho · Souldern · Fritwell · Somerton · Upper Heyford · Steeple Aston · Middle Aston · North Aston · Duns Tew · Great Tew · Nether Worton · Over Worton · Sandford St. Martin · Enstone · Chipping Norton · Heythrop · Churchill · Kingham · Bledington · Westcote · Chadlington · Spelsbury · Charlbury · Ditchley Park · Wootton · Glympton · Kiddington · Woodstock · Blenheim Palace · Bladon · Begbroke · Kidlington · Yarnton · Cassington · Eynsham · Botley · North Hinksey · OXFORD · COWLEY · New Hinksey · Littlemore · Kennington · Radley · Abingdon · Culham · Clifton Hampden · Appleford · Sutton Courtenay · Steventon · Milton · Didcot · Harwell · East Hendred · West Hendred · Chilton · Blewbury · Upton

Stow-on-the-Wold · Maugersbury · Oddington · Bourton-on-the-Water · Lower Slaughter · Upper Slaughter · Naunton · Guiting Power · Temple Guiting · Kineton · Hawling · Brockhampton · Whittington · Andoversford · Shipton · Salperton · Notgrove · Turkdean · Northleach · Hampnett · Farmington · Sherborne · Windrush · Great Rissington · Little Rissington · Wick Rissington · Clapton · Great Barrington · Little Barrington · Taynton · Burford · Fulbrook · Swinbrook · Asthall · Minster Lovell · Crawley · Witney · Ducklington · Curbridge · Brize Norton · Carterton · Kencot · Broadwell · Filkins · Langford · Little Faringdon · Lechlade · Kelmscott · Buscot · Coleshill · Faringdon · Shellingford · Stanford in the Vale · Charney Bassett · Lyford · Pusey · Buckland · Longworth · Kingston Bagpuize · Fyfield · Frilford · Marcham · Garford

Cirencester · Stratton · Baunton · Bagendon · North Cerney · Rendcomb · Colesbourne · Chedworth · Chedworth Woods · Withington · Compton Abdale · Yanworth · Coln St. Dennis · Coln Rogers · Winson · Bibury · Arlington · Ablington · Barnsley · Quenington · Coln St. Aldwyns · Hatherop · Eastleach · Southrop · Fairford · Whelford · Kempsford · Castle Eaton · Marston Meysey · Meysey Hampton · Ampney Crucis · Ampney St. Mary · Poulton · Down Ampney · Driffield · Cricklade · Latton · South Cerney · Cerney Wick · Ashton Keynes · Leigh · Minety · Hankerton · Crudwell · Oaksey · Somerford Keynes · Poole Keynes · Kemble · Ewen · Coates · Tarlton · Rodmarton · Sapperton · Oakley Wood · Stratton · Brimpsfield · Elkstone · Syde · Winstone · Daglingworth · Duntisbourne Abbots · Duntisbourne Rouse · Edgeworth

Swindon · Stratton St. Margaret · Stanton Fitzwarren · Highworth · Blunsdon · Broad Blunsdon · Purton · Purton Stoke · Hannington · Sevenhampton · Watchfield · Shrivenham · Longcot · Fernham · Uffington · Woolstone · Compton Beauchamp · Ashbury · Bishopstone · Wanborough · Liddington · Chiseldon · Draycot Foliat · Wroughton · Wootton Bassett · Lydiard Millicent · Lydiard Tregoze · Rodbourne Cheney · Haydon Wick · Blunsdon St. Andrew

Marlborough · Avebury · Beckhampton · West Kennett · East Kennett · Lockeridge · Fyfield · Clatford · Manton · Mildenhall · Axford · Ramsbury · Aldbourne · Baydon · Lambourn · Eastbury · East Garston · Great Shefford · Shefford Woodlands · Welford · Weston · Boxford · Chaddleworth · Leckhampstead · Brightwalton · Peasemore · Chieveley · Hermitage · Hampstead Norris · Beedon · Compton · East Ilsley · West Ilsley · Farnborough · Lambourn Downs

Devizes · Calne · Cherhill · Heddington · Bishops Cannings · All Cannings · Stanton St. Bernard · Alton Barnes · Alton Priors · Honey Street · Wilcot · Woodborough · Pewsey · Milton Lilbourne · Easton Royal · Burbage · Great Bedwyn · Little Bedwyn · Froxfield · Chisbury · Hungerford · Kintbury · Inkpen · Combe · Ham · Shalbourne · Newbury · Speen · Thatcham · Greenham · Crookham · Bucklebury · Savernake Forest · Collingbourne Kingston · Collingbourne Ducis · Tidcombe · Wexcombe · Oxenwood · Vernham Dean · Linkenholt · Faccombe · Netherton · Combe

Chippenham · Calne · Bromham · Sandy Lane · Heddington Wick · Rowde · Seend · Potterne · Worton · Marston · Urchfont · Chirton · Marden · Wilsford · Charlton · Rushall · North Newnton · Manningford Bruce · Manningford Bohune · Wootton Rivers · Clench Common · Burbage

Stroud · Gloucester · Bath · Chippenham · Severn Bridge · Frome

Salisbury · Andover · Salisbury · Salisbury · Adjoining page 8 · Andover · Winchester · Adjoining page 15

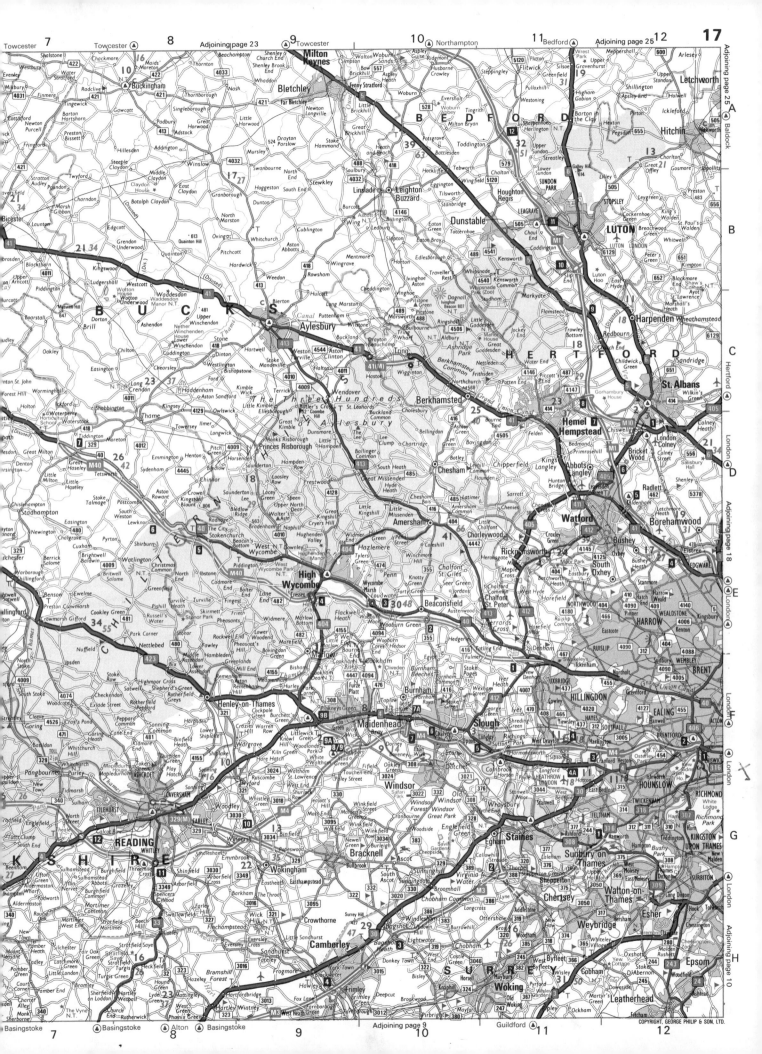

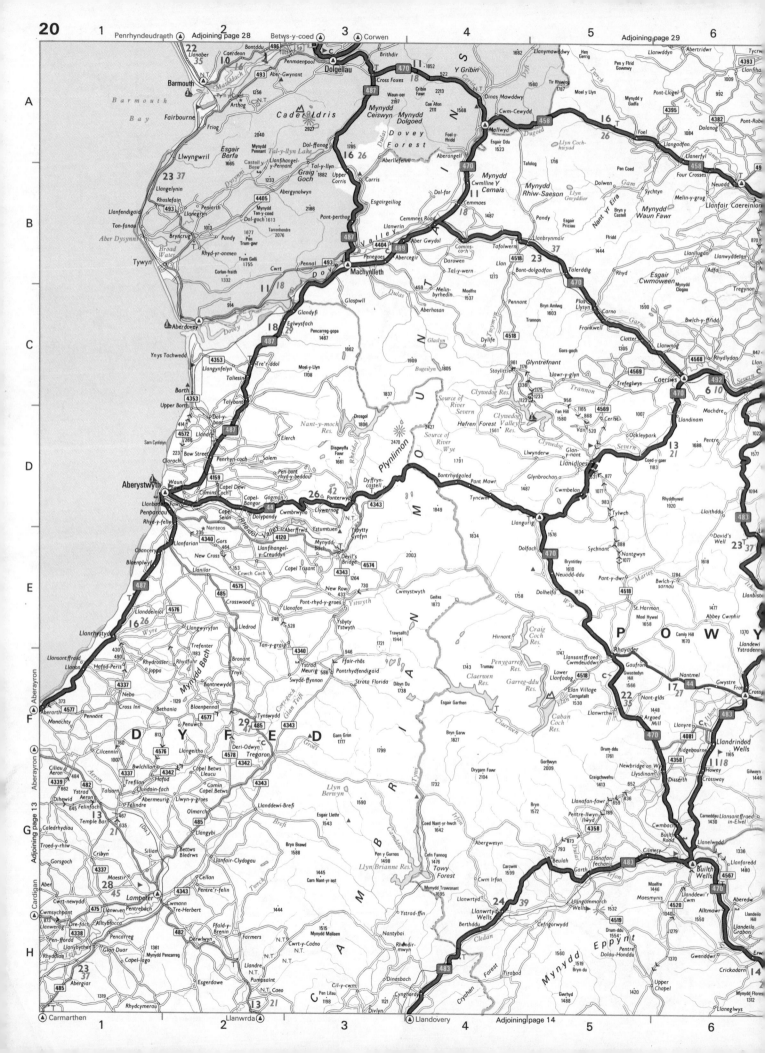

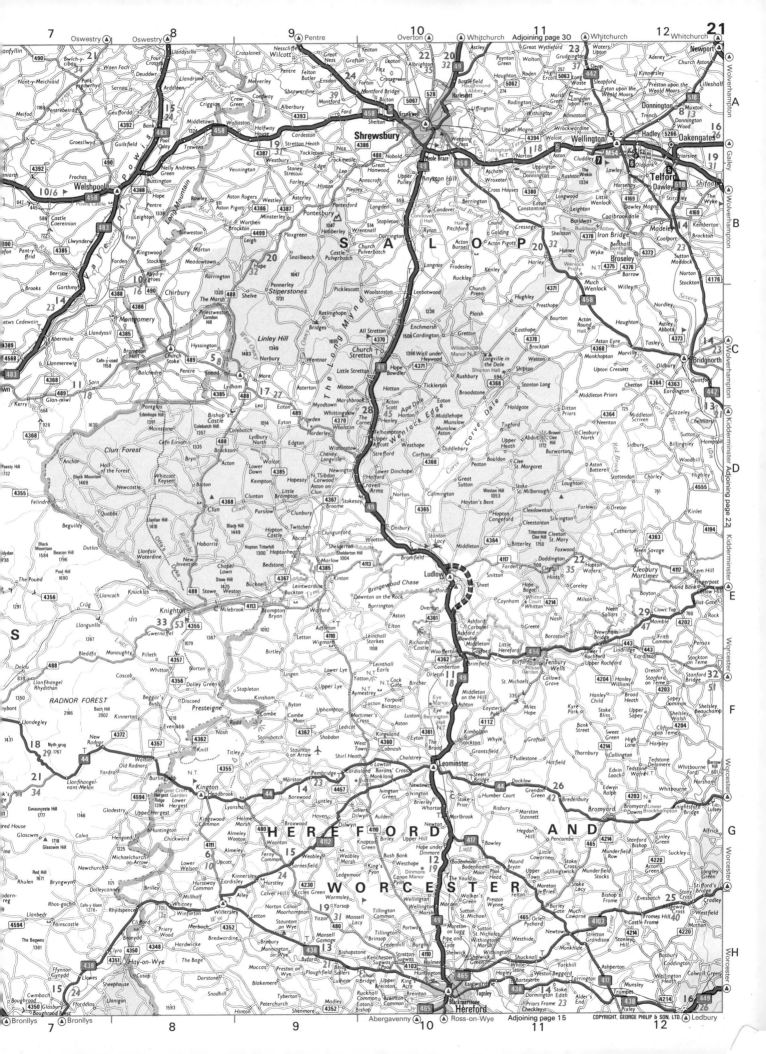

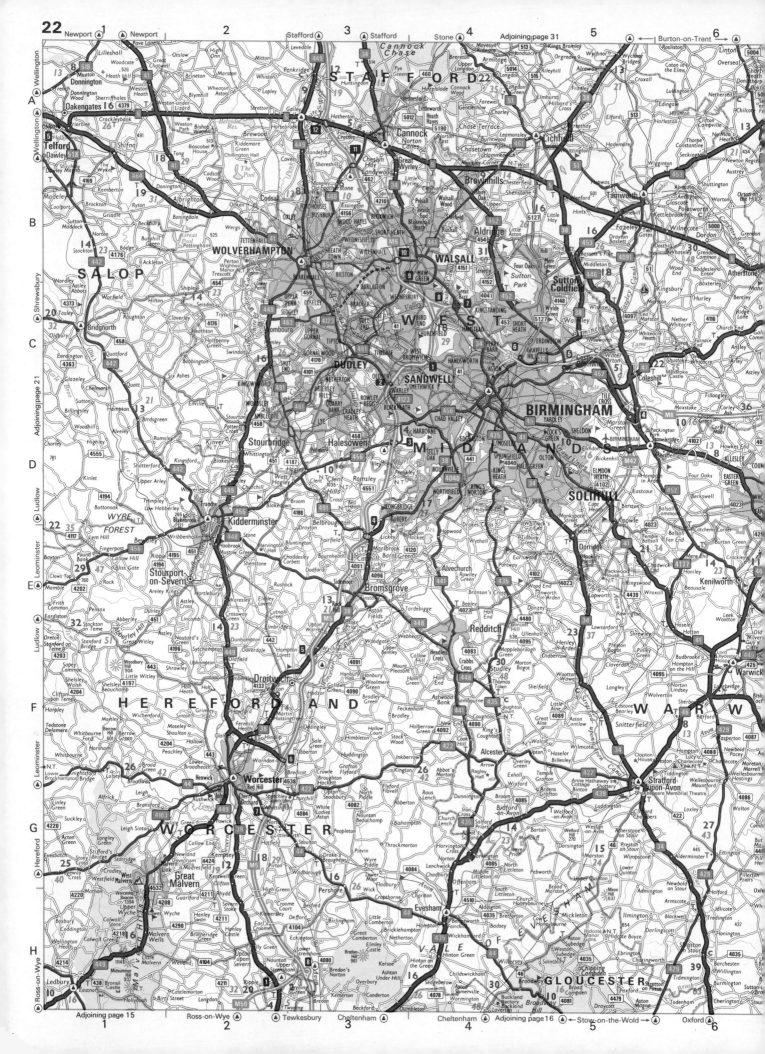

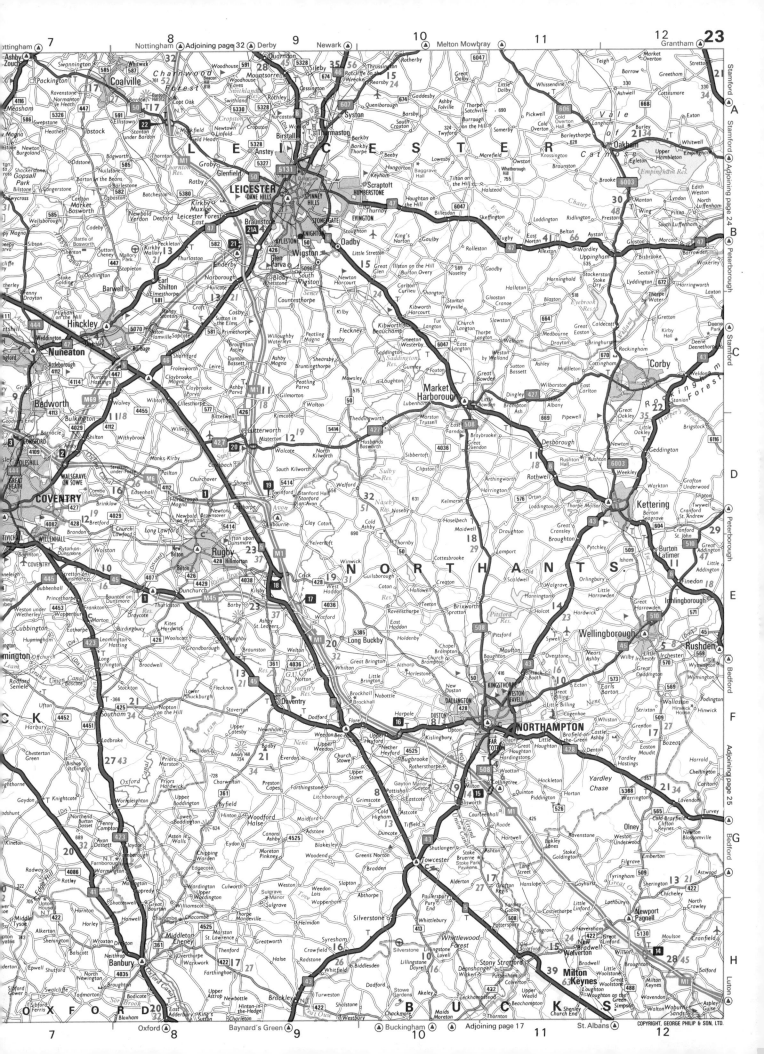

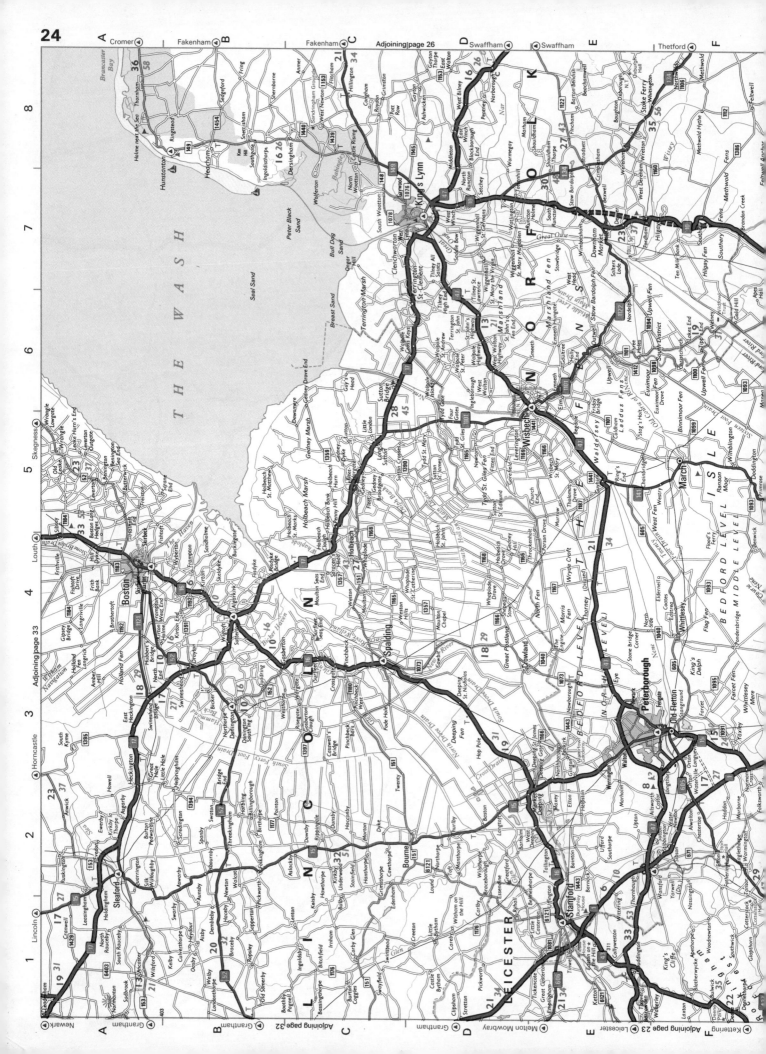

THE WASH

NORFOLK

LINCOLNSHIRE

ISLE

BEDFORD LEVEL

BEDFORD MIDDLE LEVEL

King's Lynn

Wisbech

March

Spalding

Boston

Sleaford

Peterborough

Stamford

Bourne

Adjoining page 33

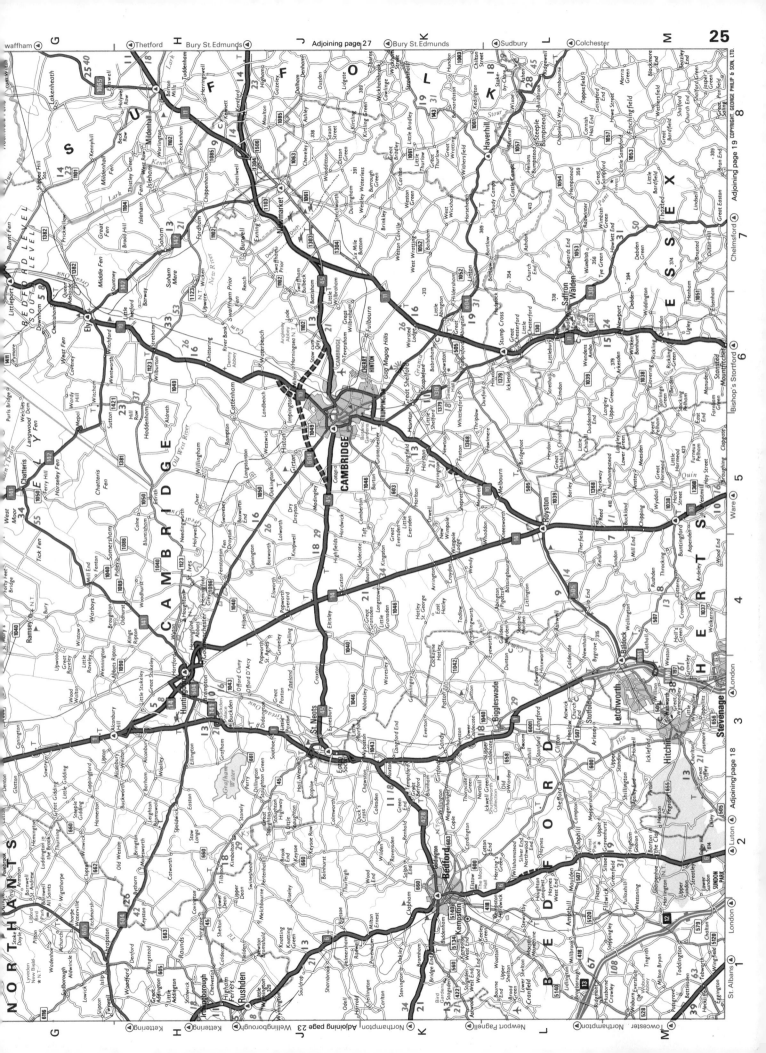

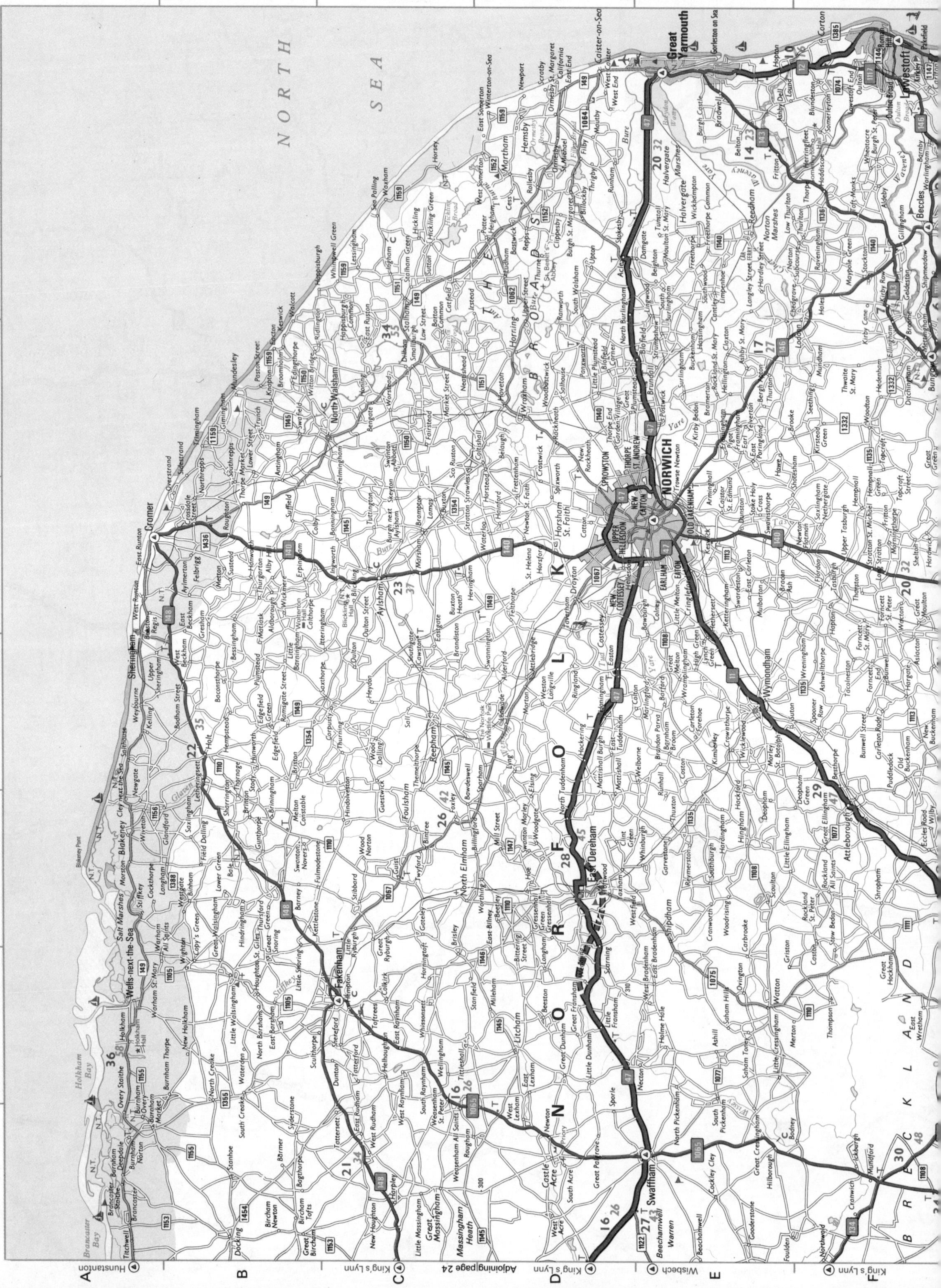

A B C D E F

8 7 6 5 4 3 2 1

NORTH SEA

Great Yarmouth
Gorleston on Sea
Lowestoft
Corton
Hopton
Caister-on-Sea
Hemsby
Winterton-on-Sea
Sea Palling
Happisburgh
Mundesley
Cromer
Sheringham
Overstrand
Weybourne
Kelling
Holt
North Walsham
Stalham
Hickling
Potter Heigham
Acle
NORWICH
Thorpe St Andrew
New Costessey
Old Catton
Upper Hellesdon
Hellesdon
Aylsham
Reepham
Fakenham
Dereham / East Dereham
Wymondham
Attleborough
Swaffham
Hingham
Wells-next-the-Sea
Blakeney
Morston
Stiffkey
Holkham
Holkham Hall
Holkham Bay
Burnham Market
Burnham Overy
Brancaster
Titchwell
Docking
Beccles
Bungay
Oulton Broad
Breydon Water

Brancaster Bay

BRECKLAND

Holkham Bay

N.T.

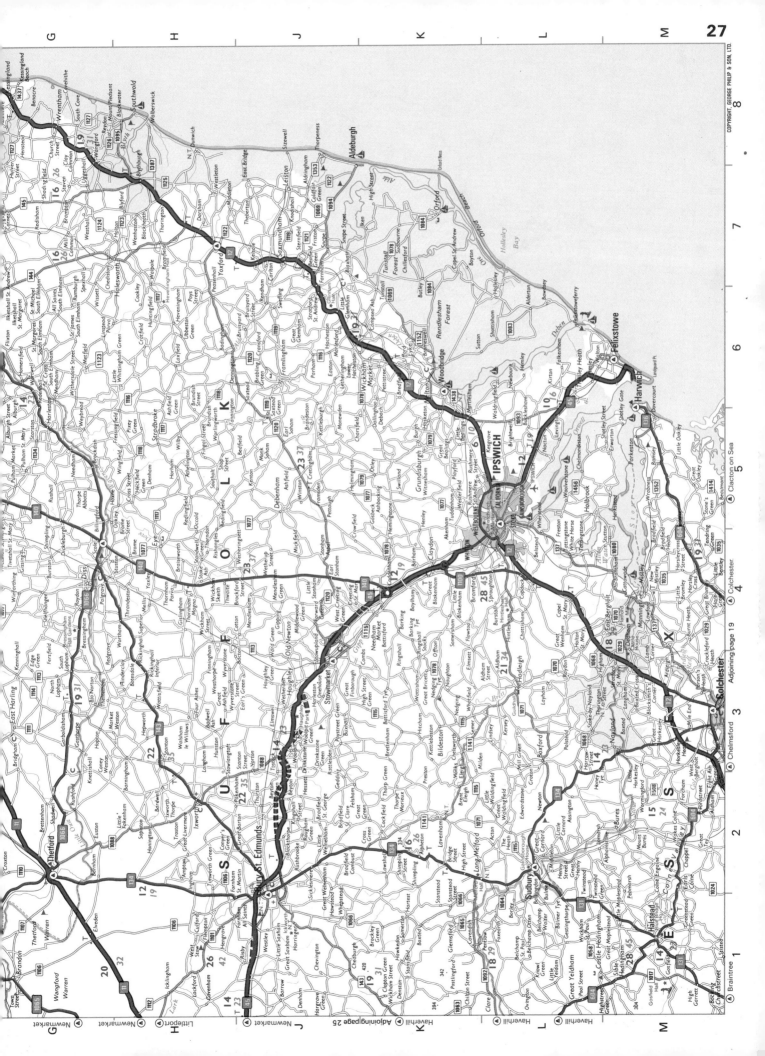

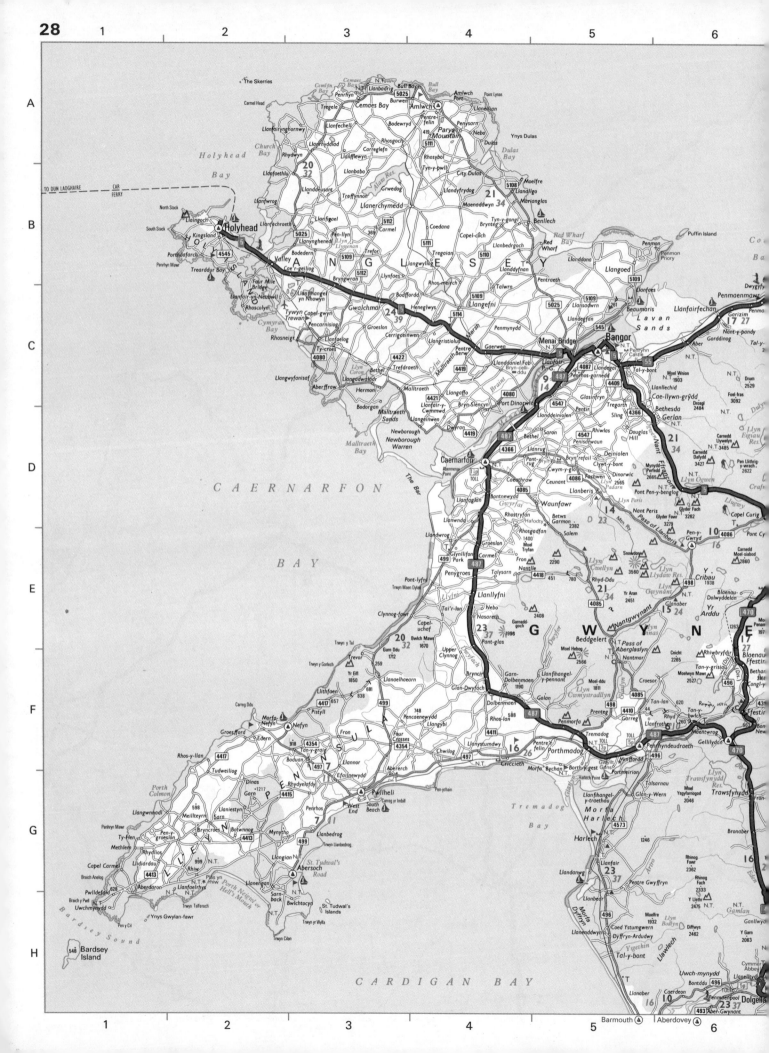

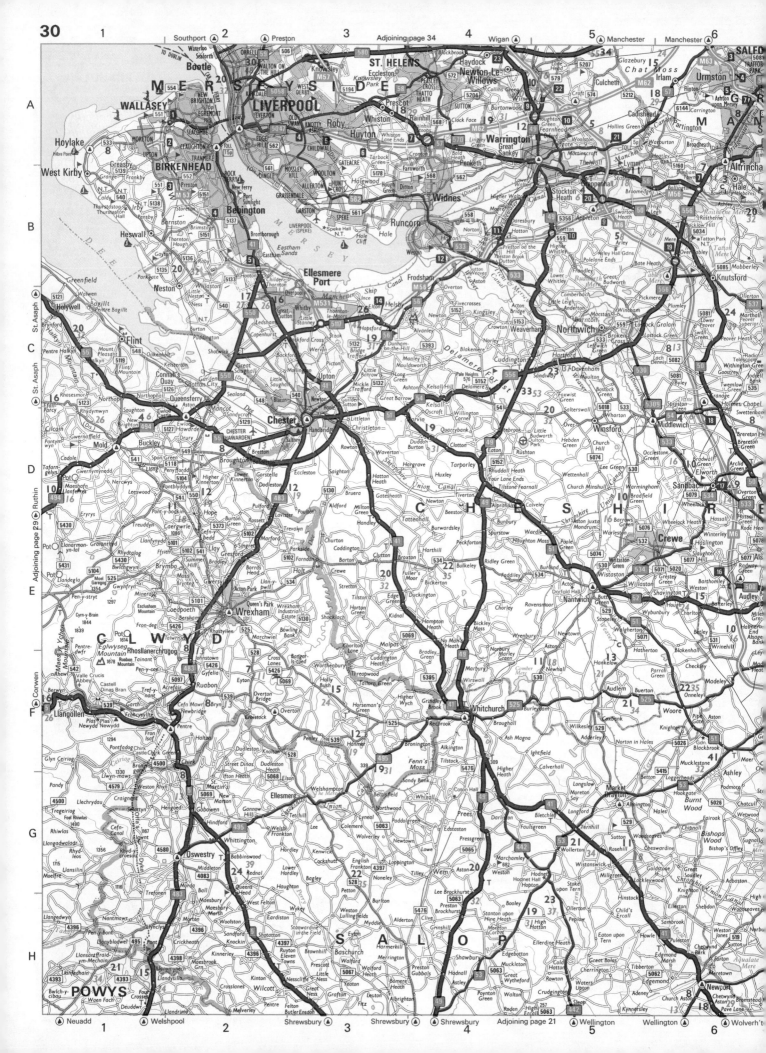

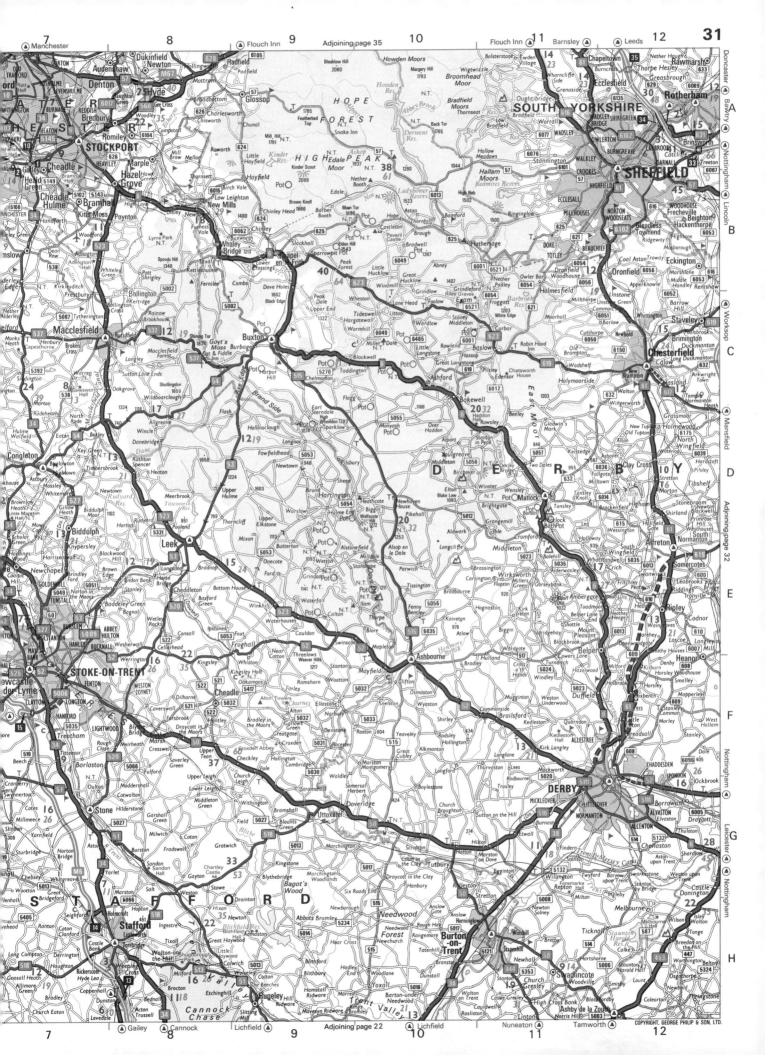

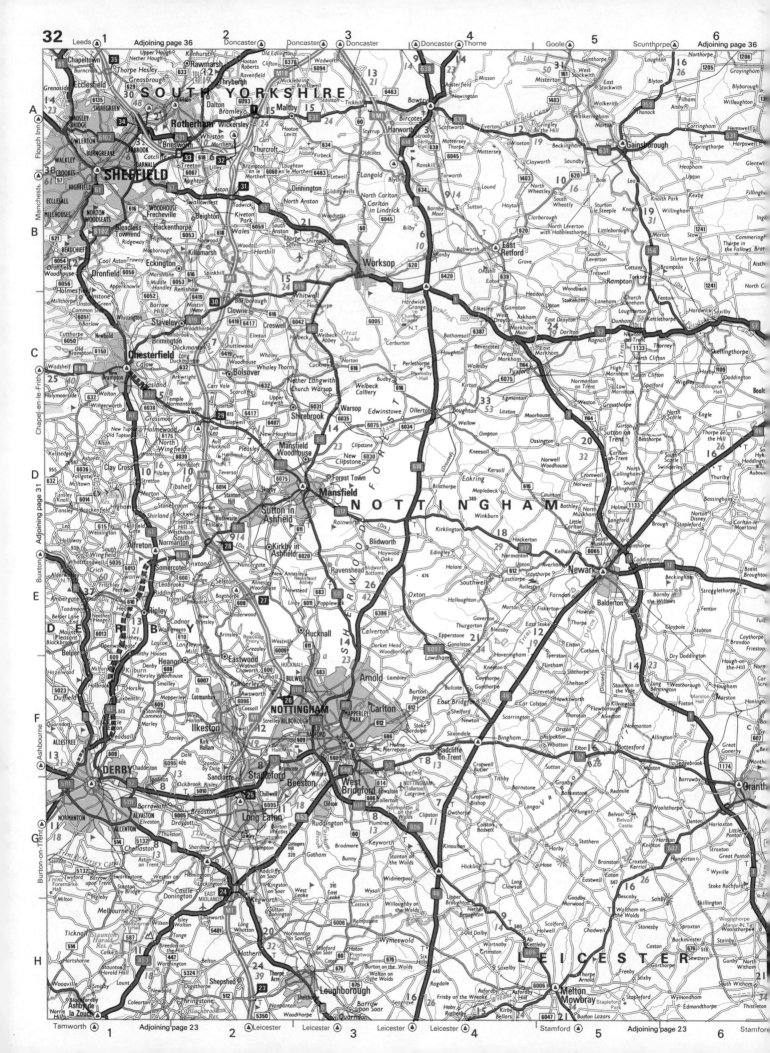

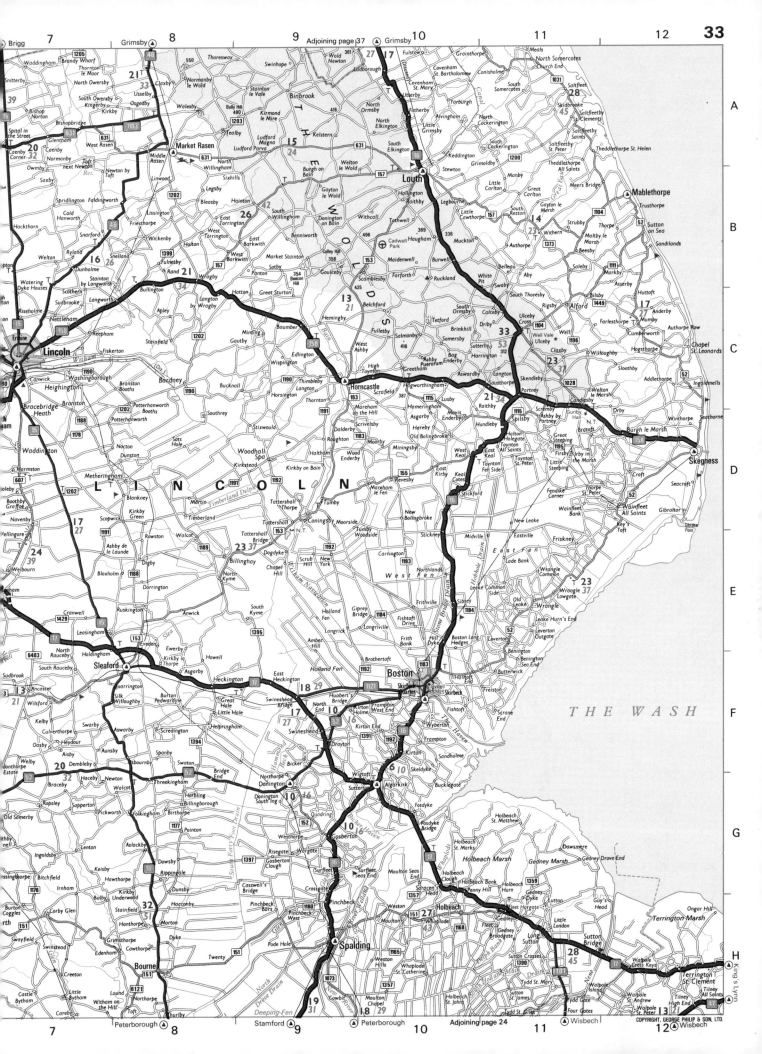

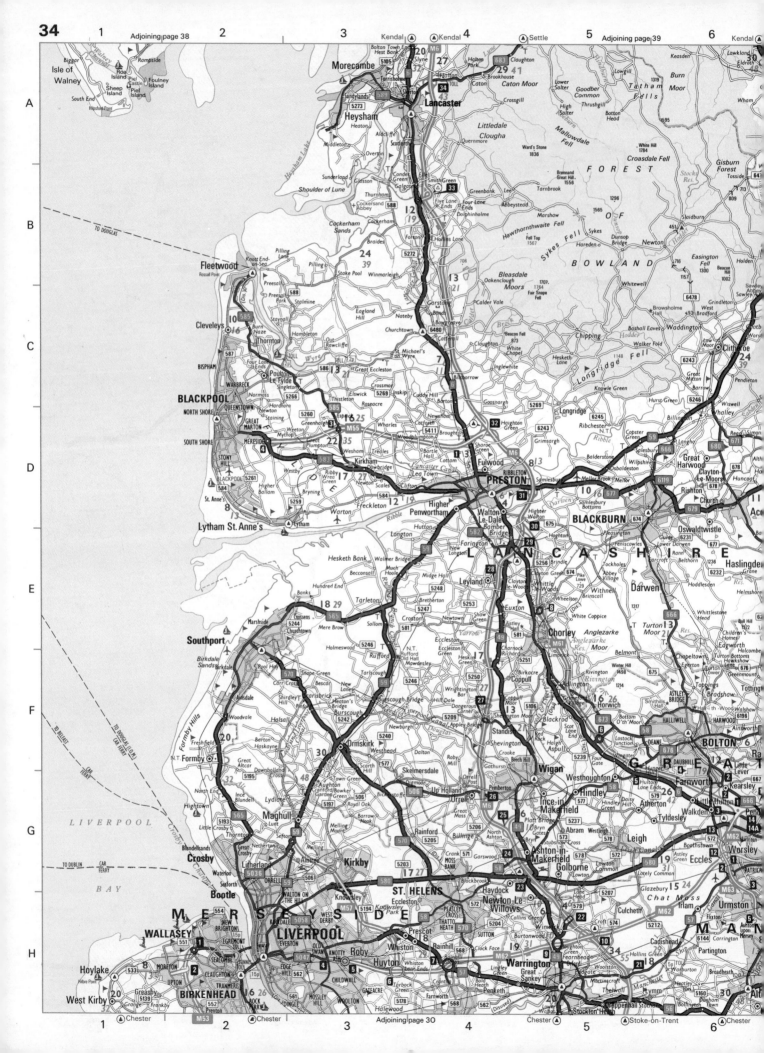

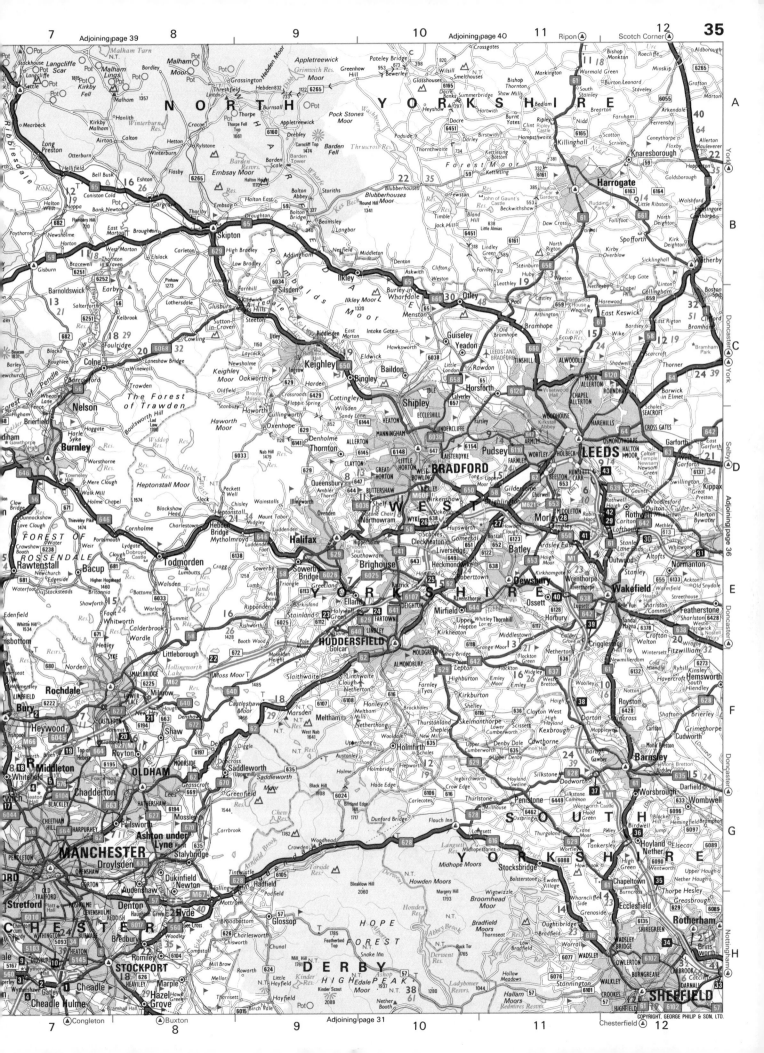

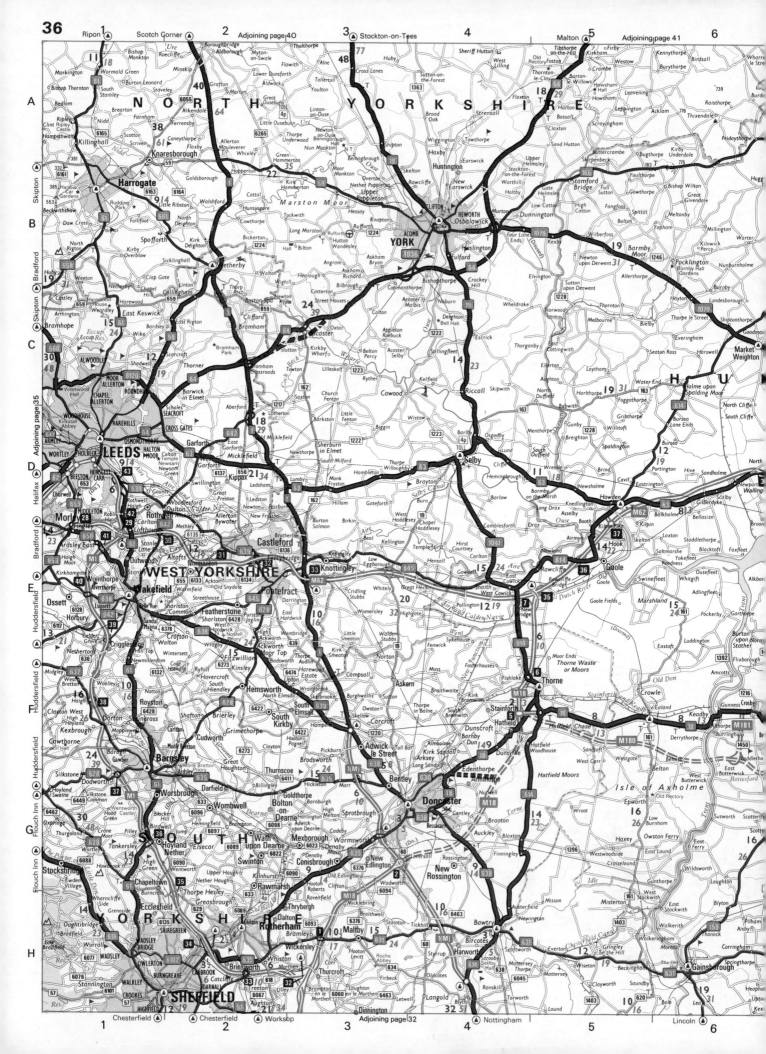

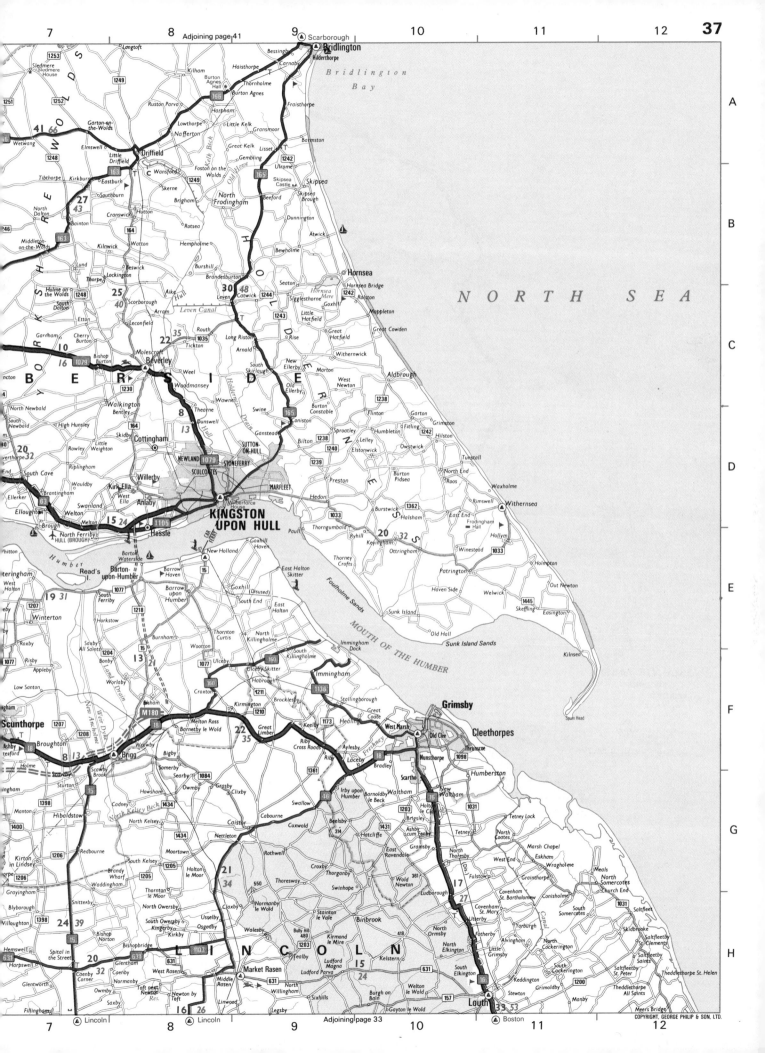

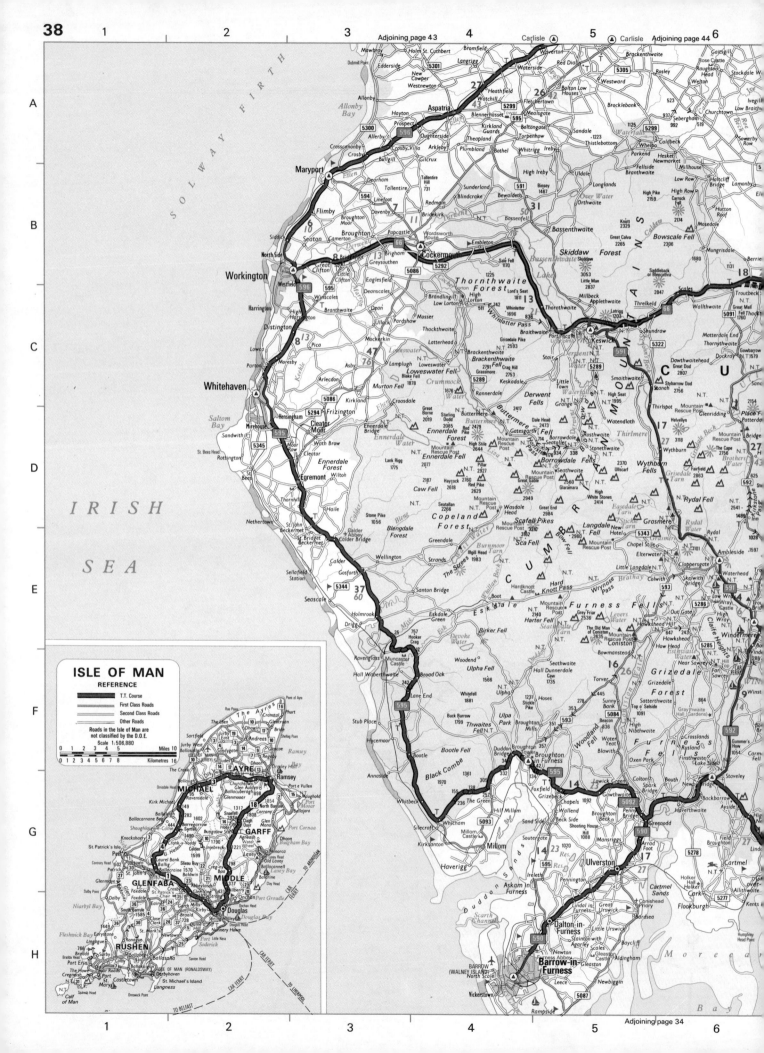

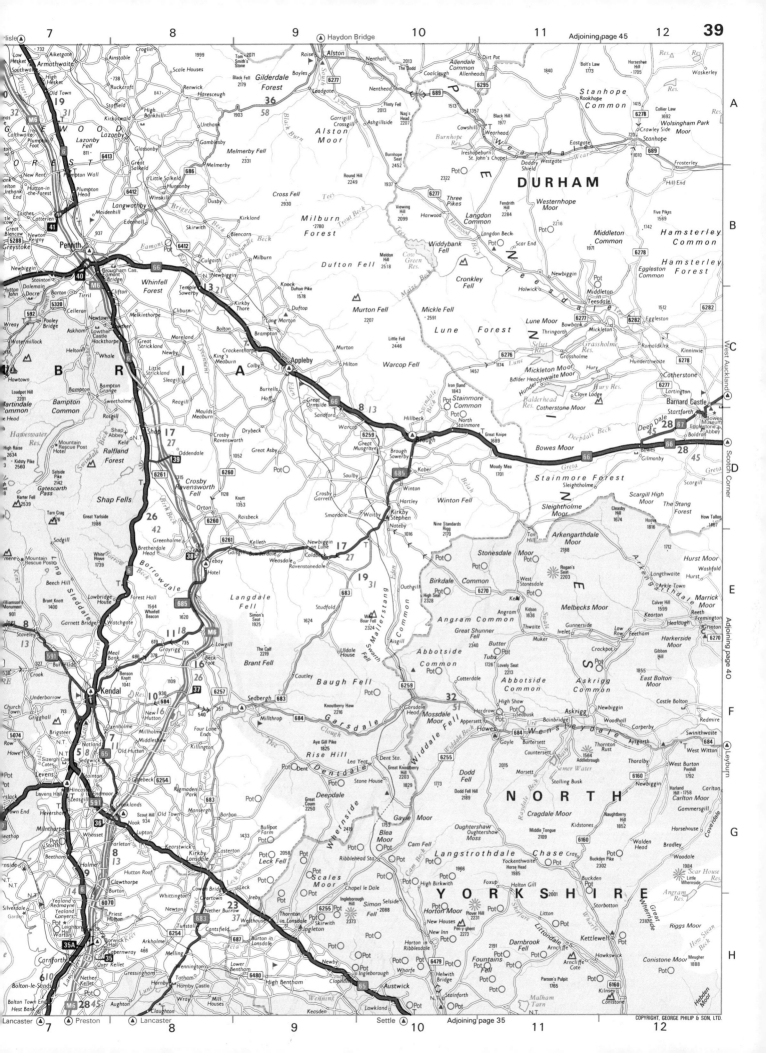

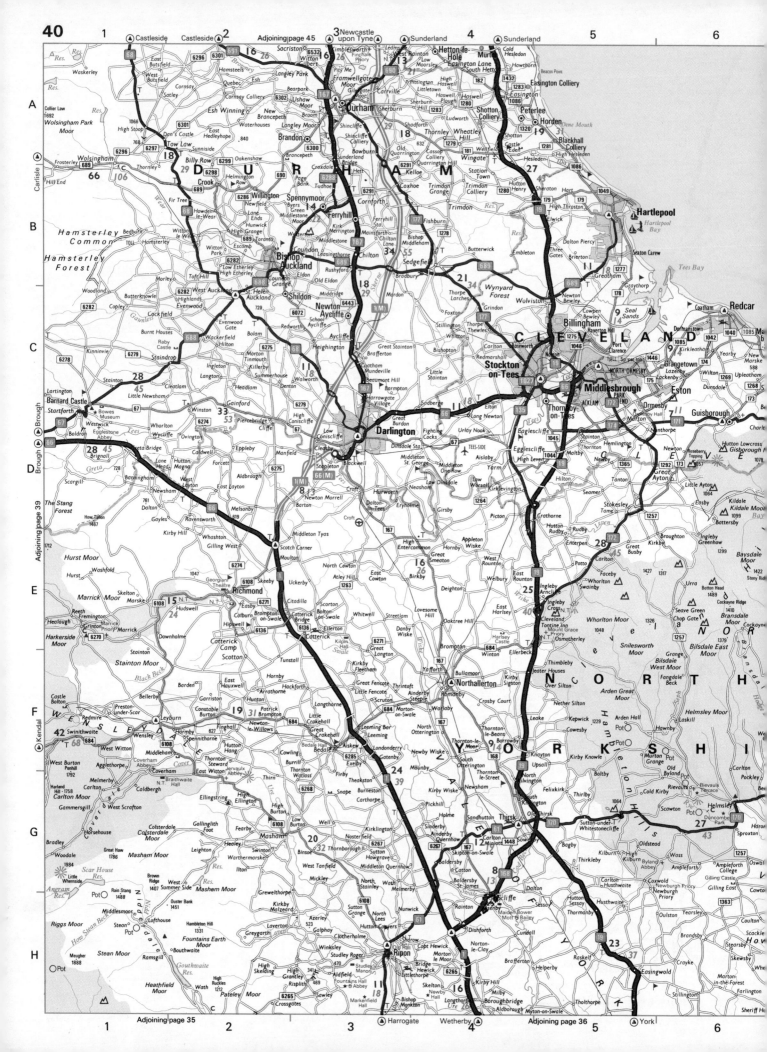

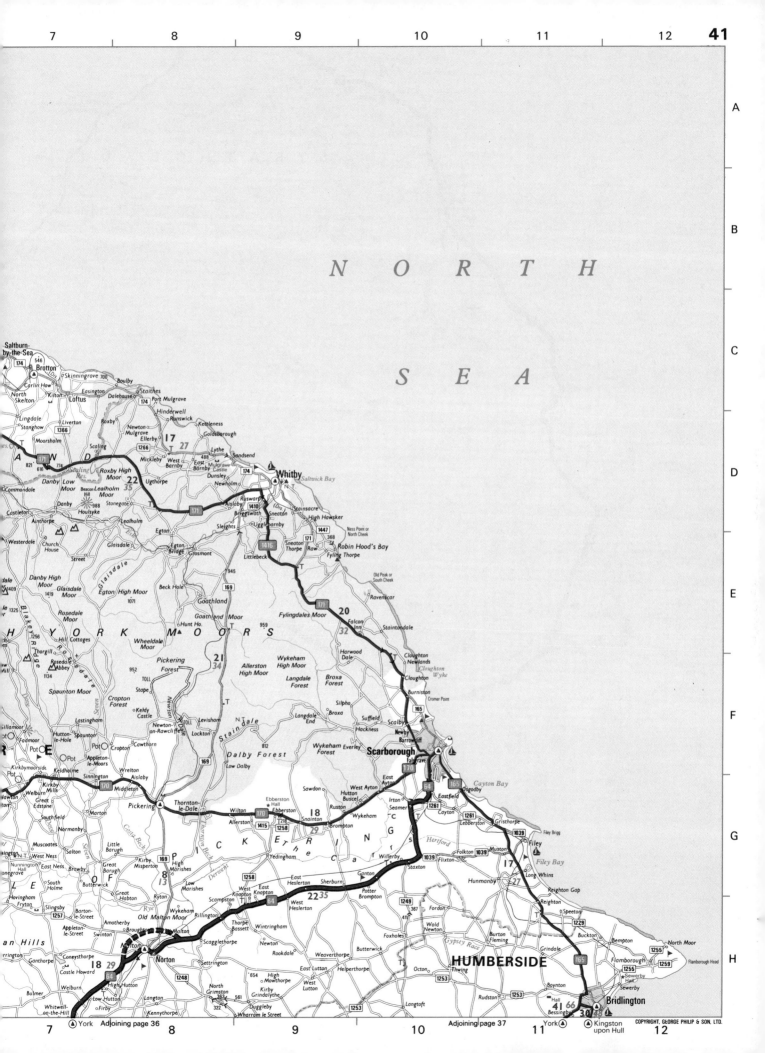

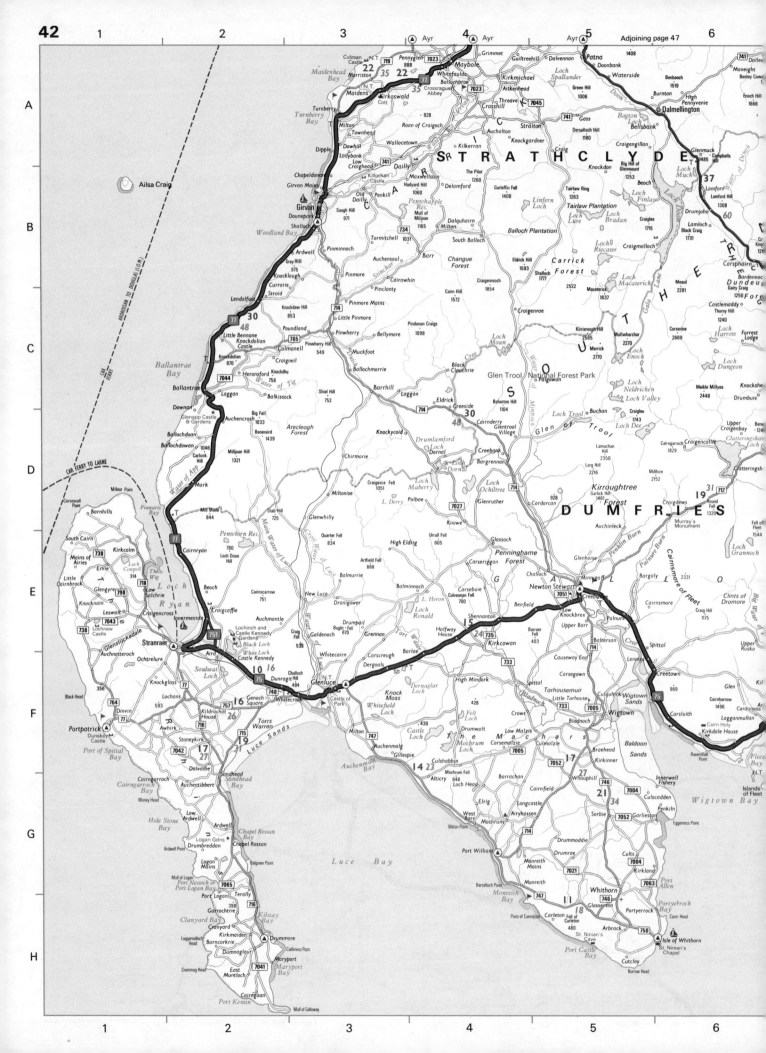

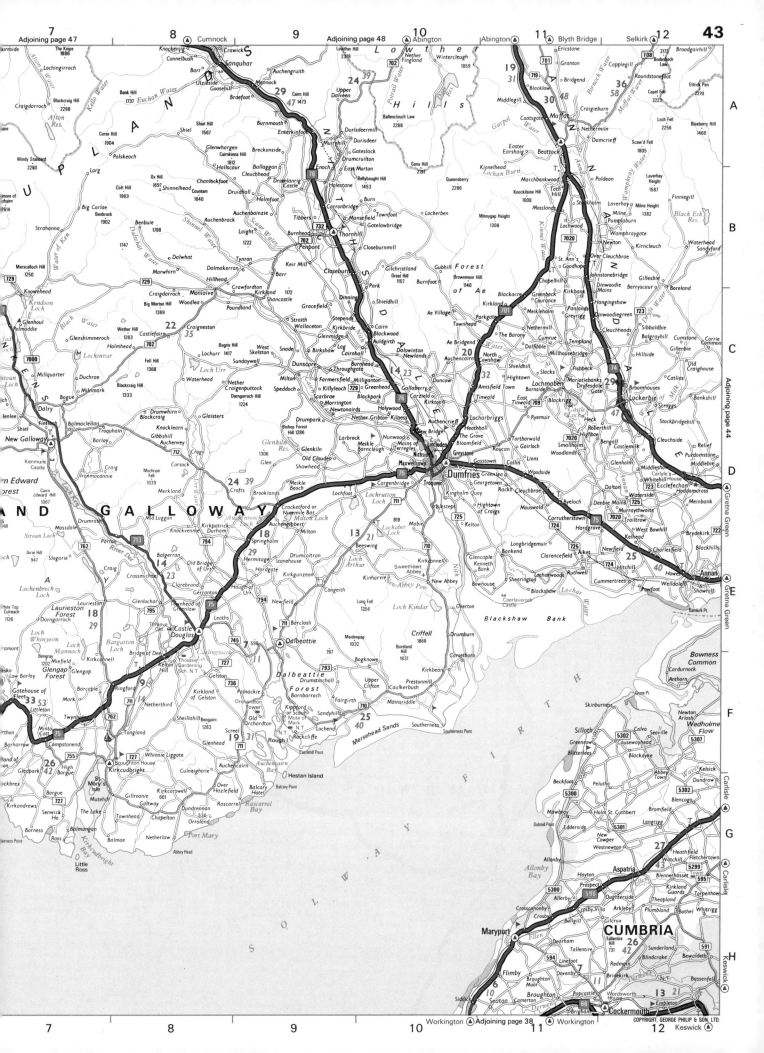

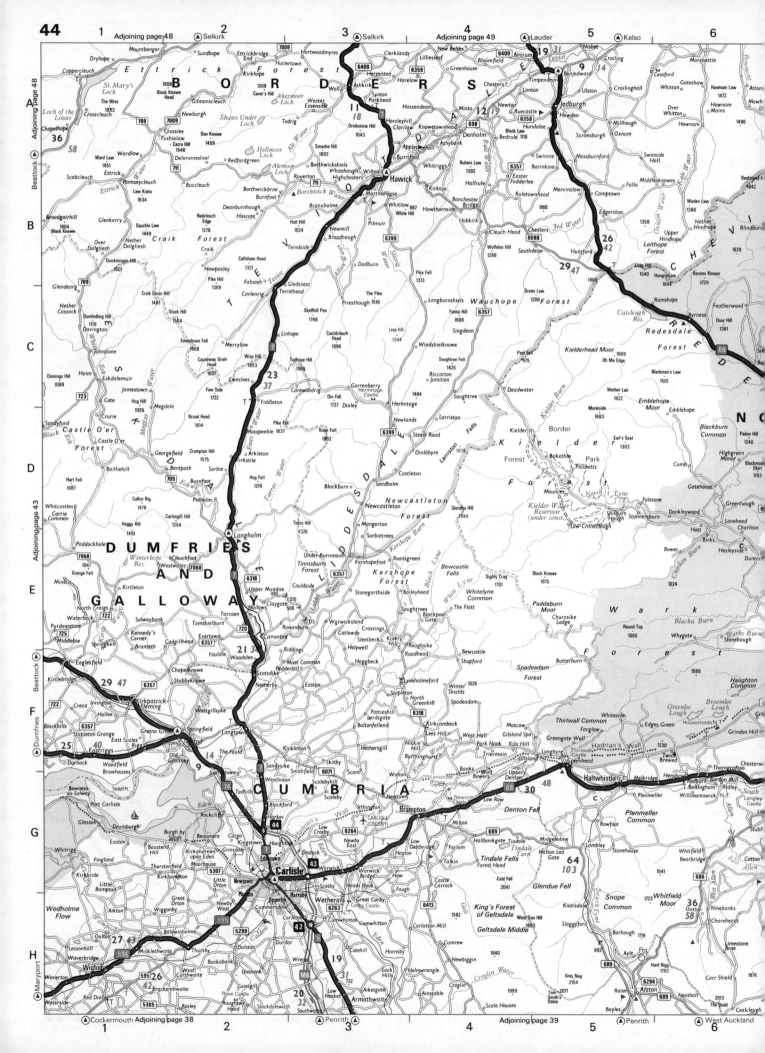

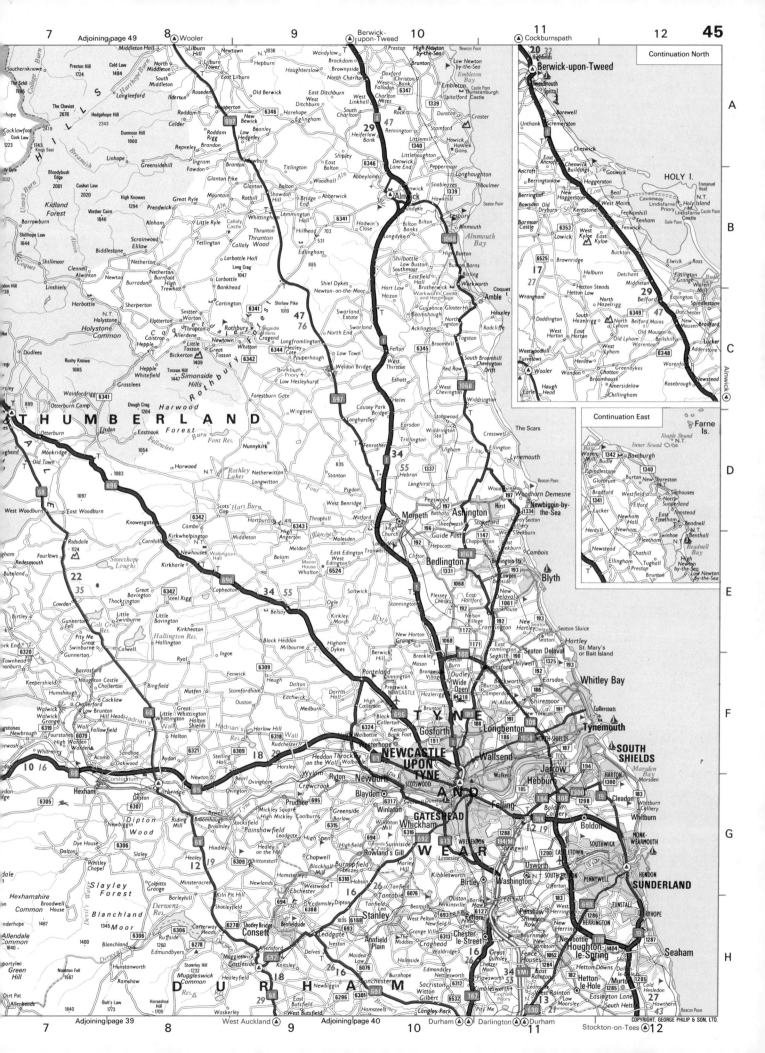

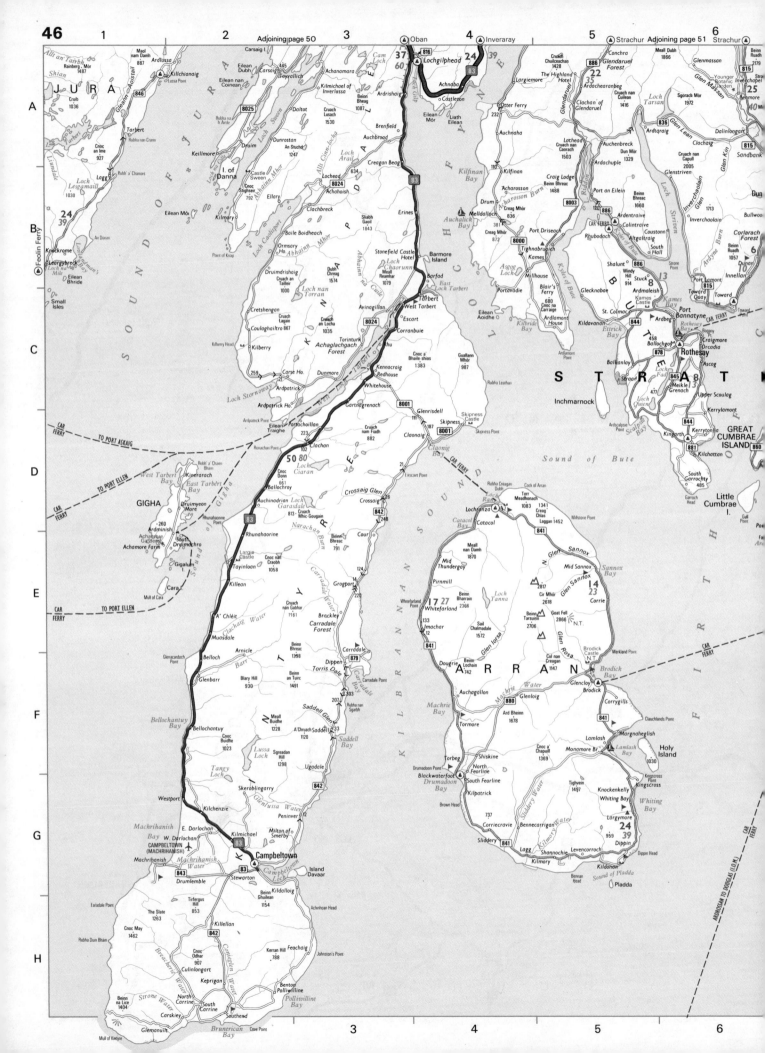

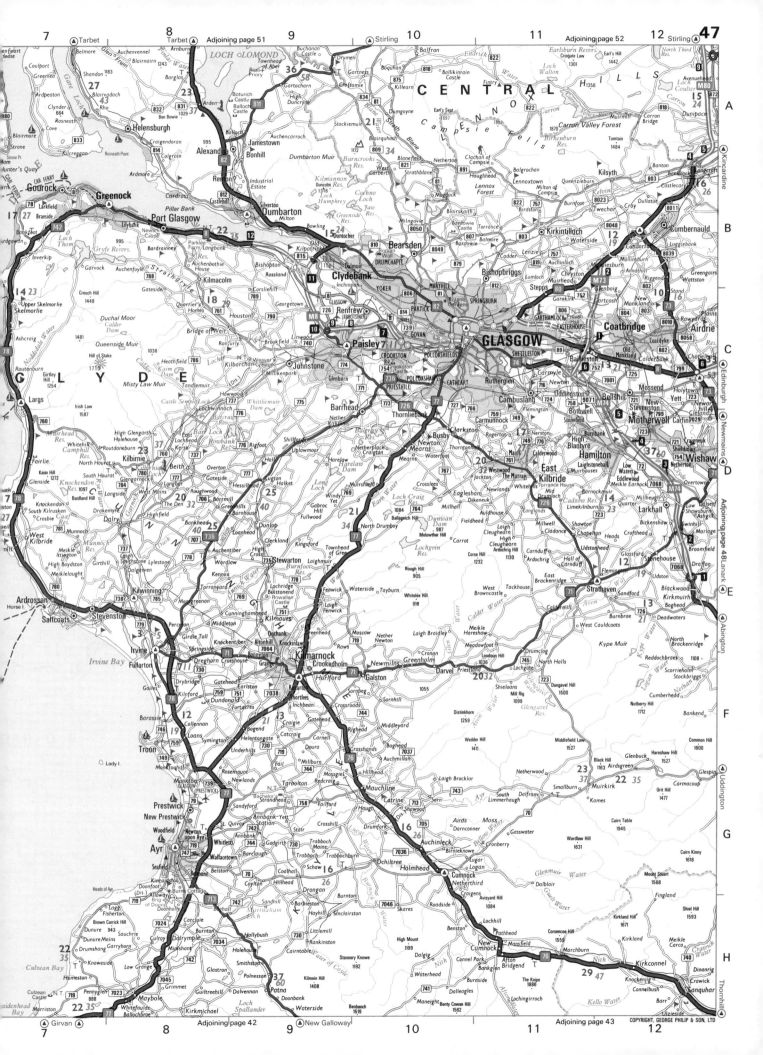

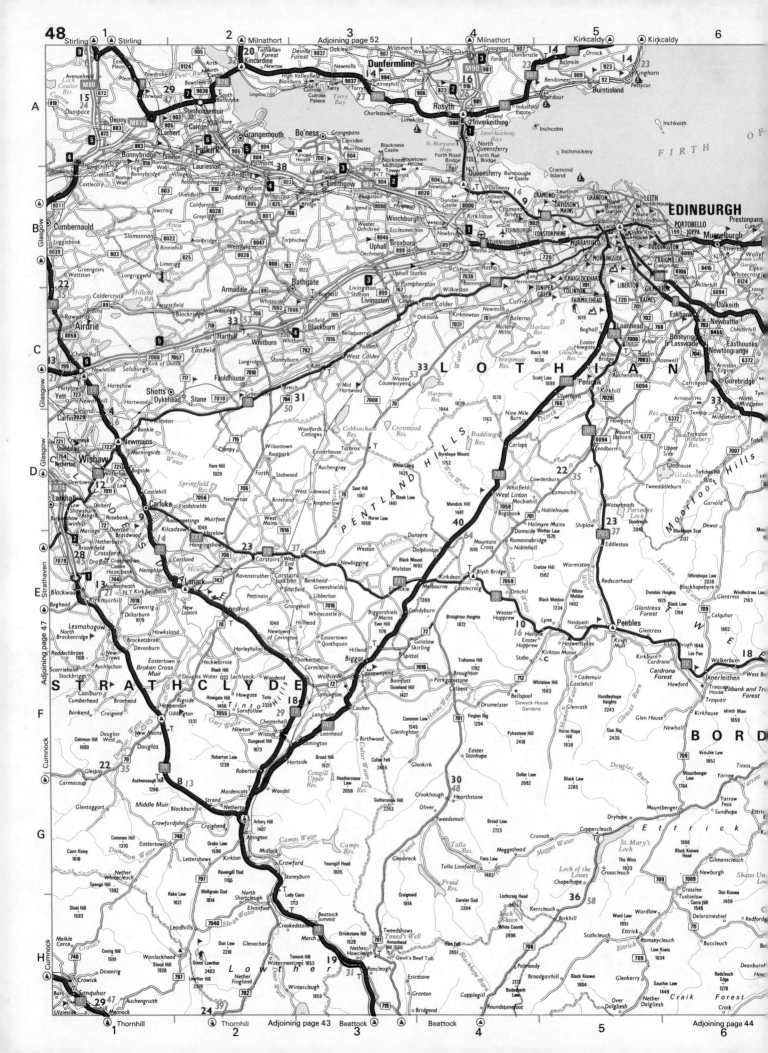

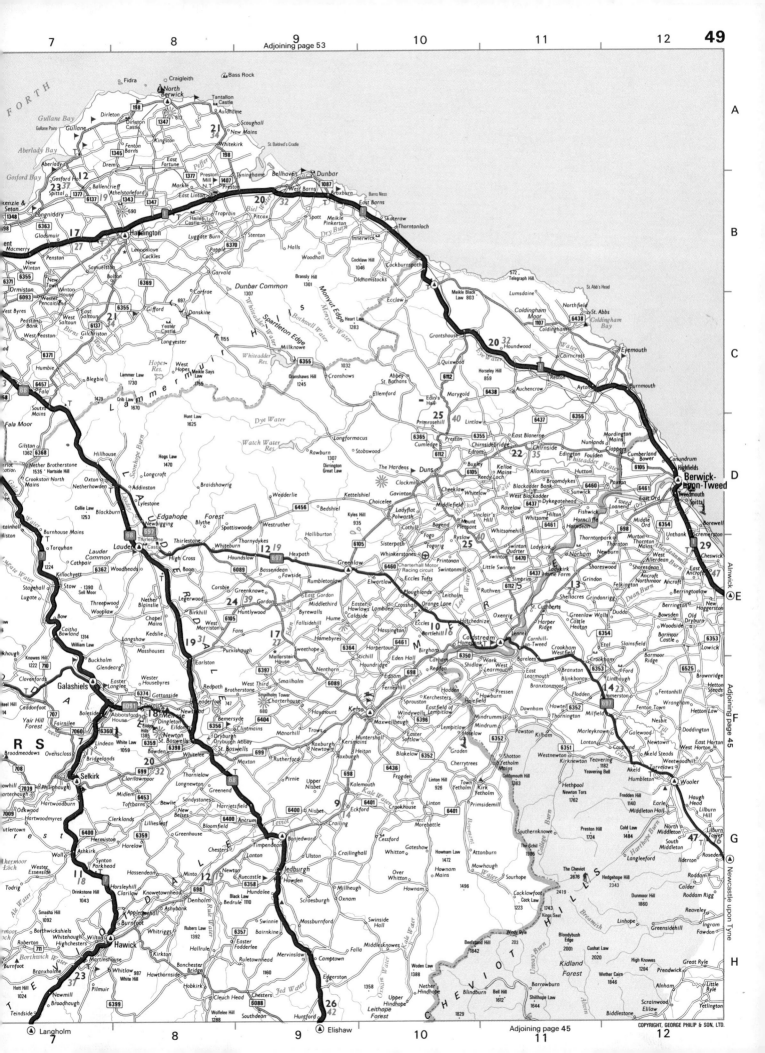

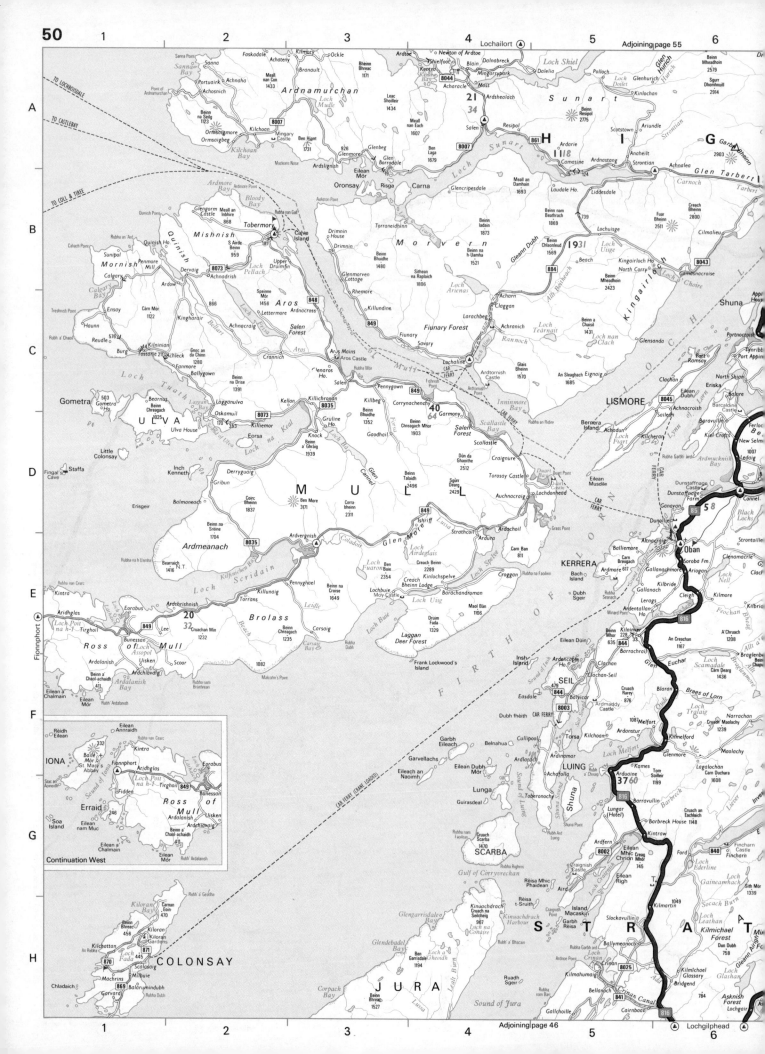

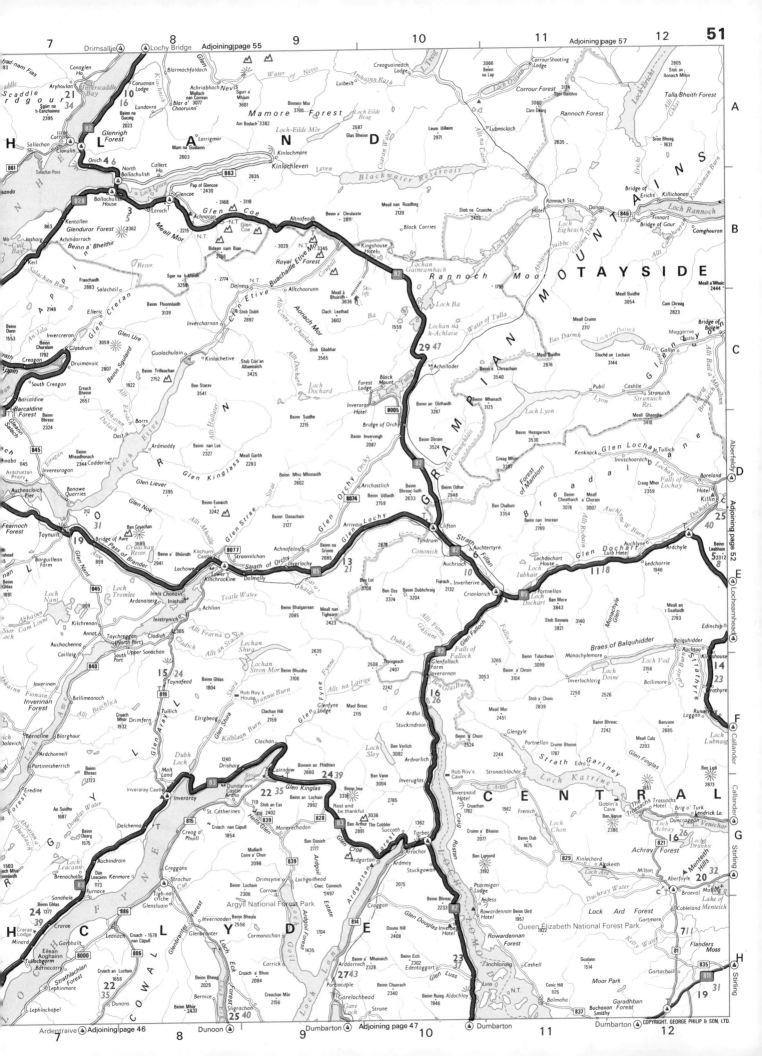

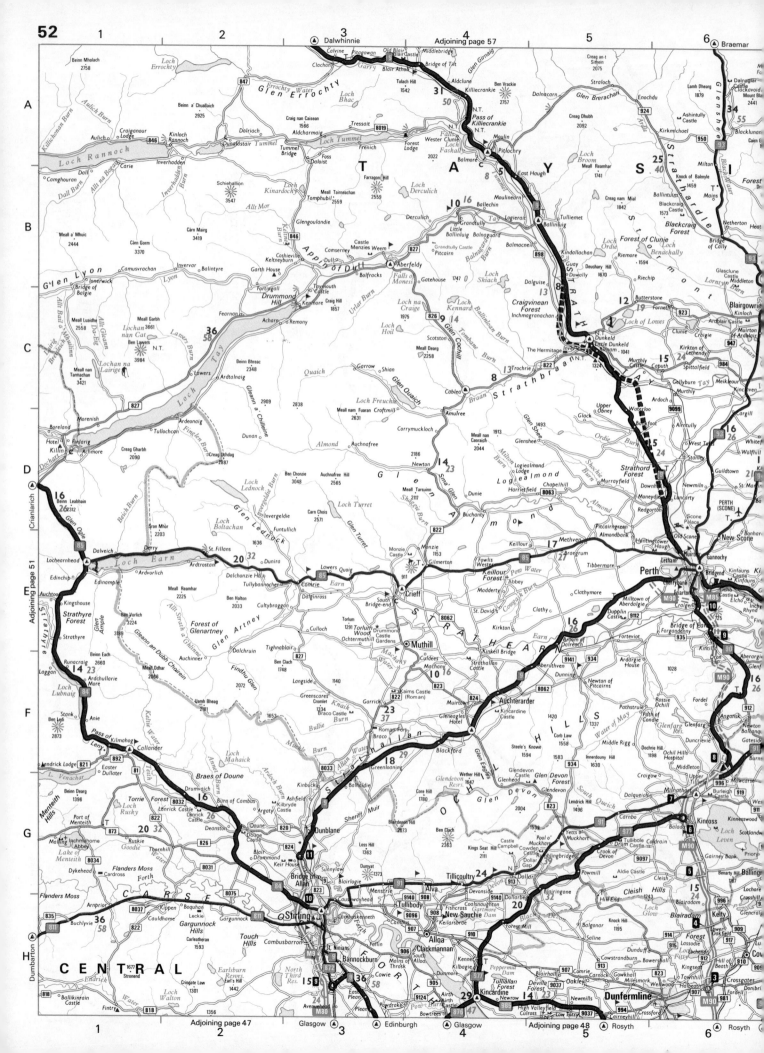

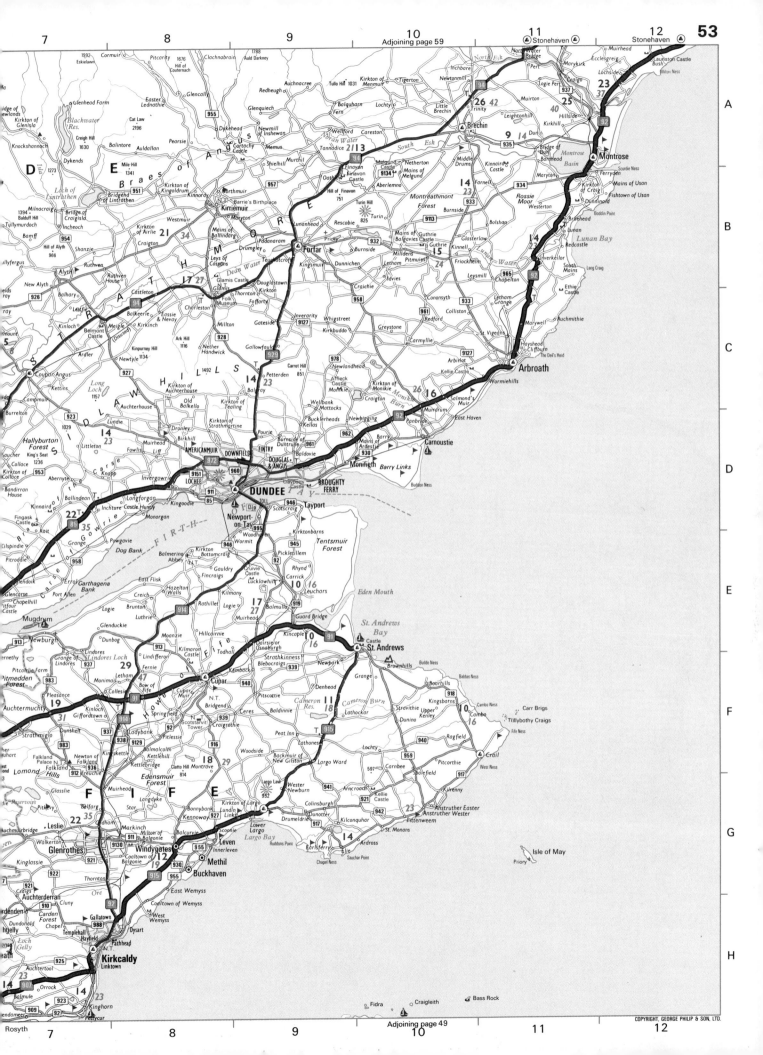

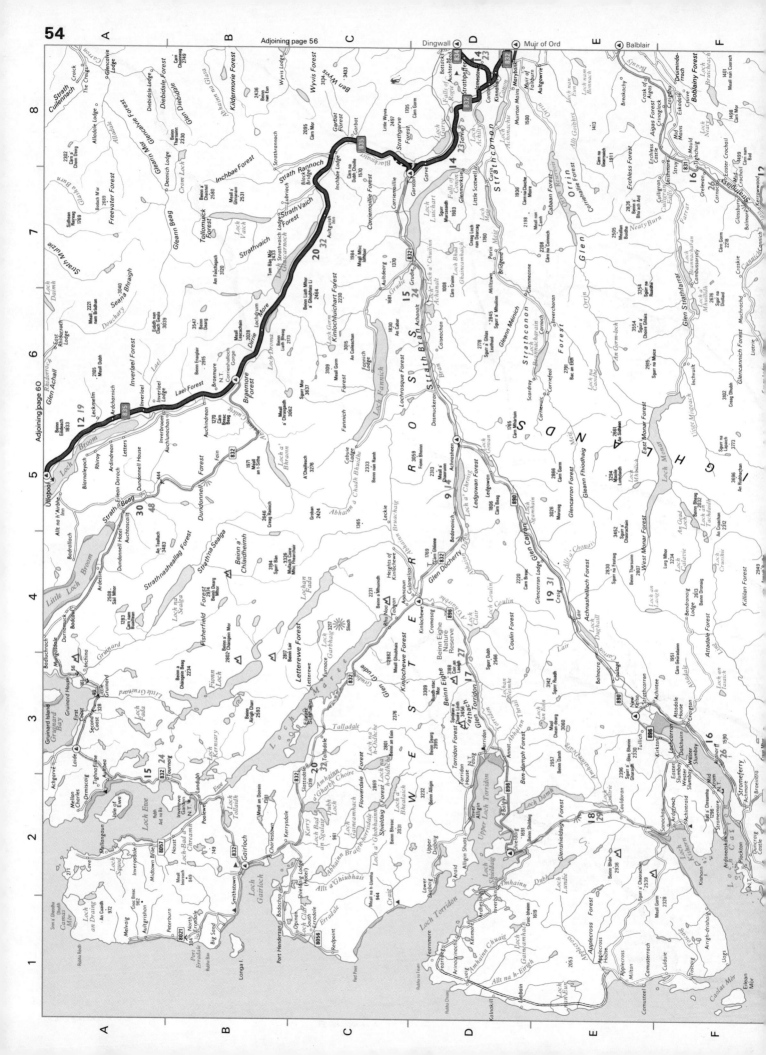

Adjoining page 58
Adjoining page 61
Adjoining page 60 Lairg
Adjoining page 54

NORTH SEA

MORAY FIRTH

GRAMPIAN

Keith · Rhynie · Keith

Lossiemouth · Branderburgh · Stotfield

Elgin · New Elgin · Bishopmill

Forres · Nairn

Inverness (DALCROSS)

Dornoch · Bonar Bridge · The Mound

Cromarty · Invergordon · Tain

Dingwall · Beauly · Muir of Ord

EASTER ROSS

BLACK ISLE

CROMARTY

The Aird

STRATHDEARN

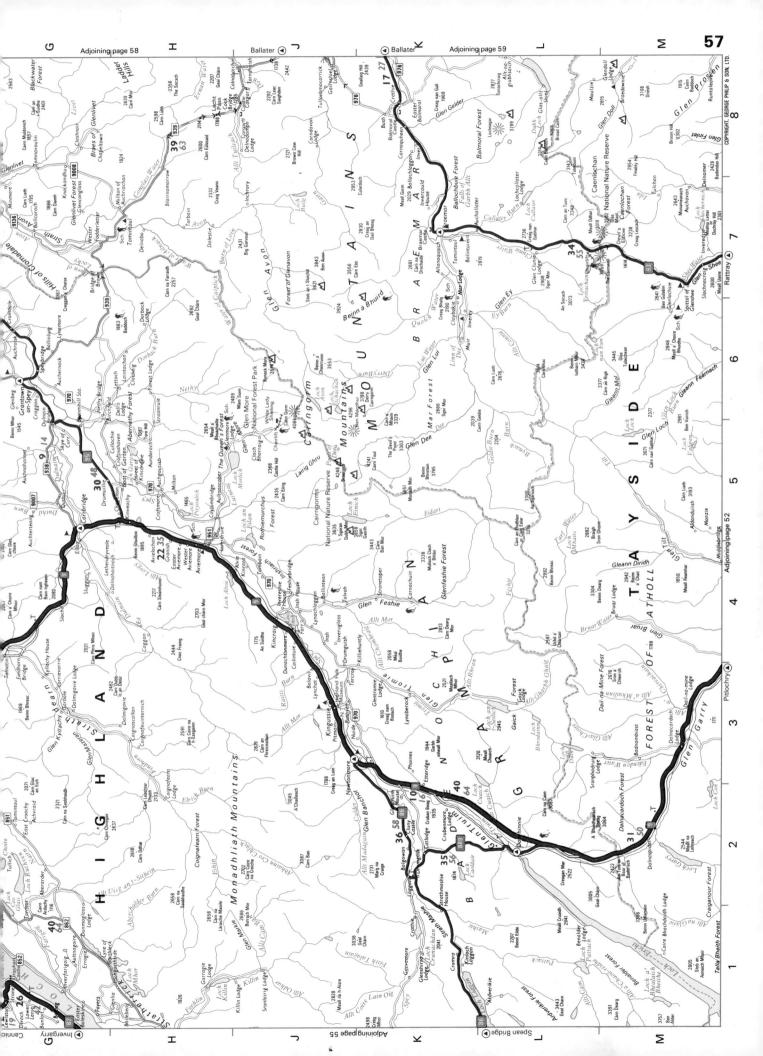

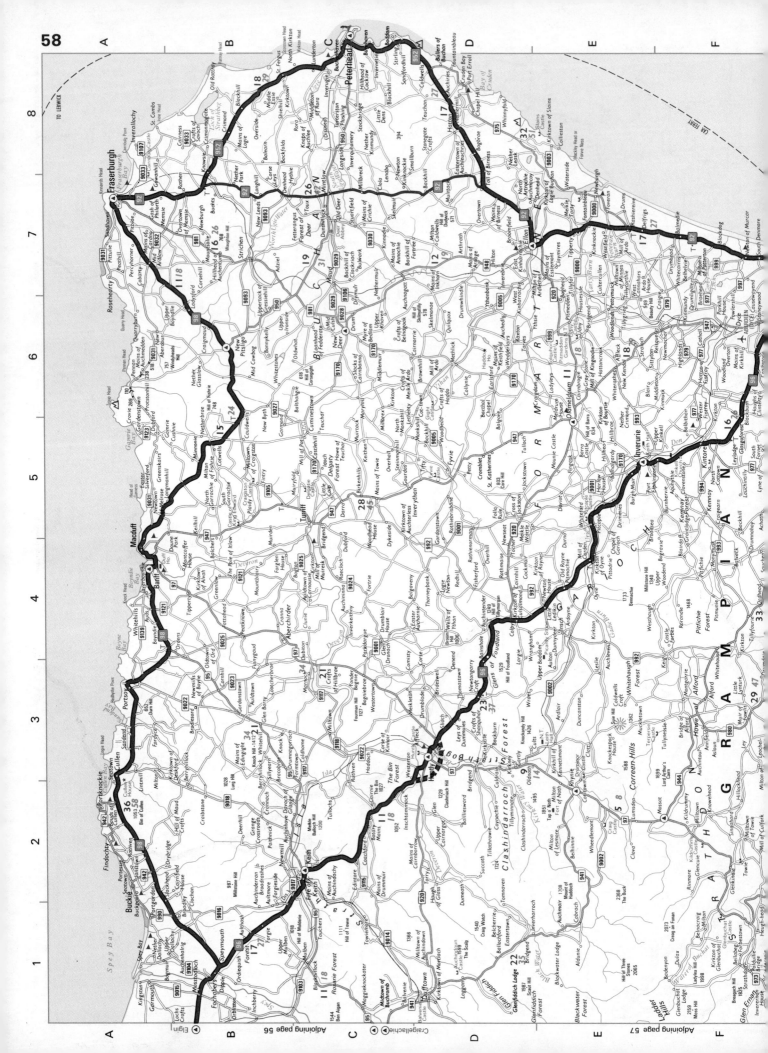

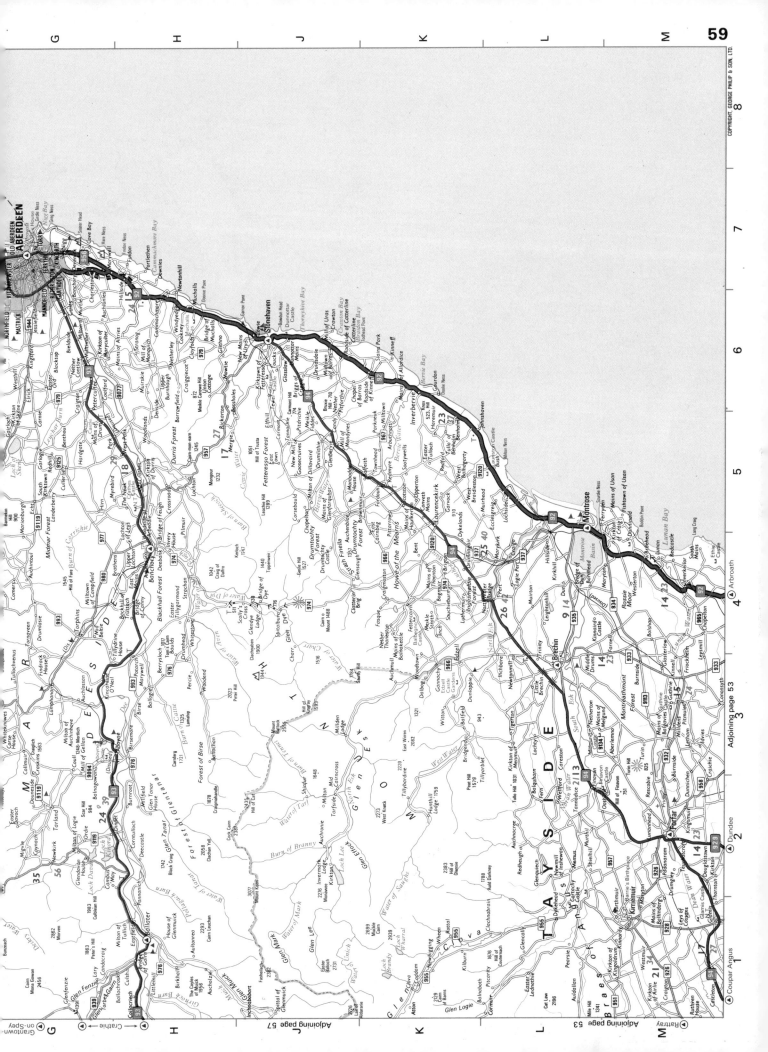

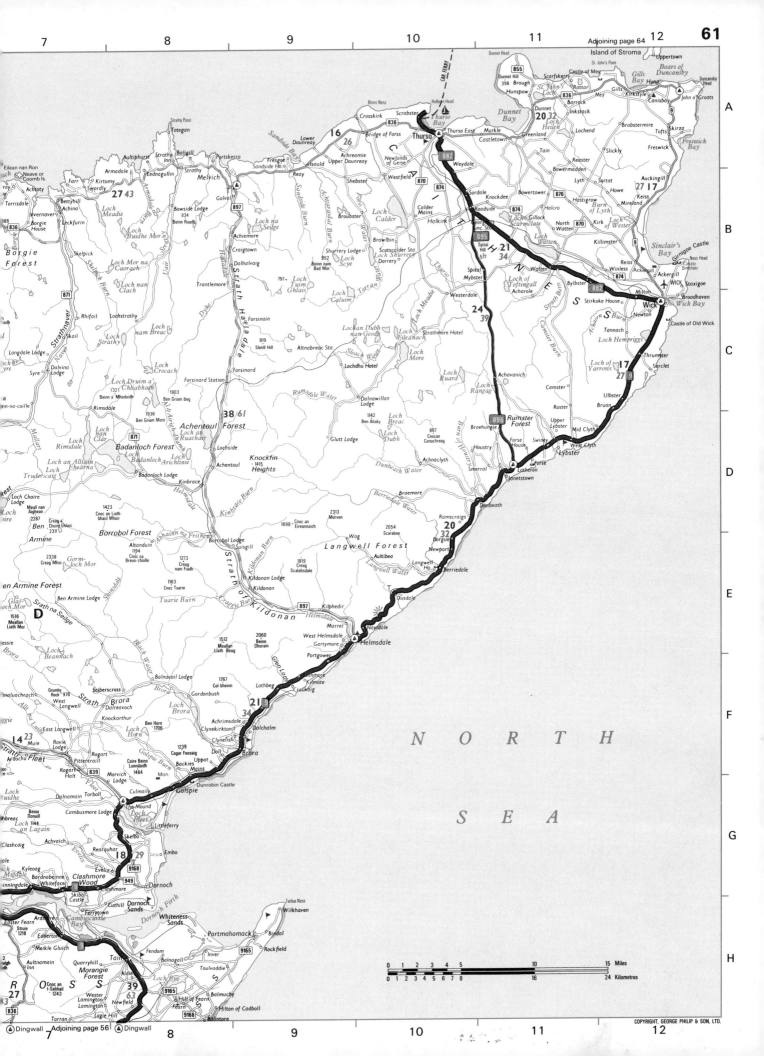

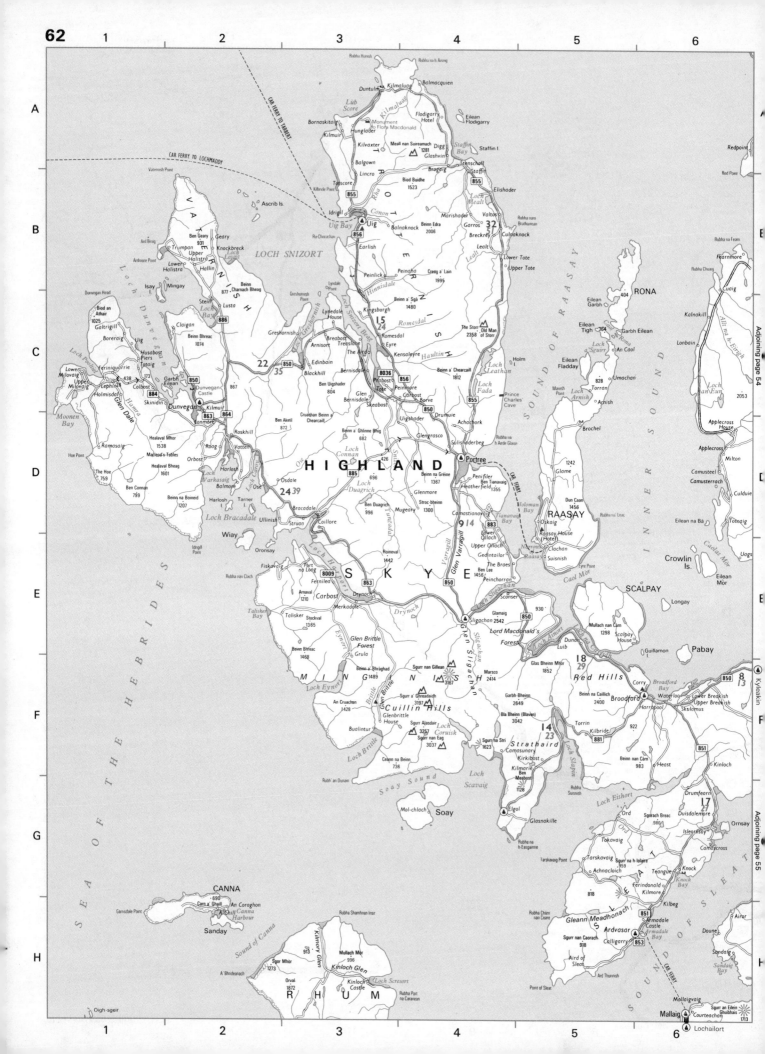

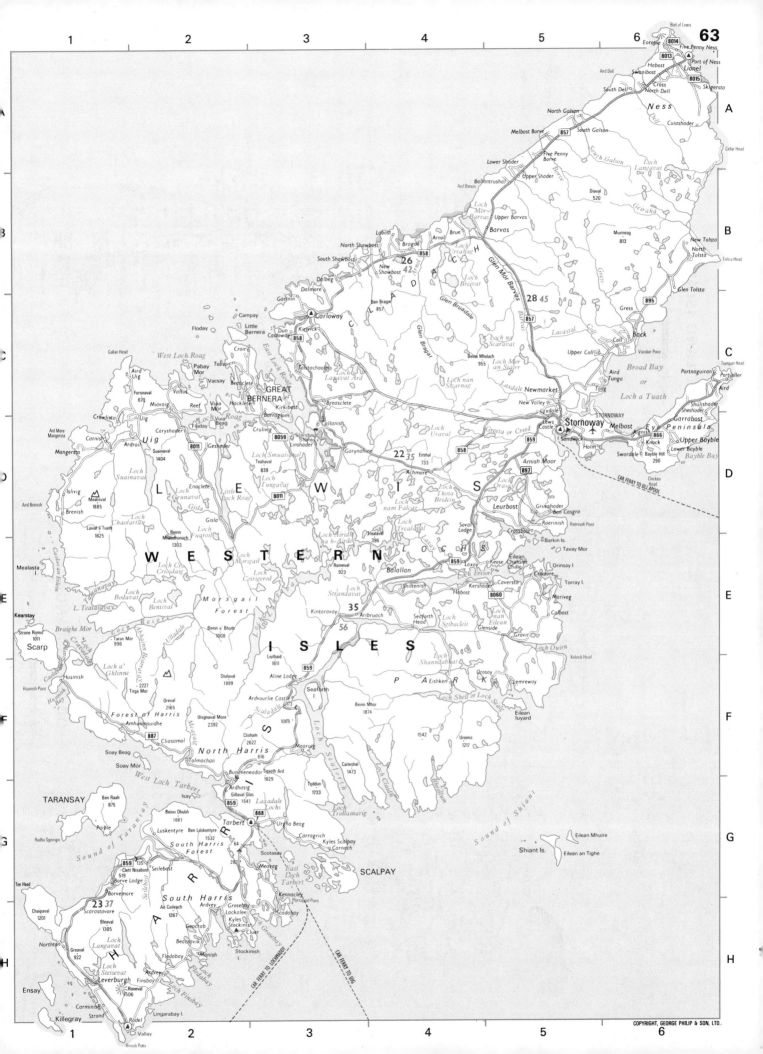

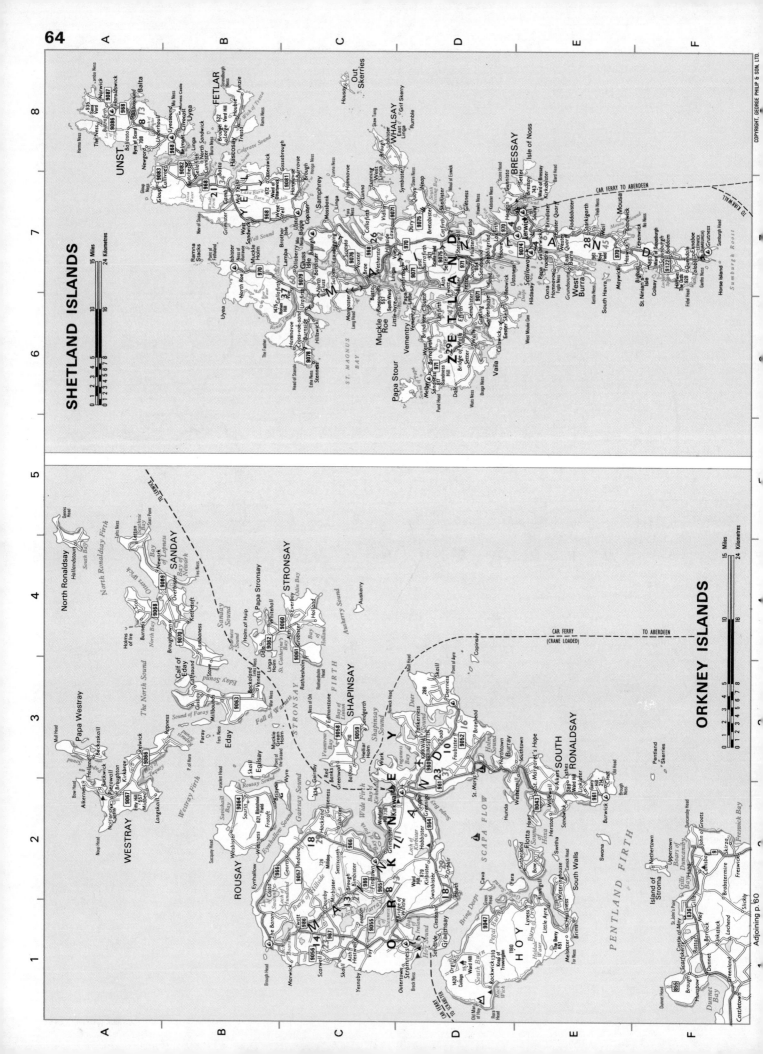

SHETLAND ISLANDS

ORKNEY ISLANDS

Adjoining p. 60

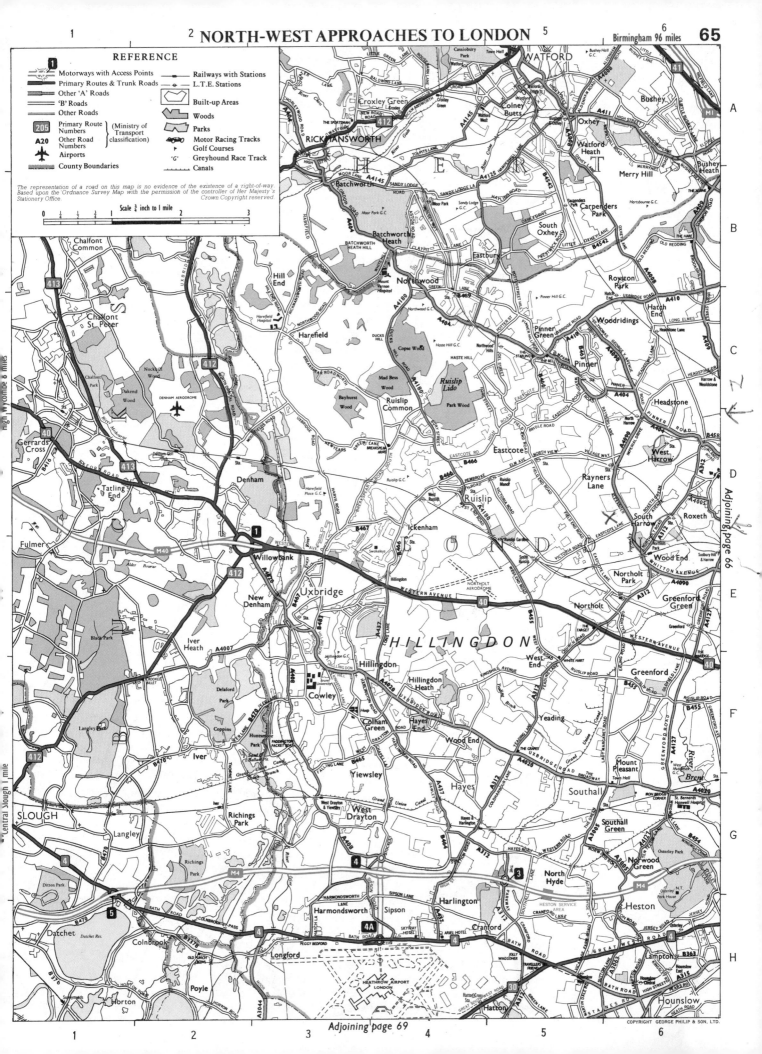

St. Albans 7 miles

Peterborough 69 miles

Hatfield 8 miles

Adjoining page 65

Adjoining page 69

Adjoining page 70

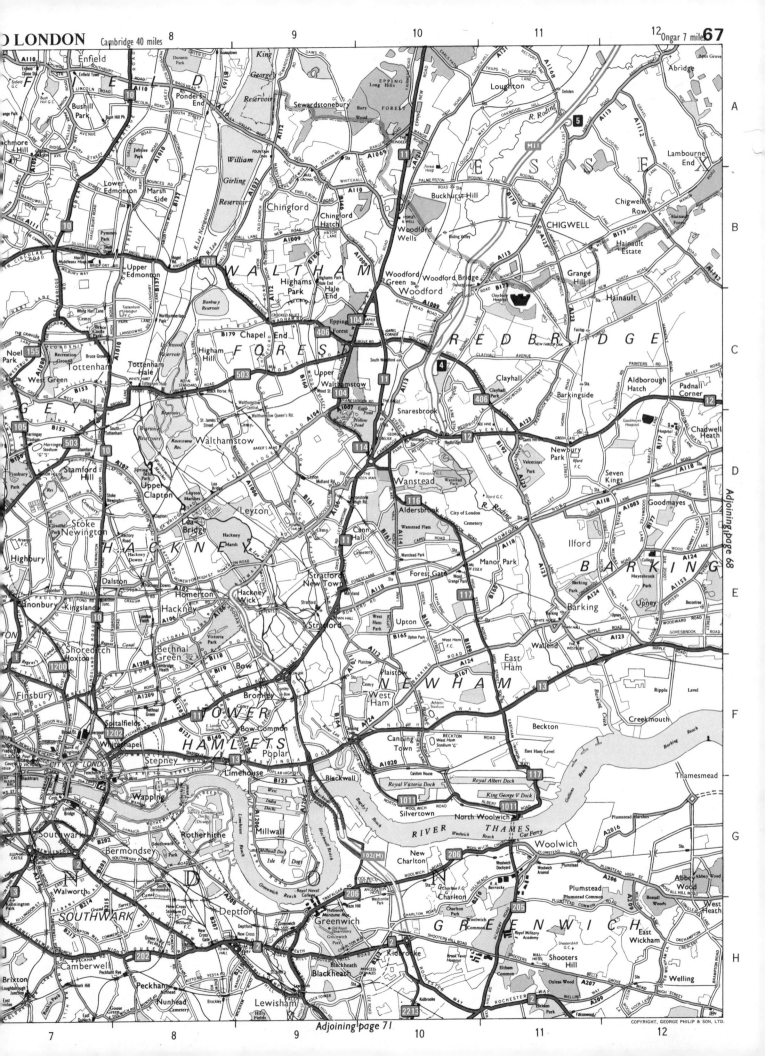

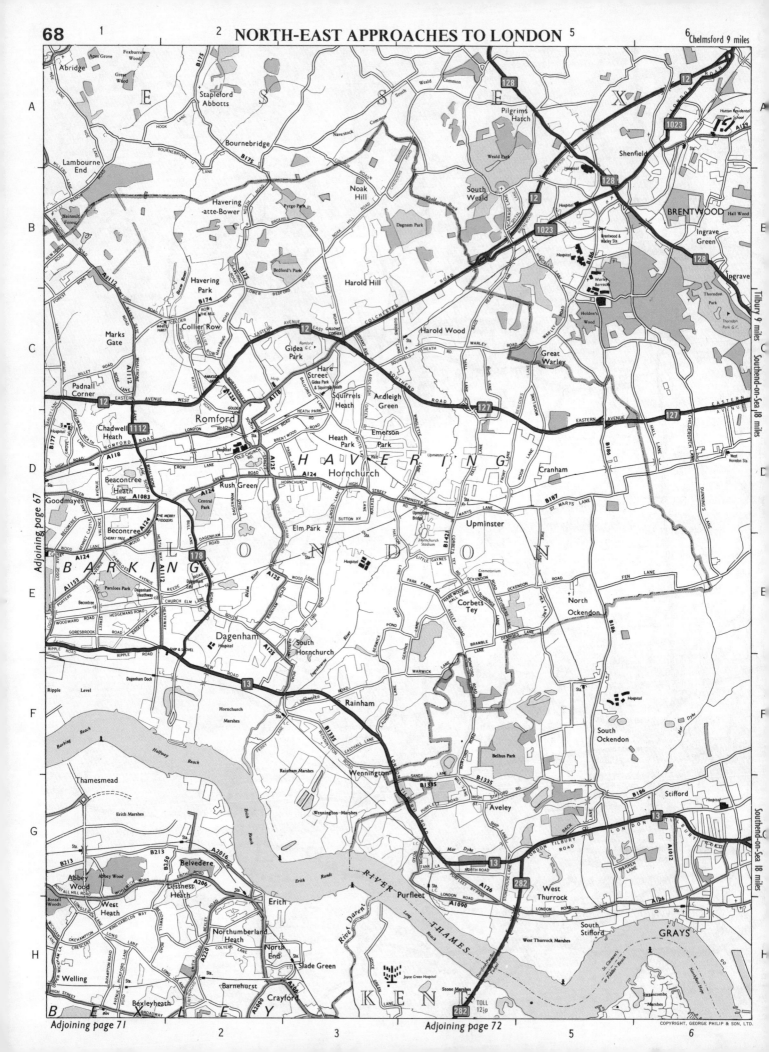

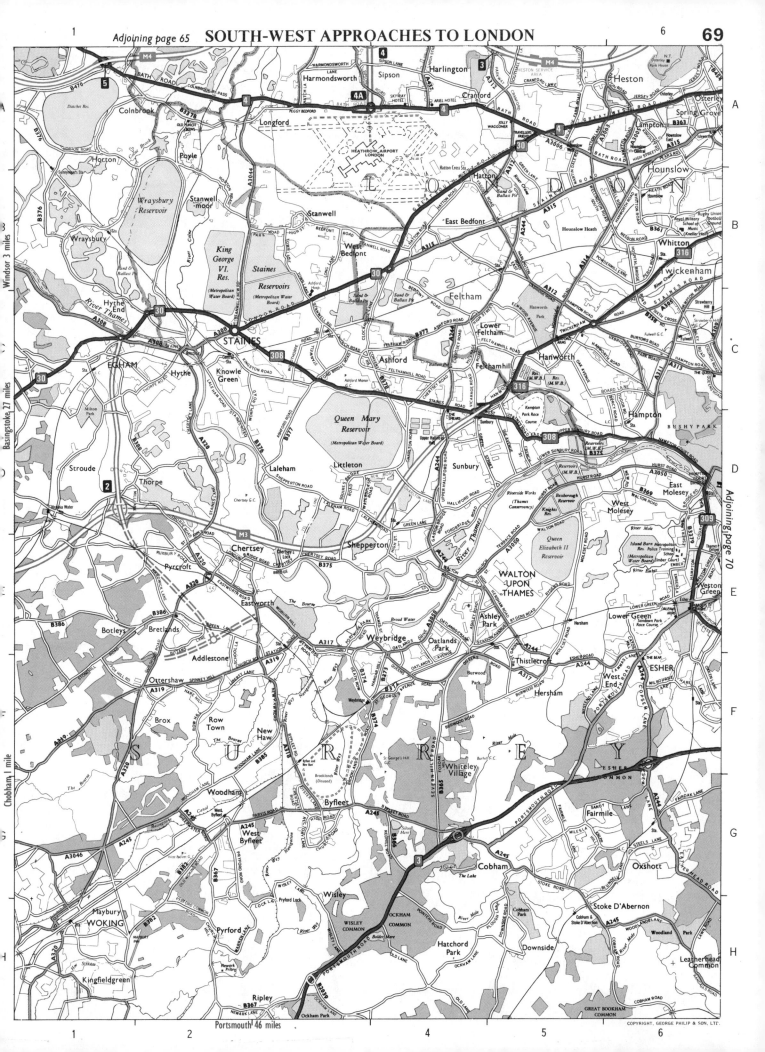

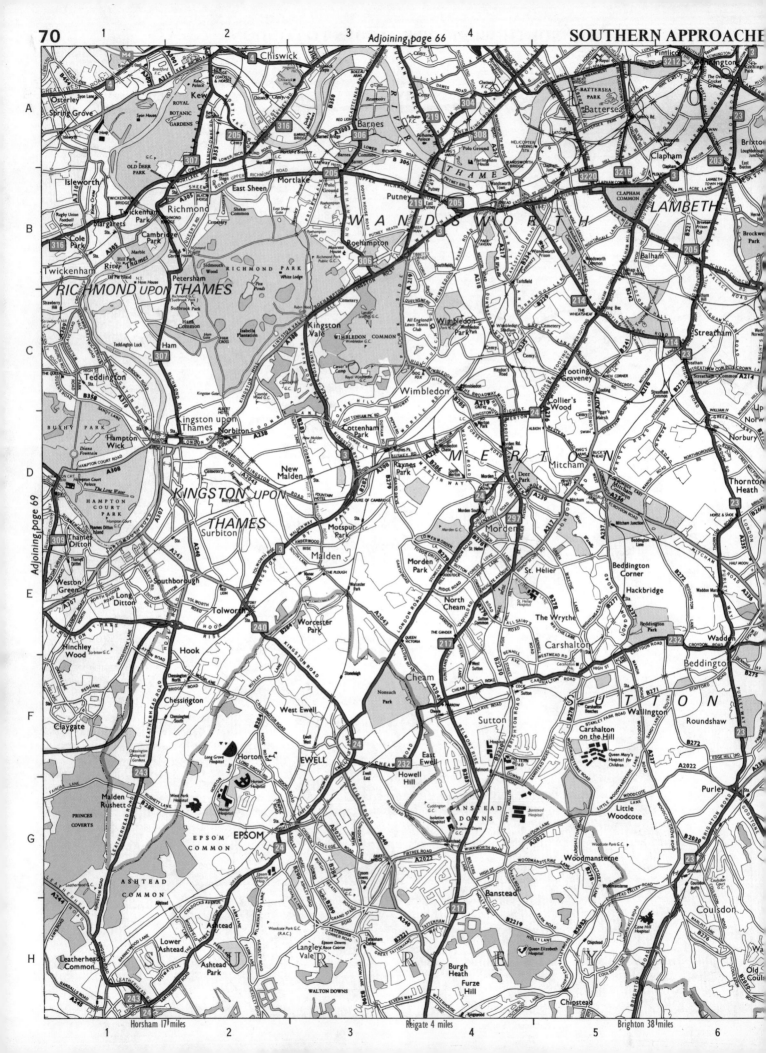

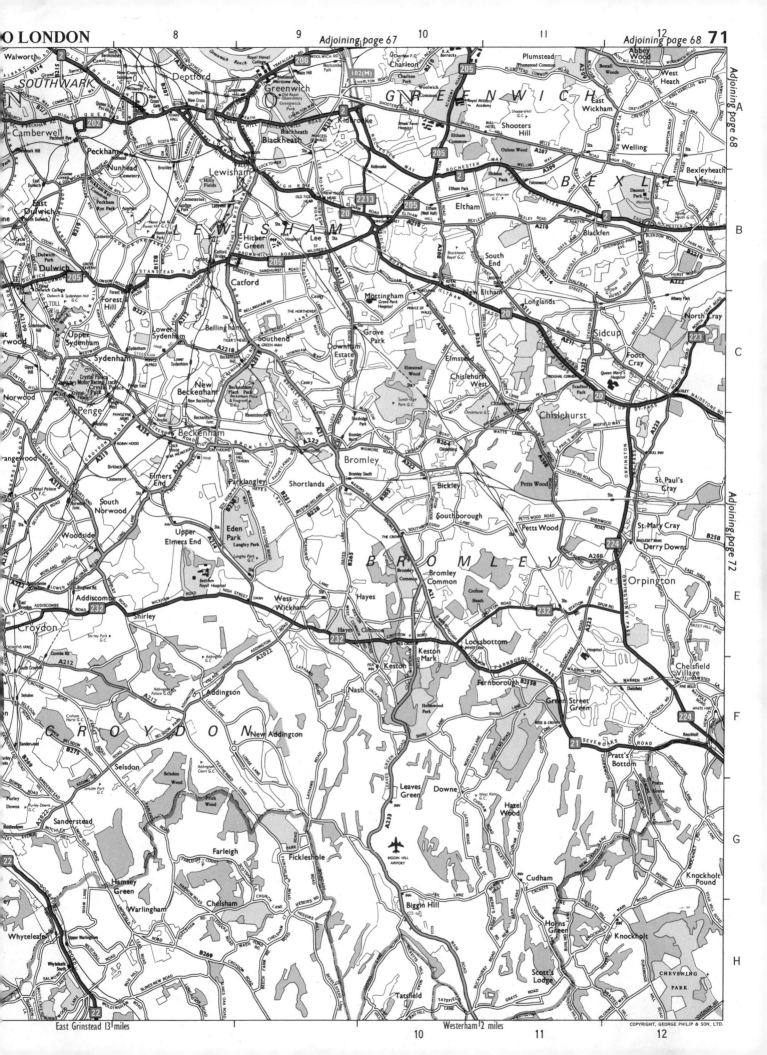

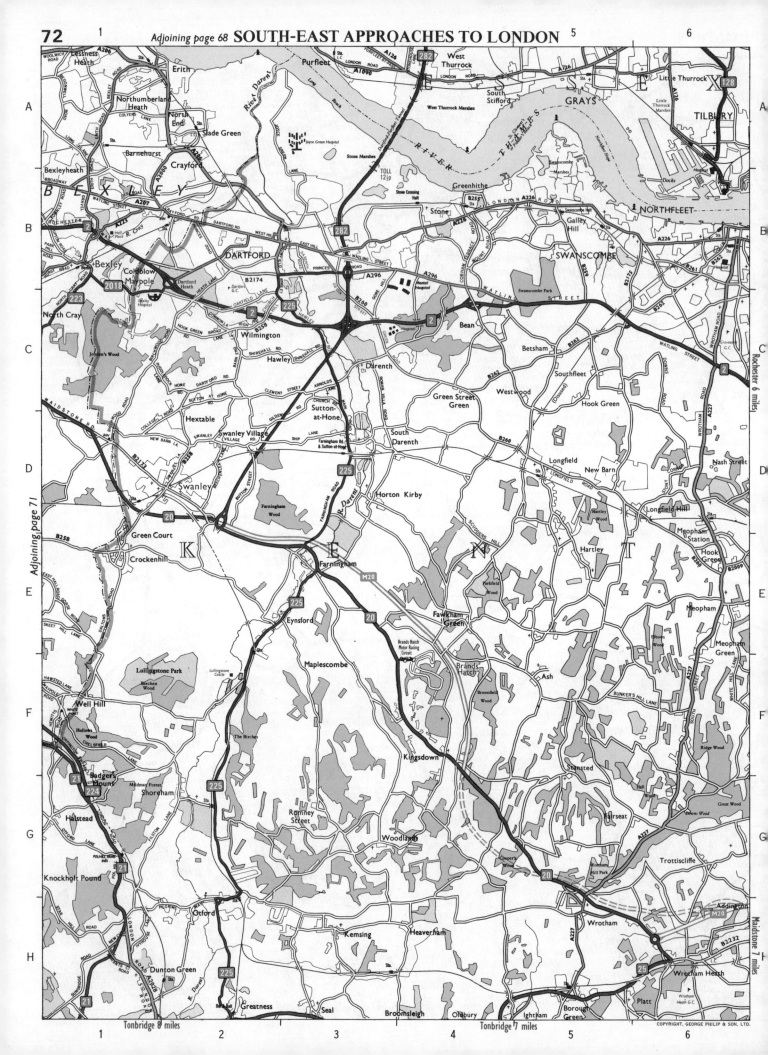

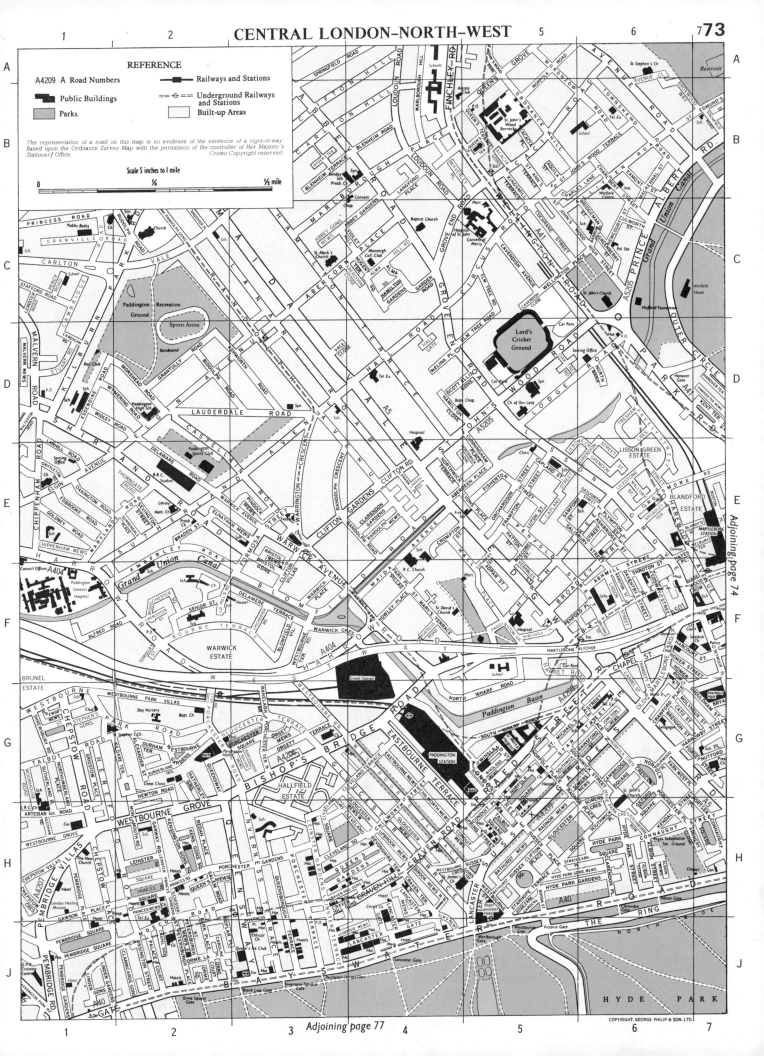

Adjoining page 74

Adjoining page 77

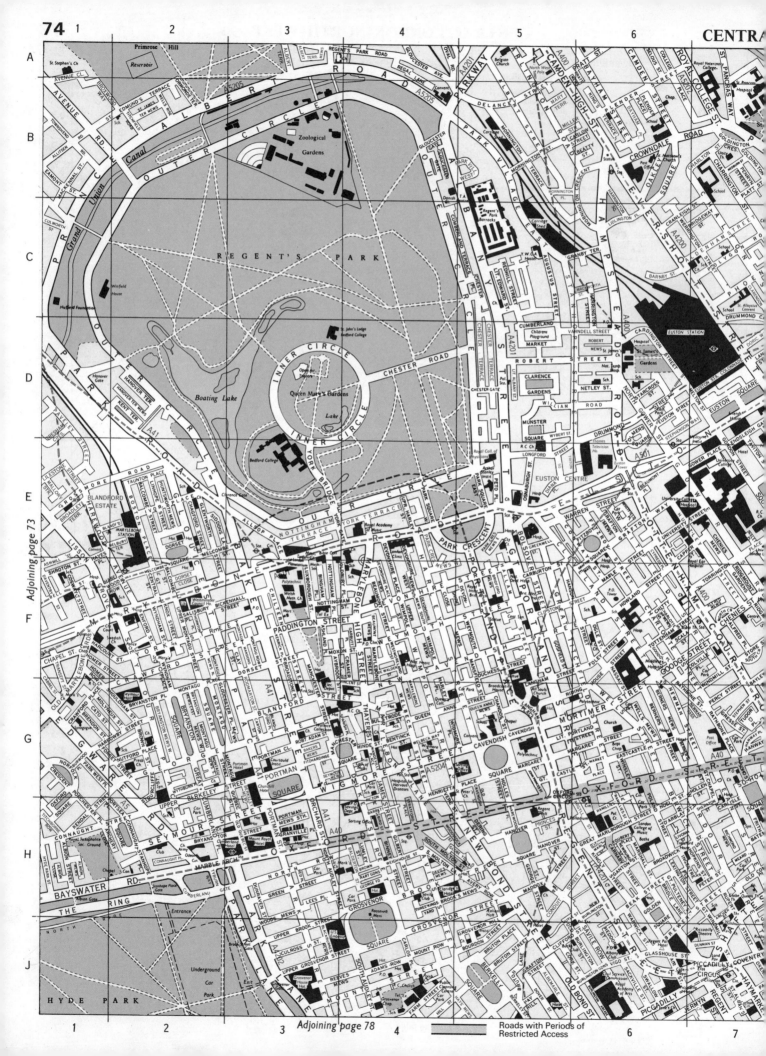

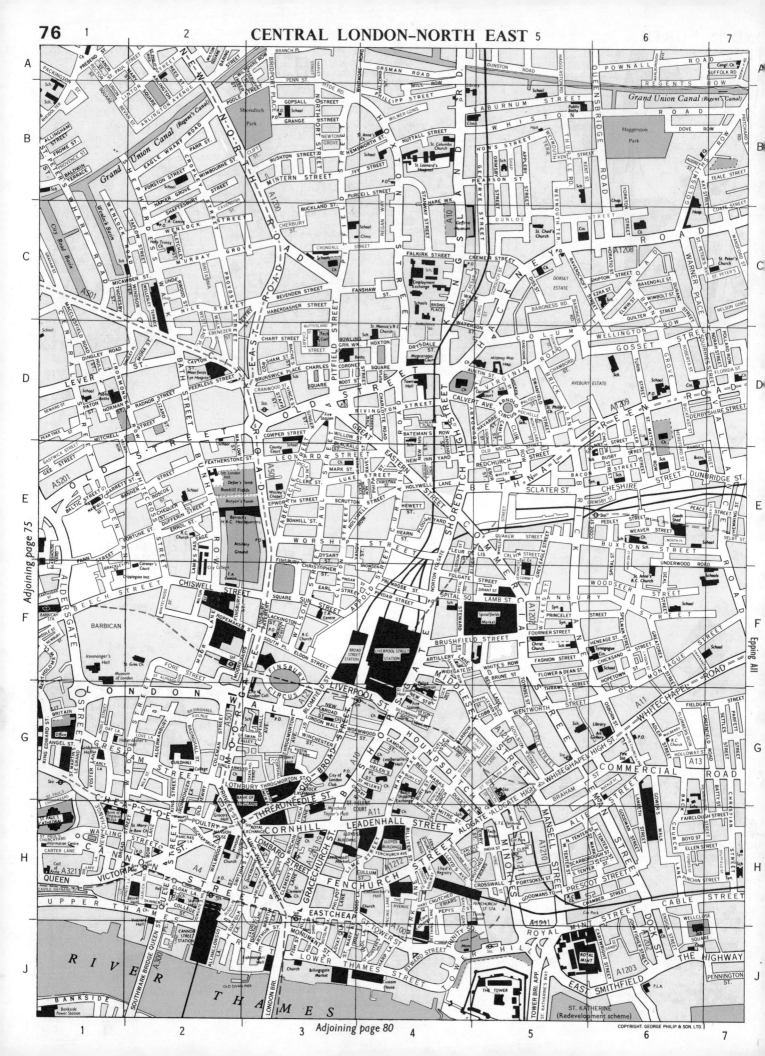

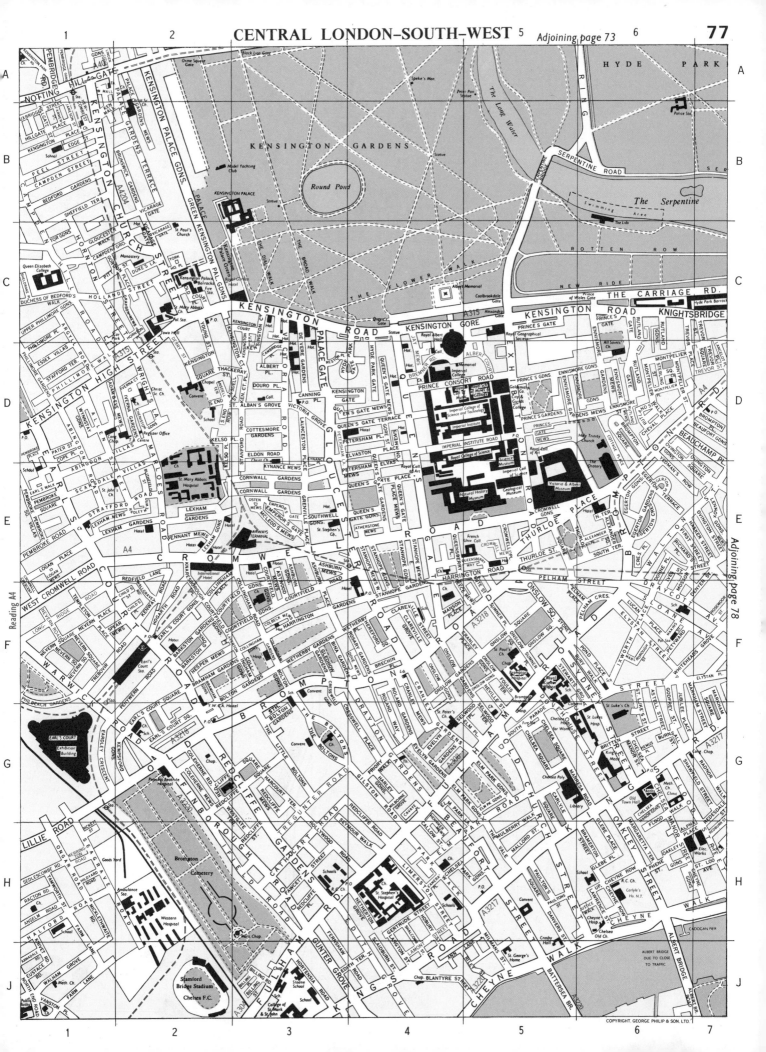

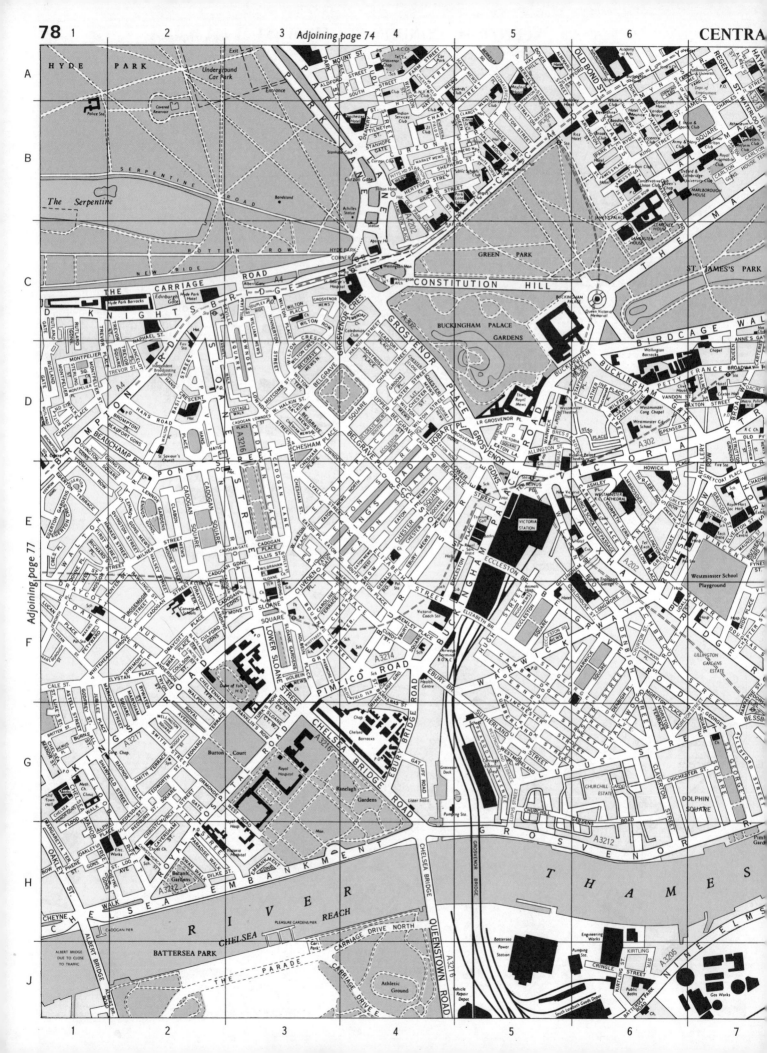

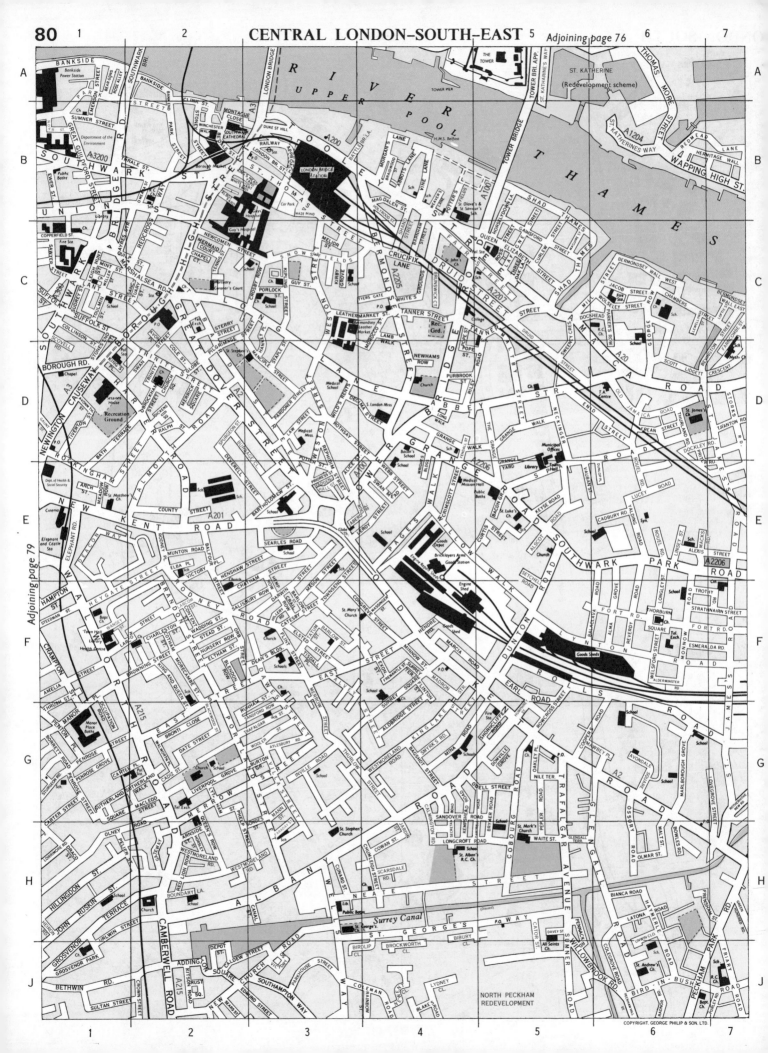

Feet – Metres

Feet	Metres or Feet	Metres
3·281	1	0·305
6·562	2	0·610
9·843	3	0·914
13·123	4	1·219
16·404	5	1·524
19·685	6	1·829
22·966	7	2·134
26·247	8	2·438
29·528	9	2·743
32·808	10	3·048
65·617	20	6·096
82·021	25	7·620
164·042	50	15·240
328·048	100	30·480

Miles – Kilometres

Miles	Km or Miles	Km
0·621	1	1·609
1·243	2	3·219
1·864	3	4·828
2·486	4	6·437
3·107	5	8·047
3·728	6	9·656
4·350	7	11·265
4·971	8	12·875
5·592	9	14·484
6·214	10	16·093
15·534	25	40·234
31·069	50	80·467
46·603	75	120·701
62·137	100	160·934

Pounds – Kilogrammes

Pounds	Kg or Pounds	Kg
2·205	1	0·454
4·409	2	0·907
6·614	3	1·361
8·819	4	1·814
11·023	5	2·268
13·228	6	2·722
15·432	7	3·175
17·637	8	3·629
19·842	9	4·082
22·046	10	4·536
44·093	20	9·072
55·116	25	11·340
110·231	50	22·680
220·462	100	45·359

Gallons – Litres

Gallons	Litres or Gallons	Litres
0·220	1	4·546
0·440	2	9·092
0·660	3	13·638
0·880	4	18·184
1·100	5	22·730
1·320	6	27·276
1·540	7	31·822
1·760	8	36·368
1·980	9	40·914
2·200	10	45·460
4·400	20	90·919
5·500	25	113·649
10·999	50	227·298
21·998	100	454·596

Tyre Pressure

Pounds per sq. inch		Kilogrammes per sq. cm.	Pounds per sq. inch		Kilogrammes per sq. cm.
14	=	0·984	24	=	1·687
15	=	1·055	25	=	1·758
16	=	1·125	26	=	1·828
17	=	1·195	27	=	1·898
18	=	1·266	28	=	1·969
19	=	1·336	29	=	2·039
20	=	1·406	30	=	2·109
21	=	1·476	35	=	2·461
22	=	1·547	40	=	2·812
23	=	1·617	45	=	3·164

Petrol Consumption

Miles per gallon		Kilometres per litre	Miles per gallon		Kilometres per litre
10	=	3·5	20	=	7·1
11	=	3·9	21	=	7·4
12	=	4·2	22	=	7·8
13	=	4·6	23	=	8·1
14	=	5·0	24	=	8·5
15	=	5·3	25	=	8·8
16	=	5·7	30	=	10·6
17	=	6·0	35	=	12·4
18	=	6·4	40	=	14·2
19	=	6·7	45	=	15·9

Temperature

Centigrade		Fahrenheit	Centigrade		Fahrenheit
−5°	=	23°	50°	=	122°
0°	=	32°	55°	=	131°
5°	=	41°	60°	=	140°
10°	=	50°	65°	=	149°
15°	=	59°	70°	=	158°
20°	=	68°	75°	=	167°
25°	=	77°	80°	=	176°
30°	=	86°	85°	=	185°
35°	=	95°	90°	=	194°
40°	=	104°	95°	=	203°
45°	=	113°	100°	=	212°

Gradients

Grade		Percentage	Grade		Percentage
1 in 3	=	33·3%	1 in 14	=	7·1%
1 in 4	=	25·0%	1 in 15	=	6·7%
1 in 5	=	20·0%	1 in 16	=	6·2%
1 in 6	=	16·7%	1 in 17	=	5·9%
1 in 7	=	14·3%	1 in 18	=	5·6%
1 in 8	=	12·5%	1 in 19	=	5·3%
1 in 9	=	11·1%	1 in 20	=	5·0%
1 in 10	=	10·0%	1 in 25	=	4·0%
1 in 11	=	9·1%	1 in 30	=	3·3%
1 in 12	=	8·3%	1 in 35	=	2·9%
1 in 13	=	7·7%	1 in 40	=	2·5%

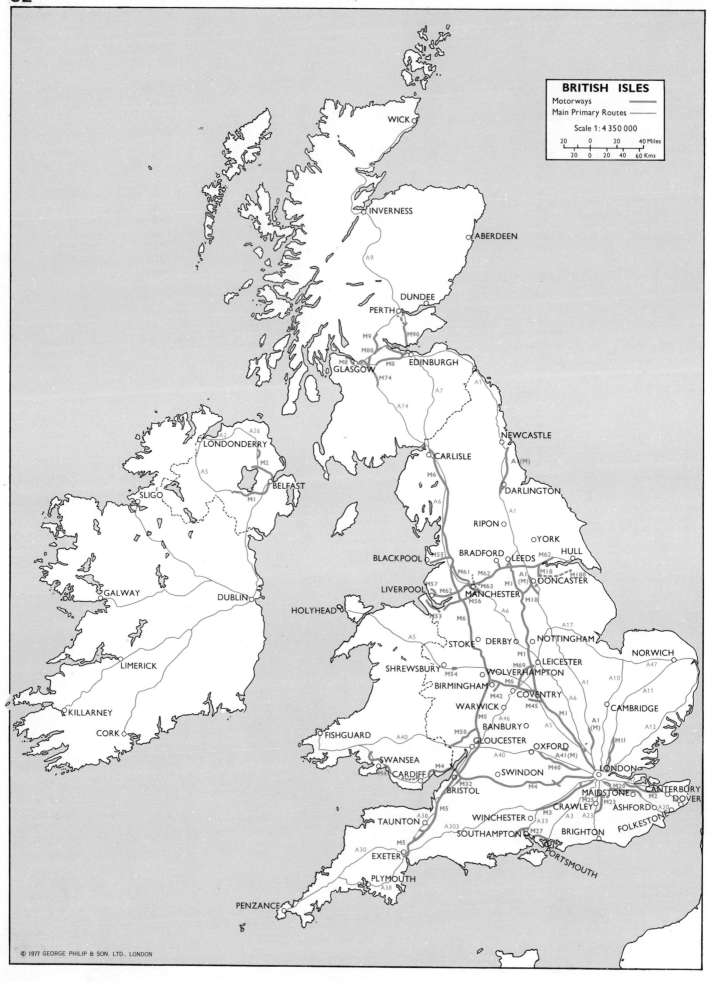

BRITISH ISLES

Motorways
Main Primary Routes

Scale 1:4 350 000

20   0   20   40 Miles
20   0   20   40   60 Kms

WICK

INVERNESS

ABERDEEN

A9

DUNDEE

PERTH

M9   M90
M80
M8   M8
GLASGOW   EDINBURGH
M74
M8

A7   A1
A74

NEWCASTLE

LONDONDERRY   A2   A26

A5   M2

BELFAST

SLIGO   M1

CARLISLE   A(M)

DARLINGTON

M6   A1

A6   RIPON

YORK

BLACKPOOL   M55   BRADFORD   M62   HULL
M61   M62   A1   M18   M180
GALWAY   M57   LEEDS   (M)   DONCASTER
LIVERPOOL   M62   M63   M1
DUBLIN   MANCHESTER   M18
M53   M56   A6

HOLYHEAD

A5   STOKE   DERBY   NOTTINGHAM   A17

LIMERICK   M1   A47
M69   LEICESTER   NORWICH
SHREWSBURY   M54   WOLVERHAMPTON   A10   A11
KILLARNEY   M6   A1
BIRMINGHAM   A6
M42   COVENTRY   CAMBRIDGE
CORK   WARWICK   M45   M1   A12
M5   A46   A1   M11
FISHGUARD   A40   M50   BANBURY   A5   (M)
GLOUCESTER   OXFORD   A41(M)
SWANSEA   A40   SWINDON   M40   LONDON
CARDIFF   M4   M4   M20
M32   MAIDSTONE   CANTERBURY
BRISTOL   M25   M23   ASHFORD   DOVER
M5   CRAWLEY   A20
A38   M3   A3   A23
TAUNTON   WINCHESTER   A33   FOLKESTONE
A303   M27   BRIGHTON
SOUTHAMPTON
M5   PORTSMOUTH
A30   EXETER

PLYMOUTH
A38

PENZANCE

⊢⊣	Overnight accommodation available	☕	Hot meals or snacks available at night
⚒	Repair facilities	⋒	Picnic area
C	Facilities for young children	𝒊	Tourist Information Centre

All motorway service areas are listed below, together with symbols indicating special facilities.

Parking, toilets and fuel are available at all times, and although all have hot meals available during the day some have only vending machine facilities at night.

M1

	Between Access Numbers
Scratchwood	2 – 4
⊢⊣ ☕ ⚒ C	
Toddington	11 – 12
☕ ⚒ C	
Newport Pagnell	14 – 15
⊢⊣ ☕ ⚒ C	
Rothersthorpe	15 – 16
Under construction	
Watford Gap	16 – 17
☕ ⚒ C	
Leicester Forest East	21 – 22
☕ ⚒ C	
Trowell	25 – 26
☕ ⚒ C	
Woodall	30 – 31
☕ ⚒ C	
Woolley Edge	38 – 39
☕ ⚒ C	

M2

	Between Access Numbers
Farthing Corner	4 – 5
☕ ⚒ ⋒	

M3

Fleet	4 – 5
☕ ⚒ C	

M4

Heston	2 – 3
☕ C ⋒	
Membury	14 – 15
☕ ⚒ C	
Leigh Delamere	17 – 18
☕ ⚒ C ⋒	
Aust	Turn off at exit 21
☕ ⚒ C ⋒	

M5

	Between Access Numbers
Exeter	Turn off at exit 30
Under construction	
Taunton Deane	25 – 26
Under construction	
⚒	
Brent Knoll Rest Area	21 – 22
Fuel not available	
Limited facilities	
⋒	
Gordano	Exit 19
☕ ⚒ C (𝒊 *Summer only*)	
Michaelwood	13 – 14
⚒	
Strensham	7 – 8
☕ ⚒	
Frankley	3 – 4
☕ ⚒ C	

M6

Corley	3 – 4
☕ ⚒ C	
Hilton Park	10 – 11
☕ ⚒ C ⋒	
Keele	15 – 16
☕ ⚒ C	
Sandbach	16 – 17
☕ ⚒	
Knutsford	18 – 19
☕ ⚒ C	
Charnock Richard	27 – 28
⊢⊣ ☕ ⚒ C	
Forton	32 – 33
☕ ⚒ C ⋒	
Burton West (*Northbound only*)	
⚒ (𝒊 *Summer only*)	35 – 36
Killington (*Southbound only*)	
⚒ ⋒	36 – 37

M6

	Between Access Numbers
Tebay West (*Northbound only*)	
⊢⊣	38 – 39
Southwaite	41 – 42
☕ ⚒ C 𝒊	

M8

Harthill	4 – 5
☕ ⚒	

M27

Rownhams	2 – 3
Under construction	
Limited facilities	

M61

Anderton	6 – 8
☕ ⚒ C	

M62

Burtonwood	7 – 9
☕ ⚒ C	
Birch	18 – 19
☕ ⚒ C	
Hartshead Moor	25 – 26
☕ ⚒ C	

A1(M)

Washington-Birtley	Tyne & Wear
☕ ⚒ C	

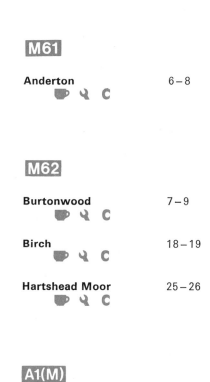

Distance Tables

Kilometres (upper-right triangle) · Miles (lower-left triangle)

	LONDON	Aberdeen	Aberystwyth	Birmingham	Bournemouth	Brighton	Bristol	Cambridge	Cardiff	Carlisle	Chester	Derby	Dover	Edinburgh	Exeter	Fishguard	Fort William	Glasgow	Harwich
LONDON		806	341	179	169	89	183	84	249	484	298	198	117	608	275	422	818	634	114
Aberdeen	501		724	658	903	895	789	742	792	349	571	634	924	198	911	795	254	241	848
Aberystwyth	212	450		193	328	425	206	354	177	375	153	222	459	526	325	90	708	525	460
Birmingham	111	409	120		237	267	132	161	163	309	117	63	296	460	259	283	642	459	267
Bournemouth	105	561	204	147		148	124	251	195	554	351	306	278	705	132	375	887	703	283
Brighton	55	556	264	166	92		217	180	288	573	386	286	130	697	275	468	906	723	203
Bristol	114	490	128	82	77	135		233	71	439	237	195	314	591	121	251	722	589	314
Cambridge	52	461	220	100	156	112	145		290	417	269	155	204	544	351	436	750	566	106
Cardiff	155	492	110	101	121	179	44	180		443	237	225	385	587	192	180	776	608	359
Carlisle	301	217	233	192	344	356	273	259	275		222	304	602	151	571	444	333	150	523
Chester	185	355	95	73	218	240	147	167	147	138		114	415	373	357	243	555	372	375
Derby	123	394	138	39	190	178	121	96	140	189	71		315	436	315	312	637	454	261
Dover	73	574	285	184	173	81	195	127	239	374	258	196		726	391	539	935	752	203
Edinburgh	378	123	327	286	438	433	367	338	365	94	232	271	451		723	616	233	72	650
Exeter	171	566	202	161	82	171	75	218	119	355	222	196	243	449		372	904	721	389
Fishguard	262	494	56	176	233	291	156	271	112	276	151	194	335	383	231		777	594	533
Fort William	508	158	440	399	551	563	480	466	482	207	345	396	581	145	562	483		183	856
Glasgow	394	150	326	285	437	449	366	352	378	93	231	282	467	45	448	369	114		673
Harwich	71	527	286	166	176	126	195	66	223	325	233	162	126	404	242	331	532	418	
Holyhead	261	430	113	153	288	316	211	243	212	212	85	156	334	304	286	169	417	303	309
Hull	168	348	229	143	255	223	226	124	244	155	132	98	251	225	301	285	362	250	181
Inverness	537	105	482	445	594	590	528	497	524	253	387	430	601	159	603	529	66	176	563
Leeds	190	322	173	111	261	251	206	148	212	115	78	74	269	199	268	229	322	210	214
Leicester	98	417	151	39	166	153	112	68	139	208	94	28	171	294	187	207	415	301	134
Lincoln	136	382	189	85	217	191	163	86	190	180	123	51	213	259	238	245	387	273	152
Liverpool	205	334	104	94	235	260	164	184	164	116	17	88	278	210	239	160	323	211	250
Manchester	192	332	133	81	228	247	167	154	172	115	38	58	265	209	242	189	322	210	220
Newcastle	271	230	270	209	348	326	295	231	310	58	175	164	344	107	370	326	257	143	297
Norwich	107	487	267	155	212	162	221	60	237	287	210	139	169	364	277	331	494	380	63
Nottingham	123	388	154	50	189	178	132	84	152	185	87	16	196	265	207	210	392	278	150
Oxford	56	464	157	62	92	99	66	79	107	256	128	98	129	341	139	207	461	340	134
Penzance	282	683	313	268	193	269	186	329	230	466	333	307	354	560	111	342	673	559	353
Plymouth	213	614	244	199	124	213	117	260	161	397	264	238	285	491	42	273	604	490	284
Preston	216	302	144	105	256	271	185	198	190	85	49	100	289	179	266	200	292	180	264
Sheffield	162	358	158	75	227	217	163	124	176	145	78	36	235	235	248	214	352	240	190
Southampton	79	530	202	128	32	60	75	136	119	322	194	164	149	416	111	231	520	415	150
Stranraer	410	235	342	301	453	465	382	368	384	109	247	298	483	133	464	385	199	85	434
Swansea	196	506	76	126	162	220	85	216	41	289	151	165	280	383	160	71	496	382	264
Worcester	114	428	98	26	131	168	60	116	75	211	88	65	187	305	135	155	418	304	182
York	196	309	197	134	273	251	215	157	242	116	102	89	269	186	290	253	323	211	223

Distances in these tables are based on Primary Routes as far as possible and are not necessarily the shortest distances between any two towns.

	Inverness	Leeds	Leicester	Lincoln	Liverpool	Manchester	Newcastle	Norwich	Nottingham	Oxford	Penzance	Plymouth	Preston	Sheffield	Southampton	Stranraer	Swansea	Worcester	York
LONDON	864	306	158	219	330	309	436	172	198	90	454	343	348	261	127	660	315	183	315
Aberdeen	169	518	671	615	538	534	370	784	624	747	1099	988	486	576	853	378	814	689	497
Aberystwyth	776	278	243	304	167	214	435	430	248	253	504	393	232	254	325	550	122	158	317
Birmingham	716	179	63	137	151	130	336	249	80	100	431	320	169	121	206	484	203	42	216
Bournemouth	956	420	267	349	378	367	560	341	304	148	311	200	412	365	51	729	261	211	439
Brighton	950	404	246	307	418	398	525	261	286	159	433	343	436	349	97	748	354	270	404
Bristol	850	332	180	262	264	269	475	356	212	106	299	188	298	262	121	615	137	97	346
Cambridge	800	238	109	138	296	248	372	97	135	127	529	418	319	200	219	592	348	187	253
Cardiff	843	341	224	306	264	277	499	381	245	172	370	259	306	283	192	618	66	121	389
Carlisle	407	185	335	290	187	185	93	462	298	412	750	639	137	233	518	175	465	340	187
Chester	623	126	151	198	27	61	282	338	140	206	536	425	79	126	312	398	243	142	164
Derby	692	119	45	82	142	93	264	224	26	158	494	383	161	58	264	480	266	105	143
Dover	967	433	275	343	447	426	554	272	315	208	570	459	465	378	240	777	451	301	433
Edinburgh	256	320	473	417	338	336	172	586	426	549	901	790	288	378	669	214	616	491	299
Exeter	970	431	301	383	385	389	595	446	333	224	179	68	428	399	179	747	257	217	467
Fishguard	851	369	333	394	257	304	525	533	338	333	550	439	322	344	372	620	114	249	407
Fort William	106	518	668	623	520	518	414	795	631	742	1083	972	470	566	837	320	798	673	520
Glasgow	283	338	484	439	340	338	230	612	447	547	900	789	290	386	668	137	615	489	340
Harwich	906	344	216	245	402	354	478	101	241	216	568	457	425	306	241	698	429	293	359
Holyhead	745	262	295	335	151	198	418	481	277	325	639	528	201	262	455	517	304	245	301
Hull	615	90	145	61	196	151	190	240	148	262	663	552	180	103	412	425	433	272	63
Inverness		579	729	673	605	604	428	842	682	816	1159	1049	555	634	925	417	872	747	552
Leeds	358		158	108	119	64	148	277	116	272	613	502	90	58	378	360	369	220	39
Leicester	453	98		82	187	138	301	187	42	119	480	369	206	105	225	510	282	109	174
Lincoln	418	67	51		192	137	245	169	56	201	562	451	185	72	307	465	340	192	124
Liverpool	376	74	116	119		55	253	360	167	251	563	452	50	119	357	362	270	169	158
Manchester	375	40	86	85	34		212	306	119	230	568	457	48	64	325	360	295	164	103
Newcastle	266	92	187	152	157	132		414	254	412	774	663	203	206	518	262	517	378	127
Norwich	523	174	116	105	224	190	257		198	224	626	515	354	241	299	637	439	283	293
Nottingham	424	72	26	35	104	74	158	123		156	512	401	167	64	262	473	283	122	134
Oxford	507	169	74	125	156	143	256	139	97		402	291	272	217	106	587	230	95	291
Penzance	720	381	298	349	350	353	481	389	318	250		126	597	560	357	925	436	396	645
Plymouth	652	312	229	280	281	284	412	320	249	181	78		486	447	246	814	325	285	534
Preston	345	56	128	115	31	30	126	220	104	169	371	302		113	375	312	322	203	126
Sheffield	394	36	65	45	74	40	128	150	40	135	348	278	70		323	490	336	163	90
Southampton	575	235	140	191	222	202	322	186	163	66	222	153	233	201		679	257	193	398
Stranraer	259	224	317	289	225	224	163	396	294	365	575	506	194	254	422		641	515	362
Swansea	542	229	175	211	168	183	321	273	176	143	271	202	200	209	160	398		161	418
Worcester	464	137	68	119	105	102	235	176	76	59	246	177	126	101	120	320	100		257
York	343	24	108	77	98	64	79	182	83	181	401	332	78	56	247	225	260	160	

National Tourist Offices

British Tourist Office
64 St James's Street
London
SW1A 1NF
☎ 01–629 9191

Isle of Man
Isle of Man Tourist Board
13 Victoria Street
Douglas, Isle of Man
☎ Douglas (0624) 4323

England
English Tourist Board
4 Grosvenor Gardens
London SW1 0DU
☎ 01–730 3400

Northern Ireland
Northern Ireland Tourist Board
River House, 48 High Street
Belfast BT1 2DS
☎ Belfast (0232) 31221

Scotland
Scottish Tourist Board
23 Ravelston Terrace
Edinburgh EH4 3EU
☎ Edinburgh 031–332 2433

Wales
Wales Tourist Board
Welcome House
Llandaff, Cardiff CF5 2YZ
☎ Cardiff (0222) 27281

In addition, there are many other information offices offering localised information both in large towns and tourist areas, but some are open only during the summer season.

All offices are indicated by this sign

Regional Tourist Offices

Northumbria Tourist Board
Prudential Building
140–150 Pilgrim Street
Newcastle upon Tyne NE1 6TQ
☎ Newcastle upon Tyne 28795

East Midlands Tourist Board
Bailgate
Lincoln LN1 3AR
☎ Lincoln 31521

South East England Tourist Board
Cheviot House, 4–6 Monson Road
Tunbridge Wells
Kent TN1 1NH
☎ Tunbridge Wells 33066

Mid-Wales Tourism Council
The Owain Glyndwr Institute
Maengwyn Street
Machynlleth, Powys
☎ Machynlleth 2401

Central Regional Council
Tourist Department
Viewforth
Stirling
☎ 0721 3111

Highlands & Islands Development Board
PO Box 7, Bridge House
Bank Street
Inverness

Cumbria Tourist Board
Ellerthwaite
Windermere
Cumbria

Heart of England Tourist Board
PO Box 15
Worcester WR1 2JT
☎ Worcester 29511

Thames and Chilterns Tourist Board
PO Box 10
8 Market Place, Abingdon
Oxon OX14 3HG
☎ Abingdon (0235) 22711

North Wales Tourism Council
Civic Centre
Colwyn Bay
Clwyd
☎ Colwyn Bay 56881

Dumfries & Galloway Tourist Association
Douglas House
Newton Stewart DG8 6DQ
☎ Newton Stewart 2549

Lothian Regional Council
Department of Recreation
40 Torphichen Street
Edinburgh EH3 8JJ

North West Tourist Board
Last Drop Village
Bromley Cross, Bolton
Lancs BL7 9PZ
☎ Bolton (0204) 591511

East Anglia Tourist Board
14 Museum Street
Ipswich IP1
☎ Ipswich (0473) 21411

London Tourist Board
4 Grosvenor Gardens
London
SW1 0DU
☎ 01–730 0791

South Wales Tourism Council
Darkgate
Carmarthen
Dyfed
☎ Carmarthen 7557

Fife Tourist Authority
High Street
Leven KY8 4QA
☎ Leven 23327

Strathclyde Regional Council
McIver House
Cadogan Street
Glasgow G2 7QG

Yorkshire and Humberside Tourist Board
312 Tadcaster Road
York YO2 2HF
☎ York 67961

West Country Tourist Board
Trinity Court, Southernhay East
Exeter EX1 1QS
☎ Exeter 76351

Southern Tourist Group
Information Centre
Canute Road
Southampton SO1 1FH
☎ 0703 20438

Borders Regional Council
Tourism Regional Office
3 Exchange Street
Jedburgh
☎ Jedburgh 2227

Grampian Regional Council
Woodhill House
Ashgrove Road West
Aberdeen AB9 2LU
☎ 0224 23401

Tayside Regional Council
Tourism Division
Tayside House
Dundee

National Trust Regional Offices

Northern Ireland
The National Trust
Malone House
Barnett Demesne
Belfast BT9 5PU
☎ Belfast 669564

West Midlands
The National Trust
Attingham Park
Nr. Shrewsbury
Shropshire
☎ Upton Magna 202

Northern Home Counties
The National Trust
Hughenden Manor
High Wycombe
Buckinghamshire
☎ High Wycombe 28051

Wessex
The National Trust
Stourhead Estate Office
Stourton, Warminster
Wilts
☎ Bourton, Dorset 224

North West
The National Trust
Broadlands, Borrans Road
Ambleside
Cumbria
☎ Ambleside 3003

East Midlands
The National Trust
Clumber Park
Worksop
Nottinghamshire
☎ Worksop 3509

Eastern
The National Trust
Blickling Estate Office
Aylsham
Norwich NOR 09Y
☎ Aylsham 3471

Devon
The National Trust
Killerton Estate Office
Budlake, Exeter
Devon
☎ Hele 228

North East
The National Trust
Cambo
Morpeth
Northumberland
☎ Scots Gap 234

Severn
The National Trust
35/36 Church Street
Tewkesbury
Gloucestershire
☎ Tewkesbury 292427

Kent and East Sussex
The National Trust
Scotney Castle, Lamberhurst
Tunbridge Wells
Kent TN3 8JN
☎ Lamberhurst 651

Cornwall
The National Trust
The Friaries
Mount Folly, Bodmin
Cornwall
☎ Bodmin 2214

Yorkshire
The National Trust
32 Goodramgate
York
☎ York 29621

South Midlands
The National Trust
22 London Street
Faringdon, Oxon
☎ Faringdon 20371

Surrey and West Sussex
The National Trust
Polesden Lacey
Dorking, Surrey
☎ Bookham 53401

South Wales
The National Trust
Napier House, Spilman Street
Carmarthen, Dyfed
☎ Carmarthen 7813

North Wales
The National Trust
Dinas, Betws-y-Coed
Gwynedd
☎ Betws-y-Coed 312

National Parks

Special information centres have been set up within the National Parks and give detailed information of facilities, walks, etc. These offices are well signposted, but a number are open only during the summer.

Corran – Ardgour A861–A82
7 cars: Frequent service
until 18.45 hours *(dusk in winter)*
Crossing time–6 mins.
☎ Ardgour 243

Cuan B8003–Isle of Luing
5 cars: Service according to demand
No Sunday service
Crossing time–20 mins.
☎ Lochgilphead 2233

Dunoon – Gourock A815–A8
40 cars: Frequent service until
22.00 hours *(19.30 hours in winter)*
Crossing time–20 mins.
☎ Gourock 34567

Hunters Quay – Cloch Pt. A815–A78
24 cars: Hourly service
until 20.30 hours
Crossing time–15 mins.
☎ Dunoon 4452

Kessock – Inverness B9161
22 cars: Frequent service
until 22.30 hours
Crossing time–4 mins.
☎ 0463 33270

Kylesku A894
6 cars: Frequent service
until 21.00 hours *(dusk in winter)*
Crossing time–5 mins.
☎ Brora 301 or Kylestrome 222

Renfrew – Yoker A741–A814
15 cars: Continuous service
Crossing time–5 mins.
☎ 041–221 8733

Bodinnick – Fowey B3269
6 cars: Continuous service
until 20.50 hours *(dusk in winter)*
Crossing time–5 mins.
☎ Polruan 453

Dartmouth Floating Bridge A379
18 cars: Frequent service
until 22.45 hours
Crossing time–5 mins.
☎ 080–43 3351

Dartmouth Lower Ferry B3205
8 cars: Frequent service until
23.30 hours *(22.45 hours in winter)*
Crossing time–3 mins.
☎ 080–425 342

Hull – New Holland A15
20 cars: Frequent service
until 21.15 hours
Crossing time–20 mins.
☎ Hull 28613

Cowes – East Cowes A3020–A3021
12 cars: Frequent service
until 23.30 hours
Crossing time–2 mins.
☎ Cowes 3041

King Harry – Philleigh B3289
28 cars: Frequent service until
21.00 hours *(18.00 hours in winter)*
Crossing time–5 mins.
☎ 0872 2463

Loddon – Reedham B1140
2 cars: Frequency according to
demand until 22.00 hours
Crossing time–3 mins.
☎ Freethorpe 429

Sandbanks – Shell Bay B3369
28 cars: Frequent service until
22.00 hours *(21.00 hours in winter)*
Crossing time–5 mins.
☎ Studland 203/216

Torpoint – Devonport A374
34 cars: Frequent service
day and night
☎ Torpoint 812233

Windermere B5285–B5284 (to A592)
10 cars: Frequent service
until 21.50 hours
(20.50 hours in winter)
Crossing time–5 mins.

Woolston – Southampton A3025
14 cars: Frequent service
day and night
Crossing time–3 mins.
☎ Southampton 24333

Woolwich A1011, A117 and A205
45 cars: Frequent service
until 22.15 hours
Crossing time–6 mins.
☎ 01–854 9857

Some of the above ferries have certain restrictions for larger vehicles and caravans, and enquiries should be made beforehand. The normal times of operation have been given, but variations may occur according to the season or local conditions. Charges have been omitted as these are liable to change.

Ferries to the islands have not been included as advanced booking is often necessary, especially in the holiday season, and application should be made direct to the operator for details.

Erskine Bridge A898
☎ Bishopton 2022

Forth Bridge A90
☎ 031–331 1699

Tay Bridge A92
☎ Dundee 21881

Dartford Tunnel A282
☎ Dartford 21222

Tyne Tunnel A108
☎ Wallsend 624451

Mersey Tunnels
Kingsway ☎ 051–638 9441
Liverpool A59–Birkenhead M53
Queensway ☎ 051–647 8814
Liverpool (Lime St.)–Birkenhead A41

Batheaston Bridge
Near Bath
A4–A36

Cleddau Bridge
Pembroke–Neyland
A77

Clifton Bridge
Bristol
B3129

Dunham Bridge
Lincoln–Worksop A57
☎ Dunham-on-Trent 222

Middlesbrough Transporter Bridge
A178
☎ Middlesbrough 48411

Briwet Bridge, Penrhyndeudraeth
A487–A496

Porthmadog Embankment
A487

Sandwich Bridge
A256
☎ Sandwich 2669

Selby Bridge
A19
☎ Selby 3126

Severn Bridge
M4
☎ Pilning 2346

Shard Bridge
Blackpool–Lancaster A588
☎ Blackpool 25515

Swinford Bridge
Oxford–Witney B4044
☎ Oxford 881325

Tamar Bridge
Plymouth–Liskeard A38
☎ Plymouth 31577

Warburton Bridge
East of Warrington B5159
☎ 061–872 2411

Whitchurch – Pangbourne Bridge
Whitchurch–Pangbourne B471
☎ Pangbourne 3126

Whitney Bridge
Hay-on-Wye B4350
☎ Kington 534

Dulwich College Road
West Dulwich
London

Aldwark Bridge
Ouseburn–Tollerton
North-west of York

There are weight and size restrictions in force at certain smaller toll bridges and these should be checked beforehand. Charges have been omitted as these are liable to change.

Local Radio Stations

Local radio stations broadcast details of road works, diversions and weather reports for their areas throughout the hours of broadcasting. Although some stations broadcast continuously day and night, the majority are only on the air from early morning until late at night. Reception varies from 10 to 30 miles from the transmitter.

Belfast
Downtown Radio   293 m and 96·0 vhf

Birmingham
BBC Radio Birmingham   206 m and 95·6 vhf
BRMB Radio   261 m and 94·8 vhf

Blackburn
BBC Radio Blackburn   351 m and 96·4 vhf

Bradford
Pennine Radio   235 m and 96·0 vhf

Brighton
BBC Radio Brighton   202 m and 95·3 vhf

Bristol
BBC Radio Bristol   194 m and 95·5 vhf

Carlisle
BBC Radio Carlisle   397 m, 206 m and 95·6 vhf

Chatham
BBC Radio Medway   290 m and 96·7 vhf

Derby
BBC Radio Derby   269 m, 96·5 and 94·2 vhf

Edinburgh
Radio Forth   194 m and 96·8 vhf

Glasgow
Radio Clyde   261 m and 95·1 vhf

Hull
BBC Radio Humberside   202 m and 96·9 vhf

Ipswich
Radio Orwell   257 m and 97·1 vhf

Leeds
BBC Radio Leeds   271 m and 92·4 vhf

Leicester
BBC Radio Leicester   188 m and 95·1 vhf

Liverpool
BBC Radio Merseyside   202 m and 95·8 vhf
Radio City   194 m and 96·7 vhf

London
BBC Radio London   206 m and 94·9 vhf
Capital Radio   194 m and 95·8 vhf
LBC   261 m and 97·3 vhf

Manchester
Piccadilly Radio   261 m and 97·0 vhf
BBC Radio Manchester   206 m and 95·1 vhf

Middlesbrough
Radio Cleveland   194 m and 96·6 vhf

Newcastle
BBC Radio Newcastle   206 m and 95·4 vhf
Metro Radio   261 m and 97·0 vhf

Nottingham
BBC Radio Nottingham   197 m and 95·4 vhf
Radio Trent   301 m and 96·2 vhf

Oxford
BBC Radio Oxford   202 m and 95·2 vhf

Plymouth
Plymouth Sound   261 m and 96·0 vhf

Portsmouth
Radio Victory   257 m and 95·0 vhf

Reading
Thames Valley Broadcasting   210 m and 97·0 vhf

Sheffield
BBC Radio Sheffield   290 m, 97·4 and 88·6 vhf
Radio Hallam   194 m   Sheffield 95·2 vhf
                            Rotherham 95·9 vhf

Southampton
BBC Radio Solent   301 m, 188 m and 96·1 vhf

Stockton-on-Tees
Radio Tees   257 m and 95·0 vhf

Stoke-on-Trent
BBC Radio Stoke-on-Trent   200 m and 96·1 vhf

Swansea
Swansea Sound   257 m and 95·1 vhf

Wolverhampton
Beacon Radio   303 m and 97·2 vhf

Additional weather information can be obtained from the Meteorological Office by telephoning any of the following numbers:

London	01–836 4311
Glasgow	041–248 3451
Manchester	061–832 6701
Newcastle	0632 26453
Nottingham	0602 3311
Southampton	0703 28844

Town Plan Section

Contents

Aberdeen, 1½ inches = 1 mile   page **91**
Bath 1½ inches = 1 mile **118**
Birmingham 1½ inches = 1 mile **108**
Birmingham City Centre 3 inches = 1 mile **109**
Blackburn, 1½ inches = 1 mile **99**
Blackpool, 1½ inches = 1 mile **99**
Bolton, 1½ inches = 1 mile **103**
Bournemouth 1½ inches = 1 mile **119**
Bradford, 1½ inches = 1 mile **98**
Brighton 1½ inches = 1 mile **120**
Bristol 1½ inches = 1 mile **116**
Bristol City Centre 3 inches = 1 mile **117**
Burnley, 1½ inches = 1 mile **99**
Cambridge 1½ inches = 1 mile **112**
Cambridge City Centre 3 inches = 1 mile **112**
Canterbury 1½ inches = 1 mile **120**
Cardiff 1½ inches = 1 mile **115**
Cardiff City Centre 3 inches = 1 mile **115**
Coventry 1½ inches = 1 mile **111**
Coventry City Centre 3 inches = 1 mile **111**

Derby 1½ inches = 1 mile **107**
Doncaster, 1½ inches = 1 mile **105**
Dundee, 1½ inches = 1 mile **93**
Edinburgh, 1½ inches = 1 mile **92**
Edinburgh, City Centre 3 inches = 1 mile **93**
Exeter, 1½ inches = 1 mile **118**
Gateshead, 1½ inches = 1 mile **95**
Glasgow, 1½ inches = 1 mile **90**
Glasgow, City Centre 3 inches = 1 mile **91**
Gloucester 1½ inches = 1 mile **117**
Halifax, 1½ inches = 1 mile **97**
Harrogate. 1½ inches = 1 mile **97**
Huddersfield, 1½ inches = 1 mile **98**
Hull, 1½ inches = 1 mile **99**
Hull, City Centre 3 inches = 1 mile **99**
Ipswich 1½ inches = 1 mile **113**
Jarrow & S. Shields, 1½ inches = 1 mile **94**
Leeds, 1½ inches = 1 mile **96**
Leeds, City Centre 3 inches = 1 mile **96**
Leicester 1½ inches = 1 mile **110**

Leicester City Centre 3 inches = 1 mile **110**
Liverpool, 1½ inches = 1 mile **100**
Liverpool, City Centre 3 inches = 1 mile **101**
Manchester, 1½ inches = 1 mile **102**
Manchester, City Centre 3 inches = 1 mile **103**
Middlesbrough, 1½ inches = 1 mile **95**
Newcastle, 1½ inches = 1 mile **94**
Newcastle, City Centre 3 inches = 1 mile **94**
Newport (Gwent) 1½ inches = 1 mile **114**
Northampton 1½ inches = 1 mile **110**
Norwich 1½ inches = 1 mile **113**
Nottingham 1½ inches = 1 mile **107**
Nottingham City Centre 3 inches = 1 mile **107**
Oldham, 1½ inches = 1 mile **103**
Oxford 1½ inches = 1 mile **112**
Oxford City Centre 3 inches = 1 mile **112**
Perth, 1½ inches = 1 mile **91**
Plymouth 1½ inches = 1 mile **117**
Portsmouth 1½ inches = 1 mile **120**
Preston, 1½ inches = 1 mile **99**

Rotherham, 1½ inches = 1 mile **105**
Sheffield, 1½ inches = 1 mile **104**
Sheffield, City Centre 3 inches = 1 mile **105**
Southampton 1½ inches = 1 mile **119**
Southend 1½ inches = 1 mile **113**
St. Helens, 1½ inches = 1 mile **101**
Stoke-on-Trent 1½ inches = 1 mile **106**
Stoke-on-Trent (Hanley)
    City Centre 3 inches = 1 mile **106**
Stratford-upon-Avon 1½ inches = 1 mile **111**
Sunderland, 1½ inches = 1 mile **95**
Swansea 1½ inches = 1 mile **114**
Swansea City Centre 3 inches = 1 mile **114**
Taunton 1½ inches = 1 mile **118**
Torquay 1½ inches = 1 mile **118**
Wallasey & Birkenhead,
    1½ inches = 1 mile **101**
Warrington, 1½ inches = 1 mile **101**
Wolverhampton 1½ inches = 1 mile **109**
York, 1½ inches = 1 mile **97**

Reference

Town Plans

Scale: 1½ inches = 1 mile

0   ¼   ½   1

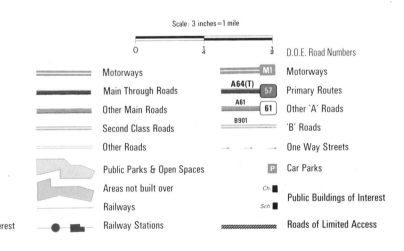

Motorways
Main Through Roads
Other Main Roads
Second Class Roads
Other Roads
Public Parks & Open Spaces
Areas not built over
Railways
Railway Stations

D.O.E. Road Numbers
M1   Motorways
A64(T)   57   Primary Routes
A61   61   Other 'A' Roads
B901   'B' Roads
43   Motorway Access Point Numbers
P   Car Parks
+   Churches of Interest
Canals
Public Buildings of Interest
Mus.   Hosp.   Sch.

City Centre Plans

Scale: 3 inches = 1 mile

0   ¼   ½

Motorways
Main Through Roads
Other Main Roads
Second Class Roads
Other Roads
Public Parks & Open Spaces
Areas not built over
Railways
Railway Stations

D.O.E. Road Numbers
M1   Motorways
A64(T)   57   Primary Routes
A61   61   Other 'A' Roads
B901   'B' Roads
→   One Way Streets
P   Car Parks
Ch. ■   Sch. ■   Public Buildings of Interest
Roads of Limited Access

Locator Maps

M1   Motorways
57   Primary Routes
621   Other 'A' Roads

Towns with Town Plans
◉ ○   Other Towns

Abbreviations in Text

Cent.	Century	Ho.	House
Ch.	Church	M.D.	
Coll.	College	Mls. m.	Miles
Dec.	Decorated	Perp.	Perpendicular
E.C.	Early Closing Day	Pop.	Population
Ed.	Educated	R.C.	Roman Catholic
E.E.	Early English	Sch.	School

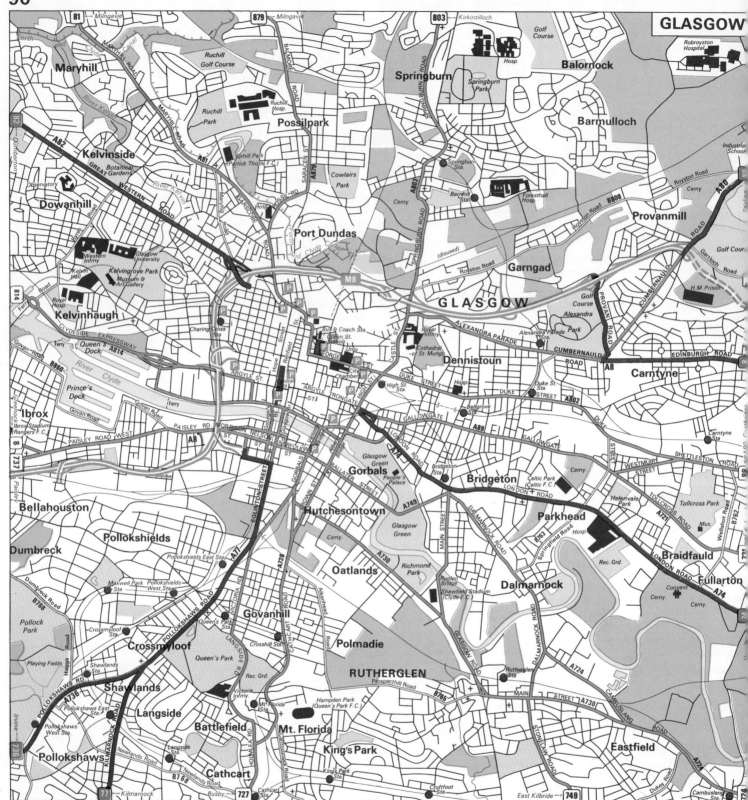

GLASGOW

Population: 861,000. E.C. Tuesday,

London 399 miles; Edinburgh 44 miles; Manchester 212 miles.

Large port, shipbuilding and industrial centre. The Cathedral is built on the site of an earlier church erected by St. Mungo; early English Gothic choir; Rood Screen. In the S.E. Chapel is St. Mungo's Well and the tomb of Bishop Wishart. People's Palace, museum devoted to the history of Glasgow. James Watt's workshop in Trongate. Art Gallery and Museum in Kelvingrove Park. The University established 1450, is housed, in Kelvingrove Park, in buildings designed by Sir George Gilbert Scott. University Library; Hunterian Museum and Library. Golf.

ABERDEEN

Population:182,006.
E.C. Wed. and Sat.
M.D. Friday.
London 501 miles,
Glasgow 150 miles,
Edinburgh 123 miles.
University city, resort
and fishing port.
Exporter of cattle
and granite. Old
Aberdeen; St.
Machar's Cathedral,
15th Cent.; King's
College 1495.
New Aberdeen 'the
Granite City'. Ancient
Market Cross, 1686.
Art Gallery and
Museum; Marischal
College; Town House,
1866, incorporating
tower of 14th Cent.
Tolbooth. E. Church
rebuilt 1837. W.
Church rebuilt 1763.
14th Cent. Bridge of
Balgownie.
Angling, golf.

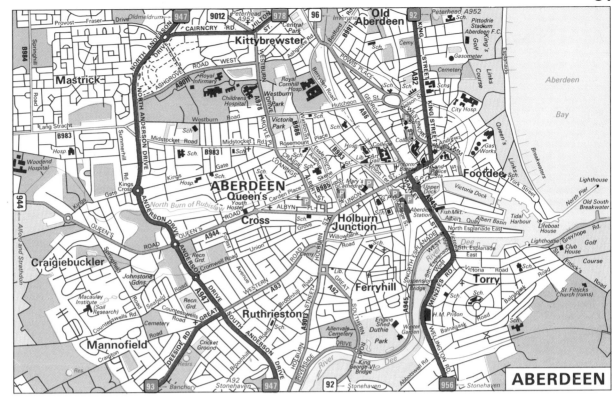

ABERDEEN

PERTH

Population:43,051. E.C. Wed. M.D. Fri.
London 415 miles, Glasgow 61 miles,
Edinburgh 42 miles. Motorail Terminal.
Capital of Scotland until 1452. St. John's
Church; square central tower surmounted by
15th Cent. steeple. South Inch, once used
for witch burnings and archery. North Inch,
scene of judicial combat in 1396. Art
Gallery and Museum; St. Ninian's Cathedral;
Fair Maid of Perth's House; ruins of Elcho
Castle 16th Cent. Angling, golf.

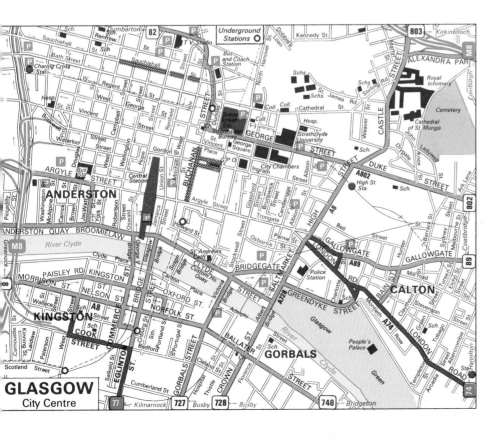

GLASGOW
City Centre

PERTH

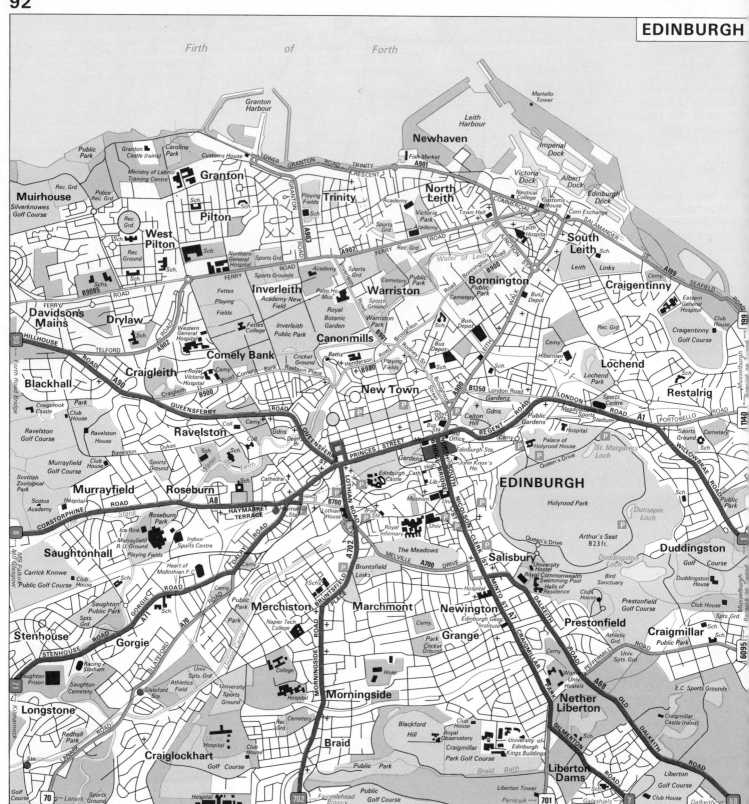

EDINBURGH
Population: 453,422
M.D. Tuesday and Wednesday.
London 377 miles; Glasgow 44 miles.
Capital of Scotland and University City with an outport at Leith. Princes Street with Scott Monument and Royal Scottish Academy. Castle; St. Margarets Chapel; and Scottish National War Memorial; National Gallery and Parliament Hall; St. Giles Cathedral; St. Mary's Cathedral; National Library of Scotland; John Knox's House; Holyrood Palace and Abbey. Greyfriars Church where National Covenant was signed in the churchyard. Angling, golf.

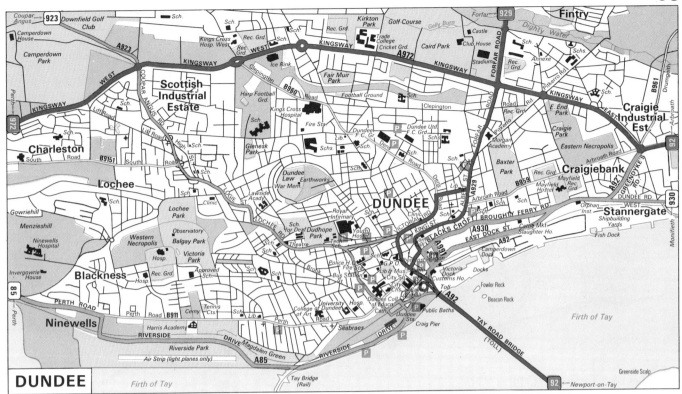

DUNDEE

DUNDEE
Population:182,084
E.C. Wednesday. M.D. Tuesday.
London 426 miles, Edinburgh 54 miles,
Glasgow 74 miles.
Port and industrial town. University; Albert Institute
and Library; Museum and Art Galleries; Caird Hall
(City Offices). Dundee Law 572 ft. Road and rail Tay
Bridges. Golf.

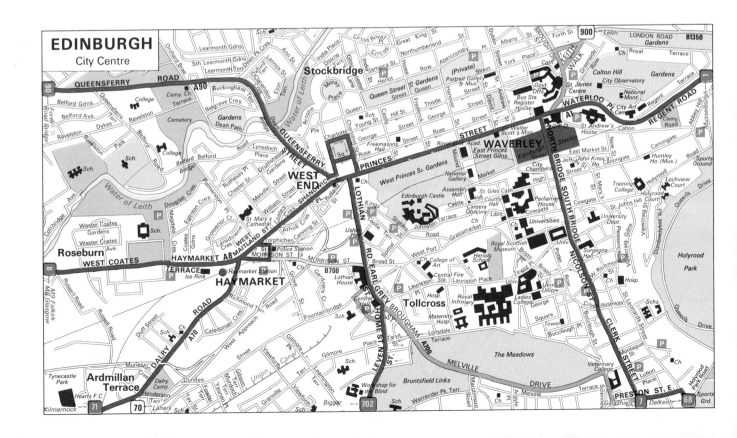

EDINBURGH
City Centre

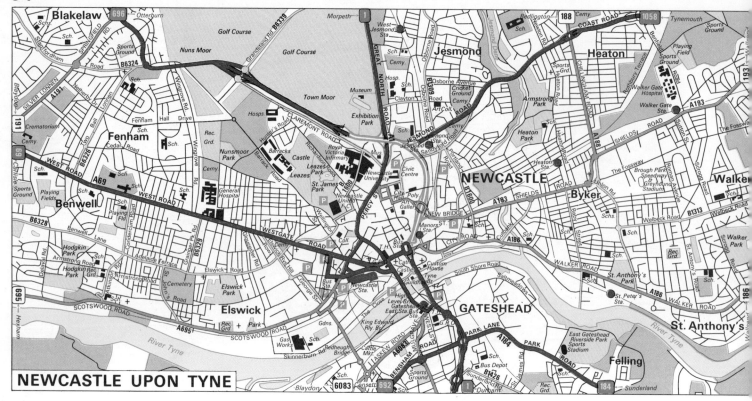

NEWCASTLE UPON TYNE

NEWCASTLE UPON TYNE
Population: 222,153
E.C. Wednesday or Saturday.
M.D. Tuesday, Thursday and Saturday.
London 271 miles, Edinburgh 107 miles,
Manchester 132 miles.
Formerly the Roman Station of Pons Ælius
but now the industrial capital of North East
England. The Cathedral was formerly one of
the largest parish churches in England with
fine spire and ancient font cover. Remains
of 12th Cent. Castle, Keep restored. The
original entrance to the castle is the Black
Gate, the upper part of which contains a
collection of Roman antiquities. Remains of
14th Cent. Town Walls. Guildhall 1658;
Trinity Hall, early 18th Cent. chapel and hall.
All Saints' Church rebuilt 1789 with 15th
Cent. German Brass. Museums and Laing
Art Galleries. Angling, golf.

JARROW
Population: 28,779 E.C. Wed. Newcastle
7 miles. Monastery where Venerable Bede
lived and worked. St. Paul's Church original
burial place of Bede. Norman Tower and
Saxon Chancel. First English glass made at
Monastery.

SOUTH SHIELDS
Population: 100,513 E.C. Wed. Newcastle
10 miles. Seaport and resort built on site of
Roman Camp. Remains of Roman Fort. Lifeboat Memorial commemorates first standard
lifeboat.

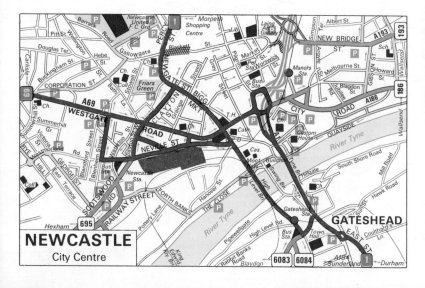

NEWCASTLE
City Centre

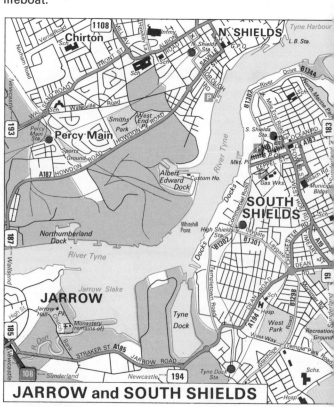

JARROW and SOUTH SHIELDS

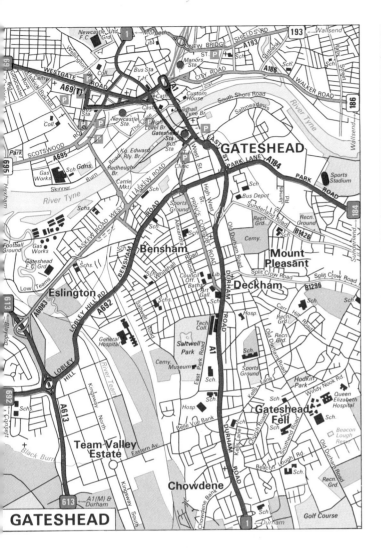

GATESHEAD

GATESHEAD

Population: 94,457. E.C. Wed. Newcastle 1 mile.
Industrial town on south bank of Tyne opposite Newcastle.
Connected with Newcastle by five bridges. High Level Bridge
1850 by R. Stephenson. 14th Cent. St. Mary's Church with
Norman Doorway and Jacobean Woodwork. Holy Trinity
Church. Industrial Museum in Saltwell Park. Shipley Art
Gallery. Golf.

MIDDLESBROUGH

Population:154,580. E.C. Wednesday. M.D. Saturday.
London 246 miles, Newcastle 37 miles.
Important port, industrial and shopping centre on River Tees.
Entirely developed since 1800. Dorman Museum; R.C.
Cathedral; Marton, birthplace of Capt. Cook 3 miles. Interesting
transporter bridge over Tees. Golf, angling.

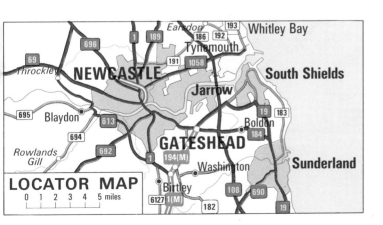

LOCATOR MAP

0 1 2 3 4 5 miles

SUNDERLAND

SUNDERLAND

Population:298,000. E.C. Wed. London 269 miles, Newcastle
12 miles. Important port with shipbuilding and marine
engineering. Saxon Monastery at Monkwearmouth also St.
Peter's Church. Museum, Art Gallery. Angling, bathing, golf.

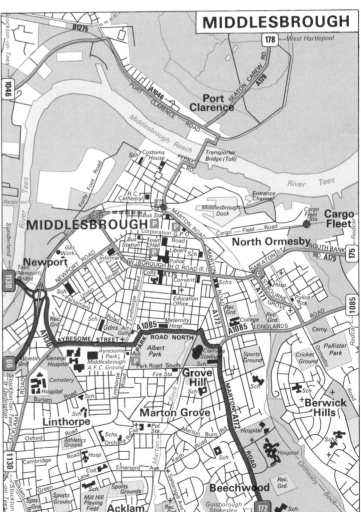

MIDDLESBROUGH

LEEDS

Pop. 501,000 E.C. Wed. London 190 mls. Manchester 40 mls. Centre 19th Cent. development of cloth industry. City Art Gallery and Museum; St. Ann's R.C. Cathedral; St. John's Church 1634 Renaissance woodwork; St. Peter's Church 10th Cent. cross. University founded 1877. Kirkstall Abbey (3½ m. N.W.) Cistercian ruins with chapter house, church and tower. Lord Darnley born at Temple Newsham now a Museum (4 miles N.). Harewood House 18th Cent. Angling, golf.

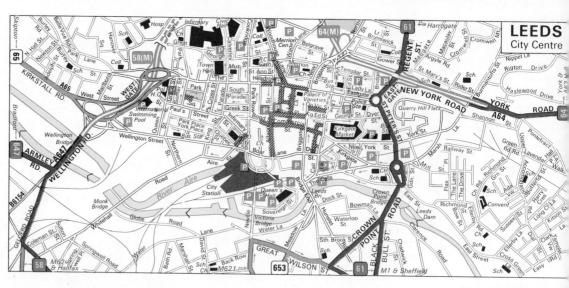

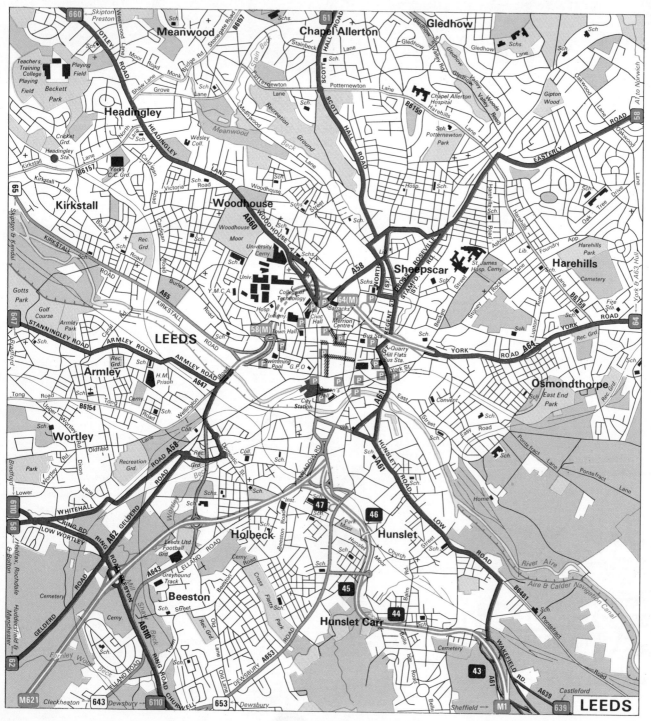

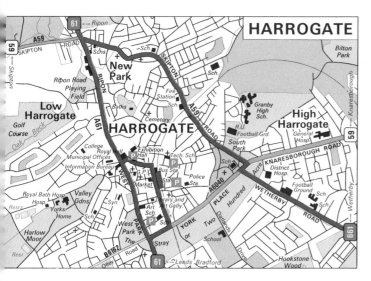

HARROGATE

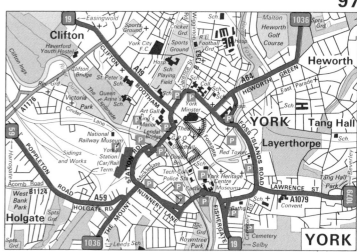

YORK

HARROGATE Population:64,280 E.C. Wed. London 207 miles, Leeds 16 miles. Popular spa and touring centre for the Dales. Grand buildings round 'The Stray'. Beautiful gardens; Baths; Pump Room; Royal Hall and Concert Room; Museum and Art Gallery. Nearby are Ripley Castle (3 m. N.W.) and Harewood House (7 m. S.). Angling, golf, riding, swimming.

YORK Population:104,513 E.C.Wed. M.D. Daily.London 196 miles, Manchester 64 miles. Roman Eboracum. Medieval walls and gates well preserved. York Minster. E.E., Dec. and Perp. begun in 11th Cent. St. Williams Coll. Jacobean. Treasurers Ho. 17th Cent. St. Mary's Abbey ruins. Shambles. St. Peter's Sch. Merchant Adventurer's Hall, St. Margaret's Church. National Railway Museum.

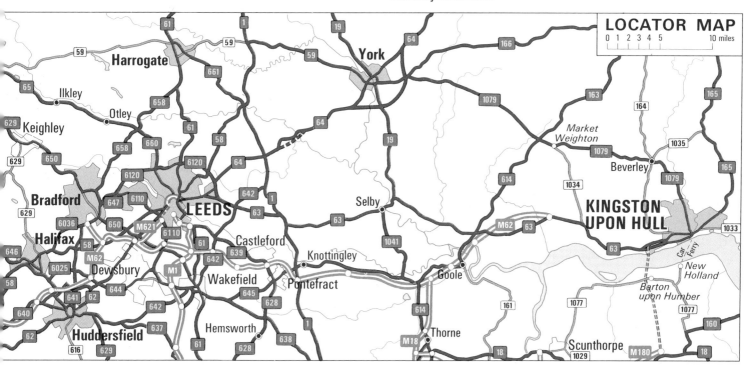

LOCATOR MAP

0 1 2 3 4 5   10 miles

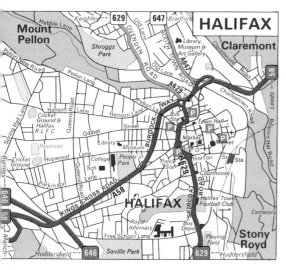

HALIFAX

HALIFAX Pop.91,171 E.C. Thur. M.D. Daily. London 193 miles, Bradford 8 miles. Woollen town. St. John's Ch. Piece Hall, Shibden Park & Hall; Folk Museum. Bankfield Art Gallery and Museum.

HUDDERS- FIELD Pop.131,190 E.C. Wed. M.D. Mon. London184 mls. Bradford 11 miles. Woollens, chemicals, engineering. Town Hall; Art Gallery; Museum; Sports Centre; Almondbury Ch. Roman remains.

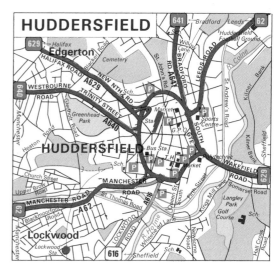

HUDDERSFIELD

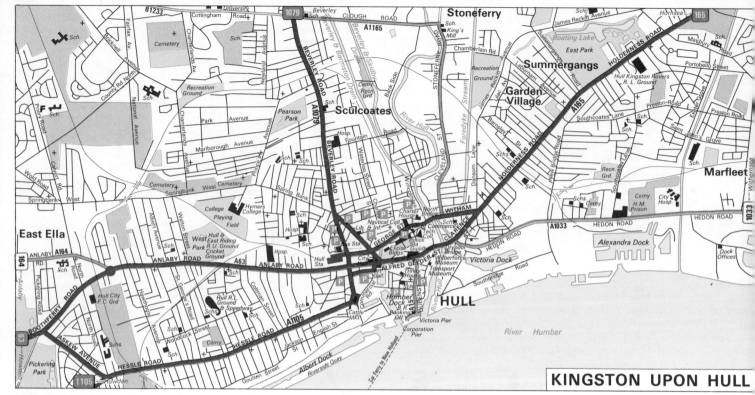

KINGSTON UPON HULL

KINGSTON UPON HULL Pop: 285,472. E.C. Thur. M.D. Tue., Fri., and Sat. London 168 miles, Manchester 94 miles. Seaport laid out by Edward I. Holy Trinity Church Dec. and Perp. Wm. Wilberforce and Andrew Marvel ed. Grammar Sch. rebuilt 1583. Wilberforce Mus. in Tudor House birthplace. St. Mary's Ch. Law Cts., University ; Ferens Art Gallery.

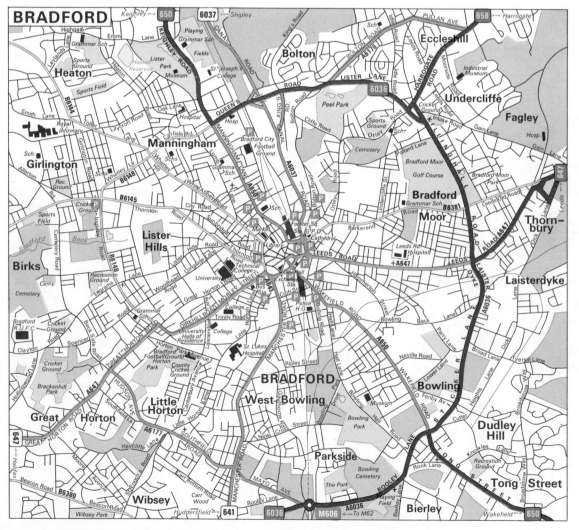

BRADFORD

BRADFORD
Population: 293,756.
E.C. Wednesday.
London 200 miles,
Manchester 34 miles,
Leeds 9 miles.
Centre of worsted trade with numerous mills and ware-houses. It is a stone-built city with a Town Hall dating from 1873. St. Peter's Church 15th Cent. has become the Cathedral of a new diocese. Cartwright Memorial Hall honours the inventor of the power loom. Natural History and Archaeological Museum; Bolling Hall 14th Cent. Delius was born here in 1863. Emily, Charlotte, Anne and Branwell Brontë born at Thornton. Industrial Museum in Moorside Road, Eccleshill. Golf.

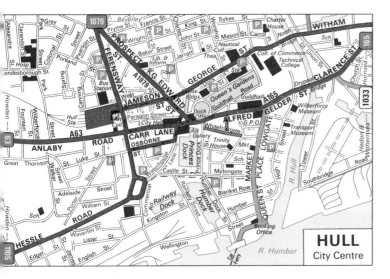

HULL
City Centre

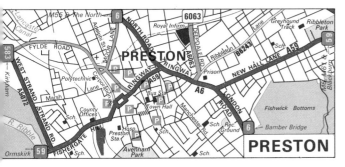

PRESTON

BLACKPOOL

PRESTON

Population: 131,900 E.C.Thur. M.D. Mon., Wed., Fri., and Sat. London 213 miles, Manchester 29 miles. Important centre of communications and engineering industry. Sir Richard Arkwright, inventor, born here 1732. Parish Church has 15th and 7th Cent. silver crosses. Harris Public Library and Museum. Avenham Park scene of egg-rolling carnival Easter Monday. Golf.

BLACKPOOL

Population: 151,311 E.C. Wednesday. London 227 miles, Manchester 45 miles. Popular holiday resort on Lancashire coast with 7 mile promenade, splendid sands, five ballrooms and three piers. Views from 520 ft. Blackpool Tower with ballroom, aquarium, aviary, zoo, roof gardens and circus on same site. Grundy Art Gallery. R.C. Church by Pugin. Stanley Park with rose and Italian gardens. Angling, boating, bathing, cricket and golf.

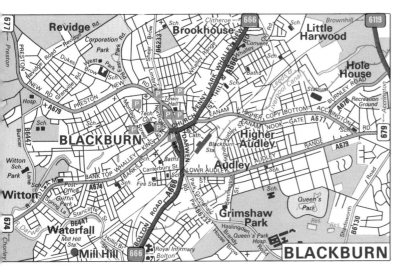

BLACKBURN

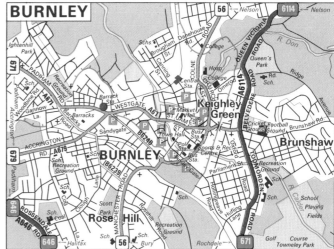

BURNLEY

BLACKBURN

Population: 101,672 E.C. Thursday. London 213 miles, Manchester 24 miles. Industrial and marketing centre and one of the world's greatest cotton manufacturing centres. 19th Cent. Cathedral; 19th Cent. Town Hall; Market Hall; Leur's Textile Museum and Museum and Art Gallery. St. Gabriel's Church built in the modern idiom. Corporation Park. Golf.

BURNLEY

Population: 96,500 E.C. Tuesday. London 206 miles, Manchester 24 miles. Set amid moorland country it is an engineering centre. Partly 15th Century Parish Church, St. Mary's R.C. Church by Pugin. Paulinas Cross Towneley Park with Towneley Hall Museum and Art Gallery. Golf.

LIVERPOOL

LIVERPOOL
Population: 574,560 E.C. Wednesday
London 205 miles, Birmingham 94 miles, Manchester 34 miles.
City and port on the Mersey with a dock frontage exceeding 7 miles. Royal Liver Building, 17 storeys with two towers surmounted by figures of the 'Liver', a mythical bird. Town Hall, the oldest public building, 1754. Public museums and Library; Walker Art Gallery; St. George's Hall; Cathedral, begun 1904, worthy of note are stained glass and great organ. R.C. Cathedral, designed by Sir Edwin Lutyens, begun 1933 and consecrated 1967. Mersey Tunnel, opened 1934. University founded in 1881. Birthplace of Gladstone. Golf, horse racing.

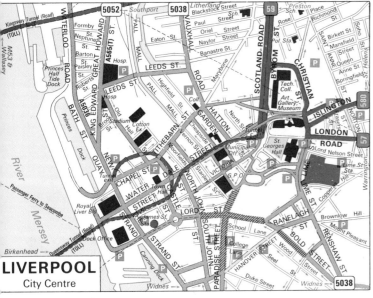

LIVERPOOL
City Centre

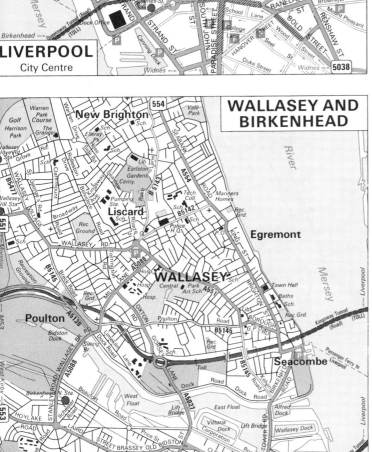

WALLASEY AND BIRKENHEAD

WALLASEY AND BIRKENHEAD
Population:234,799. E.C. Wallasey Wednesday.
Birkenhead Thursday.
London 199 miles, Birmingham 96 miles.
Birkenhead is a large port and industrial town, with
shipbuilding industry on West bank of Mersey.
Priory ruins with Chapter House and vaulted
crypts, Williamson Art Gallery and Museum.
Birkenhead and Arrowe Parks. Hamilton Square,
one of largest and finest in England. Wallasey is
large residential and holiday resort north of
Birkenhead with fine sands and fun fair. Bathing,
boating, golf.

WARRINGTON
Pop:68,262. E.C. Thur.
London 183 miles,
Manchester 17 miles.
Ancient borough on banks of
River Mersey. Rebuilt church
of St. Elphin with spire 281 ft.
high. Holy Trinity Church;
St. Mary's R.C. Church
designed by A. W. N. Pugin;
Barley Mow Inn;
Cromwell Statue; Museum;
The Old Academy, 18th Cent.
Town Hall and Wilderspool,
site of Roman Veratinum.
Boating, golf.

ST. HELENS
Pop:104,173. E.C. Thur.
London 192 miles,
Manchester 22 miles.
Famous for glass making.
St. Mary's R.C. Church.
Pilkington's Glass Museum.
The ruined 15th Cent. Chantry
Chapel of Windlesham Abbey;
17th Cent. cottage, birthplace
of R. J. Seddon, Prime
Minister of New Zealand
from 1893-1906.
An industrial town.
Rugby league, Golf and theatre.

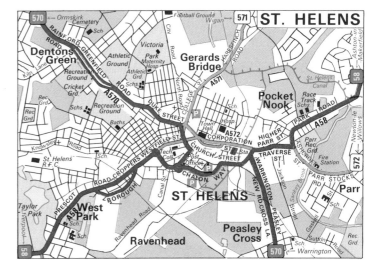

LOCATOR MAP
0 1 2 3 4 5 miles

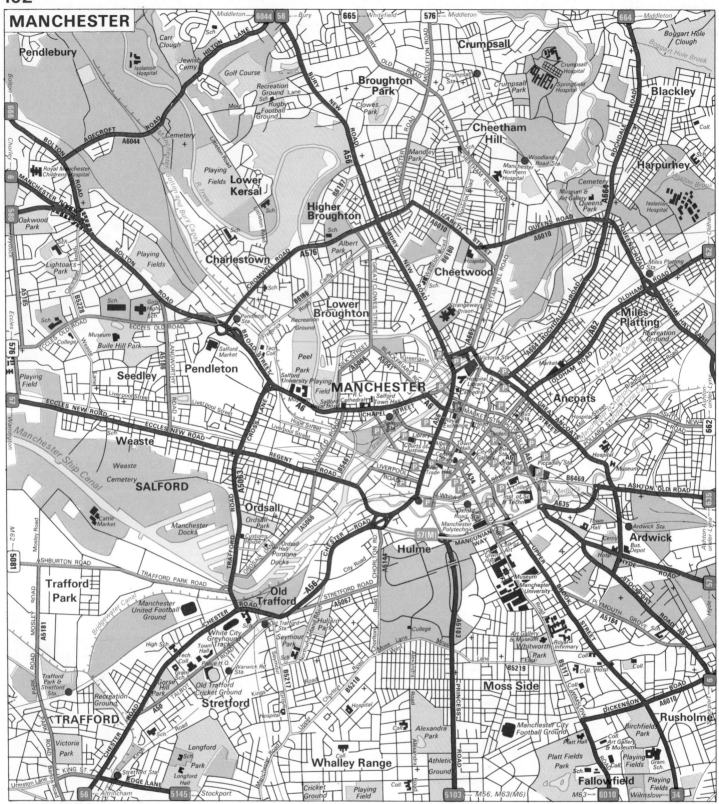

MANCHESTER

Population: 541,468

E.C. Wednesday

London 189 miles, Birmingham 80 miles.

Centre of the cotton manufacturing area and it is linked to the sea by the Ship Canal, opened 1894. Also has fine modern docks. Central Library; Town Hall; Royal Exchange. Cath. 15th Cent., mainly Perpendicular, formerly parish church, tower, choir and stalls. Chetham's Hospital, 15th Cent., with what is claimed to be the first public library in Europe; now a school. John Ryland's Library; City Art Gallery; University, founded 1880. Museum; Whitworth Art Gallery; Three halls at Platt, Heaton and Wythenshawe, now house museums. Golf.

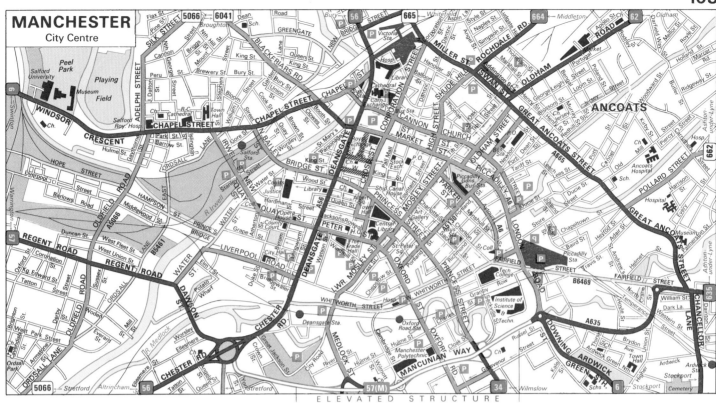

MANCHESTER
City Centre

ELEVATED STRUCTURE

BOLTON

Population:154,360.E.C. Wednesday.
London195 miles, Manchester 12 miles.
Bolton is one of the 'cotton towns' of Lancashire and is the centre of fine spinning and weaving industries. Richard Arkwright and Samuel Crompton were the inventors of spinning machinery and are especially associated with the town. St. Mary's Church Decorated and Perpendicular, modern Parish Church. Man and Scythe Inn, 17th Cent. Town Hall, 19th Cent: Art Gallery, Library and Museum. Golf.

OLDHAM

Population:105,705.
E.C. Tuesday.
London186 miles,
Manchester 7 miles.
Oldham is one of the 'cotton towns' and is a great textile and engineering centre. Art Gallery, Museum and Library, Town Hall. Golf.

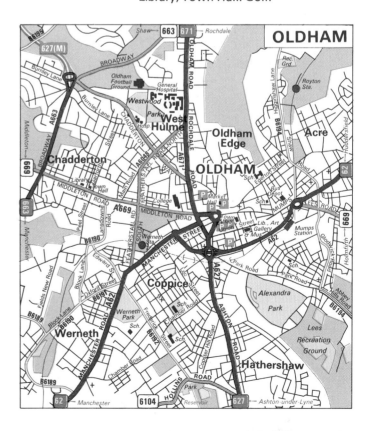

SHEFFIELD

SHEFFIELD
Population: 520,325
E.C. Thursday. M.D. Daily except Thursday.
London 162 miles, Manchester 38 miles.
Industrial and university city long famous for the manufacture of cutlery, silverware and plate. Cathedral, formerly Parish Church, with monuments in the Shrewsbury Chapel. Cutler's Hall, 1832. Town Hall, tower 210 ft., surmounted by a 7 ft. statue of Vulcan. City Hall; Central Library and Graves Art Gallery; City Museum, Manor Lodge, 16th Cent., occupied occasionally by Queen Mary when in captivity. Ruskin Museum; Beauchief Abbey ruins, partly restored, now a church. Crucible Theatre. Golf.

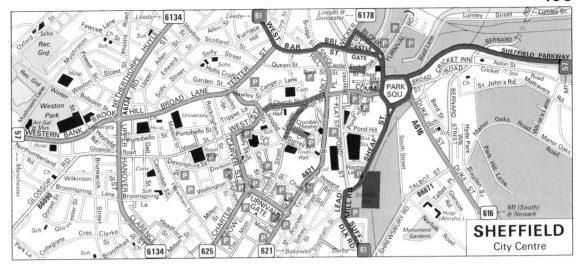

SHEFFIELD
City Centre

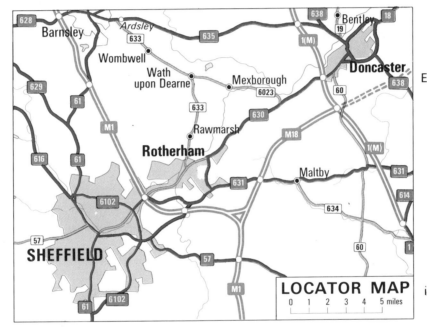

ROTHERHAM

Population:84,646
E.C. Thur.
M.D. Mon. and Sat.
London 165 miles,
Sheffield 6 miles.
Industrial town on the
banks of the River
Rother. Five-arched
Chantry Bridge with 15th
Cent. Chapel in centre.
All Saints Church 15th
Cent., with crocketed spire.
Museum and Art Gallery
in Clifton Park. Nearby
are Wentworth
Woodhouse and Roche
Abbey ruins. Golf.

LOCATOR MAP

0 1 2 3 4 5 miles

DONCASTER

Pop:82,505.
E.C. Thur. M.D. Tue. & Sat.
London 158 miles,
Sheffield 18 miles.
Old borough dating from
1194. Mansion House,
1748, houses Council
Chamber and Mayor's
Parlour. Corn Exchange
and Market Hall.
Grammar School
founded 13th Cent.
Parish Church of
St. George built 1858 to
replace earlier one burnt
down. New Museum and
Art Gallery. Many parks
including Hexthorpe Flatts.
Race course home of the
classic St. Leger race.

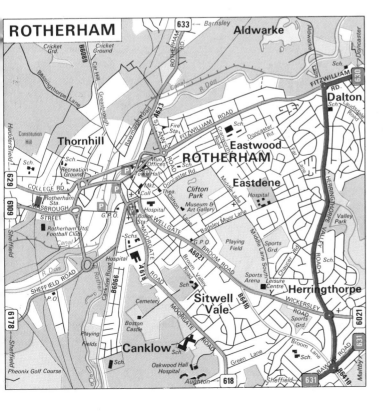

ROTHERHAM

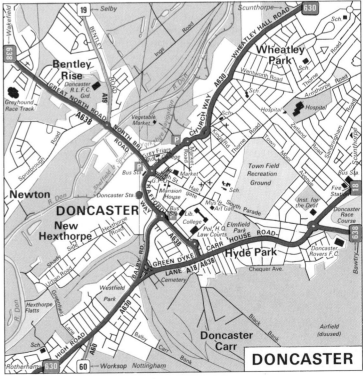

DONCASTER

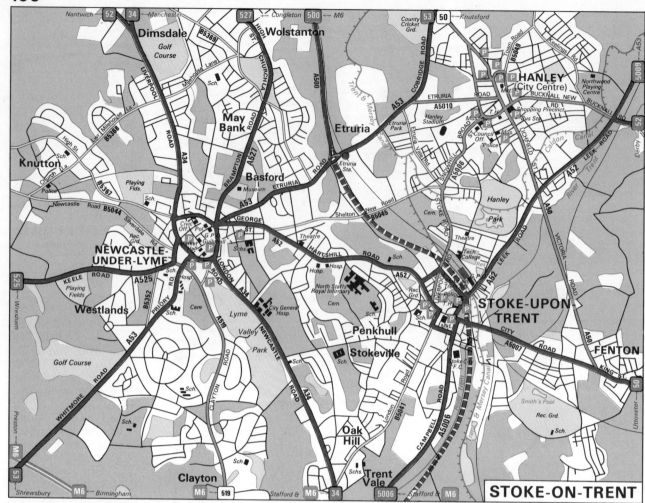

STOKE-ON-TRENT

STOKE-ON-TRENT

Population: 255,800 E.C. Thursday. M.D. Saturday.
London 152 miles, Birmingham 43 miles.
The railway centre of the Potteries and the 'Kaype'
of Arnold Bennett (born at Hanley 1867). St. Peter's
Church 1839, contains memorials to Josiah Wedg-
wood, the two Josiah Spodes and a window to
Thomas Minton. Etruria, founded 1769 by Wedgwood,
pottery works still carried on by his descendants.
Etruria Hall, his residence, now used as offices,
museum and for exhibitions of pottery. Ford Green
Hall Folk Museum. Golf.

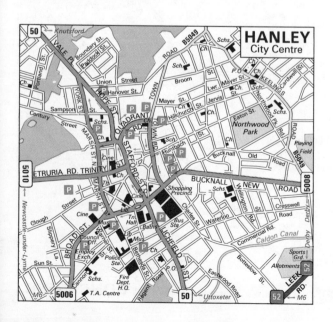

HANLEY
City Centre

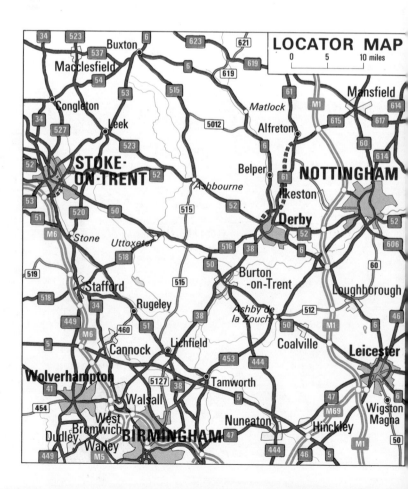

LOCATOR MAP

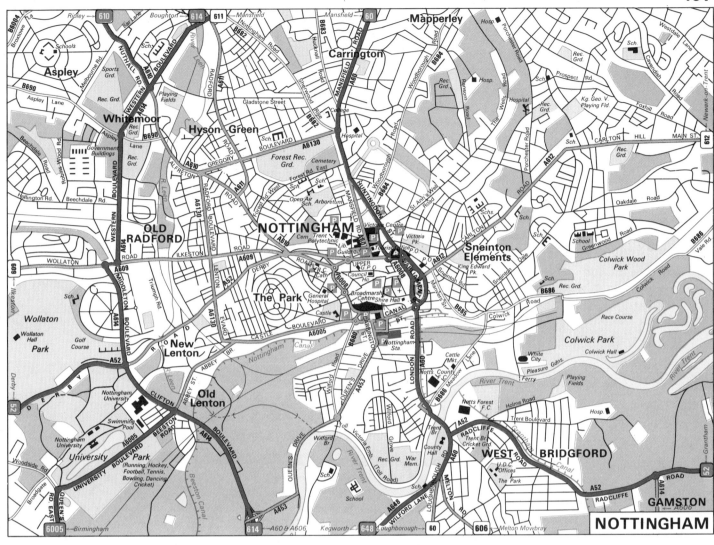

NOTTINGHAM

NOTTINGHAM
Population: 287,790   E.C. Mon. & Thurs.
London 123 miles, Birmingham 51 miles.
Industrial and university city on River Trent. 17th Cent. Castle on site of Norman Castle, now a museum and art gallery. Castle Rock pierced by passages and caves. St. Mary's Church is Perpendicular and has a fine nave and tower. Newdigate House, where Marshal Tallard resided. St. Peter's Church. R.C. Cathedral designed by Pugin. Wide range of sporting activities.

DERBY
Population: 219,580
E.C. Wednesday. M.D. Tues., Thurs., Fri., Sat.
London 126 miles, Birmingham 40 miles.
Historic county town and industrial centre. Cathedral rebuilt 1725 with 16th Cent. Perpendicular tower, 210 ft. St. Werburgh's partly rebuilt, where Dr. Johnson was married. St. Peter's Church 14th-15th Cent. Chapel of Our Lady of the Brigg (c. 1330) beside St. Mary's Bridge. Royal Crown Derby Works. Eagle Centre (Shopping) & Civic Hall. Roman Well at Chester Green. Art Gallery and Museums.

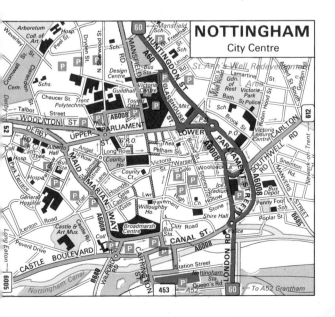

NOTTINGHAM City Centre

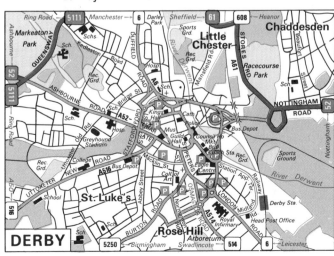

DERBY

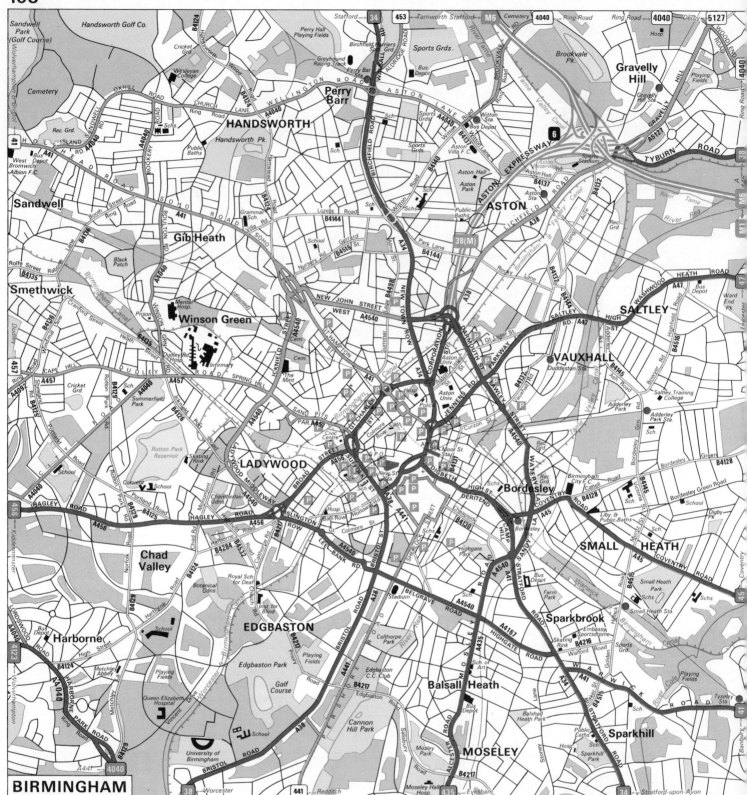

BIRMINGHAM

BIRMINGHAM
Population: 1,087,000
E.C. Wednesday.
London 110 miles, Manchester 80 miles.
Great industrial centre, university city. Feeney Galleries in Council House, 1880. Town Hall, 1850, contains fine organ. Hall of Memory; Joseph Chamberlain Museum; Boulton and Watt Museum. St. Philip Cathedral, beautiful windows by Burne-Jones. R.C. Cathedral by Pugin. Barber Institute of Fine Arts. Aston Hall, 17th Cent. mansion, now a museum and art gallery. Rotunda. Bull Ring Shopping Centre. Botanical Gardens. Golf.

BIRMINGHAM
City Centre

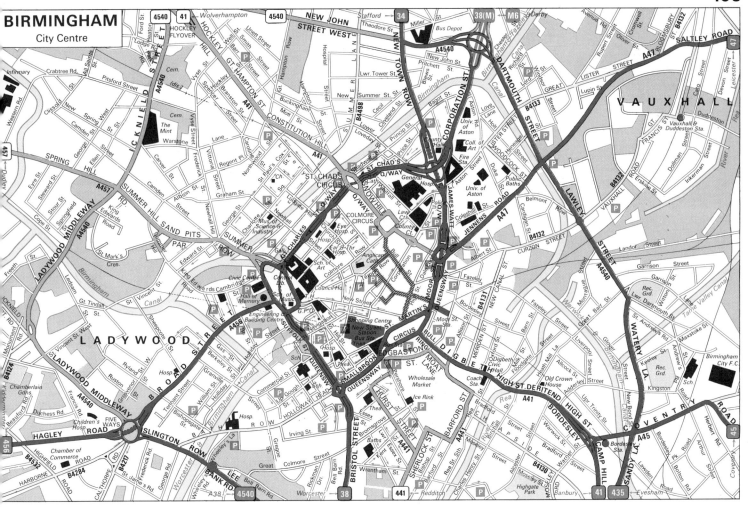

WOLVERHAMPTON

WOLVERHAMPTON
Population:268,847
E.C. Thursday.
London 125 miles, Birmingham 15 miles.
Industrial town on the western fringe of the Black Country. 18th Cent. St. John's Church in Grecian Style. 10th Cent. St. Peter's Church with some excellent Perpendicular design. Queen Square with statue of Prince Consort. Municipal Art Gallery and Museum, Public Library and 19th Cent. Town Hall. Golf.

LOCATOR MAP
0   5   10 miles

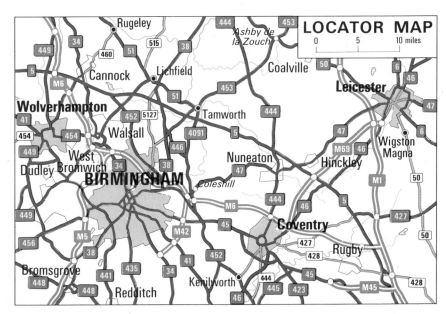

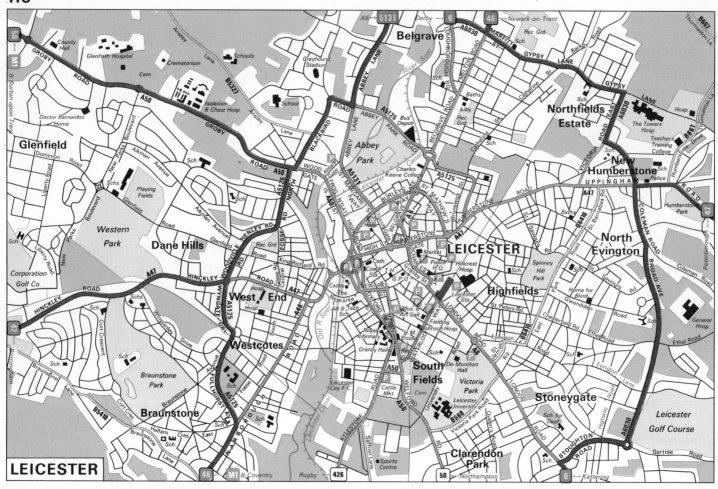

LEICESTER

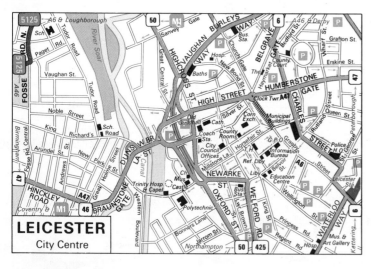

LEICESTER
City Centre

LEICESTER
Population: 287,350
E.C. Thursday.
M.D. Wednesday, Friday and Saturday.
London 99 miles, Birmingham 40 miles.
County town and industrial centre. St. Nicholas Church partly Saxon and Norman. Jewry wall of Roman Masonry. Bow Bridge, traditional burial place of Richard III. Norman Castle, ruins. St. Mary de Castro Church, Norman chancel, roof. Newarke Chantry House, 1512 (damaged 1940). Skeffington House, museum of local history. Newarke Gateway 1322, St. Martin's Church, Cathedral of new diocese. 16th Cent. Guildhall. City Museum and Art Gallery; Roman pavements; University; Leicester Abbey, remains.

NORTHAMPTON
Population:129,000 E.C. Thur. M.D. Wed. and Sat. London 65 miles, Birmingham 49 miles.
County town and centre of footwear industry. St. Peter's Church, a fine example of the Norman Period. Hazelrigge Mansion which survived the fire of 1675. Town Hall and Guildhall. Lawrence Washington was mayor in 1532 and 1545. Museum. St. Giles's Church, Perpendicular with some Norman. St. Sepulchre's, one of four round churches in England. R.C. Cathedral by Pugin, 1864. Eleanor Cross 1291 erected by Edward I.

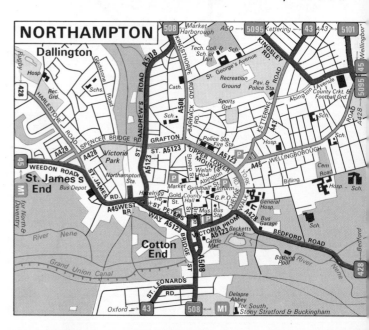

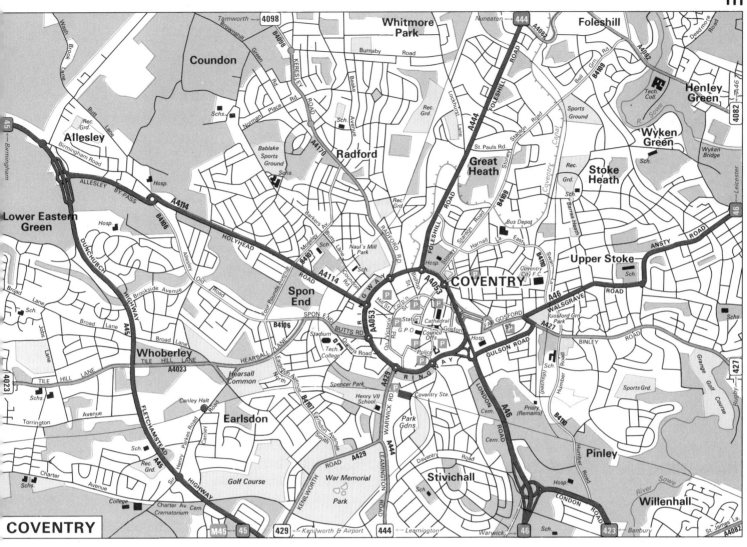

COVENTRY

COVENTRY. Population: 337,000 E.C. Thurs. M.D. Wed. Fri. & Sat. London 89 miles, Birmingham 17 miles. Industrial City associated with the motor industry. Remains of 14th Cent. cathedral include outer walls, tower and spire, 303 ft. Adjoining is new Cathedral designed by Sir Basil Spence. St. Mary's Hall founded 13th cent. for local trade guilds. Ford's almshouses; and Bond's Almshouses, 16th Cent. Bablake School & Bond's Almshouses, 16th Cent. Holy Trinity Ch., Perp. with spire 237 ft. Remains of medieval town walls & gates. Godiva statue Ellen Terry born here. The Precinct shopping centre. Golf.

STRATFORD-UPON-AVON. Pop: 21,500. E.C. Thur. M.D. Tue. & Fri. London 91 miles, Birmingham 24 miles. Market town. Shakespeare's birthplace and Museum. Royal Shakespeare Theatre. Collegiate Church, Shakespeare's burial place. Grammar School, Guildhall and Chapel. Harvard House; Town Hall and 15th Cent. Clopton Bridge over River Avon; Anne Hathaway's Cottage, Shottery, and nearby Charlecote House. Angling, boating, golf, swimming.

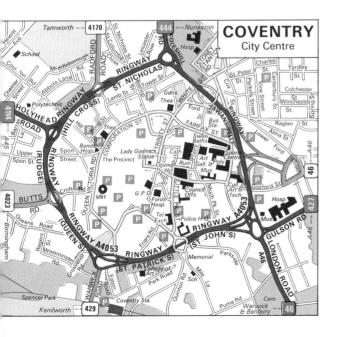

COVENTRY
City Centre

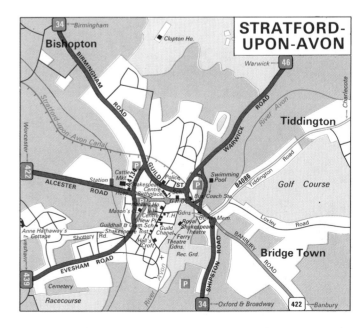

STRATFORD-UPON-AVON

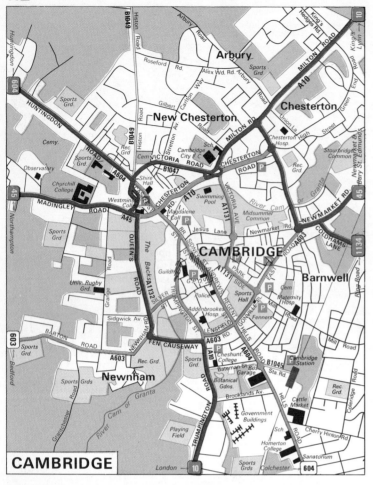

CAMBRIDGE

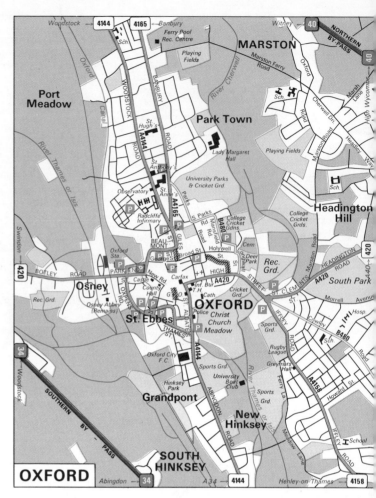

OXFORD

CAMBRIDGE
Population: 103,710
E.C. Thursday, M.D. Daily.
London 53 miles, Birmingham 99 miles.
County town and university city. Of architectural note; gateways of St. John's, Queens', Trinity College Hall; interior of King's College Chapel (late Perpendicular), Combination Room of St. John's. Gardens of Christ's, 'The Backs'. St. Mary's the Great; St. Sepulchre oldest of four round churches in England. Fitzwilliam Museum and Art Gallery. University Library. Botanical Gardens. Golf.

OXFORD
Population: 114,220 E.C. Thursday. M.D. Wednesday.
London 56 miles, Birmingham 64 miles.
County town and university city. Noteworthy colleges are: Christchurch whose chapel is now the Cathedral, mainly 12th Cent.; Merton, medieval library, the oldest college; Magdalen, Perpendicular, water walks; New College, founded 1379; Wadham College, hall and gardens. Bodleian Library. Ashmolean Museum. High Street. St. Mary's Church, Perpendicular with Decorated spire, 188 ft. Radcliffe Camera, viewpoint. University Museum, St. Peter-in-the-East Church, Norman crypt. Castle remains. Angling, boating, golf.

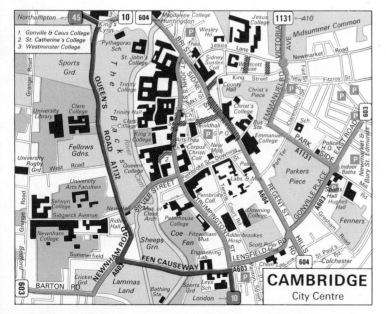

CAMBRIDGE
City Centre

1. Gonville & Caius College
2. St. Catherine's College
3. Westminster College

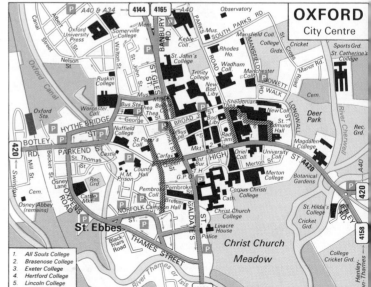

OXFORD
City Centre

1. All Souls College
2. Brasenose College
3. Exeter College
4. Hertford College
5. Lincoln College
6. Queen's College

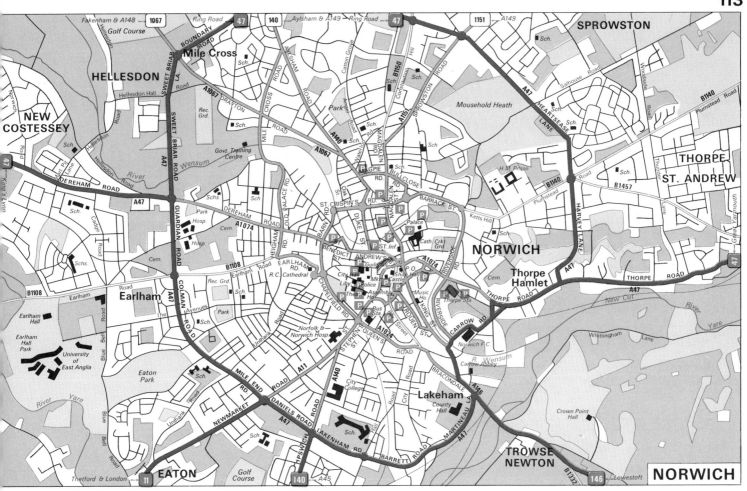

NORWICH

NORWICH. Population:122,083 E.C. Thur. M.D. Wed. & Sat. London 110 miles, Birmingham155 miles. County town. Castle c. 1130, now a museum. Cathedral mainly Norman with Decorated spire 315 ft. Guildhall. Bishop's Bridge, 13th Cent. Angling, golf, yachting.

IPSWICH. Population:122,600 E.C. Wed. and Sat. M.D. Tue. London 70 miles, Birmingham 152 miles. Angling, boating, golf.

SOUTHEND ON SEA. Pop:162,770 E.C. Wed. London 40 miles. Pier, 1⅓ miles long. Angling, bathing, boating, golf, sailing.

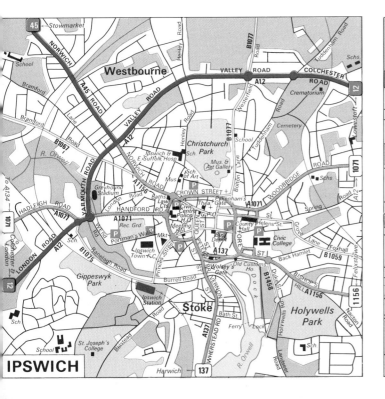

IPSWICH

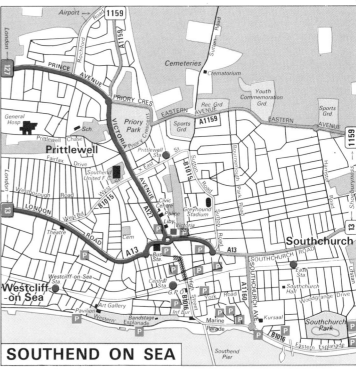

SOUTHEND ON SEA

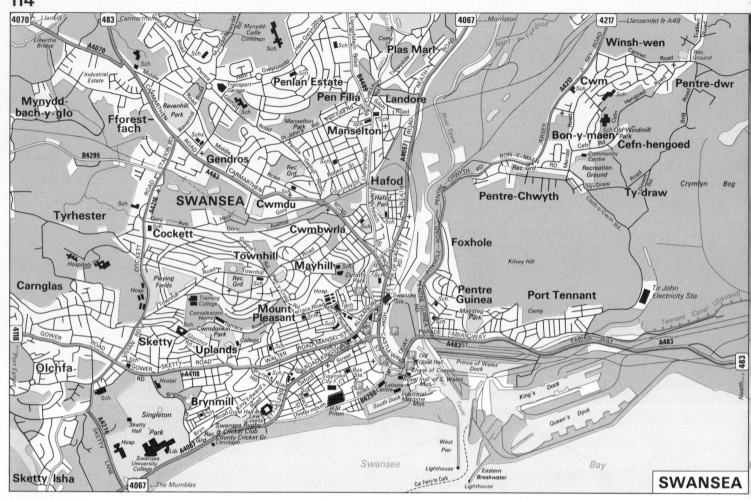

SWANSEA

SWANSEA
Population: 189,853
E.C. Thur. M.D. Wed. & Sat.
London 192 miles, Birmingham 126 miles
Industrial, administrative and university town. Port and docks. Remains of 14th Cent. Castle. Market, largest in Wales. Multi sport leisure centre. Guildhall notable as containing Brangwyn panels. Glyn Vivian Art Gallery; Royal Institution of S.Wales museum, Industrial and Maritime Museum. Nash House site of the birthplace of 'Beau' Nash. University College, Singleton Park and Clyne Gardens. Cwmdonkin Park and nearby the birthplace of Dylan Thomas. Oystermouth Castle, remains of hall, gatehouse and keep. Gower Peninsula. Bathing, sailing, surfing, caving, walking, golf.

NEWPORT
Population: 112,048.
E.C. Thursday.
London 141 miles, Birmingham 90 miles.
Once a walled town situated beside the River Usk, it is now an important industrial centre with extensive and modern docks. Remains of Norman Castle on the bank of the river. Cathedral Church of St. Woolo's, retaining Perpendicular tower, fine Norman arch and nave, early English chapel. Museum and Art Gallery containing Roman relics from Caerwent and Caerleon. Murenger House 16th Cent. Civic Centre. One of two Transporter Bridges in England, 177 ft. above the waters of the Usk.
Fishing, golf.

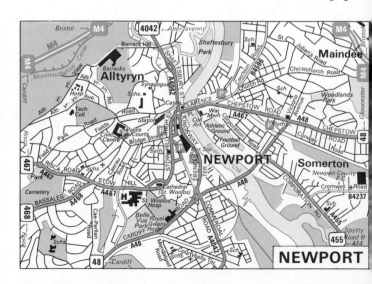

SWANSEA
City Centre

NEWPORT

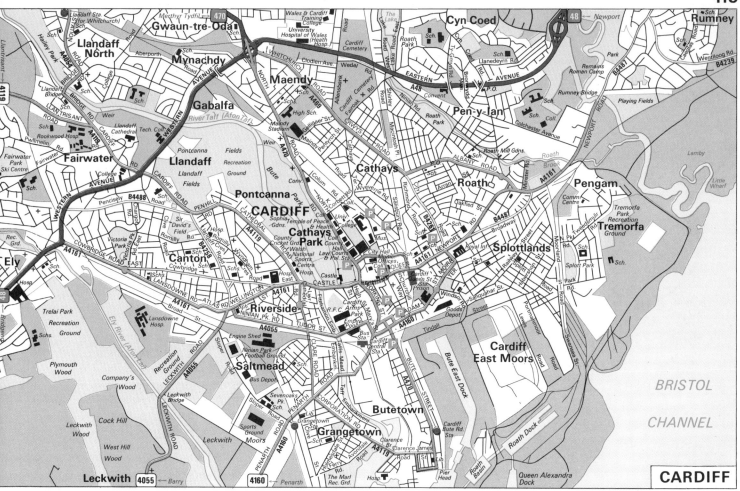

CARDIFF

CARDIFF
Population: 290,000
E.C. Wednesday.
London 154 miles,
Birmingham 101 miles,
Bristol 42 miles.
Seaport and university city.
Castle, begun 1090, on site of
Roman Castrum, Gateway
recently rebuilt, 'Black Tower',
13th Cent. In Cathays Park are
the municipal buildings,
including City and County Halls.
University College, National
Museum of Wales, Law Courts,
Welsh National War Memorial.
Llandaff Cathedral, Norman and
Early English, restored after
war damage; famous statue by
Epstein, Reredos by Rossetti,
Chapter House, Bishop's Palace
gatehouse 1300. Golf.

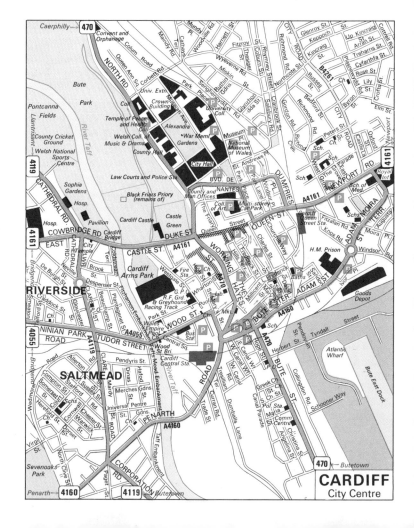

CARDIFF
City Centre

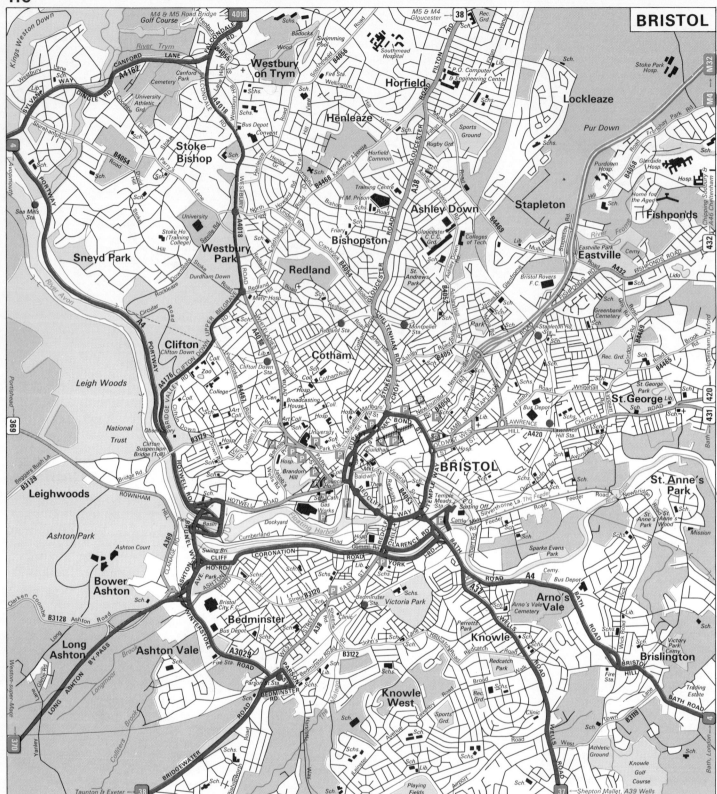

BRISTOL

BRISTOL

Population: 421,800   E.C. Wednesday and Saturday. M.D. Fri., and Sat.
London 117 miles, Birmingham 85 miles.
Industrial and university city. Docks at Bristol, Avonmouth and Portishead. Cathedral, Norman chapter house; Lady Chapel, Early English. Lord Mayor's Chapel, originally founded in 1225, it is the only civic chapel in England. Norman Abbey Gateway; St. Mary Redcliff Church, Perpendicular. Theatre Royal, oldest in England. Art Gallery and Museum. Red Lodge and Georgian House. Folk Museum at Blaise Castle Estate. Many old inns and houses. Clifton Suspension Bridge spanning the impressive Avon Gorge. Cabot Tower; he sailed west from Bristol to discover Newfoundland. Bristol Grammar School, 16th Cent. Corn-market with the famous 'nails' outside. Numerous old churches in the 'City' including John Wesley's Chapel in Broadmead. Part of Temple Meads station is the original terminus designed by I. K. Brunel for the London and Bristol Railway. Downs and Zoological Gardens at Clifton. Golf.

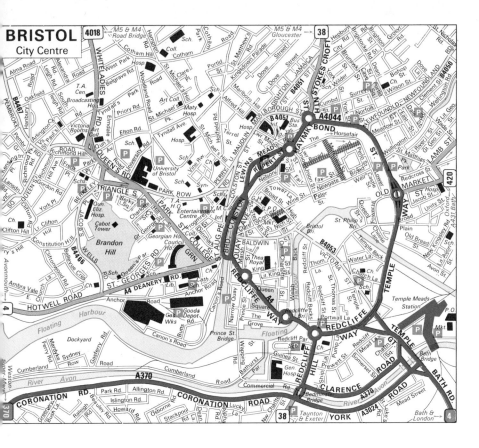

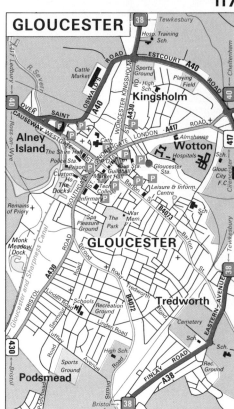

PLYMOUTH

Population: 250,000 E.C. Wednesday.
London 214 miles, Birmingham 210 miles.
Important port and naval dock. Drake, Cook, Hawkins and Chichester started voyages from here. Last port of call of Pilgrim Fathers. The Hoe, where Drake is said to have been playing bowls while the Spanish Armada approached. Smeaton's Tower, a re-erected part of the third Eddystone Lighthouse, Barbican Fish Market. Remains of 14th Cent. Castle Gatehouse. St. Andrew's Church, 15th Cent., Prysten House 15th Cent. monastic house. Art Gallery and Museum. Stonehouse in which is the Royal William Victualling Yard. Recently rebuilt Civic Centre and town centre. Angling, bathing, boating, golf.

GLOUCESTER

Population: 90,700 E.C. Thur. M.D. Mon. & Sat.
London 103 miles, Birmingham 51 miles.
Inland port and county town. Fine Cathedral, once the Benedictine Abbey church, Norman vaulting in nave, East Window, 1352; tomb of Edward II; 14th Cent. stalls, Lady Chapel, 1498. Norman Crypt, Cloisters, fan tracery vaulting. Chapter House, Norman; Library including copy of Coverdale's Bible, Abbot's House. Folk Museum. St. Nicholas Church. New Inn, 1450. Norman Church of St. Mary de Lode, on site of Roman Temple.

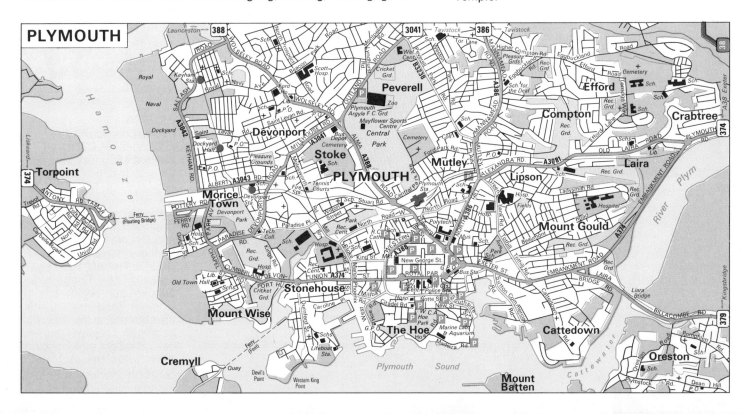

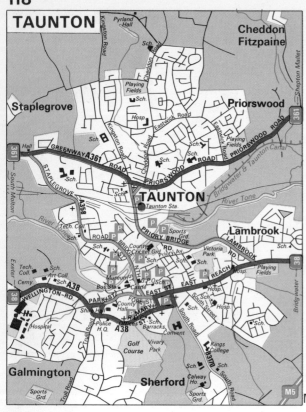

TAUNTON

BATH

Population: 84,545.
E.C. Thur. & Sat.
M.D. Wed.
London 108 miles,
Birm'ham 88 miles.
Spa and residential
town since Roman
occupation.
Roman Bath;
Pump Room.
Abbey Church,
from 1499; 'Jacob's
Ladder' flanks
West Front
window. Retains
some fine houses
of the 18th Cent.,
notably 'The
Royal Crescent'
and 'The Circus'.
Gt. Pulteney St.
Art Gallery.
Robert Adam's
Pulteney Bridge.
Holburne of
Menstrie Museum,
Sydney Gardens.
Assembly Rooms &
Museum of Costume

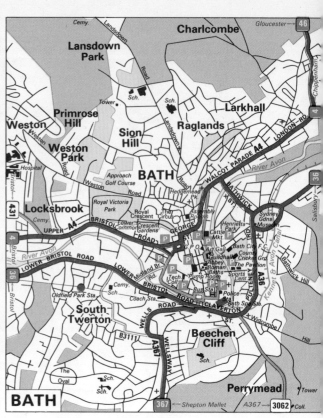

TAUNTON

Population: 37,373. E.C. Thursday. M.D. Saturday.
London 145 mls., Birmingham 131 mls., Bristol 43 mls.
County town of Somerset. St. Mary Magdalen's Ch.,
Perpendicular, sculptured tower (reconstructed 1862);
St. James's Church (rebuilt); Priory Barn, 12th Cent.
Taunton Castle, Norman, now museum; Hall was
scene of the 'Bloody Assize', 1685. White Hart has
historic associations. Market Ho., Guildhall. Golf.

TORQUAY   (Torbay Population: 108,888)

Population: 56,400 E.C. Wednesday and Saturday.
London 191 miles, Birmingham 188 miles.
Large seaside resort. Ruins of Torre Abbey with
'Spanish Barn' and Art Gallery. Torquay Natural
History Museum where prehistoric remains from
Kent's Cavern are arranged. The 12th Cent. St.
Michael's Chapel. The coastline is of much geological
interest. Angling, bathing, boating, golf, sailing.

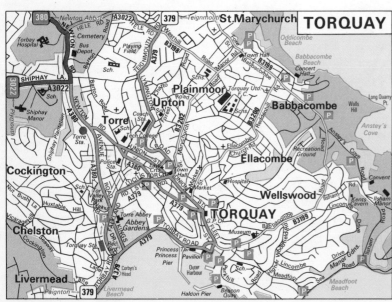

EXETER

Population: 95,729
E.C. Wed. M.D. Fri.
London 169 miles,
Plymouth 42 miles.
Formerly the Roman city Isca,
Exeter is now an historic,
cathedral and university city.
Cathedral, mainly Early English
and Decorated; Norman towers
built over transepts; West Front.
Guildhall rebuilt 1330 and
restored 1464. Rougemont
Gardens contain remains of
Norman Rougemont Castle and
the entrance to the subterranean
passages. Tucker's Hall, fine
oak panelling, guild relics.
Mols Coffee House, 16th Cent.
Numerous Georgian and Regency
houses. Angling, boating, golf.

BOURNEMOUTH

Pop:153,425.
E.C. Wed.
London
103 miles,
Birmingham
146 miles.
Renowned for
cliff walks,
sands, gardens
and chines,
Alum, Durley,
Middle and
Boscombe.
Natural
Science
Museum,
Russell Cotes Art
Gallery and
Museum. Over-
cliff Drives, Pier
and Winter
Gardens. Golf.

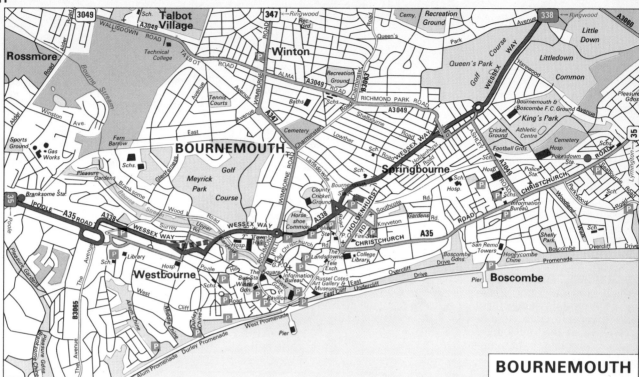

BOURNEMOUTH

SOUTHAMPTON

Pop:214,826.
E.C. Wed.
London 76 miles,
Birmingham
124 miles.
Britain's chief
passenger port,
Extensive
docks. God's
House Gate,
part of Town
Wall. Canute's
House, medieval.
West Quay,
whence the
Pilgrim Fathers'
Mayflower
sailed. Garden of
Remembrance.
St. Michael's
Church 1100,
restored. Tudor
House museum.
Three town
gates remain,
Bargate and two
posterns. Civic
Centre.
University and
Sims Library.
The ruins of
Netley Abbey.
Angling, boating
golf.

SOUTHAMPTON

PORTSMOUTH

Population: 200,380
E.C. Mon., Wed.
M.D. Fri., and Sat.
London 70 miles.
Birmingham 137 miles.
Portsmouth, a base of the Royal Navy, and the seaside resort Southsea are built on an island alongside a fine land–locked harbour. The Cathedral Church of St. Thomas of Canterbury, 12th Cent. and partly rebuilt in the 17th Cent. R.C., 19th Cent. Cathedral of St. John with an imposing Rose Window. Dickens birthplace, now a museum. H.M.S. Victory in the Dockyard also Victory Museum and Naval College. Great Smithy, Old Sally Port where Nelson and Blake sailed from. King James Gate and Landport Gate, former gateways of the old walled town. Angling, bathing, boating, golf.

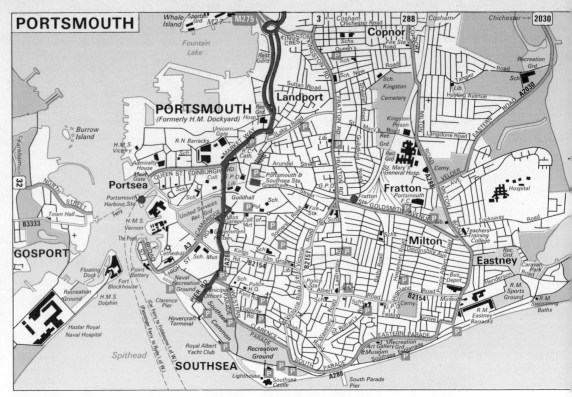

CANTERBURY Population: 36,290

E.C. Thur. M.D. Mon. and Wed.
London 58 miles, Birmingham 172 miles.
Ecclesiastical centre. West Gate. St. Peter's Church 13th Cent. St. Thomas's Hospital founded 12th Cent. 'Weavers' Houses'. St. John's Hospital founded by Lanfranc. Cathedral, 11th to 15th Cent.; 'Bell Harry' central tower; N.W. transept scene of Thomas à Becket's murder, 1170; Shrine in Trinity Chapel; Tomb of Black Prince. King's School – Norman staircase.
Angling, boating, golf.

BRIGHTON Population: 161,000

E.C. Wed., Thur.
London 52 miles, Birmingham 162 miles.
Seaside resort made famous by George IV. Royal Pavilion, 1784, built for George, Prince of Wales (who later became George IV), rebuilt 1817, in oriental style by Nash. Mrs. Fitzherbert, wife of George IV, is buried here. St. Nicholas Church, Norman font; Museums and Art Galleries; Whitehawk Camp (neolithic earthworks); Devil's Dyke, beauty spot, ringed by prehistoric entrenchment. Angling, bathing, boating, golf.

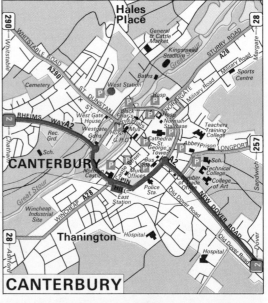

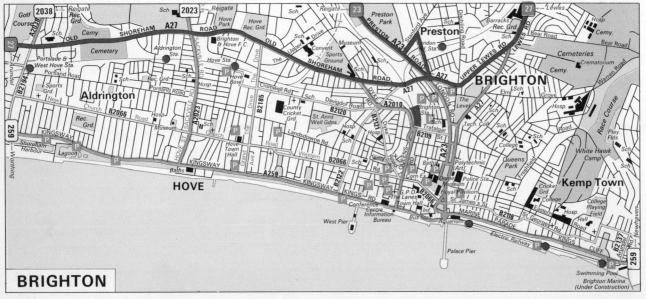

INDEX TO SECTIONAL MAP OF GREAT BRITAIN

ABBREVIATIONS

Aber. – *Aberdeen*
Angl. – *Anglesey*
Arg. – *Argyll*
Beds. – *Bedfordshire*
Berks. – *Berkshire*
Ber. – *Berwick*
Bldgs. – *Buildings*
Brec. – *Breconshire*
Bri. – *Bridge*
Bucks. – *Buckinghamshire*
Caer. – *Caernarvonshire*
Caith. – *Caithness*
Cambs. – *Cambridgeshire and Isle of Ely*
Cards. – *Cardiganshire*
Carm. – *Carmarthenshire*
Cas. – *Castle*
Ches. – *Cheshire*
Clack. – *Clackmannan*
Cnr. – *Corner*
Co. – *County*
Com. – *Common*
Corn. – *Cornwall*
Cumb. – *Cumberland*
Denb. – *Denbighshire*
Derby. – *Derbyshire*
Dumf. – *Dumfries*
Dunb. – *Dunbarton*
Dur. – *Durham*
E. Loth. – *East Lothian*
E. & W. Suff. – *East & West Suffolk*
E. & W. Sussex – *East & West Sussex*
E. Riding – *East Riding*
Flint – *Flintshire*
For. – *Forest*
Glam. – *Glamorgan*
Glos. – *Gloucestershire*
Grn. – *Green*
Gt. – *Great*
Hants. – *Hampshire*
Herefs. – *Herefordshire*
Herts. – *Hertfordshire*
Ho. – *House*
Holl. – *Holland*
Hth. – *Heath*
Hunts. – *Huntingdon and Peterborough*
Inver. – *Inverness*
I. – *Island*
I.o.M. – *Isle of Man*
I.o.W. – *Isle of Wight*
Junc. – *Junction*
Kest. – *Kesteven*
Kinc. – *Kincardine*
Kinr. – *Kinross*
Kirk. – *Kirkcudbright*
L. – *Lake*
Lan. – *Lanark*
Lancs. – *Lancashire*
Leics. – *Leicestershire*
Lincs. – *Lincolnshire*
Lind. – *Lindsey*
Lo. – *Lodge*
London – *Greater London*
Mer. – *Merionethshire*
Midloth. – *Midlothian*
Mon. – *Monmouthshire*
Mont. – *Montgomeryshire*
Norf. – *Norfolk*
Northants. – *Northamptonshire*
N. Riding – *North Riding*
Northumb. – *Northumberland*
Notts. – *Nottinghamshire*
Oxon. – *Oxfordshire*
Peeb. – *Peebles*
Pemb. – *Pembrokeshire*
Rad. – *Radnorshire*
Ren. – *Renfrew*
Ross & Crom. – *Ross & Cromarty*
Rox. – *Roxburgh*
Rut. – *Rutland*
Sel. – *Selkirk*
Salop. – *Shropshire*
Som. – *Somerset*
Staffs. – *Staffordshire*
Sta. – *Station*
Stir. – *Stirling*
Suff. – *Suffolk*
Suther. – *Sutherland*
Vill. – *Village*
War. – *Warwickshire*
Wig. – *Wigtown*
Wilts. – *Wiltshire*
W. Loth. – *West Lothian*
W. Riding – *West Riding*
Westmor. – *Westmorland*
Worcs. – *Worcestershire*
Yorks. – *Yorkshire*

The county names used to distinguish two or more places with the same name in this index are those in use prior to 1st April 1974.

MAP
32 Ab Kettleby......H 4
7 Abbas Combe....D 10
22 Abberley.........E 1
19 Abberton, Essex..B 10
22 Abberton, Worcs..G 3
45 Abberwick........B 9
18 Abbess Roding....C 6
6 Abbey...........E 5
20 Abbey Cwmhir....E 6
15 Abbey Dore......A 7
6 Abbey Hill.......D 6
31 Abbey Hulton.....E 7
49 Abbey St. Bathans C 10
32 Abbey Town.....F 12
34 Abbey Village.....E 5
38 Abbeylands, I.o.M. G 2
45 Abbeylands, Northumb.....B 10
34 Abbeystead.......B 4
4 Abbots Bickington.E 3
31 Abbots Bromley...H 9
17 Abbots Langley..D 11
22 Abbot's Morton..G 4
25 Abbots Ripton....G 3
22 Abbot's Salford...G 4
7 Abbotsbury.......H 9
4 Abbotsham.......C 3
5 Abbotskerswell....J 7
25 Abbotsley........K 3
8 Abbotswood......D 5
8 Abbotts Ann......B 5
21 Abcott..........E 9
21 Abdon.........D 11
28 Aber, Caer.......C 6
13 Aber, Cards.......B 8
13 Aberarth.........A 8
12 Aber-Cych.......C 6
20 Aber Gwydol.....B 3
28 Aber-Gwynant....H 6
14 Aber Village......B 4
13 Aberaeron.......A 8
14 Aberaman........D 3
20 Aberangell........A 4
12 Aberarad.........C 6
57 Aberarder, Inver...G 2
55 Aberarder, Inver...L 8
52 Aberargie........F 6
13 Aberavon.......H 11
13 Aber-banc........C 7
14 Aberbeeg.........D 5
14 Aberbran.........A 3
14 Abercanaid.......D 4
14 Abercarn.........E 5
12 Abercastle........D 2
20 Abercegir.........B 4
55 Aberchalder House J 7
58 Aberchirder.......B 4
14 Abercrave........C 2
14 Abercregan.......E 2
14 Abercwmboi......D 3
14 Abercynafon......C 4
14 Abercynon........E 4
14 Aberdare.........D 3
28 Aberdaron.......H 1
59 Aberdeen.........G 7
58 Aberdeen, Co.....F 4
48 Aberdour.........A 5
20 Aberdovey.......C 2
13 Aberdulais......G 11
20 Aberedw.........H 6
12 Abereiddy........D 2
28 Abererch.........G 3
14 Aberfan..........D 4
52 Aberfeldy.........B 3
28 Aberffraw........C 3
20 Aberffrwd........E 2
36 Aberford.........C 2
51 Aberfoyle.......G 12
14 Abergavenny......C 6
29 Abergele.........B 9
13 Abergiar.........C 8
13 Abergorlech......D 9
20 Abergwesyn.......G 4
13 Abergwili.........E 8
14 Abergwynfi.......E 2
20 Abergynolwyn....B 2
20 Aberhosan........C 4
14 Aberkenfig.......F 2
49 Aberlady.........A 7
53 Aberlemno.......B 10
20 Aberllefenni......A 3
20 Abermeurig......G 1
21 Abermule........C 7
13 Abernant, Carm...E 7
14 Aber-nant, Glam..D 3
53 Abernethy........E 7
53 Abernyte.........D 7
12 Aberporth........B 6
28 Abersoch.........G 3
14 Abersychan.......D 6
14 Aberthin.........G 3
14 Abertillery.......D 5
14 Abertridwr, Glam. E 4
29 Abertridwr, Mont. H 9
14 Abertysswg.......D 5
52 Aberuthven.......F 5
14 Aberyscir.........A 3
20 Aberystwyth......D 2
16 Abingdon........D 6
9 Abinger.........B 12
9 Abinger Hammer.A 12
48 Abington.........G 2
25 Abington Pigotts..L 4
16 Ablington, Glos...C 2
8 Ablington, Wilts...A 3
31 Abney..........B 10
59 Aboyne..........H 3
34 Abram...........G 5
56 Abriachan........F 1
18 Abridge.........D 5
15 Abson..........G 10
23 Abthorpe.......G 10
33 Aby............B 11
36 Acaster Malbis.. C 4
36 Acaster Selby.....C 3
4 Accott...........C 5
34 Accrington.......D 6
62 Achachork.......D 4
50 Achadun.........D 5
50 Achafolla.........F 5
46 Achahoish........B 3
51 Achallader.......C 10
46 Achamore Farm...E 1
54 Achanalt.........D 6
46 Achanamara......A 3
56 Achandunie......C 2
60 Achany..........F 6
55 Achaphubuil.....M 5
50 Acharacle........A 4
50 Acharn, Argyll....C 4
52 Acharn, Perth.... C 2
61 Acharole........C 11
46 Acharosson.......B 4
50 Achateny.........A 3
58 Achath..........F 5
61 Achavanich......C 11
56 Achavraat........E 5
60 Achavraie........F 2
13 Achddu..........G 8
61 Achentoul........D 8
60 Achfary..........C 4
60 Achgarve.........G 1
60 Achiemore, Kyle of Durness, Suther. A 4
61 Achiemore, Suther. B 9
62 A'Chill..........H 2
60 Achiltibuie.......F 2
61 Achina...........B 7
51 Achindarroch.....B 7
55 Achintee, Inver....M 5
54 Achintee, Ross and Cromarty.......F 3
54 Achintraid........F 2
55 Achlain..........H 6
50 Achleck..........C 1
46 A'Chleit.........E 2
51 Achlian..........E 8
55 Achluachrach.....L 7
60 Achlyness........B 4
60 Achmelvich.......E 2
63 Achmore, Lewis, Ross and Cromarty...D 4
52 Achmore, Perth....D 1
54 Achmore, Ross and Cromarty.......F 2
51 Achnaba, Arg.....D 7
46 Achnaba, Arg.....A 4
57 Achnabat.........G 2
60 Achnacarnin......D 2
55 Achnacarry Ho....L 5
62 Achnacloich......G 5
61 Achnaclyth.....D 10
51 Achnacon........B 8
55 Achnaconeran....H 8
50 Achnacraig.......C 2
50 Achnacroish......C 6
50 Achnadrish.......B 2
51 Achnafalnich.....E 9
55 Achnafraschoille..L 6
56 Achnaggaron....C 2
50 Achnaha.........A 2
60 Achnahanat......G 6
50 Achnalea.........A 6
61 Achnaluachrach...F 7
55 Achnanellan......L 5
60 Achnanerain......F 6
55 Achnangart......H 3
55 Achnasaul........K 5
54 Achnasheen......D 5
56 Achnastank.......F 8
50 Achosnich........A 2
50 Achranich........C 4
61 Achreamie........A 9
51 Achriabhach......A 8
60 Achriesgill.......B 4
61 Achrimsdale......F 9
61 Achtoty..........B 7
25 Achurch..........G 1
60 Achuvoldrach.....B 6
61 Achvaich.........G 7
57 Achvraid, Inver....G 2
56 Achvraid, Inver....F 2
61 Ackergill........B 12
55 Acklam, East Riding A 5
40 Acklam, North Riding C 5
22 Ackleton.........B 1
45 Acklington......C 10
36 Ackton...........E 2
36 Ackworth Moor Top F 2
26 Acle............D 7
22 Acock's Green....D 5
11 Acol...........A 11
45 Acomb, Northumb.F 7
36 Acomb, Yorks.....B 4
15 Aconbury........A 8
34 Acre............E 6
9 Acre Street.......F 9
29 Acrefair........F 12
30 Acton, Cheshire...E 5
8 Acton, Dorset....H 1
18 Acton, London....F 2
21 Acton, Salop......D 8
27 Acton, Suffolk....L 2
30 Acton Bridge.....C 4
21 Acton Burnell....B 10
21 Acton Green.....G 12
30 Acton Park...... E 2
21 Acton Pigott.....B 11
21 Acton Round.....C 11
21 Acton Scott......C 10
31 Acton Trussell....H 8
15 Acton Turville....F 11
30 Adbaston........G 6
7 Adber...........D 9
30 Adderley.........F 5
45 Adderstone......C 12
48 Addiewell........C 3
35 Addingham.......B 9
17 Addington, Bucks .A 8
10 Addington, Kent..B 5
18 Addington, London G 4
49 Addinston........D 8
17 Addlestone......H 11
33 Addlethorpe.....C 12
30 Adeney..........H 5
20 Adfa............B 6
21 Adforton.........E 9
11 Adisham........C 11
16 Adlestrop.........A 3
36 Adlingfleet.......E 6
31 Adlington, Ches...B 7
34 Adlington, Lancs..F 5
21 Admaston, Salop. A 11
31 Admaston, Staffs. H 9
22 Admington.......G 5
17 Adstock..........A 8
23 Adstone.........G 9
9 Adversane......D 12
56 Advie............F 7
36 Adwick le Street...F 3
36 Adwick upon Dearne G 3
4 Adworthy........D 6
58 Adziel...........B 7
43 Ae Bridgend......C 10
43 Ae Village.......C 10
4 Affeton Barton.... E 6
58 Affleck, Aber......D 3
58 Affleck, Aber.....E 6
7 Affpuddle.......G 11
55 Affric Lodge......G 5
29 Afon-wen.......C 10
5 Afton, Devon.....J 7
8 Afton, I.o.W......G 5
47 Afton Bridgend..H 11
40 Agglethorpe......F 1
38 Agneash.........G 2
63 Aignish..........D 6
37 Aike............C 8
64 Aikerness........A 2
64 Aikers...........E 2
43 Aiket...........E 11
39 Aiketgate........A 7
44 Aikton..........H 1
21 Ailey...........G 9
24 Ailsworth........F 2
40 Ainderby Steeple..F 4
19 Aingers Green....B 11
34 Ainsdale.........F 2
39 Ainstable........A 7
34 Ainsworth........F 6
41 Ainthorpe........D 7
34 Aintree..........G 3
50 Aird, Arg.........G 5
63 Aird, Ross & Crom. C 6
42 Aird, Wig.........F 2
62 Aird of Sleat.....H 5
63 Aird Tunga.......C 6
63 Aird Uig.........C 2
60 Airdachuilinn.....C 4
47 Airdrie.........C 12
47 Airdsgreen.......F 12
54 Airigh-drishaig....F 1
36 Airmyn..........E 5
52 Airntully.........D 6
55 Airor............J 1
52 Airth............H 4
35 Airton...........A 7
42 Airyhassen.......G 4
33 Aisby, Kest.......F 7
32 Aisby, Lind.......A 6
39 Aisgill..........E 10
5 Aish............K 6
6 Aisholt..........C 5
40 Aiskew..........F 3
40 Aislaby, Dur......D 4
41 Aislaby, N. Riding G 8
41 Aislaby, N. Riding D 8
32 Aisthorpe........B 6
64 Aith, Orkney Is...C 4
64 Aith, Shetland Is..D 7
64 Aith Hestwall.....C 1
42 Aitkenhead.......A 4
56 Aitnoch..........F 5
49 Akeld...........F 12
49 Akeld Steads.....F 12
23 Akeley.........H 10
27 Akenham.........K 5
3 Albaston........C 11
21 Alberbury........A 9
12 Albert Town......E 3
10 Albourn..........F 1
22 Albrighton, Salop..B 2
30 Albrighton, Salop. H 4
27 Alburgh..........G 6
27 Alburgh Street....G 5
18 Albury, Herts.....B 4
9 Albury, Surrey...A 12
26 Alby Hill.........B 5
56 Alcaig...........D 1
22 Alcester.........F 4
10 Alciston.........G 4
6 Alcombe, Som.....B 3
15 Alcombe, Wilts...G 11
25 Alconbury........H 3
25 Alconbury Hill....G 3
25 Alconbury Weston H 3
47 Aldandulish......M 5
26 Aldborough, Norf. B 5
40 Aldborough, Yorkshire.... H 4
16 Aldbourne........G 4
37 Aldbrough, E. Riding, C 10
40 Aldbrough, N. Riding, D 2
17 Aldbury.........C 10
52 Aldcharmaig......A 3
34 Aldcliffe.........A 3
52 Aldclune.........A 4
27 Aldeburgh........J 8
26 Aldeby...........F 7
18 Aldenham........D 1
8 Alderbury........C 3
26 Alderford....... D 4
15 Alderley.........E 11
31 Alderley Edge.....B 7
17 Aldermaston......H 7
17 Aldermaston Wharf G 7
22 Alderminster......G 6
21 Alder's End.....H 11
8 Aldershot, Dorset .E 3
9 Aldershot, Hants. A 10
16 Alderton, Glos....A 1
23 Alderton, Northants.....G 10
30 Alderton, Salop...H 4
27 Alderton, Suffolk..L 6
15 Alderton, Wilts..F 11
31 Alderwasley......E 11
40 Aldfield.........H 3
30 Aldford..........D 3
19 Aldham, Essex....A 9
27 Aldham, Suffolk ..L 3
27 Aldham Street....L 3
56 Aldie........... B 3
9 Aldingbourne....F 10
38 Aldingham.......H 5
22 Aldington........H 4
11 Aldington Corner .D 9
51 Aldochlay.......H 10
25 Aldreth.........H 5
22 Aldridge.........B 4
27 Aldringham.......J 7
16 Aldsworth........C 3
58 Aldunie..........E 1
31 Aldwark, Derby .D 10
36 Aldwark, Yorks...A 2
9 Aldwick.........F 10
25 Aldwincle........G 1
16 Aldworth.........F 6
47 Alexandria.......A 9
6 Aley............B 5
4 Alfardisworthy....E 2
6 Alfington........F 5
9 Alfold ....C 11
9 Alfold Crossways C 11
58 Alford, Aberdeen..F 3
33 Alford, Lincs....C 11
7 Alford, Somerset..C 9
32 Alfreton.........E 1
22 Alfrick..........G 1
10 Alfriston........H 4
24 Algarkirk........ B 4
7 Alhampton...... C 9
63 Aline Lodge......F 3
55 Alisary..........L 1
36 Alkborough.......E 6
23 Alkerton........ H 7
11 Alkham.........D 11
30 Alkington........F 4
31 Alkmonton......F 10
27 All Saints, South Elmham.... G 6
21 All Stretton......C 10
60 Alladale Lodge...G 5
5 Allaleigh........K 7
57 Allanaquoich.....K 7
56 Allanfearn.......E 3
56 Allangrange Ho.. E 2
49 Allanton........D 11
8 Allbrook.........D 6
16 All Cannings.....H 2
45 Allendale Town...G 7
39 Allenheads..... A 10
18 Allen's Green.... B 4
45 Allensford.......H 9
15 Allensmore......A 8

MAP
31 Allenton, Derby G 12
48 Allenton, Lan. D 1
7 Aller C 7
43 Allerby H 11
45 Allerdene C 8
6 Allerford B 3
41 Allerston G 9
36 Allerthorpe B 5
30 Allerton, Lancs. B 3
35 Allerton, Yorks. D 10
36 Allerton Bywater D 2
36 Allerton Mauleverer A 2
45 Allerwash F 7
22 Allesley D 6
31 Allestree F 11
23 Allexton B 11
31 Allgreave D 8
19 Allhallows F 8
54 Alligin Shuas D 2
31 Allimore Green H 7
32 Allington, Lincs. F 6
8 Allington, Wilts. B 4
16 Allington, Wilts. H 2
38 Allithwaite G 6
52 Alloa H 4
43 Allonby G 11
47 Alloway H 8
7 Allowenshay E 7
13 Allt G 9
55 Alltbeithe, Inver. G 4
55 Alltbeithe, Inver. J 4
51 Alltchaorunn B 9
20 Alltmawr H 6
60 Alltnacaillich C 5
57 Allt-na-giubhsaich L 8
60 Allt na h'Airbhe G 3
60 Allton Dubh F 2
55 Alltsigh H 8
13 Alltwalis D 8
13 Alltwen G 10
13 Alltyblacca B 8
7 Allweston E 10
32 Alma Park Estate F 6
21 Almeley G 9
21 Almeley Wooton G 9
7 Almer F 12
36 Almholme F 4
30 Almington G 5
4 Alminstone Cross D 2
52 Almondbank E 5
35 Almondbury F 10
15 Almondsbury F 9
45 Alndyke B 10
36 Alne A 3
56 Alness C 2
45 Alnham B 8
45 Alnmouth B 10
45 Alnwick B 10
27 Alphamstone M 2
27 Alpheton K 2
5 Alphington G 8
31 Alport D 10
30 Alpraham D 4
19 Alresford B 10
22 Alrewas A 5
30 Alsager E 6
30 Alsagers Bank E 6
31 Alsop en le Dale E 10
44 Alston, Cumb. H 5
6 Alston, Devon F 6
16 Alstone, Glos. A 1
6 Alstone, Som. B 6
31 Alstonefield E 9
4 Alswear D 6
61 Altanduin E 8
3 Altarnun B 9
60 Altassmore G 6
46 Altgaltraig B 5
34 Altham D 6
19 Althorne D 9
36 Althorpe F 6
42 Alticry G 4
61 Altnabea E 10
61 Altnabreac Sta. C 9
56 Altnacardich E 1
60 Altnacealgach Hot. F 4
50 Altnacraig E 6
51 Altnafeadh B 9
60 Altnaharra D 6
35 Altofts E 12
32 Alton, Derby D 1
9 Alton, Hants. B 8
31 Alton, Staffs. F 9
16 Alton Barnes H 2
7 Alton Pancras F 10
16 Alton Priors H 2
47 Altonhill E 9
30 Altrincham A 6
55 Altrua K 6
51 Altskeith G 11
56 Alltyre House D 6
52 Alva G 4

MAP
30 Alvanley C 4
31 Alvaston G 12
22 Alvechurch E 4
22 Alvecote B 6
8 Alvediston D 1
22 Alveley D 1
4 Alverdiscott C 4
9 Alverstoke F 7
35 Alverthorpe E 11
32 Alverton F 5
16 Alvescot D 4
15 Alveston, Glos. E 9
22 Alveston, War. F 6
9 Alverstone G 7
57 Alvie J 4
33 Alvingham A 10
15 Alvington D 9
24 Alwalton F 2
45 Alwinton B 7
35 Alwoodley C 11
53 Alyth B 7
33 Amber Hill E 9
15 Amberley, Glos. D 11
9 Amberley, Sussex E 11
31 Ambersgate E 11
45 Amble C 11
22 Amblecote D 2
35 Ambler Thorn D 9
38 Ambleside E 6
12 Ambleston D 3
17 Ambrosden B 7
36 Amcotts F 6
53 Americanmuir D 8
17 Amersham D 10
17 Amersham Com. D 10
45 Amersidelaw C 12
8 Amesbury B 3
63 Amhuinnsuidhe F 2
22 Amington B 6
43 Amisfield Town C 11
28 Amlwch A 4
28 Amlwch Port A 4
13 Ammanford F 9
41 Amotherby H 7
8 Ampfield D 5
48 Ampherlaw D 3
40 Ampleforth G 6
40 Ampleforth Coll. G 6
16 Ampney Crucis D 2
16 Ampney St. Mary D 2
16 Ampney St. Peter D 2
8 Amport B 4
25 Ampthill L 1
27 Ampton H 2
12 Amroth F 5
52 Amulree C 4
62 An Caol C 5
62 An Coroghon H 2
50 Anaheilt A 5
54 Anancaun C 4
33 Ancaster F 7
21 Anchor D 7
49 Ancroft E 12
49 Ancroft Northmoor E 12
49 Ancrum G 9
33 Anderby C 12
7 Anderson F 12
30 Anderton C 5
8 Andover B 5
8 Andover Down B 5
16 Andoversford B 1
38 Andreas F 2
52 Angansk F 6
2 Angarrak F 3
12 Angle G 2
38 Anglers' Hotel D 3
28 Anglesey C 4
9 Angmering F 12
9 Angmering-on-Sea F 12
39 Angram, N. Riding E 11
36 Angram, W. Riding B 3
53 Angus, County B 9
52 Anie F 1
56 Ankerville B 4
37 Anlaby D 8
24 Anmer C 8
8 Anna Valley B 5
43 Annan E 12
38 Annaside G 3
51 Annat, Argyll E 7
54 Annat, Ross & Crom. D 3
47 Annathill B 12
47 Annbank G 9
47 Annbank Station G 9
32 Annesley Woodhouse E 2
58 Annfield F 3
45 Annfield Plain H 10
45 Annitsford F 11

MAP
21 Annscroft B 10
45 Annstead D 12
7 Ansford C 10
22 Ansley C 6
31 Anslow H 10
31 Anslow Gate H 10
9 Anstey, Hants. B 8
25 Anstey, Herts. M 5
23 Anstey, Leics. A 9
53 Anstruther Easter G 10
53 Anstruther Wester G 10
10 Ansty, Sussex F 2
23 Ansty, War. D 7
8 Ansty, Wilts. C 1
9 Anthill Common E 8
43 Anthorn F 12
26 Antingham B 6
3 Antony D 11
4 Anvil Corner E 2
33 Anwick E 8
42 Anwoth F 6
24 Apes Hall F 6
24 Apethorpe F 1
33 Apley C 8
32 Apperknowle B 1
15 Apperley B 11
39 Appersett F 10
50 Appin House C 6
37 Appleby, Lincs. F 7
39 Appleby, Westmor. C 9
22 Appleby Magna A 6
22 Appleby Parva A 6
18 Appleby Street D 3
54 Applecross E 1
54 Applecross House E 1
4 Appledore, Devon C 3
6 Appledore, Devon E 4
11 Appledore, Kent E 8
11 Appledore Heath E 8
16 Appleford E 6
8 Appleshaw A 4
38 Applethwaite C 5
16 Appleton, Berks. D 5
30 Appleton, Ches. B 5
40 Appleton, Yorks. E 4
36 Appleton Roebuck C 3
41 Appleton-le-Moors F 7
41 Appleton-le-Street H 7
49 Appletreehall H 8
35 Appletreewick A 9
6 Appley D 4
34 Appley Bridge F 4
9 Apse Heath H 7
18 Apsley End A 1
9 Apuldram F 9
58 Aquhythie F 5
54 Araid D 2
54 Aranarff F 3
59 Arbeadie H 4
53 Arbirlot C 10
17 Arborfield G 8
17 Arborfield Cross G 8
42 Arbrack H 5
53 Arbroath C 11
59 Arbuthnott K 5
56 Archiestown E 8
30 Arclid Green D 6
60 Ardachadail G 3
46 Ardachearanbeg A 5
50 Ardachoil D 4
46 Ardachuple A 5
55 Ardachvie K 5
50 Ardalanish F 1
51 Ardanaiseig E 8
54 Ardaneaskan F 2
50 Ardanstur F 5
52 Ardargie House F 5
50 Ardarie A 5
54 Ardarroch F 2
46 Ardbeg C 6
60 Ardcharnich G 3
50 Ardchiavaig F 1
51 Ardchonnell F 7
50 Ardchrishnish E 2
52 Ardchullarie More F 1
51 Ardchyle E 12
53 Ardcross G 10
51 Arddarroch H 9
21 Arddleen A 8
18 Ardeley A 3
55 Ardelve G 2
47 Arden A 8
40 Arden Hall F 5
50 Ardencaple Ho. F 5
22 Ardens Grafton G 5
50 Ardentallan Ho. E 5
46 Ardentraive B 5
52 Ardeonaig D 2
51 Ardess H 10
60 Ardessie G 2
50 Ardfern G 5
51 Ardgartan G 10
60 Ardgay G 6

MAP
47 Ardgowan B 7
63 Ardhasig G 2
54 Ardheslaig D 2
50 Ardinamar F 5
60 Ardindrean G 3
10 Ardingly E 2
16 Ardington E 5
55 Ardintoul G 2
58 Ardlair E 3
46 Ardlamont House C 5
50 Ardlarach F 5
27 Ardleigh M 3
53 Ardler C 7
16 Ardley A 6
51 Ardlui F 10
46 Ardlussa A 2
51 Ardmaddy D 8
60 Ardmair G 3
46 Ardmaleish C 6
51 Ardmay G 10
46 Ardminish E 2
55 Ardmolich M 1
61 Ardmore, Ross & Crom. H 7
50 Ardmore, Argyll E 5
47 Ardmore, Dunb. B 8
50 Ardnacross C 3
47 Ardnadam A 7
56 Ardnagrask E 1
55 Ardnamurach K 2
50 Ardnastang A 5
47 Ardneil D 7
51 Ardno G 8
58 Ardo House E 7
52 Ardoch C 6
47 Ardochrig E 11
61 Ardochu F 7
55 Ardochy House J 6
50 Ardow B 2
58 Ardoyne E 4
46 Ardpatrick C 3
46 Ardpatrick House C 3
47 Ardpeaton A 7
46 Ardrishaig A 3
63 Ardroil D 1
56 Ardross Castle B 2
47 Ardrossan E 7
50 Ardshealach A 4
35 Ardsley G 12
35 Ardsley East E 11
50 Ardslignish A 3
52 Ardtalnaig C 2
46 Ardtaraig A 5
50 Ardtoe A 4
52 Ardtrostan E 2
50 Arduaine F 5
56 Ardullie C 1
50 Ardura E 4
62 Ardvasar H 5
50 Ardvergnish E 3
57 Ardverikie L 1
63 Ardvey, Loch Finsbay H 2
63 Ardvey, Loch Stockinish H 2
51 Ardvorlich, Dunb. F 10
52 Ardvorlich, Perth. E 1
63 Ardvourlie Castle F 3
42 Ardwell, Ayr. B 3
52 Ardwell, Wig. G 2
22 Areley Kings E 2
9 Arford B 9
52 Argaty G 2
14 Argoed D 5
20 Argoed Mill F 5
50 Argyll, Co. E 8
63 Aribruach E 6
51 Arichastlich D 10
50 Aridhglas F 1
54 Arinacrinachd D 1
50 Ariogan E 6
55 Arisaig L 1
55 Arisaig House L 1
50 Ariundle A 5
36 Arkendale A 2
25 Arkesden M 6
39 Arkholme H 8
39 Arkle Town E 12
43 Arkleby H 12
44 Arkleton D 2
18 Arkley D 2
36 Arksey F 4
32 Arkwright Town C 2
15 Arle B 12
38 Arlecdon C 3
25 Arlesey L 3
21 Arleston A 12
30 Arley, Cheshire B 5
22 Arley, War. C 6
15 Arlingham C 10
4 Arlington, Devon B 5
16 Arlington, Glos. C 2
10 Arlington, Sussex G 4

MAP
4 Arlington Beccott B 5
61 Armadale, Suther. B 8
48 Armadale, W. Loth. C 2
62 Armadale Castle H 6
39 Armathwaite A 7
26 Arminghall E 5
22 Armitage A 4
35 Armley D 11
22 Armscote H 6
25 Armston G 2
36 Armthorpe G 4
47 Arnburn A 8
39 Arncliffe H 11
39 Arncliffe Cote H 11
53 Arncroach G 10
8 Arne G 1
23 Arnesby C 9
46 Arnicle F 2
55 Arnisdale H 2
62 Arnish C 5
62 Arnisort C 3
48 Arniston Engine C 6
63 Arnol B 4
32 Arnold, Notts. F 3
37 Arnold, Yorks. C 9
52 Arnprior H 1
39 Arnside G 7
50 Aros Mains C 3
38 Arrad Foot G 5
37 Arram C 8
40 Arrathorne F 2
9 Arreton G 7
25 Arrington K 4
51 Arrivain D 10
51 Arrochar G 10
22 Arrow F 4
56 Artafallie E 2
35 Arthington C 11
23 Arthingworth D 11
20 Arthog A 2
58 Arthrath D 7
9 Arundel E 11
51 Aryhoulan A 7
38 Asby C 3
37 Asby cum Fenby G 10
46 Ascog C 6
17 Ascot G 10
16 Ascott-under-Wychwood B 4
40 Asenby H 4
32 Asfordby H 4
32 Asfordby Hill H 4
33 Asgarby D 10
24 Asgarby A 2
11 Ash, Kent B 11
10 Ash, Kent B 5
7 Ash, Somerset D 8
9 Ash, Surrey A 10
4 Ash Bullayne E 6
23 Ash Green D 7
30 Ash Magna F 4
4 Ash Mill D 6
6 Ash Priors C 5
6 Ash Thomas E 3
9 Ash Vale A 10
16 Ashampstead F 6
27 Ashbacking K 5
31 Ashbourne F 10
6 Ashbrittle D 4
5 Ashburton J 6
4 Ashbury, Devon F 4
16 Ashbury, Berks. F 4
37 Ashby F 7
33 Ashby by Partney D 11
33 Ashby de la Launde E 7
31 Ashby de la Zouch H 12
26 Ashby Dell E 8
23 Ashby Folville A 10
23 Ashby Magna C 9
23 Ashby Parva C 8
33 Ashby Puerorum C 10
23 Ashby St. Ledgers E 9
26 Ashby St. Mary E 6
15 Ashchurch A 12
14 Ashcombe, Som. H 6
6 Ashcombe, Devon H 3
7 Ashcott C 8
47 Ashcraig C 7
17 Ashcroft F 8
25 Ashdon L 7
9 Ashe A 7
19 Asheldham D 9
25 Ashen L 8
17 Ashendon C 8
13 Ashfield, Carm. D 10
27 Ashfield, E. Suffolk J 5
52 Ashfield, Perth. G 3
27 Ashfield Green H 6
31 Ashford, Derby C 10
4 Ashford, Devon C 4
8 Ashford, Hants. E 3

MAP
11 Ashford, Kent D 9
17 Ashford, Surrey G 11
21 Ashford Bowdler E 10
21 Ashford Carbonel E 10
16 Ashford Hill H 6
47 Ashgill D 12
39 Ashgillside A 10
6 Ashill, Devon E 4
26 Ashill, Norfolk E 2
6 Ashill, Somerset D 6
19 Ashingdon, Essex E 8
45 Ashington, Northumb. D 10
7 Ashington, Som. D 9
9 Ashington, Sussex E 12
49 Ashkirk G 7
8 Ashlett F 6
15 Ashleworth B 11
25 Ashley, Cambs. J 8
30 Ashley, Cheshire B 6
4 Ashley, Devon E 5
15 Ashley, Glos. E 12
8 Ashley, Hants. C 5
8 Ashley, Hants. G 4
11 Ashley, Kent C 11
23 Ashley, Northants C 11
30 Ashley, Staffs. F 6
17 Ashley Green D 10
8 Ashley Heath F 3
16 Ashmansworth H 5
4 Ashmansworthy D 2
7 Ashmore D 12
16 Ashmore Green G 6
22 Ashorne F 6
32 Ashover D 1
22 Ashow E 6
21 Ashperton H 11
5 Ashprington K 7
4 Ashreigney E 5
10 Ashtead B 1
30 Ashton, Cheshire C 4
2 Ashton, Cornwall G 3
21 Ashton, Herefs. F 10
23 Ashton, Northants. G 11
25 Ashton, Northants. G 2
15 Ashton Common H 12
16 Ashton Keynes E 2
34 Ashton-in-Makerfield G 5
22 Ashton under Hill H 3
35 Ashton under Lyne G 8
34 Ashton-upon-Mersey H 6
15 Ashton Watering G 8
8 Ashurst, Hants. E 5
10 Ashurst, Kent D 4
10 Ashurst, Sussex F 1
10 Ashurstwood D 3
4 Ashwater F 3
25 Ashwell, Herts. L 4
23 Ashwell, Rutland A 12
26 Ashwellthorpe F 4
7 Ashwick A 9
24 Ashwicken D 8
49 Ashybank H 8
38 Askam in Furness G 4
36 Askern F 3
7 Askerswell G 9
39 Askham C 7
36 Askham Bryan B 3
36 Askham Richard B 3
50 Asknish H 6
39 Askrigg F 11
35 Askwith B 10
24 Aslackby C 2
26 Aslacton F 4
32 Aslockton F 5
58 Asloun F 3
43 Aspatria G 12
18 Aspenden A 4
23 Aspley Guise H 12
17 Aspley Heath A 10
34 Aspull F 5
36 Asselby D 5
33 Asserby B 12
27 Assington L 2
56 Assynt House C 2
31 Astbury D 7
23 Astcote G 10
21 Asterley B 9
21 Asterton C 9
21 Asthall C 4
16 Asthall Leigh C 4
30 Astley, Salop H 4
22 Astley, War. C 6
22 Astley, Worcs. E 1
21 Astley Abbots C 12
34 Astley Bridge F 6
22 Astley Cross E 2
34 Astley Green G 6
17 Aston, Berks. F 9
30 Aston, Cheshire E 5

MAP

30 Aston, Cheshire...B 4
31 Aston, Derby....B 10
29 Aston, Flintshire.C 12
21 Aston, Herefs...E 10
21 Aston, Herefs....F 10
18 Aston, Herts....B 3
16 Aston, Oxon.....D 4
30 Aston, Salop....G 4
21 Aston, Salop....A 11
30 Aston, Staffs....F 6
31 Aston, Staffs....G 7
22 Aston, War.....C 4
32 Aston, Yorks....B 2
17 Aston Abbotts..B 9
16 Aston Blank....B 2
21 Aston Botterell..D 11
22 Aston Cantlow...F 5
17 Aston Clinton...C 9
15 Aston Crews....B 10
15 Aston Cross....A 12
18 Aston End......B 3
21 Aston Eyre.....C 12
22 Aston Fields...C 5
23 Aston Flamville...C 8
15 Aston Ingham..B 10
30 Aston juxta Mondrum
   D 5
23 Aston le Walls....G 8
16 Aston Magna...A 3
21 Aston on Clun..D 9
21 Aston Pigott....B 9
21 Aston Rogers...B 9
17 Aston Rowant..D 8
17 Aston Sandford..C 8
22 Aston Somerville..H 4
22 Aston Subedge..H 5
16 Aston Tirrold...F 6
31 Aston upon Trent G 12
16 Aston Upthorpe..E 6
25 Astwick.......L 3
25 Astwood.......K 1
22 Astwood Bank..F 4
24 Aswarby......B 2
33 Aswardby.....C 10
21 Atcham.......B 11
27 Athelington.....H 5
7 Athelney......C 7
49 Athelstaneford...B 8
4 Atherington, Devon
   D 5
9 Atherington, Sussex
   F 11
22 Atherstone....B 6
22 Atherstone on Stour
   G 5
34 Atherton......G 5
55 Athnamulloch...G 5
40 Atley Hill......E 3
31 Atlow........E 10
54 Attadale House..F 3
26 Attleborough, Norfolk
   F 3
23 Attleborough,
   Warwickshire..C 7
26 Attlebridge.....D 4
59 Atton........K 1
49 Attonburn.....G 10
37 Atwick.......B 9
15 Atworth.......H 11
32 Aubourn......D 6
51 Auchachenna...E 7
46 Auchagallon....F 4
57 Auchallater....K 7
42 Auchalton.....A 4
57 Auchavan.....M 7
46 Auchbroad....A 3
58 Auchedly......D 6
43 Auchenbainzie..B 9
59 Auchenblae....J 5
47 Auchenbothie Ho..B 8
43 Auchenbrack...B 8
46 Auchenbreck...A 5
43 Auchencairn,
   Dumfries....C 10
43 Auchencairn,
   Kirkcudbright...F 9
47 Auchencarroch..A 9
43 Auchencrieff...D 10
42 Auchencrosh...D 2
49 Auchencrow...C 11
48 Auchendinny...C 5
47 Auchenfoyle....B 8
43 Auchengibbert..D 9
48 Auchengray....D 3
43 Auchengruith...A 9
58 Auchenhairig...B 1
48 Auchenheath...E 1
42 Auchenmalg...F 3
42 Auchensoul....B 3
42 Auchentibbert...G 2
47 Auchentiber....E 8
47 Auchenvennel..A 8
43 Auchenvey.....D 8

MAP

57 Auchernack.....G 6
57 Auchgourish....H 5
46 Auchinadrian...D 2
58 Auchinderran...B 2
51 Auchindrain....G 6
54 Auchindrean...B 6
58 Auchinhove....B 2
58 Auchininna....C 4
47 Auchinleck, Ayr..G 10
42 Auchinleck, Kirk..D 5
47 Auchinloch....B 11
52 Auchinner.....F 2
58 Auchintender...D 4
59 Auchintoul, Aber..G 4
58 Auchintoul, Aber..F 3
58 Auchiries.......D 8
58 Auchleven......E 4
48 Auchlochan....F 1
59 Auchlossan.....G 3
60 Auchlunachan...H 3
59 Auchlunies.....G 6
51 Auchlyne......E 12
58 Auchmacoy....D 7
42 Auchmantle....E 2
47 Auchmillan.....F 10
53 Auchmithie.....C 11
53 Auchmuirbridge...G 7
59 Auchmull......K 3
57 Auchnacloich Pier.D 7
50 Auchnacraig....D 4
59 Auchnacree....L 2
55 Auchnadaull....L 5
52 Auchnafree.....D 3
56 Auchnagallin...F 6
58 Auchnagatt....C 7
46 Auchnaha......A 4
57 Auchnahannet..G 5
56 Auchnahillin...F 3
42 Auchnotteroch..F 1
59 Aucholzie.....H 1
51 Auchrioch.....E 10
57 Auchroisk.....G 6
59 Auchronie.....J 2
60 Auchtascailt....H 3
52 Auchterarder...F 4
55 Auchteraw.....J 7
53 Auchterderran...H 7
53 Auchterhouse...C 8
53 Auchtermuchty...F 7
54 Auchterneed....D 8
57 Auchterteang...G 5
53 Auchtertool....H 7
56 Auchtertyre, Moray
   D 7
51 Auchtertyre, Perth E 10
55 Auchtertyre,
   Ross & Crom...G 2
52 Auchtoo......E 1
61 Auckingill.....B 12
36 Auckley......G 4
58 Auckmair.....E 1
35 Audenshaw....G 8
30 Audlem.......F 5
30 Audley.......E 6
25 Audley End....L 6
58 Auds........A 4
36 Aughton, E. Riding
   C 5
34 Aughton, Lancs..G 3
39 Aughton, Lancs..H 8
32 Aughton, W. Rid..B 2
16 Aughton, Wilts..H 3
53 Auldallan......A 8
56 Auldearn.......D 5
21 Aulden.......G 10
43 Auldgirth......C 10
49 Auldhame.....A 8
47 Auldhouse.....D 11
58 Auldtown......B 3
58 Auldtown of
   Carnousie.....C 4
52 Aulich.......A 1
32 Ault Hucknall...D 2
55 Ault-a-chrinn...H 3
60 Aultanrynie....D 4
60 Aultbea.......G 1
54 Aultdearg......C 7
56 Aultfearn......E 1
54 Aultgowrie.....E 8
54 Aultgrishan....A 1
54 Aultguish Inn...C 7
58 Aulthash......B 5
61 Aultiphurst....A 8
58 Aultmore......B 1
57 Aultnagaire....G 1
56 Aultnamain Inn..A 5
57 Aultnancaber ..H 5
55 Aultnaslat.....J 5
58 Aulton.......E 3
59 Aultonrea.....H 1
57 Aultnadorach...H 5
6 Aunk........F 4
24 Aunsby.......B 1

MAP

15 Aust...........E 9
17 Austenwood....E 10
36 Austerfield.....H 4
35 Austonley.....F 9
22 Austrey.......B 6
39 Austwick......H 10
33 Authorpe......B 11
33 Authorpe Row...C 12
16 Avebury.......G 2
18 Aveley.......F 6
15 Avening.......E 12
52 Avenuehead....H 3
32 Averham......E 5
5 Aveton Gifford...L 6
57 Avielochan....H 5
57 Aviemore......H 4
46 Avinagillan....C 3
16 Avington, Berks..G 5
9 Avington, Hants..C 7
56 Avoch........D 3
16 Avon.........F 1
15 Avon, Co......F 9
23 Avon Dassett ....G 7
48 Avonbridge....B 2
15 Avonmouth....F 8
5 Avonwick......K 6
8 Awbridge......D 5
42 Awhirk.......F 2
15 Awkley.......F 9
6 Awliscombe....F 5
15 Awre.........D 10
32 Awsworth......F 2
7 Axbridge......A 8
9 Axford, Hants...B 7
16 Axford, Wilts...G 3
6 Axminster......F 6
6 Axmouth......G 6
40 Aycliffe.......C 3
45 Aydon........F 8
15 Aylburton.....D 9
44 Ayle.........H 5
6 Aylesbeare.....G 4
17 Aylesbury.....C 9
4 Aylescott......D 5
10 Aylesford......B 6
11 Aylesham.....C 11
23 Aylestone.....B 9
26 Aylmerton.....B 5
26 Aylsham......C 5
15 Aylton.......A 9
21 Aymestrey.....F 9
16 Aynho........A 6
18 Ayot St. Lawrence B 2
18 Ayot St. Peter...B 2
47 Ayr..........G 8
47 Ayr, County....F 9
39 Aysgarth......F 12
6 Ayshford......C 3
38 Ayside.......G 6
23 Ayston.......B 12
18 Aythorpe Roding..B 6
49 Ayton........C 11
40 Azerley.......H 3
5 Babbacombe....J 8
30 Babbinswood...G 2
7 Babcary.......C 9
7 Babington.....A 10
29 Babell.......C 11
25 Babraham.....K 6
32 Babworth......B 4
63 Back........C 6
55 Back of Keppoch..L 1
64 Backaland.....B 3
64 Backaskaill....A 3
58 Backbarrow....G 6
58 Backburn......D 3
12 Backe........E 6
58 Backfolds.....B 8
30 Backford......C 3
30 Backford Cross...C 3
58 Backhill, Aber...D 5
58 Backhill, Aber...F 5
58 Backhill, Aber...D 7
58 Backhill of
   Clackriach.....C 7
58 Backhill of Fortree D 7
59 Backhill of
   Trustach......H 4
61 Backies.......F 8
53 Backmuir of
   New Gilston....F 9
15 Backwell......G 8
45 Backworth....F 11
18 Bacon End.....B 6
26 Baconsthorpe...B 4
15 Bacton, Herefs...A 7
26 Bacton, Norfolk..B 6
27 Bacton, Suffolk..J 3
35 Bacup........G 7
54 Badachro......B 2
60 Badagyle......F 2

MAP

61 Badanloch Lodge .D 8
54 Badavanich.....D 5
16 Badbury.......F 3
23 Badby........F 9
60 Badcall,
   Ross & Crom...G 2
60 Badcall, Suther...C 3
60 Badcall, Loch Inchard,
   Sutherland....B 4
31 Baddeley Green..E 8
26 Baddesley Ensor..B 6
60 Baddidarach....E 2
15 Baddington....B 12
58 Baddock......D 4
58 Badenyon.....F 1
7 Badford Peverell .G 10
22 Badge........B 1
10 Badger's Mount..B 4
15 Badgeworth....B 12
7 Badgworth.....A 7
55 Badicaul......G 1
27 Badingham....H 6
60 Badintagairt....F 5
11 Badlesmere....C 9
60 Badluchrach....G 2
60 Badnaby......C 3
57 Badnambiast...M 3
56 Badnonan.....F 5
60 Badrallach.....G 2
22 Badsey.......H 4
9 Badshot Lea ...A 10
36 Badsworth.....F 2
27 Badwell Ash....H 3
33 Bag Enderby...C 10
7 Bagber........E 11
40 Bagby........G 5
16 Bagendon.....D 4
29 Bagillt.......C 11
23 Baginton......E 7
13 Baglan.......H 10
30 Bagley.......G 3
31 Bagnal.......E 8
16 Bagnor.......G 3
17 Bagshot, Surrey..H 10
16 Bagshot, Wilts...H 4
15 Bagstone......F 10
26 Bagthorpe, Norf..B 1
32 Bagthorpe, Notts..E 2
23 Bagworth......A 8
15 Bagwy Llydiart..B 8
35 Baildon.......C 10
46 Baile Boidheach..B 2
50 Baile Mor......F 1
57 Bailebeag.....H 1
44 Baileyhead....E 3
44 Bailliehill.....D 1
47 Baillieston....C 11
58 Bainshole.....D 4
39 Bainbridge....F 11
24 Bainton, Hunts..E 2
37 Bainton, Yorks...B 7
44 Bairnkine.....B 5
18 Baker Street....F 6
18 Baker's End....B 4
44 Bakethin......D 4
31 Bakewell......C 10
29 Bala.........G 8
52 Balado.......G 6
63 Balallan......E 4
50 Balalochan....B 1
57 Balavil.......J 3
57 Balbeg.......J 3
53 Balbeggie.....D 6
58 Balbithan.....F 5
54 Balblair, Inverness.E 1
56 Balblair,
   Ross & Crom..C 3
43 Balcary.......G 9
60 Balchedre.....C 8
58 Balchers......B 4
60 Balchladich....D 2
56 Balchraggan, Inver.F 1
56 Balchraggan, Inver.E 1
56 Balchreick.....B 3
10 Balcombe......E 2
53 Balcurvie......G 8
40 Balder Head....C 11
40 Baldersby......G 4
40 Baldersby St. James G 4
34 Balderstone....D 5
32 Balderton......D 2
53 Baldinnie......F 9
25 Baldock.......M 3
53 Baldovie.......D 9
38 Baldrine......G 2
11 Baldslow......G 7
38 Baldwin.......G 2
44 Baldwinholme...H 2
30 Baldwins Gate...F 4
26 Bale.........B 3
58 Balearn.......B 8

MAP

48 Balerno.......C 4
59 Balfeith......K 5
59 Balfield.......K 3
64 Balfour.......C 3
47 Balfron.......A 10
58 Balgaveny.....D 4
43 Balgerran.....E 8
52 Balgonar......H 5
58 Balgove.......D 6
57 Balgowan.....K 2
62 Balgown......A 3
53 Balgray.......C 9
43 Balgrayhill....C 12
47 Balgrochan....B 11
54 Balgy........D 2
52 Balhaldie.....G 3
58 Balhalgardy...E 5
53 Balharry......C 7
64 Baliasta......A 8
61 Baligill.......A 8
56 Balintore.....B 4
53 Balintore.....A 7
56 Balintraid....C 3
57 Balintuim.....K 7
52 Balintyre.....B 2
53 Balkeerie......C 8
36 Balkholme.....D 6
42 Balkissock....C 2
30 Ball.........G 2
16 Ball Hill......H 5
28 Ballabeg......H 1
38 Ballacannell...G 2
38 Ballacarnane Beg..G 1
57 Ballachlaggan...K 8
59 Ballachrosk....H 1
51 Ballachulish Ho..B 7
38 Ballacraine....G 1
38 Ballacuberagh..G 2
43 Ballaggan.....B 9
38 Ballajora......G 3
38 Ballakaigan....H 1
38 Ballaleigh.....G 1
42 Ballantrae.....C 2
63 Ballantrushal...B 5
19 Ballards Gore...E 9
38 Ballasalla, I.o.M...F 2
38 Ballasalla, I.o.M..H 1
59 Ballater.......H 1
38 Ballaugh......G 2
56 Ballchraggan...B 3
57 Ballcorah......G 7
52 Ballechin......B 4
49 Ballencrieff....B 7
46 Ballianlay.....C 5
50 Balliemore....E 5
38 Ballig........G 1
52 Balikinrain Castle .H 1
39 Ballimeanoch...F 7
51 Ballimore.....F 12
56 Ballindalloch...F 7
53 Ballindean....D 7
27 Ballingdon....L 2
17 Ballinger Com...D 10
15 Ballingham....A 9
52 Ballingry......G 6
56 Ballinlagg.....F 6
57 Ballinluig, Inver...G 6
52 Ballinluig, Perth..B 5
57 Ballintean.....J 4
52 Ballintuim.....B 6
42 Ballminnoch...E 4
56 Balloan.......E 2
56 Balloch, Inverness .E 3
47 Balloch, Dunb...A 9
59 Ballochan.....H 3
42 Ballochbroe....A 4
42 Ballochdoan...D 2
42 Ballochdowan..D 2
58 Ballochford....D 1
46 Ballochgoy....C 6
42 Ballochmorrie..C 3
46 Ballochroy....D 2
59 Ballogie.......H 3
9 Balls Cross....D 11
10 Ball's Green....D 4
50 Ballygown....C 2
50 Ballymeanoch...H 5
55 Balmacara.....G 1
43 Balmaclellan...D 7
52 Balmacneil....B 5
53 Balmacolm....F 8
62 Balmacquien...A 4
43 Balmae.......G 7
51 Balmaha......H 11
50 Balmeanach...D 2
43 Balmangan....G 7
58 Balmedie......F 7
53 Balmerino.....E 8
8 Balmerlawn....F 5
54 Balmore, Inver...F 7
62 Balmore, Skye, Inver.
   D 2

MAP

52 Balmore, Perth...A 4
47 Balmore, Stirling .B 11
56 Balmuchy......B 4
53 Balmule.......H 7
53 Balmullo......E 9
56 Balmungie.....D 3
42 Balmurrie.....E 3
59 Balnaboth.....K 1
56 Balnabruaich...C 3
56 Balnabual.....E 3
61 Balnacoil Lodge...F 8
54 Balnacra......E 3
56 Balnacraig.....F 1
56 Balnafoich.....F 2
56 Balnagall......B 4
56 Balnageith.....D 6
59 Balnagowan...G 2
52 Balnaguard....B 4
56 Balnaguisich...C 2
55 Balnain.......G 8
60 Balnakeil......A 5
62 Balnaknock....B 3
56 Balnapaling...C 4
59 Balquharn.....L 2
51 Balquhidder...E 12
22 Balsall.......E 6
22 Balsall Common..D 6
23 Balscott......H 7
25 Balsham......K 7
64 Baltasound...A 8
30 Balterley.....E 6
42 Baltersan.....E 5
32 Balterton.....E 5
58 Balthangie.....C 6
7 Baltonsborough..C 8
50 Balure.......C 6
5 Balvack......F 4
58 Balvaird......D 1
56 Balvenie......C 1
50 Balvicar......F 5
55 Balvraid, Inver...H 2
56 Balvraid, Inver...F 4
34 Bamber Bridge..E 4
18 Bamber's Green..B 6
45 Bamburgh.....D 12
58 Bamff........B 7
48 Bamflatt......F 3
31 Bamford......B 10
6 Bampton, Devon..D 3
16 Bampton, Oxon..D 4
39 Bampton,
   Westmorland...C 7
55 Bampton Grange..C 7
55 Banavie ....M 5
23 Banbury......H 8
13 Bancffosfelen...F 8
59 Banchory, Kinc...G 7
59 Banchory, Kinc...H 4
13 Bancycapel....E 7
12 Banc-y-felin...E 6
13 Banc-y-ffordd...C 7
53 Bandirran House..D 7
58 Banff........A 4
28 Bangor.......C 5
30 Bangor-Is-coed..F 3
27 Banham.......G 4
8 Bank, Hants....E 4
21 Bank, Mont....A 8
35 Bank Newton...B 8
21 Bank Street....F 11
43 Bankend, Dumf..E 11
48 Bankend, Lanark..F 1
52 Bankfoot, Perth...D 5
47 Bankfoot, Renfrew B 7
47 Bankglen......H 11
58 Bankhead, Aber..F 6
59 Bankhead, Aber..A 4
47 Bankhead, Ayr...D 8
48 Bankhead, Lanark.E 3
45 Bankhead,
   Northumberland B 8
47 Banknock......B 12
44 Banks, Cumb...F 4
34 Banks, Lancs....E 3
43 Bankshill......C 12
26 Banningham....C 5
19 Bannister Green..B 7
52 Bannockburn...H 3
10 Banstead......B 1
5 Bantham......L 5
47 Banton.......B 12
15 Banwell.......H 7
11 Bapchild......B 8
50 Barachandroman.E 4
47 Barassie......F 8
50 Baravullin.....D 6
56 Barbaraville....C 3
31 Barber Booth...B 9
47 Barbieston....H 9
39 Barbon........G 8
50 Barbreck House..G 5
4 Barbrook......A 6
23 Barby........E 9

MAP

51 Barcaldine........C 7
43 Barcaple.........F 7
22 Barchesten......H 6
47 Barclaugh.......G 9
43 Barclosh........E 9
10 Barcombe.......G 3
10 Barcombe Cross...F 3
40 Barden..........F 2
35 Barden Scale....A 9
42 Bardennoch......B 6
64 Bardister.......C 7
61 Bardnabeinne....G 7
33 Bardney........C 8
23 Bardon.........A 8
44 Bardon Mill.....G 6
47 Bardowie.......B 10
47 Bardrainney.....B 8
38 Bardsea........H 5
35 Bardsey........C 12
27 Bardwell.......H 2
49 Barelees.......F 11
21 Barewood.......G 9
46 Barfad.........B 4
26 Barford, Norfolk..E 4
22 Barford, War....F 6
16 Barford St. John..A 5
8 Barford St. Martin C 2
16 Barford St. Michael A 5
11 Barfreston......C 11
42 Bargaly.........E 5
47 Barglas........A 8
14 Bargoed.........D 5
42 Bargrennan......D 4
51 Barguillean Farm..E 7
25 Barham, Hunts...H 2
11 Barham, Kent...C 10
27 Barham, Suffolk..K 4
43 Barharrow......F 7
24 Barholm........D 2
44 Barhough.......H 5
23 Barkby.........A 9
23 Barkby Thorpe...A 9
32 Barkestone.....G 5
17 Barkham........G 9
18 Barking, Essex...E 5
27 Barking, Suffolk..K 4
27 Barking Tye.....K 4
35 Barkisland......E 9
32 Barkston, Lincs...F 6
36 Barkston, Yorks..D 3
25 Barkway........M 5
42 Barlae.........F 4
31 Barlaston......F 7
43 Barlay.........D 7
32 Barlborough....C 2
36 Barlby.........D 4
23 Barlestone.....B 8
25 Barley, Herts...L 5
35 Barley, Lancs...C 7
45 Barley Mow.....H 11
45 Barleyhill......H 8
23 Barleythorpe....A 11
19 Barling........E 9
32 Barlow, Derby...C 1
35 Barlow, Durham...G 9
36 Barlow, Yorks...D 4
36 Barmby Moor....B 5
36 Barmby on the Marsh
         D 5
26 Barmer.........B 1
49 Barmoor Castle..E 12
49 Barmoor Ridge..E 12
20 Barmouth.......A 2
40 Barmpton.......C 3
37 Barmston.......A 9
43 Barmurrie......D 7
51 Barnacarry.....H 7
24 Barnack........E 2
23 Barnacle.......D 7
51 Barnaline......F 7
39 Barnard Castle..C 12
25 Barnardiston....K 8
43 Barnbarroch....F 9
36 Barnburgh......G 3
26 Barnby.........F 8
36 Barnby Dun.....F 4
32 Barnby in the Willows
         E 6
32 Barnby Moor....B 4
42 Barncorkrie.....H 2
18 Barnes.........F 2
10 Barnes Street...C 5
18 Barnet.........D 3
37 Barnetby le Wold.F 8
26 Barney.........B 3
27 Barnham, Suffolk.G 2
9 Barnham, Sussex.F 11
26 Barnham Broom...E 4
59 Barnhead......L 4
56 Barnhill.......D 7
31 Barnhills......D 1
27 Barningham, Suff.H 3
40 Barningham, Yorks.D 1

37 Barnoldby le Beck
         G 10
35 Barnoldswick....C 7
9 Barns Green....C 12
16 Barnsley, Glos...D 2
35 Barnsley, Yorks..F 12
4 Barnstaple......C 4
30 Barnston, Cheshire B 1
18 Barnston, Essex..B 6
32 Barnstone......G 4
22 Barnt Green....E 4
30 Barnton........C 5
25 Barnwell All Saints G 2
25 Barnwell St. Andrew
         G 2
15 Barnwood.......C 11
21 Barons' Cross...G 10
47 Barr, Ayr......H 12
42 Barr, Ayr......B 4
43 Barr, Dumfries...E 8
58 Barra Castle....E 5
42 Barrachan......G 4
50 Barrachrail.....E 5
63 Barraglom......D 3
45 Barrasford......F 7
50 Barravullin.....G 5
38 Barregarrow ....J 2
47 Barrhead.......D 10
42 Barrhill.......C 2
25 Barrington, Cambs.K 5
7 Barrington, Som...D 7
2 Barripper.......F 3
55 Barrisdale.....J 3
47 Barrmill.......D 8
61 Barrock........A 11
34 Barrow, Lancs....C 6
23 Barrow, Rutland .A 12
21 Barrow, Salop...B 12
7 Barrow, Som....C 10
27 Barrow, Suffolk..J 1
15 Barrow Gurney..G 8
37 Barrow Haven....E 8
32 Barrow Hill.....C 1
38 Barrow-in-Furness H 5
34 Barrow Nook....G 3
7 Barrow Street....C 11
37 Barrow-upon-Humber
         E 8
32 Barrow-upon-Soar H 3
31 Barrow-upon-Trent
         G 12
45 Barrowburn.....B 7
32 Barrowby.......G 6
41 Barrowcliff.....F 10
23 Barrowden......B 12
35 Barrowford.....C 7
30 Barrows Green...D 5
51 Barrs..........D 8
53 Barry, Angus...D 10
14 Barry, Glam....G 4
23 Barsby.........A 10
26 Barsham........F 7
22 Barston........D 5
21 Bartestree.....H 11
58 Barthol Chapel...D 6
30 Barthomley.....D 5
34 Bartle Hall.....D 4
49 Bartlehill......E 10
8 Bartley........E 4
25 Bartlow........L 7
25 Barton, Cambs...K 5
30 Barton, Cheshire.E 3
5 Barton, Devon...J 8
16 Barton, Glos....B 2
34 Barton, Lancs...C 4
34 Barton, Lancs...F 2
7 Barton, Somerset..A 7
22 Barton, War....G 4
39 Barton, Westmor..C 7
40 Barton, Yorks...D 3
18 Bayford, Herts...C 3
24 Barton Bendish...C 7
26 Barton Common..C 7
15 Barton End.....H 4
17 Barton Hartshorn .A 7
32 Barton in Fabis...G 2
23 Barton-in-the-Beans
         B 7
25 Barton-in-the-Clay M 2
25 Barton Mills....H 11
8 Barton-on-Sea....G 4
16 Barton-on-the-Heath
         A 4
7 Barton St. David..C 3
23 Barton Seagrave .D 12
8 Barton Stacey....B 6
4 Barton Town....B 5
37 Barton Waterside..E 8
41 Barton-le-Street..H 1
36 Barton-le-Willows .A 5
31 Barton-under-
         Needwood....H 10
37 Barton-upon-Humber
         E 8

35 Barugh.........F 11
63 Barvas.........B 5
25 Barway........H 6
23 Barwell........B 8
36 Barwick in Elmet..C 2
30 Baschurch......H 3
23 Bascote........F 7
31 Basford Green...E 8
34 Bashall Eaves...C 6
8 Bashley........F 4
17 Basildon, Berks..F 7
19 Basildon, Essex..E 7
9 Basing.........A 8
9 Basingstoke....A 7
31 Baslow.........C 11
7 Bason Bridge...B 7
14 Bassaleg.......F 6
49 Bassendean.....E 9
38 Bassenfell.....B 4
38 Bassenthwaite...B 5
38 Bassenthwaite Lake
         Station.......B 4
4 Basset's Cross...F 4
8 Bassett........D 5
22 Bassett's Pole...E 5
25 Bassingbourn...L 4
32 Bassingfield....F 3
32 Bassingham....D 6
33 Bassingthorpe..G 7
64 Basta..........B 7
24 Baston.........D 2
26 Bastwick.......D 7
18 Batchworth Heath.E 1
7 Batcombe, Dorset..F 4
7 Batcombe, Som...B 10
30 Bate Heath.....B 5
15 Bath..........H 10
15 Bathampton.....H 11
15 Bathealton.....D 4
15 Batheaston.....G 11
15 Bathford.......H 11
48 Bathgate.......B 3
32 Bathley........G 6
10 Bathpool, Corn...B 10
6 Bathpool, Som...D 6
6 Bathway.........A 9
35 Batley.........E 11
16 Batsford.......A 3
32 Battersby......D 6
18 Battersea......F 3
27 Battisford.....K 4
27 Battisford Tye...K 3
10 Battle, Sussex...F 6
14 Battle, Brec....A 3
7 Battleborough...A 7
21 Battlefield.....A 10
19 Battlesbridge...D 8
18 Battlesden.....A 10
6 Battleton......C 3
8 Battramsley....F 5
9 Batt's Corner...B 9
58 Bauds of Cullen..A 2
17 Baughurst......H 7
34 Baulds.........H 4
16 Baulking.......E 4
33 Baumber........C 9
30 Baunton.......D 1
8 Baverstock.....C 2
26 Bawburgh......E 5
36 Bawdeswell....C 3
7 Bawdrip........B 7
27 Bawdsey........L 2
5 Bawtry.........A 4
34 Baxenden......E 6
22 Baxterley......B 6
38 Baybridge.......D 7
38 Baycliff.......H 5
16 Baydon.........F 4
18 Bayford, Herts....C 3
7 Bayford, Som....C 10
39 Bayles.........A 9
27 Baylham........K 4
16 Baynards' Green..A 6
21 Bayston Hill....B 10
21 Bayton.........E 12
50 Beach, Argyll...B 5
15 Beach, Glos....G 10
23 Beachampton...H 11
24 Beachamwell...E 8
15 Beachley.......E 9
10 Beacon End.....A 9
8 Beacon Hill, Dor. G 1
9 Beacon Hill, Surrey
         B 10
17 Beacon's Bottom..E 9
17 Beaconsfield....E 10
63 Beacravik......H 2
40 Beadlam.......G 6
45 Beadnell......D 12
4 Beaford........D 3
45 Beal, Northumb..B 12
36 Beal, Yorks......E 3

55 Bealachasan.....H 3
7 Beaminster......F 8
45 Beamish........H 10
35 Beamsley......B 9
10 Bean..........A 5
45 Beanacre.......H 12
45 Beanley........A 9
44 Beara Moor.....D 4
44 Bearbridge.....G 6
6 Beare..........F 3
9 Beare Green....D 1
45 Bearl..........G 9
22 Bearley........F 5
40 Bearnus........C 1
40 Bearpark.......A 3
47 Bearsden......B 10
11 Bearsted.......C 7
44 Bearwood.......F 2
43 Beattock.......A 11
48 Beattock Summit .H 3
18 Beauchamp Roding C 6
32 Beauchief......B 1
14 Beaufort.......C 5
8 Beaulieu.......F 5
56 Beauly........E 1
25 Beaumaris.....C 5
44 Beaumont, Cumb..G 2
19 Beaumont, Essex .A 11
40 Beaumont Hill...C 3
22 Beausale.......E 6
9 Beauworth.....C 7
4 Beaworthy.....F 3
9 Beazley........B 3
19 Beazley End....A 7
40 Bebington......D 5
45 Bebside........E 11
26 Beccles........F 7
11 Becconsall.....E 3
39 Beck Foot.....F 8
41 Beck Hole......E 8
5 Beck Row......H 8
38 Beck Side......G 5
22 Beckbury.......B 1
17 Beckenham.....G 4
43 Beckfoot......G 11
16 Beckford......A 1
34 Beckhampton...G 3
32 Beckingham, Lincs. E 6
32 Beckingham, Notts. A 5
7 Beckington.....A 11
16 Beckley, Hants...F 4
16 Beckley, Oxon...C 6
11 Beckley, Sussex...F 7
35 Beckwithshaw...B 11
18 Becontree.....E 5
40 Bedale.........F 3
44 Bedburn.......B 1
7 Bedchester.....D 12
28 Beddgelert.....E 5
10 Beddingham....G 3
18 Beddington.....G 3
21 Bedfield.......J 5
25 Bedford.......K 2
25 Bedfordshire, Co. .K 2
24 Bedhampton....E 8
27 Bedingfield....H 5
33 Bedlam........A 11
45 Bedlington.....E 10
14 Bedlinog.......D 4
15 Bedminster.....B 9
17 Bedmond......D 11
31 Bednall.......H 8
32 Bedrule.......H 2
49 Bedshiel.......D 9
21 Bedstone......E 9
23 Bedwas........C 7
14 Bedwellty.....D 5
23 Bedworth......C 7
23 Beeby.........A 10
23 Beech, Hants...B 8
31 Beech, Staffs...F 7
17 Beech Hill, Berks..H 8
34 Beech Hill, Lancs..F 4
39 Beech Hill,
         Westmorland...E 7
16 Beechingstoke...H 2
16 Beedon........F 6
16 Beedon Hill....F 6
37 Beeford.......B 9
31 Beeley.........C 11
27 Beelsby........G 9
17 Beenham.......G 7
2 Beeny.........B 1
7 Beer, Devon...G 6
7 Beer, Somerset..C 7
7 Beer Hackett...E 9
7 Beercrocombe...D 7
5 Beesands......M 7
33 Beesby........B 11
5 Beeson........L 7
25 Beeston, Beds...K 3
30 Beeston, Cheshire .D 4

26 Beeston, Norfolk..D 2
32 Beeston, Notts...D 3
35 Beeston, Yorks...D 11
26 Beeston Regis....A 5
43 Beeswing.......E 10
39 Beetham.......G 7
26 Beetley.......D 3
14 Began.........F 5
16 Begbroke......C 5
24 Begdale.......E 6
12 Begelly.......F 5
21 Beggar's Bush...F 8
21 Beguildy......D 7
26 Beighton, Norf...E 7
32 Beighton, Yorks..B 2
47 Beith.........D 8
11 Bekesbourne...C 10
26 Belaugh.......D 6
22 Belbroughton...D 3
27 Belchamp Otten...L 1
27 Belchamp St. Paul.L 1
27 Belchamp Walter..L 1
58 Belcherrie.....D 1
33 Belchford......C 10
53 Belfarg........G 7
45 Belford........C 12
45 Belford Mains...C 12
58 Belhelvie.......F 7
58 Belhinnie......E 2
18 Bell Bar.......C 3
35 Bell Busk......B 7
22 Bell Heath.....D 3
58 Bellabeg.......F 1
50 Bellanoch......H 5
36 Bellasize......D 6
35 Belle Vue......E 12
33 Belleau.......B 11
56 Bellehiglash....F 7
40 Bellerby.......F 1
5 Bellever.......H 5
49 Bellhaven.....E 9
17 Bellingdon.....D 10
45 Bellingham.....E 7
46 Belloch........F 2
46 Bellochantuy...F 2
10 Bells Yew Green..D 5
42 Bellsbank.....A 5
47 Bellshill, Lanark .C 12
45 Bellshill,
         Northumb.....C 12
48 Bellspool......F 4
48 Bellsquarry.....C 3
56 Belmaduthy....D 2
24 Belmesthorpe...D 1
47 Belmont, Ayr...G 8
34 Belmont, Lancs..F 5
64 Belmont, Shetland Is.
         B 8
47 Belmore.......A 7
58 Belnacraig.....F 1
3 Belowda.......D 7
31 Belper.........E 11
31 Belper Lane End .E 11
45 Belsay.........E 9
27 Belstead......L 4
47 Belston.......G 9
4 Belstone.......F 5
4 Belstone Corner..F 5
34 Belthorn......E 6
11 Beltinge......A 10
44 Beltingham.....G 6
36 Beltoft.......F 6
32 Belton, Leics...H 2
32 Belton, Kesteven .F 6
36 Belton, Lindsey...F 6
26 Belton, Norfolk...E 8
23 Belton, Rutland ..B 11
32 Belvoir........G 5
9 Bembridge......G 8
49 Bemersyde.....F 8
8 Bemerton......C 3
41 Bempton.......H 12
61 Ben Armine Lodge E 7
63 Ben Casgro......D 5
27 Benacre.......G 8
57 Benalder Lodge..L 1
43 Benbruie.......B 8
48 Bendameer.....A 5
54 Bendronaig Lodge F 4
24 Benefield......F 1
11 Benenden......E 7
42 Benfield.......E 5
27 Benfield Green...J 7
45 Benfieldside....H 9
8 Bengall........D 12
26 Bengate.......C 6
22 Bengeworth.....H 4
59 Benholm......K 5
36 Beningbrough...A 3
18 Benington, Herts..A 5
33 Benington, Lincs. E 11
33 Benington Sea End F 11

28 Benllech.......B 4
46 Benmore.......A 6
60 Benmore Lodge...F 4
5 Bennacott......G 2
46 Bennecarrigan...G 4
33 Benniworth....G 8
10 Benover.......C 6
17 Benson.........E 7
47 Benston.......H 10
59 Bent..........K 4
45 Benthall,
         Northumb.....D 12
21 Benthall, Salop...B 12
15 Bentham.......C 12
59 Benthoul......G 5
9 Bentley, Hants....B 9
22 Bentley, War.....E 8
37 Bentley, E. Riding D 8
36 Bentley, W. Riding G 3
22 Bentley Heath...D 5
4 Benton........B 5
46 Benton Polliwilline H 2
44 Bentpath......D 2
24 Bentwick......F 4
4 Bentwitchen....C 6
9 Bentworth.....B 8
42 Beoch, Ayr.....B 6
42 Beoch, Wigtown..E 2
7 Beoley........E 4
55 Beoraidberg....K 1
9 Bepton........D 10
18 Berden........A 5
5 Bere Alston.....J 3
5 Bere Ferrers.....J 3
7 Bere Regis......G 11
2 Berepper.......G 4
26 Bergh Apton....E 6
9 Berkeley.......D 10
17 Berkhamsted....C 10
7 Berkley.......A 11
16 Berkshire, Co....F 5
22 Berkswell......D 6
18 Bermondsey....F 3
55 Bernera.......G 2
62 Bernisdale.....C 3
17 Berrick Salome...E 7
61 Berriedale.....E 10
38 Berrier........B 6
21 Berriew........B 7
49 Berrington, Northumb.
         E 12
21 Berrington, Salop. B 10
49 Berringtonlaw...E 12
6 Berrow........A 6
22 Berrow Green...F 1
4 Berry Cross.....D 3
4 Berry Down Cross .B 4
15 Berry Hill, Glos...C 9
12 Berry Hill, Pem...C 4
5 Berry Pomeroy...K 7
58 Berryhillock, Banff B 2
4 Berrynarbor.....A 4
18 Berry's Green....H 4
43 Berryscaur.....B 12
59 Berrysloch.....H 3
29 Bersham.......E 12
20 Berthddu......H 4
49 Berwick, Co....D 8
10 Berwick, Dorset..G 9
10 Berwick, Sussex..H 4
16 Berwick Bassett..E 2
45 Berwick Hill....F 10
8 Berwick St. James .B 2
8 Berwick St. John..D 1
7 Berwick St. Leonard
         C 12
49 Berwick-upon-Tweed
         D 12
29 Berwyn........F 11
32 Bescaby.......G 5
34 Bescar........F 3
22 Besford.......H 3
36 Bessacarr.....H 2
10 Bessels Green...C 4
16 Bessels Leigh...D 5
37 Bessingby......A 9
26 Bessingham....B 4
10 Best Beech Hill..E 5
26 Besthorpe, Norf...F 4
32 Besthorpe, Notts..D 5
37 Beswick.......B 8
45 Betchworth....C 1
28 Bethania, Caer...F 6
20 Bethania, Cards...F 1
26 Bethel, Anglesey..C 3
28 Bethel, Caer....D 5
29 Bethel, Mer.....F 9
11 Bethersden....D 8
28 Bethesda, Caer...D 6
12 Bethesda, Pem....E 4
13 Bethlehem......D 10
18 Bethnal Green...F 3
30 Betley.........E 6

MAP

10 Betsham........A 5
11 Betteshanger.....C 11
7 Bettiscombe......F 7
30 Bettisfield.......G 3
30 Betton.........G 5
14 Bettws..........F 2
20 Bettws Bledrws..G 2
12 Bettws Evan.....B 6
15 Bettws Newydd...D 7
61 Bettyhill........B 7
13 Betws...........F 9
21 Betws Cedewain...C 7
28 Betws Garmon....D 5
29 Betws Gwerfil Goch
　　　　F 9
29 Betws-y-coed....E 7
29 Betws-yn-Rhos...C 8
20 Beulah, Brec....G 5
12 Beulah, Cards...B 6
32 Bevercotes.......C 4
37 Beverley........C 8
15 Beverstone.....E 11
15 Bevington.....E 10
38 Bewaldeth......B 4
44 Bewcastle......F 4
22 Bewdley........E 1
35 Bewerley.....A 10
37 Bewholme......B 9
49 Bewlie.........G 8
10 Bexhill.........G 6
18 Bexley.........F 5
18 Bexleyheath....F 5
24 Bexwell........E 7
27 Beyton.........J 2
27 Beyton Green.....J 2
16 Bibury.........C 2
17 Bicester........B 7
22 Bickenhill.......D 5
24 Bicker.........B 3
34 Bickerstaffe....G 3
30 Bickerton, Ches..E 4
45 Bickerton, Northumb.
　　　　C 8
36 Bickerton, Yorks..B 2
4 Bickingcott......C 6
4 Bickington, Devon C 4
5 Bickington, Devon H 7
6 Bickleigh, Devon..E 3
5 Bickleigh, Devon..J 4
4 Bickleton.......C 4
30 Bickley Moss.....E 4
19 Bicknacre.......D 8
6 Bicknoller......B 5
11 Bicknor.........B 7
8 Bickton, Hants...E 3
21 Bicton, Herefs..F 10
21 Bicton, Salop....B 8
21 Bicton, Salop...A 10
11 Biddenden......D 7
11 Biddenden Green .D 7
25 Biddenham......K 1
15 Biddestone.....G 11
7 Biddisham.......A 7
23 Biddlesden......H 9
45 Biddlestone.....B 8
31 Biddulph.......D 7
31 Biddulph Moor...D 7
4 Bideford.......C 3
22 Bidford-on-Avon..G 4
10 Bidborough.....D 4
6 Bidwell.........F 3
36 Bielby..........C 5
59 Bieldside........G 6
8 Bierley, Hants,...H 6
35 Bierley, Yorks...D 10
17 Bierton.........C 9
43 Big Corlae......B 7
54 Big Sand........B 1
5 Bigbury.........L 5
5 Bigbury-on-Sea...L 5
37 Bigby..........F 8
48 Biggar, Lanark...F 3
34 Biggar, Lancs....A 1
48 Biggarshiels Mains E 3
31 Biggin, Derby..E 11
31 Biggin, Derby...D 10
36 Biggin, Yorks...D 3
18 Biggin Hill.....H 4
25 Biggleswade.....L 3
9 Bighton.........C 7
9 Bignor..........E 11
64 Bigton.........F 7
1 Bilberry.......D 7
32 Bilborough......F 3
6 Bilbrook........B 4
36 Bilbrough.......C 3
32 Bilby..........B 4
27 Bildeston......K 3
1 Billacott.......A 9
19 Billericay......D 7
32 Billesdon.....B 10
22 Billesley.......F 5
24 Billingborough...B 2

MAP

34 Billinge........G 4
27 Billingford......G 5
26 Billingford......C 3
40 Billingham.....C 5
33 Billinghay......E 8
36 Billingley......G 2
9 Billinghurst...C 12
21 Billingsley.....D 12
17 Billington, Beds..B 10
34 Billington, Lancs..D 6
26 Billockby......D 7
40 Billy Row......A 2
34 Bilsborrow.....C 4
33 Bilsby.........C 11
9 Bilsham.........F 11
11 Bilsington......E 9
15 Bilson Green....C 9
32 Bilsthorpe......D 4
48 Bilston, Midloth..C 5
22 Bilston, Staffs...B 3
23 Bilstone.......B 7
11 Bilting.........C 9
45 Bilton, Northumb.
　　　　B 10
15 Bilton, Som. ..G 10
37 Bilton, E. Riding..D 9
36 Bilton, W. Riding..B 3
23 Bilton, War.....E 8
45 Bilton Banks....B 10
64 Bimbister.......C 2
37 Binbrook......H 10
7 Bincombe......H 10
61 Bindal.........H 9
7 Binegar........A 9
17 Binfield.......G 9
17 Binfield Heath...F 8
45 Bingfield.......F 8
32 Bingham.......F 4
7 Bingham's Melcombe
　　　　F 11
35 Bingley........C 10
26 Binham.........B 3
8 Binley.........A 6
48 Binniehill......B 1
40 Binnose.......G 3
9 Binstead.......G 7
9 Binsted........B 9
22 Binton.........G 5
26 Bintree........C 3
21 Binweston......B 8
19 Birch, Essex....B 9
35 Birch, Lancs....F 7
19 Birch Green....B 9
31 Birch Vale.....B 8
26 Bircham Newton..B 1
26 Bircham Tofts...B 1
18 Birchanger.....B 5
21 Bircher........F 10
57 Birchfield......G 5
14 Birchgrove, Cardiff,
　　Glamorgan....F 5
13 Birchgrove, Glam.G 10
11 Birchington....A 11
31 Birchover......D 10
32 Bircotes.......A 3
22 Bird End.......C 4
25 Birdbrook......L 8
9 Birdham........F 9
23 Birdingbury.....E 8
15 Birdlip.......C 12
36 Birdsall.......A 6
22 Birdsgreen......D 1
7 Birdsmoor Gate...F 7
47 Birdston.......B 11
35 Birdwell......G 12
15 Birdwood......B 10
49 Birgham........E 10
34 Birkacre........F 4
40 Birkby.........E 3
34 Birkdale.......F 2
30 Birkenhead.....A 2
58 Birkenhills.....C 5
47 Birkenshaw, Lanark
　　　　D 12
35 Birkenshaw, Yorks.
　　　　D 10
59 Birkhall.......H 1
53 Birkhill, Angus..D 8
49 Birkhill, Berwick..E 8
48 Birkhill, Dumfries.H 5
36 Birkin.........D 3
44 Birks..........E 6
43 Birkshaw.......C 9
21 Birley.........G 10
10 Birling, Kent....B 5
45 Birling, Northumb.
　　　　B 10
22 Birlingham......H 3
22 Birmingham....D 5
52 Birnam.........C 5
47 Birnieknowe....G 10
59 Birse..........H 3
59 Birsemore......H 3

MAP

23 Birstall, Leics....A 9
35 Birstall, Yorks...E 11
35 Birstwith......A 11
24 Birthorpe......B 2
48 Birthwood......F 3
45 Birtley, Durham..G 11
21 Birtley, Herefs...E 9
45 Birtley, Northumb. E 7
8 Birts Street.....A 11
23 Bisbrooke.....B 12
4 Bish Mill......C 6
17 Bisham........F 9
22 Bishampton.....G 3
40 Bishop Auckland..B 2
37 Bishop Burton...C 7
40 Bishop Middleham B 3
40 Bishop Monkton..H 3
33 Bishop Norton...A 7
15 Bishop Sutton...H 9
35 Bishop Thornton.A 10
36 Bishop Wilton...B 6
33 Bishopbridge....A 7
47 Bishopbriggs....B 11
56 Bishopmill.....C 8
16 Bishops Cannings .H 2
21 Bishop's Castle...D 8
7 Bishop's Caundle.E 10
15 Bishop's Cleeve..B 12
21 Bishop's Frome ..G 12
18 Bishop's Green...B 6
6 Bishop's Hull....D 5
23 Bishop's Itchington F 7
6 Bishop's Lydeard..C 5
4 Bishop's Nympton D 6
30 Bishop's Offley....G 6
18 Bishop's Stortford .B 5
9 Bishop's Sutton...C 7
22 Bishop's Tachbrook
　　　　F 6
4 Bishop's Tawton ..C 4
9 Bishop's Waltham.D 7
22 Bishop's Wood ...A 2
11 Bishopsbourne...C 10
5 Bishopsteignton...H 8
6 Bishopstoke.....C 6
13 Bishopston......H 9
17 Bishopstone, Bucks.
　　　　C 9
21 Bishopstone, Herefs.
　　　　H 9
10 Bishopstone, Sussex
　　　　H 4
8 Bishopstone, Wilts.C 2
16 Bishopstone, Wilts F 3
7 Bishopstrow....B 11
6 Bishopswood....E 6
15 Bishopsworth...G 9
36 Bishopthorpe....B 4
40 Bishopton, Dur...C 4
47 Bishopton, Ren...B 9
15 Bishpool.......E 7
15 Bishton, Glos....F 7
21 Bisley, Glos....D 12
17 Bisley, Surrey..H 10
34 Bispham.......C 2
2 Bissoe.........E 5
8 Bisterne Close...F 4
33 Bitchfield......G 7
4 Biteford........D 2
4 Bittadon.......B 4
5 Bittaford.......K 5
26 Bittering Street..D 2
21 Bitterley.....E 11
8 Bitterne.......E 6
23 Bitteswell......D 8
17 Bix...........F 8
64 Bixter.........D 7
32 Blaby..........B 9
16 Black Bourton...D 4
54 Black Bridge.....C 7
45 Black Callerton..F 10
42 Black Clauchrie..C 4
51 Black Corries ...B 10
50 Black Croft.....D 6
4 Black Dog......C 7
45 Black Heddon...E 9
51 Black Mount....C 10
19 Black Notley....B 7
13 Black Pill .....H 9
4 Black Torrington..E 3
43 Blackacre.....C 11
49 Blackadder Bank.D 11
5 Blackawton....L 7
6 Blackborough..E 4
24 Blackborough End D 8
10 Blackboys......F 4
31 Blackbrook, Derby
　　　　E 11
34 Blackbrook, Lancs.G 4
30 Blackbrook, Staffs. F 6
58 Blackburn, Aber..F 6
48 Blackburn, Lanark G 2
34 Blackburn, Lancs. .D 5

MAP

49 Blackburn,
　　Midlothian.....D 8
44 Blackburn, Rox. .D 3
48 Blackburn,
　　W. Lothian.....C 3
43 Blackcraig......D 8
3 Blackditch Cross ..E 6
58 Blackdog.......F 7
43 Blackdyke......F 12
35 Blacker Hill....G 12
8 Blackfield......F 6
44 Blackford, Cumb..G 2
52 Blackford, Perth..F 4
7 Blackford, Som...A 7
7 Blackford, Som. .D 10
31 Blackfordby....H 11
8 Blackgang......H 6
40 Blackhall Colliery .A 5
45 Blackhall Mill...G 9
10 Blackham......D 4
49 Blackhaugh.....E 7
19 Blackheath, Essex B 10
27 Blackheath, Suff...H 7
9 Blackheath, Surrey
　　　　B 11
22 Blackheath,Worcs. D 3
58 Blackhill, Aber...B 8
47 Blackhill, Aber...C 8
62 Blackhill, Inver...C 3
58 Blackhillock.....C 1
56 Blackhills, Moray D 8
44 Blackhills, Dumfries
　　　　F 1
15 Blackhorse.....F 10
48 Blackhopebyre...E 6
30 Blackland......G 1
43 Blacklaw.......A 11
35 Blackley........G 7
45 Blacklunans.....H 10
21 Blackmarstone...H 10
14 Blackmill.......F 3
9 Blackmoor......C 9
4 Blackmoor Gate..B 5
18 Blackmore......D 6
25 Blackmore End,
　　Essex........M 8
18 Blackmore End,
　　Hertfordshire...B 2
48 Blackness......A 3
9 Blacknest......B 9
35 Blacko.........C 7
43 Blackpark......C 10
34 Blackpool.......C 2
44 Blackpool Gate..E 4
48 Blackridge......C 2
43 Blackrigg.....C 11
14 Blackrock, Brec...C 5
15 Blackrock, Mon...E 8
34 Blackrod.......F 5
43 Blackshaw......E 11
35 Blackshaw Head..D 8
27 Blacksmith's Cnr..M 3
17 Blackstone......F 1
17 Blackthorn.....B 7
27 Blackthorpe.....J 2
17 Blacktoft......E 6
59 Blacktop.......G 6
2 Blackwater, Corn..E 4
17 Blackwater, Hants.H 9
15 Blackwater, I.o.W. G 6
6 Blackwater, Som..E 6
27 Blackwater, Suff...H 8
58 Blackwater Lodge E 1
46 Blackwaterfoot...G 4
11 Blackwell, Derby .C 10
31 Blackwell, Derby..D 2
22 Blackwell, War...H 6
43 Blackwood,
　　Dumfries......C 10
47 Blackwood,
　　Lanark........E 12
14 Blackwood, Mon. .E 5
31 Blackwood Hill...E 8
30 Blacon.........C 2
43 Bladnoch.......F 5
16 Bladon.........C 5
13 Blaen Celyn.....B 7
3 Blaen Dyryn.....A 3
12 Blaenannerch....B 6
28 Blaenau-Dolwyddelan.
　　　　E 6
28 Blaenau Ffestiniog.F 6
14 Blaenavon......C 6
14 Blaenawey......B 6
12 Blaen-ffos......C 5
14 Blaengarw......E 2
14 Blaengavenny...D 2
14 Blaengwrach....D 2
14 Blaengwynfi....E 2
20 Blaenpennal.....F 2
20 Blaenplwyf.....E 1

MAP

12 Blaenporth......B 6
12 Blaenwaun.....D 6
13 Blaen-y-Coed....D 7
14 Blaerhondda.....D 3
6 Blagdon Hill....D 5
15 Blagdon........B 8
55 Blaich.........M 4
50 Blain..........A 4
14 Blaina.........D 5
58 Blair..........E 6
52 Blair Atholl.....A 4
52 Blair Drummond .G 2
52 Blairadam......H 6
48 Blairburn......A 3
58 Blairdaff.......F 4
52 Blairgowrie.....C 6
52 Blairhall......H 5
52 Blairingone.....G 5
52 Blairlogie......G 3
47 Blairmore, Argyll A 7
60 Blairmore, Suther. B 3
47 Blairnairn......A 8
57 Blairnamarrow...H 8
52 Blairquhosh....A 10
46 Blair's Ferry....B 5
47 Blairskaith.....B 10
47 Blairvadach.....A 7
58 Blaisdon.......C 10
22 Blakebrook.....D 2
14 Blakedown......D 2
49 Blakelaw......F 10
30 Blakemere, Ches..C 4
21 Blakemere, Herefs. H 9
15 Blakeney, Glos...D 10
26 Blakeney, Norfolk.A 3
30 Blakenhall, Ches...E 6
22 Blakenhall, Staffs..B 3
22 Blakenhall Heath..B 4
22 Blakeshall......D 2
23 Blakesley......G 9
45 Blanchland.....H 8
35 Bland Hill......B 10
7 Blandford Forum E 12
7 Blandford St.Mary F 12
47 Blanefield......A 10
33 Blankney......D 8
51 Blar a' Chaoruinn .A 8
50 Blaran.........F 6
51 Blarghour......F 7
55 Blarmachfoldach,
　　Inverness......M 5
51 Blarmachfoldach,
　　Inverness......A 8
60 Blarnaleyoch...G 3
28 Blashford......E 3
23 Blaston......C 11
24 Blatherwycke....F 1
38 Blawith........F 5
27 Blaxhall.......J 7
36 Blaxton........G 4
45 Blaydon........G 10
7 Bleadon.......A 7
11 Blean.........B 10
33 Bleasby, Lincs...B 8
32 Bleasby, Notts...E 4
53 Blebocraigs.....F 9
21 Bleddfa........F 7
16 Bledington.....B 3
17 Bledlow........D 8
17 Bledlow Ridge..D 9
4 Blegberry......C 1
10 Blencarn......B 9
43 Blencogo.....G 12
9 Blendworth.....E 8
43 Blennerhasset...G 12
16 Bletchingdon...B 6
10 Bletchingley....C 2
17 Bletchley, Bucks..A 9
30 Bletchley, Salop..G 5
25 Bletherston.....E 4
25 Bletsoe........J 1
16 Blewbury......F 6
26 Blickling......C 5
32 Blidworth......E 3
32 Blidworth Bottoms E 3
44 Blindburn......B 6
38 Blindcrake.....B 4
10 Blindley Heath...C 2
49 Blinkbonny.....F 11
3 Blisland.......B 8
22 Bliss Gate......E 1
8 Blissford.......A 7
23 Blisworth.....G 10
31 Blithbury......H 9
31 Blithford......H 9
43 Blitterlees.....F 11
27 Blo Norton.....G 3
16 Blockley.......A 3
26 Blofield.......B 6
26 Blofield Corner..D 6
43 Bloomfield,
　　Dumfries.....D 10

MAP

49 Bloomfield, Rox...G 8
31 Blore..........E 10
31 Blounts Green...G 9
16 Bloxham.......A 5
33 Bloxholm......E 8
22 Bloxwich......B 3
7 Bloxworth.....G 12
35 Blubberhouses...B 10
26 Blundeston......F 8
25 Blunham.......K 3
16 Blunsdon St. Andrew
　　　　E 2
22 Bluntington.....E 2
25 Bluntisham.....H 5
3 Blunts.........C 10
37 Blyborough.....H 7
37 Blyford........H 7
22 Blymhill.......A 2
45 Blyth, Northumb. E 11
32 Blyth, Notts.....B 3
48 Blyth Bridge....E 4
27 Blythburgh.....H 7
49 Blythe.........D 8
31 Blythe Bridge...E 4
31 Blythe Marsh...F 8
31 Blythebridge....G 9
36 Blyton........H 6
53 Boarhills......F 10
4 Boarhunt......E 7
16 Boars Hill......D 6
10 Boarshead......E 4
17 Boarstall......C 7
4 Boasley Cross...F 4
57 Boat of Garten ..H 5
56 Boath..........B 1
11 Bobbing.......B 7
22 Bobbington.....C 2
18 Bobbingworth...C 5
56 Boblainy.......F 1
19 Bocking.......B 7
19 Bocking Churchstreet
　　　　A 7
3 Boconnoc.......D 8
58 Boddam, Aber...C 8
64 Boddam, Shetland Is.
　　　　F 7
7 Bodden.......B 10
28 Bodedern.....B 3
29 Bodelwyddan...C 9
21 Bodenham, Herefs.
　　　　G 10
8 Bodenham, Wilts..D 3
21 Bodenham Moor.G 11
28 Bodewryd.....A 3
29 Bodfari........C 10
28 Bodffordd.....C 4
26 Bodham Street..B 4
10 Bodiam.......E 6
23 Bodicote......H 8
3 Bodieve.......B 7
3 Bodinnick......D 8
10 Bodle Street Grn..G 5
3 Bodmin.......C 8
29 Bodnant.......C 7
26 Bodney........E 1
28 Bodorgan......C 3
11 Bodsham Green..D 9
28 Boduan........F 3
3 Bodwen........D 7
58 Bogallan.......E 2
58 Bogbrae........D 8
47 Bogend, Ayr....F 9
49 Bogend, Berwick .D 10
47 Boghall, Ayr.....H 9
48 Boghall, Midloth. .C 5
48 Boghall, W. Loth. .C 3
58 Boghead, Aber...E 7
32 Boghead, Ayr. ...F 10
47 Boghead, Lanark.E 12
56 Boghole.......D 5
43 Bogknowe......F 10
15 Bogmarsh......A 8
59 Bogmuir, Kinc...K 4
58 Bogmuir, Moray .A 1
58 Bogniebrae.....C 3
8 Bognor Regis...F 11
58 Bograxie.......F 4
48 Bogsbank......D 4
58 Bogside........D 1
56 Bogton........C 4
43 Bogue.........C 7
2 Bohortha.......F 6
55 Bohuntine......L 7
3 Bokiddick......C 7
40 Bolam, Durham..C 2
45 Bolam, Northumb. F 9

MAP
5 Bolberry M 6
30 Bold Heath A 4
45 Boldon Colliery G 11
8 Boldre F 5
40 Boldron D 1
32 Bole B 5
31 Bolehill E 11
2 Boleigh G 2
49 Boleside F 7
52 Bolfracks B 3
6 Bolham E 3
6 Bolham Water E 5
2 Bolingey D 5
31 Bollington, Ches. B 8
30 Bollington, Ches. B 6
31 Bollington Cross C 8
10 Bolney F 1
25 Bolnhurst J 2
53 Bolshan B 11
32 Bolsover C 2
35 Bolsterstone G 11
15 Bolstone A 8
40 Boltby F 5
17 Bolter End E 9
49 Bolton, E. Lothian B 7
34 Bolton, Lancs. F 6
45 Bolton, Northumb. B 9
39 Bolton, Westmor. C 8
36 Bolton, Yorks. B 5
35 Bolton Abbey B 9
35 Bolton Bridge B 9
34 Bolton by Bowland B 6
39 Bolton-le-Sands H 7
38 Bolton Low Houses A 5
36 Bolton-on-Dearne G 2
40 Bolton-on-Swale E 3
36 Bolton Percy C 3
39 Bolton Town End H 7
44 Boltonfellend F 3
3 Bolventor B 9
30 Bomere Heath H 3
60 Bonar Bridge G 6
51 Bonawe Quarries D 7
37 Bonby F 8
12 Boncath C 5
44 Bonchester Bridge B 4
9 Bonchurch H 7
4 Bondleigh E 5
34 Bonds C 4
22 Bonehill B 5
48 Bo'ness A 3
52 Bonhard D 6
47 Bonhill A 9
22 Boningdale B 2
49 Bonjedward G 9
49 Bonkle D 1
48 Bonnington B 4
53 Bonnybank G 8
48 Bonnybridge A 1
58 Bonnykelly B 6
48 Bonnyrigg and Lasswade C 6
47 Bonnyton F 9
31 Bonsall D 11
15 Bont B 7
28 Bont Newydd F 6
28 Bontddu H 6
20 Bont-dolgadfan B 4
28 Bont-newydd, Caer D 4
20 Bontnewydd, Cardiganshire F 2
29 Bontrhydgaled D 4
20 Bontuchel D 10
14 Bonvilston G 4
13 Bon-y-maen G 10
4 Boode B 4
30 Booley H 4
49 Boon E 8
41 Boosbeck C 7
4 Boot F 1
36 Booth D 5
35 Booth Wood E 9
33 Boothby Graffoe D 7
33 Boothby Pagnell G 7
34 Boothtown G 6
38 Bootle, Furness, Lancashire F 4
34 Bootle, Lancs. H 2
52 Boquhan, Stirling H 2
47 Boquhan, Stirling A 10
21 Boraston E 11
9 Borden D 9
35 Bordley A 8
9 Bordon C 9
19 Boreham, Essex C 7
10 Boreham Street G 5
18 Borehamwood D 2
43 Boreland, Dumf. B 12
52 Boreland, Perth D 1
43 Boreland of Girthon F 7
62 Boreraig C 1
49 Borewell D 12

MAP
61 Borgie House B 7
61 Borgue, Caith. E 10
43 Borgue, Kirk. G 7
27 Borley L 1
62 Bornaskitaig A 3
43 Borness G 7
10 Borough Green B 5
40 Boroughbridge H 4
30 Borras Head E 2
61 Borrobol Lodge E 8
32 Borrowash G 1
40 Borrowby F 4
38 Borrowdale D 5
59 Borrowfield H 6
20 Borth C 2
44 Borthwickbrae B 2
44 Borthwickshiels B 3
28 Borth-y-gest F 5
62 Borve C 4
63 Borve Lodge G 1
63 Borvemore G 1
39 Borwick H 7
21 Bosbury H 12
2 Boscastle A 8
8 Boscombe, Hants. G 3
8 Boscombe, Wilts. B 3
3 Boscoppa D 7
9 Bosham F 9
12 Bosherston G 3
2 Boskenna G 1
31 Bosley D 7
36 Bossall A 5
59 Bossholes H 6
3 Bossiney A 8
11 Bossingham C 10
6 Bossington A 3
30 Bostock Green C 5
24 Boston A 4
33 Boston Long Hedges E 10
36 Boston Spa C 2
3 Boswinger F 7
2 Botallack F 1
18 Botany Bay D 3
58 Botary Mains C 2
23 Botcheston B 8
27 Botesdale H 3
45 Bothal D 10
32 Bothamsall C 4
43 Bothel H 12
7 Bothenhampton G 8
47 Bothwell D 12
17 Botley, Bucks. D 10
8 Botley, Hants. E 6
16 Botley, Berks. C 6
17 Botolph Claydon B 8
10 Botolphs G 1
54 Bottacks D 8
32 Bottesford, Leics. F 5
37 Bottesford, Lincs. F 7
25 Bottisham J 6
16 Bottlesford H 2
31 Bottom House E 9
34 Bottom O'th'Moor F 5
53 Bottomcraig E 8
35 Bottoms E 8
34 Botton Head A 5
38 Bottongate A 5
4 Bottreaux Mill C 7
3 Botusfleming D 11
28 Botwnnog G 2
10 Bough Beech C 4
21 Boughrood H 7
21 Boughrood Brest. H 7
15 Boughspring E 9
24 Boughton, Norfolk E 8
32 Boughton, Notts. C 4
11 Boughton Aluph C 9
23 Boughton E 11
11 Boughton Lees C 9
11 Boughton Malherbe C 7
10 Boughton Monchelsea C 6
11 Boughton Street B 9
41 Boulby C 8
13 Bouldon D 11
45 Boulmer B 11
12 Boulston F 3
58 Boultenstone F 2
37 Boultham C 6
23 Bounton on Dunsmore E 8
25 Bourn K 4
24 Bourne D 2
25 Bourne End, Beds. L 1
17 Bourne End, Bucks. E 10
17 Bourne End, Hertfordshire D 11
18 Bournebridge D 5
8 Bournemouth G 3
19 Bournes Green, Essex E 9

MAP
15 Bournes Green, Gloucestershire D 12
22 Bournheath E 3
45 Bournmoor H 11
22 Bournville D 4
16 Bourton, Berks. E 3
7 Bourton, Dorset C 11
21 Bourton, Salop. C 11
16 Bourton-on-the-Hill A 3
16 Bourton-on-the-Water B 3
44 Boustead Hill G 1
38 Bouth G 6
40 Bouthwaite H 2
17 Boveney F 10
14 Boverton G 3
5 Bovey Tracey H 7
17 Bovingdon D 11
17 Bovingdon Green E 9
18 Bovinger C 5
4 Bow, Devon F 6
49 Bow, Midlothian E 7
64 Bow, Orkney Is. E 2
17 Bow Brickhill A 10
53 Bow of Fife F 8
20 Bow Street D 2
39 Bowbank C 11
40 Bowburn A 3
8 Bowcombe G 6
6 Bowd G 4
5 Bowden, Devon L 7
49 Bowden, Roxburgh F 8
15 Bowden Hill H 12
39 Bowderdale E 9
30 Bowdon B 6
44 Bower E 6
7 Bower Hinton D 8
8 Bowerchalke D 2
15 Bowerhill H 12
61 Bowermadden B 11
31 Bowers G 7
19 Bowers Gifford E 7
52 Bowershall H 6
61 Bowertower B 11
39 Bowers D 12
34 Bowgreave C 4
49 Bowhill G 7
43 Bowhouse E 11
3 Bowithick A 9
34 Bowker's Green G 3
38 Bowland Bridge F 6
21 Bowley G 11
9 Bowlhead Green B 10
47 Bowling B 9
22 Bowling Green G 2
38 Bowmanstead F 5
44 Bowness-on-Solway G1
38 Bowness-on-Windermere E 6
49 Bowsden E 12
61 Bowside Lodge B 8
48 Bowtrees A 2
15 Box, Glos. D 11
15 Box, Wilts. G 11
15 Boxbush C 10
16 Boxford, Berks. G 5
27 Boxford, Suffolk L 3
9 Boxgrove E 10
10 Boxley B 6
4 Box's Shop F 1
27 Boxted, Essex M 3
27 Boxted, Suffolk K 1
27 Boxted Cross M 3
25 Boxworth J 4
25 Boxworth End H 5
11 Boyden Gate B 11
31 Boylestone G 10
58 Boyndie A 4
41 Boynton H 11
7 Boys Hill E 10
5 Boyton, Cornwall G 2
27 Boyton, Suffolk K 7
8 Boyton, Wilts. B 1
18 Boyton Cross C 6
23 Bozeat F 12
6 Braaford-on-Tone D 5
38 Braaid H 2
27 Brabling Green J 6
11 Brabourne D 9
11 Brabourne Lees D 9
61 Brabstermire A 12
62 Bracadale D 3
24 Braceborough D 2
33 Bracebridge Heath C 7
33 Braceby G 7
35 Bracewell B 7
56 Brachla F 1
32 Brackenfield D 1
38 Brackenthwaite, Cumberland C 4
44 Brackenthwaite, Cumberland H 1

MAP
9 Bracklesham F 9
55 Brackletter L 6
46 Brackley, Argyll E 3
23 Brackley, Northants. H 9
60 Brackloch E 3
17 Bracknell G 9
52 Braco F 3
58 Bracobrae B 3
26 Bracon Ash E 5
55 Bracora K 1
55 Bracorina K 1
31 Bradbourne E 10
40 Bradbury B 3
38 Bradda H 1
23 Bradden G 10
17 Bradenham D 9
16 Bradenstoke F 1
17 Bradfield, Berks. G 7
6 Bradfield, Devon E 4
27 Bradfield, Essex M 4
35 Bradfield, Yorks. H 11
27 Bradfield Combust J 2
30 Bradfield Green D 5
27 Bradfield Heath M 4
27 Bradfield St. Clair J 2
27 BradfieldSt.George J 2
4 Bradford, Devon E 3
45 Bradford, Northumb. D 11
35 Bradford, Yorks. D 10
7 Bradford Abbas E 9
15 Bradford Leigh H 11
4 Bradford Mill D 7
15 Bradford-on-Avon H 11
9 Brading G 7
30 Bradley, Denb. E 2
31 Bradley, Derby F 10
9 Bradley, Hants. B 7
37 Bradley, Lincs. F 10
22 Bradley, Staffs. C 3
31 Bradley, Staffs. H 7
22 Bradley, Worcs. F 3
39 Bradley, Yorks. G 12
30 Bradley Common F 4
22 Bradley Green F 3
31 Bradley in the Moors F 9
32 Bradmore G 3
7 Bradney B 7
6 Bradninch F 3
31 Bradnop E 8
7 Bradpole G 8
34 Bradshaw F 6
5 Bradstone H 3
30 Bradwall Green D 6
31 Bradwell, Derby. B 10
19 Bradwell, Essex B 8
26 Bradwell, Suffolk E 8
23 Bradwell, Bucks. H 11
16 Bradwell Grove C 3
19 Bradwell-on-Sea C 10
19 Bradwell Waterside C 10
4 Bradworthy E 2
4 Bradworthy Cross E 2
64 Brae C 7
60 Brae Doune G 5
60 Brae of Achnahaird E 2
55 Brae Roy Lodge K 7
56 Braeantra B 1
57 Braedownie M 8
43 Braefoot A 9
52 Braegrum E 5
58 Braehead, Aber. F 7
53 Braehead, Angus B 11
48 Braehead, Lanark D 2
48 Braehead, Lanark F 1
64 Braehead, Orkney Is. D 3
42 Braehead, Wigtown F 5
61 Braehungie D 11
54 Braeintra F 2
60 Braelangwell Lodge (Hotel) G 6
57 Braemar K 7
61 Braemore, Caith. D 10
54 Braemore, Ross & Cromarty B 6
47 Braeside B 7
51 Braeval G 12
40 Brafferton, Dur. C 3
48 Brafferton, Yorks. H 4
40 Brafferton, Yorkshire H 4
23 Bradfield-on-the-Green F 11
63 Bragar B 4
18 Bragbury End B 3
50 Braglenbeg E 6
34 Braides B 3

MAP
49 Braidshawrig D 8
48 Braidwood E 1
31 Brailsford F 11
45 Brainshaugh C 10
19 Braintree B 7
27 Braiseworth H 4
8 Braishfield D 5
38 Braithwaite, Cumb. C 5
36 Braithwaite, Yorks. F 4
32 Braithwell A 3
10 Bramber G 1
32 Bramcote F 2
9 Bramdean C 7
26 Bramerton E 6
18 Bramfield, Herts. B 3
27 Bramfield, Suffolk H 7
27 Bramford K 4
31 Bramhall B 7
36 Bramham C 2
36 Bramham Crossroads C 2
35 Bramhope C 11
17 Bramley, Hants. H 7
9 Bramley, Surrey B 11
32 Bramley, Yorks. A 2
6 Brampford Speke F 3
44 Brampton, Cumb. G 4
15 Brampton, Herefs. A 7
25 Brampton, Hunts. H 3
32 Brampton, Lincs. B 6
26 Brampton, Norf. C 5
27 Brampton, Suffolk G 7
39 Brampton, Westmor. C 9
36 Brampton, Yorks. G 2
15 Brampton Abbots B 9
23 Brampton Ash C 11
21 Brampton Bryan E 9
32 Brampton en le Morthen A 2
31 Bramshall G 9
8 Bramshaw E 4
9 Bramshott C 9
18 Bran End A 6
50 Branault A 3
26 Brancaster A 1
26 Brancaster Staithe A 1
40 Brancepeth A 2
56 Branchill D 6
15 Brand Green B 10
56 Branderburgh C 8
37 Brandesburton B 9
27 Brandeston J 5
4 Brandis Corner E 3
26 Brandiston C 4
38 Brandlingill C 4
40 Brandon, Durham A 3
32 Brandon, Lincs. E 6
45 Brandon, Northumb. A 8
27 Brandon, Suffolk G 1
23 Brandon, War. D 7
24 Brandon Creek F 7
26 Brandon Parva E 4
40 Brandsby H 6
37 Brandy Wharf G 8
2 Brane G 1
8 Branksome G 2
8 Branksome Park G 2
8 Bransbury B 6
6 Branscombe G 5
22 Bransford G 1
8 Bransgore F 3
22 Branson's Cross E 4
32 Branston, Leics. G 5
33 Branston, Lincs. C 7
31 Branston, Staffs. H 10
33 Branston Booths C 8
9 Branstone H 7
32 Brant Broughton E 6
44 Branteth E 1
27 Brantham M 4
38 Branthwaite, Cumb. C 3
38 Branthwaite, Cumb. B 5
37 Brantingham D 7
45 Branton, Northumb. A 8
36 Branton, Yorks. G 4
44 Branxholme B 3
49 Branxton F 11
49 Branxtonmoor F 11
31 Brassington E 11
10 Brasted C 3
10 Brasted Chart C 3
59 Brathens H 4
33 Bratoft D 11
32 Brattleby B 6
6 Bratton, Somerset B 3
8 Bratton, Wilts. A 1
5 Bratton Clovelly G 3
4 Bratton Fleming B 5
7 Bratton Seymour C 10
18 Braughing A 4

MAP
23 Braunston, Northants. E 9
23 Braunston, Rut. A 11
23 Braunstone B 9
4 Braunton B 4
41 Brawby, Yorks. G 7
12 Brawdy, Pemb. E 2
61 Brawlbin B 10
17 Bray F 10
3 Bray Shop B 10
17 Bray Wick F 9
23 Braybrooke D 11
4 Brayford C 6
36 Brayton D 4
3 Brazacott A 9
62 Breabost C 3
11 Breach B 7
18 Breachwood Green B 2
63 Breaclete C 2
31 Breadsall F 12
15 Breadstone D 10
54 Breafield F 8
2 Breage G 3
54 Breakachy E 8
15 Bream D 9
8 Breamore D 3
15 Bream's Eaves D 9
6 Brean A 6
35 Brearton A 11
63 Breasclete C 3
32 Breaston G 2
13 Brechfa D 8
59 Brechin L 4
43 Breckonside A 9
62 Breckrey B 4
14 Brecon A 4
35 Bredbury H 8
11 Brede F 7
21 Bredenbury G 11
27 Bredfield K 6
11 Bredger B 7
11 Bredhurst B 7
22 Bredicot G 3
15 Bredon A 12
22 Bredon's Norton H 3
21 Bredwardine H 9
32 Breedon on the Hill H 1
48 Breich C 2
36 Breighton D 5
21 Breinton H 10
21 Breinton Com. H 10
16 Bremhill G 1
51 Brenachoille G 7
10 Brenchley D 5
4 Brendon A 6
46 Brenfield A 3
63 Brenish D 1
45 Brenkley F 10
18 Brent E 2
27 Brent Eleigh K 2
6 Brent Knoll A 6
25 Brent Pelham M 5
18 Brentford F 2
18 Brentwood E 6
11 Brenzett E 8
22 Brereton A 4
30 Brereton Green D 6
30 Brereton Heath D 6
64 Bressay E 7
27 Bressingham G 4
64 Bretabister D 7
31 Bretby H 11
23 Bretford D 7
22 Bretforton H 4
39 Bretherdale Head E 8
34 Bretherton E 4
6 Brett B 4
27 Brettenham, Suff. K 3
27 Brettenham, Norf. G 2
30 Bretton D 2
10 Brewer Street C 2
22 Brewood A 2
56 Briach D 6
7 Briantspuddle G 11
18 Bricket Wood D 1
22 Bricklehampton H 3
38 Bride F 2
38 Bridekirk B 4
12 Bridell C 5
5 Bridestowe G 4
58 Brideswell D 3
5 Bridford G 7
11 Bridge, Kent C 10
2 Bridge, Cornwall E 4
25 Bridge End, Bedfordshire K 1
24 Bridge End, Lincs. B 2
45 Bridge End, Northumb. B 9
40 Bridge Hewick H 4
58 Bridge of Alford F 3
52 Bridge of Allan G 3

MAP

56 Bridge of Avon....F 7
51 Bridge of Awe....E 7
51 Bridge of Balgie,
  Perth......C 12
53 Bridge of Brewlands A 7
57 Bridge of Brown..G 7
52 Bridge of Cally...B 6
59 Bridge of Canny..H 4
53 Bridge of Craigisla.B 7
43 Bridge of Dee.....F 8
56 Bridge of Derrybeg.F 8
58 Bridge of Don....F 7
59 Bridge of Dun....L 4
59 Bridge of Dye....J 4
52 Bridge of Earn...E 6
51 Bridge of Ericht..B 12
59 Bridge of Feugh..H 4
61 Bridge of Forss..A 10
59 Bridge of Gairn..H 1
51 Bridge of Gaur...B 12
53 Bridge of Lintrathen B 7
59 Bridge of Murchalls H 6
51 Bridge of Orchy.D 10
52 Bridge of Tilt....A 4
64 Bridge of Waith..D 1
64 Bridge of Walls...D 6
47 Bridge of Weir...C 9
4 Bridge Reeve....E 5
21 Bridge Sollars....H 9
27 Bridge Street......K 2
30 Bridge Trafford..C 3
25 Bridgefoot, Cambs.L 5
38 Bridgefoot, Cumb..B 3
7 Bridgehampton...D 9
49 Bridgelands......F 7
9 Bridgemary......F 7
58 Bridgend, Aber...C 5
58 Bridgend, Aber...D 3
58 Bridgend, Aber...E 6
59 Bridgend, Angus..K 3
50 Bridgend, Argyll..H 6
58 Bridgend, Banff...D 1
12 Bridgend, Cards..B 5
3 Bridgend, Corn...D 8
43 Bridgend, Dumf..A 11
53 Bridgend, Fife...F 8
14 Bridgend, Glam...F 2
52 Bridgend, Perth...E 6
54 Bridgend, Ross &
  Cromarty.....D 7
38 Bridgend, Westmor. D 6
48 Bridgend, W. Lothian B 3
4 Bridgerule.......F 1
21 Bridges.........C 9
3 Bridgetown, Corn.A 10
6 Bridgetown, Som..C 3
22 Bridgetown, Staffs.A 3
27 Bridgham.......G 3
21 Bridgnorth......C 12
7 Bridgwater......B 6
41 Bridlington.....H 12
7 Bridport........G 8
15 Bridstow........B 9
35 Brierfield.......D 7
15 Brierley, Glos....C 9
21 Brierley, Herefs..G 10
36 Brierley, Yorks...F 2
22 Brierley Hill....C 2
40 Brierton........B 5
14 Briery Hill......C 5
51 Brig o' Turk....G 12
37 Brigg..........F 8
59 Briggs of Criggie..J 6
41 Briggswath......D 9
38 Brigham, Cumb...B 3
37 Brigham, Yorks...B 8
35 Brighouse.......E 10
8 Brighstone......H 6
16 Brighthampton...D 5
31 Brightgate......D 11
10 Brightling......F 5
19 Brightlingsea....B 10
2 Brighton, Corn...D 6
10 Brighton, Sussex..H 2
48 Brightons.......B 2
16 Brightwalton.....F 5
17 Brightwell, Oxon..E 7
27 Brightwell, Suffolk.L 5
17 Brightwell Baldwin E 7
40 Brignall........D 1
37 Brigsley........G 10
39 Brigsteer.......F 7
23 Brigstock.......D 12
17 Brill, Bucks......C 6
2 Brill, Cornwall...G 4
21 Brilley.........G 8
12 Brimaston......D 3
21 Brimfield.......F 10

32 Brimington......C 1
15 Brimpsfield......C 12
16 Brimpton.......H 6
64 Brims..........E 1
15 Brimscombe.....D 11
30 Brimstage.......B 2
57 Brin..........G 2
55 Brinacory.......K 1
36 Brind.........D 5
64 Brindister, Shetland Is. D 6
64 Brindister, Shetland Is. E 7
34 Brindle........E 5
31 Brindley Ford....E 7
22 Brineton........A 2
23 Bringhurst......C 11
25 Bringsty........H 2
26 Briningham.....B 3
33 Brinkhill.......C 10
25 Brinkley.......K 7
23 Brinklow.......D 8
16 Brinkworth......F 1
34 Brinscall.......E 5
15 Brinsea........H 7
32 Brinsley........E 2
21 Brinsop........H 10
32 Brinsworth......A 1
26 Brinton........B 3
64 Brinyan........B 2
26 Brisley........C 3
15 Brislington......G 9
11 Brissenden Green .D 8
15 Bristol.........G 9
26 Briston........B 4
35 Britannia.......E 7
8 Britford........C 3
14 Brithdir, Glam...D 5
29 Brithdir, Mer....H 7
10 British Legion Village B 6
13 Briton Ferry....G 10
17 Britwell Salome...E 7
5 Brixham........K 8
5 Brixton.........K 4
7 Brixton Deverill..B 11
23 Brixworth.......E 10
16 Brize Norton....C 4
16 Broad Blunsdon...E 3
22 Broad Campden ..H 5
8 Broad Chalke....C 2
6 Broad Clyst......F 3
25 Broad Green, Beds. L 1
19 Broad Green, Essex B 8
22 Broad Green, Worcs. F 1
12 Broad Haven....F 2
21 Broad Heath....F 12
25 Broad Hill......H 7
16 Broad Hinton....F 4
16 Broad Laying....H 5
22 Broad Marston...G 5
13 Broad Oak, Carm..E 9
38 Broad Oak, Cumb. F 4
7 Broad Oak, Dorset G 8
15 Broad Oak, Herefs. B 8
11 Broad Oak, Sussex F 7
36 Broad Oak, Yorks. A 4
11 Broad Street......B 7
19 Broad Street Green C 8
16 Broad Town.....F 2
35 Broadbottom....H 8
9 Broadbridge.....E 9
9 Broadbridge Hth..E 2
12 Broadfield......G 5
62 Broadford......F 5
9 Broadford Bri....D 12
48 Broadgairhill....H 5
44 Broadhaugh.....B 3
61 Broadhaven.....C 12
30 Broadheath......A 6
7 Broadhembury...F 5
5 Broadhempston...J 7
11 Broadland Row...F 7
13 Broadlay.......F 7
58 Broadley.......B 1
58 Broadley Com....C 4
4 Broadmead......D 7
49 Broadmeadows...A 7
9 Broadmere......A 7
12 Broadmoor......F 4
4 Broadnymet.....F 6
11 Broadoak, Kent..B 10
10 Broadoak, Sussex..F 5
58 Broadrashes.....B 2
58 Broadsea.......E 5
11 Broadstairs.....A 12
8 Broadstone, Dorset F 7
21 Broadstone, Salop C 11
16 Broadtown Lane ..F 2
22 Broadwas.......G 1
18 Broadwater, Herts. B 2

9 Broadwater, Sussex F 12
12 Broadway, Carm...F 6
12 Broadway, Pemb...F 2
6 Broadway, Som...E 6
22 Broadway, Worcs..H 4
16 Broadwell, Glos...A 3
16 Broadwell, Oxon..D 3
23 Broadwell, War...F 8
45 Broadwell House..H 7
15 Broadwell Lane End C 9
7 Broadwey......H 10
7 Broadwindsor....F 8
4 Broadwood-Kelly.E 5
5 Broadwoodwidger.G 3
21 Brobury........H 9
62 Brochel........D 5
7 Brockbridge....D 7
45 Brockdam......A 9
27 Brockdish.......G 5
27 Brockenhurst....F 4
48 Brocketsbrae.....E 1
27 Brockford Street..J 4
23 Brockhall.......F 9
10 Brockham......C 1
16 Brockhampton, Glos. B 1
15 Brockhampton,
  Herefordshire...A 9
7 Brockhampton Green F 10
35 Brockholes.....F 10
31 Brockhouse......C 8
27 Brockhurst......F 7
38 Brocklebank.....A 5
37 Brocklesby......F 9
15 Brockley.......H 8
27 Brockley Green ..K 1
21 Brockton, Salop..B 1
21 Brockton, Salop..B 8
21 Brockton, Salop..C 11
15 Brockweir.......D 8
29 Brockwood......D 7
15 Brockworth.....C 12
31 Brocton........H 8
46 Brodick........F 5
58 Brodiesord......B 3
36 Brodsworth.....F 3
62 Brogaig........A 4
25 Brogborough....L 1
30 Broken Cross,
  Cheshire.....C 6
31 Broken Cross,
  Cheshire......C 7
15 Brokenborough ..E 12
30 Bromborough....B 2
27 Brome.........H 4
27 Brome Street....H 5
27 Bromeswell.....K 6
43 Bromfield, Cumb. G 12
21 Bromfield, Salop E 10
25 Bromham, Beds...K 1
16 Bromham, Wilts..H 1
18 Bromley........G 4
11 Bromley Green...D 8
10 Brompton, Kent ..A 6
41 Brompton, N. Riding G 9
40 Brompton, N. Riding E 4
21 Brompton Hall...C 8
40 Brompton-on-Swale E 2
6 Brompton Ralph..C 4
6 Brompton Regis..C 3
15 Bromsash.......B 9
15 Bromsberrow....A 10
22 Bromsgrove.....E 3
30 Bromstead Heath .H 6
21 Bromyard.......G 12
21 Bromyard Downs G 12
28 Bronaber.......G 6
20 Bronant........F 2
12 Brongest.......C 6
29 Bronington......F 4
14 Bronllys........A 5
13 Bronwydd Arms..E 7
21 Bronydd........H 8
12 Brook, Carm.....F 6
8 Brook, Hants....C 5
8 Brook, Hants....E 4
8 Brook, I.o.W.....H 5
11 Brook, Kent.....D 9
9 Brook, Surrey..B 12
9 Brook, Surrey...B 10
25 Brook End......J 2
8 Brook Hill......E 4
18 Brook Street, Essex E 6
10 Brook Street, Sussex E 2
26 Brooke, Norfolk ..E 6
23 Brooke, Rutland .B 12
15 Brookend......D 9

47 Brookfield.......C 9
31 Brookhouse, Ches. C 8
34 Brookhouse, Lancs.A 4
31 Brookhouse Green D 7
11 Brookland.......E 8
43 Brooklands......D 9
18 Brookmans Park..D 2
21 Brooks.........C 7
15 Brookthorpe.....C 11
17 Brookwood......H 10
25 Broom, Beds.....L 3
40 Broom, Durham ..A 3
22 Broom, War.....G 4
22 Broom, Worcs...D 3
8 Broom Hill......F 2
52 Broom of Dalreoch E 5
49 Broomdykes.....D 11
26 Broome, Norfolk ..F 6
21 Broome, Salop...D 9
10 Broome Park....C 1
30 Broomedge......B 5
9 Broomer's Crn...D 12
58 Broomfield, Aber..D 7
19 Broomfield, Essex.C 7
11 Broomfield, Kent A 10
11 Broomfield, Kent..C 7
48 Broomfield, Lan...E 1
6 Broomfield, Som...C 6
36 Broomfleet......D 6
17 Broomhall......G 10
45 Broomhaugh.....G 8
45 Broomhill, Northumb. C 10
56 Broomhill, Ross &
  Cromarty.......C 3
57 Broomhill Station .G 6
26 Broomholm......B 6
45 Broomhouse....C 11
43 Broomhouses...C 12
45 Broomley.......G 8
15 Brooms Green...A 10
15 Broomsberrow Heath A 10
61 Brora..........F 9
21 Broseley........B 12
22 Brotheridge Green H 2
49 Brotherstone....F 9
33 Brothertoft......F 10
36 Brotherton......E 3
45 Brotherwick....C 10
41 Brotton........C 7
64 Broubster.......B 10
61 Brough........A 11
31 Brough, Derby...B 10
32 Brough, Notts...D 5
64 Brough, Orkney Is. C 2
64 Brough, Whalasay,
  Shetland Is....C 8
64 Brough, Yell,
  Shetland Is.....C 7
64 Brough, Zetland,
  Shetland Is.....C 7
39 Brough, Westmor. D 10
37 Brough, Yorks...D 7
64 Brough Lodge....B 8
39 Brough Sowerby .D 10
30 Broughall.......F 4
23 Broughton, Bucks. H 12
38 Broughton, Cumb. B 3
30 Broughton, Flint..D 2
14 Broughton, Glam..G 2
8 Broughton, Hants. C 4
25 Broughton, Hunts. G 4
34 Broughton, Lancs..B 4
37 Broughton, Lincs..F 7
23 Broughton, Northants. A 2
64 Broughton, Orkney Is. A 2
40 Broughton, Oxon..H 3
48 Broughton, Peebles F 4
40 Broughton, N. Riding E 6
41 Broughton, N. Riding H 8
35 Broughton, W. Riding B 8
23 Broughton Astley .C 8
38 Broughton Beck...C 3
15 Broughton Com..H 12
30 Broughton Foggs .D 3
15 Broughton Gifford H 12
22 Broughton Hackett G 3
38 Broughton in Furness F 5
38 Broughton Mills..F 4
38 Broughton Moor..B 3
64 Broughtown.....B 4
53 Broughty Ferry..D 9
44 Browhouses.....G 1
9 Brown Candover..B 7

31 Brown Edge.....E 7
58 Brownhill, Aber...D 6
30 Brownhill, Salop..H 3
53 Brownhills, Fife..F 10
22 Brownhills, Staffs..B 4
31 Brownlow Heath..D 7
59 Brownmuir......K 5
45 Brownridge.....B 11
15 Brown's Hill....D 12
23 Brownsover.....D 8
5 Brownston......K 6
45 Brownyside......A 9
17 Brox..........H 11
41 Broxa.........F 9
18 Broxbourne.....C 4
49 Broxburn, E. Lothian B 9
48 Broxburn, W. Lothian B 4
18 Broxted........A 6
30 Broxton........E 3
21 Broxwood.......G 9
10 Broyle Side.....G 3
61 Bruan........C 21
57 Bruar Lodge....M 4
63 Brue..........B 4
30 Bruera.........D 3
16 Bruern Abbey....B 4
27 Bruisyard......J 6
27 Bruisyard Street..J 6
36 Brumby........F 6
31 Brund.........D 9
26 Brundhall......E 6
27 Brundish.......H 5
27 Brundish Street..H 6
55 Brunery.......M 1
45 Brunswick Village F 10
23 Bruntingthorpe...C 9
53 Brunton, Fife....E 8
45 Brunton, Northumb. A 10
16 Brunton, Wilts...H 3
6 Brushford.......D 3
4 Brushford Barton .E 5
7 Bryanston......F 12
43 Brydekirk......E 12
29 Brymbo........E 12
7 Brympton......E 8
13 Bryn, Carm.....G 9
29 Bryn, Denbigh...F 12
13 Bryn, Glam.....H 11
34 Bryn, Lancs.....G 4
21 Bryn, Salop.....D 8
34 Bryn Gates.....G 5
14 Bryn Golau.....E 3
28 Bryn-Siencyn....D 4
14 Brynamman.....F 10
12 Bryn-berian.....C 4
13 Brynbryddan....H 11
14 Bryncethin......F 2
28 Bryncir.........F 4
13 Bryn-coch......G 10
28 Bryncroes......G 2
20 Bryncrug......B 2
29 Bryneglwys.....E 10
29 Brynford.......C 11
28 Bryngwran......B 3
15 Bryngwyn, Mon...C 7
21 Bryngwyn, Rad...G 7
12 Bryn-henllan....C 4
13 Brynhoffnant....B 7
34 Bryning........D 3
14 Brynmawr......C 5
14 Brynmenyn.....C 2
13 Brynmill.......H 10
28 Bryn'refail......D 5
14 Brynsadler......F 3
29 Bryn-teg.......E 12
14 Bryn-y-Cae.....F 3
14 Bryn-y-gwenin...C 6
29 Bryn-y-maen....C 7
62 Bualintur......F 3
23 Bubbenhall.....E 7
36 Bubwith.......C 5
48 Buccleuch......H 6
42 Buchan........E 5
47 Buchanan Castle ..A 9
51 Buchanan Smithy H 11
58 Buchanhaven....D 8
52 Buchanty.......D 4
52 Buchlyvie......H 1
58 Buchts.........B 7
44 Buckabank......H 2
25 Buckden, Hunts...H 3
39 Buckden, Yorks..G 11
26 Buckenham......E 6
6 Buckerell......F 5
5 Buckfast.......J 6
5 Buckfastleigh....J 6
53 Buckhaven.....G 8
49 Buckholm......H 7
18 Buckhurst Hill...E 4

58 Buckie........A 2
17 Buckingham....A 8
17 Buckinghamshire, Co. C 8
16 Buckland, Berks...D 4
21 Buckland, Bucks...C 9
5 Buckland, Devon..L 5
15 Buckland, Glos...A 3
25 Buckland, Herts..M 5
11 Buckland, Kent..D 11
10 Buckland, Surrey..C 1
4 Buckland Brewer .D 3
17 Buckland Com...C 10
7 Buckland Dinham A 11
4 Buckland Filleigh..E 3
5 Buckland in the Moor H 6
5 Buckland Monachorum...J 4
7 Buckland Newton F 10
6 Buckland St. Mary E 6
24 Bucklegate......B 4
53 Bucklerheads....D 9
8 Bucklers Hard....F 5
27 Bucklesham.....L 5
29 Buckley.......D 12
30 Bucklow Hill....B 6
32 Buckminster....H 6
33 Bucknall, Lincs...C 9
16 Bucknell, Oxon...B 6
21 Bucknell, Salop...E 9
31 Bucknall, Staffs...E 7
58 Buckpool.......A 2
4 Buck's Cross....D 2
9 Bucks Green....C 12
9 Bucks Horn Oak ..B 9
4 Buck's Mills.....D 2
7 Buckthorn Weston D 10
21 Buckton, Herefs...E 9
45 Buckton, Northumb. B 12
41 Buckton, Yorks. .H 11
25 Buckworth......H 2
16 Buclebury......G 6
22 Budbrooke......F 6
32 Budby.........C 3
4 Budd's Titson...F 1
4 Bude..........E 1
6 Budlake........F 3
45 Budle.........D 12
6 Budleigh Salterton H 4
2 Budock Water....F 5
30 Buerton........F 5
23 Bugbrooke......F 10
31 Buglawton......D 7
3 Bugle..........D 7
36 Bugthorpe......A 5
21 Buildwas.......B 11
47 Builstonend.....E 9
20 Builth Road.....G 6
20 Builth Wells.....G 6
17 Bulbourne......C 10
24 Bulby.........C 2
32 Bulcote........F 4
8 Bulford........B 3
30 Bulkeley.......E 4
23 Bulkington, War..D 7
15 Bulkington, Wilts H 12
4 Bulkworthy......E 3
28 Bull Bay........A 4
8 Bull Hill.......F 5
40 Bullamoor......F 4
17 Bullbrook......G 9
58 Bullers of Buchan .D 8
11 Bulley.........B 11
43 Bullgill........H 11
15 Bullinghope....A 8
8 Bullington, Hants..B 6
33 Bullington, Lincs..B 8
39 Bullpot Farm....G 9
46 Bullwood.......B 6
27 Bulmer, Essex...L 2
41 Bulmer, Yorks...H 7
27 Bulmer Tye......L 1
16 Bulphan.......E 6
10 Bulverhythe.....G 6
58 Bulwark.......C 7
15 Bulwark Village ..E 1
32 Bulwell........F 3
24 Bulwick........F 1
8 Bumble's Green..C 4
55 Bunacaimb.....K 1
55 Bunarkaig......L 6
63 Bunaveneadar...H 2
30 Bunbury........D 4
56 Bunchrew......E 2
50 Bunalloch......E 1
50 Bunessan......E 1
38 Bungalow Station .G 2
26 Bungay.........F 6
57 Bunloit........G 1

MAP
32 Bunny.........G 3
54 Buntait.........F 8
18 Buntingford.....A 4
26 Bunwell.........F 4
26 Bunwell Street....F 4
31 Burbage, Derby..C 9
23 Burbage, Leics..C 8
16 Burbage, Wilts..H 3
17 Burchett's Green..F 9
8 Burcombe........C 2
16 Burcot, Oxon....E 6
22 Burcot, Worcs....E 3
17 Burcott.........B 9
36 Burdale.........A 6
27 Bures.........M 2
16 Burford, Oxon...C 4
21 Burford, Salop..F 11
50 Burg............C 1
10 Burgess Hill....F 2
27 Burgh..........K 5
44 Burgh by Sands...G 2
26 Burgh Castle....E 8
10 Burgh Heath.....B 1
33 Burgh le Marsh..D 12
58 Burgh Muir......E 5
26 Burgh next Aylsham
C 5
33 Burgh on Bain..B 9
26 Burgh St.Margaret D 7
26 Burgh St. Peter...F 8
16 Burghclere......H 6
56 Burghead........C 7
17 Burghfield......G 7
17 Burghfield Com..G 7
21 Burghill.......H 10
36 Burghwallis.....F 3
10 Burham.........B 6
9 Buriton.........D 9
30 Burland........E 5
3 Burlawn.........C 7
17 Burleigh.......G 10
6 Burlescombe.....E 4
7 Burleston......G 11
8 Burley, Hants...F 3
23 Burley, Rutland..A 12
21 Burley Gate....H 11
35 Burley in Wharfdale
C 10
8 Burley Lodge....E 4
8 Burley Street....F 3
30 Burleydam.......F 5
21 Burlingjobb.....G 8
10 Burlow.........F 4
30 Burlton.........H 3
11 Burmarsh.......E 9
22 Burmington.....H 6
6 Burn, Devon.....D 5
43 Burn, Dumfries..B 10
36 Burn, Yorks.....D 4
34 Burn Naze......C 2
52 Burn of Cambus..G 2
35 Burnage........H 7
31 Burnaston......G 11
47 Burnbank.......D 11
47 Burnbrae......E 12
36 Burnby.........C 6
35 Burncross......G 12
39 Burneside......F 7
64 Burness........A 4
40 Burneston......G 3
15 Burnett.......H 10
43 Burnfoot, Dumf..B 10
44 Burnfoot, Dumf..D 2
45 Burnfoot, Northumb.
B 8
44 Burnfoot, Rox....A 3
44 Burnfoot, Rox....B 2
47 Burnfoot, Stirling B 11
32 Burngreave.....A 1
17 Burnham, Bucks..F 10
37 Burnham, Lincs...E 8
17 Burnham Beeches F 10
26 BurnhamDeepdale A 1
18 Burnham Green...B 3
26 Burnham Market..A 1
26 Burnham Norton..A 1
26 Burnham Overy...A 1
26 Burnham Thorpe..B 2
6 Burnham-on-Sea..A 6
19 Burnham-on-Crouch
D 9
58 Burnhaven......C 8
43 Burnhead, Dumf. C 10
43 Burnhead, Dumf..B 9
58 Burnhervie......F 5
22 Burnhill Green...B 1
45 Burnhope......H 10
47 Burnhouse.......D 8
49 Burnhouse Mains D 7
41 Burniston......F 10
35 Burnley........D 7
49 Burnmouth, Ber..C 12
43 Burnmouth, Dumf. A 9

MAP
45 Burnopfield......G 10
59 Burnroot........H 2
35 Burnsall........A 9
53 Burnside, Angus..B 9
47 Burnside, Ayr....H 10
43 Burnside, Dumf..C 11
32 Burnside, Fife...F 6
56 Burnside, Nairn...F 5
64 Burnside, Shetland Is.
C 6
48 Burnside, W. Lothian
D 9
53 Burnside of Duntrune
19 Burnt Heath.....A 10
40 Burnt Houses....C 2
35 Burnt Yates....A 11
2 Burnthouse......F 5
48 Burntisland.....A 5
22 Burntwood......A 4
9 Burpham, Surrey..A 12
9 Burpham, Sussex.E 11
45 Burradon, Northumb.
B 8
45 Burradon, Northumb.
F 11
64 Burrafirth.......A 8
2 Burras.........F 4
64 Burravoe.......C 7
39 Burrells........C 9
53 Burrelton.......C 7
4 Burridge, Devon..C 4
9 Burridge, Hants...E 7
40 Burrill.........F 3
36 Burringham......F 6
4 Burrington, Devon D 5
21 Burrington, Herefs.
E 10
15 Burrington, Som..A 6
25 Burrough Green...K 7
23 Burrough on the Hill
A 10
6 Burrow, Devon..G 4
6 Burrow, Somerset .B 3
7 Burrow Bridge....C 7
17 Burrowhill......H 10
9 Burrows Cross....A 12
13 Burry...........H 8
13 Burry Port......G 8
13 Burrygreen.....H 8
34 Burscough.......F 3
34 Burscough Bridge..F 3
36 Bursea.........D 6
36 Bursea Lane Ends..D 6
37 Burshill........B 8
8 Bursledon......E 6
31 Burslem........E 7
27 Burstall........L 4
7 Burstock.......F 7
27 Burston, Norfolk..G 4
31 Burston, Staffs...G 8
10 Burstow.......D 2
37 Burstwick......D 10
39 Burtersett.....F 11
44 Burthinghurst....F 4
30 Burton, Cheshire..C 2
30 Burton, Cheshire..D 4
7 Burton, Dorset ..G 10
8 Burton, Hants....G 3
33 Burton, Lincs....C 7
45 Burton, Northumb.
D 12
12 Burton, Pemb....F 3
6 Burton, Somerset..B 5
39 Burton, Westmor..G 8
39 Burton, Westmor..C 9
15 Burton, Wilts....F 11
37 Burton Agnes....A 9
7 Burton Bradstock .G 8
33 Burton Coggles ..H 7
37 Burton Constable .C 9
23 Burton Dassett ..G 7
41 Burton Fleming .H 11
30 Burton Green, Denb.
D 2
22 Burton Green, War.
E 6
23 Burton Hastings ..C 7
39 Burton in Lonsdale H 9
32 Burton Joyce....H 2
23 Burton Latimer .E 12
32 Burton Lazars ...H 5
35 Burton Leonard..A 11
32 Burton on the Wolds
H 3
31 Burton-on-Trent .H 10
23 Burton Overy...B 10
24 Burton Pedwardine
A 2
37 Burton Pidsea ...D 10

MAP
36 Burton Salmon....D 3
36 Burton upon Stather
E 6
34 Burtonwood......H 4
30 Burwardsley.....D 4
21 Burwarton......D 11
10 Burwash........F 5
10 Burwash Common.F 5
10 Burwash Weald..F 5
25 Burwell, Cambs....J 7
33 Burwell, Lincs...B 10
28 Burwen.........A 4
64 Burwick........E 2
25 Bury, Hunts......G 4
35 Bury, Lancs.....F 7
6 Bury, Somerset..C 3
9 Bury, Sussex....E 11
18 Bury Green......B 4
27 Bury St. Edmunds .J 2
36 Burythorpe......A 6
36 Busby.........D 10
41 Buscel.........G 9
16 Buscot.........D 3
59 Bush..........L 5
21 Bush Bank......G 10
27 Bush Green......G 5
57 Bush..........K 8
22 Bushbury.......B 3
18 Bushey.........D 1
18 Bushey Heath....E 2
15 Bushley.......A 11
16 Bushton.........F 2
8 Busta..........C 7
45 Buston Barns...B 10
18 Butcher's Pasture..B 6
15 Butcombe.......H 8
45 Buteland.......E 7
7 Butleigh........C 8
7 Butleigh Wootton..C 8
17 Butler's Cross....C 9
22 Butlers Marston...G 6
27 Butley.........K 7
30 Butt Green......E 5
44 Butterburn.....F 5
36 Buttercrambe....A 5
40 Butterknowle....C 1
6 Butterleigh.....E 3
38 Buttermere, Cumb.D 4
16 Buttermere, Wilts. H 4
30 Butters Green....E 6
35 Buttershaw.....D 10
52 Butterstone.....C 5
31 Butterton......E 9
40 Butterwick, Dur...B 4
41 Butterwick, E. Riding
H 10
24 Butterwick, Lincs..A 5
41 Butterwick, N. Riding
G 7
21 Buttington.....B 8
23 Buttock's Booth..F 11
22 Buttonoak......D 1
8 Butt's Green....C 4
8 Buttsash.......E 6
27 Buxhall.........J 3
49 Buxley.........D 10
10 Buxted.........F 4
31 Buxton, Derby....C 9
26 Buxton, Norfolk..C 5
26 Buxton Heath....C 5
14 Bwlch..........B 5
29 Bwlchgwyn......E 11
20 Bwlchllan......F 1
28 Bwlchtocyn.....H 3
29 Bwlch-y-cibau ..H 11
29 Bwlch-y-ddâr ...H 11
13 Bwlchyfadfa ....B 8
20 Bwlch-y-ffridd....C 6
12 Bwlch-y-groes....C 6
20 Bwlch-y-sarnau...E 6
43 Byeloch.......D 11
40 Byers Green......B 2
23 Byfield........G 8
31 Byfleet........H 11
21 Byford.........H 9
25 Bygrave........L 4
61 Bylbster.......B 11
29 Bylchau........D 9
30 Byley..........C 6
13 Bynea..........G 9
49 Byrewalls.....E 9
44 Byrness........C 6
32 Bythorn.......H 2
21 Byton..........F 9
45 Bywell.........G 8
9 Byworth.......D 11
52 Cablea.........C 4
37 Cabourne......G 9
58 Cabrach........E 1
54 Cabuie Lodge...C 5
6 Cadbury........F 3
4 Cadbury Barton..D 6
59 Caddam........K 1

MAP
47 Cadder.........B 11
51 Cadderlie......D 7
17 Caddington....B 11
49 Caddonfoot......F 7
10 Cade Street......F 5
23 Cadeby, Leics....B 7
36 Cadeby, Yorks....G 3
6 Cadeleigh......E 3
44 Cademuir......F 5
44 Cadgillhead.....E 2
2 Cadgwith.......H 4
53 Cadham.........G 7
34 Cadishead.......H 6
13 Cadle..........G 9
16 Cadley, Wilts....G 3
8 Cadley, Wilts....A 4
17 Cadmore End....E 8
8 Cadnam.........E 5
37 Cadney.........G 8
29 Cadole........D 11
13 Cadoxton-Juxta-Neath
G 11
60 Cadubh........G 3
14 Cae Hopkin.....C 2
28 Caeathraw......D 4
28 Cae-lwyn-grydd...C 5
33 Caenby.........A 7
33 Caenby Corner...A 7
13 Caeo..........C 10
14 Caer Farchell...D 1
14 Caerau........E 2
13 Cae'r-bryn....F 9
28 Cardeon........H 6
28 Cae'r-geiliog....B 3
29 Caergwrle.....D 12
12 Caerlleon......E 6
14 Caernarvon.....D 4
14 Caerphilly.....F 5
20 Caersws.......C 6
13 Caerwedros....A 7
15 Caerwent.......E 8
29 Caerwys......C 10
57 Caggan........H 4
43 Cairn.........C 10
50 Cairnbaan.....H 5
58 Cairnbrogie....E 6
49 Cairncross....C 11
42 Cairnderry.....D 4
51 Cairndow.......F 9
58 Cairness.......B 8
48 Cairneyhill.....A 3
59 Cairnfield.....G 5
58 Cairnfield House..B 2
42 Cairngaan.....H 2
42 Cairngarroch...G 1
43 Cairnhall......C 10
58 Cairnhill.......D 4
58 Cairnie, Aber....C 2
59 Cairnie, Aber....G 5
58 Cairnorrie......D 6
42 Cairnryan......E 2
42 Cairnsmore.....E 5
47 Cairntable.....H 9
58 Cairnwhin......B 3
54 Caiseachan.....D 6
26 Caister-on-Sea....D 8
37 Caistor.......C 11
26 Caistor St.Edmund E 5
45 Caistron.......C 8
49 Caitha Bowland..F 7
61 Caithness, Co....C 10
63 Calbost........E 5
8 Calbourne......G 6
33 Calceby........C 11
22 Calchems Corner..E 6
15 Calcot Farm....E 11
17 Calcot Row......G 7
56 Calcots Station....C 8
11 Calcott........B 10
38 Caldbeck.......A 6
40 Caldbergh......G 1
25 Caldecote,
Bedfordshire....L 3
25 Caldecote,
Cambridgeshire K 4
24 Caldecote, Hunts. .F 2
25 Caldecott, Hunts. .H 1
23 Caldecott, Rut. .C 12
38 Calder, Cumb....E 3
49 Calder, Northumb.
G 12
38 Calder Bridge....E 3
35 Calder Grove....E 11
61 Calder Mains ..B 10
34 Calder Vale.....C 4
47 Calderbank.....C 12
35 Calderbrook.....E 8
48 Caldercruix....C 1
47 Caldermill......E 11
47 Calderwood....D 11
15 Caldicot.......E 8

MAP
49 Caldside........E 9
40 Caldwell.......D 2
30 Caldy..........B 1
13 Caledfwlch ....D 10
13 Caledrhydiau....B 8
64 Calfsound......B 3
50 Calgary........B 1
56 Califer.........D 6
26 California, Norf..D 8
48 California, Stir..B 2
27 California, Suff...L 5
5 California Cross ..K 6
31 Calke.........H 12
45 Callaly........B 9
52 Callander.......F 1
63 Callanish......D 3
51 Callert House....A 8
3 Callington....C 10
15 Callow.........A 8
21 Callow End.....G 2
22 Callow Hill, Worcs.
E 1
22 Callow Hill, Worcs.
F 4
16 Callow Hill....F 1
17 Callowhill.....G 11
21 Callows Grave...F 11
8 Calmore........E 5
16 Calmsden......C 1
16 Calne.........G 1
32 Calow.........C 1
3 Calstock......C 11
16 Calstone Wellington
G 1
26 Calthorpe......B 5
38 Calthwaite.....A 7
35 Calton, Yorks...A 8
31 Calton, Staffs...E 9
30 Calveley......D 4
31 Calver........C 11
21 Calver Hill......G 9
30 Calverhall.....F 5
6 Calverleigh....E 3
35 Calverley......C 10
23 Calverton, Bucks.H 11
32 Calverton, Notts...E 3
52 Calvine........A 3
43 Calvo.........F 12
48 Calzeat.......F 4
15 Cam...........D 10
62 Camascross.....G 6
50 Camasine.......A 5
50 Camasnacroise...B 6
54 Camasterach....E 1
62 Camastianavaig ..D 4
62 Camasunary.....F 4
64 Camault Muir....F 1
11 Camber.........F 8
17 Camberley......H 9
18 Camberwell.....F 3
36 Camblesforth.....D 4
45 Cambo, Northumb.
D 8
45 Cambois......E 11
2 Camborne......F 4
25 Cambridge, Cambs.J 5
15 Cambridge, Glos. D 10
25 Cambridgeshire and
Isle of Ely, Co. .K 5
52 Cambus........H 3
59 Cambus o'May ...G 2
52 Cambusbarron...H 3
52 Cambuskenneth..H 3
47 Cambuslang....C 11
61 Cambusmore Lo. .G 8
54 Cambussorray...F 7
18 Camden........F 3
15 Cameley.......H 9
3 Camelford......A 8
48 Camelon.......A 2
9 Camelsdale....C 10
54 Camerory......F 6
38 Camerton, Cumb..B 3
7 Camerton, Som. .A 10
55 Camisky........L 5
59 Cammachmore..H 6
22 Cammeringham..B 6
56 Campbeltown or
Ardersier......D 3
46 Campbeltown....G 2
45 Camperdown...F 11
53 Campmuir......C 7
35 Camps Green...L 7
36 Campsall......F 3
27 Campsey Ash....K 6
25 Campton.......L 2
44 Camptown......B 5

MAP
12 Camrose........E 3
52 Camserney......B 3
61 Camster......C 11
55 Camus-luinie...G 3
54 Camusteel......E 1
52 Camusvrachan..B 1
8 Canada........D 4
59 Candacraig......G 1
58 Candacraig House F 1
33 Candlesby.....C 11
59 Candy.........J 5
48 Candyburn......E 3
17 Cane End.......F 8
19 Canewdon......D 9
18 Canfield End....B 6
8 Canford Bottom..F 2
8 Canford Magna..F 2
61 Canisbay.....A 12
7 Cann..........D 12
7 Cann Common ..D 12
7 Cannards Grave..B 9
54 Cannich.......F 7
6 Cannington.....B 6
22 Cannock......A 3
22 Cannock Wood...A 4
15 Canonpy.......C 9
21 Canon Bridge...H 10
21 Canon Pyon....G 10
44 Canonbie......E 2
23 Canons Ashby...G 9
2 Canonstown....F 2
11 Canterbury....B 10
26 Cantley, Norfolk..E 7
36 Cantley, Yorks...G 4
14 Canton........G 5
56 Cantraybruich...E 3
56 Cantraydoune...E 3
56 Cantraywood...E 3
39 Cantsfield.....H 8
19 Canvey.......F 8
33 Canwick......C 7
2 Canworthy Water .B 2
55 Caol.........M 5
55 Caonich......K 4
10 Capel..........D 1
20 Capel-Bangor...D 2
20 Capel Betws Lleucu
G 2
28 Capel Carmel...G 1
28 Capel Curig....D 6
13 Capel Cynon....B 7
13 Capel Dewi, Carm. E 8
20 Capel Dewi, Cards.
D 2
13 Capel Dewi, Cards.
C 8
29 Capel Garmon...E 7
13 Capel Gwyn....E 8
13 Capel Gwynfe...E 10
13 Capel Hendre....F 9
13 Capel Isaac....D 9
12 Capel Iwan.....C 6
11 Capel le Ferne ..D 11
14 Capel Llanilterne ..F 4
27 Capel St. Andrew .K 7
27 Capel St. Mary...L 4
20 Capel Seion....D 2
20 Capel Trisant....E 3
12 Capel Tygwydd...C 6
28 Capel-côch.....B 4
28 Capel-gwyn....C 3
13 Capel-iago.....C 9
28 Capel-uchaf....E 4
29 Capelulo.......C 7
14 Capel-y-ffin....A 6
30 Capenhurst.....C 2
39 Capernwray....H 8
45 Capheaton......E 8
48 Cappercleuch....G 5
48 Capplegill......H 4
5 Capton, Devon...K 7
6 Capton, Somerset .B 4
52 Caputh........C 6
32 Car Colston.....F 4
2 Carbis Bay......F 2
62 Carbost, Skye...E 3
62 Carbost, Skye....C 4
60 Carbreck......B 4
32 Carbrooke.....E 3
32 Carburton.....C 3
3 Carclaze......D 7
47 Carcluie......H 8
36 Carcroft......F 3
53 Cardenden.....H 7
21 Cardeston......A 9
14 Cardiff.......G 5
12 Cardigan......B 5
25 Cardington,
Bedfordshire....K 2
21 Cardington, Salop.
C 10

MAP
3 Cardinham C 8
42 Cardorcan D 5
56 Cardow E 7
48 Cardrona F 6
47 Cardross B 8
43 Cardurnock F 12
24 Careby D 1
59 Careston L 3
12 Carew G 4
12 Carew Cheriton G 4
12 Carew Newton F 4
44 Carewoodrig C 3
15 Carey A 9
47 Carfin D 12
49 Carfrae B 8
43 Cargenbridge D 10
52 Cargill C 6
44 Cargo G 2
3 Cargreen C 11
49 Carham F 10
6 Carhampton B 3
2 Carharrack F 4
52 Carie A 1
8 Carisbrooke G 6
38 Cark G 6
3 Carkeel D 11
2 Carland D 5
44 Carlatton Mill H 4
24 Carlby D 2
35 Carlecotes G 10
2 Carleen G 3
44 Carlenrig C 2
44 Carleton, Cumb. H 3
42 Carleton, Wig. H 5
35 Carleton, Yorks. B 8
26 Carleton Forehoe E 4
26 Carleton Rode F 4
2 Carlidnack G 5
41 Carlin How C 7
15 Carlingcott H 10
44 Carlisle G 2
48 Carlops D 4
63 Carloway C 3
25 Carlton, Beds. K 1
25 Carlton, Cambs. K 7
40 Carlton, Durham C 4
23 Carlton, Leics. B 7
40 Carlton, N. Riding E 5
40 Carlton, N. Riding F 6
40 Carlton, N. Riding G 1
32 Carlton, Notts. F 3
27 Carlton, Suffolk J 7
36 Carlton, W. Riding E 4
35 Carlton, W. Riding D 1
35 Carlton, W. Riding F 12
26 Carlton Colville F 8
23 Carlton Curlieu B 10
40 Carlton Husthwaite G 5
32 Carlton in Lindrick B 3
40 Carlton Miniott G 4
32 Carlton Scroop F 6
32 Carlton-le-Moorland D 6
32 Carlton-on-Trent D 5
48 Carluke D 1
3 Carlyon Bay D 7
48 Carmacoup G 1
13 Carmarthen E 7
13 Carmel, Carm. E 9
28 Carmel, Caer. E 4
28 Carmel, Anglesey B 3
29 Carmel, Flintshire C 11
13 Carmel Chapel D 10
38 Carmel Fell F 6
63 Carminish H 1
59 Carmont J 5
47 Carmunnock D 11
47 Carmyle C 11
53 Carmyllie C 10
37 Carnaby A 9
63 Carnach, Harris G 3
55 Carnach, Inver. L 1
55 Carnach, Ross & Cromarty G 4
57 Carnachuin K 4
57 Carnaquheen K 8
53 Carnbee F 10
52 Carnbo G 5
55 Carndu G 3
47 Carnduff E 11
2 Carne F 6
47 Carnell F 9
14 Carnetown E 4
39 Carnforth H 7
55 Carn-gorm G 3
12 Carnhedryn Uchaf D 2
2 Carnhell Green F 3
63 Carnish D 1
2 Carnkie F 4
20 Carno C 5
55 Carnoch, Inver. K 2
54 Carnoch, Inver. F 7
54 Carnoch, Ross & Cromarty E 6
52 Carnock H 5
2 Carnon Downs F 5
53 Carnoustie D 10
48 Carnwath E 3
29 Carog E 7
39 Carperby F 12
32 Carr A 2
34 Carr Cross F 3
44 Carr Shield H 6
32 Carr Vale C 2
46 Carradale E 3
63 Carragrich G 3
57 Carrbridge G 5
35 Carrbrook G 8
28 Carreglefn A 3
12 Carregwen C 6
51 Carrick, Argyll H 9
53 Carrick, Fife E 9
48 Carriden A 3
34 Carrington, Ches. H 6
33 Carrington, Lincs. E 10
48 Carrington, Midloth. C 6
29 Carrog F 10
56 Carron, Moray E 8
48 Carron, Stirling A 2
47 Carron Bridge A 12
43 Carronbridge B 9
48 Carronshore A 2
47 Carrot E 10
15 Carrow Hill E 7
43 Carrutherstown D 11
40 Carrville A 3
46 Carsaig, Argyll A 2
50 Carsaig, Argyll E 3
42 Carscreugh F 3
46 Carse House C 2
42 Carsebuie E 4
42 Carsegown F 5
42 Carseriggan E 4
43 Carsethorn F 10
18 Carshalton G 3
31 Carsington E 11
46 Carskiey H 2
42 Carsluith F 6
42 Carsphairn B 6
48 Carstairs E 2
48 Carstairs Junction E 2
49 Carterhaugh G 7
8 Carter's Clay D 4
16 Carterton C 4
45 Carterway Heads H 8
3 Carthew D 7
40 Carthorpe G 3
45 Cartington C 8
48 Cartland E 1
38 Cartmel G 6
13 Carway F 8
7 Cary Fitzpaine D 9
63 Caryshader D 2
43 Carzield C 10
21 Cascob F 8
51 Cashell H 11
51 Cashlie C 12
8 Cashmoor E 1
16 Cassey Compton C 1
16 Cassington, Oxon C 5
7 Cassington, Som. B 7
40 Cassop Colliery A 4
24 Casswell's Bridge C 3
14 Castell-y-bwch E 6
39 Casterton G 8
26 Castle Acre D 1
23 Castle Ashby F 11
31 Castle Bank H 7
39 Castle Bolton F 12
22 Castle Bromwich C 5
24 Castle Bytham D 1
21 Castle Caereinion B 7
25 Castle Camps L 7
44 Castle Carrock G 4
7 Castle Cary C 10
15 Castle Combe F 11
32 Castle Donington G 2
43 Castle Douglas E 8
16 Castle Eaton E 2
40 Castle Eden A 4
58 Castle Forbes F 4
21 Castle Frome H 12
17 Castle Green H 10
31 Castle Gresley H 11
49 Castle Heaton E 11
27 Castle Hedingham L 1
10 Castle Hill D 6
41 Castle Howard H 7
53 Castle Huntly D 8
42 Castle Kennedy F 2
12 Castle Morris D 3
44 Castle O'er D 1
21 Castle Pulverbatch B 9
24 Castle Rising C 8
56 Castle Stuart E 3
12 Castlebythe D 4
47 Castlecary B 12
48 Castlecraig, Peeb. E 4
56 Castlecraig, Ross & Cromarty C 4
43 Castlefairn C 8
36 Castleford E 2
58 Castlehill, Aber. C 5
47 Castlehill, Dunb. B 9
48 Castlehill, Lanark D 1
48 Castlehill, Peeb. F 5
42 Castlemaddy C 6
12 Castlemartin G 3
43 Castlemilk D 12
15 Castlemorton A 11
45 Castleside H 9
23 Castlethorpe H 11
53 Castleton, Angus C 8
46 Castleton, Argyll A 4
31 Castleton, Derby B 10
35 Castleton, Lancs. F 7
14 Castleton, Mon. F 6
44 Castleton, Rox. D 3
41 Castleton, Yorks. D 7
61 Castletown, Caith. A 11
7 Castletown, Dorset H 7
45 Castletown, Dur. G 11
56 Castletown, Inver. E 3
38 Castletown, I.o.M. H 1
35 Castley C 11
26 Caston, Norfolk F 2
24 Castor, Hunts. F 2
43 Castramont E 7
13 Caswell H 9
31 Cat and Fiddle Inn C 8
46 Catacol D 4
15 Catbrain F 9
15 Catbrook D 8
2 Catchall G 2
32 Catcliffe A 2
7 Catcott B 7
7 Catcott Burtle B 7
47 Catcraig F 9
10 Caterham C 2
26 Catfield C 7
64 Catfirth D 7
18 Catford G 4
34 Catforth D 4
17 Cathays F 5
47 Cathcart C 10
14 Cathedine B 5
9 Catherington E 8
7 Catherston Leweston G 7
21 Catherton E 12
49 Cathpair E 7
43 Catlins C 12
57 Catlodge K 2
44 Catlowdy E 3
16 Catmore F 5
34 Caton A 4
5 Cator Court H 5
47 Catrine G 10
15 Cat's Ash E 7
10 Catsfield G 6
22 Catshill E 3
36 Cattal B 2
27 Cattawade M 4
34 Catterall C 4
40 Catterick E 3
40 Catterick Bridge E 3
40 Catterick Camp E 2
39 Catterlen B 7
59 Catterline J 6
36 Catterton C 3
9 Catteshall B 11
23 Catthorpe D 9
7 Cattistock F 9
26 Catton, Norfolk D 5
44 Catton, Northumb. G 6
40 Catton, Yorks. G 4
37 Catwick C 9
25 Catworth H 2
16 Caulcot B 6
52 Cauldhame H 1
31 Cauldon E 9
44 Cauldside E 3
31 Cauldwell H 11
58 Cauldwells B 5
43 Caulkerbush F 10
7 Caundle Marsh E 10
22 Caunsall D 2
32 Caunton D 5
42 Causeway End F 5
58 Causewayend, Aber. F 7
48 Causewayend, Lanark F 3
43 Causewayhead, Cumb. F 12
52 Causewayhead, Stir. H 3
45 Causey Park Bri. D 10
39 Cautley F 9
27 Cavendish K 1
27 Cavenham H 1
17 Caversfield B 7
17 Caversham G 8
63 Caversta E 5
31 Caverswall F 8
36 Cavil D 5
56 Cawdor E 4
3 Cawsand E 11
26 Cawston C 4
41 Cawthorn F 8
35 Cawthorne F 11
24 Cawthorpe C 2
36 Cawood C 3
40 Cawton G 6
25 Caxton J 4
21 Caynham E 11
32 Caythorpe, Lincs. E 6
32 Caythorpe, Notts. F 4
41 Cayton G 10
61 Ceann-na-coille C 7
29 Cefn-Berain C 9
29 Cefn-Canol G 11
29 Cefn Coch, Mer. G 10
29 Cefn Coch, Mont. H 10
14 Cefn Cribbwr F 2
14 Cefn Cross F 2
21 Cefn Einion D 8
14 Cefn Fforest D 5
15 Cefn Llaithan B 7
29 Cefn Mawr F 12
14 Cefn Rhigos D 2
29 Cefn-brith E 8
13 Cefn-bryn-brain F 10
14 Cefn-coed-y-cymmer C 3
29 Cefn-ddwysarn F 9
20 Cefngorwydd H 5
29 Cefn-y-bedd E 12
12 Cefn-y-pant D 5
13 Cellan B 9
31 Cellarhead E 8
39 Celleron C 7
28 Cemaes Bay A 3
20 Cemmaes B 4
20 Cemmaes Road B 4
12 Cenarth C 6
53 Ceres F 9
20 Cerist D 5
7 Cerne Abbas F 10
16 Cerney Wick E 2
28 Cerrigceinwen C 4
29 Cerrigydrudion E 9
26 Cess D 7
49 Cessford G 10
28 Ceunant D 5
15 Chaceley A 11
2 Chacewater E 5
17 Chackmore A 8
23 Chacombe H 8
22 Chad Valley D 4
22 Chadbury G 4
35 Chadderton G 7
31 Chaddesden F 12
22 Chaddesley Corbett E 2
16 Chaddleworth F 5
16 Chadlington B 4
23 Chadshunt G 7
32 Chadwell H 5
18 Chadwell St. Mary F 6
22 Chadwick End E 5
7 Chaffcombe E 7
5 Chagford G 6
10 Chailey F 3
24 Chainbridge E 5
10 Chainhurst C 6
8 Chalbury E 2
8 Chalbury Com. E 2
10 Chaldon C 2
7 Chaldon Herring or East Chaldon H 11
8 Chale H 6
8 Chale Green H 6
17 Chalfont St. Giles E 10
17 Chalfont St. Peter E 11
15 Chalford D 12
17 Chalford Com. E 11
17 Chalgrove D 7
10 Chalk A 5
4 Challacombe, Devon B 6
4 Challacombe, Devon D 6
42 Challoch E 5
11 Challock Lees C 8
17 Chalton, Beds. B 11
9 Chalton, Hants. E 8
17 Chalvey F 10
10 Chalvington G 4
48 Champany B 3
20 Chancery E 1
17 Chandler's Cross D 11
8 Chandler's Ford D 6
43 Chanlockfoot B 8
7 Chantry B 10
53 Chapel H 7
7 Chapel Allerton A 7
35 Chapel Allerton C 11
3 Chapel Amble B 7
23 Chapel Brampton E 10
30 Chapel Chorlton F 6
23 Chapel End C 7
22 Chapel Green D 6
36 Chapel Haddlesey D 4
58 Chapel Hill, Aber. D 8
33 Chapel Hill, Lincs. E 9
15 Chapel Hill, Mon. D 8
35 Chapel Hill, Yorks. C 12
21 Chapel Lawn E 8
39 Chapel le Dale G 9
49 Chapel Mains E 8
59 Chapel of Barras J 6
58 Chapel of Garioch E 5
42 Chapel Rossan G 2
16 Chapel Row, Berks. G 6
10 Chapel Row, Sussex G 5
33 Chapel St. Leonards C 12
38 Chapel Stile E 5
25 Chapeland Way L 8
42 Chapeldonan B 3
31 Chapel-en-le-Frith B 9
47 Chapelhall C 12
43 Chapelhill, Dumf. B 11
53 Chapelhill, Perth E 7
52 Chapelhill, Perth D 5
48 Chapelhope G 5
44 Chapelknowe F 2
38 Chapels G 5
53 Chapelton, Angus B 11
4 Chapelton, Devon C 5
59 Chapelton, Kinc. J 5
43 Chapelton, Kirk. G 8
47 Chapelton, Lan. E 11
57 Chapelton, Inver. H 5
57 Chapeltown, Banff G 8
34 Chapeltown, Lancs. F 6
35 Chapeltown, Yorks. G 12
5 Chapmans Well G 2
7 Chapmanslade B 11
18 Chapmore End B 3
19 Chappel A 9
7 Chard E 7
6 Chardstock F 6
44 Chareheads H 6
15 Charfield E 10
11 Charing C 8
8 Charing Cross E 3
11 Charing Heath C 8
22 Charingworth H 5
16 Charlbury B 5
15 Charlcombe H 10
16 Charlcutt G 1
22 Charlecote F 6
4 Charles C 6
43 Charlesfield E 12
53 Charleston C 8
59 Charlestown, Aber. G 7
3 Charlestown, Corn. E 7
7 Charlestown, Dorset H 9
48 Charlestown, Fife A 3
54 Charlestown, Ross & Cromarty B 2
56 Charlestown, Ross & Cromarty E 2
35 Charlestown, Yorks. D 8
56 Charlestown of Aberlour E 8
35 Charlesworth H 9
5 Charleton, Devon L 6
16 Charleton, Oxon A 6
6 Charlinch B 6
18 Charlton, Herts. A 2
44 Charlton, Northumb. D 6
9 Charlton, Sussex E 10
8 Charlton, Wilts. A 3
8 Charlton, Wilts. D 3
16 Charlton, Wilts. H 2
7 Charlton, Wilts. D 12
16 Charlton, Wilts. E 1
22 Charlton, Worcs. H 4
40 Charlton, Yorks. D 6
16 Charlton Abbots B 1
7 Charlton Adam C 9
7 Charlton Horethorne D 10
16 Charlton Kings B 1
7 Charlton Mackrell C 8
7 Charlton Marshall F 12
45 Charlton Mires A 10
7 Charlton Musgrove C 10
16 Charlton-on-Otmoor C 6
7 Charlton-on-the-Hill F 12
9 Charlwood, Hants. C 8
10 Charlwood, Surrey D 1
7 Charminster G 10
7 Charmouth G 7
17 Charndon B 7
16 Charney Bassett E 5
34 Charnock Richard F 4
27 Charsfield J 5
11 Chart Sutton C 7
17 Charter Alley H 7
49 Charterhouse, Roxburgh F 9
7 Charterhouse, Som. A 8
16 Charterville Allotments C 4
11 Chartham C 9
11 Chartham Hatch B 9
8 Charton A 5
17 Chartridge D 10
23 Charwelton G 8
22 Chase Terrace A 4
22 Chasetown A 4
16 Chastleton A 3
4 Chasty F 2
34 Chatburn C 6
30 Chatcull G 6
10 Chatham B 6
45 Chathill E 12
10 Chattenden A 6
25 Chatteris G 5
27 Chattisham L 4
45 Chatton C 12
17 Chaul End B 11
4 Chawleigh E 6
25 Chawston K 3
9 Chawton B 8
31 Cheadle, Cheshire A 7
31 Cheadle, Staffs. F 8
31 Cheadle Hulme B 7
18 Cheam G 2
17 Cheapside G 10
17 Chearsley C 8
31 Chebsey G 7
17 Checkendon F 7
30 Checkley, Cheshire F 6
21 Checkley, Herefs. H 11
31 Checkley, Staffs. F 9
27 Chedburgh J 1
7 Cheddar A 8
17 Cheddington B 10
31 Cheddleton E 8
6 Cheddon Fitzpaine C 6
26 Chedgrave E 7
7 Chedington F 8
27 Chediston G 7
16 Chedworth C 2
7 Chedzoy B 7
49 Cheeklaw D 10
35 Cheetham Hill G 7
4 Cheglinch B 4
4 Cheldon Barton E 6
31 Chelford C 7
31 Chellaston G 12
25 Chellington K 1
22 Chelmarsh C 1
27 Chelmondiston L 5
31 Chelmorton C 9
19 Chelmsford C 7
18 Chelsea F 3
18 Chelsfield Village G 5
27 Chelsworth K 3
14 Cheltenham, Brec. C 5
15 Cheltenham, Glos. B 12
25 Chelveston H 1
15 Chelvey G 8
15 Chelwood H 9
10 Chelwood Com. E 3
10 Chelwood Gate E 3
21 Cheney Longville D 9
17 Chenies D 11
15 Chepstow E 8
16 Cherhill G 1
15 Cherington, Glos. D 12
22 Cherington, War. H 6
13 Cheriton, Glam. H 8

MAP
9 Cheriton, Hants...C 7
11 Cheriton, Kent...D 11
4 Cheriton, Som.....A 6
4 Cheriton Bishop...F 6
5 Cheriton Cross....G 6
6 Cheriton Fitzpaine.F 2
12 Cheriton or Stackpole Elidor.........G 3
30 Cherrington.......H 5
37 Cherry Burton....C 7
25 Cherry Hinton.....K 6
22 Cherry Orchard...G 2
52 Cherrybank.......E 6
49 Cherrytrees.......F 10
17 Chertsey.........G 11
7 Cheselbourne.....F 11
17 Chesham.........D 10
17 Chesham Bois...D 10
30 Cheshire, Co. ....D 5
18 Cheshunt.........D 4
22 Cheslyn Hay......A 3
18 Chessington......H 2
30 Chester..........D 3
45 Chester Moor....H 11
7 Chesterblade......B 10
32 Chesterfield.......C 1
22 Chesterfield.......B 4
48 Chesterhall.......F 2
48 Chesterhill.......C 6
45 Chester-le-Street .H 11
44 Chesters, Rox.....B 5
49 Chesters, Rox.....G 8
24 Chesterton, Hunts. F 2
16 Chesterton, Oxon .B 6
31 Chesterton, Staffs..E 7
23 Chesterton Green..F 7
44 Chesterwood......F 6
11 Chestfield........B 10
30 Cheswardine......G 6
45 Cheswick.........A 11
45 Cheswick Bldgs...A 11
7 Chetnole..........E 9
6 Chettiscombe......E 3
25 Chettisham.......G 6
8 Chettle...........E 1
21 Chetton..........C 12
30 Chetwynd Aston..H 6
30 Chetwynd Park...H 6
25 Cheveley..........J 8
10 Chevening.........B 4
27 Chevington........J 1
45 Chevington Drift.C 11
6 Chevithorne......E 3
15 Chew Magna......H 9
15 Chew Stoke......H 9
15 Chewton Keynsham H 9
7 Chewton Mendip..A 9
23 Chicheley.......G 12
9 Chichester.......F 10
7 Chickerell........H 9
7 Chicklade........C 12
21 Chickward........G 8
9 Chidden..........D 8
9 Chiddingfold....C 11
10 Chiddingly.......G 4
10 Chiddingstone...D 4
10 Chiddingstone Causeway......C 4
10 Chiddingstone Hoath D 4
7 Chideock.........G 7
6 Chidgley..........C 4
9 Chidham.........F 9
16 Chieveley.........G 5
18 Chignall St. James.C 6
18 Chignall Smealy...C 6
18 Chigwell.........E 4
18 Chigwell Row.....E 5
8 Chilbolton........B 5
8 Chilcomb.........C 6
7 Chilcombe........G 9
7 Chilcompton......A 9
22 Chilcote..........A 6
7 Child Okeford....E 11
30 Childer Thornton .B 2
34 Children's Homes .E 6
16 Childrey.........E 5
30 Child's Ercall.....H 5
22 Childswickham ...H 4
30 Childwall.........A 3
18 Childwick Green..C 1
7 Chilfrome........F 9
9 Chilgrove.........E 9
11 Chilham..........C 9
8 Chilhampton.....C 3
4 Chilla............F 3
5 Chillaton.........H 3
11 Chillenden.......C 11
8 Chillerton........H 6
27 Chillesford.......K 7
45 Chillingham.....C 12
5 Chillington, Devon L 7
MAP
7 Chillington, Somerset.......E 7
32 Chillwell.........G 2
8 Chilmark.........C 1
16 Chilson..........B 4
3 Chilsworthy, Cornwall B 11
4 Chilsworthy, Devon E 2
7 Chilthorne Domer D 8
16 Chilton, Berks.....F 6
17 Chilton, Bucks....C 8
4 Chilton, Devon....E 7
40 Chilton, Durham..B 3
9 Chilton Candover .B 7
7 Chilton Cantelo...D 9
16 Chilton Foliat....G 4
40 Chilton Lane .....B 3
7 Chilton Polden....B 7
27 Chilton Street.....K 1
6 Chilton Trinity....B 6
8 Chilworth, Hampshire.....D 5
9 Chilworth, Surrey A 11
16 Chimney..........D 4
9 Chineham.........A 8
18 Chingford.........E 4
31 Chinley...........B 9
31 Chinley Head.....B 9
17 Chinnor...........D 8
30 Chipnall..........G 6
25 Chippenham, Oxon H 8
15 Chippenham, Wilts. G 12
17 Chipperfield.....D 11
25 Chipping, Herts...M 5
34 Chipping, Lancs...C 5
22 Chipping Campden H 5
16 Chipping Norton..B 4
15 Chipping Sodbury F 10
23 Chipping Warden .G 8
6 Chipstable.........D 4
10 Chipstead, Kent...B 4
10 Chipstead, Surrey .B 2
21 Chirbury.........C 8
29 Chirk............F 12
29 Chirk Green......F 12
42 Chirmorie.........D 3
49 Chirnside........D 11
49 Chirnsidebridge..D 11
16 Chirton...........H 2
16 Chisbury..........G 4
7 Chiselborough....E 8
16 Chiseldon.........F 3
17 Chislehampton....D 7
18 Chislehurst.......G 4
11 Chislet...........B 11
35 Chisley...........D 9
18 Chiswell Green....C 1
18 Chiswick.........F 2
35 Chisworth.........H 8
11 Chitcombe.........F 7
9 Chithurst.........D 9
25 Chittering.........H 6
8 Chitterne..........B 2
4 Chittlehamholt....D 5
4 Chittlehampton...C 5
15 Chittoe..........H 12
5 Chivelstone......M 6
17 Chobham.......H 10
49 Choicelee........D 10
8 Cholderton.......B 4
17 Cholesbury.......C 10
45 Chollerford........F 7
45 Chollerton........F 7
17 Cholsey..........E 7
21 Cholstrey........F 10
40 Chop Gate........E 5
45 Choppington.....E 10
45 Chopwell.........G 9
30 Chorley, Cheshire .E 4
34 Chorley, Lancs. .E 5
21 Chorley, Salop...D 12
22 Chorley, Staffs....A 4
17 Chorleywood.....E 11
30 Chorlton..........E 6
35 Chorlton cum Hardy H 7
30 Chorlton Lane....E 3
25 Chrishall.........L 5
24 Christchurch, Cambs. F 6
8 Christchurch, Hants. G 3
15 Christchurch, Mon.E 7
16 Christian Malford .F 1
30 Christleton.......D 3
17 Christmas Com....E 12
7 Christon...........A 7
45 Christon Bank...A 10
5 Christow..........G 7
9 Christ's Hospital .C 12
MAP
47 Chryston........B 11
5 Chudleigh........H 7
5 Chudleigh Knighton H 7
4 Chulmleigh.......E 6
35 Chunal..........H 9
34 Church...........D 6
30 Church Aston....H 6
23 Church Brampton E 10
31 Church Broughton G 10
9 Church Crookham A 9
31 Church Eaton....H 7
25 Church End, Beds. L 3
19 Church End, Essex A 7
25 Church End, Essex.L 7
17 Church End, Hampshire.....H 7
17 Church End, Hertfordshire..C 12
37 Church End, Kent..........G 12
18 Church End, London........E 3
24 Church End, Norf. E 5
22 Church End, War..C 6
16 Church End, Wilts. F 1
16 Church Enstone...B 5
36 Church Fenton....C 3
6 Church Green....G 5
31 Church Gresley..H 11
16 Church Hanborough C 5
30 Church Hill......D 5
22 Church Honeybourne H 5
41 Church House....E 7
41 Church Houses....E 7
8 Church Knowle...H 1
32 Church Laneham..C 5
23 Church Langton .C 10
23 Church Lawford ..D 8
31 Church Lawton...E 7
31 Church Leigh.....G 9
22 Church Lench.....G 4
30 Church Minshull..D 5
21 Church Preen....C 11
21 Church Pulverbatch B 9
21 Church Stoke.....C 8
23 Church Stowe.....F 9
10 Church Street, Kent A 6
27 Church Street, Suffolk G 8
21 Church Stretton..C 10
39 Church Town.....F 7
14 Church Village....F 4
32 Church Warsop...C 3
15 Churcham.......B 11
15 Churchdown.....B 12
18 Churchend, Essex .B 6
19 Churchend, Essex E 10
15 Churchend, Glos. E 10
22 Churchfield.......C 4
4 Churchill, Devon..B 5
6 Churchill, Devon..F 6
22 Churchill, Salop...D 2
16 Churchill, Oxon...B 4
15 Churchill, Som....H 7
22 Churchill, Worcs. .G 3
22 Churchingford....E 5
23 Churchover.......D 8
6 Churchstanton....E 5
15 Churchstow.......L 6
38 Churchtown, Cumb. A 6
4 Churchtown, Dev. .F 3
38 Churchtown, I.o.M. G 2
34 Churchtown, Lancs. C 4
34 Churchtown, Lancs. E 3
44 Churnsike Lodge..E 5
5 Churston Ferrers..K 8
9 Churt............B 10
30 Churton..........E 3
35 Churwell.........D 11
8 Chute Standen....A 5
28 Chwilog..........F 4
29 Cilcain...........D 11
13 Cilcennin.........A 8
13 Cilfrew..........G 11
14 Cilfynydd..........E 4
12 Cilgerran.........C 5
12 Cilgwyn..........C 4
13 Ciliau Aeron......A 8
13 Cilmaengwyn....F 10
50 Cilmalieu.........B 6
20 Cilmery...........G 5
12 Cilrhedyn........D 6
MAP
13 Cilsan............E 9
29 Ciltalgarth........F 8
12 Cilwendeg........C 6
13 Cilybebyll........F 10
13 Cil-y-cwm........C 11
15 Cinderford.......C 10
12 Cippyn...........B 5
16 Cirencester.......D 1
40 Citadilla..........E 2
28 City Dulas........B 4
57 Clach Bharraig....J 5
46 Clachaig, Argyll...A 6
57 Clachaig, Inver....H 6
50 Clachan, Argyll...C 6
50 Clachan, Argyll...F 5
51 Clachan, Argyll...F 9
46 Clachan, Argyll...D 3
62 Clachan, Inver.....E 5
52 Clachan, Perth.....A 3
47 Clachan of Campsie A 11
46 Clachan of Glendaruel A 5
50 Clachan-Seil......F 5
46 Clachbreck........B 3
59 Clachnabrain.....L 1
60 Clachtoll..........D 2
52 Clackavoid.......A 6
52 Clackmannan......H 4
52 Clackmannan, Co. G 4
56 Clackmarras......D 8
19 Clacton on Sea...B 11
47 Cladance........E 11
51 Cladich...........E 8
50 Claggan..........C 4
62 Claigan..........C 2
22 Claines...........F 2
60 Clais Charnach....A 4
60 Claisfearn.........C 3
7 Clandown.......A 10
9 Clanfield, Hants...D 8
16 Clanfield, Oxon...D 4
8 Clanville..........A 5
46 Claonaig.........D 4
35 Clap Gate........B 12
11 Clap Hill..........D 9
8 Clapgate, Dorset ..F 2
13 Clapgate, Herts....A 4
25 Clapham, Beds....K 1
6 Clapham, Devon..H 2
18 Clapham, London .F 3
9 Clapham, Sussex .E 12
39 Clapham, Yorks...H 9
49 Clappers.........D 12
38 Clappersgate.......E 6
16 Clapton, Glos.....B 3
7 Clapton, Somerset .F 7
7 Clapton, Som....A 10
15 Clapton-in-Gordano G 8
4 Clapworthy.......D 5
20 Clarach...........D 2
12 Clarbeston........E 4
12 Clarbeston Road..E 4
32 Clarborough.......B 4
27 Clare.............L 1
43 Clarebrand........E 8
43 Clarencefield.....E 11
49 Clarilaw..........G 8
49 Clarilawmoor.....F 8
9 Clarken Green....A 7
47 Clarkston.......D 10
61 Clashcoig.........G 7
58 Clashindarroch....D 2
61 Clashmore.........G 7
61 Clashnessie.......D 2
57 Clashnoir.........G 8
52 Clathy............E 5
52 Clathymore.......E 5
58 Clatt.............E 3
20 Clatter............C 5
8 Clatterford........G 6
59 Clattering Bridge ..J 4
42 Clatteringshawes ..D 6
6 Clatworthy........C 4
30 Claughton, Ches...A 2
34 Claughton, Lancs..A 4
34 Claughton, Lancs..C 4
6 Clavelshay........C 6
22 Claverdon........F 5
15 Claverham.......H 8
25 Clavering.........M 6
22 Claverley.........C 2
15 Claverton.......H 11
14 Clawdd-coch......F 4
29 Clawddnewydd ..E 10
39 Clawthorpe.......G 8
4 Clawton...........F 2
37 Claxby, Lincs.....H 9
37 Claxby, Lincs....C 11
26 Claxton, Norfolk..E 6
36 Claxton, Yorks....A 5
23 Clay.............D 9
MAP
27 Clay Common....G 8
32 Clay Cross.......D 1
57 Claybokie........K 6
23 Claybrooke Magna C 8
23 Claybrooke Parva .C 8
23 Claydon, Oxon....G 8
27 Claydon, Suffolk..K 4
59 Clayfolds.........H 6
44 Claygate, Dumf. ..E 2
10 Claygate, Kent....D 6
17 Claygate, Surrey .H 12
6 Clayhanger, Devon D 4
22 Clayhanger, War. .B 4
6 Clayhidon.........E 5
8 Clayhill, Hants....E 5
11 Clayhill, Sussex....F 7
58 Claymires.........E 7
32 Claypole..........E 6
31 Clayton, Staffs.....F 7
10 Clayton, Sussex...G 2
35 Clayton, Yorks...D 10
36 Clayton, Yorks....F 2
34 Clayton Green....E 5
35 Clayton West....F 11
34 Clayton-le-Moors .D 6
34 Clayton-le-Woods .E 4
32 Clayworth........A 4
45 Cleadon.........G 12
5 Clearbrook.......J 4
15 Clearwell.........D 9
40 Cleasby..........D 3
64 Cleat.............E 2
40 Cleatlam..........C 1
38 Cleator...........D 3
38 Cleator Moor.....D 3
35 Cleckheaton.....E 10
21 Clee St. Margaret.D 11
21 Cleedownton....D 11
21 Cleehill..........E 11
21 Cleestanton.......D 11
37 Cleethorpes......F 10
21 Cleeton St. Mary.E 11
17 Cleeve, Berks.....F 7
15 Cleeve, Somerset ..H 8
16 Cleeve Hill.......A 1
22 Cleeve Prior.....G 4
22 Clehonger........A 8
50 Cleigh...........E 6
52 Cleish...........G 6
48 Cleland..........D 1
50 Clenamacrie.......E 6
16 Clench Common..H 3
24 Clenchwarton.....C 7
45 Clennell..........B 7
22 Clent............D 3
21 Cleobury Mortimer E 12
21 Cleobury North..D 11
56 Clephanton.......E 4
47 Clerkland.........E 9
47 Clerklands.......G 7
64 Clestran..........D 1
44 Cleuch Head.......B 4
43 Cleuchbrae......D 11
44 Cleuchfoot.......E 2
43 Cleuchhead.......B 9
43 Cleuchheads.....C 12
43 Cleuchside.......D 12
16 Clevancy.........G 2
15 Clevedon.........G 7
40 Cleveland, Co.....C 5
40 Cleveland Tontine Inn E 5
34 Cleveleys.........C 2
16 Cleverton.........F 1
14 Clevis............G 2
7 Clewer............A 8
26 Cley-next-the-Sea..A 3
63 Cliasamol.........F 2
39 Cliburn...........C 8
9 Cliddesden........A 7
30 Cliff..............A 4
11 Cliff End.........G 7
10 Cliff Woods.......A 6
53 Cliffburn.........C 11
19 Cliffe, Kent.......F 7
36 Cliffe, Yorks......D 4
40 Cliffe, Yorks......D 2
4 Clifford, Devon...D 2
21 Clifford, Herefs. ..H 8
36 Clifford, Yorks....C 2
22 Clifford Chambers G 5
15 Clifford's Mesne .B 10
11 Cliffsend.........B 12
25 Clifton, Beds......L 3
31 Clifton, Derby...F 10
15 Clifton, Glos......G 9
34 Clifton, Lancs.....D 4
48 Clifton, Midloth...B 4
45 Clifton, Northumb. E 10
32 Clifton, Notts.....G 3
MAP
16 Clifton, Oxon.....A 6
51 Clifton, Perth.....D 10
35 Clifton, W. Riding B 10
36 Clifton, W. Riding G 3
39 Clifton, Westmor..C 8
22 Clifton, Worcs....G 2
36 Clifton, Yorks.....B 4
22 Clifton Campville .A 6
16 Clifton Hampden..E 6
23 Clifton Reynes...G 12
23 Clifton upon Dunsmore......D 8
21 Clifton upon Teme F 12
11 Cliftonville......A 12
9 Climping........F 11
48 Climpy...........D 2
7 Clink............A 11
35 Clint............A 11
26 Clint Green.......D 3
49 Clintmains........F 8
26 Clippesby.........D 7
24 Clipsham.........D 1
4 Clipston, Devon...F 5
23 Clipston, N'thants D 10
32 Clipston, Notts...G 4
32 Clipstone.........D 3
34 Clitheroe.........C 6
30 Clive.............H 4
64 Clivocast.........B 8
37 Clixby............G 8
29 Clocaenog.......E 10
58 Clochan..........B 1
13 Clochyrie.........F 8
30 Clock Face.......A 4
49 Clockmill.......D 10
14 Clodock..........B 6
7 Cloford..........B 10
13 Cloigyn...........F 8
58 Clola.............C 7
25 Clophill..........L 2
25 Clopton..........G 2
27 Clopton Green....K 1
38 Close Clark.......H 1
43 Closeburn........B 9
43 Closeburnmill....B 10
6 Closworth........E 9
25 Clothall.........M 4
40 Clotherholme.....H 3
30 Clotton..........D 4
35 Clough..........F 9
35 Clough Foot......E 8
41 Cloughton.......F 10
41 Cloughton Newlands F 10
64 Clousta..........D 6
58 Clova, Aberdeen ..E 2
59 Clova, Angus.....K 1
39 Clove Lodge.....C 11
4 Clovelly..........D 2
49 Clovenfords......F 7
58 Clovenstone......F 5
56 Cloves...........D 7
51 Clovulin..........A 7
35 Clow Bridge.......D 7
32 Clowne...........C 2
21 Clows Top.......E 12
55 Cluanie Inn.......H 4
55 Cluanie Lodge....H 5
21 Cluddley........A 11
63 Cluer............H 2
21 Clun.............D 8
56 Clunas...........E 4
21 Clunbury.........D 9
56 Clune............E 7
55 Clunes...........K 6
21 Clungunford......E 9
58 Clunie, Banff.....C 4
52 Clunie, Perth.....C 6
21 Clunton..........D 9
53 Cluny............H 7
57 Cluny Castle......K 2
30 Clutton, Cheshire .E 3
15 Clutton, Som.....H 9
29 Clwyd, Co........E 10
14 Clydach, Brec.....C 5
13 Clydach, Glam...G 10
14 Clydach Vale......E 3
47 Clydebank.......B 10
12 Clydey...........C 6
16 Clyffe Pypard......F 2
47 Clynder...........A 7
12 Clynderwen.......E 5
13 Clyne............G 11
61 Clynekirkton.......F 8
61 Clynelish..........E 8
28 Clynnog-fawr.....E 4
21 Clyro............H 7
6 Clyst Honiton....G 3
6 Clyst Hydon......F 4
6 Clyst St. George ..G 3
6 Clyst St. Lawrence.F 4
6 Clyst St. Mary....G 3

MAP

28 Clywt-y-bont.....D 5
20 Cnwch Coch.....E 2
58 Coachford.......C 2
3 Coad's Green.....B 10
32 Coal Aston.......B 1
21 Coalbrookdale...B 12
14 Coalbrookvale....C 5
48 Coalburn.........F 1
45 Coalburns........G 9
39 Coalcleugh.....A 10
15 Coaley.........D 11
59 Coalford.........G 6
47 Coalhall.........G 9
19 Coalhill.........D 7
15 Coalpit Heath....F 10
31 Coalpit Hill.....E 7
21 Coalport.......B 12
52 Coalsnaughton....H 4
53 Coaltown of Balgonie
    G 8
53 Coaltown of Wemyss
    H 8
23 Coalville.........A 8
15 Coalway Lane End D 8
7 Coat.............D 8
47 Coatbridge......C 12
47 Coatdyke........C 12
16 Coate, Wilts....H 2
16 Coate, Wilts....F 3
15 Coates, Glos....D 1
24 Coates, Hunts....F 4
9 Coates, Sussex...D 11
40 Coatham.........C 6
40 Coatham Mundeville
    C 3
43 Coatsgate.......A 11
4 Cobbaton........C 5
15 Coberley........C 12
10 Cobham, Kent....A 5
17 Cobham, Surrey .H 11
51 Cobleland......H 12
21 Cobnash.........F 10
58 Coburty.........A 7
57 Cock Bridge.....H 8
19 Cock Clarks.....D 8
21 Cock Gate......F 10
40 Cockayne........E 6
25 Cockayne Hatley..K 4
49 Cockburnspath...B 10
49 Cockenzie and
    Port Seton.....B 7
34 Cockerham.......B 3
38 Cockermouth.....B 4
18 Cockernhoe Green B 1
40 Cockfield, Durham C 2
27 Cockfield, Suffolk .K 2
9 Cocking.........D 10
5 Cockington.......J 8
7 Cocklake.........A 8
45 Cocklaw.........F 7
49 Cocklawfoot.....G 11
49 Cockles.........B 8
26 Cockley Cley.....E 1
58 Cockmuir........D 4
17 Cockpole Green...F 9
30 Cockshutt.......G 3
26 Cockthorpe......A 3
6 Cockwood........H 3
15 Cockyard........A 7
3 Codda.........B 9
27 Coddenham......K 4
30 Coddington, Ches..E 3
21 Coddington, Her. H 12
32 Coddington, Notts.E 5
8 Codford St. Mary .B 1
8 Codford St. Peter .B 1
18 Codicote........B 2
9 Codmore Hill...D 12
32 Codnor..........E 1
15 Codrington......F 10
32 Codsall.........B 2
22 Codsall Wood....B 2
14 Coed Ely.........F 4
15 Coed Morgan.....C 7
28 Coed Ystumgwern H 5
28 Coedana........B 4
14 Coedkernew......F 5
29 Coedpoeth......E 12
21 Coedway........A 9
13 Coed-y-bryn.....C 7
15 Coed-y-fedw.....C 7
14 Coed-yr-ynys....B 5
12 Coelbren........C 2
5 Coffinswell......J 8
6 Cofton.........H 3
22 Cofton Hacket...E 3
14 Cogan...........G 5
23 Cogenhoe.......F 11
19 Coggeshall......B 8
19 Coggeshall Hamlet B 8
57 Coignafearn Lo...H 2
57 Coignafeuinternich H 3
57 Coignascallan.....H 3

59 Coilacriech........H 1
57 Coilintuie.........J 4
51 Coillaig..........E 7
55 Coille Mhorgil....J 5
62 Coillore..........D 3
55 Coiltry...........J 7
57 Coire Bhachdaidh
    Lodge........M 1
14 Coity............F 3
60 Colaboll.........F 6
2 Colan............D 6
6 Colaton Raleigh..G 4
62 Colbost.........C 1
40 Colburn.........E 2
8 Colbury.........E 5
38 Colby, I.o.M......H 1
26 Colby, Norfolk...B 5
39 Colby, Westmor...C 9
19 Colchester......A 10
14 Colcot..........G 4
16 Cold Ash........G 6
23 Cold Ashby......D 10
15 Cold Ashton.....G 10
12 Cold Blow.......F 5
23 Cold Brayfield...G 12
33 Cold Hanworth...B 7
30 Cold Hatton.....H 5
45 Cold Hesleden...H 12
35 Cold Hiendly....F 12
23 Cold Higham.....G 10
40 Cold Kirby......G 5
3 Cold Northcott...A 9
19 Cold Norton.....D 8
23 Cold Overton....A 11
39 Coldbeck.......E 9
60 Coldbackie......B 6
10 Coldean.........G 2
5 Coldeast........H 7
8 Colden Common...D 6
27 Coldfair Green...J 7
24 Coldham........E 5
15 Coldharbour, Glos.D 8
10 Coldharbour, Kent C 4
58 Coldhome........C 3
49 Coldingham....C 11
52 Coldrain.........G 6
11 Coldred........C 11
4 Coldridge.......E 6
49 Coldstream.....E 11
9 Coldwaltham....D 11
58 Coldwells........D 8
58 Coldwells Croft..E 3
7 Cole...........C 10
18 Cole Green......C 3
8 Cole Henley.....A 6
21 Colebatch.......D 8
6 Colebrook.......F 3
4 Colebrooke......F 6
56 Coleburn........D 8
37 Coleby, Lincs....E 7
33 Coleby, Lincs....D 7
4 Coleford, Devon .F 6
15 Coleford, Glos...C 9
7 Coleford, Som...A 10
8 Colehill.........F 2
30 Colemere........G 3
9 Colemore........C 8
32 Coleorton.......H 1
15 Colerne........G 11
16 Colesbourne......C 1
25 Colesden........K 2
16 Coleshill, Berks...E 3
17 Coleshill, Bucks...E 10
52 Coleshill, War....C 5
6 Colestocks......F 4
10 Colgate.........E 1
47 Colgrain........A 8
53 Colinsburgh.....G 9
48 Colinton........C 5
46 Colintraive......B 5
26 Colkirk.........C 2
63 Coll............C 6
53 Collace.........D 7
57 Collafirth........C 7
2 Collamoor Head..B 2
5 Collaton.........L 4
5 Collaton St. Mary.K 7
47 Collenan........F 8
53 Collesie........F 7
5 Colleton Mills...D 5
18 Collier Row.....E 5
10 Collier Street....C 6
18 Collier's End....B 4
58 Collieston.......E 8
43 Collin..........D 11
53 Collingbourne Ducis
    A 4
8 Collingbourne
    Kingston.....A 4
35 Collingham......C 12
21 Collington......F 12
23 Collingtree......G 11

34 Collins Green.....H 4
53 Colliston........C 10
16 Collyin.........F 4
59 Collmuir........G 3
58 Collynie.........D 6
24 Collyweston.....E 1
42 Colmonell.......C 3
25 Colmworth......J 2
16 Coln Rogers.....C 2
16 Coln St. Aldwyn..D 2
16 Coln St. Dennis...C 2
17 Colnabaichin....H 8
17 Colnbrook......F 11
25 Colne, Hunts....H 5
35 Colne, Lancs....C 7
27 Colne Engaine....M 2
26 Colney..........E 5
18 Colney Heath....C 2
18 Colney Street....D 2
45 Colpitts Grange..G 8
58 Colpy...........D 4
48 Colquhar.......E 6
4 Colscott........D 2
32 Colsterdale......G 2
32 Colsterworth....H 6
32 Colston Bassett..G 4
56 Coltfield.........C 7
26 Coltishall.......D 6
38 Colton, Lancs....G 5
26 Colton, Norfolk...D 4
31 Colton, Staffs....H 9
36 Colton, W. Riding C 3
35 Colton, W. Riding D 12
21 Colva...........G 7
22 Colwall Green....H 1
22 Colwall Stone....H 1
45 Colwell.........E 8
31 Colwich.........H 8
14 Colwinston......G 3
38 Colwith.........E 5
9 Colworth........F 10
29 Colwyn Bay......B 8
6 Colyford........G 6
6 Colyton.........G 6
44 Comb...........D 6
16 Combe, Berks....H 5
21 Combe, Herefs...F 9
16 Combe, Oxon....H 5
9 Combe Common..B 10
21 Combe Moor.....F 9
6 Combe Florey....C 5
4 Combe Martin...A 5
6 Combe Raleigh...F 5
6 Combe St.Nicholas E 6
5 Combebow.......G 4
5 Combeinteignhead .J 8
30 Comberbach.....C 5
27 Comberton, Cambs.K 5
21 Comberton, Herefs.
    F 10
6 Combpyne......G 6
31 Combridge.......F 9
22 Combrook........G 6
27 Combs, Derby...B 9
27 Combs, Suffolk...K 3
4 Combwich.......B 6
59 Comers.........G 4
20 Comin Capel Betws G 2
20 Comins-coch.....D 2
20 Comins-coch.....B 4
58 Comisty.........C 3
12 Commercial......E 5
14 Common Coed-y-paen
    D 6
32 Common Side.....C 1
41 Commondale......D 7
3 Common Moor...C 9
31 Commonside......F 11
31 Compstall.......A 8
43 Compstonend....F 7
16 Compton, Berks...F 6
5 Compton, Devon .J 7
8 Compton, Hants...C 6
9 Compton, Surrey .A 11
9 Compton, Sussex .E 9
8 Compton, Wilts...A 3
7 Compton Abbas .D 12
16 Compton Abdale .C 2
16 Compton Bassett..G 1
16 Compton Beauchamp
    E 4
7 Compton Bishop .A 7
7 Compton
    Chamberlayne ..C 2
15 Compton Dando..H 9
7 Compton Dundon.C 8
15 Compton Greenfield
    F 9
7 Compton Martin..A 7
7 Compton Pauncefoot
    D 10
7 Compton Valence .G 9
52 Comrie, Fife.....H 5

52 Comrie, Perth....E 3
51 Conaglen House ..A 7
46 Conchra.........A 5
34 Conder Green....B 3
16 Condicote........A 3
47 Condorrat........B 12
21 Condover........B 10
27 Coney Weston....G 3
9 Coneyhurst Com. D 12
41 Coneysthorpe....H 7
35 Coneythorpe...A 12
58 Confundentand...F 3
3 Congdon's Shop .B 10
43 Congeith........E 9
23 Congerstone......B 7
24 Congham........C 8
31 Congleton........D 7
28 Congl-y-wal......F 6
15 Congresbury......H 7
56 Conicavel.......D 5
33 Coningsby........D 9
25 Conington, Cambs.J 4
25 Conington, Hunts. G 3
36 Conisbrough......G 8
37 Conisholme......H 11
37 Coniston, Yorks...D 9
35 Coniston, Lancs...E 5
35 Coniston Cold....B 7
35 Conistone.......H 12
29 Connah's Quay ..C 12
50 Connel..........D 6
47 Connel Park....H 11
47 Connelbush......H 12
2 Connor Downs...F 3
56 Cononbridge.....D 1
35 Cononley........B 8
53 Cononsyth.......C 10
31 Consall.........E 8
45 Consett.........H 9
40 Constable Burton..F 2
2 Constantine......G 4
2 Constantine Bay..G 3
54 Contin..........D 8
56 Contullich.......C 2
49 Conundrum......D 12
59 Conveth Mains...K 5
56 Convinth........F 1
29 Conwy..........B 7
11 Conyer..........B 8
27 Conyer's Green...H 2
10 Cooden..........G 6
22 Cook Hill........F 4
4 Cookbury........E 3
17 Cookham........F 10
17 Cookham Dean...F 9
17 Cookham Rise...F 9
22 Cookley, Worcs...D 2
27 Cookley, Suffolk ..H 6
17 Cookley Green....E 8
59 Cookney.........H 5
10 Cooksbridge.....G 3
18 Cooksmill Green..C 6
9 Coolham........D 12
10 Cooling, Kent....A 6
19 Cooling, Kent....F 7
10 Cooling Street....A 6
2 Coombe, Cornwall D 6
4 Coombe, Cornwall E 1
6 Coombe, Devon ..D 3
8 Coombe, Wilts...A 3
8 Coombe Bissett...C 3
15 Coombe Down...H 11
15 Coombe Hay....H 10
15 Coombe Hill....B 12
7 Coombe Keynes .H 11
10 Coombes........G 1
12 Coombs.........F 4
56 Cooperhill......D 6
10 Coopers' Corner..C 4
10 Cooper's Green..F 4
18 Coopersale Com...D 5
9 Cootham........E 12
27 Copdock........L 4
19 Copford Green...B 9
64 Copister.........C 7
25 Cople...........K 2
40 Copley..........C 1
36 Copmanthorpe....B 3
2 Coppathorne.....A 2
31 Coppenhall......H 7
2 Copperhouse.....F 3
25 Coppingford.....G 3
7 Coppleridge.....D 11
4 Copplestone.....F 6
34 Coppull.........F 4
34 Coppull Moor....F 4
10 Copsale.........F 1
34 Copster Green....D 5
40 Copt Hewick....H 4
23 Copt Oak........A 8
10 Copthorne......D 2
26 Copy's Green....B 2

8 Copythorne.......E 5
45 Corbridge........G 8
23 Corby..........C 12
33 Corby Glen.......H 7
21 Coreley.........E 11
17 Cores End.......E 10
6 Corfe...........D 6
8 Corfe Castle.....H 1
8 Corfe Mullen....F 1
21 Corfton.........D 10
57 Corgariff.........J 8
9 Corhampton......D 7
10 Cork's Pond......D 5
22 Corley...........D 6
22 Corley Ash......C 6
22 Corley Moor......D 6
48 Cormiston........F 3
51 Cormonachan....H 9
53 Cormuir.........A 8
57 Corndavon Lodge .J 8
40 Cornforth........B 3
58 Cornhill.........B 3
49 Cornhill-on-Tweed E 11
45 Cornhills........E 8
35 Cornholme........D 8
37 Cornish Hall End..L 8
40 Cornsay.........A 2
40 Cornsay Colliery .A 2
14 Corntown, Glam. .G 3
56 Corntown, Ross &
    Cromarty.....D 1
59 Corntulloch......H 2
3 Cornwall, County .C 8
16 Cornwell........A 4
5 Cornwood.......K 5
5 Cornworthy.....K 7
55 Corpach.........M 5
26 Corpusty........C 4
51 Corran, Argyll...A 7
55 Corran, Inver.....J 2
46 Corranbuie......C 3
38 Corrany.........G 2
55 Corribeg........L 4
46 Corrie..........E 5
43 Corrie Common .C 12
46 Corriecravie......G 4
54 Corriefeol.......E 6
55 Corriegour......K 6
54 Corriemoillie.....C 7
60 Corriemulzie Lo...G 4
57 Corrievorrie......G 3
54 Corrievuic.......E 6
55 Corrimony......C 7
19 Corringham, Essex F 7
32 Corringham, Lincs.A 6
20 Corris..........B 3
51 Corrour Shooting
    Lodge......A 11
51 Corrow.........G 9
62 Corry...........F 6
56 Corry of Ardnagrask
    E 1
46 Corrygills......F 5
55 Corryhully......L 3
60 Corrykinloch....E 5
52 Corrymuckloch...D 4
50 Corrynachenchy...C 4
49 Corsbie.........E 8
7 Corscombe.......F 8
58 Corse, Aberdeen .D 3
58 Corse, Aberdeen ..B 7
59 Corse House.....D 3
58 Corse of Kinnoir..C 3
58 Corsehill........B 7
42 Corsemalzie......F 4
15 Corsham.......G 11
59 Corsindae.......G 4
7 Corsley.........B 11
7 Corsley Heath...B 11
47 Corsliehill......C 9
43 Corsock........D 8
15 Corston, Glos....F 12
15 Corston, Som...H 10
48 Corstorphine.....B 5
59 Cortachy Castle...L 1
27 Corton, Suffolk...F 8
8 Corton, Wilts....B 1
7 Corton Denham ..D 9
51 Coruanan Lodge ..A 8
29 Corwen.........F 10
7 Coryates.........H 9
6 Coryton, Devon...G 3
19 Coryton, Essex...F 7
23 Cosby..........C 9
22 Coseley.........C 3
23 Cosgrove.......H 11
9 Cosham.........F 8
12 Cosheston......G 3
32 Cossall.........F 2
10 Cossington......A 9
64 Costa...........B 2

26 Costessey........D 5
32 Costock.........H 3
32 Coston, Leics....H 6
26 Coston, Norfolk...E 4
44 Cote............C 1
30 Cotebrook.......D 4
44 Cotehill.........H 3
31 Cotes, Staffs....G 7
39 Cotes, Westmor...F 7
23 Cotesbach.......D 8
32 Cotgrave........G 3
58 Cothall.........F 6
32 Cotham.........E 5
6 Cothelstone.....C 5
39 Cotherstone.....C 12
16 Cothill, Berks....D 6
49 Cothill, Berwick .D 10
5 Cotleigh........F 5
32 Cotmanhay......F 2
25 Coton, Cambs....J 5
23 Coton, Northants.E 10
31 Coton, Staffs.....H 7
31 Coton, Staffs.....G 8
31 Coton Clanford ..H 7
31 Coton in the Clay G 10
22 Coton in the Elms.A 6
5 Cott............K 6
34 Cottam, Lancs...D 4
32 Cottam, Notts....B 5
56 Cottartown.......F 6
25 Cottenham......H 5
39 Cotterdale......F 10
18 Cottered........A 3
24 Cotterstock......F 1
32 Cottesbrooke....E 10
32 Cottesmore.....A 12
6 Cotteylands......E 3
23 Cottingham,
    Northants.....C 11
37 Cottingham, Yks. .D 8
35 Cottingley......C 9
17 Cottisford........A 7
27 Cotton..........J 4
25 Cotton End......L 2
58 Cot-town, Aber....E 2
58 Cot-town, Aber...D 6
31 Cotwalton.......G 8
58 Cotwells........B 5
3 Couchsmill......D 8
15 Coughton, Herefs..B 9
22 Coughton, War...F 4
46 Coulaghailtro....C 2
54 Coulags.........E 3
54 Couldoran......E 2
54 Coulin Lodge.....D 4
59 Coull...........G 3
47 Coulport........A 7
18 Coulsdon........H 3
5 Coulston.........A 1
48 Coulter.........F 3
40 Coulton.........H 6
21 Cound.........B 11
40 Coundon, Durham B 3
22 Coundon, War...D 6
40 Coundon Grange..B 2
39 Countersett.....F 11
23 Countesthorpe....C 9
8 Countess........B 3
6 Countess Wear...G 3
4 Countisbury......A 6
53 Coupar Angus...C 7
49 Coupland.......F 12
6 Couple Cross....B 3
54 Cour............E 3
43 Courance.......C 11
17 Court Corner....H 7
3 Court Henry.....E 9
55 Courteachan.....K 1
23 Courteenhall....G 11
19 Courtsend.......E 10
4 Courtway........C 5
48 Cousland........C 6
22 Cousleywood.....E 5
58 Couston........B 6
6 Cove, Devon ....D 3
47 Cove, Dunbarton .A 7
8 Cove, Hampshire A 10
54 Cove, Ross & Crom.
    A 2
59 Cove Bay.......G 7
27 Covehithe.......G 8
22 Coven..........A 3
25 Coveney........G 6
37 Covenham St.
    Bartholomew..H 11
37 Covenham St. Mary
    H 11
23 Coventry........D 7
2 Coverack.......H 5
40 Coverham......F 1
15 Covington......C 7
22 Cow Honeybourne H 5
39 Cowan Bridge...G 8

MAP
10 Cowbeech.......G 5
24 Cowbit.........D 4
14 Cowbridge, Glam..G 3
6 Cowbridge, Som...B 3
10 Cowden, Kent....D 3
45 Cowden, Northumb.
　　　　　　　　　　E 7
52 Cowdenbeath....H 6
48 Cowdenburn.....D 5
8 Cowes.........F 6
40 Cowesby........F 5
10 Cowfold........F 1
59 Cowie, Kinc...J 6
52 Cowie, Stirling..H 3
45 Cowpen........E 11
40 Cowpen Bewley...C 5
31 Cowers Lane.....E 11
6 Cowley, Devon...G 3
15 Cowley, Glos....C 12
18 Cowley, London...F 1
16 Cowley, Oxon....D 6
40 Cowling, N. Riding F 3
35 Cowling, W. Riding
　　　　　　　　　　C 8
25 Cowlinge.......K 8
9 Cowplain.......E 8
39 Cowshill......A 10
52 Cowstrandburn..H 5
36 Cowthorpe.....B 2
17 Cox Green......F 9
30 Coxbank.......F 5
31 Coxbench.....F 12
10 Coxheath......C 6
11 Coxhill.......C 11
40 Coxhoe.......B 3
7 Coxley.......B 8
18 Coxtie Green....D 5
40 Coxwold.......G 5
14 Coychurch......F 3
47 Coylton.......G 9
57 Coylumbridge...H 5
59 Coynach.......G 2
58 Coynachie.....D 2
14 Coytrahen......F 2
54 Cozae Lodge....F 6
22 Crabbs Cross....F 4
10 Crabtree.......F 1
61 Crackaig......F 9
39 Crackenthorpe...C 9
2 Crackington.....B 2
2 Crackington Haven B 2
22 Crackley.......E 6
22 Crackley bank....A 1
39 Crackpot......E 12
35 Cracoe........A 8
6 Craddock......E 4
22 Cradley.......G 1
22 Cradley Heath...D 3
14 Cradoc........A 3
3 Crafthole.....D 10
45 Cragend.......C 9
35 Cragg........E 8
51 Craggan, Dunb. .H 10
57 Craggan, Moray..G 6
60 Craggan, Ross &
　　Cromarty......G 4
56 Craggiemore....F 3
45 Craghead......H 10
58 Craibstone, Aber. .F 6
58 Craibstone, Banff..B 2
53 Craichie......B 10
42 Craig, Ayr.....A 5
43 Craig, Kirk.....D 7
43 Craig, Kirk.....E 8
54 Craig, Ross & Crom.
　　　　　　　　　　E 4
46 Craig Lodge....B 5
14 Craig Penllyn....F 3
13 Craig Trebanos ..G 10
52 Craiganour Lodge..A 1
55 Craigard.......J 7
55 Craigbeg......L 8
42 Craigcaffie.....E 2
13 Craig-cefn-parc ..G 10
58 Craigdam......E 6
43 Craigdarroch,Dumf C8
43 Craigdarroch, Ayr .A 7
42 Craigdews......D 6
54 Craigdhu......F 8
58 Craigearn......F 5
56 Craigellachie....E 8
42 Craigencallie....D 6
42 Craigencross....E 1
48 Craigend, Lanark .F 1
52 Craigend, Perth...E 6
47 Craigendoran....A 8
42 Craigengillan....A 5
42 Craigenrae.....C 4
47 Craigens.......G 10
59 Craiggiecat......H 6
56 Craighead, Banff .F 8
43 Craighead, Lanark G 2
58 Craigie, Aberdeen .F 6

47 Craigie, Ayr......F 9
52 Craigie, Perth...C 6
43 Craigieburn.....A 11
48 Craiglockhart....B 5
42 Craimalloch.....B 5
58 Craigmaud......B 6
46 Craigmore......C 6
59 Craigmoston....K 4
30 Craignant......G 1
42 Craigneil......C 2
43 Craigneston....C 8
47 Craigneuk.....D 12
50 Craignure......D 4
59 Craigo.........L 4
52 Craigow........F 6
53 Craigrothie.....F 8
53 Craigs.........G 7
59 Craigton, Aber...G 6
53 Craigton, Angus .C 10
53 Craigton, Angus...B 8
47 Craigton, Lanark D 10
54 Craigton, Ross &
　　Cromarty......F 3
56 Craigton, Ross &
　　Cromarty......E 2
61 Craigtown......B 9
13 Craig-y-Duke...G 10
14 Craig-y-nos....C 2
44 Craik.........B 2
53 Crail.........F 11
49 Crailing.......G 9
49 Crailinghall....G 9
36 Craiselound....G 5
48 Cramalt.......G 5
36 Crambe........A 5
45 Cramlington....E 11
48 Cramond.......B 5
48 Cramond Bridge ..B 4
55 Cranachan......L 7
30 Cranage.......C 6
31 Cranberry......G 7
58 Cranbog.......F 7
8 Cranborne......E 2
17 Cranbourne....G 10
10 Cranbrook......D 6
10 Cranbrook Com...D 6
35 Crane Moor....G 11
25 Cranfield......L 1
18 Cranford......F 1
23 Cranford St. Andrew
23 Cranford St. John D 12
15 Cranham, Glos...C 12
18 Cranham, London.E 6
34 Crank........G 4
9 Cranleigh......B 12
8 Cranmore......G 5
58 Cranna.......B 4
58 Crannach......B 2
50 Crannich......C 2
23 Cranoe.......C 11
27 Cransford......J 6
49 Cranshaws.....C 9
38 Cranstal......F 2
37 Cranswick.....B 8
2 Crantock......D 5
33 Cranwell......E 7
26 Cranwich......F 1
26 Cranworth.....E 3
42 Cranyard.......H 2
5 Crapstone.....J 4
51 Crarae........H 7
60 Crask Inn......E 6
54 Crask of Aigas...E 8
54 Craskie.......F 7
59 Craskins......G 3
45 Craster.......A 10
27 Cratfield......H 6
59 Crathes.......H 5
57 Crathie.......K 1
40 Crathorne.....D 5
21 Craven Arms....D 10
45 Crawcrook.....G 9
48 Crawford......G 2
48 Crawfordjohn...G 2
43 Crawfordton....B 9
47 Crawick......H 12
8 Crawley, Hants...C 6
16 Crawley, Oxon...C 4
10 Crawley, Sussex...D 1
10 Crawley Down...D 2
39 Crawley Side....A 12
35 Crawshaw Booth..B 4
59 Crawton.......J 6
14 Cray, Brec.....B 2
39 Cray, Yorks.....G 11
18 Crayford......F 5
40 Crayke.......H 6
19 Crays Hill......E 7
17 Cray's Pond....F 7
17 Crazies Hill....F 9
50 Creach Bheinn Lodge
　　　　　　　　　　E 4

4 Creacombe......D 7
51 Creag a' Phuill...G 8
51 Creagan.......C 7
46 Creagan Beag....A 3
51 Creaguaineach Lodge
　　　　　　　　　　A 10
23 Creaton.......E 10
44 Creca.........F 1
21 Credenhill......H 10
4 Crediton.......F 7
42 Creebank......D 4
42 Creebridge.....E 5
6 Creech Heathfield .D 6
6 Creech St. Michael D 6
2 Creed.........E 6
18 Creekmouth.....F 5
42 Creeside.......C 4
27 Creeting St. Mary..J 4
24 Creeton.......D 1
42 Creetown......F 6
21 Cregerina......G 7
51 Creggans......G 8
38 Cregneish......H 1
38 Creg-ny-Baa....G 2
53 Creich........E 8
14 Creigiau.......F 4
54 Crelevan......F 7
3 Cremyll........D 11
21 Cressage......B 11
12 Cresselly.......F 4
17 Cressex........E 9
19 Cressing.......B 8
45 Cresswell, Northumb.
　　　　　　　　　　D 11
12 Cresswell, Pemb...F 4
31 Cresswell, Staffs...E 8
32 Creswell.......C 2
27 Cretingham.....J 5
46 Cretshengan....C 2
21 Crew Green.....A 8
30 Crewe, Cheshire..E 3
30 Crewe, Cheshire..E 6
7 Crewkerne.....E 7
51 Crianlarich.....E 11
13 Cribyn........B 8
28 Criccieth.......F 4
31 Crich, Derby....E 12
15 Crick, Mon.....E 8
23 Crick, Northants...E 9
20 Crickadarn.....H 6
7 Cricket Malherbie .E 7
7 Cricket St. Thomas E 7
30 Crickheath.....H 2
14 Crickhowell.....B 5
16 Cricklade......E 2
36 Cridling Stubbs ..E 3
52 Crieff.........E 3
21 Criggian......A 8
35 Crigglestone....E 11
58 Crimond.......B 8
58 Crimonmogate...B 8
24 Crimplesham....E 7
54 Crinaglack......F 8
50 Crinan........H 5
26 Cringleford.....E 5
12 Crinow.........F 5
8 Cripplestyle.....E 3
10 Cripp's Corner...F 6
38 Croasdale......C 3
7 Crock Street.....E 7
10 Crockenhill.....A 4
5 Crockernwell....G 6
7 Crockerton.....B 11
36 Crockey Hill....B 4
10 Crockham Hill...C 3
10 Crockhurst Street .D 5
19 Crockleford Hth..A 10
21 Crockmeole.....A 9
14 Croes-Hywel....C 6
14 Croeserw......E 2
12 Croes-goch....D 2
13 Croes-lan......C 7
28 Croesor.......F 6
14 Croes-y-ceiliog...E 6
13 Croesyceiliog....V 7
14 Croes-y-mwyalch..E 6
12 Croft, Cards....C 5
34 Croft, Lancs.....H 5
23 Croft, Leics.....C 8
33 Croft, Lincs....D 12
40 Croft, Yorks.....D 3
47 Croftamie.....A 9
47 Crofthead......E 12
52 Croftmill......C 3
57 Croftmore.....H 5
57 Croftnahaven....H 5
16 Crofton, Wilts...H 5
35 Crofton, Yorkshire
　　　　　　　　　　E 12
43 Crofts.........D 8
58 Crofts of Belnagoak C 6

58 Crofts of Haddo ..D 6
58 Crofts of Hillbrae .C 3
58 Crofts of Meikle Ardo
　　　　　　　　　　D 6
58 Crofts of Savoch..B 8
58 Crofts of Shanquhar
　　　　　　　　　　D 3
13 Crofty.........G 8
54 Croggan.......E 4
44 Croglin........H 4
43 Crogo.........D 8
60 Croick........C 2
63 Croir.........C 2
56 Cromarty......C 3
54 Cromasag......D 4
58 Cromblet.......D 5
57 Cromdale......G 6
21 Cromer, Herts...A 3
26 Cromer, Norfolk...A 5
31 Cromford......E 11
15 Cromhall......E 10
15 Cromhall Com...E 10
63 Cromore.......E 5
57 Cromra........K 1
32 Cromwell......D 5
47 Cronan........E 10
47 Cronberry......G 11
9 Crondall......A 9
38 Cronk-y-Voddy...G 2
30 Cronton.......A 4
40 Crook, Durham...B 2
39 Crook, Westmor...F 7
56 Crook of Alves...D 7
52 Crook of Devon...G 5
34 Crooke........F 4
47 Crookedholm....F 9
48 Crookedstane....H 2
32 Crookes.......B 1
16 Crookham, Berks..H 6
49 Crookham, Northumb.
　　　　　　　　　　F 11
9 Crookham Village..A 9
49 Crookham Westfield
　　　　　　　　　　F 11
10 Crouch........C 5
7 Crouch Hill....E 10
8 Croucheston....D 2
16 Croughton.....A 6
58 Crovie........A 5
8 Crow.........F 3
35 Crow Edge.....G 10
15 Crow Hill......B 9
3 Crowan........F 4
10 Crowborough....E 4
10 Crowborough Town
　　　　　　　　　　E 4
6 Crowcombe....C 5
35 Crowden.......G 10
17 Crowell.......D 8
23 Crowfield, Northants.
　　　　　　　　　　H 9
27 Crowfield, Suffolk .J 5
10 Crowhurst, Surrey.C 3
10 Crowhurst, Sussex.G 6
10 Crowhurst Lane End
　　　　　　　　　　C 3
24 Crowland......D 3
2 Crowlas.......F 2
36 Crowle, Lincs....F 5
22 Crowle, Worcs...G 3
63 Crowlista......D 1
17 Crowmarsh Gifford
　　　　　　　　　　E 7
2 Crown Town....G 3
5 Crownhill......K 4
26 Crownthorpe....E 4
42 Crows........F 4
2 Crows-an-wra...G 1
10 Crowthorne....H 9
30 Crowton......C 4
22 Croxall.......A 5
37 Croxby.......G 9
40 Croxdale......B 3
31 Croxden......F 9
12 Croxley Green...E 11
25 Croxton, Hunts....J 3
37 Croxton, Lincs...F 8
27 Croxton, Norfolk .G 2
31 Croxton, Staffs...G 6
32 Croxton Kerrial...G 5
47 Croy, Dunb.....B 12
56 Croy, Inver.....E 4
4 Croyde.......B 3
4 Croyde Bay.....B 3
25 Croydon, Cambs..K 4
18 Croydon, London .G 3
58 Crubenmore Lo...K 2
58 Cruden Bay.....D 8
16 Crudwell.......E 1
21 Crug.........E 1
8 Crugmeer......B 6
13 Crugybar......C 10
54 Cruive........F 8
63 Cruivig........D 3

14 Crumlin........D 5
3 Crumplehorn....E 9
11 Crundale, Kent ..C 9
12 Crundale, Pemb...E 3
44 Crurie........D 1
6 Cruwys Morchard .E 2
16 Crux Easton....H 5
13 Crwbin........F 8
17 Cryers Hill.....D 9
12 Crymmych......D 5
13 Crynant.......F 11
54 Cuaig........D 1
23 Cubbington....E 7
2 Cubert.......D 5
17 Cublington.....B 9
10 Cuckfield......F 2
7 Cucklington....D 10
32 Cuckney.......C 3
17 Cuddesdon.....D 7
17 Cuddington, Bucks.
　　　　　　　　　　C 8
30 Cuddington, Ches. C 4
30 Cuddington Heath.F 3
34 Cuddy Hill.....C 4
18 Cudham......H 4
5 Cudlipptown....H 4
7 Cudworth, Som...E 7
36 Cudworth, Yorks..F 2
12 Cuffern.......E 2
18 Cuffley.......D 3
10 Cuiashader.....A 6
54 Culaneilan......D 4
56 Culbo.........D 2
56 Culbokie......D 2
64 Cross-voe-sand...C 6
56 Culburnie......E 1
56 Culcabock......E 2
56 Culcairn.......C 2
56 Culcharry......E 4
34 Culcheth.......H 5
56 Culcraggie.....C 2
52 Culdees.......F 4
58 Culdrain......D 3
54 Culduie.......F 1
27 Culford.......H 1
39 Culgaith......B 8
16 Culham.......E 6
46 Culinlongart....H 2
60 Culkein.......D 2
60 Culkein Drumbeg .D 3
15 Culkerton.....E 12
57 Cullachie......G 5
56 Cullen.......A 3
45 Cullercoats....F 12
59 Cullerlie......G 5
56 Cullicudden....C 2
54 Culligran......F 7
35 Cullingworth...D 9
50 Cullipool......F 5
64 Cullivoe......B 8
52 Culloch.......E 3
56 Culloden House..E 3
6 Cullompton....E 4
6 Culm Davy.....E 5
61 Culmaily......G 8
42 Culmalzie.....D 10
21 Culmington....D 10
6 Culmstock.....E 4
60 Culnacraig.....F 2
54 Culnaightrie....F 8
62 Culnaknock....B 4
42 Culquhirk......F 5
60 Culrain.......G 6
48 Culross......A 3
47 Culroy.......H 8
47 Culscadden....G 5
59 Culsh........H 1
42 Culshabbin.....F 4
56 Culswick......D 6
58 Cultercullen....E 7
58 Cults, Aberdeen..D 3
59 Cults, Aberdeen..G 6
42 Cults, Wigtown..G 5
52 Cultybraggan....E 3
10 Culverstone Green.B 5
33 Culverthorpe....F 7
23 Culworth......G 9
56 Culzie Lodge....C 1
47 Cumberhead....F 12
49 Cumberland Bower
　　　　　　　　　　D 12
47 Cumbernauld....B 12
33 Cumberworth...C 12
58 Cumbria, Co....C 6
58 Cuminestown....C 5
49 Cumledge.....D 10
44 Cummersdale...H 2
43 Cummertrees...E 12
56 Cummingstown...C 7
47 Cumnock......G 10
16 Cumnor.......D 5
44 Cumrew.......H 4
43 Cumrue.......C 11

MAP

43 Cumstone.......C 12
44 Cumwhinton....H 3
44 Cumwhitton....H 3
40 Cundall.........H 4
47 Cunninghamhead..E 8
64 Cunnister......B 7
53 Cupar..........F 8
53 Cupar Muir.....F 8
8 Cupernnam......D 5
31 Curbar.........C 11
16 Curbridge, Oxon..C 4
9 Curdbridge, Hants.E 7
22 Curdworth......C 5
54 Curian.........D 7
6 Curland........E 6
42 Currarie.......B 2
16 Curridge.......G 6
48 Currie.........C 4
7 Curry Mallet...D 7
7 Curry Rivel....D 7
10 Curtisden Green..D 6
2 Cury...........G 4
58 Cushnie........B 5
6 Cushuish.......C 5
21 Cusop..........H 8
64 Cusvie.........B 3
42 Cutcloy........H 5
6 Cutcombe.......B 3
48 Cuthill, Midloth..B 6
61 Cuthill, Suther...H 8
22 Cutnall Green...E 2
16 Cutsdean.......A 2
31 Cutthorpe......C 11
17 Cuxham.........E 7
10 Cuxton.........A 6
37 Cuxwold........G 9
29 Cwm, Flint....C 10
14 Cwm, Mon.....D 5
20 Cwm-Cewydd....A 4
12 Cwm Cych......C 6
13 Cwm-Duad......D 7
14 Cwm Ffrwd Oer..D 6
20 Cwm Irfon.....G 4
13 Cwm-Mawr.....F 8
12 Cwm-Morgan...D 6
29 Cwm-Penmachno..E 7
14 Cwmaman.......D 3
13 Cwmann.........B 9
13 Cwmavon.......H 11
12 Cwm-bach, Carm.D 6
14 Cwm-bach, Glam..D 4
20 Cwm-bach, Rad..G 6
21 Cwm-bach, Rad...H 7
20 Cwmbelan......D 5
14 Cwmbran.......E 6
20 Cwmbrwyno....D 3
14 Cwmcarn.......E 5
15 Cwmcarvan.....D 8
12 Cwmcoy........C 6
14 Cwmdare.......D 3
14 Cwm-du, Brec...B 5
13 Cwm-du, Carm...D 9
14 Cwmfelin, Glam...D 4
14 Cwmfelin, Glam...E 2
12 Cwmfelin Boeth..E 5
14 Cwmfelin-fach....E 5
12 Cwmfelin-Mynach.E 6
13 Cwm-ffrwd......D 6
13 Cwmgiedd.......C 1
13 Cwmgors.......F 10
13 Cwmgwili......F 9
13 Cwmifor......D 10
13 Cwmisfael.......E 8
20 Cwmlline.......B 4
13 Cwmllyfri......F 7
13 Cwmllynfell...F 10
12 Cwmmiles......E 5
13 Cwm-parc......E 3
13 Cwm-pengraig...C 7
14 Cwm-rhos......B 5
13 Cwmsychpant....B 8
14 Cwmtillery.....D 5
14 Cwmysg........A 2
14 Cwm-y-glo.....F 9
14 Cwmyoy........B 6
20 Cwmystwyth....E 3
20 Cwrt..........B 2
13 Cwrt-newydd...B 8
13 Cwrt-y-Cadno..C 10
13 Cwrt-y-defaid..F 1
14 Cwrt-y-gollen...C 6
29 Cwym-y-glo...D 9
29 Cyffilliog....D 10
14 Cymmer, Glam...E 3
14 Cymmer, Glam...E 2
14 Cyncoed........F 5
13 Cynghordy, Glam.G 10
13 Cynghordy, Carm.C 11
13 Cyneidre.......F 8
14 Cynonville.....E 2
29 Cynwyd.......F 10
13 Cynwyl Elfed...D 7
35 Dacre Banks....A 10

MAP

23 Dadford.......H 10
23 Dadlington......B 7
13 Dafen.........G 8
18 Dagenham......F 5
16 Daglingworth...D 1
17 Dagnall........C 10
51 Dail...........D 8
42 Dailly.........B 3
57 Dail-na-mine Lo..M 3
53 Dairsie or Osnaburgh
              E 9
34 Daisy Hill......G 5
51 Dalavich.......F 7
43 Dalbeattie.....E 9
63 Dalbeg.........B 3
47 Dalblair.......G 11
59 Dalbog.........K 3
38 Dalby..........H 1
61 Dalchalm.......F 9
51 Dalchenna......G 8
52 Dalchonzie Ho...E 2
60 Dalchork.......F 6
55 Dalchreichart...H 7
52 Dalchruin......E 2
54 Dalchuirn......F 3
56 Dalcross Station...E 3
33 Dalderby........D 9
32 Dale, Derby....F 2
12 Dale, Pembroke..F 2
64 Dale, Shetland Is..D 6
39 Dale Head......D 7
41 Dalehouse......C 8
50 Dalelia........A 5
57 Dalestie.......H 7
43 Dalfibble......C 11
47 Dalfram.......G 11
47 Dalgarven......E 8
47 Dalgig.........H 10
52 Dalginross.....E 3
52 Dalguise.......B 5
61 Dalhalvaig.....B 9
25 Dalham.........J 8
46 Dalinlongart...A 6
48 Dalkeith.......C 6
52 Dall...........B 1
56 Dallas.........D 7
47 Dalleagles.....H 10
27 Dallinghoo.....K 5
10 Dallington, Sussex.F 5
23 Dallington, Northants.
              F 10
39 Dalmain Dacre...C 7
43 Dalmakerran....B 8
51 Dalmally.......E 9
42 Dalmellington...A 6
48 Dalmeny........B 4
48 Dalmeny Rows...B 4
60 Dalmichy.......F 6
57 Dalmigavie.....H 3
57 Dalmigavie Lodge.G 3
63 Dalmore, Lewis...B 3
56 Dalmore, Ross &
       Cromarty......C 2
56 Dalmore, Ross &
       Cromarty......B 1
47 Dalmuir........B 10
56 Dalmunach......E 8
50 Dalnabreck.....A 4
57 Dalnacardoch Lo. M 3
52 Dalnacarn......A 5
57 Dalnahaitnach...H 4
61 Dalnamain......G 7
57 Dalnaspidal....M 2
61 Dalnawillan Lo. .C 10
51 Dalness........B 9
61 Dalnessie......E 7
52 Daloist........A 3
52 Dalqueich......G 6
42 Dalquhairn.....B 4
61 Dalreavoch.....F 7
52 Dalriach.......A 2
47 Dalry, Ayr.....D 8
43 Dalry, Kirk....C 7
47 Dalrymple......H 8
48 Dalserf........D 1
44 Dalston........H 2
43 Dalswinton.....C 10
52 Dalton, Dumf...D 12
45 Dalton, Northumb.F 9
45 Dalton, Northumb.G 7
40 Dalton, N. Riding G 4
40 Dalton, N. Riding D 1
32 Dalton, W. Riding A 2
40 Dalton Piercy...B 5
38 Dalton-in-Furness.H 5
45 Dalton-le-Dale...H 12
40 Dalton-on-Tees...D 3
46 Daltot.........A 3
42 Dalvadie.......F 2
52 Dalveich.......E 1
47 Dalvennan......H 9
61 Dalvina Lodge...C 7

MAP

57 Dalwhat........B 8
57 Dalwhinnie.....L 2
6 Dalwood.......F 6
8 Damerham......D 3
26 Damgate.......E 7
42 Damnaglaur....H 2
18 Damside........D 4
11 Danaway Borden..B 7
19 Danbury........C 8
41 Danby.........D 7
40 Danby Wiske....E 3
56 Dandaleith.....E 8
48 Danderhall.....B 6
18 Dane End.......B 3
23 Dane Hills.....B 9
31 Danebridge.....D 8
10 Danehill.......E 3
34 Dangerous Corner.F 4
40 Dan's Corner...A 1
49 Danskine......C 8
22 Danzey Green...E 5
14 Daren-felen....C 5
10 Darenth.......A 4
30 Daresbury......B 4
36 Darfield.......G 2
11 Dargate........B 9
45 Dargues........D 7
3 Darite.........C 9
22 Darlaston......C 3
35 Darley.......A 10
31 Darley Bridge...D 11
22 Darlingscott...H 6
40 Darlington.....D 3
30 Darliston......G 4
32 Darlton........C 5
32 Darnall........A 1
56 Darnaway Castle..D 5
47 Darnconner....G 10
43 Darngarroch...E 7
49 Darnick........F 8
20 Darowen.......B 4
58 Darra..........C 5
4 Darracott, Corn..D 1
4 Darracott, Devon.B 3
45 Darras Hall....F 9
36 Darrington.....B 3
23 Darsham........H 7
10 Dartford.......A 4
5 Dartington.....J 6
5 Dartmeet.......H 5
5 Dartmouth......K 7
57 Darton.........F 11
47 Darvel.........F 10
34 Darwen.........E 6
17 Datchet........F 10
18 Datchworth.....B 3
18 Datchworth Green B 3
34 Daubhill.......F 6
16 Dauntsey.......F 1
16 Dauntsey Green...F 1
16 Dauntsey Lock...F 1
30 Davenham.......C 5
23 Daventry.......F 9
20 David's Well...E 6
48 Davidson's Mains B 5
56 Davidston......C 3
3 Davidstow......A 8
44 Davington......C 1
58 Daviot, Aberdeen .E 5
56 Daviot, Inverness.F 3
17 Davis Street...G 9
58 Davoch of Grange .C 2
35 Daw Cross.....B 11
30 Dawesgreen.....C 1
21 Dawley........B 12
21 Dawley Bank...B 12
21 Dawley Magna...B 12
5 Dawlish.......H 8
7 Dawlish Wake...E 7
5 Dawlish Warren..H 3
29 Dawn...........C 8
19 Daws Heath....D 5
3 Daw's House...A 10
24 Dawsmere.......C 5
16 Dawthwaitehead..C 6
16 Daylesford.....B 3
44 Deadwater......C 4
45 Deadwaters.....E 12
11 Deal..........C 12
38 Dean, Cumb....C 3
4 Dean, Devon...B 4
4 Dean, Devon...B 5
5 Dean, Devon...J 6
8 Dean, Dorset...D 1
9 Dean, Hants....D 7
7 Dean, Somerset..B 10
5 Dean Prior.....J 6
31 Dean Row......B 7
10 Dean Street....C 6
44 Deanburnhaugh...B 2
5 Deane..........A 7
60 Deanich Lodge ..H 5
8 Deanland......D 2

MAP

38 Deanscales.....C 3
23 Deanshanger Hill H 11
52 Deanston......G 2
38 Dearham.......B 3
27 Debach........K 5
25 Debden, Essex..M 7
18 Debden Estate...D 4
25 Debden Green...M 7
27 Debenham......J 5
48 Dechmont......B 3
16 Deddington.....A 6
27 Dedham........M 4
59 Deebank.......H 4
59 Deecastle.....H 2
23 Deene.........C 12
24 Deenethorpe...F 1
17 Deepcut......H 10
24 Deeping Gate...E 3
24 Deeping St. James.E 3
24 Deeping St. Nicholas
             D 3
58 Deerhill......B 2
15 Deerhurst.....A 11
64 Deerness......D 3
23 Deighton, N. Riding
             E 4
35 Deighton, W. Riding
             E 10
36 Deighton......C 4
28 Deiniolen.....D 5
3 Delabole......A 8
30 Delamere......C 4
42 Delamford.....B 4
56 Delchirach....F 7
58 Delfrigs......E 7
57 Dell Lodge....H 6
56 Dellifure.....F 6
57 Delnabo.......H 7
57 Delnadamph Lo..J 8
48 Deloraineshiel..H 6
35 Delph.........F 8
43 Delves........H 9
24 Dembleby......B 1
36 Denaby........G 3
36 Denaby Main...G 3
43 Denbie Mains...D 11
29 Denbigh.......D 10
5 Denbury.......J 7
32 Denby.........F 1
35 Denby Dale....F 11
16 Denchworth....E 5
58 Denend........D 3
25 Denford.......H 1
19 Dengie........D 9
17 Denham, Bucks..E 11
27 Denham, Suffolk..H 5
27 Denham, Suffolk..J 1
58 Denhead, Aber..B 7
58 Denhead, Aber..E 7
53 Denhead, Fife...F 9
49 Denholm.......G 8
35 Denholme......D 9
9 Denmead.......E 8
27 Dennington....H 6
48 Denny.........A 1
10 Denny Bottom...D 4
8 Denny Lodge....E 5
48 Dennyloanhead...A 1
35 Denshaw.......F 8
59 Denside.......H 5
27 Denston.......K 1
31 Denstone......F 9
39 Dent..........F 9
39 Dent Station...F 10
25 Denton, Hunts..G 2
11 Denton, Kent..C 11
35 Denton, Lancs..H 8
32 Denton, Lincs..G 6
27 Denton, Norfolk..G 6
23 Denton, Northants.
             F 11
17 Denton, Oxon..D 7
10 Denton, Sussex..H 3
40 Denton, N. Riding C 2
35 Denton, W. Riding B 10
24 Denver........E 7
45 Denwick.......B 8
45 Denwick Lane End
             A 10
26 Deopham.......E 3
26 Deopham Green...F 3
4 Deptford, Devon..D 5
4 Deptford, Devon..B 1
18 Deptford, London.F 4
8 Deptford, Wilts..B 2
31 Derby.........G 11
38 Derbyhaven....H 1
32 Derbyshire, Co..D 11
52 Derculich.....B 4

MAP

42 Dergoals......F 3
14 Deri..........D 5
20 Deri-Odwyn....F 2
52 Derry.........F 1
15 Derry Hill.....G 12
50 Derryguaig....D 2
11 Derringstone...C 10
31 Derrington....H 7
36 Derrythorpe....F 6
24 Dersingham.....C 8
50 Dervaig........B 2
29 Derwen.......E 10
13 Derwlwyn......C 9
23 Desborough....D 11
23 Desford.......B 8
45 Detchant......B 12
11 Detling.......B 7
29 Deuddwr......H 11
15 Devauden......D 8
59 Devenick......G 7
20 Devil's Bridge...E 3
16 Devizes.......H 1
4 Devon, County..F 5
48 Devonburn.....E 1
3 Devonport.....D 11
52 Devonside.....G 4
2 Devoran.......F 5
48 Dewar.........D 6
7 Dewlish.......F 11
15 Dewsall Court...A 8
35 Dewsbury.....E 11
38 Dhoon.........G 2
38 Dhoor.........F 2
38 Dhowin........F 2
9 Dial Post.....D 12
8 Dibden.........E 5
8 Dibden Purlieu...E 5
27 Dickleburgh...G 4
16 Didbrook......A 2
16 Didcot........E 6
25 Diddington....J 3
21 Diddlebury....D 10
15 Didley........A 7
9 Didling.......D 10
15 Didmarton.....F 11
5 Didworthy.....J 5
60 Diebidale Lodge ..H 5
33 Digby.........E 8
62 Digg..........A 4
35 Diggle........F 9
34 Digmoor......G 4
18 Digswell Water...B 3
13 Dihewid.......A 8
47 Dikeneuk......D 11
26 Dilham........C 6
31 Dilhorne......F 8
48 Dillarburn....E 1
25 Dillington....J 2
45 Dilston.......G 8
7 Dilton Marsh...A 11
21 Dilwyn........G 9
48 Dinanrig......H 1
28 Dinas, Caer...G 3
12 Dinas, Carm...D 6
12 Dinas, Pemb....C 4
20 Dinas Mawddwy..A 4
14 Dinas Powis...G 5
13 Dinasbach.....C 11
7 Dinder........B 9
15 Dinedor.......A 8
15 Dinedor Cross..A 8
15 Dingestow.....C 7
30 Dingle........B 2
49 Dingleton.....F 8
23 Dingley.......C 11
56 Dingwall......D 1
44 Dinlabyre.....D 4
44 Dinley........C 3
59 Dinnet........H 2
43 Dinning.......C 9
45 Dinnington,
    Northumb......F 10
7 Dinnington, Som. .E 7
28 Dinorwic......D 5
40 Dinsdale Station..D 4
17 Dinton, Bucks..C 8
8 Dinton, Wilts..C 2
42 Dinvin........F 1
43 Dinwoodie Mains C 11
43 Dinwoodiegreen .C 11
4 Dinworthy.....D 2
46 Dippen........F 3
9 Dippenhall....A 9
46 Dippin........G 5
42 Dipple, Ayr....A 3
58 Dipple, Moray...B 1
5 Diptford......K 6
45 Dipton........H 9
49 Dirleton......A 8
21 Discoed.......F 8
32 Diseworth.....H 2
40 Dishforth.....H 4

MAP

31 Disley........B 8
27 Diss..........G 4
20 Disserth......G 6
38 Distington....C 2
8 Ditchampton...C 2
7 Ditcheat......C 9
26 Ditchingham...F 6
10 Ditchling.....F 2
15 Ditteridge....G 11
5 Dittisham.....K 7
10 Ditton, Kent...B 6
30 Ditton, Lancs...B 3
25 Ditton Green...J 8
21 Ditton Priors...D 11
57 Divach........G 1
13 Divlyn........C 11
16 Dixton, Glos...A 1
15 Dixton, Mon...C 8
35 Dobcross......F 8
3 Dobwalls......C 9
5 Doccombe.....G 6
56 Dochfour House ..F 2
56 Dochgarroch...F 2
26 Docking.......B 1
21 Docklow......G 11
38 Dockray.......C 6
44 Dodburn.......B 3
18 Doddinghurst..D 6
24 Doddington, Cambs.
             F 5
11 Doddington, Kent.B 8
32 Doddington,
    Lincolnshire....C 6
49 Doddington,
    Northumb.....F 12
21 Doddington, Salop.
             E 11
6 Doddiscombsleigh.H 2
23 Dodford, Northants.
             F 9
22 Dodford, Worcs...E 3
15 Dodington, Glos..F 10
6 Dodington, Som..B 5
30 Dodleston.....D 2
35 Dodworth......G 11
32 Doe Lea.......D 2
6 Dog Village...G 3
33 Dogdyke.......E 9
9 Dogmersfield...A 9
20 Dolanog.......A 6
14 Dolau, Glam.....F 3
21 Dolau, Rad.....F 7
28 Dolbenmaen...F 4
20 Dolfach.......E 5
20 Dol-ffanog....A 3
20 Dol-for, Mont..B 4
20 Dol-for, Mont..D 6
29 Dolgarrog.....C 7
28 Dolgellau.....H 6
13 Dolgerdd......B 7
20 Dol-goch......B 2
13 Dol-gran......D 8
20 Dolhelfa......E 5
61 Doll..........F 8
52 Dollar........G 4
52 Dollarbeg.....G 4
21 Dolley Green...F 8
21 Dolleycanney...G 7
34 Dolphinholme .B 4
48 Dolphinton....E 4
4 Dolton........E 4
29 Dolwen, Denb...C 8
20 Dolwen, Mont...B 5
29 Dolwyd........B 7
29 Dolwyddelan...E 7
20 Dol-y-bont....D 2
20 Dolypandy.....D 2
36 Doncaster.....G 4
8 Donhead St. Andrew
             D 1
7 Donhead St. Mary
             D 12
52 Donibristle...H 6
6 Doniford......B 4
24 Donington, Lincs. B 3
22 Donington, Salop. B 2
33 Donington on Bain B 9
24 Donington South Ing
             B 3
22 Donisthorpe.....A 6
17 Donkey Town....H 10
44 Donkleywood...D 6
16 Donnington, Berks.
             E 5
16 Donnington, Glos. A 3
21 Donnington, Salop.
             B 11
21 Donnington, Salop.
             A 12
9 Donnington, Sussex
             F 10
15 Donnington, Worcs.
             A 10

MAP
21 Donnington Wood
      A 12
7 Donyatt.........E 7
47 Doonbank......H 9
47 Doonfoot......G 8
57 Dorback Lodge..H 6
7 Dorchester, Dorset
      G 10
17 Dorchester, Oxon .E 7
22 Dordon.........B 6
31 Dore...........B 11
56 Dores..........F 2
32 Dorket Head......E 3
10 Dorking.........C 1
10 Dormans Land....D 3
40 Dormanstown....C 6
21 Dormington.....H 11
17 Dorney.........F 10
55 Dornie.........G 3
61 Dornoch.........G 8
44 Dornock........F 1
61 Dorrery......B 10
22 Dorridge.......E 5
33 Dorrington, Lincs. E 8
21 Dorrington, Salop.
      B 10
7 Dorset, County..F 10
22 Dorsington ......G 5
21 Dorstone........H 8
17 Dorton.........C 7
55 Dorusduain......G 3
54 Dosmuckeran....D 6
22 Dosthill........B 6
7 Dottery.........G 8
3 Doublebois.......C 9
15 Doughton.......E 12
38 Douglas, I.o.M...H 2
48 Douglas, Lanark ..F 1
53 Douglas & Angus .D 9
28 Douglas Hill.....D 5
48 Douglas Water...F 2
48 Douglas West....F 1
53 Douglastown....B 9
46 Dougrie.........F 4
7 Doulting......B 10
64 Dounby.........C 1
55 Doune, Inverness .J 1
52 Doune, Perth....G 2
42 Dounepark......B 3
59 Douneside.......G 2
60 Dounie.........G 6
58 Dounie Park.....B 4
47 Doura..........F 9
5 Dousland........J 4
31 Dove Holes......B 9
38 Dovenby........B 3
11 Dover..........D 12
27 Dovercourt.....M 6
22 Doverdale......F 2
31 Doveridge......G 9
52 Dowally.........B 5
34 Dowbridge......D 3
16 Dowdeswell....B 1
42 Dowhill........A 3
14 Dowlais........D 4
4 Dowland........E 4
16 Down Ampney..D 2
15 Down Hatherley .B 11
4 Down St. Mary...E 6
5 Down Thomas...L 4
42 Downan, Ayr.....C 2
56 Downan, Banff...F 7
3 Downderry.....D 10
18 Downe ....H 4
16 Downend, Berks..G 6
15 Downend, Glos. ..G 9
9 Downend, I.o.W. .G 7
53 Downfield.......D 8
3 Downgate......B 10
25 Downham, Cambs.G 6
19 Downham, Essex .D 7
34 Downham, Lancs. C 6
49 Downham, Northumb.
      F 11
24 Downham Market E 7
7 Downhead, Som..D 9
7 Downhead, Som. B 9
52 Downhill........D 6
34 Downholland Cross
      F 2
40 Downholme.....E 1
59 Downies........H 7
17 Downley........F 8
7 Downside, Som. .A 10
7 Downside, Som. .B 9
15 Downside, Som. .H 8
17 Downside, Surrey H 12
8 Downton, Hants. .G 4
8 Downton, Wilts...D 3
21 Downton on the Rock
      E 9
24 Dowsby.........C 2

MAP
45 Doxford........A 10
15 Doynton........G 10
14 Draethen........F 5
48 Draffan.........E 7
9 Dragons Green...D 12
5 Drakeland Corner .K 4
47 Drakemyre......D 8
22 Drake's Broughton G 4
22 Drakes Cross.....D 4
3 Drakewalls .....C 11
42 Dranigower......E 3
23 Draughton, Northants.
      D 11
35 Draughton, Yorks. B 9
36 Drax...........D 5
16 Draycot Foliat....F 3
23 Draycote........E 8
32 Draycott, Derby ..G 2
16 Draycott, Glos....A 3
7 Draycott, Som....A 8
31 Draycott in the Clay
      F 8
31 Draycott in the Moors
      F 8
4 Drayford........E 6
16 Drayton, Berks...E 6
9 Drayton, Hants...E 8
23 Drayton, Leics. ..C 11
24 Drayton, Lincs...B 4
26 Drayton, Norfolk .D 5
23 Drayton, Oxon...H 8
22 Drayton, Salop...E 3
7 Drayton, Som....D 7
22 Drayton Bassett...A 8
17 Drayton Beauchamp
      C 10
17 Drayton Parslow .C 10
17 Drayton St. Leonard
      D 7
35 Drebley.........A 9
12 Dreenhill.......F 3
13 Dre-fach, Cards. ..B 8
13 Drefach, Carm....C 7
13 Drefach, Carm....E 6
47 Dreghorn.......F 8
11 Drellingore......N 11
49 Drem...........A 8
5 Drewsteignton....G 6
33 Driby...........C 11
16 Driffield, Glos....D 2
37 Driffield, Yorks...A 8
38 Drigg..........E 3
35 Drighlington....D 11
51 Drimfern........F 8
58 Drimmies.......E 5
50 Drimnin........B 3
50 Drimnin House...B 3
7 Drimpton.......F 7
55 Drimsallie......L 3
51 Drimsynie.......G 9
27 Drinkstone......J 3
27 Drinkstone Green .J 3
51 Drishaig........F 8
48 Drochil.........E 4
31 Droitton........G 9
22 Droitwich ....F 2
52 Dron...........F 6
32 Dronfield.......B 1
31 Dronfield Woodhouse
      B 11
47 Drongan........G 9
53 Dronley.........D 8
14 Drope..........G 4
9 Droxford.......D 7
29 Druid..........F 9
43 Druidhall........B 9
13 Druidsdale......J 6
12 Druidston.......E 2
46 Druim..........A 2
55 Druimarbin.....M 5
12 Druimavuic......C 7
54 Druimdhu.......D 5
46 Druimdrishaig...B 2
54 Druimindarroch...F 8
46 Druimyeon More .D 2
58 Drum, Aberdeen .C 6
46 Drum, Argyll....B 4
52 Drum, Kinc.....G 5
56 Drum, Ross &
      Cromarty.....D 2
60 Drumbeg........D 3
58 Drumblade.....D 3
58 Drumblair House .C 4
42 Drumbreddan....G 2
55 Drumbuie, Ross &
      Cromarty.....G 2
42 Drumbuie, Kirk...G 6
44 Drumburgh......G 1
43 Drumburn.......E 10
47 Drumchapel....B 10
56 Drumchardine...E 1
47 Drumclog......E 11
43 Drumcoltran....E 9

MAP
56 Drumcroy.......F 1
43 Drumcruilton.....A 9
58 Drumdaig.......F 3
56 Drumdyre.......D 2
53 Drumeldrie......G 9
48 Drumelzier......F 4
62 Drumfearn......G 6
47 Drumfork.......G 10
57 Drumgask......K 2
53 Drumgley.......D 9
57 Drumguish, Inver. .J 4
56 Drumguish, Moray F 6
55 Drumhead, Aber..D 6
59 Drumhead, Aber..H 4
42 Drumjohn......B 6
43 Drumlanrig Castle .B 9
59 Drumlasie.......G 4
46 Drumlemble.....G 2
42 Drumligair.......F 6
59 Drumlithie......J 5
42 Drummoddie.....G 5
56 Drummond......C 2
42 Drummore......H 2
57 Drumnadrochit...G 1
59 Drumnagair.....K 4
58 Drumnagorrach...B 3
58 Drumnahoy.....F 4
43 Drumpail.......E 3
42 Drumpark......D 9
42 Drumrae........G 5
43 Drumrash.......D 7
60 Drumrunie Lodge .F 3
58 Drums.........E 7
43 Drumshang.....H 7
43 Drumstinchall....F 9
59 Drumtochty Castle J 4
62 Drumuie........D 4
57 Drumuillie......G 5
52 Drumvaich......G 2
42 Drumwalt.......F 4
58 Drumwhindle....D 7
43 Drumwhirn......D 8
29 Drury..........D 12
32 Dry Doddington ..F 6
25 Dry Drayton.....J 5
19 Dry Street.......E 7
39 Drybeck........D 9
47 Drybridge......F 8
58 Drybridge.......A 2
15 Drybrook.......C 9
49 Dryburgh.......F 8
43 Dryfesdale Gate..C 11
48 Dryhope........G 5
47 Drymen........A 9
58 Drymuir........C 6
62 Drynoch........E 3
60 Duag Bridge.....G 4
58 Dubford, Aber....C 5
58 Dubford, Banff...A 5
58 Dubiton........C 4
60 Duchally.......E 5
43 Duchrae........C 7
8 Duck Street......A 5
30 Duckington.....E 4
16 Ducklington.....C 4
32 Duckmanton....C 2
25 Duck's Cross....K 2
25 Duddenhoe End...L 6
48 Duddingston....B 6
24 Duddington......E 1
10 Duddleswell.....E 3
49 Duddo.........E 12
30 Dudleston.......F 2
30 Dudleston Heath ..F 2
45 Dudley, Northants.F 10
22 Dudley, Staffs....C 3
12 Dudwells.......E 3
31 Duffield........F 11
14 Duffryn.........E 2
58 Dufftown.......D 1
56 Duffus.........C 7
41 Duggleby.......H 9
62 Duisdalemore.....G 6
15 Dusky.........M 4
14 Dukestown......C 5
35 Dukinfield......G 8
56 Dularich........F 1
28 Dulas..........A 4
58 Dulax..........F 1
7 Dulcote........B 9
6 Dulford........F 4
52 Dull...........B 3
47 Dullatur......B 12
25 Dullingham.....J 7
57 Dulnain Bridge ..G 5
3 Duloe, Cornwall ..D 9
25 Duloe, Hunts....J 3
56 Dulsie.........E 5
6 Dulverton......C 3

MAP
18 Dulwich.........G 3
47 Dumbarton......B 9
16 Dumbleton......A 1
58 Dumcrieff......A 11
58 Dumeath........D 2
43 Dumfries.......D 10
47 Dumgoyne......A 10
9 Dummer........B 7
59 Dun...........L 4
43 Dun Carloway....C 3
57 Dunachtonmore...J 4
56 Dunain House....E 2
52 Dunalastair......A 2
52 Dunan, Perth....D 2
51 Dunan, Perth....B 11
46 Dunan, Ross &
      Cromarty.......B 6
62 Dunan, Skye.....E 5
51 Dunans.........H 7
49 Dunbar.........B 9
61 Dunbeath......D 11
52 Dunblane.......G 3
53 Dunbog........E 7
6 Dunboll........B 6
8 Dunbridge......F 10
61 Duncansby Head .A 12
58 Duncanston, Aber. E 3
56 Duncanston, Ross &
      Cromarty.......D 2
6 Dunchideock....G 2
22 Dunchurch......E 8
23 Duncote........G 10
43 Duncow........C 10
57 Duncraggan.....G 12
54 Duncraig Castle...F 2
52 Duncrievie......F 6
61 Duncton........D 11
53 Dundee........D 9
7 Dundon........C 8
47 Dundonald, Ayr..F 8
53 Dundonald, Fife..H 7
60 Dundonnell Hotel.H 2
60 Dundonnell House H 3
43 Dundraw......G 12
55 Dundreggan.....H 7
43 Dundrennan.....G 8
15 Dundry........H 8
52 Dunduff........H 6
57 Dunecht.........J 4
48 Dunfermline.....A 4
35 Dunford Bridge..G 10
3 Dunge.........A 12
32 Dunham........C 5
30 Dunham Town....B 6
30 Dunham-on-the-Hill
      C 3
22 Dunhampton....E 2
33 Dunholme......B 7
52 Dunie..........D 4
53 Dunino........F 10
48 Dunipace.......A 1
52 Dunira.........E 2
52 Dunkeld........C 5
15 Dunkerton......H 10
6 Dunkeswell.....E 5
11 Dunkirk........B 9
10 Dunk's Green....C 5
59 Dunlappie.......K 3
22 Dunley.........E 1
56 Dunlichity Lodge..F 2
47 Dunlop........D 9
57 Dunmaglass Lodge G 2
3 Dunmere........B 7
52 Dunmore, Stirling.H 4
46 Dunmore, Argyll..C 3
11 Dunn Street.....B 7
61 Dunnet........A 11
53 Dunnichen.....B 10
58 Dunninald......B 11
52 Dunning........F 5
22 Dunnington, War..G 4
37 Dunnington, E. Riding
      B 9
36 Dunnington, E. Riding
      B 4
35 Dunnockshaw....D 7
59 Dunnottar Mains .J 6
58 Dunnydeer.....C 5
50 Dunollie.......D 6
46 Dunoon........B 6
53 Dunotter......G 9
42 Dunragit........F 2
46 Dunrostan......A 2
49 Duns..........D 10
16 Duns Tew......A 5
24 Dunsby........C 2
43 Dunscore.......C 10
36 Dunscroft......F 4
40 Dunsdale......C 6
17 Dunsden Green...F 8
9 Dunsfold.......B 11
5 Dunsford.......G 7
53 Dunshelt.......F 7

MAP
58 Dunshillock......C 7
41 Dunsley.........D 8
17 Dunsmore......D 9
34 Dunsop Bridge...B 5
17 Dunstable.......B 11
50 Dunstaffnage Fm. D 6
31 Dunstall.......H 10
6 Dunster........D 3
45 Dunston, Dur...G 10
33 Dunston, Lincs...D 8
26 Dunston, Norfolk .E 5
45 Dunston, Northumb.
      A 10
31 Dunston, Staffs...H 8
5 Dunstone......H 6
36 Dunsville.......F 4
37 Dunswell........D 8
48 Dunsyre........E 3
44 Dunterley......E 6
5 Dunterton.......H 2
16 Duntisbourne Abbots
      C 1
16 Duntisbourne Rouse
      D 1
7 Duntish........F 10
47 Duntocher......B 9
17 Dunton, Bucks...B 9
26 Dunton, Norfolk..C 2
25 Dunton, Oxon...L 3
23 Dunton Bassett...C 9
10 Dunton Green....B 4
18 Dunton Wayletts .E 6
62 Duntulm.......A 3
47 Dunure.........H 7
47 Dunure Mains....H 7
13 Dunvant........H 9
62 Dunvegan......C 2
60 Durness........A 5
65 Durno.........E 5
9 Durrington, Sussex
      F 12
8 Durrington, Wilts..B 3
15 Dursley.......D 10
6 Durston........C 6
7 Durweston......E 11
64 Dury..........D 7
23 Duston.........F 10
31 Duthil.........G 5
21 Dutlas.........E 7
18 Duton Hill......A 6
3 Dutson.......A 10
30 Dutton.........B 4
25 Duxford........L 6
28 Dwygyfylchi.....C 7
28 Dwyran........D 4
58 Dyce..........F 6
45 Dye House......G 7
13 Dyfatty........G 8
12 Dyfed.........D 6
14 Dyffryn, Carm....E 6
14 Dyffryn, Glam....F 4
14 Dyffryn, Glam....E 2
14 Dyffryn, Glam....G 4
12 Dyffryn, Pemb....C 3
28 Dyffryn-Ardudwy .H 5
14 Dyffryn Cellwen ..C 2
20 Dyffryn-castell....D 3
4 Dyke, Devon....D 2
24 Dyke, Lincs......C 2
56 Dyke, Moray....D 5
59 Dykehead, Angus .L 1
48 Dykehead, Lanark C 2
52 Dykehead, Perth..G 1
59 Dykelands......K 5
53 Dykends........A 7
58 Dykeside.......C 5
20 Dylife.........C 4
11 Dymchurch.....E 9
15 Dymock......A 10
14 Dyrham........G 10
53 Dysart.........H 8
29 Dyserth.......B 10
45 Eachwick.......F 9
34 Eagland Hill.....C 3
29 Eagle..........D 6
40 Eaglescliffe Junc. .D 4
38 Eaglesfield, Cumb..B 3
44 Eaglesfield, Dumf..F 1
14 Eaglesham......D 10
24 Eaglethorpe.....F 2
38 Eairy...........H 1

MAP
23 Eakley Lanes....G 11
32 Eakring.........D 4
36 Ealand.........F 6
18 Ealing.........F 2
39 Eamont Bridge...B 7
35 Earby.........C 8
34 Earcroft........E 6
21 Eardington.....C 12
21 Eardisland......F 9
21 Eardisley.......G 8
21 Eardiston, Worcs. F 12
30 Eardiston, Salop..H 2
25 Earith.........H 5
23 Earl Shilton.....B 8
27 Earl Soham......J 5
31 Earl Sterndale...C 9
27 Earl Stonham....J 4
49 Earle..........G 12
17 Earley.........G 8
26 Earlham.......E 5
62 Earlish.........B 3
23 Earls Barton....F 12
19 Earls Colne......A 8
22 Earl's Croome...H 2
27 Earl's Green.....J 3
42 Earlsdon.......D 6
53 Earlsferry.......G 9
58 Earlsford.......D 6
47 Earlston, Ayr....F 9
49 Earlston, Berwick. F 8
22 Earlswood......E 5
15 Earlswood Com. ..E 8
9 Earnley.........F 9
47 Earnockmuir....D 11
45 Earsdon, Northumb.
      D 10
45 Earsdon, Northumb.
      F 11
26 Earsham........F 6
36 Earswick........A 4
3 Eartham......E 10
38 Earystane.......H 1
40 Easby, Yorks....D 6
40 Easby, Yorks....E 2
50 Easdale........F 5
9 Easebourne....D 10
23 Easenhall......D 8
9 Eashing......B 11
17 Easington, Bucks. .C 8
40 Easington, Dur...A 4
45 Easington, Northumb.
      C 12
17 Easington, Oxon..D 7
37 Easington, Yorks. E 11
41 Easington, Yorks..C 7
40 Easington Colliery .A 4
64 Easington Grange B 12
45 Easington Lane..H 12
40 Easingwold......H 5
11 Easole Street....C 11
53 Eassie & Nevay...C 8
14 East Aberthaw...H 4
16 East Adderbury ..A 6
5 East Allington...L 6
45 East Ancroft....A 11
4 East Anstey.....C 7
9 East Ashling.....E 9
58 East Auchronie...C 6
41 East Ayton.....G 10
14 East Bank.......D 5
33 East Barkwith....B 9
10 East Barming....C 6
41 East Barnby......D 8
18 East Barnet.....D 3
49 East Barns......B 9
26 East Barsham.....B 2
26 East Beckham....B 5
18 East Bedfont....F 1
27 East Bergholt....M 4
26 East Bilney.....D 3
49 East Blanerne....D 11
10 East Blatchington .H 4
9 East Bloxworth..G 12
45 East Boldon.....G 11
8 East Boldre......F 5
45 East Bolton......D 9
47 East Brackenridge E 11
26 East Bradenham..E 2
7 East Brent......A 7
27 East Bridge......J 7
32 East Bridgford...F 4
45 East Brunton....F 10
4 East Buckland...C 5
6 East Budleigh....H 4
64 East Burra......E 7
64 East Burrafirth...D 7
7 East Burton.....G 11
40 East Butsfield....A 1
36 East Butterwick..G 6
59 East Cairnbeg....K 5
48 East Calder......C 4
26 East Carleton....E 5
23 East Carlton .....C 11

MAP
16 East Challow.....E 5
7 East Chelborough .F 9
10 East Chiltington ..G 3
7 East Chinnock....E 8
8 East Chisenbury...A 3
9 East Clandon....A 12
17 East Claydon.....B 8
15 East Clevedon....G 7
7 East Coker.......E 9
6 East Combe......C 5
7 East Compton....B 9
36 East Cottingwith..C 5
8 East Cowes.......F 6
36 East Cowick......E 4
40 East Cowton......E 3
45 East Cramlington E 11
7 East Cranmore...B 10
8 East Creech......H 1
57 East Croachy.....G 2
46 East Darlochan....G 2
8 East Dean, Hants..C 4
9 East Dean, Sussex E 10
26 East Dereham....D 3
45 East Ditchburn....A 9
4 East Down.......B 5
32 East Drayton.....C 5
15 East Dundry......H 9
45 East Edington....E 10
8 East End, Dorset..F 2
16 East End, Hants. .H 5
9 East End, Hants...D 8
8 East End, Hants...F 5
18 East End, Herts...A 4
11 East End, Kent....E 7
26 East End, Norfolk D 8
16 East End, Oxon...C 5
15 East End, Som....G 8
37 East End, Yorks. D 10
8 East Erlestoke.....A 1
10 East Farleigh.....C 6
23 East Farndon....D 10
36 East Ferry........G 6
45 East Fleetham...D 12
53 East Flisk........E 8
49 East Fortune......A 8
36 East Garforth.....D 2
16 East Garston......F 5
49 East Gordon......E 9
16 East Grafton.....H 4
8 East Grimstead...C 4
16 East Gringe.......E 5
10 East Grinstead....D 3
11 East Guldeford....F 8
23 East Haddon....E 10
16 East Hagbourne...E 6
37 East Halton.......E 9
37 East Halton Skitter E 9
18 East Ham........F 4
16 East Hanney......E 5
19 East Hanningfield .D 7
36 East Hardwick....E 2
27 East Harling......G 3
40 East Harlsey......E 4
8 East Harnham....C 3
7 East Harptree.....A 9
45 East Hartford....E 11
9 East Harting......D 9
7 East Hatch.......C 12
25 East Hatley.......K 4
52 East Haugh.......B 4
40 East Hauxwell.....F 2
53 East Haven.......D 10
24 East Heckington ..A 3
40 East Hedleyhope..A 2
16 East Hendred.....E 5
41 East Heslerton....G 9
10 East Hoathly......F 4
7 East Horrington...B 9
7 East Horsley.....A 12
45 East Horton.....C 11
7 East Huntspill....B 7
17 East Hyde.......B 12
4 East Ilkerton......A 6
16 East Ilsley........F 6
53 East Keal.......D 11
16 East Kennett.....G 2
35 East Keswick....C 12
47 East Kilbride.....D 11
58 East Kinharrachie.D 7
33 East Kirby......D 10
41 East Knapton.....G 9
7 East Knighton...H 11
4 East Knowstone ..D 7
7 East Knoyle.....C 12
45 East Kyloe.......B 12
7 East Lambrook...D 7
11 East Langdon....C 12
23 East Langton....C 10
61 East Langwell.....F 7
9 East Lavant.....E 10
40 East Layton......D 2
32 East Leake.......H 3
4 East Leigh........E 6

MAP
49 East Learmouth ..F 11
26 East Lexham.....D 2
45 East Lilburn......A 8
49 East Linton.......B 8
9 East Liss.........C 9
47 East Lockhead....D 8
3 East Looe........D 9
49 East Lothian, Co..B 8
36 East Lound.......G 6
9 East Lovington ..E 10
7 East Lulworth...H 12
41 East Lutton......H 9
7 East Lydford.....C 9
59 East Mains.......H 4
10 East Malling......B 6
9 East Marden......E 9
32 East Markham....C 5
35 East Marton......B 8
9 East Meon.......D 8
6 East Mere........E 3
19 East Mersea.....C 10
17 East Molesey....G 12
7 East Mordon....G 12
43 East Morton, Dumf.
B 9
35 East Morton, Yorks.
C 9
42 East Muntloch....H 2
41 East Ness........G 7
23 East Norton.....B 11
6 East Nynehead....D 5
9 East Oakley......A 7
5 East Ogwell.......J 7
7 East Orchard....D 11
49 East Ord........D 12
5 East Panson.....G 2
10 East Peckham.....C 5
12 East Pennar......G 3
7 East Pennard.....C 9
52 East Plean.......H 3
26 East Poringland...E 6
5 East Portlemouth .M 6
5 East Prawle......M 6
9 East Preston.....F 12
6 East Quantoxhead.B 5
45 East Rainton....H 11
37 East Ravendale..G 10
26 East Raynham...C 2
32 East Retford......B 4
37 East Riding, Co...C 8
35 East Rigton......C 12
40 East Rounton.....E 4
26 East Rudham.....C 1
26 East Runton......A 5
26 East Ruston......C 6
49 East Saltoun......C 7
44 East Scales.......F 1
16 East Shefford......G 5
45 East Sleekburn...E 11
26 East Somerton....D 8
36 East Stockwith ...H 6
7 East Stoke, Dorset
H 12
32 East Stoke, Notts. .E 5
7 East Stour.......D 11
11 East Stourmouth .B 11
4 East Stowford.....C 5
9 East Stratton.....B 7
11 East Studdal.....C 11
10 East Sussex, Co....F 5
3 East Taphouse ...C 9
19 East Tilbury......F 7
43 East Tinwald.....C 11
9 East Tistead......C 8
33 East Torrington...B 8
59 East Town........J 5
26 East Tuddenham..D 4
8 East Tytherley....C 4
8 East Tytherton....G 1
4 East Village.......E 7
24 East Walton......D 8
4 East Warlington...E 6
5 East Week.......G 5
8 East Wellow......D 5
53 East Wemyss.....G 8
48 East Whitburn....C 2
19 East Wick.......D 10
12 East Williamston..F 4
24 East Winch.......D 8
9 East Wittering.....F 9
40 East Witton......G 2
45 East Woodburn...D 7
16 East Woodhay ...H 5
9 East Worldham...B 9
26 East Wretham.....F 2
4 East Youlstone....D 1
10 Eastbourne ......H 5
37 Eastburn.........B 7
18 Eastbury, Herts...E 1
16 Eastbury, Berks....F 4
11 Eastchurch.......A 8
15 Eastcombe.......D 12
18 Eastcote, London .E 1

MAP
23 Eastcote, Northants.
G 10
22 Eastcote, War.....D 5
4 Eastcott, Devon...D 1
8 Eastcott, Wilts....A 2
16 Eastcourt, Wilts...H 3
16 Eastcourt, Wilts. ..E 1
10 Eastdean.........H 4
19 Eastend..........E 9
56 Easter Ardross....B 2
58 Easter Aucharnie..D 4
57 Easter Aviemore .H 4
56 Easter Balcroy....E 4
57 Easter Balmoral...K 8
57 Easter Boleskine ..G 1
56 Easter Brae.......C 2
15 Easter Compton...F 9
54 Easter Crochail....F 8
56 Easter Culbo......D 2
59 Easter Davoch....G 2
55 Easter Drummond H 8
52 Easter Dullater....F 1
43 Easter Earshaig ..A 11
61 Easter Fearn......H 7
44 Easter Fodderlee ..B 4
56 Easter Galcantray .E 4
22 Easter Green.....D 6
48 Easter Happrew...E 4
48 Easter Howgate...C 5
49 Easter Howlaws..E 10
56 Easter Kinkell....D 1
49 Easter Langlee....F 8
53 Easter Lednathie..A 8
56 Easter Milton.....D 5
56 Easter Moniack...E 1
56 Easter Muckovie..E 3
59 Easter Ord.......G 6
64 Easter Quarff.....E 7
58 Easter Silverford ..A 5
64 Easter Skeld......D 6
54 Easter Slumbay....F 3
49 Easter Softlaw ...F 10
48 Easter Stanhope...F 4
59 Easter Tillygarmond
H 4
59 Easter Tulloch....K 5
56 Easterfield.......E 3
9 Eastergate.......F 11
47 Easterhouse, Lan. C 11
48 Easterhouse, Peeb..D 3
8 Easterton.........A 2
58 Eastertown, Banff. D 1
48 Eastertown, Lan...F 2
48 Eastertown, Lan...E 3
48 Eastertown, Lan...G 1
7 Eastertown, Som. .A 7
58 Eastertown of
Auchleuchries ..D 8
59 Eastfield, Aber. ...H 1
48 Eastfield, Lanark..C 2
48 Eastfield, Lanark ..E 2
41 Eastfield, Yorks..G 10
45 Eastfield Hall....B 10
49 Eastfield of Lempitlaw
F 10
39 Eastgate, Dur....A 11
26 Eastgate, Norfolk .C 4
30 Eastham.........B 2
17 Easthampstead....G 9
17 Eastheath.........G 9
4 East-the-Water....C 3
21 Easthope........C 11
19 Easthorpe, Essex ..B 9
32 Easthorpe, Notts. .E 4
48 Easthouses.......C 6
4 Eastington, Devon.E 6
15 Eastington, Glos..D 11
15 Eastington, Glos...C 2
16 Eastleach Martin..D 3
16 Eastleach Turville .D 3
4 Eastleigh, Devon ..C 4
8 Eastleigh, Hants...B 8
11 Eastling..........B 8
45 Eastnook.........D 8
15 Eastnor.........A 10
36 Eastoft...........E 6
9 Eastoke..........F 8
44 Easton, Cumb.....G 1
44 Easton, Cumb.....F 3
5 Easton, Devon....G 6
7 Easton, Dorset ...H 7
8 Easton, Hants.....C 6
25 Easton, Hunts.....H 2
8 Easton, I.o.W.....G 5
32 Easton, Leics.....G 6
26 Easton, Norfolk..D 4
7 Easton, Somerset..A 8
27 Easton, Suffolk....J 6
15 Easton, Wilts....G 12
15 Easton Grey.....E 12
15 Easton-in-GordanoG 8
23 Easton Maudit...F 12
24 Easton-on-the-Hill.E 1

MAP
16 Easton Royal.....H 3
24 Eastrea..........F 4
44 Eastriggs........F 1
36 Eastrington.......D 5
11 Eastry..........C 11
33 Eastville.........E 11
32 Eastwell.........G 5
18 Eastwick.........C 4
19 Eastwood, Essex ..E 8
32 Eastwood, Notts...F 2
23 Eathorpe.........E 7
16 Eaton, Berks......D 5
30 Eaton, Cheshire...D 4
31 Eaton, Cheshire...D 7
32 Eaton, Leics.......B 4
32 Eaton, Leics......G 5
26 Eaton, Norfolk....E 5
21 Eaton, Salop......C 9
21 Eaton, Salop.....C 10
21 Eaton Bishop....H 10
17 Eaton Bray......B 10
21 Eaton Constantine
B 11
17 Eaton Green.....B 10
16 Eaton Hastings...D 4
25 Eaton Socon......J 3
30 Eaton upon Tern .H 5
41 Ebberston........G 9
8 Ebbesbourne Wake
D 2
14 Ebbw Vale.......C 5
45 Ebchester........G 9
15 Ebdon...........H 7
6 Ebford...........G 3
15 Ebley...........D 11
22 Ebrington........H 5
5 Ebsworthy Town..G 4
16 Ecchinswell ......H 6
49 Ecclaw..........C 10
43 Ecclefechan.....D 12
49 Eccles, Berwick ..E 10
10 Eccles, Kent......B 6
34 Eccles, Lancs.....G 6
21 Eccles Green.....H 9
26 Eccles Road.......F 3
49 Eccles Tofts.....E 10
32 Ecclesall..........B 1
35 Ecclesfield......H 12
59 Ecclesgreig........L 5
31 Eccleshall.........G 7
35 Eccleshill........D 10
48 Ecclesmachan.....B 3
30 Eccleston, Ches....D 3
34 Eccleston, Lancs. .H 4
34 Eccleston, Lancs...E 4
34 Eccleston Green...E 4
35 Eccup...........C 11
59 Echt.............G 5
49 Eckford..........G 9
22 Eckington ....H 3
23 Ecton...........F 11
31 Edale............B 9
10 Edburton.........G 1
43 Edderside.......G 11
61 Edderton.........H 7
16 Eddington, Berks..G 4
11 Eddington, Kent .A 10
4 Eddistone........D 1
48 Eddleston.........E 5
47 Eddlewood.......D 12
49 Eden Hall.......F 10
10 Edenbridge.......C 3
35 Edenfield.........E 7
39 Edenhall.........B 8
24 Edenham.........C 2
31 Edensor.........C 11
51 Edentaggart.....H 10
36 Edenthorpe.......F 4
44 Edentown........G 2
28 Edern...........F 2
7 Edgarley.........C 8
22 Edgbaston.......D 4
17 Edgcott, Bucks....B 8
6 Edgcott, Som......B 2
21 Edge............B 9
15 Edge End.........C 9
30 Edge Green, Ches..E 3
27 Edge Green, Norf. G 3
30 Edge Hill.........A 2
30 Edgebottom......H 4
26 Edgefield.........B 4
26 Edgefield Green ..B 6
30 Edgemond ....H 6
44 Edgerston.........B 5
44 Edges Green......F 5
35 Edgeside.........E 7
15 Edgeworth......D 12
4 Edgeworthy......E 7
30 Edgmond Marsh..H 6
21 Edgton..........D 9
18 Edgware.........E 2
34 Edgworth........E 6
52 Edinample.......E 1

MAP
62 Edinbain.........C 3
48 Edinburgh........B 5
52 Edinchip.........E 1
22 Edingale.........A 6
32 Edingley.........E 4
26 Edingthorpe......B 6
49 Edington, Ber. ..D 11
7 Edington, Som. ...B 7
8 Edington, Wilts. ..A 1
7 Edington Burtle ...B 7
7 Edingworth.......A 7
58 Edintore.........C 2
23 Edith Weston....B 12
6 Edithmead........A 6
17 Edlesborough....B 10
45 Edlingham, Northumb.
B 9
33 Edlington, Lind. ..C 9
8 Edmondsham.....E 2
45 Edmondsley.....H 10
32 Edmondthorpe...H 6
64 Edmonstone......C 3
18 Edmonton........E 3
45 Edmundbyers.....H 8
49 Ednam..........F 10
51 Edra............F 11
49 Edrom..........D 11
30 Edstaston........G 4
22 Edstone..........F 5
21 Edvin Loach.....G 12
32 Edwalton.........G 3
27 Edwardstone......L 2
13 Edwinsford.......D 9
32 Edwinstowe......D 3
25 Edworth..........L 3
21 Edwyn Ralph....G 12
59 Edzell...........K 3
14 Efail Isaf.........F 4
29 Efail-Parcy......C 11
23 Efail-fâch.......G 11
28 Efailnewydd......G 3
29 Efail-rhyd.......H 11
12 Efailwen.........D 5
29 Efenechtyd......E 10
9 Effingham.......A 12
64 Effirth..........D 6
4 Efford...........F 8
11 Egerton, Kent.....C 8
34 Egerton, Lancs....F 6
5 Egg Buckland.....K 4
17 Eggington.......B 10
40 Egglescliffe.......D 4
39 Eggleston.......C 12
17 Egham..........G 11
23 Egleton.........A 12
45 Eglingham........A 9
3 Egloshayle........C 7
3 Egloskerry........A 9
14 Eglwys-Brewis....G 3
29 Eglwysbach.......C 7
29 Eglwysfach.......C 3
12 Eglwyswrw.......C 5
32 Egmanton........C 4
32 Egremont, Cumb. .D 3
30 Egremont, Lancs. .A 2
41 Egton...........D 8
41 Egton Bridge......E 8
17 Egypt..........F 10
19 Eight Ash Green ..A 9
50 Eignaig..........C 5
57 Eil..............H 4
55 Eilanreach.......H 2
49 Eildon...........F 8
60 Eilean Darach....H 3
56 Eileanach Lodge ..C 1
63 Eishken..........F 4
20 Elan Village......F 5
15 Elberton.........E 9
5 Elburton.........K 4
52 Elcho............E 6
16 Elcombe.........F 2
24 Eldernell.........F 4
15 Eldersfield.......A 11
40 Eldon............B 3
42 Eldrick..........C 4
34 Eldroth..........A 6
35 Eldwick.........C 10
20 Elerch...........D 2
59 Elfhill............J 5
45 Elford, Northumb.
D 12
22 Elford, Staffs......A 5
56 Elgin............C 8
62 Elgol............G 4
11 Elham..........D 10
53 Elie.............G 9
45 Elilaw...........B 8
8 Eling............E 5
62 Elishader.........B 4
45 Elishaw..........D 7
32 Elkesley.........C 4
16 Elkstone.........C 1
57 Ellan............G 5

MAP
35 Elland..........E 10
46 Ellary............B 2
31 Ellastone.........F 9
34 Ellel.............B 4
49 Ellemford.......C 10
31 Ellenhall.........G 7
9 Ellen's Green....C 12
40 Ellerbeck.........E 4
41 Ellerby...........D 8
30 Ellerdine Heath...H 5
6 Ellerhayes........F 3
51 Elleric...........C 7
37 Ellerker..........D 7
30 Ellerton, Salop....H 6
40 Ellerton, N. Riding E 3
36 Ellerton, E. Riding C 5
17 Ellesborough......C 9
30 Ellesmere.........G 2
30 Ellesmere Port....C 3
8 Ellingham, Hants...E 3
26 Ellingham, Norf...F 6
45 Ellingham, Northumb.
E 12
40 Ellingstring.......G 2
25 Ellington, Hunts. .H 3
45 Ellington, Northumb.
D 11
9 Ellisfield.........B 8
23 Ellistown.........A 8
58 Ellon............D 7
38 Ellonby..........B 6
37 Elloughton ......D 7
15 Ellwood..........C 9
24 Elm.............E 6
7 Elm............D 11
18 Elm Park.........E 5
22 Elmbridge........E 2
25 Elmdon, Essex....L 6
22 Elmdon, War.....D 5
22 Elmdon Heath....D 5
18 Elmers End.......G 4
23 Elmesthorpe......C 8
9 Elmfield.........G 7
22 Elmhurst.........A 5
22 Elmley Castle.....H 3
22 Elmley Lovett.....E 2
15 Elmore..........C 11
15 Elmore Back.....C 10
4 Elmscott.........D 1
27 Elmsett..........K 3
19 Elmstead Market.B 10
11 Elmstone........B 11
15 Elmstone Hardwicke
B 12
27 Elmswell, Suffolk ..J 3
37 Elmswell, Yorks...A 7
32 Elmton..........C 2
60 Elphin...........F 3
48 Elphinstone.......B 6
59 Elrick...........G 6
42 Elrig............G 4
51 Elrigbeag.........F 8
45 Elsdon..........D 7
35 Elsecar.........G 12
18 Elsenham.........A 5
16 Elsfield..........C 6
37 Elsham..........F 8
26 Elsing...........D 4
35 Elslack..........B 8
30 Elson............G 2
48 Elsrickle..........E 3
9 Elstead, Surrey...B 10
9 Elsted, Sussex....D 9
32 Elston, Notts.....E 5
8 Elston, Wilts......B 2
4 Elstone..........D 5
37 Elstonwick......D 10
25 Elstow...........K 2
18 Elstree..........D 2
33 Elswick..........C 3
25 Elsworth.........J 4
38 Elterwater........E 5
18 Eltham...........F 4
25 Eltisley..........J 4
30 Elton, Cheshire ...C 3
31 Elton, Derby ....D 10
40 Elton, Durham....C 4
15 Elton, Glos......C 10
21 Elton, Herefs.....E 10
24 Elton, Hunts......F 2
32 Elton, Notts......F 5
48 Elvanfoot........H 2
31 Elvaston.........G 12
27 Elveden..........G 1
11 Elvington, Kent..C 11
36 Elvington, Yorks. .B 5
49 Elwartlaw.......E 10
40 Elwick, Durham...B 5
45 Elwick, Northumb.
B 12
30 Elworth.........D 6
6 Elworthy.........C 4
25 Ely, Cambs.......G 6

MAP

14 Ely, Glam. . . . . . . .G 5
23 Emberton . . . . .G 12
44 Emblehope . . . . .D 6
38 Embleton, Cumb.. B 4
40 Embleton, Dur.. . .B 4
45 Embleton, Northumb.
A 10
61 Embo . . . . .G 8
35 Embsay . . . . .B 8
8 Emery Down . . . . .E 4
35 Emley. . . . . .F 11
35 Emley Moor . . . .F 11
17 Emmbrook . . . . . . .G 8
17 Emmington . . . . . .D 8
24 Emneth . . . . .E 6
24 Emneth Hungate . .E 6
23 Empingham . . . . .A 12
9 Empshott . . . . .C 9
9 Emsworth . . . . . . .E 9
63 Enaclete . . . . .D 2
16 Enborne . . . . .G 5
16 Enborne Row . . . . .H 5
21 Enchmarsh . . . . . .C 10
7 Encombe . . . . . . .H 12
23 Enderby . . . . .B 8
39 Endmoor . . . . .G 7
31 Endon . . . . .E 7
31 Endon Bank . . . . . .E 8
18 Enfield . . . . .D 3
8 Enford . . . . .A 3
15 Engine Common . .F 10
17 Englefield . . . . . . .G 7
17 Englefield Green . G 10
15 English Bicknor . . .C 9
30 English Frankton . .G 3
15 Englishcombe . . . .H 10
8 Enham Alamein . .A 5
6 Enmore . . . . .C 6
38 Ennerdale Bridge..D 3
43 Enoch . . . . .B 9
52 Enochdu . . . . .A 5
50 Ensay . . . . .C 1
8 Ensbury . . . . .F 2
21 Ensdon . . . . .A 9
4 Ensis . . . . .C 4
16 Enstone . . . . .B 5
43 Enterkinfoot. . . . . .A 9
40 Enterpen . . . . .E 5
22 Enville. . . . . .C 2
50 Eorabus . . . . .E 1
63 Eoropie . . . . .A 6
15 Epney. . . . . .C 11
32 Epperstone . . . . . . .D 4
18 Epping . . . . .D 4
18 Epping Green . . . . .C 3
18 Epping Green . . . . .C 4
18 Epping Upland . . .C 4
40 Eppleby. . . . . .D 2
10 Epsom . . . . .B 1
23 Epwell . . . . .H 7
36 Epworth . . . . .G 5
29 Erbistock . . . . . . .F 12
55 Erbusaig . . . . .G 1
54 Erchless Castle . . .E 8
22 Erdington . . . . . . .C 5
51 Eredine . . . . .G 7
60 Eriboll . . . . .B 5
48 Ericstane . . . . .H 3
10 Eridge Green . . . . .E 4
46 Erines . . . . .B 4
25 Eriswell . . . . .G 8
18 Erith. . . . . .F 5
33 Ermine . . . . .C 7
5 Ermington . . . . . .K 5
26 Erpingham . . . . . . .B 5
55 Errocht . . . . .L 5
57 Errogie . . . . .G 1
53 Errol. . . . . .E 7
42 Ervie . . . . .E 1
27 Erwarton . . . . .M 5
20 Erwood . . . . .H 6
40 Eryholme . . . . .D 3
29 Eryrys . . . . .D 11
46 Escart . . . . .C 3
40 Escomb . . . . .B 2
36 Escrick . . . . .C 4
13 Esgair . . . . .D 7
13 Esgairgeiliog . . . . .B 3
13 Esgerdawe. . . . . . . .C 9
40 Esh . . . . .A 2
40 Esh Winning. . . . . .A 2
17 Esher . . . . .H 12
45 Eshott . . . . .C 10
35 Eshton. . . . . .B 8
54 Eskadale . . . . .F 8
48 Eskbank . . . . .C 6
38 Eskdale Green . . . .E 4
44 Eskdalemuir . . . . . .C 1
37 Eskham . . . . .G 11
34 Esprick . . . . .D 3
31 Essendine . . . . .D 1
18 Essendon . . . . .C 3
19 Essex, Co. . . . . . . .C 7

MAP

56 Essich . . . . .F 2
22 Essington . . . . .B 3
40 Eston . . . . .C 6
49 Etal . . . . .E 11
16 Etchilhampton . . . .H 2
10 Etchingham . . . . . . .E 6
11 Etchinghill, Kent.D 10
31 Etchinghill, Staffs..H 8
17 Eton . . . . .F 10
17 Eton Wick . . . . . . .F 10
57 Etteridge . . . . .K 3
22 Ettington . . . . .G 6
24 Etton, Hunts. . . . . .E 2
37 Etton, Yorks. . . . . .C 7
48 Ettrick . . . . .H 5
48 Ettrickbridge End .G 6
31 Etwall . . . . .G 11
27 Euston . . . . .G 2
24 Euximoor Drove . .F 6
34 Euxton. . . . . .E 4
14 Evanstown . . . . . . .E 3
56 Evanton . . . . .C 2
33 Evedon . . . . .E 8
61 Evelix . . . . .G 7
21 Evenjobb . . . . .F 8
17 Evenley . . . . .A 7
16 Evenlode . . . . .A 3
40 Evenwood . . . . .C 2
40 Evenwood Gate. . . .C 2
64 Everbay . . . . .C 4
7 Evercreech . . . . . . .B 9
23 Everdon . . . . .F 9
36 Everingham . . . . . . .C 6
8 Everleigh . . . . .A 3
41 Everley . . . . .F 10
25 Eversholt . . . . .M 1
7 Evershot . . . . .F 9
17 Eversley. . . . . .H 8
17 Eversley Cross . . . .H 9
37 Everthorpe . . . . . . .D 7
25 Everton, Beds. . . . .K 3
8 Everton, Hants. . . .G 4
30 Everton, Lancs. . . .A 2
32 Everton, Notts. . . .A 4
44 Evertown . . . . .E 2
21 Evesbatch . . . . . . .H 12
22 Evesham . . . . .H 4
23 Evington . . . . .B 10
35 Ewden Village . . .G 11
10 Ewell . . . . .B 1
11 Ewell Minnis . . . .D 11
17 Ewelme . . . . .E 7
16 Ewen . . . . .D 1
14 Ewenny . . . . .G 2
33 Ewerby . . . . .E 8
44 Eweslees . . . . .C 2
9 Ewhurst, Surrey . .B 12
11 Ewhurst, Sussex . .F 7
9 Ewhurst Green . .B 12
29 Ewloe . . . . .D 12
4 Eworthy . . . . .F 3
9 Ewshot. . . . . .A 9
15 Ewyas Harold . . . .B 7
8 Exbourne . . . . .F 5
6 Exbury . . . . .F 6
6 Exebridge . . . . . . .D 3
40 Exelby . . . . .F 3
6 Exeter . . . . .G 3
6 Exford . . . . .B 2
22 Exhall . . . . .G 4
17 Exlade Street . . . . .F 7
6 Exminster . . . . . . .G 3
6 Exmouth . . . . .H 4
64 Exnaboe . . . . .F 7
25 Exning . . . . .J 7
6 Exton, Devon. . . . .H 3
9 Exton, Hants. . . . .D 7
23 Exton, Rutland . .A 12
6 Exton, Somerset. .C 3
6 Exwick . . . . .G 3
31 Eyam . . . . .C 10
23 Eydon . . . . .G 9
21 Eye, Herefs. . . . . .F 10
24 Eye, Hunts. . . . . . .E 3
27 Eye, Suffolk . . . . . .H 4
49 Eyemouth . . . . . . .C 12
25 Eyeworth . . . . .L 4
11 Eyhorne Street . . . .C 7
27 Eyke . . . . .K 6
25 Eynesbury . . . . . . .J 3
10 Eynsford . . . . .B 4
16 Eynsham . . . . .C 5
7 Eype . . . . .G 8
62 Eyre . . . . .C 3
11 Eythorne . . . . . . .C 11
29 Eyton, Denbigh . .F 12
21 Eyton, Herefs. . .F 10
21 Eyton, Salop. . . . .D 9
30 Eyton, Salop. . . . .H 3
21 Eyton upon the Weald
Moors . . . . .A 12
16 Faccombe. . . . . . . .H 5
40 Faceby. . . . . .E 5

MAP

28 Fachwen . . . . .D 5
35 Facit. . . . . .E 7
30 Faddiley. . . . . .E 4
55 Faddoch . . . . .G 3
41 Fadmoor. . . . . .F 7
31 Fagginton . . . . . . .G 11
13 Fagwyr . . . . .G 10
47 Fail. . . . . .F 9
15 Failand . . . . .G 8
47 Failford . . . . .G 9
35 Failsworth . . . . . . .E 3
54 Fain. . . . . .B 5
6 Fair Oak . . . . .D 4
8 Fair Oak . . . . .D 6
17 Fair Oak Green . . .H 7
35 Fairburn . . . . .D 2
20 Fairbourne . . . . . . .A 2
36 Fairburn . . . . .D 2
22 Fairchild . . . . .H 4
22 Fairfield . . . . .E 3
16 Fairford . . . . .D 3
43 Fairgirth . . . . .F 9
47 Fairlie . . . . .D 7
11 Fairlight. . . . . .G 7
11 Fairlight Cove . . . .G 7
6 Fairmile . . . . .F 4
48 Fairmilehead . . . . .C 5
49 Fairnilee . . . . .F 7
30 Fairoak . . . . .G 6
10 Fairseat . . . . .B 5
26 Fairstead, Norfolk C 6
19 Fairstead, Sussex . .B 7
10 Fairwarp . . . . .E 3
4 Fairy Cross. . . . . . .D 3
26 Fakenham . . . . . . .C 2
49 Fala . . . . .C 7
48 Falahill . . . . .D 6
41 Falcon Inn . . . . . .E 10
33 Faldingworth . . . . .B 8
15 Falfield . . . . .E 10
27 Falkenham . . . . . . .L 6
48 Falkirk . . . . .A 2
53 Falkland . . . . .F 7
44 Falla . . . . .B 5
32 Fallgate. . . . . .D 1
52 Fallin . . . . .H 3
45 Fallowfield . . . . . . .F 7
49 Fallsidehill . . . . . . .E 9
10 Falmer. . . . . .G 2
2 Falmouth . . . . .F 5
44 Falnash . . . . .B 2
41 Falsgrave . . . . . . .F 10
44 Falstone . . . . .D 5
60 Fanagmore . . . . . . .C 3
40 Fangdale Beck . . . .F 6
36 Fangfoss . . . . .B 5
50 Fanmore . . . . .C 2
54 Fannich Lodge . . . .C 6
49 Fans . . . . .E 9
17 Far Bletchley . . . . .A 9
23 Far Cotton . . . . . .F 11
38 Far Sawrey . . . . . . .F 6
24 Farcet . . . . .F 3
21 Farden . . . . .E 11
9 Fareham . . . . .F 7
22 Farewell. . . . . .A 4
33 Farforth . . . . .B 10
44 Farglow . . . . .F 5
16 Faringdon . . . . . . .E 4
34 Farington . . . . .E 4
44 Farlam . . . . .G 4
15 Farleigh, Som. . . . .G 8
10 Farleigh, Surrey. .B 3
7 Farleigh Hungerford
A 11
9 Farleigh Wallop. .A 8
15 Farleigh Wick . . .H 11
33 Farlesthorpe . . . . .C 11
39 Farleton . . . . .G 8
31 Farley, Cheshire..F 9
21 Farley, Salop. . . . .B 9
15 Farley, Somerset . .G 7
8 Farley, Wiltshire. .C 4
9 Farley Green . . . .B 12
17 Farley Hill . . . . . .H 8
15 Farleys End . . . . .C 11
21 Farlow. . . . . .D 11
29 Farm Yard. . . . . . . .D 7
9 Farmborough . . . .H 10
16 Farmcote . . . . .A 2
13 Farmers . . . . .C 10
43 Farmersfield. . . . . .C 9
16 Farmington . . . . . .C 4
16 Farmoor . . . . .C 5
58 Farmtown. . . . . .A 5
16 Farnborough, Berks.
F 5
18 Farnborough, London
G 4
23 Farnborough, War.
G 8

MAP

17 Farnborough Grn. H 9
9 Farncombe..B 11
30 Farndon, Denbigh.E 3
32 Farndon, Notts....E 5
53 Farnell. . . . . .B 11
31 Farnham, Dorset. .E 1
18 Farnham, Essex.. .A 5
27 Farnham, Suffolk. .J 7
9 Farnham, Surrey. .B 9
35 Farnham, Yorks.. .A 12
17 Farnham Com.. . .F 10
18 Farnham Green. . .A 5
17 Farnham Royal . .F 10
35 Farnhill. . . . . .C 9
10 Farningham . . . . . .A 4
13 Farnley, Yorks.. .B 11
35 Farnley, Yorks.. .D 11
35 Farnley Tyas. . . . .F 10
34 Farnworth, Lancs..B 4
34 Farnworth, Yorks. G 6
8 Farringdon . . . . . . .G 4
9 Farrington. . . . . . . .C 8
7 Farrington Gurney A 9
35 Farsley . . . . .D 10
22 Farthinghoe. . . . . . .H 8
11 Farthingloe . . . . . .D 11
23 Farthingstone . . . . .G 9
35 Fartown. . . . . .E 10
4 Farway . . . . .G 5
54 Fasag. . . . . .D 3
2 Faskadale . . . . .A 2
55 Fasnakyle . . . . .G 7
59 Fasque . . . . .K 4
55 Fassfern. . . . . .L 4
45 Fatfield . . . . .H 11
58 Fattahead . . . . .B 4
46 Faugh. . . . . .G 3
48 Fauldhouse . . . . . . .C 2
44 Fauldie. . . . . .F 2
19 Faulkbourne. . . . . .B 6
11 Faulkland. . . . . . . .A 10
30 Faulsgreen. . . . . . . .G 4
11 Faversham. . . . . . . .B 9
56 Favillar . . . . .F 8
45 Fawdon. . . . . .B 8
5 Fawfieldhead . . . . .D 9
10 Fawkham Green . .B 5
16 Fawler. . . . . .B 5
16 Fawley, Berks.. . . .F 5
17 Fawley, Bucks.. . .E 8
8 Fawley, Hants.. . .F 6
11 Fawley Chapel. . . .A 9
49 Fawside. . . . . .E 9
36 Faxfleet . . . . .E 6
10 Faygate. . . . . .E 1
22 Fazeley. . . . . .B 5
40 Fearby . . . . .G 2
56 Fearn. . . . . .B 4
60 Fearn Lodge . . . . .H 6
52 Fearnan. . . . . .C 2
41 Fearnbeg. . . . . .D 1
30 Fearnhead. . . . . . . .A 5
54 Fearnmore. . . . . . . .D 1
22 Featherstone, War..B 3
36 Featherstone, Yorks.
E 2
44 Featherwood . . . . .C 6
22 Feckenham . . . . . . .F 4
56 Feddan. . . . . .D 5
9 Feering. . . . . .B 8
39 Feetham. . . . . .E 12
10 Felbridge. . . . . . . .D 3
11 Felbrigg. . . . . .B 5
10 Felcourt. . . . . .D 3
17 Felden. . . . . .D 11
1 Feldownhead. . . . .H 2
21 Felhampton . . . . . .D 10
12 Felin-Wnda. . . . . .B 6
14 Felindre, Brec.. . .B 5
20 Felindre, Cards.. .G 1
13 Felindre, Carm...D 10
13 Felindre, Carm.. .G 9
13 Felindre, Glam.. .E 9
21 Felindre, Radnor..D 7
13 Felin-fach, Brec. . .A 4
13 Felinfach, Cards.. .A 8
13 Felinfoel. . . . . .G 8
13 Felin-gwm Isaf..E 8
13 Felin-gwm Uchaf..E 8
40 Felixkirk. . . . . .G 5
27 Felixstowe. . . . . . .M 6
27 Felixstoweferry....L 6
49 Felkington . . . . . . .E 12
45 Felling. . . . . .G 11
38 Fellside. . . . . .B 5
25 Felmersham . . . . . .J 1
26 Felmingham....C 5
9 Felpham. . . . . .F 11
27 Felsham. . . . . .J 2

MAP

19 Felstead. . . . . .B 7
18 Feltham. . . . . .G 1
26 Felthorpe . . . . .D 5
21 Felton, Herefs.. .G 11
15 Felton, Somerset. .H 8
21 Felton Butler . . . . .A 9
24 Feltwell . . . . .F 8
25 Fen Drayton. . . . . .H 4
22 Fen End. . . . . .E 6
35 Fenay Bridge. . . . .F 10
35 Fence. . . . . .C 7
45 Fence Houses. . . . .H 11
33 Fendike Corner. .D 11
56 Fendom. . . . . .B 4
24 Fengate . . . . .F 3
45 Fenham. . . . . .B 12
45 Fenhamhill. . . . . . .B 12
34 Feniscowles. . . . . . .E 5
6 Feniton . . . . .F 4
31 Fenny Bentley. . . . .E 10
23 Fenny Compton . .G 7
23 Fenny Drayton . . .B 7
17 Fenny Stratford. . .A 10
45 Fenrother. . . . . . . .D 10
25 Fenstanton . . . . . . .H 4
24 Fenton, Hunts. . . . .G 4
32 Fenton, Lincs.. . . .C 6
32 Fenton, Notts.. . . .E 6
31 Fenton, Staffs.. . . .F 7
49 Fenton Barns . . . . .A 8
49 Fenton Town. . . . .F 12
49 Fentonhill . . . . . . .F 12
47 Fenwick, Ayr.. . . .E 9
45 Fenwick, Northumb.
F 9
45 Fenwick, Northumb.
B 12
36 Fenwick, Yorks.. .E 4
46 Feochaig. . . . . .H 3
2 Feock. . . . . .F 5
62 Ferindonald . . . . . .G 6
62 Feriniquarrie. . . . . .C 1
62 Ferlochan. . . . . . . .D 6
13 Ferryside. . . . . .F 7
61 Ferrytown. . . . . . . .H 7
26 Fersfield. . . . . .G 4
55 Fersit. . . . . .L 7
57 Feshiebridge. . . . . .J 4
17 Fetcham. . . . . .H 12
58 Fetterangus. . . . . . .C 7
59 Fettercairn. . . . . . .K 4
38 Fewston. . . . . .B 10
14 Ffairfach. . . . . .E 9
20 Ffair-rhôs. . . . . . . .F 3
13 Ffald-y-Brenin. . .C 9
14 Ffawyddog. . . . . . .B 5
16 Ffestiniog.. . . :. . .F 6
29 Ffordd-las, Denb..C 7
21 Fforddlas, Rad.. .H 7
13 Fforest. . . . . .G 9
13 Fforest fach . . . . . .G 9
13 Fforest Goch. . . .G 10
13 Ffosrasol. . . . . .B 7
13 Ffos-y-ffin. . . . . . .A 8
29 Ffrith. . . . . .E 12
21 Ffynnon Gynydd .H 7
13 Ffynnon-ddrain. . .E 7
29 Ffynnongroew. . .B 10
60 Fiag Bridge. . . . . . .E 5
60 Fiag Lodge. . . . . . .D 5
50 Fidden. . . . . .G 1
15 Fiddington, Glos. A 12
15 Fiddington, Som.. B 5
7 Fiddleford. . . . . . . .E 11
18 Fiddlers Hamlet. .D 5
44 Fiddleton. . . . . .C 2
31 Field. . . . . .G 9
26 Field Broughton . .G 6
26 Field Dalling. . . . .B 3
23 Field Head. . . . . . .A 8

MAP

47 Fieldhead . . . . . . .D 11
53 Fife, County. . . . . .G 7
58 Fife of Keith. . . . .C 2
7 Fifehead Magdalen
D 11
7 Fifehead Neville .E 11
7 Fifehead St. Quintin
E 11
17 Fifield, Berks.. . .F 10
16 Fifield, Glos.. . . . .B 3
8 Fifield, Wilts.. . . .A 3
8 Fifield Bavant. . . .D 2
8 Figheldean . . . . . . .A 3
40 Fighting Cocks.. .D 4
26 Filby. . . . . .D 8
41 Filey . . . . .G 11
23 Filgrave. . . . . .G 12
16 Filkins . . . . .D 3
4 Filleigh, Devon . .E 6
4 Filleigh, Devon . .C 5
32 Fillingham . . . . . . .B 6
22 Fillongley . . . . . . .C 6
32 Filton. . . . . .F 9
37 Fimber. . . . . .A 7
59 Finavon. . . . . .L 2
24 Fincham . . . . .E 8
17 Finchampstead . . .H 9
50 Fincharn. . . . . .G 6
4 Finchdean. . . . . . . .E 9
25 Finchingfield . . . . .M 8
18 Finchley. . . . . .E 3
53 Fincraigs. . . . . .E 8
31 Findern. . . . . .G 11
56 Findhorn . . . . .C 6
57 Findhorn Bridge . G 4
58 Findochty. . . . . . . .A 2
59 Findon, Kinc.. . . .H 7
9 Findon, Sussex . .E 12
56 Findon Mains. . . . .D 2
59 Findrack House. .G 3
23 Findon. . . . . .E 12
27 Fingal Street. . . . .H 5
58 Fingask, Aber.. . .E 5
52 Fingask, Perth . . .E 6
22 Fingerpost. . . . . . .E 1
17 Fingest. . . . . .E 8
40 Finghall. . . . . .F 2
44 Finglang, Cumb.. G 1
47 Finland, Dumf. .H 12
11 Finglesham . . . . .C 12
19 Fingringhoe. . . . .B 10
55 Finiskaig. . . . . . . .K 2
52 Finlarig. . . . . .D 1
17 Finmere. . . . . .A 7
51 Finnart. . . . . .B 12
43 Finniegill. . . . . . .B 12
27 Finningham . . . . . .H 3
36 Finningley. . . . . . .G 4
58 Finnygaud. . . . . . .B 3
63 Finsbay. . . . . .H 2
18 Finsbury. . . . . . . .F 3
22 Finstall. . . . . .E 3
38 Finsthwaite . . . . . .F 6
16 Finstock. . . . . .C 4
64 Finstown. . . . . . . .C 2
43 Fintloch. . . . . .D 7
58 Fintry, Aberdeen ..B 5
53 Fintry, Angus.. . .D 9
47 Fintry, Stirling. .A 11
50 Fionnphort. . . . . . .F 1
40 Fir Tree . . . . .B 2
32 Firbeck . . . . .A 3
41 Firby, E. Riding. . .H 7
40 Firby, N. Riding . .G 3
33 Firsby . . . . .D 11
60 First Coast . . . . . .G 1
36 Fishlake. . . . . .F 4
43 Fishbeck . . . . .C 11
9 Fishbourne, Hants
G 7
9 Fishbourne, Sussex
F 10
40 Fishburn . . . . .B 4
52 Fishcross. . . . . .H 4
58 Fisherford. . . . . . . .D 4
7 Fisher's Pond. . . . .D 6
9 Fisherstreet. . . . . .C 11
47 Fisherton, Ayr.. .H 7
56 Fisherton, Inver.. .B 2
8 Fisherton de la Mere
B 2
12 Fishguard . . . . .C 3
15 Fishponds. . . . . . . .G 9
35 Fishpool, Lancs.. .F 7
32 Fishpool, Notts.. .C 5
24 Fishtoft . . . . .A 5
33 Fishtoft Drive. . . .E 10
53 Fishtown of Usan B 12
49 Fishwick . . . . . . .D 11
62 Fiskavaig. . . . . . . .E 2
33 Fiskerton, Lincs.. .C 7
32 Fiskerton, Notts.. .E 4
37 Fitling. . . . . .D 10

MAP
24 Fitten End......D 5
8 Fittleton......A 3
9 Fittleworth.....D 11
30 Fitz.......H 3
6 Fitzhead......C 5
36 Fitzwilliam......F 2
50 Fiunary......C 3
15 Five Acres......C 9
10 Five Ashes......F 4
34 Five Lane Ends...B 4
3 Five Lanes......B 9
10 Five Oak Green...D 5
9 Five Oaks......C 12
63 Five Penny Borve .A 5
63 Five Penny Ness ..A 6
13 Five Roads......F 8
30 Fivecrosses......C 4
7 Fivehead......D 7
19 Flack's Green...B 7
17 Flackwell Heath...E 9
22 Fladbury......G 3
64 Fladdabister......E 7
31 Flagg......C 10
41 Flamborough....H 2
17 Flamstead......C 11
9 Flansham......F 11
35 Flappit Spring...C 9
35 Flasby......B 8
31 Flash......C 8
17 Flaunden......D 11
32 Flawborough....F 5
36 Flawith......A 3
15 Flax Bourton....G 8
35 Flaxby......A 12
15 Flaxley......C 10
6 Flaxpool......C 5
36 Flaxton......A 4
23 Fleckney......C 10
23 Flecknoe......F 8
7 Fleet, Dorset....H 9
9 Fleet, Hants....A 9
9 Fleet, Hants....F 8
24 Fleet, Lincs....C 5
33 Fleet Hargate...H 11
45 Fleetham......E 12
34 Fleetwood......B 2
14 Flemingston....G 3
47 Flemington, Lan..C 11
47 Flemington, Lan..E 12
27 Flempton......H 1
38 Fletchertown....A 4
10 Fletching......F 3
4 Flexbury......E 1
9 Flexford......A 10
38 Flimby......B 3
10 Flimwell......E 6
29 Flint......C 11
29 Flint Mountain ..C 11
32 Flintham......F 5
37 Flinton......D 10
24 Flitcham......C 8
25 Flitton......L 2
4 Flitton Barton...C 6
25 Flitwick......M 1
36 Flixborough......F 6
34 Flixton, Lancs....H 6
27 Flixton, Suffolk..G 6
41 Flixton, Yorks...G 10
35 Flockton......F 11
35 Flockton Green ..F 11
49 Flodden......F 11
63 Flodabay......H 2
62 Flodigarry Hotel..A 4
24 Flood's Ferry....F 5
38 Flookburgh......H 6
26 Flordon......F 5
23 Flore......F 9
45 Flotterton......C 8
35 Flouch Inn......G 10
27 Flowton......K 4
58 Flushing, Aber....C 8
2 Flushing, Cornwall F 5
6 Fluxton......G 4
22 Flyford Flavell...G 3
19 Fobbing......E 7
58 Fochabers......B 1
14 Fochriw......D 4
36 Fockerby......E 6
56 Fodderty......D 1
7 Foddington......C 9
20 Foel......A 5
13 Foelgastell......E 9
53 Foffarty......C 9
36 Foggathorpe....C 5
49 Fogo......D 10
49 Fogorig......E 10
60 Foindle......C 3
53 Folda......A 7
31 Fole......D 9
23 Foleshill......D 7
7 Folke......E 10
11 Folkestone......E 11
24 Folkingham......B 2

10 Folkington......H 4
24 Folksworth......F 2
41 Folkton......G 10
58 Folla Rule......D 5
35 Follifoot......B 12
4 Folly Gate......F 4
9 Folly Hill......A 9
14 Fonmon......G 4
8 Fonthill Bishop...C 1
12 Fonthill Gifford..C 12
7 Fontmell Magna .E 12
9 Fontwell......E 10
31 Foolow......C 10
18 Foots Cray......G 5
58 Forbestown......F 1
6 Forches Corner...D 5
50 Ford, Argyll......G 6
17 Ford, Bucks......C 8
5 Ford, Devon ....L 7
4 Ford, Devon....D 3
16 Ford, Glos......A 2
49 Ford, Northumb..F 12
21 Ford, Salop......A 9
6 Ford, Somerset...C 4
31 Ford, Staffs......E 9
9 Ford, Sussex......F 11
15 Ford, Wilts......G 11
6 Ford Barton......D 3
19 Ford End......B 7
6 Ford Street......D 5
6 Fordcombe......D 5
52 Fordel......F 6
52 Fordell......H 6
19 Fordham, Essex...A 9
24 Fordham, Norfolk E 7
22 Fordhouses......B 3
8 Fordingbridge....E 3
41 Fordon......H 10
59 Fordoun......K 5
19 Fordstreet......A 9
16 Fordwells......C 4
11 Fordwich......B 10
58 Fordyce......A 3
31 Forebridge......H 8
9 Forest Green......B 12
39 Forest Hall......E 8
44 Forest Head......G 4
17 Forest Hill......C 7
51 Forest Lo., Argyll C 10
57 Forest Lo., Inver..H 6
57 Forest Lo., Kirk..C 10
52 Forest Lo., Perth..A 4
52 Forest Mill......H 4
10 Forest Row.....,D 3
32 Forest Town......D 3
45 Forestburn Gate..C 9
56 Foresterseat......D 7
9 Forestside......E 9
53 Forfar......B 9
52 Forgandenny......E 6
14 Forge Hammer....E 6
14 Forge Side......D 6
58 Forgie......B 1
58 Forgieside......B 1
58 Forglen House....B 4
34 Formby......F 2
26 Forncett End......F 4
26 Forncett St. Mary.F 4
26 Forncett St. Peter.F 5
26 Forneth......C 6
27 Fornham All Saints J 1
27 Fornham St. Martin H 2
58 Forres......D 6
48 Forrestfield......C 1
31 Forsbrook......F 8
61 Forse......D 11
61 Forse House......D 11
61 Forsinain......C 9
61 Forsinard......C 9
61 Forsinard Station .C 8
7 Forston......G 10
55 Fort Augustus....J 7
56 Fort George......D 3
55 Fort William......M 5
61 Fortacres......F 9
52 Forteviot......E 5
48 Forth......D 2
11 Forthampton....A 11
52 Fortingall......B 2
8 Forton, Hants....B 6
34 Forton, Lancs....B 8
21 Forton, Salop....A 9
7 Forton, Somerset..E 7
31 Forton, Staffs....H 6
58 Fortrie......C 4
56 Fortrose......D 3
7 Fortuneswell.....H 7
17 Forty Green......E 10
25 Forty Feet Bridge.G 4
27 Forward Green...J 4

16 Fosbury......H 4
24 Fosdyke......B 4
24 Fosdyke Bridge ..B 4
52 Foss......A 3
11 Fossebridge......C 2
18 Foster Street......C 5
31 Fosterhouses......F 4
31 Foston, Derby...G 10
32 Foston, Lincs......F 6
36 Foston, Yorks......A 5
37 Foston on the Wolds
......B 8
33 Fotherby......A 10
24 Fotheringhay......F 2
64 Foubister......D 3
18 Foul Mile......F 5
49 Foulden, Berwick D 11
26 Foulden, Norfolk .E 1
55 Foulis Castle......C 1
36 Foulridge......C 7
26 Foulsham......C 3
58 Fountainbleau, Aber.
......D 8
58 Fountainbleau, Aber.
......E 7
49 Fountainhall......D 7
27 Four Ashes ......H 3
28 Four Crosses, Caer.F 3
29 Four Crosses, Mont.
......H 12
20 Four Crosses, Mont.
......B 6
22 Four Crosses, Staffs.
......A 3
10 Four Elms......C 3
6 Four Forks......C 6
34 Four Gate......F 5
24 Four Gotes ......D 5
30 Four Lane Ends, Ches.
......D 4
34 Four Lane Ends,
Lancashire......B 4
34 Four Lane Ends,
Lancashire......C 2
36 Four Lane Ends,
Yorkshire......B 4
39 Four Lane Ends,
Yorkshire......F 8
2 Four Lanes......F 4
9 Four Marks......C 8
28 Four Mile Bridge..B 2
15 Four Oaks, Glos. B 10
11 Four Oaks, Sussex.F 7
22 Four Oaks, War...D 6
22 Four Oaks, War...B 4
13 Four Roads, Carm.F 8
38 Four Roads, I.o.M.H 1
10 Four Throws......E 6
30 Fourlanes End......D 6
45 Fourlaws......E 7
45 Fourstones......F 7
58 Fovant......C 2
58 Foveran......E 7
1 Fowey......D 8
58 Fowlershill......F 7
10 Fowlhall......C 6
31 Fowlis......D 8
52 Fowlis Wester......E 4
25 Fowlmere......L 5
15 Fownhope......A 9
9 Fox Corner......A 11
17 Fox Lane......H 9
10 Foxcote......A 10
38 Foxdale......H 1
27 Foxearth......L 1
16 Foxfield......G 5
16 Foxham......F 1
3 Foxhole......D 7
41 Foxholes......H 10
17 Foxhunt Green...F 4
26 Foxley, Norfolk...C 3
15 Foxley, Wilts......F 12
31 Foxt......E 9
25 Foxton, Cambs....K 5
40 Foxton, Durham..C 4
23 Foxton, Leics. ..C 10
39 Foxup......G 11
30 Foxwist Green....C 5
21 Foxwood......E 11
15 Foy......A 9
57 Foyers......G 1
52 Foys......E 9
17 Fraddam......F 3
22 Fraddon......D 6
22 Fradley......A 5
31 Fradswell......G 8
31 Fraisthorpe......A 9
10 Framfield......F 4
26 Framingham Earl .E 6
26 Framingham Pigot .E 6
27 Framlingham......J 6
7 Frampton, Dorset.G 9
24 Frampton, Lincs...B 4

15 Frampton Cotterell F 9
15 Frampton Mansell
......D 12
15 Frampton on Severn
......D 10
24 Frampton West End
......B 4
27 Framsden......J 5
40 Framwellgate Moor
......A 3
22 Franche......D 2
30 Frandley......B 5
30 Frankby......B 1
22 Frankley......D 3
21 Frank's Bridge...G 7
23 Frankton......E 7
20 Frankwell, Mont...C 5
21 Frankwell, Salop. A 10
10 Frant......E 5
58 Fraserburgh......A 7
19 Frating......B 10
19 Frating Green....B 10
3 Freathy......D 11
32 Frecheville......B 1
25 Freckenham......H 8
34 Freckleton......D 3
32 Freeby......H 5
16 Freeland......C 5
26 Freethorpe......E 7
26 Freethorpe Com...E 7
24 Freiston......B 4
4 Fremington, Devon C 4
40 Fremington, Yorks.E 1
15 Frenchay......F 9
5 Frenchbeer......G 5
51 Frenich, Perth...G 11
52 Frenich, Perth ...A 3
9 Frensham......B 9
61 Fresgoe......A 9
34 Freshfield......F 2
8 Freshwater......G 5
12 Freshwater East...G 4
27 Fressingfield......H 6
61 Freswick......A 12
15 Fretherne ....C 10
26 Frettenham......D 5
53 Freuchie......F 7
12 Freystrop Cross...F 3
7 Friar Waddon...H 10
52 Friarton......E 6
24 Friday Bridge......E 6
10 Friday Street......H 5
36 Fridaythorpe......A 6
18 Friern Barnet......E 3
33 Friesthorpe......B 8
32 Frieston......E 6
17 Frieth......E 9
16 Frilford......D 5
16 Frilsham......G 6
17 Frimley......H 9
17 Frimley Green ...H 10
10 Frindsbury......A 6
24 Fring......B 8
17 Fringford......A 7
11 Frinsted......B 7
19 Frinton......B 12
53 Friockheim......B 10
20 Friog......A 2
32 Frisby on the Wreake
......H 4
33 Friskney......E 11
27 Friston, Suffolk...J 7
10 Friston, Sussex...H 4
32 Fritchley......E 1
33 Frith Bank ......E 10
21 Frith Common...E 12
8 Fritham......E 4
4 Frithelstock......D 3
4 Frithelstock Stone.D 3
17 Frithsden......C 11
33 Frithville......E 10
11 Frittenden......D 7
26 Fritton, Norfolk...F 5
26 Fritton, Norfolk...E 7
38 Frizington......D 3
15 Frocester......D 11
21 Frochas......B 7
21 Frodesley......B 10
37 Frodingham......F 7
30 Frodsham......B 4
49 Frogden......G 10
31 Froggatt......C 11
7 Frogham, Hants...H 9
15 Frogland Cross...F 9
5 Frogmore, Devon .L 6
17 Frogmore, Hants..H 9
7 Frome......B 11
5 Frome St. Quintin F 9
21 Fromes Hill......H 12
28 Fron, Caer......E 4
28 Fron, Caer......F 3

13 Fron, Carm......D 11
21 Fron, Mont......B 8
20 Fron, Rad......F 6
29 Fron Isaf......F 12
29 Froncysyllte .....F 12
29 Fron-deg......E 12
29 Frongoch......F 8
28 Fron-oleu......G 6
39 Frosterley......A 12
64 Frotoft......B 2
16 Froxfield......G 4
9 Froxfield Green...D 8
6 Froyle......B 9
18 Fryerning......D 6
41 Fryton......H 7
32 Fulbeck......E 6
25 Fulbourn......K 6
16 Fulbrook......C 4
6 Fulford, Somerset .C 5
31 Fulford, Staffs......F 8
36 Fulford, Yorks......B 4
18 Fulham......F 2
10 Fulking......G 1
36 Full Sutton......B 5
4 Fullaford......B 6
47 Fullarton......F 8
19 Fuller Street......B 7
30 Fuller's Moor......E 4
8 Fullerton......B 5
33 Fulletby......C 10
58 Fulwood......A 5
47 Fullwood......D 9
17 Fulmer......F 10
26 Fulmodeston......B 3
33 Fulnetby......B 5
37 Fulstow......G 11
34 Fulwood, Lancs...D 4
6 Fulwood, Som...D 5
9 Funtington......E 9
9 Funtley......E 7
52 Funtullich......D 2
64 Funzie......B 8
6 Furley......F 6
51 Furnace, Argyll...G 7
54 Furnace, Ross &
Cromarty......C 3
22 Furnace End......C 6
10 Furner's Green ...E 3
36 Furness......E 5
31 Furness Vale......B 8
18 Furneux Pelham ..A 4
17 Furze Platt......F 9
7 Furzebrook......H 12
4 Furzehill......B 6
6 Fyfett......E 6
16 Fyfield, Berks....D 5
18 Fyfield, Essex....C 6
16 Fyfield, Glos....D 3
8 Fyfield, Hants....A 4
16 Fyfield, Wilts....G 2
41 Fyling Thorpe...E 9
58 Fyvie......D 5
47 Gabroc Hill......D 9
23 Gaddesby......A 10
47 Gadgirth......G 9
14 Gaer......B 5
28 Gaerwen......C 4
16 Gagingwell......B 5
57 Gaick Lodge......L 3
47 Gailes......F 8
22 Gailey......A 3
40 Gainford......C 2
32 Gainsborough, Lincs.
......A 5
27 Gainsborough, Suffolk
......L 5
25 Gainsford End....L 8
59 Gairloch, Aber....G 5
43 Gairloch, Dumf..D 11
54 Gairloch, Ross &
Cromarty......B 2
55 Gairlochy......L 6
52 Gairney Bank....G 6
57 Gairnshiel Lodge ..J 8
39 Gaisgill......E 8
44 Gaitsgill......H 2
48 Galalaw......E 3
49 Galashiels......F 7
21 Galdenoch......B 3
49 Galewood......F 12
34 Galgate......B 4
7 Gallampton......B 9
43 Gallaberry......C 10
50 Gallanach......E 5
50 Gallanachmore...E 5
22 Galley Common ..C 6
19 Galleyend......D 7
19 Galleywood......D 7
51 Gallin......C 12
53 Gallowfauld......C 9
22 Gallows Green....F 3
31 Gallows Green....F 9

55 Galltair......G 2
5 Galmpton, Devon .K 7
5 Galmpton, Devon M 6
40 Galphay......H 3
47 Galston......F 10
62 Galtrigill......C 1
43 Galtway......G 8
39 Gamblesby......A 8
25 Gamlingay......K 3
4 Gammaton Moor .D 4
40 Gammersgill......G 1
58 Gamrie......A 5
32 Gamston, Notts...C 4
32 Gamston, Notts...F 3
15 Ganarew......C 8
50 Ganavan......D 6
28 Ganllwyd......H 6
59 Gannachy......K 3
52 Gannochy......E 6
30 Gannow Hill......G 2
37 Ganstead......D 9
41 Ganthorpe......H 7
41 Ganton......G 10
50 Gaodhail......D 3
54 Garbat......C 8
51 Garbhallt......H 7
26 Garboldisham.....G 3
57 Garbole......G 3
29 Garden City......C 12
58 Gardenstown......A 5
64 Garderhouse......D 5
37 Gardham......C 7
7 Gare Hill......B 11
51 Garelochhead ...H 9
16 Garford......E 5
36 Garforth......D 2
35 Gargrave......B 8
52 Gargunnock......H 2
63 Garinin......C 3
28 Garizim......C 6
42 Garlieston......G 5
11 Garlinge Green...C 9
58 Garlogie......B 5
58 Garmond......B 5
50 Garmony......D 4
58 Garmouth......A 1
28 Garn......G 2
28 Garn-Dolbenmaen F 4
13 Garnant......F 10
14 Garndiffaith......D 6
39 Garnett Bridge...E 7
47 Garnkirk......C 11
14 Garnlydan......C 5
13 Garnswllt......F 9
13 Garn-yr-erw......C 5
63 Garrabost......D 6
57 Garragie......H 1
2 Garras......G 4
28 Garreg......F 5
52 Garrick......F 3
39 Garrigill......A 9
40 Garriston......F 2
43 Garroch......C 7
42 Garrochtrie......B 4
62 Garros......B 4
52 Garrow......C 3
47 Garryhorn......H 8
39 Garsdale Head...F 10
16 Garsdon......E 1
31 Garshall Green ...G 8
17 Garsington......D 7
34 Garstang......C 4
30 Garston......B 3
34 Garswood......G 4
51 Gartachoil......H 12
47 Gartcosh......C 11
20 Garth, Brec......G 5
29 Garth, Denb. ...F 11
30 Garth, Glam......E 2
38 Garth, I.o.M......H 2
52 Garth House......B 2
14 Garth Place......E 5
47 Garthamlock......C 11
14 Garthbrengy......A 4
59 Garthdee......C 7
21 Garthmyl......C 7
32 Garthorpe, Leics. .H 5
37 Garthorpe, Lincs..E 6
58 Gartly......D 3
51 Gartmore......H 12
46 Gartnagrenach....C 3
47 Gartness......A 10
47 Gartocharn......A 9
21 Garton......D 10
37 Garton-on-the-Wolds
......A 7
61 Gartymore......E 9
49 Garvald, E. Loth. .B 8
48 Garvald, Midloth. .D 6
54 Garvamore......K 1
55 Garvan......M 3
50 Garvard......H 1
54 Garve......D 8

MAP

26 Garvestone......E 3
59 Garvock, Kinc...K 5
47 Garvock, Renfrew.B 7
15 Garway........B 8
63 Garynahine .....D 3
58 Gash of Philorth..A 7
55 Gaskan..........M 2
7 Gaspar..........C 11
42 Gass............A 5
43 Gasstown......D 10
47 Gasswater......G 11
15 Gastard......G 12
27 Gasthorpe......G 3
8 Gatcombe ......H 6
36 Gate Helmsley...B 5
30 Gateacre......A 3
39 Gatebeck......G 8
36 Gateforth......D 3
47 Gatehead, Ayr...F 9
44 Gatehouse, Northumb.
                    D 6
52 Gatehouse, Perth..B 4
43 Gatehouse of Fleet F 7
43 Gatelawbridge ...B 10
26 Gateley..........C 3
40 Gatenby......F 3
38 Gatesgarth......D 4
49 Gateshaw......G 10
45 Gateshead......G 10
30 Gatesheath......D 3
53 Gateside, Angus...C 9
47 Gateside, Ayr...D 8
52 Gateside, Fife...F 6
56 Gateside, Moray..D 7
47 Gateside, Renfrew B 8
43 Gateslack......A 10
34 Gathurst........F 4
31 Gatley..........A 7
10 Gatton..........C 3
49 Gattonside......F 8
20 Gaufron......F 5
23 Gaulby........B 10
53 Gauldry......E 6
24 Gaultree......E 6
8 Gaunt's Common..F 2
33 Gautby........C 9
49 Gavinton......D 10
58 Gawanhill......A 8
35 Gawber........F 11
17 Gawcott......A 8
38 Gawthwaite......G 5
23 Gaydon......G 7
23 Gayhurst......G 11
39 Gayle........F 11
40 Gayles..........D 1
30 Gayton, Cheshire.B 1
24 Gayton, Norfolk..D 8
23 Gayton, Northants.
                    G 10
31 Gayton, Staffs...G 8
33 Gayton le Marsh.B 11
33 Gayton le Wold..B 9
24 Gayton Thorpe..D 8
24 Gaywood......C 7
25 Gazeley......J 8
62 Geary..........B 2
56 Geddes House...D 4
27 Gedding......J 2
23 Geddington...D 12
62 Gedintailor......E 4
24 Gedney......C 5
24 Gedney Broadgate.C 5
24 Gedney Drove End
                    C 6
24 Gedney Dyke...C 5
24 Gedney Hill......D 4
35 Gee Cross......H 8
60 Geisgeil......C 3
26 Geldeston......F 7
29 Gell............C 8
14 Gelli..........E 3
14 Gellideg........D 3
14 Gelligaer......E 5
28 Gellilydan......F 6
13 Gellinudd......G 10
29 Gellioedd......F 8
52 Gellyburn......C 6
43 Gelston......F 8
37 Gembling......A 9
42 Genoch Square...F 2
22 Gentleshaw......A 4
63 Geocrab......H 2
17 George Green....F 11
4 George Nympton .D 6
44 Georgefield......D 1
4 Georgeham......B 3
43 Georgetown, Dumf.
                    D 10
14 Georgetown, Mon.C 5
47 Georgetown, Ren..C 9
61 Georgmas Junction
    Station......B 11
64 Georth..........C 2

28 Gerlan..........C 6
4 Germansweek....F 3
2 Germoe..........G 3
2 Gerrans......F 6
43 Gerranton......E 8
17 Gerrards Cross...E 11
63 Geshader......D 2
27 Gestingthorpe...L 1
21 Geuffordd......A 7
43 Gibbshill......D 8
33 Gibraltar......D 12
15 Giddeahall......G 11
18 Gidea Park......E 5
5 Gidleigh........G 5
49 Gifford........C 8
53 Giffordtown......F 7
35 Giggleswick......A 7
36 Gilberdyke......D 6
43 Gilchristland....B 10
49 Gilchriston......C 7
43 Gilcrux ......H 12
35 Gildersome......D 11
32 Gildingwells......B 3
40 Gilesgate Moor...A 3
14 Gileston......H 3
14 Gilfach......D 5
14 Gilfach Goch......E 3
13 Gilfachrheda......A 7
41 Gillamoor......F 7
43 Gillenbie......C 12
43 Gillesbie......B 12
42 Gillespie......F 3
40 Gilling East......G 6
40 Gilling West......E 2
7 Gillingham, Dorset
                    D 11
11 Gillingham, Kent .A 7
26 Gillingham,
    Norfolk......F 7
61 Gillock......B 11
31 Gillow Heath......D 7
43 Gillroanie........G 8
61 Gills..........A 12
26 Gill's Green ......E 6
48 Gilmanscleuch....G 6
48 Gilmerton, Midloth.
                    C 5
52 Gilmerton, Perth ..E 4
39 Gilmonby......D 12
23 Gilmorton......C 9
44 Gilsland......F 5
44 Gilsland Spa......F 5
49 Gilston......D 7
14 Gilwern......C 6
26 Gimingham......B 6
27 Gipping......J 4
33 Gipsey Bridge...E 10
47 Girdle Toll......E 8
64 Girlsta........D 7
40 Girsby........D 4
25 Girtford......K 3
14 Girthill......E 7
43 Girthon........F 7
25 Girton, Cambs...J 5
32 Girton, Notts...D 5
42 Girvan........B 3
42 Girvan Mains......B 3
35 Gisburn......B 7
63 Gisla..........D 2
26 Gisleham......F 8
27 Gislingham......H 4
27 Gissing......G 4
6 Gittisham......F 5
10 Givons Grove...C 1
52 Glack........D 5
56 Glackbea......F 1
56 Glackossian......F 2
11 Gladdish......C 7
21 Gladestry......G 8
28 Gladhouse......D 6
49 Gladsmuir......B 7
31 Gladwin's Mark .D 11
33 Glais........G 10
41 Glaisdale......E 8
43 Glaisters......D 8
53 Glamis........B 8
13 Glan Duar......C 8
28 Glan-Dwyfach......F 4
28 Glanaber......E 6
13 Glanamman....F 10
26 Glandford......B 3
14 Glandwr........D 5
12 Glan-dwr......D 5
20 Glandyfi......C 3
14 Glangrwyney......C 5
14 Glanllynfi........E 2
21 Glan-miwl......C 7
12 Glanryd........C 5
14 Glan-ryd, Brec...C 1
12 Glan-ryd, Pemb...D 5
25 Glanton........B 9
45 Glanton Pike......B 9
7 Glanvilles WoottonE10

29 Glan-y-don......B 11
20 Glan-y-nant......D 5
29 Glanyrafon......F 9
28 Glan-y-Wern......G 5
24 Glapthorn......F 1
32 Glapwell........D 2
57 Glas-allt Shiel....L 8
21 Glasbury......H 7
56 Glaschoil......F 6
38 Glascoe........F 2
29 Glascoed......C 9
58 Glascoforest......F 5
22 Glascote........B 6
21 Glascwm........G 7
51 Glasdrum......C 7
29 Glasfryn......E 8
47 Glasgow......C 10
62 Glashvin......A 4
28 Glasinfryn......C 5
59 Glaslaw........J 6
55 Glasnacardoch, Inver.
                    K 1
55 Glasnacardoch, Inver.
                    K 1
62 Glasnakille......G 5
20 Glaspwll........C 3
54 Glassburn......F 7
42 Glasserton......H 5
47 Glassford......E 12
15 Glasshouse Hill..B 10
35 Glasshouses......A 10
53 Glasslie........G 7
42 Glassoch......E 4
44 Glasson, Cumb...G 1
34 Glasson, Lancs...B 3
39 Glassonby......A 8
53 Glasterlaw......B 10
23 Glaston......B 12
7 Glastonbury......B 8
47 Glastron......H 8
25 Glatton......G 2
34 Glazebury......G 5
21 Glazely........D 12
32 Gleadless Townend B 1
38 Gleaston......H 5
46 Glecknabae......C 5
43 Gledpark......F 7
44 Gledsnest......B 3
46 Glemanuilt......H 1
27 Glemsford......K 1
58 Glen, Banff....D 2
42 Glen, Kirk.....F 6
43 Glen, Kirk.....D 9
52 Glen, Perth....E 6
38 Glen Auldyn....G 2
58 Glen Barry....B 3
62 Glen Bernisdale...C 3
50 Glen Borrodale...A 3
57 Glen Clunie Lodge L 7
58 Glen Dronoch....C 4
48 Glen House....F 6
38 Glen Mona....G 2
55 Glen Nevis House.M 5
23 Glen Parva....B 9
59 Glen Tanar House H 2
63 Glen Tolsta....B 6
48 Glen Village....B 2
38 Glen Vine....G 2
55 Glenancross....K 1
50 Glenaros House...C 3
46 Glenbarr......F 2
50 Glenbeg, Argyll ..A 3
57 Glenbeg, Moray...B 6
59 Glenbervie......J 5
47 Glenboig......C 12
51 Glenbranter......H 8
48 Glenbreck......G 3
55 Glenbrein Lodge .H 8
62 Glenbrittle House .F 3
58 Glenbuchat Lodge.F 1
47 Glenbuck......F 12
47 Glenburn......C 9
59 Glencally......L 1
60 Glencalvie Lodge .G 5
60 Glencanisp Lodge..E 3
43 Glencaple......E 10
54 Glencarron Lodge .E 4
53 Glencarse......B 9
60 Glencassley Castle.F 5
46 Glencloy......F 5
51 Glencoe........B 8
57 Glenconglass....G 7
52 Glencraig......H 6
50 Glencripesdale....B 4
58 Glencuie......F 2
59 Glendavan House .G 2
44 Glendearg, Dumf..C 1
49 Glendearg, Selkirk.F 8
52 Glendevon......G 5
55 Glendoe Lodge .H 8
55 Glendoebeg.....J 8
53 Glendoik......E 7
57 Glendoll Lodge...M 8

53 Glenduckie......E 7
59 Glendye Lodge....J 4
52 Gleneagles Hotel ..F 4
55 Gleneig........H 2
56 Glenerney......E 6
51 Glenfalloch Farm F 10
52 Glenfarg......F 6
59 Glenfenzie......G 1
56 Glenferness House.E 5
58 Glenfiddich Lodge D 1
23 Glenfield......B 9
47 Glenfinart House..A 7
55 Glenfinnan......L 3
55 Glenfintaig Lodge .L 6
52 Glenfoot......F 6
55 Glenforslan......M 1
51 Glenfyne Lodge .F 9
43 Glengap......F 7
29 Glengarnock......D 8
52 Glengoulandie...B 3
62 Glengrasco......D 4
51 Glengyle......F 11
42 Glengyre......E 1
43 Glenhead, Kirk...F 8
52 Glenhead, Perth ..G 4
53 Glenhead Farm...A 7
48 Glenhighton......F 4
42 Glenhoise......E 5
43 Glenholm......D 12
43 Glenhoul......C 7
50 Glenhurich......A 5
48 Glenkerry......H 5
43 Glenkiln......D 9
58 Glenkindie......F 2
48 Glenkirk......F 3
13 Glenlatterach......D 7
43 Glenlee......C 7
57 Glenlia......H 1
57 Glenlochsie......M 6
46 Glenloig......G 4
42 Glenluce......F 3
57 Glenmarksie......D 7
46 Glenmassan......A 6
38 Glenmaye......G 1
54 Glenmeanne......D 7
43 Glenmidge......C 9
38 Glenmooar......G 2
50 Glenmore, Argyll .F 6
50 Glenmore, Argyll .A 3
62 Glenmore, Inver...D 4
55 Glenmore Lodge .H 5
50 Glenmorven Cott..B 3
42 Glenmuck......A 6
48 Glenochar......H 2
59 Glenquiech......L 2
48 Glenrath......F 5
59 Glenridding......D 4
46 Glenrisdell......D 4
60 Glenrossal......F 5
53 Glenrothes......G 7
42 Glenruther......C 9
50 Glensanda......C 5
47 Glensaugh......J 4
52 Glenshee......D 5
43 Glenshimmeroch..C 7
57 Glenshirra Lodge .K 1
47 Glenside, Ayr...D 7
63 Glenside, Ross &
    Cromarty......E 5
51 Glensluain......H 8
46 Glenstriven......B 6
55 Glensulaig......L 4
48 Glentaggart......G 1
33 Glentham......A 7
48 Glentress, Peebles .E 5
48 Glentress, Peebles .E 6
57 Glentromie Lodge.K 3
42 Glentrool Village .D 4
38 Glentruan......F 2
57 Glentruim House..K 2
32 Glentworth......A 6
56 Glenurquhart....C 3
43 Glenwhargen......A 8
42 Glenwhilly......D 3
48 Glespin......G 1
43 Glewstone......B 9
64 Gletness......D 7
59 Glewstone......B 9
24 Glinton......E 3
59 Glithno........H 6
23 Glooston......C 11
35 Glossop......H 9
45 Gloster Hill......C 10
15 Gloucester......C 11
15 Gloucestershire, Co.
                    D 10
64 Gloup........A 7
2 Gloweth......A 5
35 Glusburn......C 8
53 Glutt Lodge ...D 9
2 Gluvian......C 5
16 Glympton......B 5
29 Glyn..........D 7

12 Glyn-Arthen......B 6
29 Glyn Ceiriog......F 11
20 Glynbrochan......D 5
14 Glyncoch......E 4
14 Glyncorrwg......D 2
10 Glynde......G 3
10 Glyndebourne....G 3
29 Glyndyfrdwy....F 10
28 Glynllifon Park...E 4
14 Glynneath......D 2
14 Glyntaff......E 4
13 Glynteg......C 7
31 Gnosall......H 7
31 Gnosall Heath ...H 7
23 Goadby......B 11
32 Goadby Marwood.H 5
14 Goat Lees......C 9
16 Goatacre......F 1
7 Goathill......E 10
41 Goathland......E 8
10 Goathurst......C 6
10 Goathurst Com....C 4
60 Gobernuisgach Lodge
                    C 5
30 Gobowen......G 2
9 Godalming......B 11
11 Goddard's Green .E 7
10 Godden Green....C 4
5 Godford Cross....F 5
25 Godmanchester...H 3
7 Godmanston....F 10
11 Godmersham....C 9
9 Godney........B 8
2 Godolphin Cross .F 3
9 Godre'r-graig....F 11
56 Godshill, Hants...E 3
9 Godshill, I.o.W...H 7
10 Godstone......C 2
8 Godwinscroft......F 3
14 Goetre......D 6
18 Goff's Oak......D 3
48 Gogar......B 4
20 Gogfnan......D 2
28 Golan........F 5
3 Golant......D 8
3 Golberdon ......C 10
35 Golborne......G 5
35 Golcar........E 9
24 Gold Hill, Cambs..F 6
7 Gold Hill, Dorset E 11
15 Goldcliff......F 7
16 Golden Balls......D 6
10 Golden Cross.....G 4
10 Golden Green....C 5
13 Golden Grove....E 9
8 Golden Hill, Hants.F 4
12 Golden Hill, Pem..G 3
9 Golden Pot......B 8
15 Golden Valley ..B 12
31 Goldenhill......E 7
18 Golders Green...E 3
19 Goldhanger......C 9
21 Golding........B 11
25 Goldington......K 2
41 Goldsborough,
    N. Riding......D 8
36 Goldsborough,
    W. Riding......B 5
2 Goldsithney......G 3
30 Goldstone......G 6
36 Goldthorpe......G 3
4 Goldworthy......D 3
56 Gollanfield......D 4
15 Gollinglith Foot ..G 2
6 Golsoncott......B 4
61 Golspie......G 8
9 Golval........B 9
8 Gomeldon......C 3
35 Gomersal......E 10
54 Gometra House...C 1
9 Gomshall......A 12
32 Gonalston......E 4
64 Gonfirth......D 7
18 Good Easter......C 6
26 Gooderstone......E 1
43 Goodhope......B 11
10 Goodleigh......C 5
36 Goodmanham....C 6
11 Goodnestone, Kent
                    C 11
11 Goodnestone, KentB 9
23 Goodrich......C 9
5 Goodrington......K 8
12 Goodwick......C 3
8 Goodworth Clatford
                    B 5
23 Goodyers End....D 7
36 Goole..........E 5
36 Goole Fields ....E 5
2 Goonbell......E 4
2 Goonhavern......D 5
10 Goose Green....C 5
59 Goosecruives......J 5

4 Gooseham........D 1
43 Goosehill......A 8
5 Goosewell......K 4
16 Goosey........E 4
34 Goosnargh......C 4
30 Goostrey......C 6
22 Gorcott Hill......E 4
28 Gorddinog......C 6
49 Gordon........E 9
61 Gordonbush......F 8
58 Gordonstown,
    Aberdeen......D 5
58 Gordonstown, Banff
                    B 3
48 Gorebridge......C 6
24 Gorefield......D 5
17 Goring........F 7
9 Goring-by-Sea....F 12
17 Goring Heath....F 7
26 Gorleston on Sea..B 8
22 Gornalwood......C 3
3 Gorran Churchtown
                    E 7
3 Gorran Haven....E 7
44 Gorrenberry......C 3
20 Gors..........E 2
16 Gorse Hill......E 3
29 Gorsedd......C 10
13 Gorseinon......G 9
64 Gorseness......C 2
31 Gorseybank......E 11
13 Gorsgoch......B 8
13 Gorslas........F 9
15 Gorsley......B 10
54 Gorstan......D 7
55 Gorstanvorran....M 2
30 Gorstella......D 2
15 Gorsty Common ..A 8
35 Gorton........G 7
27 Gosbeck......K 5
24 Gosberton......B 3
24 Gosberton Clough.C 3
27 Gosfield......M 1
21 Gosford......F 10
49 Gosford House....B 7
38 Gosforth, Cumb...E 3
45 Gosforth, Northumb.
                    F 10
18 Gosmore......A 2
9 Gosport......F 7
21 Gossabrough......C 8
45 Goswick......B 12
32 Gotham......G 3
16 Gotherington......A 1
10 Goudhurst......D 6
33 Goulceby......B 9
47 Gourock......B 7
58 Gourdas......C 5
59 Gourdon......K 6
47 Govan......C 10
32 Goverton......E 4
5 Goveton......L 6
14 Govilon......C 6
36 Gowdall......E 4
9 Gower........D 1
13 Gowerton......G 9
52 Gowkhall......H 5
36 Gowthorpe......B 5
33 Goxhill, Lincs...E 9
37 Goxhill, Yorks...C 9
37 Goxhill Haven....E 9
31 Goytre........H 11
43 Gracefield......C 9
49 Graden......F 10
21 Graffham......D 10
25 Grafham, Hunts. .H 3
9 Grafham, Surrey .B 11
23 Grafton, Herefs...A 8
16 Grafton, Oxon....D 4
30 Grafton, Salop...H 3
21 Grafton, Worcs..F 11
36 Grafton, Yorks...A 2
22 Grafton Flyford...G 3
23 Grafton Regis. G 11
23 Grafton Underwood
                    D 12
11 Grafty Green....C 7
29 Graianrhyd......E 11
29 Graig..........C 7
29 Graig-fechan....E 10
48 Graigmillar......B 6
19 Grain..........F 9
13 Grainsby......G 10
37 Grainthorpe......G 11
2 Grampound......E 6
2 Grampound Road.E 6
17 Granborough......B 8
32 Granby........G 5
23 Grandborough....E 8
52 Grandtully......B 4
34 Grane..........E 6
15 Grange, Ayr......F 9
30 Grange, Cheshire.B 1

MAP
38 Grange, Cumb....C 5
53 Grange, Fife.....F 10
53 Grange, Perth....E 7
40 Grange, Yorks.....F 6
58 Grange Crossroads B 2
7 Grange Gate....H 12
56 Grange Hall......D 6
35 Grange Moor......E 11
53 Grange of Lindores E 7
45 Grange Villa....H 10
48 Grangehall.......E 2
31 Grangemill......D 11
48 Grangemouth.....A 2
38 Grange-over-Sands G 6
48 Grangepans......A 3
14 Grangetown, Glam. G 5
40 Grangetown, Yks..C 6
57 Granish..........H 5
37 Gransmoor........A 9
12 Granston........D 2
25 Grantchester......K 5
32 Grantham........G 6
58 Grantlodge.......F 5
48 Granton, Dumf...H 3
48 Granton, Midloth..B 5
57 Grantown-on-Spey G 6
21 Grantsfield......F 10
49 Grantshouse.....C 10
30 Grappenhall......B 5
37 Grasby..........G 8
38 Grasmere........D 6
35 Grasscroft........G 8
30 Grassendale.......B 3
39 Grassholme......C 11
35 Grassington......A 9
45 Grasslees.........C 8
25 Grassmoor.......D 1
32 Grassthorpe......C 5
8 Grateley..........B 4
31 Gratwich.........G 9
18 Graveley, Herts...A 2
25 Graveley, Hunts...J 4
22 Gravelly Hill......C 5
11 Graveney.........B 9
10 Gravesend........A 5
63 Gravir...........E 5
37 Grayingham......G 7
39 Grayrigg.........E 8
18 Grays............F 6
9 Grayshott.......C 10
9 Grayswood.......C 10
40 Graythorp........B 5
17 Grazeley.........G 8
36 Greasbrough.....H 2
30 Greasby..........B 1
32 Greasley.........E 2
25 Great Abington...K 6
25 Great Addington..H 1
22 Great Alne.......F 5
34 Great Altcar......F 2
18 Great Amwell.....C 4
39 Great Asby.......D 9
27 Great Ashfield....H 3
40 Great Ayton......D 6
19 Great Baddow....C 7
15 Great Badminton.F 11
25 Great Bardfield...M 8
25 Great Barford.....K 2
22 Great Barr.......C 4
16 Great Barrington..C 3
30 Great Barrow......C 3
27 Great Barton.......J 2
41 Great Barugh.....G 7
45 Great Bavington..E 8
27 Great Bealings....K 5
26 Great Bedwyn....H 4
19 Great Bentley....B 11
23 Great Billing.....F 11
26 Great Bircham....B 1
27 Great Blakenham .K 4
39 Great Blencow.....B 7
30 Great Bolas.......H 5
9 Great Bookham..A 12
23 Great Bourton ...H 8
23 Great Bowden....C 11
25 Great Bradley.....K 8
19 Great Braxted.....C 8
27 Great Bricett......K 3
17 Great Brickhill...A 10
31 Great Bridgeford..G 7
23 Great Brington...F 10
19 Great Bromley....A 10
30 Great Budworth...B 5
40 Great Burdon.....D 3
19 Great Burstead....E 7
40 Great Busby.......E 5
18 Great Canfield....B 6
33 Great Carlton....B 11
24 Great Casterton...E 1
15 Great Chalfield...H 4
11 Great Chart......D 8

MAP
22 Great Chatwell....A 1
25 Great Chesterford .L 6
8 Great Cheverell...A 1
25 Great Chishill.....L 5
19 Great Clacton....B 11
38 Great Clifton.....B 3
37 Great Coate......F 10
22 Great Comberton .H 3
44 Great Corby .....H 3
27 Great Cornard....L 2
37 Great Cowden...C 10
16 Great Coxwell....E 4
40 Great Crakehall...F 3
23 Great Cransley ..D 11
26 Great Cressingham E 1
34 Great Crosby.....G 2
31 Great Cubley....F 10
23 Great Dalby.....A 10
23 Gt. Doddington ..F 12
6 Great Dorweeke...F 3
15 Great Doward.....C 9
26 Great Dunham....D 2
18 Great Dunmow....B 6
8 Great Durnford....B 3
18 Great Easton, Essex A 6
23 Great Easton, Leics. C 11
34 Great Eccleston....C 3
41 Great Edstone....G 7
26 Great Ellingham...F 3
7 Great Elm.......A 10
25 Great Eversden ...K 5
40 Great Fencote.....F 3
27 Great Finborough .J 3
26 Great Fransham ..D 2
17 Great Gaddesden C 11
25 Great Gidding.....G 2
36 Great Givendale ..B 6
27 Great Glemham ...J 6
23 Great Glen......B 10
32 Great Gonerby.....F 6
15 Great Graig.......B 7
25 Great Gransden....K 4
26 Great Green, Norf.F 6
27 Great Green, Suff..K 2
41 Great Habton.....G 8
24 Great Hale.......A 2
18 Great Hallingbury.B 5
21 Great Hanwood .B 10
23 Great Harrowden.E 12
34 Great Harwood...D 6
27 Great Haseley....D 7
37 Great Hatfield....C 9
31 Great Haywood...H 8
23 Great Heath.......D 7
36 Great Heck.......E 4
27 Great Henny......L 2
15 Great Hinton ....H 12
26 Great Hockham...F 2
19 Great Holland....B 12
27 Great Horkesley..M 3
25 Great Hormead ..M 5
35 Great Horton ....D 10
17 Great Horwood...A 8
23 Great Houghton, Northants.......F 11
36 Great Houghton, Yorkshire.......F 2
31 Great Hucklow ..B 10
37 Great Kelk.......A 8
17 Great Kimble ....D 9
17 Great Kingshill...D 9
40 Great Langton ....F 3
19 Great Leighs......B 7
37 Great Limber.....F 9
23 Great Linford ...H 12
27 Great Livermere ..H 2
31 Great Longstone .C 10
45 Great Lumley....H 11
22 Great Malvern....G 2
27 Great Maplestead.M 1
34 Great Marton ....D 2
26 Great Massingham C 1
26 Great Melton.....E 4
17 Great Milton.....D 7
17 Great Missenden D 10
34 Great Mitton.....C 6
11 Great Mongeham C 12
34 Great Moss........G 4
39 Great Musgrave .D 10
30 Great Ness ....H 3
19 Great Oakley, Essex A 11
23 Great Oakley, Northants.....D 12
18 Great Offley......A 1
39 Great Ormside....C 9
44 Great Orton......H 2
36 Great Ouseburn...A 2
23 Great Oxendon...D 10
18 Great Oxney Grn..C 6
26 Great Palgrave ...D 1

MAP
18 Great Parndon....C 4
25 Great Paxton......J 3
34 Great Plumpton ..D 3
26 Great Plumstead ..D 6
32 Great Ponton.....G 6
36 Great Preston ....D 2
25 Great Raveley....G 4
16 Great Rissington..B 3
16 Great Rollright...A 4
12 Great Rudbaxton .E 3
26 Great Ryburgh ...C 3
45 Great Ryle.......B 8
19 Great Saling.......A 7
39 Great Salkeld.....B 8
25 Great Sampford...L 7
30 Great Sankey.....A 4
30 Great Saughall....C 2
27 Great Saxham......J 1
16 Great Shefford....G 5
25 Great Shelford....K 6
40 Great Smeaton....E 4
26 Great Snoring.....B 2
16 Great Somerford ..F 1
30 Great Soudley ....G 6
40 Great Stainton....C 3
19 Great Stambridge .E 9
25 Great Staughton...J 2
33 Great Steeping...D 11
11 Great Stonar....B 12
39 Great Strickland ..C 8
25 Great Stukeley....H 3
33 Great Sturton.....C 9
30 Gt. Sutton, Ches. .C 2
21 Gt. Sutton, Salop. D 10
45 Great Swinburne ..E 7
19 Great Tarpots ....E 7
16 Great Tew........A 5
19 Great Tey........A 9
25 Great Thurlow....K 8
4 Great Torrington .D 4
45 Great Tosson.....C 8
19 Great Totham ....C 8
38 Great Urswick ....H 5
19 Great Wakering....E 9
27 Great Waldingfield L 2
26 Great Walsingham B 2
19 Great Waltham ...C 7
18 Great Warley.....E 6
16 Great Washbourne A 1
27 Great Welnetham..J 2
27 Great Wenham....L 4
45 Great Whittington.F 8
19 Great Wigborough B 9
25 Great Wilbraham..J 6
8 Great Wishford ...C 2
15 Great Witcombe .C 12
22 Great Witley......E 1
16 Great Wolford....A 3
23 Great Woolstone .H 12
25 Great Wratting....K 8
18 Great Wymondley.A 2
22 Great Wyrley .....A 3
30 Great Wytheford..H 4
26 Great Yarmouth ..E 8
27 Great Yeldam.....L 1
18 Greater London,Co.F3
35 Greater Manchester, Co.............G 7
24 Greatford ....D 2
31 Greatgate.........F 9
40 Greatham, Dur....B 5
9 Greatham, Hants..C 9
9 Greatham, Sussex E 11
11 Greatstone-on-Sea.F 9
23 Greatworth ......H 9
25 Green End........K 2
36 Green Hammerton A 2
7 Green Ore........A 9
10 Green Street Green A 5
18 Green Tye........B 4
34 Greenbank ....B 4
43 Greenbeck.......C 11
48 Greenburn ....C 2
38 Greendale........E 4
7 Greendown........A 9
45 Greendykes......C 12
49 Greenend.........G 8
25 Greenfield, Beds. .M 2
29 Greenfield, Ches..B 11
55 Greenfield, Inver...J 6
17 Greenfield, Oxon. .E 8
35 Greenfield, Yorks..G 8
18 Greenford........F 1
48 Greengairs........B 1
48 Greengate Well....F 5
34 Greenhalgh.......D 3
16 Greenham, Berks. H 6
6 Greenham, Som...D 4
44 Greenhaugh ......D 6
47 Greenhead, Ayr...E 9
43 Greenhead, Dumf.C 10
44 Greenhead, Northumb......F 5

MAP
11 Greenhill, Kent..A 10
48 Greenhill, Stirling .B 1
47 Greenhills........D 8
10 Greenhithe.......A 5
47 Greenholm......F 10
39 Greenholme.......E 8
49 Greenhouse......G 8
35 Greenhow Hill....A 9
64 Greenigo ....D 2
49 Greenknowe......E 9
61 Greenland.......A 11
17 Greenlands.......F 8
58 Greenlaw, Banff...B 4
49 Greenlaw, Berwick E 9
49 Greenlaw Walls..E 12
43 Greenlea, Dumf..D 11
47 Greenlea, Dunb...A 7
52 Greenloaning.....F 3
34 Greenmount......F 6
47 Greenock.........B 8
38 Greenodd.........G 5
48 Greenrig.........E 1
43 Greenrow.......F 11
23 Greens Norton ..G 10
52 Greenscares.......F 3
48 Greenshields......E 3
45 Greenside........G 9
45 Greensidehill......A 8
58 Greenskairs......A 5
19 Greenstead Green.A 8
18 Greensted Green..D 5
64 Greenwall........C 3
14 Greenway, Glam. .G 4
12 Greenway, Pem. ..D 4
18 Greenwich........F 4
16 Greet............A 1
21 Greete..........E 11
33 Greetham, Lincs..C 10
23 Greetham, Rut...A 12
35 Greetland........E 9
7 Greinton.........C 7
23 Grendon,N'thants F 12
22 Grendon, War.....B 6
22 Grendon Common B 6
21 Grendon Green..G 11
17 Grendon Underwood B 8
42 Grennan.........E 3
5 Grenofen.........J 4
35 Grenoside.......H 11
30 Gresford.........E 2
26 Gresham..........B 5
62 Greshornish......C 3
63 Gress............C 6
26 Gressenhall ....D 3
26 Gressenhall Grn...D 3
39 Gressingham.....H 8
30 Grestey Green....E 6
44 Gretna...........F 2
40 Greta Bridge.....D 1
44 Gretna Green.....F 1
16 Gretton, Glos.....A 1
23 Gretton, N'thants C 12
21 Gretton, Salop...C 10
40 Grewelthorpe.....G 2
58 Grey Stone.......E 6
40 Greygarth ....H 2
13 Greynor..........F 9
43 Greyrigg, Dumf. .C 11
48 Greyrigg, Stirling. B 2
38 Greysouthen......B 3
53 Greystoke, Angus C 10
39 Greystoke, Cumb. .B 7
43 Greystone.......D 10
9 Greywell.........A 8
4 Gribbleford Bridge F 4
36 Gribthorpe.......D 5
50 Gribun...........D 2
5 Gridley Corner....G 2
23 Griff.............C 7
14 Griffithstown.....D 6
39 Grigghall.........F 7
64 Grimbister........C 2
34 Grimeford Village .F 5
36 Grimethorpe.......F 2
22 Grimley..........F 2
47 Grimmet ....H 8
33 Grimoldby.......A 11
34 Grimsargh ....D 5
37 Grimsby.........F 10
23 Grimscote.......G 10
4 Grimscott.........E 1
63 Grimshader.......D 5
24 Grimsthorpe.......C 2
32 Grimston, Leics. .H 4
24 Grimston, Norfolk C 8
37 Grimstone, Yorks. D 10
7 Grimstone........G 9
5 Grinacombe Moor G 3
41 Grindale ....H 11
22 Grindle ....B 1
31 Grindleford.......B 11
34 Grindleton ....C 6

MAP
30 Grindley Brook ...F 4
31 Grindlow........B 10
40 Grindon, Durham. C 4
44 Grindon, Northumb. F 6
49 Grindon, Northumb. E 11
31 Grindon, Staffs....E 9
44 Grindon Hill.......F 6
49 Grindonrigg.....E 11
32 Gringley on the Hill A 4
44 Grinsdale........G 2
30 Grinshill ....H 4
40 Grinton..........E 1
41 Gristhorpe......G 11
26 Griston..........E 2
16 Grittenham.......F 1
15 Grittleton.......F 11
38 Grizebeck ....G 5
38 Grizedale.........F 6
64 Grobister ....C 4
23 Groby............A 8
29 Groes, Denb.......D 9
13 Groes, Glam.....H 11
14 Groesfaen........F 4
28 Groesffordd........F 2
29 Groesffordd.......C 7
29 Groesffordd Marli.C 9
21 Groesllwyd........A 7
28 Groeslon, Angl....C 3
28 Groeslon, Caer....E 4
46 Grogport..........E 3
29 Gronant.........B 10
10 Groombridge......D 4
63 Grosebay ....H 2
15 Grosmont, Mon...B 7
41 Grosmont, Yorks. .E 8
27 Groton...........L 2
16 Grove, Berks......E 5
7 Grove, Dorset....H 7
32 Grove, Notts. ....B 4
13 Grovesend........G 9
30 Grudgington .....H 5
54 Grudie...........D 7
60 Gruids...........F 6
60 Gruinard House ..G 1
62 Grula............E 3
50 Gruline House....D 3
2 Grumbla..........G 1
27 Grundisburgh.....K 5
64 Grundsound ......E 7
64 Gruting...........D 6
64 Grutness.........F 7
28 Grwedog.........B 3
51 Gualachulain.....C 6
60 Gualin House.....B 4
53 Guard Bridge.....E 9
22 Guarlford.........H 2
52 Guay.............B 5
43 Gubhill.........B 10
11 Guestling Green ..G 7
11 Guestling Icklesham F 7
26 Guestwick........C 3
34 Guide............E 6
45 Guide Post ......E 10
25 Guilden Morden ..L 4
30 Guilden Sutton ...C 3
9 Guildford ....A 11
52 Guildtown.........D 6
23 Guilsborough....E 10
21 Guilsfield.........A 8
11 Guilton..........B 11
47 Guiltreehill.......H 8
4 Guineaford........B 4
55 Guisachan House .G 7
40 Guisborough .....D 6
35 Guiseley.........C 10
26 Guist.............C 3
16 Guiting Power....B 2
64 Gulberwick.......E 7
49 Gullane...........A 7
2 Gulval...........F 2
5 Gulworthy........H 3
12 Gumfreston.......G 4
23 Gumley..........C 10
2 Gummow's Shop .D 6
32 Gunby, Lincs.....H 6
36 Gunby, Yorks.....D 5
9 Gundleton........C 7
4 Gunn.............C 5
39 Gunnerside......E 11
45 Gunnerton........F 7
45 Gunnerton Fell....E 7
36 Gunness..........F 6
3 Gunnislake......C 11
64 Gunnista.........D 7
36 Gunthorpe, Lincs..G 6
26 Gunthorpe, Norf. .B 3
32 Gunthorpe, Notts..F 4
6 Gunville..........G 6
6 Gupworthy........C 3
8 Gurnard..........F 6

MAP
7 Gurney Slade.....A 9
14 Gurnos...........C 1
8 Gussage All Saints E 2
8 Gussage St.AndrewE 1
8 Gussage St.MichaelE 1
11 Guston.........D 11
64 Gutcher..........B 8
53 Guthrie.........B 10
24 Guy's Head.......C 6
7 Guy's Marsh.....D 11
24 Guyhirn..........E 5
45 Guyzance.......C 10
14 Gwaelod-y-garth ..F 4
29 Gwaenysgor .....B 10
28 Gwalchmai........C 3
12 Gwastad..........D 4
13 Gwaun-cae-Gurwen F 10
12 Gwbert-on-Sea....B 5
2 Gweek...........G 4
15 Gwehelog Com....D 7
20 Gwenddwr.......H 6
2 Gwennap.........F 4
14 Gwent, Co........D 6
2 Gwenter.........H 4
29 Gwernaffield.....D 11
21 Gwernaffel........E 8
15 Gwernesney......D 7
13 Gwernogle.......D 8
29 Gwernymynydd..D 11
14 Gwern-y-Steeple ..G 4
30 Gwersyllt.........E 2
29 Gwespyr.........B 10
2 Gwinear..........F 3
2 Gwithian..........F 3
29 Gwyddelwern ....F 10
19 Gwyddgrug.......C 8
29 Gwynfryn........E 11
28 Gwynedd, Co. .....E 5
20 Gwystre..........F 6
29 Gwytherin.........D 8
29 Gyfelia..........F 12
29 Gyffin............C 7
29 Gyffylliog ....D 10
21 Habberley........B 9
63 Habost, Lewis.....E 4
63 Habost, Lewis....A 6
37 Habrough.........F 9
24 Hacconby.........C 2
24 Haceby...........B 1
27 Hacheston.........J 6
32 Hackenthorpe.....B 1
18 Hacketts..........C 3
26 Hackford..........E 3
40 Hackforth.........F 3
64 Hackland.........C 2
63 Hacklete..........C 2
23 Hackleton.......G 11
41 Hackness........F 10
18 Hackney..........E 4
33 Hackthorn........B 7
39 Hackthorpe.......C 7
18 Hacton...........E 5
49 Hadden..........F 10
17 Haddenham, Bucks. C8
25 Haddenham, Cambs. H 6
49 Haddington, E. Loth. B 8
32 Haddington, Lincs. D 6
26 Haddiscoe.........F 7
58 Haddoch..........C 3
24 Haddon...........F 2
35 Hade Edge......G 10
22 Hademore.........A 5
35 Hadfield..........G 9
18 Hadham Cross....B 4
18 Hadham Ford....B 4
19 Hadleigh, Essex...E 8
27 Hadleigh, Suffolk..L 3
21 Hadley.........A 12
31 Hadley End ....H 10
18 Hadley Wood.....D 3
10 Hadlow...........C 5
10 Hadlow Down....F 4
30 Hadnall..........H 4
25 Hadstock.........L 7
45 Hadwin's Close..B 10
22 Hadzor...........F 3
11 Haffenden Quarter D 7
20 Hafod............G 1
29 Hafod-Dinbych...E 8
20 Hafod-Peris.......F 1
35 Haggate..........D 7
44 Haggbeck.........F 3
45 Haggerston.......B 11
21 Hagley, Herefs. .H 11
22 Hagley, Worcs....D 3
33 Hagworthingham C 10
34 Haigh, Lancs......F 5
35 Haigh, Yorks.....F 11
35 Haigh Moor.....E 11
34 Haighton Green ..D 4

MAP

25 Hail Weston.....J 3
38 Haile...........D 3
18 Hailey, Herts.....C 4
16 Hailey, Oxon.....C 4
10 Hailsham........G 5
18 Hainault........E 4
26 Hainford........D 5
33 Hainton.........B 9
37 Haisthorpe......A 9
32 Halam..........E 4
52 Halbeath ....H 6
6 Halberton.......E 3
61 Halcro.........B 11
30 Hale, Cheshire..B 6
8 Hale, Hants.....D 3
30 Hale, Lancs.....B 3
9 Hale, Surrey....A 10
30 Hale Cliff......B 3
10 Hale Street.....C 5
30 Halebarns......B 6
26 Hales, Norfolk...F 7
30 Hales, Staffs.....G 6
22 Halesowen......D 3
27 Halesworth......H 7
30 Halewood........B 3
22 Halford, War....H 6
21 Halford, Salop...D 10
12 Halfpenny Furze..F 6
22 Halfpenny Green..C 2
16 Halfway, Berks..G 5
13 Halfway, Carm..D 11
13 Halfway, Carm..D 10
3 Halfway House,
   Cornwall....C 8
6 Halfway House,
   Devon......G 4
21 Halfway House,
   Salop.......A 9
42 Halfway House,
   Wigtown....E 4
11 Halfway Houses ..A 8
35 Halifax.........E 9
47 Halket.........D 9
61 Halkirk........B 10
29 Halkyn........C 11
47 Hall...........D 9
38 Hall Dunnerdale .F 5
22 Hall Green.....D 5
47 Hall of Carnduff .E 11
21 Hall of the Forest .D 7
38 Hall Waberthwaite F 3
10 Halland.........F 4
23 Hallaton.......B 11
7 Hallatrow......A 10
44 Hallbankgate.....G 4
15 Hallen.........F 8
32 Hallfield Gate....D 1
49 Halliburton .....D 9
62 Hallin.........B 2
10 Halling.........B 6
33 Hallington,
   Lincs.......B 10
45 Hallington,
   Northumb.....E 8
34 Halliwell......F 6
32 Halloughton....E 4
22 Hallow........F 2
44 Hallrule.......B 4
49 Halls..........B 9
18 Hall's Green.....A 3
5 Hallsands......M 7
43 Hallscaur......B 8
24 Halltoft End.....A 5
49 Halltree.......D 7
3 Hallworthy.....A 9
48 Hallyne.......E 5
30 Halmer End.....E 6
15 Halmore.......D 10
48 Halmyre Mains ..D 4
9 Halnaker.....E 10
34 Halsall.........F 2
23 Halse, Northants..H 9
6 Halse, Somerset ..C 5
2 Halsetown......F 2
37 Halsham.......D 10
4 Halsinger......B 4
27 Halstead, Essex..M 1
10 Halstead, Kent...B 4
23 Halstead, Leics..B 11
7 Halstock.......E 8
38 Haltcliff Bridge....B 6
33 Haltham.......D 9
17 Halton, Bucks..C 9
30 Halton, Cheshire..B 4
29 Halton, Denb...F 12
34 Halton, Lancs...A 4
45 Halton, Northumb. F 8
35 Halton East.....B 9
39 Halton Gill....G 11
33 Halton Holegate .D 11
44 Halton Lea Gate..G 5
35 Halton Moor...D 12
34 Halton Park.....A 4

45 Halton Shields....F 8
35 Halton West......B 7
44 Haltwhistle......C 5
26 Halvergate......E 7
5 Halwell........K 6
4 Halwill.........F 3
4 Halwill Junction...F 3
6 Ham, Devon....F 6
15 Ham, Glos. ....D 10
11 Ham, Kent....C 12
18 Ham, London....G 2
16 Ham, Wilts......H 4
11 Ham Green, Kent .A 7
15 Ham Green, Som. G 8
22 Ham Green, Worcs.
                F 4
10 Ham Hill........B 6
11 Ham Street, Kent .E 8
7 Ham Street, Som. .C 9
8 Hamble.........E 6
17 Hambleden......E 8
9 Hambledon, Hants.E 8
9 Hambledon, Surrey
                B 11
34 Hambleton, Lancs. C 3
36 Hambleton, Yorks.D 3
7 Hambridge......D 7
9 Hambrook.......C 9
33 Hameringham ...C 10
25 Hamerton.......G 2
47 Hamilton.......D 12
9 Hammer........C 10
9 Hammerpot.....F 11
18 Hammersmith....F 2
22 Hammerwich.....A 4
7 Hammoon.......E 11
64 Hamnavoe, W. Burra
                E 7
64 Hamnavoe, Yell...C 7
64 Hamnavoe, Zet...C 6
64 Hamnavoe, Zet...C 7
10 Hampden ....H 5
17 Hampden Row....D 9
16 Hampnett.......C 2
36 Hampole........F 3
8 Hampreston.....F 2
8 Hampshire, Co....C 6
18 Hampstead......E 3
16 Hampstead Norris .F 6
35 Hampsthwaite ...A 11
18 Hampton, London G 1
22 Hampton, Salop. .D 1
22 Hampton, Worcs. H 4
15 Hampton Bishop..A 9
30 Hampton Heath...E 4
22 Hampton in Arden D 5
22 Hampton Lovett ..F 2
22 Hampton Lucy....D 5
22 Hampton on the Hill
                F 6
16 Hampton Poyle...E 1
31 Hamstall Ridware.H 9
8 Hamstead, Hants..G 5
22 Hamstead, War....C 4
16 Hamstead Marshall
                H 5
40 Hamsteels......A 2
40 Hamsterley, Dur..B 1
45 Hamsterley, Dur. .G 9
8 Hamworthy......G 1
31 Hanbury, Staffs. .G 10
22 Hanbury, Worcs...F 3
30 Handbridge.....D 3
10 Handcross......E 2
31 Handforth......B 7
30 Handley, Cheshire D 3
8 Handley, Dorset..D 2
22 Handsacre......A 4
22 Handsworth.....C 4
17 Handy Cross, Bucks.
                E 9
4 Handy Cross, Devon
                C 3
31 Hanford........F 7
8 Hanging Langford.B 2
4 Hangingshaw, Dumf.
                C 11
48 Hangingshaw, Lan. E 2
30 Hankelow.......F 5
16 Hankerton.......E 1
10 Hankham.......G 5
31 Hanley.........E 7
22 Hanley Castle...H 2
21 Hanley Child ....F 12
22 Hanley Swan ...H 2
21 Hanley William ..F 12
58 Hanlith........A 8
30 Hanmer........F 3
9 Hannington, Hants.
                A 7
23 Hannington,
   Northants......E 11
16 Hannington, Wilts. E 3

16 Hannington Wick .E 3
23 Hanslope........G 11
24 Hanthorpe......C 2
18 Hanwell, London..F 1
23 Hanwell, Oxon...H 8
18 Hanworth, Lond. .G 1
26 Hanworth, Norf...B 5
48 Happendon......F 1
26 Happisburgh.....B 7
26 Happisburgh Com. C 7
30 Hapsford........C 4
34 Hapton, Lancs...D 6
26 Hapton, Norfolk ..F 5
5 Harberton......K 6
5 Harbertonford...K 6
11 Harbledown......B 10
22 Harborne.......D 4
23 Harborough Magna
                D 8
45 Harbottle......C 7
5 Harbourneford....J 6
23 Harbury........F 7
32 Harby, Leics.....G 5
32 Harby, Notts.....C 6
6 Harcombe, Devon H 2
6 Harcombe, Devon G 5
2 Harcourt........F 5
35 Harden.........C 9
15 Hardenhuish ...G 12
59 Hardgate, Aber....G 5
43 Hardgate, Kirk....E 9
43 Hardgrove......D 11
9 Hardham ....D 11
34 Hardhorn.......C 2
26 Hardingham.....E 3
31 Hardings Wood...E 7
23 Hardingstone ...F 11
7 Hardington.....A 10
7 Hardington
   Mandeville.....E 8
8 Hardington Marsh E 8
4 Hardisworthy .....D 1
8 Hardley........F 6
26 Hardley Street....E 7
18 Hardmondsworth..F 1
39 Hardrow........F 11
32 Hardstoft......D 2
7 Hardway........C 10
17 Hardwick, Bucks..B 9
25 Hardwick, Cambs. J 5
32 Hardwick, Lincs...C 6
26 Hardwick, Norf...F 5
23 Hardwick, Northants.
                E 11
16 Hardwick, Oxon ..D 5
17 Hardwick, Oxon ..A 7
32 Hardwick Grange .C 4
15 Hardwicke, Glos. B 12
15 Hardwicke, Glos. C 11
21 Hardwicke, Herefs.H 8
19 Hardy's Green....B 9
6 Hare & Hounds Inn G 5
19 Hare Green.....A 10
17 Hare Hatch.....F 9
18 Hare Street, Essex .C 4
18 Hare Street, Herts. A 4
10 Harebeating.....G 5
33 Hareby.........D 10
34 Hareden........B 5
16 Harefield.......E 1
17 Harefield Moor ..E 11
35 Harehills ....D 11
45 Harehope......A 9
48 Harelaw, Lanark ..E 2
47 Harelaw, Renfrew.D 9
49 Harelaw, Rox....G 8
59 Haremuir.......K 5
39 Haresceugh......A 8
15 Harescombe ....C 11
15 Haresfield ......C 11
48 Hareshaw.......C 1
35 Harewood......C 12
15 Harewood End...B 8
36 Harewood Estate ..F 3
4 Harford, Devon...F 7
5 Harford, Devon...K 5
26 Hargate........F 4
31 Hargatewall....C 9
30 Hargrave, Ches...D 3
25 Hargrave, Northants.
                H 1
27 Hargrave Green ..J 1
18 Haringey.......E 3
44 Harker.........G 2
17 Harkstead .....M 5
22 Harlaston......A 5
58 Harlaw House....E 5
32 Harlaxton.......G 6
35 Harle Syke.....D 7
28 Harlech........G 5
21 Harlescott......A 10
18 Harlesden......F 2
27 Harleston, Norf...G 5

27 Harleston, Suffolk .J 3
23 Harlestone......F 10
21 Harley.........B 11
45 Harleyholm.....F 2
25 Harlington, Beds..M 1
18 Harlington, Lond..F 1
36 Harlington, Yorks. G 3
62 Harlosh........D 2
18 Harlow.........C 5
45 Harlow Hill.....F 9
36 Harlthorpe......C 5
25 Harlton........K 5
8 Harman's Cross...H 1
40 Harmby........F 2
18 Harmer Green....B 3
31 Harmerhill......H 3
33 Harmston.......D 7
16 Harnhill........D 2
18 Harold Hill.....E 5
18 Haroldston West..E 2
64 Haroldswick.....A 8
40 Harome........G 6
17 Harpenden......C 12
49 Harper Ridge...E 11
49 Harpertoun.....E 10
6 Harpford.......G 4
37 Harpham........A 8
26 Harpley, Norfolk..C 1
21 Harpley, Worcs. F 12
23 Harpole........F 10
17 Harpsden.......F 8
32 Harpswell......A 6
31 Harpur Hill.....C 9
35 Harpurhey......G 7
64 Harra..........B 7
44 Harraby........H 3
4 Harracott......C 4
62 Harrapool......F 6
52 Harrietfield.....D 5
49 Harrietsfield......G 9
11 Harrietsham.....C 7
38 Harrington, Cumb.C 2
33 Harrington, Lincs.C 10
23 Harrington,
   Northants......D 11
22 Harringworth....B.12
31 Harriseahead....E 7
35 Harrogate.......B 12
22 Harrold........F 12
18 Harrow.........E 2
27 Harrow Street....L 3
18 Harrow Weald...E 2
3 Harrowbarrow....C 11
3 Harrowbridge....B 9
40 Harrowgate VillageC 3
25 Harston, Cambs...K 5
32 Harston, Leics....G 5
36 Harswell.......C 6
40 Hart..........B 5
45 Hart Law.......C 10
45 Hartburn......D 9
27 Hartest........K 1
7 Hartfoot Lane ...F 11
30 Hartford, Ches....C 5
25 Hartford, Hunts...H 4
19 Hartford End....B 7
17 Hartfordbridge...H 8
30 Harthill, Cheshire .E 4
48 Harthill, Lanark ..C 2
32 Harthill, Yorks....B 2
31 Hartington......D 9
4 Hartland.......D 1
22 Hartlebury.......E 2
40 Hartlepool......B 5
10 Hartley, Kent....A 5
10 Hartley, Kent....E 6
45 Hartley, Northumb.
                E 11
39 Hartley, Yorks...D 10
10 Hartley Green ...A 5
17 Hartley Wespall...H 8
17 Hartley Wintney .H 8
11 Hartlip........B 7
45 Harton, Durham.G 12
21 Harton, Salop...D 10
36 Harton, Yorks....A 5
15 Hartpury......B 11
35 Hartshead......E 10
23 Hartshill......C 7
31 Hartshorne....H 11
48 Hartside.......F 2
38 Hartsop.......D 6
17 Hartwell, Bucks...C 9
23 Hartwell, Northants.
                G 11
35 Hartwith ....A 11
48 Hartwood.......C 1
49 Hartwoodburn...G 7
49 Hartwoodmyres...G 7
10 Harvel.........B 5
22 Harvington......G 4
22 Harvington Cross .G 4
16 Harwell........E 6

27 Harwich........M 6
39 Harwood, Dur...B 8
34 Harwood, Lancs..F 6
45 Harwood, Northumb.
                D 8
41 Harwood Dale...F 9
32 Harworth......A 3
9 Hascombe.....B 11
23 Haselbech......D 10
7 Haselbury Plucknett
                E 8
22 Haseley........E 6
22 Haselor........F 5
15 Hasfield.......B 11
12 Hasguard.......F 2
12 Hasguard Cross...F 2
34 Haskayne......K 5
27 Hasketon.......K 5
32 Hasland........C 1
9 Haslemere......C 10
34 Haslingden.....E 6
25 Haslingfield....K 5
30 Haslington......E 6
30 Hassall........D 6
30 Hassall Green...D 6
11 Hassell Street....C 9
49 Hassendean.....G 8
26 Hassingham.....E 6
49 Hassington.....B 10
10 Hassocks......F 2
31 Hassop........C 10
61 Hastigrow......B 11
11 Hastingleigh....D 9
11 Hastings.......G 7
11 Hastingwood....C 5
17 Hastoe........C 10
40 Haswell........A 4
40 Haswell Plough...A 4
48 Haswellsykes....E 5
9 Hatch..........A 8
18 Hatch End......E 1
6 Hatch Green....D 6
49 Hatchednize.....E 10
8 Hatchet Gate....F 5
37 Hatcliffe.......G 10
18 Hatfield, Herefs. F 11
18 Hatfield, Herts...C 2
22 Hatfield, Worcs. .G 2
36 Hatfield, Yorks...F 4
18 Hatfield Broad OakB 5
18 Hatfield Heath...B 5
8 Hatfield Peverel...C 8
36 Hatfield Woodhouse
                F 5
16 Hatford........D 4
8 Hatherden......A 5
4 Hatherleigh.....E 4
32 Hathern........H 2
16 Hatherop.......D 3
31 Hathersage....B 10
35 Hathershaw.....G 8
30 Hatherton, Ches..E 5
22 Hatherton, Staffs. A 3
25 Hatley St. George .K 4
3 Hatt..........C 11
9 Hattingley......B 8
58 Hatton, Aberdeen .D 8
30 Hatton, Cheshire..B 4
31 Hatton, Derby...G 10
33 Hatton, Lincs....C 9
18 Hatton, London...F 1
21 Hatton, Salop...C 10
22 Hatton, War.....E 6
58 Hatton Fintray...F 6
30 Hatton Heath...D 3
30 Hattoncrook.....E 6
18 Haultwick......B 3
54 Haunn.........C 1
22 Haunton.......A 6
45 Hauxley.......C 11
25 Hauxton.......K 5
47 Haugh, Ayr....G 10
35 Haugh, Lancs...F 8
49 Haugh Head...G 12
58 Haugh of Glass...D 2
43 Haugh of Urr....E 9
30 Haugham......B 10
47 Haughhead....B 11
27 Haughley......J 3
27 Haughley Green..J 3
58 Haughs of ClintertyF 6
45 Haughterslaw...A 9
32 Haughton, Notts. C 4
21 Haughton, Salop. A 11
21 Haughton, Salop. C 12
30 Haughton, Salop. G 2
31 Haughton, Staffs. .H 1
45 Haughton Castle .F 7
35 Haughton Green .H 8
30 Haughton Moss...E 4
17 Havant.........F 8
21 Haven..........G 9

37 Haven Side......E 10
9 Haven Street.....G 7
36 Havercroft......F 2
12 Haverfordwest....E 3
25 Haverhill.......L 8
38 Haverigg.......G 4
18 Havering.......E 5
18 Havering-atte-Bower
                E 5
18 Havering's Grove .D 6
23 Haversham......H 11
38 Haverthwaite....G 6
40 Haverton Hill....C 5
29 Hawarden......D 12
19 Hawbush Green..B 8
13 Hawen.........B 7
39 Hawes.........F 11
22 Hawford........F 2
44 Hawick.........B 3
31 Hawk Green.....B 8
7 Hawkchurch.....F 7
27 Hawkedon.......K 1
10 Hawkenbury.....D 5
7 Hawkeridge.....A 11
22 Hawkes End....D 6
15 Hawkesbury.....F 7
15 Hawkesbury Upton
                F 11
45 Hawkhill.......B 10
10 Hawkhurst......E 6
9 Hawkley.......C 8
6 Hawkridge.....C 2
34 Hawkshaw Lane ..F 6
38 Hawkshead.....E 6
38 Hawkshead Hill...E 6
48 Hawksland......E 1
39 Hawkswick .....H 12
32 Hawksworth, Notts.
                F 5
35 Hawksworth, Yorks.
                C 10
19 Hawkwell .....E 8
10 Hawley........A 4
17 Hawling.......H 9
16 Hawling.......B 2
40 Hawnby.......F 5
35 Haworth.......D 9
27 Hawstead......J 1
40 Hawthorn, Dur...A 4
15 Hawthorn, Wilts. G 11
44 Hawthornside....B 4
24 Hawthorpe......C 2
32 Hawton.......E 5
36 Haxby.........A 4
36 Haxey.........G 5
10 Haxted........D 3
21 Hay-on-Wye....H 8
18 Hay Street......A 4
12 Haycastle......D 2
12 Haycastle Cross..D 3
34 Haydock.......G 4
7 Haydon, Dorset..E 10
45 Haydon, Northumb.
                F 7
45 Haydon Bridge ..G 7
16 Haydon Wick....E 2
3 Haye..........C 10
18 Hayes, Kent....G 4
18 Hayes, London...F 1
31 Hayfield, Derby ..B 9
53 Hayfield, Fife...H 7
17 Hayhill........H 9
2 Hayle.........F 3
17 Hayling Island ..F 8
49 Haymount......F 9
6 Hayne.........F 2
25 Haynes.......L 2
25 Haynes West End .L 2
10 Haysden.......D 4
53 Hayshead......C 11
59 Hayton, Aberdeen G 7
43 Hayton, Cumb...G 11
44 Hayton, Cumb...G 3
32 Hayton, Notts....B 4
36 Hayton, Yorks....C 6
21 Hayton's Bent ...D 10
5 Haytor Vale ....H 6
10 Hayward's Heath .F 2
32 Haywood Oaks...E 3
31 Hazel Grove....B 8
48 Hazelbank.....E 1
7 Hazelbury Bryan.E 11
17 Hazeley.......H 8
22 Hazelslade.....A 4
53 Hazelton Walls ..D 3
31 Hazelwood....F 11
17 Hazlemere.....E 10
45 Hazlerigg....H 10
16 Hazleton......B 2
45 Hazon........C 10
24 Heacham......E 3
8 Headbourne Worthy
                C 6

MAP
21 Headbrook......G 8
11 Headcorn......D 7
16 Headington......C 6
40 Headlam......C 2
22 Headless Cross...F 4
9 Headley, Hants...C 9
16 Headley, Hants...H 6
10 Headley, Surrey...C 1
9 Headley Down...B 10
32 Headon......C 5
47 Heads......E 12
44 Heads Nook.....G 3
32 Heage......E 1
39 Healaugh, N. Riding
    E 12
36 Healaugh, W. Riding
    B 3
31 Heald Green.....B 7
4 Heale, Devon.....A 5
7 Heale, Somerset..B 10
35 Healey, Lancs.....E 7
45 Healey, Northumb.G 8
40 Healey, Yorks....G 2
45 Healey Cote....C 9
45 Healeyfield.....H 9
37 Healing......F 10
2 Heamoor......G 2
32 Heanor......F 2
4 Heanton Punchardon
    B 4
32 Heapham......A 6
48 Hearthstone.....G 4
4 Heasley Mill.....C 6
62 Heast......F 6
32 Heath......C 2
17 Heath and Reach.A 10
4 Heath Cross......F 7
17 Heath End, Berks. H 7
22 Heath End, Staffs..B 4
9 Heath End, Surrey
    A 10
22 Heath Hayes......A 4
22 Heath Hill......A 1
7 Heath House......B 7
6 Heath Pault Cross.C 3
22 Heath Town......B 3
31 Heathcote......D 10
23 Heather......A 7
62 Heatherfield......D 4
52 Heatheryhaugh....B 6
43 Heathfield, Cumb.G 12
5 Heathfield, Devon.H 7
47 Heathfield, Ren...C 8
6 Heathfield, Som...D 5
10 Heathfield, Sussex..F 4
43 Heathhall......D 10
22 Heathton......C 2
30 Heatley......A 5
35 Heaton, Lancs...H 7
34 Heaton, Lancs.....A 3
31 Heaton, Staffs...D 8
35 Heaton, Yorks...D 10
34 Heaton's Bridge...F 3
10 Heaverham......B 4
31 Heaviley......A 7
6 Heavitree......G 3
45 Hebburn......G 11
35 Hebden......A 9
35 Hebden Bridge...D 8
30 Hebden Green....D 5
12 Hebron, Carm...D 5
45 Hebron, Northumb.
    D 10
43 Heck......D 11
17 Heckfield......H 8
27 Heckfield Green..H 5
24 Heckington......A 2
48 Hecklebirnie......F 2
35 Heckmondwike ..E 10
16 Heddington......G 1
16 Heddington Wick .G 1
4 Heddon......C 5
45 Heddon on the Wall
    F 9
26 Hedenham......F 6
5 Hedge Cross......G 4
8 Hedge End......E 6
17 Hedgerley......E 10
6 Hedging......C 6
45 Hedley on the Hill G 9
22 Hednesford......A 3
37 Hedon......D 9
17 Hedsor......E 10
21 Hedgon Hill......G 11
45 Heiferlaw Bank .. A 10
40 Heighington, Dur..C 3
33 Heighington, Lincs. C 7
56 Heights of Brae...D 1
54 Heights of Kinlochewe
    C 4
60 Heilam......B 5
49 Heiton......F 9
6 Hele, Devon......F 3

MAP
4 Hele, Devon......A 4
5 Hele, Devon......G 2
6 Hele, Somerset....D 5
4 Hele Lane......E 7
47 Helensburgh......A 8
47 Helentongate......F 9
2 Helford......G 5
2 Helford Passage...G 5
26 Helhoughton.....C 2
25 Helions Bumpstead L 7
3 Helland......C 8
3 Hellandbridge....C 8
26 Hellesdon......D 5
23 Hellidon......F 8
35 Hellifield......B 7
10 Helling......G 4
26 Hellington......E 6
45 Helm......C 10
43 Helmdon......H 9
27 Helmingham......J 5
40 Helmington Row..B 2
61 Helmsdale......E 10
34 Helmshore......E 6
40 Helmsley......G 6
40 Helperby......H 5
41 Helperthorpe......H 9
24 Helpringham......B 2
24 Helpston......E 2
30 Helsby......C 3
2 Helston......G 4
3 Helstone......B 8
39 Helton......C 7
39 Helwith Bridge .H 10
17 Hemel Hempstead
    D 11
36 Hemingbrough....D 4
33 Hemingby......C 9
36 Hemingfield......G 2
25 Hemingford Abbots
    H 4
25 Hemingford Grey H 4
27 Hemingstone.....K 5
32 Hemington, Leics..G 2
25 Hemington,
    Northants.....G 2
7 Hemington, Som. A 10
27 Hemley......L 6
40 Hemlington......D 5
37 Hempholme......B 8
26 Hempnall......F 5
26 Hempnall Green...F 5
26 Hempstead, Essex .L 7
10 Hempstead, Kent..B 6
26 Hempstead, Norf..B 4
26 Hempsted......C 11
26 Hempton, Norfolk C 2
16 Hempton, Oxon...A 5
26 Hemsby......D 8
32 Hemswell......A 6
36 Hemsworth......F 2
6 Hemyock......E 5
31 Henbury, Ches....C 7
15 Henbury, Glos....F 9
4 Henderbarrow Corner
    F 3
18 Hendon, London .E 2
45 Hendon, Dur. ...G 12
15 Hendre......C 8
14 Hendreforgan.....E 3
12 Hendre-wen......D 3
13 Hendy......G 9
28 Heneglwys.......C 4
12 Hen-feddau......D 6
15 Henfield, Glos...F 10
10 Henfield, Sussex...F 1
18 Hengherst......D 8
14 Hengoed, Glam...E 5
21 Hengoed, Rad....G 8
30 Hengoed, Salop...G 2
27 Hengrave......H 1
18 Henham......A 5
21 Heniarth......B 7
6 Henlade......D 6
45 Henlaw......C 11
7 Henley, Dorset..F 10
21 Henley, Salop....D 10
7 Henley, Somerset..C 8
27 Henley, Suffolk ...K 5
9 Henley, Sussex...D 10
22 Henley-in-Arden..E 5
17 Henley-on-Thames.F 8
10 Henley Street......A 5
13 Henllan, Cards...C 7
29 Henllan, Denb...C 9
12 Henllan Amgoed..E 5
14 Henllys......C 9
25 Henlow......L 3
5 Hennock......H 7
27 Henny Street......L 2
29 Henryd......C 7
12 Henry's Moat......D 4
36 Hensall......E 4

MAP
44 Henshaw......G 6
38 Hensingham......D 2
27 Henstead......G 8
7 Henstridge......D 10
7 Henstridge Ash ..D 10
7 Henstridge Bowden
    D 10
17 Henton, Oxon.....D 8
7 Henton, Som......B 8
7 Hentstridge Marsh
    D 11
22 Henwick......G 2
3 Henwood......B 9
64 Heogan......D 7
14 Heol Senni......B 3
13 Heol-las......G 10
14 Heol-y-Cyw......F 3
45 Hepburn......A 9
36 Hepple......C 8
45 Hepple Whitefield C 8
45 Hepscott......E 10
31 Hepstonstall......D 8
27 Hepworth, Suff...H 3
35 Hepworth, Yorks. F 10
35 Herbrandston......F 2
21 Hereford......H 10
22 Hereford &
    Worcester, Co...F 2
48 Heriot......D 6
49 Heriot Station ....D 7
9 Hermiston......G 8
16 Hermitage, Berks. G 6
7 Hermitage, Dor...F 10
43 Hermitage, Kirk..E 9
44 Hermitage, Rox...C 3
9 Hermitage, Sussex.F 9
28 Hermon, Anglesey.C 3
13 Hermon, Carm...D 10
12 Hermon, Pemb...D 5
11 Herne......B 10
11 Herne Bay......A 10
4 Herner......C 5
11 Hernhill......B 9
3 Herodsfoot......D 9
11 Heronden......C 11
42 Heronsford......C 2
17 Heronsgate......E 11
7 Herriard......B 8
26 Herringfleet......F 8
25 Herring's Green...L 2
25 Herringswell......H 8
18 Herrington......H 11
11 Hersden......B 10
11 Hersham......H 12
10 Herstmonceux .....G 5
8 Herston, Dorset...H 2
64 Herston, Orkney Is.E 2
18 Hertford......C 3
18 Hertford Heath ...C 3
18 Hertfordshire, Co..B 2
18 Hertingfordbury ...C 3
38 Hesket Newmarket A 6
34 Hesketh Bank.....E 3
34 Hesketh Lane.....C 5
34 Heskin Green.....F 4
40 Hesleden......A 4
43 Hesleyside......E 6
36 Heslington......B 4
36 Hessay......B 3
3 Hessenford......D 10
27 Hessett......J 2
47 Hessilhead......D 9
36 Hessle......E 8
34 Hest Bank......A 3
18 Heston......F 1
30 Heswall......B 1
17 Hethe......A 7
26 Hethersett......E 5
43 Hethersgill......F 3
49 Hethpool......G 11
40 Hett......B 3
35 Hetton......A 8
45 Hetton Downs ..H 11
45 Hetton Law....C 11
45 Hetton Steads ....B 11
45 Hetton-le-Hole ..H 11
45 Heugh......F 9
58 Heugh-head......F 1
27 Heveningham......H 6
10 Hever......D 4
39 Heversham......G 7
26 Hevingham......C 5
15 Hewelsfield......D 9
15 Hewish, Somerset H 7
7 Hewish, Somerset .E 7
36 Heworth......B 4
45 Hexham......G 7
49 Hexpath......E 9
10 Hextable......A 4
5 Hexworthy......H 5
19 Heybridge, Essex C 8
18 Heybridge, Essex ..D 6

MAP
19 Heybridge Basin ..C 8
5 Heybrook Bay......L 4
25 Heydon, Cambs...L 5
26 Heydon, Norfolk..C 4
33 Heydour......F 7
34 Heysham......A 3
35 Heyshaw......A 10
9 Heyshott......D 10
8 Heytesbury......B 1
16 Heythrop......A 4
7 Heywood, Lancs..F 7
7 Heywood, Wilts..A 12
37 Hibaldstow......G 7
36 Hickleton......G 3
26 Hickling, Norfolk .C 7
32 Hickling, Notts...G 4
26 Hickling Green....C 7
22 Hidcote Boyce...H 5
36 High Ackworth...E 2
39 High Angerton....E 9
39 High Bankhill......A 8
18 High Beach......D 4
39 High Bentham....H 9
4 High Bickington...D 5
39 High Birkwith...G 10
47 High Blantyre...D 11
48 High Bonnybridge.B 1
43 High Borgue......F 7
47 High Boydston....E 7
35 High Bradley......B 9
4 High Bray......C 6
10 High Brooms......D 5
4 High Bullen......D 4
40 High Burton......G 2
45 High Buston......B 10
45 High Callerton....F 10
36 High Catton......B 5
45 High Church......E 10
47 High Cleughearn .E 11
16 High Cogges......C 5
40 High Coniscliffe ..D 3
47 High Cross, Ayr...E 9
49 High Cross, Ber...E 8
9 High Cross, Hants.C 8
18 High Cross, Herts. B 4
31 High Cross Bank H 11
47 High Duncryne ...A 9
18 High Easter......B 6
42 High Eldrig......E 3
40 High Ellington....G 2
40 High Entercommon
    E 4
21 High Ercall......A 11
40 High Etherley......B 2
19 High Garrett......A 7
47 High Glengarth ...D 8
40 High Grange......B 2
40 High Grantley....H 3
26 High Green, Norf..E 4
22 High Green, Worcs.
    H 2
35 High Green, Yorks.
    G 12
11 High Halden......D 8
10 High Halstow......A 6
7 High Ham......C 8
38 High Harrington...C 3
40 High Haswell......A 4
30 High Hatton......H 5
41 High Hawsker....D 9
39 High Hesket......A 7
40 High Hesleden....A 5
35 High Hoyland......F 11
37 High Hursley......D 7
10 High Hurstwood..E 4
41 High Hutton......H 8
38 High Ireby......B 5
40 High Kilburn......G 5
31 High Lane, Ches...B 8
21 High Lane, Herefs.
    F 12
18 High Laver......C 5
30 High Legh......B 5
40 High Leven......D 5
15 High Littleton......C 11
38 High Lorton......C 4
41 High Marishes.....G 8
32 High Marnham.....C 5
36 High Melton......G 3
35 High Mickley......G 8
42 High Mindork......F 4
41 High Mowthorpe .H 9
38 High Newton......G 6
45 High Newton by-the-
    Sea......E 12
38 High Nibthwaite ..F 5
30 High Offley......G 6
18 High Ongar......D 5
22 High Onn......A 2
42 High Pennyvenie..A 6
18 High Roding......B 6
38 High Row......B 6
34 High Salter......A 5

MAP
39 High Shaw......F 11
40 High Skelding......H 2
45 High Spen......G 9
40 High Stoop......A 1
3 High Street, Corn. D 7
27 High St., E. Suff...K 7
27 High St., W. Suff..K 2
27 High Street Green .K 3
40 High Throston......B 5
33 High Toynton......C 10
45 High Trewhitt......B 8
48 High Valleyfield....A 3
45 High Warden......F 7
38 High Wray......E 6
18 High Wych......C 5
17 High Wycombe...E 9
32 Higham, Derby...D 1
27 Higham, E. Suffolk L 3
10 Higham, Kent......A 6
35 Higham, Lancs...D 7
25 Higham, W. Suff..J 8
45 Higham Dykes....B 9
25 Higham Ferrers ..H 1
25 Higham Gobion ..M 2
23 Higham on the Hill
    C 7
10 Higham Wood....C 5
9 Highampton......E 4
10 Highbrook......B 2
35 Highburton......F 10
7 Highbury......A 10
44 Highchesters......B 3
16 Highclere......H 5
8 Highcliffe......G 4
7 Higher Alham ..B 10
7 Higher Ansty......F 11
6 Higher Ashton....H 2
34 Higher Ballam...D 2
2 Higher Boscaswell .F 1
6 Higher Combe....C 3
30 Higher Heath......G 4
29 Higher Kinnerton D 12
7 Higher Nyland ...D 10
34 Higher Penwortham
    D 4
2 Higher Town......C 2
30 Higher Walton, Ches.
    B 4
34 Higher Walton, Lancs.
    D 5
7 Higher Whatcombe
    F 11
30 Higher Whitley ...B 5
30 Higher Wych ....F 3
47 Highfield, Ayr....D 8
4 Highfield, Devon..F 6
45 Highfield, Dur....G 9
32 Highfield, Yorks...B 1
25 Highfields, Cambs. J 5
49 Highfields, Northumb.
    D 12
18 Highgate, London .E 3
36 Highgate, Yorks...E 4
44 Highgreen Manor D 6
58 Highlands, Aber...F 6
40 Highlands, Dur....C 2
32 Highlane......B 1
15 Highleadon......B 11
9 Highleigh......F 9
22 Highley......D 1
17 Highmoor Cross ..F 8
15 Highmoor Hill......E 8
15 Highnam Green..B 11
4 Highridge......D 6
11 Highsted......B 8
27 Highstreet Green .M 1
43 Hightae......D 11
31 Hightown, Ches...D 7
43 Hightown, Dumf. C 11
34 Hightown, Lancs. .G 2
43 Hightown of Craigs
    D 11
2 Highway, Corn...E 4
16 Highway, Wilts....G 2
5 Highweek......J 7
16 Highworth......E 3
26 Hilborough......E 1
32 Hilcote......D 2
16 Hilcott......H 2
10 Hilden Park......C 4
10 Hildenborough....C 4
25 Hildersham......K 6
31 Hilderstone......G 8
37 Hilderthorpe......A 9
21 Hilfarrance......D 5
7 Hilfield......F 9
24 Hilgay......F 7
4 Hill, Devon......C 6
15 Hill, Glos......E 9
22 Hill, Warwick....B 5
9 Hill Brow......D 9

MAP
41 Hill Cottages....E 7
34 Hill Dale......F 4
33 Hill Dyke......E 10
39 Hill End, Dur....B 12
52 Hill End, Fife ....H 5
15 Hill Gate......B 8
9 Hill Head, Hants. .F 7
45 Hill Head, Northumb.
    F 7
38 Hill Millom......G 4
12 Hill Mountain....F 3
52 Hill of Beath......H 6
56 Hill of Fearn......B 4
58 Hill of Maud Crofts B 2
31 Hill Ridware......H 9
25 Hill Row......H 5
8 Hill Top, Hants...F 5
35 Hill Top, Yorks. .F 12
8 Hill View......F 1
36 Hillam......D 3
35 Hillbeck......D 10
35 Hillberry......G 2
11 Hillborough.....A 10
8 Hillbourne......G 2
58 Hillbrae......E 5
8 Hillbutts......F 1
53 Hillcairnie......E 8
6 Hillcommon......D 5
48 Hillend, Fife......A 4
48 Hillend, Lanark...E 3
15 Hillersland......C 9
17 Hillesden......A 8
15 Hillesley......E 11
6 Hillfarrance......D 5
58 Hillhead, Aber....E 5
47 Hillhead, Ayr....F 10
47 Hillhead, Ayr....G 9
5 Hillhead, Devon .K 8
43 Hillhead, Dumf...B 8
48 Hillhead, Lanark..E 3
45 Hillhead, Northumb.
    B 9
58 Hillhead of
    Auchentumb ...B 7
58 Hillhead of Cocklaw
    C 8
49 Hillhouse......D 7
22 Hilliard's Cross ...A 5
18 Hillingdon......F 1
24 Hillington......C 8
23 Hillmorton......C 8
59 Hillockhead, Aber.G 1
58 Hillockhead, Aber. F 2
7 Hillpound......D 7
59 Hillside, Angus...L 4
43 Hillside, Dumf...C 12
59 Hillside, Kinc....H 7
64 Hillside, Shetlands C 7
8 Hillstreet......D 5
45 Hillswick......C 6
9 Hillway......G 8
64 Hillwell......F 7
16 Hilmarton......G 1
15 Hilperton......H 12
15 Hilperton Marsh.H 11
9 Hilsea......F 8
37 Hilston......D 10
25 Hilton......J 4
58 Hilton, Aberdeen .D 7
49 Hilton, Berwick. D 11
31 Hilton, Derby....G 11
7 Hilton, Dorset ...F 11
40 Hilton, Durham...C 2
22 Hilton, Salop....C 1
39 Hilton, Westmor...C 7
40 Hilton, Yorkshire .D 5
56 Hilton of Cadboll .B 4
22 Himbleton......F 3
22 Himley......C 2
39 Hincaster......G 7
16 Hinchwick......A 2
23 Hinckley......C 7
27 Hinderclay......H 3
41 Hinderwell......D 8
30 Hindford......G 2
9 Hindhead......C 10
34 Hindley, Lancs....G 5
45 Hindley, Northumb.
    G 8
34 Hindley Green....G 5
22 Hindlip......F 2
26 Hindolveston......C 3
7 Hindon......C 12
26 Hindringham......B 3
26 Hingham......E 3
30 Hinstock......H 5
27 Hintlesham......L 4
15 Hinton, Glos.....G 10
8 Hinton, Hants....C 8
15 Hinton, Herefs...H 9
23 Hinton, Northants.G 8
21 Hinton, Salop....B 9
9 Hinton Ampner...C 7

MAP

7 Hinton Blewett....A 9
15 Hinton Charterhouse H 11
22 Hinton Green....H 4
23 Hinton-in-the-Hedge H 9
9 Hinton Marsh....C 7
8 Hinton Martell....E 2
22 Hinton on the Green H 4
16 Hinton Parva....F 3
7 Hinton St. George.E 7
7 Hinton St. Mary .E 11
16 Hinton Waldrist ..D 5
21 Hints, Salop....E 11
22 Hints, Staffs.....B 5
23 Hinwick.......F 12
11 Hinxhill.......D 9
25 Hinxton.......L 6
25 Hinxworth.......L 3
35 Hipperholme..E 10
40 Hipswell.......E 2
12 Hiraeth.......E 5
59 Hirn.......G 5
29 Hirnant, Mont. .H 10
20 Hirnant, Rad.....E 4
45 Hirst.......D 11
36 Hirst Courtney...E 4
29 Hirwaen.......D 10
14 Hirwaun.......D 3
4 Hiscott.......C 4
25 Histon.......J 5
27 Hitcham.......K 3
43 Hitchill.......E 12
18 Hitchin.......A 2
18 Hither Green.....F 4
4 Hittisleigh Cross...F 6
36 Hive.......D 6
31 Hixon.......H 8
11 Hoaden.......B 11
15 Hoaldalbert......B 7
31 Hoar Cross....H 10
15 Hoarwithy.......A 8
11 Hoath.......B 10
21 Hobarris.......E 8
64 Hobbister.......D 2
18 Hobbs Cross....D 5
44 Hobkirk.......B 4
45 Hobson.......G 10
32 Hoby.......H 4
26 Hockering.......D 4
32 Hockerton.......E 4
19 Hockley.......E 8
22 Hockley Heath...E 5
17 Hockliffe....A 10
25 Hockwold cum Wilton G 8
6 Hockworthy.....D 4
18 Hoddesdon.......C 4
34 Hoddlesden.......E 6
43 Hoddomcross....D 12
12 Hodgeston.......G 4
30 Hodnet.......G 5
10 Hodsoll Street....B 5
16 Hodson.......F 3
32 Hodthorpe.......C 3
9 Hoe, Hampshire ..D 7
26 Hoe, Norfolk....D 3
9 Hoe Gate.......E 8
39 Hoff.......C 9
17 Hoggeston.......B 9
34 Hoghton.......E 5
31 Hognaston.....E 11
33 Hogsthorpe.....C 12
24 Holbeach.......C 5
24 Holbeach Bank...C 5
24 Holbeach Clough..C 4
24 Holbeach Drove...D 4
24 Holbeach Hurn...C 5
24 Holbeach St.Johns D 4
24 Holbeach St.Marks C 5
24 Holbeach St. Matthew B 5
32 Holbeck, Notts...C 3
35 Holbeck, Yorks. .D 11
22 Holberrow Green..F 4
5 Holbeton.......L 5
31 Holbrook, Derby F 12
27 Holbrook, Suffolk .L 5
8 Holbury.......F 6
45 Holburn.......B 11
5 Holcombe, Devon.H 8
34 Holcombe, Lancs..E 6
7 Holcombe, Som. .A 10
34 Holcombe Brook..F 6
6 Holcombe Rogus .D 4
23 Holcot.......E 11
34 Holden.......B 6
23 Holdenby.......E 10
8 Holdenhurst.....G 3
21 Holdgate.......C 11
33 Holdingham.....E 7
7 Holditch.......F 7

MAP

49 Holefield.......F 10
47 Holehouse, Ayr ..H 9
47 Holehouse, Ayr ...D 8
15 Hole-in-the-Wall ..A 9
43 Holestane.......B 9
6 Holford.......B 5
38 Holker.......G 6
26 Holkham.......A 2
4 Hollacombe.......F 2
64 Holland, Papa Westray Orkney Is.....A 3
64 Holland, Stronsay, Orkney Is.....C 4
33 Holland Fen.....E 9
19 Holland-on-Sea ..B 11
64 Hollandstoun....A 4
44 Hollee.......F 1
27 Hollesley.......L 6
11 Hollingbourne....C 7
10 Hollingrove.......F 6
31 Hollington,Derby F 10
31 Hollington, Staffs..F 9
10 Hollington, Sussex G 6
35 Hollingworth.....G 8
35 Hollins.......F 7
30 Hollins Green....A 5
34 Hollins Lane.....B 4
31 Hollinsclough....D 9
4 Hollocombe.......E 5
22 Hollow Court.....F 3
31 Hollow Meadows A 11
31 Holloway.......E 11
23 Hollowell.......E 10
44 Hollows.......C 4
30 Holly Bush, Flint..F 3
14 Holly Bush, Mon..D 5
24 Holly End.......E 6
22 Holly Green ....H 2
47 Hollybush, Ayr ..H 9
15 Hollybush, Worcs. A 10
37 Hollym.......E 11
22 Hollywood.......D 4
44 Holm, Dumf.....C 1
63 Holm, Ross & Cromarty.....D 5
43 Holm St. Cuthbert G 12
4 Holmacott.......C 4
35 Holmbridge......F 10
9 Holmbury St. Mary B 12
3 Holmbush.......D 7
31 Holmcroft.......H 8
25 Holme, Hunts....G 3
37 Holme, Lincs.....F 7
40 Holme, N. Riding.G 4
32 Holme, Notts.....D 5
39 Holme, Westmor..G 7
35 Holme, W. Riding.F 9
35 Holme Chapel....D 7
26 Holme Hale.....E 2
15 Holme Lacy....A 9
21 Holme Marsh....G 9
24 Holme next the Sea A 8
37 Holme on the Wolds C 7
32 Holme Pierrepont .F 3
36 Holm upon Spalding Moor.......C 6
21 Holmer.......H 10
17 Holmer Green ...D 10
30 Holmes Chapel....C 6
64 Holmesfield......B 11
34 Holmeswood......E 3
32 Holmewood......D 2
35 Holmfirth.......F 10
43 Holmfoot.......B 9
47 Holmhead.......G 10
62 Holmisdal.......C 1
37 Holmpton.......E 11
38 Holmrook.......E 3
45 Holmside.......H 10
44 Holmwrangle.....H 4
5 Holne.......J 6
4 Holsworthy.......F 2
4 Holsworthy Beacon E 2
30 Holt, Denb.......E 3
8 Holt, Dorset.....F 2
26 Holt, Norfolk....H 8
15 Holt, Wilts.....H 11
22 Holts, Worcs.....F 2
9 Holt End, Hants..B 8
22 Holt End, Worcs..E 4
22 Holt Heath.....F 2
16 Holt Wood.....E 2
36 Holtby.......B 4
33 Holton, Lincs....B 8
17 Holton, Oxon....F 6
7 Holton, Som.....D 10
27 Holton, Suffolk...H 7
8 Holton Heath....G 1

MAP

37 Holton le Clay...G 10
37 Holton le Moor...G 8
27 Holton St. Mary ..L 4
10 Holtye.......D 3
7 Holwell, Dorset .E 10
18 Holwell, Herts.....A 2
32 Holwell, Leics.....H 5
16 Holwell, Oxon....C 3
39 Holwick.......C 11
7 Holworth.......H 11
22 Holy Cross.......D 3
45 Holy Island.....B 12
9 Holybourne.......B 9
28 Holyhead.......B 2
31 Holymoorside....C 11
17 Holyport.......F 10
45 Holystone.......C 8
47 Holytown.......C 12
2 Holywell, Corn...D 5
44 Holywell, Cumb..E 3
7 Holywell, Dorset ..F 9
29 Holywell, Flint...C 11
25 Holywell, Hunts..H 4
45 Holywell, Northumb. F 11
35 Holywell Green...E 9
6 Holywell Lake...D 5
25 Holywell Row....H 8
43 Holywood.......C 10
15 Hom Green.......B 9
11 Honey Hill.....B 10
16 Honey Street....H 2
27 Honey Tye.....L 2
12 Honeyborough....F 3
4 Honeychurch....F 5
22 Honiley.......E 6
26 Honing.......C 6
26 Honingham.......D 4
32 Honington, Lincs..F 6
27 Honington, Suff...H 2
22 Honington, War...H 8
6 Honiton.......F 5
35 Honley.......F 10
24 Hoo.......A 6
22 Hoobrook.......E 2
35 Hood Green....G 11
5 Hooe, Devon....K 4
10 Hooe, Sussex....G 6
10 Hooe Common...G 6
9 Hook, Hants....A 8
18 Hook, London...G 2
12 Hook, Pemb.....F 3
16 Hook, Wilts.....F 2
36 Hook, Yorks.....E 5
10 Hook Green, Kent A 5
10 Hook Green, Kent.D 5
16 Hook Norton....A 4
7 Hooke.......F 9
30 Hookgate.......G 6
4 Hookway.......F 7
10 Hookwood.....D 2
30 Hooley.......C 3
10 Hooley.......B 2
30 Hooton.......B 2
32 Hooton Levitt...A 2
36 Hooton Pagnell..F 3
36 Hooton Roberts ..G 3
64 Hoove.......D 7
24 Hop Pole.......D 3
31 Hope, Derby....B 10
5 Hope, Devon....M 5
29 Hope, Flint.....D 12
21 Hope, Mont.....B 8
21 Hope, Salop.....B 9
60 Hope, Sutherland .B 5
21 Hope Bagot....E 11
21 Hope Bowdler...C 10
15 Hope Mansell...B 9
21 Hope under Dinmore G 10
56 Hopeman.......C 7
21 Hopesay.......D 9
36 Hopperton.......B 2
31 Hopton, Derby .E 11
30 Hopton, Salop...G 4
31 Hopton, Staffs...B 8
26 Hopton, E. Suffolk E 8
27 Hopton, W. Suff. .G 3
21 Hopton Cangeford D 11
21 Hopton Castle...E 9
21 Hopton Wafers .E 11
21 Hoptonheath.....E 9
22 Hopwas.......B 5
22 Hopwood.......E 4
10 Horam.......F 4
24 Horbling.......B 2
35 Horbury.......E 11

MAP

40 Horden.......A 5
21 Horderley.......D 9
8 Hordle.......F 4
30 Hordley.......G 2
5 Hordon.......H 4
13 Horeb, Cards.....C 7
13 Horeb, Carm.....D 8
15 Horfield.......F 9
27 Horham.......H 5
19 Horkesley Heath ..A 9
37 Horkstow.......E 7
23 Horley, Oxon.....H 7
10 Horley, Surrey...D 2
7 Hornblotton Grn. .C 9
39 Hornby, Lancs....H 8
40 Hornby, Yorks...F 2
40 Hornby, Yorks...E 4
33 Horncastle.......C 9
18 Hornchurch.....E 5
49 Horncliffe.......D 11
49 Horndean, Ber...D 11
9 Horndean, Hants. .E 8
18 Horndon on the Hill F 6
10 Horne.......D 2
6 Horner.......B 3
26 Horning.......D 6
23 Horninghold.....B 11
31 Horninglow.....H 10
25 Horningsea.......J 6
7 Horningsham.....B 11
26 Horningtoft......C 2
3 Horningtops.....D 9
4 Horns Cross, Devon D 3
11 Horns Cross, Sussex F 7
44 Hornsby.......H 3
37 Hornsea.......B 9
37 Hornsea Bridge ..B 9
18 Hornsey.......E 3
23 Hornton.......H 7
5 Horrabridge.....J 4
27 Horringer.......J 1
9 Horringford.....H 7
48 Horsburgh.......E 6
31 Horse Bridge....E 8
8 Horsebridge.....C 5
22 Horsebrook.....A 2
15 Horsecastle.....H 7
21 Horsehay.......B 12
25 Horseheath.....K 7
39 Horsehouse......G 12
17 Horsell.......H 10
30 Horseman's Grn...F 3
17 Horsenden......D 9
26 Horsey.......C 8
35 Horsforth.......C 11
10 Horsham, Sussex..E 1
22 Horsham, Worcs..F 1
26 Horsham St. Faith D 5
33 Horsington, Lincs..C 9
7 Horsington, Som. D 10
32 Horsley, Derby...F 1
15 Horsley, Glos. ...E 11
45 Horsley, Northumb. C 7
45 Horsley, Northumb. F 9
19 Horsley Cross...A 11
19 Horsleycross St...A 11
49 Horsleyhill.......G 8
32 Horsley Woodhouse F 1
10 Horsmonden......D 6
17 Horspath.......D 7
26 Horstead.......D 5
10 Horsted Keynes...E 3
17 Horton, Bucks...B 10
17 Horton, Bucks...F 11
8 Horton, Dorset...E 2
13 Horton, Glam...H 8
15 Horton, Glos.....F 10
23 Horton, Northants. G 11
6 Horton, Somerset .E 6
31 Horton, Staffs...D 8
16 Horton, Wilts...H 2
35 Horton, Yorks...B 7
7 Horton Cross....E 7
30 Horton Green....E 3
8 Horton Heath...D 6
39 Horton in Ribblesdale H 10
10 Horton Kirby....A 4
34 Horwich.......F 5
4 Horwood.......C 4
44 Hoscote.......B 2
32 Hose.......G 5
49 Hoselaw.......F 10
38 Hoses.......F 5
64 Hoswick.......E 7

MAP

52 Hotel, Perth......D 1
60 Hotel, Sutherland .E 5
37 Hotham.........D 7
11 Hothfield.......D 8
30 Hoton.......H 3
44 Hott.......D 6
64 Houbie.......B 8
30 Hough.......E 6
30 Hough Green....B 3
32 Hough-on-the-Hill.F 6
32 Hougham.......F 6
44 Houghton, Cumb..G 2
8 Houghton, Hants..C 5
25 Houghton, Hunts..H 4
12 Houghton, Pemb. .F 3
9 Houghton, Sussex E 11
25 Houghton Conquest L 2
30 Houghton Green..B 3
17 Houghton Regis .B 11
26 Houghton St. Giles B 2
45 Houghton-le-Spring H 11
23 Houghton on the Hill B 10
41 Houlsyke.......D 7
8 Hound.......E 6
17 Hound Green....H 8
49 Houndridge......F 10
49 Houndslow......E 9
6 Houndsmoor....D 5
49 Houndwood....C 11
8 Hounsdown....E 5
49 Hounslow.......F 2
64 Housay.......C 8
59 House of Glenmuick H 1
58 Housieside......E 6
47 Houston.......C 9
61 Houstry.......D 10
10 Hove.......H 2
32 Hoveringham....E 4
26 Hoveton.......D 6
41 Hovingham......H 7
44 How.......G 3
16 How Caple......A 9
10 How Green......C 4
38 How Head......E 6
49 Howbrook......G 11
45 Howburn.......F 10
49 Howden, Rox....G 9
36 Howden, Yorks..D 5
35 Howden Clough .D 11
40 Howden-le-Wear ..B 2
61 Howe, Caith....B 12
61 Howe, Norfolk...E 6
39 Howe, Westmor..F 7
19 Howe Green......D 7
58 Howe of Teuchar .C 5
19 Howe Street, Essex B 7
25 Howe Street, Essex M 8
33 Howell.......F 8
43 Howes.......E 12
20 Howey.......F 6
48 Howford.......F 6
48 Howgate, Lanark..F 2
48 Howgate, Midloth. D 5
45 Howick.......A 10
30 Howle.......H 5
15 Howle Hill......H 3
25 Howlett End.....M 7
6 Howley.......E 6
30 Howliston.......D 7
49 Hownam.......G 10
49 Hownam Mains .G 10
37 Howsham, Lincs. .G 8
36 Howsham, Yorks. .A 5
15 Howtel.......F 11
64 Howth.......D 2
15 Howton, Herefs. ..A 7
39 Howtown, Westmor. C 7
47 Howwood.......C 9
27 Hoxne.......G 5
30 Hoylake.......A 1
35 Hoyland Nether ..G 12
35 Hoyland Swaine .G 11
12 Hubberston......F 2
24 Hubbert's Bridge. A 4
36 Huby, N. Riding..A 3
35 Huby, W. Riding.B 11
35 Hucclecote.....C 12
11 Hucking.......B 7
32 Hucknall.......E 3
35 Huddersfield.....E 10
22 Huddington......F 3
40 Hudswell.......E 2
36 Huggate.......B 6
2 Hugh Town......B 1
17 Hughenden Valley.D 9
21 Hughley.......C 11

MAP

4 Huish, Devon.....E 4
16 Huish, Wilts.....H 2
6 Huish Barton....B 4
6 Huish Champflower C 4
7 Huish Episcopi....D 8
17 Hulcott.......B 9
31 Hulland.......F 11
15 Hullavington....F 12
19 Hullbridge.......D 8
31 Hulme End......D 9
31 Hulme Walfield...D 7
34 Hulton Lane Ends G 6
27 Hulver Street....G 8
8 Hulverstone ....H 5
21 Humber Court...G 1
37 Humberside, Co. ..C 7
37 Humberston....G 10
23 Humberstone....B 10
49 Humbie.......C 7
49 Humbleton, Northumb. G 12
37 Humbleton, Yorkshire.....D 10
49 Hume.......E 9
47 Humeston......H 7
45 Humshaugh....F 7
61 Huna.......A 12
34 Huncoat.......D 6
23 Huncote.......B 8
49 Hundalee.......G 9
39 Hunderthwaite ...C 12
33 Hundleby.......D 11
12 Hundleton.......G 3
25 Hundon.......K 8
9 Hundred Acres...E 7
34 Hundred End.....E 3
21 Hundred House...G 7
23 Hungarton.....A 10
34 Hunger Hill.....F 5
16 Hungerford, Berks. G 4
8 Hungerford, Hants.E 3
16 Hungerford Newtown G 5
32 Hungerton......G 6
62 Hunglader......A 3
63 Hunisish.......F 1
41 Hunmanby.....G 11
23 Hunningham....E 7
8 Hunny Hill.....G 6
18 Hunsdon.......C 4
36 Hunsingore......B 2
35 Hunslett Carr...D 11
39 Hunsonby......B 8
61 Hunspow......A 11
24 Hunstanton.....G 5
45 Hunstanworth ...H 8
27 Hunston, Suffolk .H 3
9 Hunston, Sussex .F 10
15 Hunstrete.......H 9
35 Hunsworth......D 10
22 Hunt End.......F 4
41 Hunt Ho.......E 7
47 Hunter's Quay...B 7
49 Huntershall.....F 10
47 Hunterston Works.D 7
44 Huntford.......B 5
59 Hunthill Lodge ..K 2
25 Huntingdon, Hunts. H 3
22 Huntingdon, Staffs. A 3
25 Huntingdon and Peterborough, Co. H 3
27 Huntingfield.....H 6
21 Huntington, Herefs. G 8
21 Huntington, Herefs. H 10
36 Huntington, Yorks. H 3
52 Huntingtower Haugh E 5
15 Huntley, Glos...B 10
31 Huntley, Staffs...F 8
58 Huntly.......D 3
49 Huntlywood.....E 9
10 Hunton, Kent....C 6
40 Hunton, Yorks...F 2
17 Hunton Bridge..D 11
30 Hunt's Cross....B 3
6 Huntscott......B 3
6 Huntsham......D 3
8 Huntspill......B 6
7 Huntworth.....C 7
40 Hunwick.......B 2
26 Hunworth.......B 4
7 Hurcott.......E 7
8 Hurdcott.......C 3
22 Hurley, Berks...F 9
22 Hurley, War. ....C 6
47 Hurlford.......F 9
64 Hurliness......E 1
8 Hurn.......F 3
31 Hursdfield......C 8

MAP
8 Hursley..........D 6
17 Hurst, Berks......G 9
35 Hurst, Lancs.....G 8
7 Hurst, Somerset...D 8
40 Hurst, Yorks.....E 1
10 Hurst Green......C 3
34 Hurst Green, Lancs.
............C 6
10 Hurst Green, Sussex
............E 6
10 Hurst Wickham...F 2
8 Hurstbourne Priors A 6
8 Hurstbourne Tarrant
............A 5
21 Hurstley.........G 9
10 Hurstpierpoint....F 2
21 Hurstway Com....G 8
9 Hurtmore........B 11
40 Hurworth........D 3
39 Hury...........C 11
62 Husabost Piers....C 1
23 Husbands Bosworth
............D 10
25 Husborne Crawley.L 1
40 Husthwaite......H 5
32 Huthwaite.......D 2
49 Hutlerton.......G 7
33 Huttoft.........C 12
49 Hutton, Berwick .D 11
39 Hutton, Cumb....C 7
18 Hutton, Essex.....D 6
34 Hutton, Lancs....D 4
15 Hutton, Somerset .H 7
37 Hutton, Yorks....B 8
41 Hutton Buscel....G 9
40 Hutton Conyers...H 3
39 Hutton End.....A 7
40 Hutton Hang......F 2
40 Hutton Henry....B 4
39 Hutton-in-the-Forest
............B 7
39 Hutton John.....C 7
41 Hutton-le-Hole...F 7
40 Hutton Lowcross .D 6
40 Hutton Magna....D 2
38 Hutton Roof, Cumb.
............B 6
39 Hutton Roof,
Westmorland...G 8
40 Hutton Rudby....E 5
40 Hutton Sessay....H 5
36 Hutton Wandesley.B 3
4 Huxford.........D 6
6 Huxham.........F 3
30 Huxley..........D 4
64 Huxter..........D 7
30 Huyton..........A 3
38 Hycemoor.......F 3
35 Hyde, Cheshire...H 8
15 Hyde, Glos......D 12
17 Hyde Heath.....D 10
31 Hyde Lea........H 7
9 Hydestile.......B 11
38 Hydro...........F 2
48 Hyndford........E 2
21 Hyssington......C 8
8 Hythe, Hants....E 5
11 Hythe, Kent.....E 10
7 Hythe, Somerset ..A 8
17 Hythe End......G 11
58 Hythie..........C 7
58 Ianstown........A 2
7 Ibberton........E 11
31 Ible...........D 11
8 Ibsley..........E 3
23 Ibstock.........A 7
17 Ibstone.........E 8
8 Ibthorpe........A 5
9 Ibworth.........A 7
15 Icelton.........H 7
26 Ickburgh........F 1
18 Ickenham.......A 7
17 Ickford.........C 7
11 Ickham.........B 11
18 Ickleford.......A 2
25 Ickleton.......L 6
27 Icklingham.....H 3
25 Ickwell Green....L 3
16 Icomb..........B 3
16 Idbury.........B 3
4 Iddesleigh......E 4
6 Ide...........G 2
10 Ide Hill........C 4
8 Ideford.........H 8
11 Iden...........F 8
10 Iden Green, Kent .D 6
11 Iden Green, Kent .E 7
35 Idle...........C 10
22 Idlicote........H 5
58 Idoch...........C 5
13 Idole..........E 7
31 Idridgehay......E 11
62 Idrigil.........B 3

16 Idstone.........F 4
53 Idvies.........B 10
10 Ifield..........D 1
9 Ifold..........C 11
10 Iford..........G 3
15 Ifton..........E 8
30 Ifton Heath......G 2
30 Ightfield.......F 5
10 Ightham.......B 5
27 Iken..........K 7
31 Ilam..........E 10
11 Ilchester.......D 8
49 Ilderton.......G 12
18 Ilford..........E 4
4 Ilfracombe......A 4
32 Ilkeston........F 2
27 Ilketshall St. Andrew
............G 6
27 Ilketshall St. Margaret
............G 6
35 Ilkley.........B 9
35 Illingworth......D 9
22 Illey..........D 3
2 Illogan.........E 4
2 Illogan Highway ..E 4
23 Illston on the Hill .B 10
17 Ilmer..........D 8
22 Ilmington......H 5
7 Ilminster.......E 7
5 Ilsington.......H 9
13 Ilston.........H 9
7 Ilton, Somerset...D 7
40 Ilton, Yorkshire. . G 2
46 Imachar.........E 4
37 Immingham......F 9
37 Immingham Dock .E 9
25 Impington.......J 5
55 Inbhireala or
Strathossian Ho.M 8
30 Ince...........C 3
34 Ince Blundell.....G 2
30 Ince-in-Makerfield.G 5
59 Inch...........K 4
54 Inchbae Lodge...C 8
30 Inchbare........L 3
47 Inchbean........F 9
58 Inchberry.......B 1
53 Incheoch........B 7
16 Inchina.........G 2
47 Inchinnan.......B 9
60 Inchkinloch......C 6
55 Inchlaggan.......J 5
56 Inchlumpie......B 1
59 Inchnabobart....J 1
55 Inchnacardoch (Hotel)
............H 7
60 Inchnadamph....E 4
47 Inchrory........J 7
53 Inchture........D 7
54 Inchvuilt.......F 6
52 Inchyra.........E 6
2 Indian Queens...D 6
4 Indicott........B 4
47 Industrial Estate,
Dunbarton....B 9
48 Industrial Estate, Fife
............A 4
18 Ingatestone......D 6
35 Ingbirchworth...G 10
18 Ingestre........H 8
32 Ingham, Lincs....B 6
26 Ingham, Norfolk .C 7
27 Ingham, Suffolk.H 2
24 Ingleborough, Norfolk
............D 6
39 Ingleborough, Yorks.
............H 10
31 Ingleby.........G 12
40 Ingleby Arncliffe .E 5
40 Ingleby Cross....E 5
40 Ingleby Greenhow.E 6
31 Inglesbatch.....H 10
16 Inglesham.......D 3
40 Ingleton, Durham .C 2
39 Ingleton, Yorks..H 9
34 Inglewhite......C 4
45 Ingoe..........F 8
33 Ingoldmells....C 12
33 Ingoldsby.......G 7
34 Inglewhite......C 4
45 Ingoe..........F 8
33 Ingoldmells....C 12
33 Ingoldsby.......G 7
24 Ingoldsthorpe....B 8
45 Ingram.........A 8
18 Ingrave.........E 6
35 Ingrow.........C 9
39 Ings...........E 7
15 Ingst..........E 9
26 Ingworth.......C 5
51 Inistrynich......E 8
38 Injebreck.......G 2
22 Inkberrow.......F 4

16 Inkpen........H 4
61 Inkstack.......A 11
30 Innellan.......B 6
48 Innerleithen.....F 6
53 Innerleven......G 8
42 Innermessan.....E 2
42 Innerwell Fishery .G 6
49 Innerwick, E.Loth.B 10
51 Innerwick, Perth ..B 1
51 Innis Chonain...E 8
51 Innischoarach....D 12
38 Insch..........E 4
58 Inschtammack....C 2
57 Insh...........J 4
51 Insh House......J 4
51 Inshaig........B 7
60 Inshore.........A 4
34 Inskip.........C 3
26 Instow.........C 3
35 Intake Gate......C 10
57 Inver, Aberdeen..K 8
52 Inver, Perth.....C 5
56 Inver, Ross &
Cromarty......B 4
54 Inver Alligin.....D 2
55 Inver Mallie.....K 5
55 Inverailort.....L 1
60 Inverallochy....A 8
60 Inveran.........G 6
51 Inveraray.......G 8
53 Inverarity......C 9
51 Inverarnan......F 10
54 Inverasdale......A 2
54 Inverbain.......D 2
51 Inverbeg Hotel ..H 10
59 Inverbervie......K 6
58 Inverboyndie....A 4
60 Inverbroom.....H 3
57 Invercauld House .K 7
46 Inverchaolain....B 6
46 Inverchapel......A 6
51 Invercharnan....C 8
54 Inverchoran.....E 6
51 Invercreran......C 7
57 Inverdruie......H 5
58 Inverebrie......D 7
57 Inveredrie......M 7
57 Invereshie House ..J 4
48 Inveresk........B 6
51 Inveresragan.....D 7
54 Inverewe House...B 2
51 Inverey.........K 6
57 Inverfarigaig....G 1
55 Invergarry......J 7
52 Invergeldie......D 2
55 Invergloy.......L 6
56 Invergordon.....C 3
53 Invergowrie.....D 8
55 Inverguseran....J 1
52 Inverhadden.....A 2
58 Inverharroch....D 1
51 Inverherive.....E 10
55 Inverie.........J 1
51 Inverinan......F 7
55 Inverinate......G 3
53 Inverkeilor.....B 11
48 Inverkeithing....A 4
58 Inverkeithny....C 4
47 Inverkip.......B 7
60 Inverkirkaig.....E 2
60 Inverlael.......H 3
60 Inverlael Lodge...H 3
55 Inverlair.......L 7
51 Inverlochlarig....F 11
51 Inverlochy......E 9
59 Invermark Lodge..J 2
55 Invermoriston...H 8
58 Invernan House...F 1
61 Invernaver......B 7
56 Inverness.......E 2
57 Inverness, Co.....H 3
58 Invernetie......C 8
51 Invernoaden....H 8
51 Inveroran Hotel..C 10
60 Inverpolly Lodge..E 2
58 Inverquhomery...C 8
55 Inverroy.......L 6
50 Inversanda......B 7
55 Invershiel......H 3
60 Inversnaid......G 6
60 Invershin Station .G 6
55 Inverskilavulin ...L 5
51 Inversnaid Hotel .G 10
58 Inverugie, Aber...C 8
56 Inverugie, Moray .C 7
51 Inveruglas......G 10
57 Inveruglass......J 4
58 Inverurie.......E 5
52 Invervar........B 2
59 Invery House....H 4
58 Inverythan.....C 5
4 Inwardleigh......F 4
19 Inworth........B 8

9 Iping..........D 10
5 Ipplepen........J 7
18 Ippollits.......A 2
17 Ipsden.........F 7
31 Ipstones........E 8
27 Ipswich........L 5
30 Irby...........B 1
33 Irby in the Marsh.D 11
37 Irby upon Humber G 9
23 Irchester.......E 12
39 Ireby..........H 9
38 Ireleth.........G 5
39 Ireshopeburn....A 11
55 Irine..........L 1
34 Irlam..........H 6
33 Irnham.........G 7
15 Iron Acton......F 10
21 Iron Bridge.....B 12
22 Iron Cross......G 4
43 Ironmacannie....D 7
32 Ironville.......E 2
26 Irstead.........C 7
23 Irthlingborough .E 12
44 Irthington......G 3
41 Irton..........G 10
47 Irvine.........E 8
44 Irvington......F 1
61 Isauld.........A 9
64 Isbister, Orkney..C 2
64 Isbister, Zetland..B 7
64 Isbister, Zetland..C 8
10 Isfield.........F 3
47 Isham..........E 12
23 Isham..........E 12
50 Ishriff.........D 4
7 Isle Abbotts.....D 7
7 Isle Brewers.....D 7
18 Isle of Dogs.....F 4
42 Isle of Whithorn .H 6
25 Isleham........H 7
62 Isleornsay......G 6
43 Islesteps.......D 10
18 Isleworth.......F 2
32 Isley Walton.....H 2
18 Islington........E 3
25 Islip, Northants. .G 1
16 Islip, Oxon......C 6
63 Islivig.........D 1
8 Itchen..........E 6
9 Itchen Abbas....C 7
9 Itchen Stoke....C 7
15 Itchingfield....C 12
15 Itchington......F 10
26 Itteringham.....C 4
27 Itton Common....E 8
38 Ivegill.........A 6
39 Ivelet.........E 11
51 Iver...........F 11
17 Iver Heath......F 11
45 Iveston........H 9
17 Ivinghoe.......B 10
17 Ivinghoe Aston .B 10
21 Ivington.......G 10
21 Ivington Green...G 10
10 Ivy Hatch......C 5
5 Ivybridge......K 5
11 Ivychurch.......E 9
11 Iwade..........A 7
7 Iwerne Courtney or
Shroton......E 12
7 Iwerne Minster..E 12
27 Ixworth........H 2
27 Ixworth Thorpe...H 2
35 Jack Hill.......B 10
32 Jacksdale.......E 2
58 Jackstown.......D 5
47 Jackton........D 10
2 Jacobstow......B 2
1 Jacobstowe.....F 5
9 Jacobswell......A 11
12 Jameston........G 4
44 Jamestown, Dumf. C 1
47 Jamestown, Dunb. A 9
54 Jamestown, Ross &
Cromarty......D 8
61 Janetstown......D 11
45 Jarrow.........F 11
19 Jasper's Green....A 7
48 Jawcraig........B 1
33 Jaywick Sands...C 11
17 Jealott's Hill....G 9
40 Jeater Houses....F 4
9 Jedburgh.......G 9
12 Jeffreston......F 4
56 Jemimaville....C 3
24 Jersey Marine...H 10
59 Jessiefield......G 6
10 Jevington......H 4
17 Jockey End.....C 11
30 Jodrell Bank....C 6
35 John O'Gaunts ..D 12
61 John o'Groats ..A 12
38 Johnby.........B 6

10 John's Cross......F 6
59 Johnshaven......K 6
12 Johnston........F 3
44 Johnstone, Dumf. .C 1
47 Johnstone, Ren....C 9
43 Johnstonebridge .B 11
13 Johnstown, Carm. .E 7
29 Johnstown, Denb. F 12
10 Joppa, Cards.....F 1
48 Joppa, Midloth....B 6
17 Jordans........E 10
12 Jordanston......D 3
19 Jordons........E 8
35 Jump...........G 12
9 Jumpers Green...G 3
48 Juniper Green...B 5
38 Jurby East......F 2
38 Jurby West......F 2
44 Justicetown.....G 2
39 Kaber.........D 10
58 Kaecloch.......C 4
48 Kaimes.........C 5
54 Kalemouth......G 9
54 Kalnakill.......D 1
46 Kames, Argyll...B 5
50 Kames, Argyll...F 5
47 Kames, Argyll .G 11
36 Keadby.........F 6
33 Keal Cotes.....D 10
34 Kearsley.......G 6
39 Kearstwick......G 8
39 Kearton........E 12
60 Kearvaig.......A 4
39 Keasden........H 9
33 Keddington......A 10
25 Kedington......K 8
31 Kedleston.......F 11
49 Kedslie........E 8
37 Keelby.........F 9
25 Keeley Green....L 1
45 Keepershield....F 7
12 Keeston........E 3
15 Keevil.........H 12
32 Kegworth.......G 2
3 Kehelland......F 3
58 Keig...........F 3
35 Keighley........C 9
56 Keil...........B 7
52 Keilarsbrae.....H 4
58 Keilhill.........B 5
46 Keillmore......A 2
52 Keillour........E 5
52 Keir House......G 3
43 Keir Mill.......B 9
24 Keisby.........C 1
61 Keiss..........B 12
58 Keith..........C 2
58 Keithen........C 5
35 Kelbrook.......C 8
33 Kelby..........F 7
39 Keld, Westmor...D 8
39 Keld, Yorkshire..E 11
41 Keldholme......F 7
41 Keldy Castle.....F 8
16 Kelfield, Oxon....D 4
36 Kelfield........E 5
32 Kelham........E 5
43 Kelhead........E 12
50 Kellan.........C 3
53 Kellas, Angus....D 9
56 Kellas, Moray....D 7
5 Kellaton.......M 7
16 Kellaways......G 1
39 Kelleth.........E 9
30 Kelling........A 4
36 Kellingley......E 3
36 Kellington......E 3
40 Kelloe.........B 4
49 Kelloe Mains....D 11
5 Kelly..........H 3
3 Kelly Bray......C 10
23 Kelmarsh......D 10
16 Kelmscot......D 3
30 Kelsale........J 7
30 Kelsall........C 4
30 Kelsall Hill.....C 4
25 Kelshall.......L 4
43 Kelsick........F 12
49 Kelso..........F 10
31 Kelstedge......D 11
33 Kelstern.......A 9
29 Kelsterton.....C 12
15 Kelston.......H 10
43 Kelton........D 10
43 Kelton Hill.....F 8
43 Kelty..........G 1
19 Kelvedon.......B 8
18 Kelvedon Hatch .D 6
2 Kelynack......G 1
53 Kemback........F 9
22 Kemberton......B 1
16 Kemble.........D 1
22 Kemerton......H 3

15 Kemeys Commander
............D 7
58 Kemnay.........F 5
10 Kemp Town......H 2
60 Kempie.........B 5
15 Kempley........A 10
22 Kempsey........G 2
16 Kempsford......D 3
9 Kempshott......A 7
25 Kempston......K 1
25 Kempston Hardwick
............L 1
25 Kempston West End
............K 1
21 Kempton......D 9
10 Kemsing.......B 4
11 Kemsley........A 8
11 Kenardington....E 8
21 Kenchester Sugwas
............H 10
16 Kencot.........D 4
39 Kendal.........F 7
15 Kenderchurch....A 7
2 Kenfig.........F 1
14 Kenfig Hill......F 2
21 Kenilworth......E 6
51 Kenknock......D 11
21 Kenley........B 11
52 Kenmore, Argyll ..G 8
52 Kenmore, Perth...C 3
54 Kenmore, Ross &
Cromarty......D 1
6 Kenn, Devon....H 3
15 Kenn, Somerset..G 7
63 Kennacley......G 3
46 Kennacraig.....C 3
3 Kennards House .A 10
44 Kennedy's Corner .E 1
2 Kenneggy Downs .G 3
4 Kennerleigh....E 7
52 Kennet.........H 4
58 Kenneth Bank ..E 10
25 Kennett........H 8
6 Kennford.......G 3
27 Kenninghall.....G 3
16 Kennington, Berks.D 6
11 Kennington, Kent .D 9
18 Kennington, London
............F 3
53 Kennoway......G 8
47 Kennox........E 8
25 Kennyhill......G 8
36 Kennythorpe....A 6
62 Kensaleyre.....C 3
18 Kensington......F 3
17 Kensworth......B 11
17 Kensworth Com..B 11
11 Kent, County....C 8
10 Kent Street.....C 5
51 Kentallen.......B 7
15 Kentchurch.....B 7
25 Kentford.......J 8
6 Kentisbeare.....E 4
4 Kentisbury.....B 5
4 Kentisburyford...B 5
39 Kentmere.......E 7
6 Kenton, Devon ..H 3
18 Kenton, London..E 2
27 Kenton, Suffolk ..J 5
45 Kenton Bank Foot F 10
50 Kentra........A 4
39 Kents Bank......H 6
15 Kent's Green....B 10
8 Kent's Oak.....D 5
58 Kentstone......B 11
30 Kenwick.......G 3
2 Kenwyn.......E 5
60 Keoldale.......A 5
63 Keose.........E 5
55 Keppoch........G 3
46 Keprigan......H 2
45 Kepwick........F 5
49 Kerchesters....F 10
23 Keresley.......D 7
15 Kerne Bridge....B 9
48 Kerrcleuch.....H 5
31 Kerridge.......C 8
2 Kerris.........G 2
54 Kerrowwood....F 7
21 Kerry.........C 7
46 Kerrylamont....D 6
15 Kerry's Gate....A 7
46 Kerrysdale......B 2
54 Kerrytonlia.....D 6
32 Kersall........D 4
8 Kersbrooke.....H 4
4 Kerscott.......C 5
47 Kerse.........D 8
21 Kersey.........L 5
63 Kershader......E 4
44 Kershopefoot....E 3
49 Kersmains......F 9
22 Kersoe........H 3

MAP
6 Kerswell........F 4
22 Kerswell Green...G 2
27 Kesgrave.......L 5
38 Keskadale.......C 4
27 Kessingland.....G 8
27 Kessingland Beach.G 8
2 Kestle Mill.......D 5
18 Keston.........G 4
38 Keswick, Cumb..C 5
26 Keswick, Norfolk B 6
26 Keswick, Norfolk .E 5
21 Ketley.........A 12
49 Kettelshiel......D 9
23 Kettering......D 12
26 Ketteringham.....E 5
53 Kettins........C 7
27 Kettlebaston....K 3
53 Kettlebridge.....F 8
22 Kettlebrook.....B 6
27 Kettleburgh....J 5
53 Kettlehill.......F 8
41 Kettleness......D 8
31 Kettleshulme....B 8
35 Kettlesing....B 11
35 Kettlesing Bottom
      A 11
26 Kettlestone......B 3
32 Kettlethorpe....C 6
64 Kettletoft......B 4
39 Kettlewell.....H 11
24 Ketton.........E 1
18 Kew...........F 2
14 Kewstoke.......H 6
35 Kexbrough.....F 11
32 Kexby, Lincs....B 6
36 Kexby, Yorks....B 5
31 Key Green......D 7
11 Key Street......B 7
23 Keyham......B 10
8 Keyhaven......G 5
37 Keyingham....E 10
10 Keymer.........F 2
15 Keynsham.....G 9
33 Key's Toft......D 12
25 Keysoe........J 2
25 Keysoe Roe.....J 2
25 Keyston.......H 1
32 Keyworth......G 3
45 Kibblesworth...G 10
23 Kibworth Beauchamp
      C 10
23 Kibworth Harcourt
      C 10
18 Kidbrooke......F 4
22 Kiddemore Green .A 2
22 Kidderminster...D 2
16 Kiddington.....B 5
16 Kidlington......C 6
17 Kidmore End....F 8
30 Kidnal.........E 3
58 Kidrummy.......F 2
31 Kidsgrove......E 7
39 Kidstones.....G 11
13 Kidwelly......F 7
50 Kiel Crofts ....D 6
44 Kielder.........D 4
52 Kilbagie.......H 4
47 Kilbarchan....C 9
62 Kilbeg........H 6
46 Kilberry.......C 2
47 Kilbirnie......D 8
50 Kilbride........E 6
50 Kilbride, Argyll ..E 6
62 Kilbride, Inver....F 5
59 Kilburn, Angus ..K 1
32 Kilburn, Derby .F 1
40 Kilburn, Yorks...G 5
23 Kilby..........C 9
48 Kilcadzow......D 2
50 Kilchattan, Arg. .H 1
46 Kilchattan, Bute..D 6
46 Kilchenzie......G 2
50 Kilcheran.......D 5
50 Kilchoan, Argyll .A 2
50 Kilchoan, Argyll .F 5
55 Kilchoan, Inver....K 2
51 Kilchrenan......E 7
53 Kilconquhar....G 9
15 Kilcot........B 10
56 Kilcoy.........E 1
47 Kilcreggan......A 7
40 Kildale........D 6
46 Kildalloig......G 4
46 Kildavanan.....C 5
56 Kildermorie Lodge B 1
46 Kildonan, Arran..G 5
61 Kildonan, Suther..E 9
61 Kildonan Lodge...E 9
42 Kildrochat House .F 2
35 Kildwick.......C 9
46 Kilfinan........B 4
55 Kilfinnan.......K 6
29 Kilford........D 10

MAP
12 Kilgetty.........F 5
49 Kilham, Northumb.
      F 11
37 Kilham, Yorks...A 8
42 Kilkerran........A 4
4 Kilkhampton......E 1
32 Killamarsh......B 2
13 Killay.........H 9
50 Killbeg........C 3
46 Killchianaig.....A 1
46 Killean........E 2
47 Killearn......A 10
46 Killellan.......H 2
56 Killen.........D 2
40 Killerby.......C 2
42 Killern.......F 6
51 Killichonan....B 12
50 Killichronan....C 3
55 Killiechanate...L 6
57 Killiehuntly....K 4
50 Killiemor......D 2
55 Killilan.......G 3
61 Killimster....B 12
52 Killin.........D 1
57 Killin Lodge....J 1
35 Killinghall....A 11
39 Killington......F 8
49 Killochyett.....E 7
50 Killunaig......E 2
50 Killundine.....C 3
43 Killyleoch......C 9
47 Kilmacolm.....B 8
52 Kilmahog......F 1
50 Kilmahumaig....H 5
62 Kilmaluag......A 4
62 Kilmany.......E 8
62 Kilmarie.......F 5
47 Kilmarnock....F 9
53 Kilmaron Castle .E 8
50 Kilmartin......H 5
50 Kilmaurs......E 9
50 Kilmelford.....F 6
7 Kilmersdon.....A 10
9 Kilmeston......D 7
46 Kilmichael......G 2
50 Kilmichael Glassary
      H 6
46 Kilmichael of
    Inverlussa......A 3
6 Kilmington, Devon F 6
7 Kilmington, Wilts.C 11
7 Kilmington Street C 11
52 Kilmorack......E 1
50 Kilmore, Argyll ..E 6
62 Kilmore, Inver...G 6
50 Kilmory, Argyll ..A 3
46 Kilmory, Argyll ..B 2
46 Kilmory, Arran...G 4
51 Kilmote........F 9
62 Kilmuir, Inver...A 3
62 Kilmuir, Inver.....C 2
56 Kilmuir, Ross &
    Cromarty......B 3
56 Kilmuir, Ross &
    Cromarty......C 2
46 Kilmun........A 6
17 Kiln Green......F 9
44 Kiln Hill.......F 4
45 Kiln Pit Hill....H 8
10 Kilndown......E 6
43 Kilness.......D 10
47 Kilnford........F 8
36 Kilnhurst......G 2
50 Kilninian.......C 1
50 Kilninver......E 5
37 Kilnsea.......F 11
39 Kilnsey......H 12
37 Kilnwick.......B 7
36 Kilnwick Percy...B 6
50 Kiloran........H 1
46 Kilpatrick......G 4
15 Kilpeck........A 7
61 Kilphedir.......E 9
36 Kilpin.........D 5
36 Kilpin Pike.....D 5
53 Kilrenny......G 10
23 Kilsby.........E 9
53 Kilspindie......E 7
48 Kilsyth......B 12
6 Kilton, Somerset .B 5
41 Kilton, Yorks....C 7
62 Kilvaxter......A 3
6 Kilve..........B 5
32 Kilvington......F 5
47 Kilwinning......E 8
26 Kimberley, Norf..E 4
32 Kimberley, Notts..F 2
17 Kimble Wick....G 9
45 Kimblesworth....H 11
21 Kimbolton, Herefs.
      F 10
25 Kimbolton, Hunts. H 2

MAP
23 Kimcote.........C 9
7 Kimmeridge.....H 12
49 Kimmerston.....F 12
8 Kimpton, Hants..A 4
18 Kimpton, Herts. .B 2
61 Kinbrace.......D 8
55 Kinbreack......K 4
52 Kinbuck.......G 3
47 Kincaidston.....G 8
53 Kincaple.......E 9
59 Kincardine, Co. ...J 5
52 Kincardine, Fife ..D 8
60 Kincardine, Ross &
    Cromarty......G 6
59 Kincardine O'Neil.G 3
52 Kinclaven.......C 6
59 Kincorth........G 7
56 Kincorth House ..D 6
57 Kincraig.......J 4
52 Kindallachan.....B 5
56 Kindrummond....F 2
46 Kinerarach......D 2
16 Kineton, Glos....B 2
23 Kineton, War....G 7
52 Kinfauns.......E 6
15 King Stanley....D 11
50 Kingairloch Ho...B 6
46 Kingarth.......D 6
15 Kingcoed......D 7
33 Kingerby........A 7
4 Kingford......D 5
16 Kingham......B 3
50 Kingharair......C 2
43 Kingholm Quay...D 10
48 Kinghorn......A 5
53 Kinglassie......G 7
58 Kingoodie, Aberdeen
      E 6
53 Kingoodie .Angus.D 8
21 King's Acre....H 10
31 Kings Bromley...H 9
15 Kings Caple....A 9
24 King's Cliffe....F 1
22 King's Coughton .F 4
22 Kings Heath.....D 4
17 Kings Langley ..D 11
24 King's Lynn....D 7
39 King's Meaburn...C 8
48 Kings Muir.....E 5
23 King's Norton, Leics.
      B 10
22 King's Norton, War.
      D 4
4 King's Nympton ..D 6
21 King's Pyon....G 10
25 Kings Ripton....H 4
8 King's Samborne..C 5
7 King's Stag....E 10
16 King's Sutton...A 6
18 King's Walden...B 2
11 Kings Wood....C 7
8 Kings Worth....C 6
3 Kingsand......E 11
53 Kingsbarns....F 10
5 Kingsbridge, Devon
      L 6
6 Kingsbridge, Som..C 3
62 Kingsburgh.....C 3
18 Kingsbury, London E 2
22 Kingsbury, War. ..C 6
7 Kingsbury Episcopi
      D 8
16 Kingsclere......H 6
15 Kingscote.....E 11
4 Kingscott.......D 4
46 Kingscross......G 5
7 Kingsdon......D 8
11 Kingsdown....C 12
52 Kingseat......H 6
17 Kingsey........C 8
10 Kingsfold......D 1
59 Kingsford, Aber...G 6
47 Kingsford, Ayr...E 9
22 Kingsford, Worcs. D 2
27 Kingshall Street...J 2
4 Kingsheanton....B 4
52 Kingshouse.....E 1
51 Kingshouse Hotel B 10
5 Kingskerswell....J 7
53 Kingskettle......F 8
28 Kingsland, Angl..B 2
21 Kingsland, Herefs. F 10
30 Kingsley, Ches...C 4
9 Kingsley, Hants..B 9
31 Kingsley, Staffs..F 8
9 Kingsley Green ..C 10
31 Kingsley Holt...F 9
53 Kingsmuir......B 9
11 Kingsnorth.....D 9
22 Kingstanding....C 4
5 Kingsteignton ..H 7
15 Kingsthorne....A 8
8 Kinson........F 2
23 Kingsthorpe....F 11

MAP
25 Kingston, Cambs. .K 4
5 Kingston, Devon ..L 5
7 Kingston, Dorset.E 11
8 Kingston, Dorset .H 1
49 Kingston, E. Loth..A 8
8 Kingston, Hants...F 3
8 Kingston, I.o.W...H 6
11 Kingston, Kent ..C 10
58 Kingston, Moray...A 1
9 Kingston, Sussex .F 12
16 Kingston Bagpuize D 5
17 Kingston Blount ..D 8
10 Kingston by Sea..H 1
7 Kingston Deverill C 11
16 Kingston Lisle....E 4
10 Kingston near Lewes
      G 3
32 Kingston on Soar..G 2
7 Kingston Russell .G 9
6 Kingston St. Mary C 6
15 Kingston Seymour H 7
37 Kingston upon Hull
      D 8
18 Kingston upon Thames
      G 2
18 Kingston Vale....G 2
15 Kingstone, Herefs..A 7
7 Kingstone, Som...E 7
31 Kingstone, Staffs..G 9
44 Kingstown......A 2
5 Kingswear......K 7
22 Kingswinford....C 2
17 Kingswood, Bucks.B 8
15 Kingswood, Glos. E 10
15 Kingswood, Glos. G 9
21 Kingswood, Mont. B 8
22 Kingswood, War...E 5
21 Kingswood Com. .G 8
21 Kington, Herefs...G 8
22 Kington, Worcs. .G 3
15 Kington Langley .G 12
7 Kington Magna ..C 11
15 Kington St. Michael
      F 12
57 Kingussie.......J 3
7 Kingweston......C 8
43 Kinharvie......E 10
52 Kinkell Bridge...E 4
58 Kinknockie, Aber..C 7
58 Kinknockie, Aber..E 7
44 Kinkry Hill......E 3
22 Kinlet.........D 1
53 Kinloch, Fife....F 7
62 Kinloch, Inver.....F 6
52 Kinloch, Perth....C 6
53 Kinloch, Perth....C 7
60 Kinloch, Suther..D 4
62 Kinloch Castle ...H 3
55 Kinloch Hourn...J 3
57 Kinloch Laggan..K 1
60 Kinloch Lodge...B 6
52 Kinloch Rannoch .A 2
50 Kinlochan......A 5
51 Kinlochard....G 11
55 Kinlochbeoraid...L 2
60 Kinlochbervie....B 3
55 Kinlocheil......L 4
51 Kinlochetive....C 8
54 Kinlochewe.....D 4
51 Kinlochleven....A 9
55 Kinlochmoidart ..M 1
55 Kinlochmorar....K 2
51 Kinlochmore....A 9
55 Kinlochnanuagh ..L 1
55 Kinlochspelve....E 4
55 Kinloid.........L 1
56 Kinloss........D 6
29 Kinmel Bay......B 9
58 Kinmuck.......F 6
58 Kinnadie.......C 7
58 Kinnahaird......D 8
59 Kinnaird Castle ..L 4
53 Kinnaird.......D 7
59 Kinneff.......K 6
43 Kinnelhead....B 11
53 Kinnell........B 10
30 Kinnerley......F 1
21 Kinnersley, Herefs.G 9
22 Kinnersley, Worcs. H 2
21 Kinnerton......F 8
52 Kinnesswood....G 6
40 Kinninvie......C 1
53 Kinnordy........B 8
32 Kinoulton......G 4
57 Kinrara........J 4
59 Kinross, Co......G 6
52 Kinross, Co.....G 6
53 Kinrossie........D 7
21 Kinsham........F 9
36 Kinsley........F 2
8 Kinson.........F 2
56 Kinsteary Lodge .D 5

MAP
63 Kintaravay......E 3
16 Kintbury.......G 5
56 Kintessack......D 6
52 Kintillo.........E 6
59 Kintocher.......G 3
21 Kinton, Herefs....E 9
30 Kinton, Salop....H 2
58 Kintore........F 5
50 Kintra.........F 1
56 Kintrae.........C 7
50 Kintraw........G 5
50 Kinuachdrach ...H 4
57 Kinveachy.....H 5
22 Kinver.........D 2
36 Kippax.........D 2
52 Kippen.........H 1
43 Kippford or Scaur .F 9
10 Kipping's Cross ..D 5
64 Kirbister.......D 2
38 Kirby..........H 2
26 Kirby Bedon.....E 6
32 Kirby Bellars....H 4
26 Kirby Cane......F 7
19 Kirby Cross ....B 12
41 Kirby Grindalythe.H 9
40 Kirby Hill, Yorks..E 2
40 Kirby Hill, Yorks..H 4
7 Kirby Knowle....F 5
19 Kirby le Soken...B 12
41 Kirby Misperton..G 8
23 Kirby Muxloe....B 8
35 Kirby Overblow..B 12
26 Kirby Row......F 7
40 Kirby Sigston....F 4
36 Kirby Underdale..A 6
40 Kirby Wiske.....G 4
9 Kirdford......C 11
63 Kirivick.......C 3
61 Kirk..........B 11
36 Kirk Bramwith...F 4
35 Kirk Deighton...B 12
37 Kirk Ella.......D 8
32 Kirk Hallam.....F 2
36 Kirk Hammerton..B 3
31 Kirk Ireton.....E 11
31 Kirk Langley...F 11
40 Kirk Merrington..B 3
38 Kirk Michael.....G 1
58 Kirk of Shotts....C 1
36 Kirk Sandall....F 4
36 Kirk Smeaton....E 3
49 Kirk Yetholm ..G 11
64 Kirkabister.....E 7
43 Kirkandrews....G 7
44 Kirkandrews upon
    Eden.........G 2
44 Kirkbampton....G 1
43 Kirkbank......C 11
43 Kirkbean.......F 10
64 Kirkbrae.......A 2
44 Kirkbride, Cumb..G 1
43 Kirkbride, Dumf..C 9
53 Kirkbudd.......C 9
48 Kirkburn, Peeb...F 5
37 Kirkburn, Yorks..B 7
35 Kirkburton.....F 10
34 Kirkby, Lancs....G 3
33 Kirkby, Lincs.....A 8
40 Kirkby, Yorks....E 5
40 Kirkby Fleetham..F 3
33 Kirkby Green....D 8
32 Kirkby in Ashfield.E 2
24 Kirkby le Thorpe .A 2
39 Kirkby Lonsdale .G 8
35 Kirkby Malham..A 7
23 Kirkby Mallory...B 8
40 Kirkby Malzeard .H 2
41 Kirkby Mills....G 7
33 Kirkby on Bain..D 9
39 Kirkby Stephen..D 10
39 Kirkby Thore....C 9
24 Kirkby UnderwoodC 2
36 Kirkby Wharf....C 3
41 Kirkbymoorside...F 7
53 Kirkcaldy......H 7
44 Kirkcambeck....F 4
43 Kirkcarswell....G 8
42 Kirkcolm......E 1
47 Kirkconnel.....H 12
43 Kirkconnell, Kirk.
      E 10
43 Kirkconnell, Kirk. .F 7
42 Kirkcowan......E 4
43 Kirkcudbright....F 8
43 Kirkcudbright, Co. E 7
30 Kirkdale.......A 2
43 Kirkdale House...B 8
48 Kirkdean.......E 4
48 Kirkfieldbank....E 1
43 Kirkgunzeon....E 9
34 Kirkham, Lancs...D 3
36 Kirkham, Yorks...A 5
35 Kirkhamgate....E 11

MAP
45 Kirkharle......E 8
45 Kirkheaton,
    Northumb.....E 8
35 Kirkheaton, Yorks.
      E 10
59 Kirkhill, Angus ...L 4
48 Kirkhill, Midloth. .C 5
56 Kirkhill, Ross &
    Cromarty......E 1
58 Kirkhill of
    Kennethmont...E 3
48 Kirkhope.......G 6
48 Kirkhouse......F 6
62 Kirkibost, Inver...F 5
63 Kirkibost, Lewis ..C 3
53 Kirkinch.......C 8
42 Kirkinner......F 5
47 Kirkintilloch....B 11
39 Kirkland, Cumb...B 8
38 Kirkland, Cumb...C 3
43 Kirkland, Dumf...C 9
43 Kirkland, Dumf. .C 11
47 Kirkland, Dumf. H 12
42 Kirkland, Wig....G 5
43 Kirkland Guards.G 12
43 Kirkland of Gelston F 8
40 Kirkleatham.....C 6
40 Kirklevington....D 4
26 Kirkley........F 8
45 Kirkley March...E 9
31 Kirkleyditch....B 8
32 Kirklington, Notts.D 4
40 Kirklington, Yorks.G 3
44 Kirklinton.......F 3
38 Kirkliston......B 4
42 Kirkmaiden.....H 2
42 Kirkmichael, Ayr..A 4
52 Kirkmichael, Perth A 6
47 Kirkmuirhill....E 12
48 Kirknewton, Midloth.
      C 4
49 Kirknewton,
    Northumb.....F 11
58 Kirkney........D 3
42 Kirkoswald, Ayr..A 3
39 Kirkoswald, Cumb. A 8
43 Kirkpatrick, Dur. .D 8
44 Kirkpatrick-Fleming
      F 1
38 Kirksanton......G 4
33 Kirkstead......D 9
48 Kirkstile, Aber...D 3
44 Kirkstile, Dumf. .D 2
61 Kirkstyle......A 12
58 Kirkton, Aber....C 6
58 Kirkton, Aber....E 4
58 Kirkton, Aber....F 6
58 Kirkton, Aber....F 4
53 Kirkton, Angus ..C 9
59 Kirkton, Angus ..J 2
58 Kirkton, Banff...C 4
43 Kirkton, Dumf. .C 10
53 Kirkton, Fife....E 8
56 Kirkton, Inver....F 2
48 Kirkton, Lanark ..G 2
52 Kirkton, Perth ...E 4
56 Kirkton, Ross &
    Cromarty......C 3
54 Kirkton, Ross &
    Cromarty......F 3
44 Kirkton, Rox....B 4
48 Kirkton Manor ..D 5
53 Kirkton of Airlie..B 8
53 Kirkton of
    Auchterhouse...C 8
56 Kirkton of Barevan E 4
53 Kirkton of Collace.D 7
53 Kirkton of Craig .B 11
59 Kirkton of Durris.H 5
58 Kirkton of Glenbuchat
      F 1
53 Kirkton of Glenisla A 7
53 Kirkton of
    Kingoldrum....B 8
53 Kirkton of Largo .G 9
52 Kirkton of Lethendy
      C 6
58 Kirkton of Logie
    Buchan.......E 7
59 Kirkton of Menmuir
      L 3
53 Kirkton of Monikie
      C 10
58 Kirkton of Oyne ..E 4
59 Kirkton of Skene .G 5
53 Kirkton of
    Strathmartine...D 8
53 Kirkton of Tealing.C 9
53 Kirktonbarns....D 9
58 Kirktown.......B 8
58 Kirktown of Alvah.B 4

MAP
58 Kirktown of Auchterless.....C 5
58 Kirktown of Bourtie E 5
58 Kirktown of Deskford B 2
59 Kirktown of Fetteresso J 6
58 Kirktown of Mortlach D 1
58 Kirktown of Rayne E 4
58 Kirktown of Slains. E 8
64 Kirkwall.........D 2
45 Kirkwhelpington ..E 8
37 Kirmington.......F 9
33 Kirmond le Mire ..A 9
47 Kirn............B 7
43 Kirncleuch......B 12
53 Kirriemuir........B 8
26 Kirstead Green....F 6
44 Kirtlebridge ......F 1
44 Kirtleton ....E 1
25 Kirtling...........J 8
25 Kirtling Green.....K 8
16 Kirtlington........B 6
61 Kirtomy..........B 7
56 Kirton, Inverness .D 3
24 Kirton, Lincs......B 4
32 Kirton, Notts.....C 4
27 Kirton, Suffolk....L 6
24 Kirton End........B 4
24 Kirton Holme......A 4
37 Kirton in Lindsey .G 7
23 Kislingbury.......F 10
23 Kites Hardwick...E 8
6 Kittisford........D 4
13 Kittle............H 9
31 Kitts Moss.......B 7
59 Kittybrewster.....G 7
9 Kitwood..........C 8
4 Kiverley..........D 4
15 Kivernoll.........A 8
32 Kiveton Park.....B 2
60 Klibreck.........D 6
60 Klibreck Lodge...D 6
32 Knaith...........B 5
32 Knaith Park......B 5
7 Knap Corner....D 11
17 Knaphill.........H 10
53 Knapp, Angus....D 7
6 Knapp, Somerset .D 6
58 Knaps of Auchlee .C 8
26 Knapton, Norfolk .B 6
36 Knapton, Yorks...B 3
21 Knapton Green..G 10
25 Knapwell..........J 4
35 Knaresborough ..A 12
44 Knarsdale........H 5
49 Knayton..........F 4
18 Knebworth.......B 3
36 Knedlington.......D 5
32 Kneesall.........D 4
25 Kneesworth.......L 4
32 Kneeton..........F 4
13 Knelston ....H 8
27 Knettishall.......G 3
4 Knightacott.......B 5
23 Knightcote.......G 7
5 Knighton, Devon..L 4
7 Knighton, Dorset .E 9
23 Knighton, Leics...B 9
21 Knighton, Rad.....E 8
30 Knighton, Staffs...F 6
30 Knighton, Staffs...G 6
16 Knighton, Wilts...G 4
22 Knightsfold Bridge G 1
21 Knill.............F 8
32 Knipton..........G 5
45 Knitsley..........H 9
31 Kniveton........E 10
50 Knock, Argyll....D 3
58 Knock, Banff......B 3
62 Knock, Inverness ..G 6
63 Knock, Lewis......D 6
39 Knock, Westmor. .B 9
60 Knockan.........F 3
56 Knockando........E 7
57 Knockandhu......G 8
60 Knockanrock.....F 3
61 Knockarthur.......F 7
56 Knockbain.......D 2
62 Knockbreck......B 2
63 Knockbrex........G 7
61 Knockdee........B 11
42 Knockdolian Cas.. C 2
42 Knockdon........B 5
60 Knockendon......D 7
47 Knockenjig .....H 12
46 Knockenkelly.....G 5
47 Knockentiber.....E 9
58 Knockespock Ho..E 3
42 Knockgardner.....A 4

MAP
42 Knockglass.......F 1
10 Knockholt.........B 3
10 Knockholt Pound .B 4
55 Knockie Lodge ..H 8
30 Knockin..........H 2
47 Knockinlaw......E 9
42 Knocklaugh.......B 3
43 Knocklearn.......D 8
42 Knocknain........E 1
46 Knockrome.......B 1
53 Knockshannoch...A 7
38 Knocksharry......G 1
42 Knocksheen ......C 6
43 Knockvennie......D 8
42 Knockycoid.......D 3
27 Knodishall........J 7
7 Knole............D 8
15 Knole Park.......F 9
30 Knolls Green.....B 6
30 Knolton..........F 2
8 Knook...........B 1
23 Knossington.....A 11
34 Knott End-on-Sea B 2
25 Knotting..........J 1
25 Knotting Green ...J 1
36 Knottingley.......E 3
39 Knotts...........C 7
30 Knotty Ash.......A 3
17 Knotty Green....E 10
42 Knowe...........D 4
58 Knowhead, Aber. .F 2
43 Knowehead, Kirk. C 7
45 Knowesgate......D 8
47 Knoweside.......H 7
49 Knowetownhead..G 8
27 Knowl Green.....L 1
17 Knowl Hill.......F 9
6 Knowle, Devon ..H 4
4 Knowle, Devon ..F 6
4 Knowle, Devon...B 4
15 Knowle, Glos......G 9
7 Knowle, Somerset .B 7
22 Knowle, War......D 5
34 Knowle Green.....C 5
8 Knowlton, Dorset E 2
11 Knowlton, Kent .C 11
58 Knowsie..........B 8
34 Knowsley ....H 3
4 Knowstone.......D 7
10 Knox Bridge......D 6
21 Knucklas.........E 8
30 Knutsford........B 6
31 Knypersley.......E 7
2 Kuggar..........H 4
55 Kyle of Lochalsh..G 1
55 Kyleakin.........G 1
55 Kylechorky Lodge G 8
61 Kyleoag..........G 7
55 Kylerhea.........G 2
63 Kyles Scalpay.....G 3
63 Kyles Stockinish..H 2
55 Kylesbeg.........M 1
55 Kylesknoydart....K 2
60 Kylesku..........D 3
55 Kylesmorar.......K 2
60 Kylestrome.......D 4
57 Kyllachy House...G 3
15 Kymin............C 8
15 Kynaston.........B 8
21 Kynnersley......A 12
21 Kyre Park.......F 11
63 Labost............B 7
37 Laceby...........F 10
17 Lacey Green......D 9
30 Lach Dennis......C 5
63 Lackalee.........H 2
40 Lackenby.........C 6
27 Lackford..........H 1
15 Lacock...........G 12
23 Ladbroke.........F 7
10 Laddingford......C 6
33 Lade Bank........E 11
2 Ladock...........E 6
42 Ladybank, Ayr....A 3
53 Ladybank, Fife....F 8
3 Ladycross.......A 10
49 Ladyflat.........D 10
49 Ladykirk.........E 11
58 Ladyleys.........E 6
58 Ladysford........B 6
43 Lag..............C 9
50 Lagalochan.......F 6
46 Lagg, Argyll......B 1
47 Lagg, Ayr........H 7
46 Lagg, Bute.......G 4
42 Laggan, Ayr......C 2
42 Laggan, Ayr......C 3
58 Laggan, Banff.....D 1
55 Laggan, Inver.....K 7
57 Laggan, Inver.....K 2
52 Laggan, Perth.....F 1
42 Lagganmullan.....F 6

MAP
50 Lagganulva.......C 2
60 Laid.............B 3
60 Laide............G 1
47 Laigh Braidley...E 10
47 Laigh Brocklar...G 10
47 Laigh Cleughearn D 11
47 Laigh Fenwick...E 9
47 Laigh Smithstone..E 8
47 Laighmuir........E 9
47 Laighstonehall...D 12
43 Laight...........B 9
19 Laindon..........E 7
57 Laintachan.......H 6
54 Lair.............E 4
60 Lairg............F 6
60 Lairg Muir.......F 6
60 Lairg Station.....F 6
51 Lairigmor........A 8
35 Laisterdyke......D 10
39 Laithes...........B 7
8 Lake............B 3
56 Lake of Moy.....D 6
38 Lake Side.........F 6
25 Lakenheath.......G 8
24 Lakes End........F 6
17 Laleham........G 11
14 Laleston..........F 2
48 Lamancha........D 5
27 Lamarsh..........L 2
26 Lamas............C 5
27 Lamb Corner.......M 3
64 Lambaness.......B 4
49 Lambden........E 10
10 Lamberhurst......D 5
10 Lamberhurst Quarter........D 5
18 Lambeth..........F 3
32 Lambley..........F 3
44 Lambley...........G 5
16 Lambourn.........F 4
18 Lambourne End...D 5
10 Lambs Green.....D 1
12 Lambston.........E 3
3 Lamellion.........C 9
5 Lamerton.........H 3
45 Lamesley........G 10
42 Lamford..........B 6
48 Lamington, Lan...F 3
56 Lamington, Ross & Cromarty.......B 3
46 Lamlash..........F 5
42 Lamloch..........B 6
38 Lamonby..........B 6
2 Lamorna..........G 2
2 Lamorran.........E 6
13 Lampeter.........B 9
12 Lampeter Velfrey..F 5
12 Lamphey..........G 4
38 Lamplugh.........C 3
23 Lamport..........E 11
7 Lamyatt..........C 10
4 Lana, Devon......F 2
4 Lana, Devon......E 2
48 Lanark...........E 2
48 Lanark, Co........E 1
34 Lancashire, Co....E 5
34 Lancaster.........A 4
45 Lanchester......H 10
6 Landacre.........C 2
25 Landbeach........J 6
4 Landcross.........D 3
59 Landerberry......G 5
2 Landewednack....H 4
8 Landford..........D 4
8 Landford Manor..D 4
13 Landimore........H 8
4 Landkey..........C 5
13 Landore.........G 10
3 Landrake, Corn..D 10
6 Landrake, Devon..D 3
12 Landshipping.....F 4
3 Landulph.........D 11
22 Landywood.......B 3
2 Lane.............D 5
17 Lane End, Bucks. .E 9
38 Lane End, Cumb. .F 3
9 Lane End, Hants. .D 7
9 Lane End, Hants. .G 8
10 Lane End, Kent...A 4
40 Lane Ends........B 2
31 Lane Head.......C 10
34 Lane Head, Lancs. G 5
40 Lane Head, Yorks.D 1
3 Laneast...........A 9
32 Laneham..........C 5
44 Lanehead.........D 6
35 Laneshaw Bridge..C 8
32 Langar...........G 4
47 Langbank........B 8
35 Langbar..........B 9
44 Langburnshiels....C 4
35 Langcliffe........A 7
41 Langdale End.....F 9

MAP
61 Langdale Lodge...C 7
2 Langdon, Corn....B 2
3 Langdon, Corn...A 10
15 Langdon, Worcs..A 11
39 Langdon Beck...B 11
19 Langdon Hills.....E 7
53 Langdyke.........G 8
19 Langenhoe.......B 10
25 Langford, Beds....L 3
6 Langford, Devon..F 4
19 Langford, Essex...C 8
32 Langford, Notts...D 5
16 Langford, Oxon...D 3
6 Langford Budville.D 4
25 Langford End.....K 3
27 Langham, Essex ..M 3
26 Langham, Norf....B 3
23 Langham, Rut....A 11
27 Langham, Suffolk .H 3
34 Langho...........D 6
44 Langholm, Dumf. .E 2
48 Langholm, Lan.....F 3
47 Langlands.......D 11
49 Langleeford.....G 12
17 Langley, Bucks...F 11
31 Langley, Ches.....C 8
8 Langley, Hants....F 6
18 Langley, Herts....B 2
11 Langley, Kent.....C 7
44 Langley,Northumb.G 6
6 Langley, Som.....C 4
9 Langley, Sussex ..C 9
22 Langley, War......F 5
15 Langley Burrell ..G 12
10 Langley Green....D 1
11 Langley Heath....C 7
25 Langley Lower Green..........M 5
32 Langley Mill......E 2
40 Langley Moor....A 3
40 Langley Park.....A 2
26 Langley Street.....E 7
25 Langley Upper Green.........M 5
10 Langney.........H 5
32 Langold..........B 3
3 Langore.........A 10
7 Langport.........D 7
33 Langrick..........E 9
15 Langridge........G 10
4 Langridge Ford...D 4
43 Langrigg.........G 12
9 Langrish.........D 8
33 Langriville.......E 10
35 Langsett.........G 10
49 Langshaw........E 8
47 Langside, Ayr.....D 8
52 Langside, Perth....F 3
64 Langskaill........A 2
9 Langstone........F 8
40 Langthorne, N. Riding......F 3
40 Langthorpe, N. Riding......H 4
39 Langthwaite.....E 12
24 Langtoft, Lincs....D 2
41 Langtoft, Yorks..H 10
40 Langton, Dur......C 2
33 Langton, Lincs....C 9
33 Langton, Lincs...C 11
41 Langton, Yorks...H 8
33 Langton by Wragby.......C 8
10 Langton Green....D 4
7 Langton Herring..H 9
8 Langton Matravers H 2
4 Langtree.........D 3
39 Langwathby......B 8
60 Langwell.........G 5
61 Langwell Hotel ..E 10
33 Langworth........C 8
3 Lanivet..........C 7
3 Lank............B 8
3 Lanlivery........D 8
2 Lanner...........F 4
3 Lanreath.........D 9
52 Lanrick Castle....G 2
3 Lansallos.........E 9
16 Lansdown, Glos...B 3
15 Lansdown, Som...G 10
3 Lanteglos Highway D 8
49 Lanton,Northumb.F 11
49 Lanton, Rox......G 9
4 Lapford..........E 6
22 Lapley...........A 2
22 Lapworth.........E 5
50 Larachbeg........C 4
48 Larbert...........A 1
43 Larbreck.........D 9
58 Largie...........D 4
46 Largiemore........A 4
53 Largo Ward.......F 9
47 Largs............C 7

MAP
46 Largymore........G 5
10 Larkfield, Kent....B 6
47 Larkfield, Ren.....B 7
47 Larkhall.........D 12
8 Larkhill...........B 3
26 Larling...........F 3
52 Laroch...........B 8
44 Larriston.........D 4
39 Lartington.......C 12
59 Lary.............G 1
9 Lasham..........B 8
40 Laskill...........F 6
15 Lassington.......B 11
52 Lassodie.........H 6
41 Lastingham.......F 7
19 Latchingdon & Snoreham......D 8
3 Latchley.........B 11
17 Latchmore Green .H 7
34 Lately Common...G 5
23 Lathbury........H 11
61 Latheron........D 11
53 Lathockar........F 9
53 Lathones.........F 9
17 Latimer.........D 10
38 Latterhead........C 4
15 Latteridge.......F 10
7 Lattiford........D 10
16 Latton...........E 2
58 Lauchintilly.......F 5
50 Laudale House....B 5
49 Lauder...........E 8
12 Laugharne........F 6
32 Laughterton.......C 5
23 Laughton, Leics. .C 10
36 Laughton, Lincs...G 6
10 Laughton, Sussex..G 4
32 Laughton en le Morthen.......A 2
4 Launcells.........E 1
3 Launceston......A 10
7 Launcherley......B 9
17 Launton..........B 7
38 Laurel Bank.......G 1
59 Laurencekirk......K 5
43 Laurieston, Kirk...E 7
48 Laurieston, Stir....A 2
23 Lavendon.......G 12
27 Lavenham........K 2
43 Laverhay........B 12
14 Lavernock.........G 5
8 Laverstock.......C 3
8 Laverstoke........A 6
16 Laverton, Glos....A 2
7 Laverton, Som....A 11
40 Laverton, Yorks...H 2
30 Lavister..........D 2
48 Law.............D 1
52 Lawers, Perth.....C 2
52 Lawers, Perth.....E 3
27 Lawford.........M 4
3 Lawhitton.......A 10
39 Lawkland........H 10
21 Lawley..........B 12
31 Lawnhead........H 7
12 Lawrenny........F 4
27 Lawshall.........K 2
21 Lawton..........F 10
63 Laxay............E 4
63 Laxdale..........C 5
38 Laxey............G 2
27 Laxfield..........H 6
64 Laxfirth..........D 7
60 Laxford Bridge....C 4
64 Laxo.............C 7
64 Laxobigging......C 7
24 Laxton, Northants. F 1
32 Laxton, Notts.....D 4
36 Laxton, Yorks.....E 6
35 Laycock..........C 9
19 Layer Breton......B 9
19 Layer-de-la-Haye..B 9
19 Layer Marney.....B 9
27 Layham..........L 3
16 Layland's Green ..G 5
7 Laymore.........F 7
21 Laysters Pole.....F 11
36 Laytham.........C 5
40 Lazenby..........C 6
39 Lazonby..........A 8
31 Lea, Derby.......D 11
15 Lea, Herefs......B 10
32 Lea, Lincs........B 5
21 Lea, Shropshire...B 9
21 Lea, Shropshire...C 9
15 Lea, Wilts........F 12
22 Lea Marston......C 5
34 Lea Town.........D 4
39 Lea Yeat........F 10
32 Leabrooks........E 1
55 Leacachan........G 3
56 Leachkin.........E 2
48 Leadburn.........D 5

MAP
18 Leaden Roding....C 6
23 Leadenham.......E 7
49 Leaderfoot........F 8
39 Leadgate, Cumb...A 9
45 Leadgate, Dur.....G 9
45 Leadgate, Dur.....H 9
48 Leadhills.........H 2
16 Leafield..........C 4
17 Leagrave........B 11
40 Leake............F 4
33 Leake Common Side.........E 11
33 Leake Hurn's End E 11
41 Lealholm.........D 8
62 Leatt.............B 4
23 Leamington.......E 7
23 Leamington Hasting........E 8
22 Leamonsley.......A 4
45 Leamside........H 11
51 Leanach.........H 7
55 Leanachan........L 6
56 Leanaig..........D 1
46 Leargybreck......B 1
39 Leasgill..........G 7
33 Leasingham.......E 7
40 Leasingthorne.....B 3
17 Leatherhead.....H 12
35 Leathley.........B 11
43 Leaths...........E 8
30 Leaton...........H 3
11 Leaveland........C 8
36 Leavening........A 5
18 Leaves Green.....H 4
18 Leavesden Green..D 1
45 Leazes..........G 10
41 Lebberston......G 10
16 Lechlade.........D 3
39 Leck............G 9
8 Leckford.........B 5
61 Leckfurin.........B 7
16 Leckhampstead, Berks...........G 5
23 Leckhampstead, Bucks.........H 10
16 Leckhampstead Street..........F 5
16 Leckhampstead Thicket.........F 5
15 Leckhampton....B 12
54 Leckie...........C 5
60 Leckmelm.......G 3
55 Leckroy..........K 7
14 Leckwith.........G 5
37 Leconfield.......C 8
50 Ledaig...........D 6
17 Ledburn.........B 10
15 Ledbury.........A 10
51 Ledcharrie.......E 12
21 Ledgemoor.......G 9
54 Ledgowan.........D 5
21 Ledicot...........F 9
60 Ledmore..........F 4
61 Lednagullin.......B 8
30 Ledsham, Ches....C 2
36 Ledsham, Yorks...D 2
36 Ledston..........D 2
16 Ledwell...........A 5
50 Lee, Argyll.......E 1
4 Lee, Devon.......A 4
8 Lee, Hampshire...D 5
34 Lee, Lancashire ..B 4
30 Lee, Shropshire...G 3
30 Lee Brockhurst...G 4
17 Lee Clump......D 10
30 Lee Green........D 5
5 Lee Mill Bridge...K 5
5 Lee Mill Estate....K 5
5 Lee Moor.........J 4
9 Lee-on-the-Solent..F 7
21 Leebotwood.....C 10
38 Leece............H 5
11 Leeds, Kent......C 7
35 Leeds, Yorks.....D 11
2 Leedstown........F 3
31 Leek.............E 8
22 Leek Wootton....E 6
40 Leeming.........F 3
40 Leeming Bar......F 3
31 Lees, Derby......F 11
35 Lees, Lancashire ..G 8
44 Lees Hill.........F 4
29 Leeswood.......D 12
30 Leftwich Green...C 5
33 Legbourne.......B 10
49 Legerwood.......E 8
33 Legsby...........B 8
23 Leicester.........B 9
23 Leicestershire, Co..B 9
23 Leicester For. East.B 8
7 Leigh, Dorset.....E 9
15 Leigh, Glos......B 11
10 Leigh, Kent.......C 4

MAP

34 Leigh, Lancs....G 5
21 Leigh, Shropshire..B 9
10 Leigh, Surrey.....C 1
16 Leigh, Wiltshire..E 2
22 Leigh, Worcs....G 1
19 Leigh Beck......F 8
15 Leigh Delamere..F 12
11 Leigh Green.....E 8
19 Leigh-on-Sea....E 8
9 Leigh Park......G 8
22 Leigh Sinton....G 1
7 Leigh upon
    Mendip......B 10
6 Leighland Chapel..C 4
15 Leighterton......E 11
21 Leighton, Mont....B 8
21 Leighton, Salop..B 11
7 Leighton, Som....B 10
40 Leighton, Yorks..G 2
25 Leighton
    Bromswold.....H 2
17 Leighton Buzzard.B 10
59 Leightonhill......L 4
15 Leighwoods......G 9
21 Leinthall Earls...F 10
21 Leinthall Starkes.E 10
21 Leintwardine.....E 9
23 Leire............C 8
60 Leirinmore......A 5
54 Leishmore.......F 8
27 Leiston.........J 7
53 Leitfie..........C 7
48 Leith...........B 5
49 Leitholm......E 10
2 Lelant..........F 3
37 Lelley..........D 10
22 Lem Hill........E 1
56 Lemlair.........D 1
45 Lemmington Hall..B 9
49 Lempitlaw......F 10
63 Lemreway.......F 5
18 Lemsford........C 2
58 Lenabo.........C 8
22 Lenchwick......G 4
42 Lendalfoot......C 2
51 Lendrick......G 12
11 Lenham........C 7
11 Lenham Heath...C 8
49 Lennel.........E 11
42 Lennies........F 5
47 Lennoxtown....B 11
17 Lent Rise.......F 10
24 Lenton.........C 1
26 Lenwade........D 4
47 Lenzie.........B 11
58 Leochel-Cushnie..F 3
21 Leominster.....F 10
15 Leonard Stanley..D 11
8 Lepe...........F 6
62 Lephin.........C 1
51 Lephinchapel...H 7
51 Lephinmore.....H 7
36 Leppington......A 5
35 Lepton.........F 10
50 Lerags.........E 6
3 Lerryn.........D 8
64 Lerwick........E 7
45 Lesbury........B 10
58 Leslie, Aberdeen..E 3
53 Leslie, Fife......G 7
48 Lesmahagow....E 1
2 Lesnewth.......B 2
26 Lessingham.....C 7
44 Lessonhall......H 1
42 Leswalt........E 1
18 Letchmore Heath..D 2
25 Letchworth.....M 3
16 Letcombe Bassett..F 5
16 Letcombe Regis...E 5
53 Letham, Angus..B 10
53 Letham, Fife....F 8
52 Letham, Perth....E 6
53 Letham Grange..C 11
56 Lethen House....D 5
57 Lethendryveole...H 5
58 Lethenty.......D 5
27 Letheringham....J 6
26 Letheringsett....B 4
5 Lettaford.......G 6
64 Lettan.........A 4
54 Letterewe......C 3
55 Letterfearn.....G 3
55 Letterfinlay.....K 6
55 Lettermorar.....K 1
50 Lettermore.....C 2
60 Letters.........H 3
48 Lettershaws....G 2
12 Letterston......D 3
57 Lettoch, Inver....H 6
56 Lettoch, Moray...H 5
21 Letton, Herefs...E 9
21 Letton, Herefs...H 9
18 Letty Green.....C 3

MAP

32 Letwell..........B 3
53 Leuchars.........E 9
56 Leuchars House...C 8
63 Leurbost.........D 5
22 Levedale.........A 3
53 Leven, Fife.......G 8
37 Leven, Yorks.....C 8
46 Levencorroch....G 5
39 Levens..........G 7
35 Levenshulme.....H 7
64 Levenwick.......F 7
63 Leverburgh......H 1
24 Leverington......D 5
16 Leverton, Berks..G 4
33 Leverton, Lincs...E 11
33 Leverton Outgate.E 11
27 Levington.......L 5
41 Levisham........F 8
16 Lew............D 4
3 Lewannick......B 9
5 Lewdown........G 3
16 Lewes..........G 3
12 Leweston.......E 3
18 Lewisham.......G 3
57 Lewiston........G 1
14 Lewistown.......E 3
17 Lewknor.........D 8
4 Leworthy.......B 5
63 Lews Castle.....D 5
11 Lewson Street...B 8
5 Lewtrenchard....G 3
58 Ley, Aberdeen...F 3
3 Ley, Cornwall....C 9
10 Leybourne......B 5
40 Leyburn.........F 1
30 Leycett.........E 6
18 Leygreen.......B 2
17 Leyhill Com....D 10
34 Leyland........E 4
58 Leylodge.......F 5
58 Leys...........B 7
56 Leys Castle.....F 2
53 Leys of Cossans..B 8
58 Leys of Dummuies.D 3
11 Leysdown-on-Sea..A 9
53 Leysmill........B 10
18 Leyton.........E 4
18 Leytonstone.....E 4
3 Lezant.........B 10
54 Liatrie.........F 6
14 Libanus........B 3
48 Liberton, Lan....E 3
48 Liberton, Midloth..B 5
22 Lichfield.......A 5
22 Lickey.........E 3
22 Lickey End.....E 3
9 Lickfold.......D 10
50 Liddesdale.....B 5
16 Liddington......F 3
25 Lidgate........J 8
25 Lidlington.....L 1
16 Lidstone.......B 4
55 Lienassie.......G 3
53 Liff...........D 8
5 Lifton.........G 3
5 Liftondown.....G 2
23 Lighthorne......G 7
17 Lightwater......H 10
31 Lightwood......F 7
23 Lilbourne......D 9
49 Lilburn Hill...G 12
45 Lilburn Tower...A 8
22 Lilleshall......A 1
16 Lilley, Berks....F 5
18 Lilley, Herts.....A 1
49 Lilliesleaf.......G 8
23 Lillingstone
    Dayrell......H 10
23 Lillingstone
    Lovell........H 10
7 Lillington, Dorset..E 9
23 Lillington, War....E 7
8 Lilliput.........G 2
6 Lilstock........B 5
47 Lilybank.......B 8
34 Limbrick.......F 5
35 Limefield......F 7
47 Limekilnburn...D 12
48 Limekilns......A 3
48 Limerigg......B 1
8 Limestone......H 6
44 Limestone Brae..H 6
7 Limington......D 8
26 Limpenhoe.....E 7
15 Limpley Stoke...H 11
10 Limpsfield......C 3
32 Linby..........E 3
9 Linchmere......C 10
43 Lincluden.....D 10
33 Lincoln........C 7
33 Lincolnshire, Co..D 8
22 Lincomb.......E 2
62 Lincro.........B 3

MAP

38 Lindal in Furness.H 5
38 Lindale.........G 6
49 Lindean........F 7
10 Lindfield.......E 2
9 Lindford.......C 9
53 Lindifferon.....E 8
35 Lindley.........E 10
35 Lindley Green...B 11
53 Lindores.......E 7
21 Lindridge.....E 12
18 Lindsell........A 6
27 Lindsey........L 3
38 Linefoot.......B 3
19 Linford, Essex...F 7
8 Linford, Hants..E 3
38 Lingague.......H 1
41 Lingdale.......D 7
21 Lingen.........F 9
10 Lingfield.......D 3
10 Lingfield Com...D 3
30 Lingley Green...A 4
26 Lingwood.......E 7
45 Linhope, N'thumb. A 8
44 Linhope, Rox....C 2
3 Linkinhorne....B 10
64 Linklater.......E 2
53 Linktown.......H 7
21 Linley Green...G 12
48 Linlithgow.....B 3
48 Linlithgow Bridge.B 3
60 Linneraineach...F 3
12 Linney.........G 2
43 Linns..........D 11
63 Linshader......D 3
45 Linshiels.......B 7
60 Linsidemore....G 6
17 Linslade.......B 10
27 Linstead Parva..G 6
44 Linstock.......G 3
49 Linthaugh.....F 12
22 Linthurst......E 3
35 Linthwaite.....F 9
49 Lintlaw........D 11
58 Lintmill........A 3
25 Linton, Cambs...K 7
22 Linton, Denb....A 6
15 Linton, Herefs...B 9
10 Linton, Kent....C 6
49 Linton, Rox....G 10
35 Linton, W. Riding B 12
35 Linton, W. Riding.A 8
36 Linton-on-Ouse..A 3
8 Linwood, Hants..E 3
33 Linwood, Lincs...B 8
47 Linwood, Ren....C 9
29 Lioc..........C 10
63 Lionel.........A 6
9 Liphook........C 9
6 Liscombe......C 2
3 Liskeard......C 9
9 Liss...........C 9
9 Liss Forest......C 9
37 Lisset.........A 9
33 Lissington.....B 8
14 Lisvane........F 5
15 Liswerry.......F 7
26 Litcham.......D 2
23 Litchborough...G 9
7 Litchett.......A 6
34 Litherland......G 2
25 Litlington, Cambs..L 4
11 Litlington, Sussex.H 4
25 Little Abington...K 6
25 Little Addington..H 1
22 Little Alne......A 5
18 Little Amwell....C 3
60 Little Assynt....E 3
22 Little Aston.....B 4
8 Little Atherfield..H 6
64 Little Ayre......E 1
40 Little Ayton.....D 6
19 Little Baddow....C 7
15 Little Badminton.F 11
52 Little Ballinluig..B 4
44 Little Bampton...G 1
25 Little Bardfield...M 3
25 Little Barford....J 3
26 Little Barningham.B 4
16 Little Barrington..C 3
30 Little Barrow....C 3
41 Little Barugh....E 8
45 Little Bavington..E 8
27 Little Bealings...K 5
16 Little Bedwyn...F 5
42 Little Bennane...C 2
19 Little Bentley...A 11
18 Little Berkhampsted
              C 3
23 Little Billing...F 11
15 Little Birch....A 8
27 Little Blakenham..K 4
39 Little Blencow...B 7

MAP

9 Little Bookham...A 12
23 Little Bowden....C 11
25 Little Bradley....K 8
21 Little Brampton..D 9
19 Little Braxted....B 8
59 Little Brechin....L 3
7 Little Bredy.....G 9
17 Little Brickhill...A 10
23 Little Brington...F 10
19 Little Bromley...A 10
30 Little Budworth..D 5
18 Little Burstead...E 6
24 Little Bytham....D 1
42 Little Cairnbrock..E 1
33 Little Carlton,
      Lincs.........B 11
32 Little Carlton,
      Notts.........D 5
24 Little Casterton...E 1
33 Little Cawthorpe.B 10
17 Little Chalfont...D 11
11 Little Chart......D 8
25 Little Cheney....G 9
25 Little Chesterford..L 6
8 Little Cheverell...A 2
25 Little Chishill....L 5
19 Little Clacton...B 11
23 Little Clifton.....B 3
58 Little Colp......C 5
22 Little Comberton..H 3
16 Little Compton...A 4
27 Little Cornard....L 2
21 Little Cowarne...G 11
16 Little Coxwell....E 4
40 Little Crakehall..F 3
26 Little Cressingham.E 2
23 Little Crosby.....G 2
23 Little Dalby.....A 11
58 Little Dens......C 8
5 Little Dewchurch..A 8
37 Little Driffield...A 8
26 Little Dunham...D 2
52 Little Dunkeld...C 5
18 Little Dunmow...B 6
18 Little Easton.....B 6
31 Little Eaton.....F 12
26 Little Ellingham..E 3
7 Little Elm......B 10
18 Little End.......D 5
25 Little Eversden...K 5
27 Little Fakenham..H 2
16 Little Faringdon...D 3
40 Little Fencote....F 3
36 Little Fenton....D 3
17 Little Fransham...D 2
17 Little Gaddesden.C 11
15 Little Garway....B 8
25 Little Gidding...G 2
27 Little Glemham...J 6
25 Little Gransden..K 4
7 Little Green....A 10
33 Little Grimsby...A 10
60 Little Gruinard...G 1
18 Little Hadham....B 4
24 Little Hale......B 2
18 Little Hallingbury.B 5
17 Little Hampden...D 7
23 Little Harrowden..E 12
17 Little Haseley...D 7
37 Little Hatfield...C 9
12 Little Haven....F 2
22 Little Hay......B 5
31 Little Hayfield...A 9
31 Little Haywood...H 8
21 Little Hereford...F 11
27 Little Horkesley..M 2
18 Little Hormead...A 4
10 Little Horsted...F 3
23 Little Horton....D 10
17 Little Horwood...A 9
23 Little Houghton..F 11
34 Little Hucklow...B 10
34 Little Hulton....G 6
17 Little Hungerford.G 8
45 Little Irchester...E 12
37 Little Kelk.....A 8
17 Little Kimble....C 9
17 Little Kingshill...D 10
38 Little Langdale...E 5
8 Little Langford...C 2
58 Little Ledikin....E 4
30 Little Leigh....C 5
19 Little Leighs....B 7
34 Little Lever.....G 6
23 Little Linford....H 11
8 Little London,
      Hants........A 5
17 Little London,
      Hants........H 7
24 Little London,
      Lincs.........C 5
10 Little London,
      Sussex.......F 4

MAP

35 Little London,
      Yorks........C 10
31 Little Longstone..C 10
58 Little Lynturk....F 3
22 Little Malvern....H 1
27 Little Maplestead.M 1
15 Little Marcle....A 10
16 Little Marlow....E 9
26 Little Massingham.C 1
26 Little Melton....E 5
12 Little Milford....F 3
14 Little Mill......D 6
17 Little Milton....D 7
17 Little Missenden.D 10
30 Little Ness.......H 3
30 Little Neston....C 2
12 Little Newcastle..D 3
40 Little Newsham...C 1
19 Little Oakley,
      Essex.........A 12
23 Little Oakley,
      Northants.....D 12
44 Little Orton.....G 2
36 Little Ouseburn..A 2
25 Little Paxton....J 3
2 Little Petherick...B 6
42 Little Pinmore...C 3
26 Little Plumstead..D 6
32 Little Ponton....G 6
4 Little Potheridge..E 4
25 Little Raveley....G 4
35 Little Ribson....B 12
16 Little Rissington..B 3
26 Little Ryburgh...C 3
45 Little Ryle......B 8
39 Little Salkeld....B 8
8 Little Samborne...C 5
25 Little Sampford...M 7
17 Little Sandhurst..H 9
30 Little Saughall...C 2
25 Little Saxham....J 1
54 Little Scatwell...D 7
25 Little Shelford...K 5
4 Little Silver.....F 7
6 Little Silver.....E 3
36 Little Smeaton...E 3
26 Little Snoring....B 2
15 Little Sodbury...F 10
16 Little Somerford..F 1
40 Little Stainton...C 4
30 Little Stanney...C 3
25 Little Staughton..J 2
33 Little Steeping...D 11
27 Little Stonham...J 4
23 Little Stretton,
      Leics.........B 10
21 Little Stretton,
      Shropshire....C 10
39 Little Strickland..C 8
25 Little Stukeley...H 3
45 Little Swinburne..E 8
49 Little Swinton...E 11
16 Little Tew.......A 5
25 Little Thetford...H 6
25 Little Thurlow...K 8
18 Little Thurrock...F 6
42 Little Torhouse...F 5
4 Little Torrington..D 4
45 Little Tosson....C 8
19 Little Totham....C 9
38 Little Town.....C 5
56 Little Urchany...E 4
38 Little Urswick...H 5
19 Little Wakering...E 9
27 Little Waldingfield.L 2
26 Little Walsingham.B 2
19 Little Waltham...C 7
18 Little Warley....E 6
37 Little Weighton...D 7
27 Little Welnetham..J 2
21 Little Wenlock...B 12
27 Little Whittingham
      Green........H 6
45 Little Whittington.F 8
25 Little Wilbraham..J 6
8 Little Wishford...B 2
22 Little Witley.....F 1
16 Little Wittenham..E 6
16 Little Wolford....A 3
23 Little Woolstone.H 12
25 Little Wymington..J 1
18 Little Wymondley.A 2
22 Little Wyrley....B 4
27 Little Yeldam....L 1
64 Little-ayre......C 6
41 Littlebeck......E 9
35 Littleborough,
      Lancashire....F 8
32 Littleborough,
      Notts.........B 5
11 Littlebourne....B 10
25 Littlebury......L 6
34 Littledale......A 4

MAP

15 Littledean......C 10
61 Littleferry......G 8
4 Littleham, Devon..D 3
6 Littleham, Devon..H 4
9 Littlehampton...F 11
5 Littlehempston...J 7
45 Littlehoughton...A 10
59 Littlemill, Aber...H 1
47 Littlemill, Ayr....H 9
56 Littlemill, Nairn...E 5
45 Littlemill,
      Northumb.....A 10
16 Littlemore......D 6
31 Littleover.....G 11
25 Littleport.......G 7
25 Littleport Bridge..G 7
11 Littlestone-on-Sea.F 9
40 Littlethorpe.....H 3
30 Littleton, Ches....D 3
8 Littleton, Hants...C 6
43 Littleton, Kirk....F 7
53 Littleton, Perth...D 7
7 Littleton, Som....C 8
9 Littleton, Surrey..A 11
17 Littleton, Surrey..G 11
15 Littleton Drew...F 11
8 Littleton Panell...A 2
15 Littleton upon
      Severn.......E 9
40 Littletown.......A 4
17 Littlewick Green..F 9
16 Littleworth, Berks..D 4
15 Littleworth, Glos. D 11
22 Littleworth, Staffs..A 4
31 Littleworth, Staffs..H 8
10 Littleworth, Sussex.F 1
22 Littleworth, Worcs.G 2
31 Litton, Denb....C 10
7 Litton, Som.....A 9
39 Litton, Yorks....H 11
30 Liverpool......A 2
35 Liversedge.....E 10
5 Liverton, Devon..H 7
41 Liverton, Yorks...D 7
48 Livingston......C 3
48 Livingston Station.C 3
29 Lixwm.........C 11
2 Lizard.........H 4
28 Llaingoch......B 2
20 Llaithddu......D 6
20 Llan...........B 4
14 Llan-Rumney....F 5
28 Llanaber.......H 5
28 Llanaelhaearn...F 3
20 Llanafan.......E 2
20 Llanafan-fawr...G 5
20 Llanafan-fechan...G 5
28 Llanallgo.......B 4
29 Llanarmon Dyffryn
      Ceiriog.......G 10
29 Llanarmon-yn-Ial.E 11
13 Llanarth, Cards...A 7
15 Llanarth, Mon....C 7
13 Llanarthney......E 8
29 Llanasa........B 10
28 Llanbabo.......B 3
20 Llanbadarn Fawr..D 2
20 Llanbadarn Fynyda E 6
21 Llanbadarn-y-
      garreg........G 7
15 Llanbadoc.......D 7
28 Llanbadrig......A 3
15 Llanbeder......E 7
14 Llanbedr, Brec...B 6
28 Llanbedr, Mer...H 5
21 Llanbedr, Rad....H 5
29 Llanbedr-Dyffryn-
      Clwyd.......D 10
28 Llanbeder-goch...B 4
28 Llanbedrog......G 3
29 Llanbedr-y-cennin.C 7
28 Llanberis......D 5
14 Llanbethery.....G 4
20 Llanbister......E 6
14 Llanblethian....G 3
12 Llanboidy......E 5
14 Llanbradach....E 5
56 Llanbryde......D 8
20 Llanbrynmair...B 5
14 Llancadle......G 4
14 Llancaiach.....E 4
14 Llancarfan.....G 4
15 Llancayo......D 7
15 Llancloudy.....B 8
21 Llancoch......E 7
14 Llandaff......F 5
28 Llandanwg.....G 5
13 Llandarcy......G 10
12 Llandawke......F 6
28 Llanddaniel Fab...C 4
13 Llanddarog.....E 8
20 Llanddeiniol.....E 1
28 Llanddeiniolen...D 5

MAP
29 Llandderfel......F 9
28 Llanddeusant,
    Anglesey......B 3
13 Llanddeusant,
    Carm......E 11
14 Llanddew......A 4
13 Llanddewi......H 8
20 Llanddewi-Brefi...G 2
15 Llanddewi
    Rhydderch......C 7
12 Llanddewi Velfrey.E 5
20 Llanddewi'r Cwm.G 6
29 Llanddoget......D 7
28 Llanddona......B 5
12 Llanddowror......F 6
29 Llanddulas......B 8
28 Llanddyfnan......B 4
14 Llandefaelog Fach.A 4
14 Llandefaelog
    ter-graig......A 4
14 Llandefalle......A 4
28 Llandegai......C 5
28 Llandegfan......C 5
15 Llandegfedd......E 7
29 Llandegla......E 11
21 Llandegley......F 7
13 Llandeilo......E 9
20 Llandeilo Graban.H 6
14 Llandeilo'r Fan...A 2
12 Llandeloy......D 2
15 Llandenny......D 7
15 Llandevenny......F 7
20 Llandewi
    Ystradenny......E 6
12 Llandilo......D 4
15 Llandinabo......A 8
20 Llandinam......D 6
12 Llandissilio......E 5
15 Llandogo......D 8
14 Llandough, Glam..G 5
14 Llandough, Glam..G 3
13 Llandovery......D 11
14 Llandow......G 3
20 Llandre, Cards...D 2
13 Llandre, Carm...C 10
29 Llandrillo......F 9
29 Llandrillo-yn-Rhos.B 7
20 Llandrindod Wells.F 6
21 Llandrinio......A 8
29 Llandudno......B 7
29 Llandudno Junc...B 7
28 Llandwrog......E 4
13 Llandybie......E 9
13 Llandyfaelog......F 7
13 Llandyfan......E 9
14 Llandyfodwg......F 3
13 Llandyfriog......C 7
28 Llandyfrydog......B 4
12 Llandygwydd......C 6
29 Llandyrnog......D 10
29 Llandysilio......H 12
21 Llandyssil......C 7
13 Llandyssul......C 7
14 Llanedeyrn......F 5
20 Llaneglwys......H 6
20 Llanegryn......B 2
13 Llanegwad......E 8
28 Llaneilian......A 4
29 Llanelian-yn-Rhos.C 8
29 Llanelidan......E 10
14 Llanelieu......A 5
14 Llanellen......C 6
14 Llanelli, Brec....C 5
13 Llanelli, Carm..G 8
28 Llanelltyd......H 6
14 Llanelwedd......G 6
28 Llanenddwyn......H 5
28 Llanengan......G 2
28 Llanerchymedd...B 4
20 Llanerfyl......A 6
28 Llanfachraeth....B 3
29 Llanfachreth....H 7
28 Llanfaelog......C 3
28 Llanfaelrhys......G 2
15 Llanfaenor......C 7
28 Llanfaes, Angl....C 5
14 Llanfaes, Brec....B 4
28 Llanfaethlu......A 3
28 Llanfaglan......D 4
28 Llanfair......G 5
20 Llanfair-Caereinion B 6
20 Llanfair-Clydogau.G 2
29 Llanfair Dyffryn
    Clwyd......E 10
12 Llanfair
    Nant-Gwyn.....C 5
29 Llanfair Talhaiarn.C 8
21 Llanfair Waterdine.E 8
28 Llanfairfechan....C 6
28 Llanfair-P.G.....C 5
28 Llanfair-y-
    Cwmmwd.....D 4
28 Llanfairynghornwy A 3

MAP
28 Llanfair-yn-
    Neubwll......C 2
12 Llanfallteg......E 5
12 Llanfallteg West...E 5
20 Llanfaredd......G 6
20 Llanfarian......E 2
21 Llanfechain......H 11
28 Llanfechell......A 3
20 Llanfendigaid.....B 1
29 Llanferres......D 11
28 Llanfflewyn......A 3
28 Llanfigael......B 3
20 Llanfihangel......A 6
14 Llanfihangel
    Crucorney......B 6
29 Llanfihangel Glyn
    Myfyr......E 9
14 Llanfihangel
    Llantarnam......E 6
14 Llanfihangel Nant
    Bran......A 3
21 Llanfihangel
    Rhydithon......F 7
15 Llanfihangel Rogiet F 8
14 Llanfihangel
    Tal-y-llyn......A 4
13 Llanfihangel
    ar-arth......C 8
21 Llanfihangel-nant-
    Melan......G 7
13 Llanfihangel-
    uwch-Gwili......E 8
20 Llanfihangel-y-
    Creuddyn......E 2
28 Llanfihangel yn
    Nhowyn......C 3
20 Llanfihangel-y-
    Pennant......B 2
28 Llanfihangel-y-
    pennant......F 5
28 Llanfihangel-y-
    traethau......G 5
14 Llanfilo......A 4
14 Llanfoist......C 6
29 Llanfor......G 8
28 Llanfrechfa......E 6
28 Llanfrothen......F 5
14 Llanfrynach......B 4
28 Llanfwrog, Angl...B 2
29 Llanfwrog, Denb. D 10
29 Llanfyllin......H 10
13 Llanfynydd, Carm.D 9
29 Llanfynydd, Flint.E 12
12 Llanfyrnach......D 6
20 Llangadfan......A 6
13 Llangadog, Carm.D 10
13 Llangadog, Carm..F 7
28 Llangadwaladr,
    Anglesey......C 3
29 Llangadwaladr,
    Denbigh......G 11
28 Llangaffo......C 4
13 Llangain......E 7
20 Llangammarch
    Wells......H 5
14 Llangan......G 3
14 Llangarron......B 8
14 Llangasty-Tal-y-
    llyn......B 5
13 Llangathen......E 9
14 Llangattock......C 5
15 Llangattock
    Lingoed......B 7
14 Llangattock nigh
    Usk......C 6
15 Llangattock Vibon-
    Avel......C 8
29 Llangedwyn......H 11
28 Llangefni......C 4
14 Llangeinor......F 2
28 Llangeinwen......D 4
20 Llangeitho......F 2
13 Llangeler......C 7
13 Llangelynin......B 1
13 Llangendeirne......F 8
13 Llangennech......G 9
13 Llangennith......H 7
14 Llangenny......C 6
29 Llangernyw......C 8
28 Llangian......G 2
13 Llangiwg......F 10
12 Llangloffan......D 3
12 Llanglydwen......D 5
12 Llangoed......B 5
12 Llangoedmor......B 5
29 Llangollen......F 11
14 Llangolman......D 5
14 Llangorse......B 4
15 Llangoven......D 8
29 Llangower......G 7
12 Llangranog......B 6
28 Llangristiolus......C 4
15 Llangrove......B 8

MAP
15 Llangua......B 7
21 Llangunllo......E 7
13 Llangunnor......E 8
20 Llangurig......D 5
29 Llangwm, Denb..F 9
15 Llangwm, Mon...D 7
15 Llangwm, Pemb..F 3
15 Llangwm-isaf......D 7
28 Llangwnnadl......G 2
29 Llangwyfan......D 10
14 Llangwyfanisaf....C 3
28 Llangwyllog......B 4
20 Llangwyryfon......E 2
28 Llangybi, Caer....F 4
20 Llangybi, Cards..G 2
15 Llangybi, Mon...E 7
13 Llangyfelach......G 10
20 Llangynfelyn......C 2
29 Llangynhafal...D 10
14 Llangynidr......B 5
12 Llangynin......E 6
13 Llangynllo......C 7
13 Llangynog, Carm.E 7
29 Llangynog, Mont..H 9
14 Llangynwyd......E 2
14 Llanhamlach......B 4
14 Llanharan......F 3
14 Llanharry......F 3
15 Llanhennock......E 7
14 Llanhilleth......D 5
20 Llanidloes......D 5
28 Llaniestyn......G 2
21 Llanigan......H 7
20 Llanilar......E 2
14 Llanilid......F 3
14 Llanilterne......F 4
14 Llanishen, Glam..F 5
15 Llanishen, Mon...D 8
13 Llanllawddog......D 8
28 Llanllechid......C 5
20 Llanllugan......B 6
21 Llanllwchaiarn....C 7
14 Llanllwch......E 7
28 Llanllyfni......E 4
15 Llanllywel......D 7
14 Llanmadoc......H 8
14 Llanmaes......G 3
15 Llanmartin......E 7
21 Llanmerewig......C 7
14 Llanmihangel......G 3
12 Llanmiloe......F 6
14 Llanmorlais......G 8
29 Llannefydd......C 9
13 Llannon......F 9
29 Llannor......F 3
20 Llanon......F 1
13 Llanpumsaint......D 7
28 Llanreithan......D 2
29 Llanrhaeadr......D 10
29 Llanrhaeadr-ym-
    Mochnant.....H 10
13 Llanrhidian......H 8
29 Llanrhos......B 7
14 Llanrhyddlad......A 3
20 Llanrhystyd......E 1
12 Llanrian......D 2
13 Llanrug......D 5
29 Llanrwst......D 7
12 Llansadurnen......F 6
28 Llansadwrn, Angl..C 5
13 Llansadwrn,
    Carm......D 10
13 Llan-saint......F 7
13 Llansamlet......G 10
29 Llansannan......D 8
14 Llansannor......G 3
14 Llansantffraed...B 5
20 Llansantffraed
    Cwmdeuddwr..F 5
20 Llansantffraed-in-
    Elvel......G 6
20 Llansantffraid......F 1
29 Llansantffraid Glan
    Conway......C 7
29 Llansantffraid-ym-
    Mechain......H 11
13 Llansawel......C 9
13 Llansilin......G 11
15 Llansoy......D 7
14 Llanspyddid......B 3
12 Llanstadwell......F 3
12 Llanstephan......F 7
12 Llanteg......F 5
14 Llanthony......A 6
15 Llantilio Crossenny C 7
14 Llantilio Pertholey.C 6
14 Llantood......C 5
14 Llantrisant, Glam..F 4
15 Llantrisant, Mon..E 7
14 Llantrithyd......G 4
14 Llantwit Fardre...F 4
14 Llantwit-Major...G 3
29 Llanuwchllyn......G 8

MAP
15 Llanvaches......E 7
15 Llanvair Discoed..E 8
15 Llanvapley......C 7
15 Llanvetherine......C 7
14 Llanveynoe......A 6
15 Llanvihangel
    Gobion......C 7
14 Llanvihangel
    Pontymoel......D 6
15 Llanvihangel Ystern-
    Llewern......C 7
15 Llanwarne......B 8
29 Llanwddyn......H 9
14 Llanwenarth......C 6
13 Llanwenog......B 8
15 Llanwern......E 7
12 Llanwinio......D 6
28 Llanwnda,
    Caernarvon...D 4
12 Llanwnda,
    Pembroke......C 3
13 Llanwnen......B 8
20 Llanwnog......C 6
13 Llanwrda......D 10
20 Llanwrin......B 3
14 Llanwrthwl......F 5
20 Llanwrtyd......H 4
20 Llanwrtyd Wells..H 4
28 Llanwyddelan......B 6
30 Llanyblodwel......H 1
13 Llanybri......F 7
13 Llanybyther......C 8
12 Llanycefn......E 4
12 Llanychaer Bridge.C 3
29 Llanymawddwy...H 8
30 Llanymynech......H 1
28 Llanynghenedl....B 3
29 Llanynys......D 10
30 Llan-y-pwll......E 2
20 Llanyre......F 6
29 Llanystumdwy....F 4
14 Llanywern......A 4
12 Llawhaden......E 4
14 Llawnt......G 1
20 Llawr-y-glyn......C 5
30 Llay......E 2
14 Llechfaen......A 4
12 Llechryd, Cards...C 5
14 Llechryd, Mon....C 4
14 Llechrydau......G 11
13 Llethrid......H 8
20 Lledrod......E 2
15 Llidiad-Nenog...C 9
28 Llidiardau, Caer..G 1
29 Llidiardau, Mer....F 8
37 Llidiart-y-parc...F 10
28 Llithfaen......F 3
29 Llong......D 12
21 Llowes......H 7
20 Llundain-fach......G 1
14 Llwydcoed......D 3
13 Llwyn-Celyn......A 8
13 Llwyn Dafydd......B 7
21 Llwynderw, Mont..B 7
20 Llwynderw, Mont.D 5
12 Llwyn-drain......D 6
20 Llwyngwril......A 2
14 Llwyn-hendy......G 9
29 Llwyn-mawr......G 11
14 Llwyn-on......C 3
15 Llwyn-y-groes...G 2
14 Llwyn-y-pia......E 3
30 Llynclys......H 1
28 Llynfaes......B 3
20 Llysdinam......F 6
29 Llysfaen......C 8
14 Llyswen......A 4
14 Llysworney......G 3
12 Llys-y-fran......E 4
14 Llywel......A 2
20 Llywernog......D 3
49 Loanend......D 12
20 Loanhead, Ayr...D 9
48 Loanhead, Lan....F 3
48 Loanhead, Midloth.C 5
58 Loanhead of
    Fedderate......C 6
36 Londesborough...C 6
18 London......F 3
3 London Apprentice E 7
18 London Colney...D 2
40 Londonderry......F 3
33 Londonthorpe......F 7
54 Londubh......B 2
60 Lone......C 4
15 Long Ashton......G 9
32 Long Bennington..F 5
7 Long Bredy......G 9
23 Long Buckby......B 9
7 Long Burton......E 10
32 Long Clawson......G 4
8 Long Common......E 6
31 Long Compton,
    Staffordshire...H 7

MAP
54 Lochcarron......F 3
61 Lochdhu Lodge...C 9
51 Lochdochart Ho..E 11
50 Lochdonhead......D 5
54 Lochdrum......B 6
46 Lochead, Argyll...B 3
46 Lochead, Argyll...A 5
52 Lochearnhead......E 1
53 Lochee......D 8
61 Lochend, Caith...A 11
52 Lochend, Fife......H 6
56 Lochend, Inver...F 2
43 Lochend, Kirk....F 9
43 Locherben......B 10
43 Lochfoot......D 9
50 Lochgair......H 6
57 Lochgarthside......H 1
47 Lochgate......F 11
53 Lochgelly......H 7
46 Lochgilphead......A 4
51 Lochgoilhead......G 9
56 Loch-hill......C 8
47 Lochhill......H 11
56 Lochindorb Lo...F 5
47 Lochingirroch...H 11
60 Lochinver......E 3
48 Lochlycock......F 2
43 Lochmaben......C 11
60 Lochmore Lodge..D 4
52 Lochore......G 6
46 Lochranza......D 4
47 Lochridge......E 9
58 Lochs Crofts......B 1
56 Lochside, Inver....D 4
59 Lochside, Kinc...L 5
61 Lochside, Suther...D 8
60 Lochstack Lodge..C 4
61 Lochstrathy......C 8
59 Lochton......H 5
59 Lochton of Leys..H 4
59 Lochty, Angus...L 3
53 Lochty, Fife.....F 10
50 Lochuisge......B 5
43 Lochurr......C 8
47 Lochwinnoch......C 8
43 Lochwood......B 11
55 Lochy Bridge...M 5
44 Lock Hills......H 3
3 Lockengate......D 7
43 Lockerbie......C 12
16 Lockeridge......G 3
8 Lockerley......C 4
15 Locking......H 7
16 Lockinge......E 5
32 Lockington, Leics..G 2
37 Lockington, Yorks.B 7
30 Lockleywood......G 5
8 Lock's Heath......E 6
41 Lockton......F 8
23 Loddington, Leics.B 11
23 Loddington,
    Northants.....D 11
5 Loddiswell......L 6
26 Loddon......F 6
25 Lode......J 6
7 Loders......C 8
9 Lodsworth......D 10
35 Lofthouse,
    W. Riding...E 12
40 Lofthouse,
    W. Riding......H 1
41 Loftus......F 3
47 Logan......G 10
42 Logan Mains......G 2
30 Loggerheads......G 6
53 Logie, Fife......E 7
53 Logie, Fife......E 9
56 Logie Hill......B 3
58 Logie Newton......D 4
59 Logie Pert......L 4
52 Logiealmond Lo...D 4
52 Logierait......B 5
12 Login......E 5
25 Lolworth......J 5
54 Lonbain......D 1
18 London......F 3
60 Loch Loyal Lo....C 6
55 Lochailort......L 2
50 Lochaline......C 4
62 Lochans......F 2
43 Locharbriggs......D 10
43 Locharwoods......E 11
60 Lochassynt Lodge.D 3
51 Lochawe......E 8
50 Lochbuie......E 3
57 Lochcallater......L 7

MAP
16 Long Compton,
    Warwickshire...A 4
17 Long Crendon......C 8
8 Long Crichel......E 1
17 Long Ditton......G 12
36 Long Drax......D 5
32 Long Duckmanton C 2
32 Long Eaton......G 2
30 Long Green......C 3
16 Long Hanborough.C 5
48 Long Hermiston...B 4
23 Long Itchington..F 7
23 Long Lawford......D 8
7 Long Load......D 8
17 Long Marston,
    Herts.......C 9
36 Long Marston,
    Yorks.......B 3
29 Long Marton......C 9
27 Long Melford......K 2
15 Long Newnton...E 12
40 Long Newton......D 4
35 Long Preston......A 7
37 Long Riston......C 9
36 Long Sandall......F 4
25 Long Stanton All
    Saints.........J 5
25 Long Stanton
    St. Michael.....J 5
26 Long Stratton......F 5
23 Long Street......G 11
9 Long Sutton,
    Hampshire.....A 9
24 Long Sutton, Lincs.C 5
7 Long Sutton,
    Somerset......D 8
21 Long Waste......A 11
32 Long Whatton.....H 2
41 Long Whins......G 11
16 Long Wittenham..E 6
47 Longbar......D 8
45 Longbenton......F 11
16 Longborough......A 3
22 Longbridge, War..D 3
22 Longbridge, War..F 6
7 Longbridge
    Deverill......B 11
54 Longbridgemuir..E 11
44 Longbyre......F 5
42 Longcastle......G 5
31 Longcliffe......E 10
16 Longcot......E 4
49 Longcroft, Ber....D 8
48 Longcroft, Stir....A 1
17 Longcross......H 10
21 Longden......B 10
22 Longdon......A 4
22 Longdon Green...A 4
21 Longdon upon
    Tern......A 11
6 Longdown......G 2
2 Longdowns......F 4
45 Longdyke......B 10
10 Longfield......A 5
10 Longfield Hill......A 5
31 Longford, Derby..F 10
15 Longford, Glos...B 11
18 Longford, London.F 1
30 Longford, Salop..G 5
23 Longford, War....D 7
53 Longforgan......D 8
49 Longformacus....D 9
45 Longframlington..C 9
8 Longham, Dorset.F 2
26 Longham, Norf...D 2
58 Longhill......B 7
45 Longhirst......D 10
15 Longhope......B 10
45 Longhorsley......D 9
45 Longhoughton......B 10
38 Longlands......B 5
16 Longlane, Berks...G 6
31 Longlane, Derby..F 11
15 Longlevens......B 11
22 Longley Green....G 1
58 Longmanhill......A 5
9 Longmoor Camp..C 9
56 Longmorn......D 8
49 Longnewton......G 8
15 Longney......C 11
49 Longniddry......B 7
31 Longnor......D 9
21 Longnot......B 10
8 Longparish......B 6
34 Longridge, Lancs..D 5
48 Longridge,
    W. Lothian....C 2
48 Longriggend......B 1
31 Longsdon......E 8
58 Longside......C 8
30 Longslow......G 5
8 Longstock......B 5
3 Longstone......B 7

MAP

25 Longstowe........K 4
24 Longthorpe........F 3
34 Longton, Lancs.........E 4
31 Longton, Staffs.........F 7
44 Longtown, Cumb.........F 2
14 Longtown, Herefs.........A 6
21 Longville in the Dale........C 11
15 Longwell Green........G 10
17 Longwick........D 8
45 Longwitton........D 9
21 Longwood........B 11
16 Longworth........D 5
49 Longyester........C 8
62 Lonmore........D 2
10 Loose........C 6
17 Loosley Row........D 9
58 Lootcherbrae........B 3
8 Lopcombe Corner........C 4
7 Lopen........E 8
30 Loppington........G 3
45 Lorbottle........B 8
45 Lorbottle Hall........B 8
9 Lordington........E 9
44 Lordsgate........F 3
43 Lorg........B 7
32 Loscoe........E 2
56 Lossiemouth........C 8
30 Lostock Gralam........C 5
30 Lostock Green........C 5
34 Lostock Junction........F 5
3 Lostwithiel........D 8
61 Lothbeg........F 9
35 Lothersdale........C 8
61 Lothmore........F 9
7 Lottisham........C 9
17 Loudwater........E 10
32 Loughborough........H 3
13 Loughor........G 9
23 Loughton, Bucks.........H 11
18 Loughton, Essex........D 4
21 Loughton, Salop........D 11
24 Lound, Lincs.........D 2
32 Lound, Notts.........B 4
26 Lound, Suffolk........E 8
31 Lount........H 12
33 Louth........B 10
35 Love Clough........D 7
9 Lovedean........E 8
4 Loveacott........C 4
8 Lover........D 4
36 Loversall........G 4
18 Loves Green........C 6
40 Lovesome Hill........E 4
12 Loveston........F 4
7 Lovington........C 9
42 Low Ardwell........G 2
43 Low Barlay........F 7
35 Low Bradfield........H 11
35 Low Bradley........B 9
38 Low Braithwaite........A 6
45 Low Brunton........F 7
36 Low Burnham........G 5
40 Low Burton........G 3
45 Low Buston........B 10
36 Low Catton........B 5
40 Low Coniscliffe........D 3
42 Low Craighead........A 3
44 Low Cranecleugh........D 5
44 Low Crosby........G 3
41 Low Dalby........F 8
40 Low Dinsdale........D 4
36 Low Eggborough........E 3
40 Low Etherley........B 2
44 Low Geltbridge........G 4
47 Low Grange........H 8
22 Low Habberley........D 2
7 Low Ham........C 8
45 Low Hedgeley........A 9
39 Low Hesket........A 7
45 Low Hesleyhurst........C 9
41 Low Hutton........H 8
42 Low Knockbrex........E 5
31 Low Leighton........B 8
38 Low Lorton........C 4
42 Low Malzie........F 4
41 Low Marishes........G 8
32 Low Marnham........C 5
41 Low Mill........F 7
34 Low Moor........C 6
45 Low Moorsley........H 11
45 Low Newton-by-the-Sea........A 10
44 Low Row, Cumb.........G 4
38 Low Row, Cumb.........B 6
39 Low Row, Yorks.........E 12
42 Low Salchrie........E 1
37 Low Santon........F 7
47 Low Shawsburn........D 12
26 Low Street........C 6
26 Low Thurlton........E 7
48 Low Torry........A 3
45 Low Town........C 9
47 Low Waters........D 12
40 Low Worsall........D 4
38 Low Wray........E 6
39 Lowbridge House........E 7
38 Lowca........C 2
32 Lowdham........F 4
30 Lowe........G 4
6 Lower Aisholt........C 5
7 Lower Ansty........F 11
6 Lower Ashton........H 2
17 Lower Assendon........F 8
63 Lower Bayble........D 6
10 Lower Beeding........E 1
39 Lower Bentham........H 9
7 Lower Bockhampton........G 10
23 Lower Boddington........G 8
2 Lower Boscaswell........F 1
9 Lower Bourne........B 10
22 Lower Brailes........H 6
62 Lower Breakish........F 6
22 Lower Broadheath........F 2
15 Lower Bullingham........A 8
25 Lower Caldecote........K 3
15 Lower Cam........D 10
14 Lower Chapel........A 4
8 Lower Chicksgrove........C 1
8 Lower Chute........A 4
10 Lower Cokeham........H 1
31 Lower Crossings........B 9
35 Lower Cumberworth........F 11
14 Lower Cwm-twrch........C 1
34 Lower Darwen........E 6
25 Lower Dean........H 2
54 Lower Diabaig........D 2
10 Lower Dicker........G 4
21 Lower Dinchope........D 10
61 Lower Dounreay........A 9
21 Lower Down........D 9
2 Lower Drift........G 2
36 Lower Dunsforth........A 2
8 Lower Everleigh........A 3
15 Lower Failand........G 8
9 Lower Farringdon........C 8
38 Lower Foxdale........G 1
12 Lower Freystrop........F 3
9 Lower Froyle........B 9
60 Lower Gledfield........G 6
10 Lower Green, Kent........D 5
26 Lower Green, Norf.........B 3
27 Lower Hacheston........J 6
62 Lower Halistra........B 2
11 Lower Halstow........A 7
11 Lower Hardres........C 10
56 Lower Hempriggs........C 7
21 Lower Hergest........G 8
16 Lower Heyford........B 6
10 Lower Higham........A 6
30 Lower Hordley........G 3
10 Lower Horsebridge........G 4
51 Lower Kinchrackine........E 8
7 Lower Kingcombe........F 9
10 Lower Kingswood........C 1
30 Lower Kinnerton........D 2
15 Lower Langford........H 8
53 Lower Largo........G 9
31 Lower Leigh........G 8
57 Lower Lenie........G 1
20 Lower Llanfadog........F 5
4 Lower Loxhore........B 5
15 Lower Lydbrook........C 9
21 Lower Lye........F 9
14 Lower Machen........E 5
15 Lower Maes-coed........A 7
19 Lower Mayland........D 9
62 Lower Milovaig........C 1
22 Lower Moor........G 3
18 Lower Nazeing........C 4
52 Lower Oakfield........H 6
62 Lower Ollach........D 4
14 Lower Penarth........G 5
22 Lower Penn........C 2
8 Lower Pennington........G 5
30 Lower Peover........C 6
35 Lower Place........F 8
22 Lower Quinton........G 5
21 Lower Rochford........F 11
34 Lower Salter........A 5
16 Lower Seagry........F 1
63 Lower Shader........A 5
25 Lower Shelton........L 1
17 Lower Shiplake........F 8
23 Lower Shuckburgh........F 8
16 Lower Slaughter........B 3
15 Lower Stanton St. Quintin........F 12
11 Lower Stoke........A 7
26 Lower Street........B 6
22 Lower Strensham........H 3
17 Lower Sundon........A 11
8 Lower Swanwick........E 6
16 Lower Swell........B 3
62 Lower Tote........B 4
12 Lower Town........C 3
23 Lower Tysoe........H 7
9 Lower Upham........D 7
6 Lower Vexford........C 5
34 Lower Walton........H 5
7 Lower Waterston........G 10
7 Lower Weare........A 7
21 Lower Welson........G 8
30 Lower Whitley........B 5
9 Lower Wield........B 8
17 Lower Winchendon........C 8
17 Lower Woodend........E 9
8 Lower Woodford........C 3
22 Lower Wyche........H 1
23 Lowesby........A 10
26 Lowestoft........F 8
26 Lowestoft End........F 8
38 Loweswater........C 4
10 Lowfield Heath........D 2
34 Lowgill, Lancs.........A 5
39 Lowgill, Westmor.........E 8
25 Lowick, Northants.........G 1
45 Lowick, Northum.........B 11
38 Lowick Green........G 5
14 Lowlands........E 6
22 Lowsonford........E 5
39 Lowther........C 8
37 Lowthorpe........A 8
34 Lowton, Lancs.........G 5
6 Lowton, Som.........D 5
34 Lowton Common........G 5
6 Loxbeare........E 3
9 Loxhill........B 11
4 Loxhore........B 5
22 Loxley........G 6
7 Loxton........A 7
9 Loxwood........C 11
60 Lubachoinnich........G 5
60 Lubcroy........F 4
23 Lubenham........C 10
51 Lubnaclach........A 11
54 Lubriach........B 7
6 Luccombe........B 3
9 Luccombe Village........H 7
45 Lucker........D 11
3 Luckett........B 11
15 Luckington........F 11
53 Lucklawhill........E 9
6 Luckwell Bridge........B 2
21 Lucton........F 10
37 Ludborough........H 10
12 Ludchurch........F 5
35 Luddenden........E 9
35 Luddenden Foot........E 9
10 Luddesdown........B 5
36 Luddington, Lincs.........E 6
22 Luddington, War.........G 5
25 Luddington in the Brook........G 2
21 Ludford........E 10
33 Ludford Magna........A 9
33 Ludford Parva........A 9
17 Ludgershall........B 7
8 Ludgershall........A 4
2 Ludgvan........F 2
26 Ludham........D 7
21 Ludlow........E 10
7 Ludwell........D 12
40 Ludworth........A 4
4 Luffincott........F 2
47 Lugar........G 10
49 Lugate........E 7
49 Luggate Burn........B 8
47 Luggiebank........B 12
47 Lugton........D 9
21 Lugwardine........H 11
62 Luib........E 5
51 Luib Hotel........E 12
51 Luibeilt........A 9
21 Lulham........H 9
22 Lullington, Derby........A 6
7 Lullington, Som.........A 11
22 Lulsey........G 1
15 Lulsgate Bottom........H 8
35 Lumb........E 9
35 Lumbutts........E 8
36 Lumby........D 3
47 Lumloch........B 11
59 Lumphanan........G 3
52 Lumphinnans........H 6
49 Lumsdaine........B 11
58 Lumsden........E 2
53 Lunan........B 11
53 Lunanhead........B 9
52 Luncarty........D 6
37 Lund, E. Riding........B 7
36 Lund, E. Riding........D 4
51 Lundavra........A 8
58 Lunderton........C 8
53 Lundie, Angus........D 8
55 Lundie, Inverness........H 5
53 Lundin Links........G 9
50 Lungar (Hotel)........G 5
64 Lunna........C 7
64 Lunning........C 7
13 Lunnon........H 9
10 Lunsford........B 6
10 Lunsford's Cross........G 6
34 Lunt........G 2
21 Luntley........G 9
6 Luppitt........F 5
35 Lupsett........E 11
39 Lupton........G 8
9 Lurgashall........C 10
56 Lurgmore........F 1
33 Lusby........C 10
51 Luss........H 10
62 Lusta........C 2
5 Lustleigh........H 6
21 Luston........F 10
59 Luthermuir........K 4
53 Luthrie........E 8
17 Luton, Beds.........B 12
5 Luton, Devon........H 8
10 Luton, Kent........A 6
23 Lutterworth........D 9
5 Lutton, Devon........K 5
24 Lutton, Lincs.........C 5
25 Lutton, Northants.........G 2
6 Luxborough........B 3
3 Luxulyan........D 7
61 Lybster........D 11
21 Lydbury North........D 9
11 Lydd........F 9
11 Lydd-on-Sea........F 9
11 Lydden........D 11
23 Lyddington........B 12
17 Lyde Green........H 8
6 Lydeard St. Lawrence........C 4
5 Lydford........G 4
35 Lydgate........E 8
21 Lydham........C 9
16 Lydiard Millicent........F 2
34 Lydiate........G 2
7 Lydlinch........E 10
15 Lydney........D 9
12 Lydstep........G 4
22 Lye........D 3
15 Lye Cross........H 8
17 Lye Green, Bucks.........D 10
10 Lye Green, Sussex........E 4
16 Lyford........E 5
47 Lylestone, Ayr.........E 8
49 Lylestone, Ber.........D 8
11 Lymbridge Green........D 10
7 Lyme Regis........G 7
11 Lyminge........D 10
8 Lymington........F 4
9 Lyminster........F 11
30 Lymm........B 5
8 Lymore........G 4
11 Lympne........E 10
6 Lympsham........A 6
6 Lympstone........H 3
57 Lynaberack........K 3
57 Lynachlaggan........J 4
6 Lynch........B 3
26 Lynch Green........E 4
57 Lynchat........J 3
8 Lyndhurst........E 4
23 Lyndon........B 12
48 Lyne, Peebles........E 5
17 Lyne, Surrey........G 11
15 Lyne Down........A 9
57 Lyne of Gorthleck........H 1
58 Lyne of Skene........F 5
30 Lyneal........G 3
62 Lynedale House........C 3
16 Lyneham, Oxon.........B 4
16 Lyneham, Wilts.........F 1
44 Lyneholmeford........F 4
57 Lynemore........G 6
45 Lynemouth........D 11
64 Lyness........E 1
26 Lyng, Norfolk........D 4
7 Lyng, Somerset........C 7
4 Lynmouth........A 6
11 Lynsted........B 8
4 Lynton........A 6
7 Lyon's Gate........F 10
21 Lyonshall........G 9
8 Lytchett Matravers........G 1
8 Lytchett Minster........G 1
61 Lyth........B 11
34 Lytham........D 3
34 Lytham St. Anne's........D 2
41 Lythe........D 8
64 Lythes........E 3
63 Maaruig........F 3
2 Mabe Burnthouse........F 5
43 Mabie........D 10
33 Mablethorpe........B 12
48 Macbiehill........D 4
31 Macclesfield........C 7
31 Macclesfield For.........C 8
58 Macduff........A 4
52 Machany........F 4
14 Machen........E 5
46 Machrihanish........G 1
50 Machrins........H 1
20 Machynlleth........B 3
13 Mackworth........F 11
49 Macmerry........B 7
52 Madderty........E 4
48 Maddiston........B 2
9 Madehurst........E 11
21 Madeley, Salop........B 12
30 Madeley, Staffs.........F 6
30 Madeley Heath........F 6
25 Madingley........J 5
21 Madley........H 9
22 Madresfield........G 2
2 Madron........F 2
28 Maenaddwyn........B 4
12 Maenclochog........D 4
14 Maendy........G 3
28 Maentwrog........F 6
13 Maen-y-groes........A 7
30 Maer........F 6
13 Maerdy, Carm.........D 10
29 Maerdy, Denbigh........F 9
14 Maerdy, Glam.........D 3
15 Maerdy, Mon.........B 7
30 Maesbrook Green........H 2
30 Maesbury........H 2
30 Maesbury Marsh........H 2
12 Maesgwynne........E 5
29 Maeshafn........D 11
13 Maesllyn........C 7
20 Maesmynis........H 6
14 Maesteg........E 2
13 Maestir........B 9
13 Maestwynog........C 10
13 Maes-y-bont........E 9
13 Maesycrugiau........C 8
14 Maes-y-cwmmer........E 5
13 Maesymeillion........B 7
18 Magdalen Laver........C 5
58 Maggieknockater........C 1
10 Magham Down........G 5
34 Maghull........G 3
15 Magor........F 7
7 Maiden Bradley........B 11
45 Maiden Law........H 10
7 Maiden Newton........F 9
12 Maiden Wells........G 3
5 Maidencombe........J 8
48 Maidencots........G 2
17 Maidenhead........F 10
39 Maidenhill........B 7
42 Maidens........A 3
17 Maiden's Green........G 9
33 Maidenwell........B 10
23 Maidford........G 9
17 Maids' Moreton........A 8
10 Maidstone........C 6
23 Maidwell........D 10
64 Mail........E 7
14 Maindee........E 6
47 Mains, Lanark........D 11
52 Mains, Perth........B 6
61 Mains, Sutherland........F 8
42 Mains of Airies........E 1
59 Mains of Allardice........K 6
59 Mains of Altries........H 6
58 Mains of Annochie........C 7
53 Mains of Ardestie........D 10
58 Mains of Arnage........D 7
58 Mains of Auchindachy........C 2
58 Mains of Auchmedden........A 6
53 Mains of Balgavies........B 10
53 Mains of Ballindarg........B 9
59 Mains of Balnakettle........K 4
58 Mains of Birness........D 7
56 Mains of Bunachton........F 2
58 Mains of Cairnborrow........D 2
58 Mains of Cardno........A 7
58 Mains of Crichie........C 7
56 Mains of Dalvey........F 7
59 Mains of Drum........G 5
58 Mains of Drummuir........C 2
56 Mains of Drynie........E 2
58 Mains of Edingight........B 3
58 Mains of Esslemont........E 7
59 Mains of Glenfarquhar........J 5
59 Mains of Haulkerton........K 5
58 Mains of Inkhorn........D 7
58 Mains of Keithfield........D 6
58 Mains of Kirkhill........F 6
58 Mains of Logie........B 8
59 Mains of Melgund........L 3
56 Mains of Newhall........C 3
43 Mains of Terregles........D 10
59 Mains of Thornton........K 4
52 Mains of Throsk........H 3
56 Mains of Tore........D 2
58 Mains of Towie........C 5
53 Mains of Usan........B 12
40 Mainsforth........B 3
43 Mainsriddle........F 10
21 Mainstone........D 8
15 Maisemore........B 11
5 Malborough........M 6
18 Malden Rushett........H 2
19 Maldon........C 8
35 Malham........A 8
55 Mallaig........K 1
55 Mallaigvaig........K 1
48 Malleny Mills........C 4
52 Malling........G 1
28 Malltraeth........C 3
20 Mallwyd........A 4
15 Malmesbury........F 12
4 Malmsmead........A 7
30 Malpas, Cheshire........E 3
2 Malpas, Corn.........E 5
14 Malpas, Mon.........E 6
51 Malt Land........F 8
40 Maltby, N. Riding........D 5
40 Maltby, W. Riding........A 3
33 Maltby le Marsh........B 11
11 Maltman's Hill........D 8
41 Malton........H 8
22 Malvern Link........G 1
22 Malvern Wells........H 1
21 Mamble........E 12
14 Mamhilad........D 6
2 Manaccan........G 5
21 Manafon........B 7
5 Manaton........H 6
33 Manby........B 11
22 Mancetter........C 6
35 Manchester........G 7
29 Mancot........D 12
24 Manea........F 6
42 Maneight........A 6
40 Manfield........D 2
64 Mangaster........C 7
63 Mangersta........D 1
44 Mangerton........D 3
15 Mangotsfield........G 10
12 Manian Fawr........B 5
63 Manish........H 2
30 Manley........C 4
14 Manmoel........D 5
16 Manningford Bohune........H 2
16 Manningford Bruce........H 2
35 Manningham........D 10
10 Mannings Heath........E 1
8 Mannington........F 2
27 Manningtree........M 4
59 Mannofield........G 6
12 Manorbier........G 4
12 Manorbier Newton........G 4
49 Manorhill........F 9
12 Manorowen........C 3
43 Mansefield........B 9
13 Manselfield........H 9
21 Mansell Gamage........H 9
21 Mansell Lacy........H 9
39 Mansergh........G 8
47 Mansfield, Ayr.........H 11
32 Mansfield, Notts.........D 3
32 Mansfield Woodhouse........D 3
38 Mansriggs........G 5
7 Manston, Dorset........E 11
11 Manston, Kent........B 12
8 Manswood........E 2
24 Manthorpe, Lincs.........D 2
32 Manthorpe, Lincs.........F 6
37 Manton, Lincs.........G 7
23 Manton, Rutland........B 12
16 Manton, Wilts.........G 3
18 Manuden........A 5
50 Maolachy........F 6
7 Maperton........D 10
17 Maple Cross........E 11
32 Maplebeck........D 4
17 Mapledurham........F 7
9 Mapledurwell........A 8
10 Maplehurst........F 1
10 Maplescombe........B 4

MAP
31 Mapleton.......E 10
32 Mapperley........F 2
32 Mapperley Park..F 3
7 Mapperton,
   Dorset.........F 12
7 Mapperton,
   Dorset.........F 8
22 Mappleborough
   Green.........E 4
37 Mappleton......C 10
35 Mapplewell.....F 12
7 Mappowder.....F 10
57 Mar Lodge.......K 7
2 Marazion........G 2
30 Marbury........F 4
24 March, Cambs....F 5
48 March, Lan.....H 3
16 Marcham........D 5
30 Marchamley.....G 4
43 Marchbankwood.B 11
47 Marchburn.....H 11
31 Marchington.....G 9
31 Marchington
   Woodlands.....G 9
30 Marchwiel.......E 2
8 Marchwood......E 5
14 Marcross.......G 3
21 Marden, Herefs..H 10
10 Marden, Kent....D 6
16 Marden, Wilts..H 2
10 Marden Beech...D 6
10 Marden Thorn...D 6
14 Mardy..........C 6
7 Mare Green.....D 7
17 Marefield, Bucks..E 9
23 Marefield, Leics..A 11
33 Mareham le Fen.D 10
33 Mareham on the
   Hill...........C 10
32 Marehey........E 1
10 Maresfield.....F 3
37 Marfleet.......D 9
30 Marford........E 2
13 Margam........H 11
7 Margaret Marsh.D 11
18 Margaret Roding..C 6
18 Margaretting.....D 6
11 Margate........A 12
46 Margnaheglish....F 5
24 Marham........D 8
4 Marhamchurch..F 1
24 Marholm........E 2
28 Marianglas......B 4
28 Mariansleigh....D 6
59 Marionburgh.....G 5
62 Marishader......B 4
63 Mariveg........E 5
43 Marjoriebanks..C 11
42 Mark, Ayr.......D 2
43 Mark, Kirk......F 7
7 Mark, Somerset..A 7
7 Mark Causeway..B 7
10 Mark Cross.....E 5
10 Markbeech......D 4
33 Markby.........B 12
23 Market Bosworth..B 7
24 Market Deeping..E 2
30 Market Drayton..G 5
23 Market
   Harborough...C 10
8 Market Lavington.A 2
23 Market Overton..A 12
33 Market Rasen.....A 8
33 Market Stainton..B 9
26 Market Street...C 6
36 Market Weighton..C 6
27 Market Weston..G 3
23 Markfield......A 8
14 Markham........D 5
32 Markham Moor...C 4
53 Markinch.......G 8
35 Markington......A 10
49 Markle.........B 8
19 Marks Tey......B 9
15 Marksbury.....H 10
17 Markyate.......C 11
48 Marlage........D 1
16 Marlborough....G 3
21 Marlbrook,
   Herefs.........G 10
22 Marlbrook, Worcs.
           E 3
22 Marlcliff......G 4
5 Marldon.......J 7
27 Marlesford.....J 6
30 Marley Green....F 4
45 Marley Hill.....G 10
8 Marley Mount....F 4
49 Marleyknowe....F 12
26 Marlingford.....E 4
35 Marloes........F 1
17 Marlow, Bucks...E 9
21 Marlow, Herefs..E 9

17 Marlow Bottom...E 9
10 Marlpit Hill.....C 3
7 Marnhull......D 11
58 Marnoch........C 3
31 Marple.........A 8
36 Marr..........G 3
61 Marrel.........E 9
40 Marrick........E 1
12 Marros.........F 5
45 Marsden, Dur...G 12
35 Marsden, Yorks..F 9
39 Marsett........F 11
6 Marsh, Devon....E 6
6 Marsh, Somerset..C 4
16 Marsh Baldon...D 6
16 Marsh Benham..G 5
37 Marsh Chapel...G 11
17 Marsh Gibbon...B 7
6 Marsh Green,
   Devon.........G 4
10 Marsh Green,
   Kent.........D 3
21 Marsh Green,
   Shropshire.....A 11
6 Marsh Street....B 3
18 Marshall's Heath..B 2
26 Marsham........C 5
34 Marshaw.......B 5
11 Marshborough...B 11
21 Marshbrook.....C 10
15 Marshfield, Glos..G 11
14 Marshfield, Mon..F 5
2 Marshgate......B 2
32 Marshlane......B 1
34 Marshside......E 2
7 Marshwood......F 7
40 Marske.........E 1
40 Marske-by-the-Sea C 6
30 Marston, Ches...C 5
21 Marston, Herefs..G 9
32 Marston, Lincs...F 6
16 Marston, Oxon...C 6
22 Marston, Staffs..A 2
31 Marston, Staffs..G 8
22 Marston, War....C 5
22 Marston, War.....G 5
16 Marston, Wilts...H 1
22 Marston Green...D 5
7 Marston Magna...D 9
16 Marston Meysey..D 2
31 Marston
   Montgomery...F 10
25 Marston Moretaine L 1
31 Marston on Dove.G 11
23 Marston St. Lawrence
           H 8
21 Marston Stannett G 11
23 Marston Trussell.D 10
15 Marstow........B 9
17 Marsworth......C 10
16 Marten........H 4
30 Marthall.......C 6
26 Martham........D 8
8 Martin, Hants...D 2
11 Martin, Kent...C 12
33 Martin, Lincs...D 8
8 Martin Drove End.D 2
22 Martin Hussingtree F 2
4 Martinhoe......A 5
4 Martinhoe Cross..A 6
30 Martinscroft.....A 5
44 Martinshouse....B 3
7 Martinstown....G 10
27 Martlesham.....K 6
12 Martletwy......F 4
22 Martley........F 1
7 Martock.......D 8
31 Marton, Ches...C 7
37 Marton, E. Riding.C 9
32 Marton, Lincs...B 5
40 Marton, N. Riding D 5
41 Marton, N. Riding G 7
21 Marton, Salop...B 5
36 Marton, W. Riding A 2
23 Marton, War.....E 7
40 Marton le Moor..H 4
40 Marton-in-the-
   Forest.........H 6
8 Martyr Worthy...C 2
17 Martyr's Green..H 11
43 Marwhirn........B 8
64 Marwick........C 1
4 Marwood........B 4
4 Marwood Middle..B 4
5 Mary Tavy......H 4
54 Marybank.......D 8
56 Maryburgh......D 1
59 Maryculter......G 8
49 Marygold.......C 10
58 Maryhill, Aber....C 6
47 Maryhill, Lan...B 10
59 Marykirk.......L 4
56 Marypark.......F 7

38 Maryport, Cumb..B 3
42 Maryport, Wig...H 2
53 Maryton, Angus..B 8
53 Maryton, Angus..B 11
59 Marywell, Aber...H 3
53 Marywell, Angus..C 11
59 Marywell, Kinc...G 7
40 Masham........G 2
45 Mason :.........F 10
32 Mastin Moor.....C 2
59 Mastrick.......G 6
18 Matching.......C 5
18 Matching Green...C 5
18 Matching Tye....C 5
45 Matfen.........F 8
10 Matfield.......D 5
18 Mathern........E 8
22 Mathon.........H 1
12 Mathry.........D 2
26 Matlask........B 5
31 Matlock.......D 11
31 Matlock Bath...D 11
26 Matson........C 11
38 Matterdale End...C 6
32 Mattersey......A 4
32 Mattersey Thorpe.A 4
17 Mattingley.....H 8
26 Mattishall......D 4
26 Mattishall Burgh..D 4
53 Mattocks.......C 9
47 Mauchline......G 10
58 Maud..........C 7
13 Maudsland......D 7
16 Maugersbury....B 3
38 Maughold......G 3
54 Mauld.........F 8
25 Maulden.......L 2
39 Mauls Meaburn...D 8
40 Maunby........F 4
21 Maund Bryan...G 11
6 Maundown......C 4
26 Mautby........D 8
22 Mavesyn Ridware.A 4
33 Mavis Enderby..D 10
56 Maviston.......D 5
22 Maw Green......B 4
43 Mawbray.......G 11
52 Mawcarse.......G 6
34 Mawdesley......F 4
14 Mawdlam.......F 1
2 Mawgan........G 4
2 Mawla..........E 4
2 Mawnan........G 5
2 Mawnan Smith..G 5
24 Maxey.........E 2
22 Maxstoke......C 6
11 Maxton, Kent...D 11
49 Maxton, Rox.....F 8
49 Maxwellheugh...F 10
42 Maxwellston.....B 4
43 Maxwelltown...D 10
5 Maxworthy......G 1
31 May Bank......E 7
13 Mayals........H 9
47 Maybole.......H 8
17 Maybury.......H 11
31 Mayfield, Staffs..F 10
10 Mayfield, Sussex..E 5
17 Mayford.......H 10
19 Mayland.......D 9
10 Maynard's Green..F 5
15 Maypole, Mon...C 8
2 Maypole,
   Is. of Scilly....D 2
26 Maypole Green..F 7
64 Maywick.......E 7
64 Mead..........E 1
15 Meadgate......H 10
47 Meadowfoot....E 11
21 Meadowtown....B 5
39 Meal Bank......F 8
37 Meals.........G 11
38 Mealsgate......A 4
35 Mearbeck......A 7
7 Meare.........B 8
6 Meare Green....D 6
47 Mearns........D 10
23 Mears Ashby....E 11
25 Measham.......A 7
10 Meath Green....D 2
39 Meathop.......G 7
63 Meavag........G 3
5 Meavy.........J 4
23 Medbourne.....C 11
45 Medburn.......F 9
4 Meddon........D 2
17 Medmenham....F 9
45 Medmosley.....H 9
9 Medstead......B 8
31 Meerbrook.....D 8
33 Meers Bridge...B 12
25 Meesden.......M 5
4 Meeth.........E 4

44 Megdale.........C 1
48 Meggethead.....G 4
12 Meidrim........E 6
21 Meifod.........A 7
53 Meigle.........C 7
43 Meikle
   Barncleugh....D 10
43 Meikle Beoch...C 8
47 Meikle Carco...H 12
47 Meikle Earnock..D 12
59 Meikle Fiddes...J 5
52 Meikle Forter....A 6
61 Meikle Gluich...H 7
46 Meikle Grenach..C 6
47 Meikle Hareshaw.E 11
47 Meikle Ittington..E 7
56 Meikle
   Kildrummie....D 4
49 Meikle Pinkerton..B 9
59 Meikle Strath...K 4
52 Meikle Tarty....E 7
58 Meikle Wartle...D 5
47 Meikleholm....C 11
47 Meikielaught....E 7
52 Meikleour......C 6
58 Meikleton......C 3
14 Meillteyrn.....G 2
43 Meinbank......D 12
31 Meinciau......F 8
31 Meirheath......F 8
63 Melbost........D 6
43 Melbost Borve...A 5
25 Melbourn......L 5
31 Melbourne,
   Derby........H 12
48 Melbourne, Lan..E 4
36 Melbourne, Yorks.C 5
7 Melbury Abbas..D 12
7 Melbury Bubb...F 9
7 Melbury Osmond..E 9
7 Melbury Sampford.F 9
64 Melby.........D 6
25 Melchbourne....J 1
7 Melcombe Regis .H 10
5 Meldon, Devon..G 4
45 Meldon, N'thumb. E 9
25 Meldreth.......L 5
29 Meliden.......B 10
14 Melin Court.....D 2
29 Melin-byrhedin...C 4
29 Melin-y-coed....D 7
20 Melin-y-grug....B 6
29 Melin-y-wig.....E 9
39 Melkinthorpe...C 8
44 Melkridge......G 5
15 Melksham......H 12
54 Mellangaun.....A 2
46 Melldalloch.....B 4
52 Melling, Lancs...H 8
34 Melling, Lancs...G 3
34 Melling Mount...G 3
27 Mellis.........H 4
60 Mellon Charles..G 1
60 Mellon Udrigle..G 1
34 Mellor, Cheshire..A 8
34 Mellor, Lancs...D 5
34 Mellor Brook...D 5
7 Mells.........A 10
39 Melmerby, Cumb..B 8
40 Melmerby,
   N. Riding.....G 4
40 Melmerby,
   N. Riding.....G 1
7 Melplash.......F 8
49 Melrose.......F 8
64 Melsetter.......E 1
45 Melsonby......D 2
35 Meltham......F 9
35 Meltham Mills...F 10
47 Melton, E. Riding.D 7
27 Melton, Suffolk..K 6
26 Melton Constable..B 3
32 Melton Mowbray.H 5
37 Melton Ross....F 8
36 Meltonby......B 6
14 Melvaig........A 1
21 Melverley......A 9
61 Melvich........B 8
6 Membury.......F 6
58 Memsie........A 7
59 Memus.........L 2
28 Menai Bridge...C 5
27 Mendham.......G 6
27 Mendlesham....J 4
27 Mendlesham Green
           J 4
3 Menheniot.....C 10
43 Mennock.......A 9
35 Menston.......C 10

52 Menstrie.......G 3
36 Menthorpe.....D 5
17 Mentmore......B 10
55 Meoble........L 2
21 Meole Brace...A 10
9 Meonstoke.....D 7
10 Meopham.......B 5
10 Meopham Green..B 5
10 Meopham Station.A 5
25 Mepal.........G 5
25 Meppershall....L 2
21 Merbach.......H 8
30 Mere, Cheshire..B 6
7 Mere, Wilts....C 11
34 Mere Brow.....E 3
35 Mere Clough...D 7
22 Mere End......E 6
22 Mere Green.....B 5
11 Meresborough..B 7
34 Mereside.......D 2
30 Meretown......H 6
10 Mereworth.....C 5
59 Mergie.........H 5
22 Meriden.......D 6
62 Merkadale.....E 3
43 Merkland......D 8
60 Merkland Lodge..D 5
12 Merlin's Bridge..F 3
30 Merrington.....H 3
12 Merrion........G 3
7 Merriot.......E 8
5 Merrivale......H 4
9 Merrow........A 11
44 Merrylaw......C 2
3 Merrymeet.....C 10
34 Merseyside, Co...H 3
11 Mersham.......D 9
10 Merstham......C 2
9 Merston.......F 10
8 Merstone......H 6
2 Merther.......E 6
13 Merthyr.......E 7
14 Merthyr Cynog..A 3
14 Merthyr Mawr...F 2
14 Merthyr Tydfil..D 4
14 Merthyr Vale...D 4
4 Merton, Devon..E 4
18 Merton, London..G 3
26 Merton, Norfolk..F 2
17 Merton, Oxon...B 7
44 Mervinslaw.....B 5
19 Messing........B 9
37 Messingham....G 7
27 Metfield.......G 6
33 Metheringham..D 8
53 Methil.........G 8
28 Methlem.......G 1
35 Methley......D 12
58 Methlick.......D 6
52 Methven.......E 5
24 Methwold.......F 8
24 Methwold Hythe..F 8
26 Mettingham....F 6
26 Metton........B 5
3 Mevagissey.....E 7
36 Mexborough.....G 3
61 Mey..........A 12
16 Meysey Hampton.D 2
63 Miavaig........C 2
58 Michael Muir....D 6
15 Michaelchurch...B 8
14 Michaelchurch
   Escley.........A 6
21 Michaelchurch-on-
   Arrow........G 8
14 Michaelston-le-Pit.G 5
14 Michaelston-super-
   Ely...........G 4
14 Michaelstone-y-
   Vedw........F 6
3 Michaelstow....B 8
8 Michelmersh....C 5
27 Mickfield......J 4
30 Mickle Trafford..C 3
36 Micklebring....H 3
41 Mickleby.......D 8
36 Micklefield....D 2
10 Mickleham.....C 11
31 Mickleover.....G 11
44 Micklethwaite...H 1
22 Mickleton, Glos..H 5
39 Mickleton, Yorks.C 12
35 Mickletown....D 12
35 Mickley.......G 3
45 Mickley Square..G 9
58 Mid Ardlaw.....A 7
58 Mid Beltie.....G 5
59 Mid Cairncross..J 2
48 Mid Calder.....C 3
61 Mid Clyth......D 11
58 Mid Cowbog....B 6
54 Mid Crochail...F 7

58 Mid Culsh......C 6
47 Mid Drumloch...D 11
14 Mid Glamorgan, Co.
           E 4
48 Mid Hartwood...C 3
43 Mid Laggan....D 8
9 Mid Lavant....E 10
54 Mid Mains.....F 8
46 Mid Sannox....E 5
54 Mid Strom.....F 2
46 Mid Thundergay..E 4
64 Mid Yell.......B 7
64 Midbea........A 2
17 Middle Assendon..F 8
16 Middle Aston...A 6
16 Middle Barton..B 5
15 Middle Bridge...G 8
7 Middle Chinnock..E 8
59 Middle Drums...L 3
58 Middle Essie....B 8
32 Middle Handley..B 1
17 Middle Claydon..B 8
22 Middle Littleton..G 4
12 Middle Mill....D 2
49 Middle Ord....D 12
33 Middle Rasen...A 8
52 Middle Rigg....F 5
15 Middle Street...D 11
23 Middle Tysoe...H 7
8 Middle Wallop..B 4
8 Middle Winterslow C 4
8 Middle Woodford.C 3
43 Middlebie.....D 12
57 Middlebridge...M 4
49 Middlefield....D 10
43 Middlegill.....A 11
40 Middleham.....F 2
21 Middlehope.....D 10
7 Middlemarsh...E 10
58 Middlemuir....C 6
58 Middlemuir House.E 7
40 Middlesbrough..C 5
43 Middleshaw,
   Dumfries......D 12
39 Middleshaw,
   Westmorland...F 8
44 Middlesknowes..B 6
40 Middlesmoor....H 1
40 Middlestone....B 3
40 Middlestone Moor.B 3
35 Middlestown....E 11
49 Middlethird....E 9
58 Middleton, Aber..E 6
47 Middleton, Ayr..E 8
31 Middleton, Derby E 11
31 Middleton, Derby D 10
27 Middleton, Essex..L 2
13 Middleton, Glam..H 7
8 Middleton, Hants..B 6
21 Middleton, Herefs. E 11
52 Middleton, Kinr...F 6
34 Middleton, Lancs..A 3
35 Middleton, Lancs..F 7
48 Middleton,
   Midlothian.....D 6
24 Middleton, Norf...D 8
41 Middleton,
   N. Riding......G 8
25 Middleton,
   Northants......C 11
45 Middleton,
   Northumberland E 9
45 Middleton,
   Northumb......B 12
52 Middleton, Perth..B 6
21 Middleton, Salop.E 11
30 Middleton, Salop..G 2
15 Middleton, Som..G 8
27 Middleton, Suffolk H 7
22 Middleton, War...B 5
35 Middleton,
   W. Riding....D 11
35 Middleton,
   W. Riding....B 10
23 Middleton Cheney.H 8
31 Middleton Green.G 8
49 Middleton Hall..G 12
39 Middleton in
   Teesdale......C 11
58 Middleton of Rora C 8
9 Middleton-on-Sea F 11
21 Middleton on the
   Hill...........F 11
37 Middleton-on-the-
   Wolds........B 7
40 Middleton One
   Row..........D 4
21 Middleton Priors.C 11
40 Middleton
   Quernhow.....G 3
40 Middleton St. George
           D 4
21 Middleton Scriven D 12

MAP
16 Middleton Stoney . . B 6
40 Middleton Tyas . . E 3
21 Middletown . . . . . . A 8
30 Middlewich . . . . . . D 6
27 Middlewood Green J 4
47 Middleyard . . . . . . F 10
7 Middlezoy . . . . C 7
40 Middridge . . . . C 3
60 Midfield . . . . A 6
15 Midford . . . . H 10
34 Midge Hall . . . . . . E 4
44 Midgeholme . . . . . G 5
35 Midgeley . . . . F 11
16 Midgham . . . . G 6
35 Midgley . . . . D 9
35 Midhopestones . . G 11
9 Midhurst . . . . D 10
49 Midlem . . . . G 8
48 Midlock . . . . G 2
48 Midlothian, Co. . . . C 5
7 Midsomer Norton A 10
60 Midtown . . . . B 6
54 Midtown Brae . . . . A 2
59 Midtown of Barras J 6
58 Midtown of
    Buchromb . . . . . . C 1
33 Midville . . . . E 11
43 Miefield . . . . F 7
61 Migdale . . . . G 7
59 Migvie . . . . G 2
7 Milborne Port . . . . D 10
7 Milborne St. Andrew
                F 11
7 Milborne Wick . . D 10
45 Milbourne . . . . E 9
50 Milbuie . . . . H 1
39 Milburn . . . . B 9
15 Milbury Heath . . E 10
40 Milby . . . . H 4
16 Milcombe . . . . A 5
27 Milden . . . . K 3
25 Mildenhall, Suff. . H 8
16 Mildenhall, Wilts. . G 3
16 Mile Elm . . . . G 1
19 Mile End, Essex . . A 9
26 Mile End, Suffolk . . F 6
21 Milebrook . . . . E 8
26 Mileham . . . . D 2
15 Miles End . . . . C 9
30 Miles Green . . . . . . E 6
21 Miles Hope . . . . . . F 11
52 Milesmark . . . . . . H 5
49 Milfield . . . . F 12
31 Milford, Derby . F 12
4 Milford, Devon . . D 1
31 Milford, Staffs. . . H 8
9 Milford, Surrey . B 11
8 Milford, Wilts. . . . . C 3
12 Milford Haven . . . . F 4
8 Milford on Sea . . G 4
47 Milhall . . . . D 10
15 Milkwall . . . . C 9
8 Milkwell . . . . D 1
35 Mill Bank . . . . E 9
31 Mill Brow . . . . A 8
27 Mill Common . . . . G 7
17 Mill End, Bucks. . . F 9
17 Mill End, Herts. . . E 11
25 Mill End, Herts. . M 4
25 Mill End, Hunts. . . G 4
18 Mill Green, Essex D 6
27 Mill Green, Suffolk L 3
18 Mill Hill . . . . E 2
39 Mill Houses . . . . . H 8
9 Mill Lane . . . . A 9
58 Mill of Ardo,
    Aberdeen . . . . . . E 7
58 Mill of Ardo,
    Aberdeen . . . . . . D 6
58 Mill of Carden . . E 4
58 Mill of Culfork . . F 2
59 Mill of Gellan . . . G 3
59 Mill of Mondynes. J 5
59 Mill of Monquich. H 6
58 Mill of Muiresk . . C 4
58 Mill of Pot . . . . . C 5
59 Mill of Uras . . . . . J 6
26 Mill Street . . . . . . D 3
38 Millbach . . . . C 5
64 Millbounds . . . . . . B 3
58 Millbreck . . . . C 7
58 Millbrex . . . . C 6
9 Millbridge . . . . . . B 10
25 Millbrook, Beds. . L 1
3 Millbrook, Corn. . D 11
4 Millbrook, Devon. C 6
8 Millbrook, Hants. E 5
47 Millburn . . . . F 9
5 Millcombe . . . . . . L 7
11 Millcorner . . . . . . F 7
31 Milldale . . . . E 10
58 Millden Lodge . . . J 3
53 Milldens . . . . B 10

MAP
48 Millerhill . . . . B 6
31 Miller's Dale . . . . C 10
31 Millers Green . . . E 11
59 Millfield . . . . H 2
30 Millgreen . . . . G 5
21 Millhalf . . . . H 8
6 Millhayes . . . . E 5
47 Millheugh, Lan. . D 12
49 Millheugh, Rox. . . G 9
39 Millholme . . . . . . F 8
46 Millhouse, Arg. . . B 4
38 Millhouse, Cumb. . B 6
35 Millhouse, Yorks. G 11
43 Millhousebridge . . C 11
32 Millhouses . . . . . . B 1
43 Milliganton . . . . . . C 10
47 Millikenpark . . . . . C 9
36 Millington . . . . . . B 6
49 Millknowe . . . . . . C 9
31 Millmeece . . . . . . G 7
38 Millom . . . . G 4
3 Millpool . . . . C 8
46 Millport . . . . D 6
43 Millquarter . . . . . . C 7
31 Millthorpe . . . . . . C 11
39 Millthrop . . . . F 9
59 Milltimber . . . . . . G 6
53 Millton . . . . C 8
57 Millton of
    Auchriachan . . . H 7
58 Milltown, Aber. . . F 2
58 Milltown, Aber. . . F 7
59 Milltown, Aber. . . G 4
58 Milltown, Banff. . C 3
32 Milltown, Derby. . D 1
4 Milltown, Devon. . B 4
54 Milltown, Ross &
    Cromarty . . . . . . D 7
52 Milltown of
    Aberdalgie . . . . . E 5
58 Milltown of
    Auchindown . . . D 1
59 Milltown of
    Campfield . . . . . G 4
58 Milltown of
    Craigston . . . . . B 5
56 Milltown of
    Edinvillie . . . . . F 8
58 Milltown of
    Minnes . . . . E 7
58 Milltown of Towie. F 2
47 Millwall . . . . D 11
53 Milnacraig . . . . . . B 7
52 Milnathort . . . . . . G 6
43 Milne . . . . B 12
47 Milngavie . . . . . . B 10
43 Milnmark . . . . C 7
35 Milnrow . . . . F 8
39 Milnthorpe . . . . . . G 7
21 Milson . . . . E 11
11 Milstead . . . . B 7
8 Milston . . . . B 3
58 Milton, Aber. . . . . E 1
59 Milton, Angus . . . J 2
42 Milton, Ayr. . . . . . B 4
42 Milton, Ayr. . . . . . A 3
58 Milton, Banff. . . . A 3
16 Milton, Berks. . . . E 6
61 Milton, Caith. . . C 12
25 Milton, Cambs. . . J 6
44 Milton, Cumb. . . G 4
31 Milton, Derby . . G 11
43 Milton, Dumf. . . C 9
47 Milton, Dunb. . . B 9
9 Milton, Hants. . . . F 8
57 Milton, Inver. . . . H 5
57 Milton, Inver. . . . G 1
43 Milton, Kirk. . . . . D 9
23 Milton,
    Northants. . . . . G 10
16 Milton, Oxon. . . . A 5
12 Milton, Pemb. . . . G 4
52 Milton, Perth. . . . A 6
51 Milton, Perth. . . G 12
56 Milton, Ross &
    Cromarty . . . . . D 2
56 Milton, Ross &
    Cromarty . . . . . E 1
56 Milton, Ross &
    Cromarty . . . . . . B 3
54 Milton, Ross &
    Cromarty . . . . . E 1
7 Milton, Som. . . . . D 8
14 Milton, Som. . . . . H 6
42 Milton, Wig. . . . . F 3
7 Milton Abbas . . . F 11
5 Milton Abbot . . . D 1
48 Milton Bridge . . . C 5
25 Milton Bryan . . . M 1
7 Milton Clevedon . C 10
58 Milton Coldwells. D 7
4 Milton Damerel . . E 3

MAP
16 Milton End . . . . . . D 2
25 Milton Ernest . . . . K 1
30 Milton Green . . . . . D 3
16 Milton Hill . . . . . . E 6
23 Milton Keynes . . . H 12
16 Milton Lilbourne . . H 3
58 Milton of
    Ardlethen . . . . D 6
59 Milton of
    Auchinhove . . . . G 3
53 Milton of Balgonie G 8
56 Milton of
    Braicklaich . . . . D 3
47 Milton of Campsie B 11
58 Milton of Cushnie . F 3
59 Milton of
    Dillavaird . . . . . J 5
56 Milton of Farr . . . F 2
58 Milton of Fishrie . B 5
58 Milton of Lesmore E 2
59 Milton of Logie . . G 2
59 Milton of Murtle . G 6
58 Milton of Noth . . E 2
46 Milton of Smerby . G 2
59 Milton on Tullich . H 1
7 Milton on Stour . . C 11
11 Milton Regis . . . . B 7
16 Milton under
    Wychwood . . . . B 4
7 Miltoncombe . . . . . J 4
56 Miltonduff . . . . . . D 7
42 Miltonise . . . . D 3
6 Milverton . . . . D 4
31 Milwich . . . . G 8
51 Minard . . . . H 7
15 Minchinhampton . D 12
49 Mindrum . . . . F 11
49 Mindrummill . . . . F 11
6 Minehead . . . . B 3
29 Minera . . . . E 12
16 Minety . . . . E 1
28 Minffordd . . . . F 5
50 Mingarrypark . . . . A 4
33 Miningsby . . . . . . D 10
3 Minions . . . . C 9
47 Minishant . . . . H 8
57 Minmore . . . . G 7
42 Minnigaff . . . . E 5
58 Minnonie . . . . B 5
50 Minorca . . . . G 2
44 Minsca . . . . E 1
36 Minskip . . . . A 2
8 Minstead . . . . E 4
11 Minster, Kent. . . B 11
11 Minster, Kent. . . . A 8
16 Minster Lovell . . . C 4
45 Minsteracres . . . . . G 8
21 Minsterley . . . . . . B 9
15 Minsterworth . . . C 11
7 Minterne Magna . F 10
33 Minting . . . . C 9
58 Mintlaw . . . . C 7
49 Minto . . . . G 8
43 Minto Cott. . . . . . F 7
21 Minton . . . . C 9
12 Minwear . . . . F 4
22 Minworth . . . . C 5
64 Mirbister . . . . C 1
38 Mirehouse . . . . . . D 2
61 Mireland . . . . B 12
35 Mirfield . . . . E 10
15 Miserden . . . . C 12
14 Miskin, Glam. . . . F 4
14 Miskin, Glam. . . . D 4
36 Misson . . . . H 5
36 Misterton,
    Nottinghamshire H 5
7 Misterton,
    Somerset . . .   E 8
23 Misterton,
    Warwickshire. . D 9
27 Mistley . . . . M 4
13 Mitcham . . . . J 5
15 Mitcheldean . . . . . B 9
8 Mitcheldever . . . . B 6
15 Mitchel Troy . . . . C 8
2 Mitchell . . . . D 6
15 Mitcheltroy Com. . C 8
45 Mitford . . . . D 10
2 Mithian . . . . E 4
22 Mitton . . . . A 2
17 Mixbury . . . . A 7
31 Mixon . . . . D 9
53 Moanzie . . . . E 8
44 Moat Common . . . F 3
30 Mobberley . . . . . . B 6
21 Moccas . . . . H 9
57 Mochdre, Den. . . B 7
20 Mochdre, Mont. . D 6
42 Mochrum . . . . G 4
42 Mochrum . . . . C 6
10 Mockbeggar . . . . . A 6
56 Mockbeggar . . . . . D 6
38 Mockerkin . . . . . . C 3

MAP
5 Modbury . . . . K 5
31 Moddershall . . . . . G 8
61 Modsarie . . . . B 7
28 Moelfre, Angl. . . . B 4
29 Moelfre, Denb. . . G 11
43 Moffat . . . . A 11
25 Moggerhanger . . . . K 2
60 Moin House . . . . . . B 6
22 Moira . . . . A 6
11 Molash . . . . C 9
62 Mol-chlach . . . . . . G 4
29 Mold . . . . D 11
35 Moldgreen . . . . . . F 10
45 Molehill Green . . . A 5
37 Molescroft . . . . . . C 8
45 Molesden . . . . E 9
25 Molesworth . . . . . . H 2
4 Molland . . . . C 7
4 Molland Cross . . . C 6
30 Mollington, Ches. . C 2
23 Mollington, Oxon. G 8
47 Mollinsburn . . . . . B 12
19 Molting Green . . . B 9
13 Monachty . . . . A 8
51 Monachylemore . . F 11
46 Monamore Bridge . F 5
21 Monaughty . . . . . . F 8
59 Monboddo House . J 5
51 Monevechadan . . . G 9
27 Moneyden . . . . . . J 5
52 Moneydie . . . . D 5
58 Moniaive . . . . C 8
53 Monifieth . . . . D 9
53 Monikie . . . . C 9
58 Monimail . . . . F 8
12 Monington . . . . . . C 5
35 Monk Bretton . . . F 12
36 Monk Fryston . . . D 3
17 Monk Sherborne . . H 7
27 Monk Soham . . . . J 5
45 Monk-
    Wearmouth . . . G 12
21 Monkhide . . . . H 11
21 Monkhopton . . . . C 11
21 Monkland . . . . . . G 10
4 Monkleigh . . . . . . D 3
15 Monknash . . . . . . G 3
4 Monkokehampton E 5
45 Monkridge . . . . . . D 7
27 Monks Eleigh . . . . K 3
10 Monk's Gate . . . . E 1
31 Monks' Heath . . . . C 7
23 Monks Kirby . . . . D 8
17 Monks Risborough D 9
58 Monkshill . . . . . . D 5
4 Monksilver . . . . . . C 4
15 Monkswood . . . . . . D 7
47 Monkton, Ayr. . . . G 8
26 Monkton, Devon. F 5
11 Monkton, Kent. . B 11
12 Monkton, Pemb. . G 3
6 Monkton, Som. . . C 6
15 Monkton
    Coombe . . . . . . H 11
7 Monkton Deverill B 11
15 Monkton
    Farleigh . . . . . H 11
6 Monkton
    Heathfield . . . . D 6
8 Monkton Up
    Wimborne . . . . E 2
7 Monkton Wyld . . F 7
47 Monktonhill . . . . . F 8
47 Monkwood . . . . . . C 8
15 Monmouth . . . . . . C 8
15 Monmouth Cap. . B 7
21 Monnington on
    Wye . . . . H 9
53 Monorgan . . . . . . D 8
42 Monreith . . . . G 4
42 Monreith Mains . . G 4
58 Montcoffer House . B 4
21 Montford . . . . A 9
21 Montford Bridge . A 9
58 Montgarrie . . . . . . F 3
21 Montgomery . . . . C 8
47 Montgreenan . . . . E 8
47 Montrave . . . . F 8
59 Montrose . . . . L 5
8 Monxton . . . . B 5
31 Monyash . . . . D 10
58 Monymusk . . . . . F 4
52 Monzie, Perth. . . . C 5
57 Monzie, Perth. . . M 5
47 Moodiesburn . . . . B 11
35 Moor Allerton . . C 11
16 Moor Crichel . . . E 2
36 Moor Ends . . . . . . F 5
58 Moor Monkton . . B 3
56 Moor of Granary . D 6
38 Moor Row . . . . . . D 3

MAP
11 Moor Street . . . . . B 7
33 Moorby . . . . D 10
8 Moordown . . . . . . G 3
30 Moore . . . . B 4
15 Moorend . . . . D 10
8 Moorgreen . . . . . . E 6
31 Moorhall . . . . C 11
21 Moorhampton . . . H 9
44 Moorhouse,
    Cumb. . . . . G 2
32 Moorhouse, Notts. D 5
7 Moorlinch . . . . . . C 7
41 Moorsholm . . . . . . D 7
5 Moorshop . . . . H 4
33 Moorside, Lancs. F 8
33 Moorside, Lincs. . D 9
8 Moortown, Hants. F 3
8 Moortown, I. of
    Wight, Hants. . . H 6
37 Moortown, Lincs. G 8
55 Morar . . . . K 1
56 Moray, Co. . . . . . . E 7
6 Morebath . . . . D 3
49 Morebattle . . . . . . G 10
34 Morecambe . . . . . . A 3
7 Morecombelake . . G 7
60 Morefield . . . . G 3
39 Moreland . . . . C 8
5 Moreleigh . . . . K 6
52 Morenish . . . . D 1
38 Moresby . . . . C 2
8 Morestead . . . . . . D 6
17 Moreton, Dorset. . G 12
18 Moreton, Essex . . C 5
17 Moreton, Oxon. . . D 8
16 Moreton-in-Marsh A 3
21 Moreton Jeffries . G 11
22 Moreton Morrell . F 6
21 Moreton on Lugg H 10
23 Moreton Pinkney . G 9
30 Moreton Say . . . . G 5
15 Moreton Valence . C 11
5 Moretonhampstead G 6
13 Morfa . . . . F 9
22 Morfa'Bychan . . . F 5
14 Morfa Glas . . . . . D 2
28 Morfa-Nefyn. . . . F 2
13 Morriston, Glam. G 10
26 Morston . . . . A 3
4 Mortehoe . . . . B 3
32 Morthen . . . . A 2
17 Mortimer Com. . . H 7
17 Mortimer West
    End . . . . H 7
21 Mortimer's Cross . F 9
18 Mortlake . . . . F 2
44 Morton, Cumb. . . H 2
32 Morton, Derby. . . D 1
15 Morton, Glos. . . . E 9
24 Morton, Kesteven,
    Lincs. . . . . C 2
32 Morton, Lindsey,
    Lincs. . . . . A 5
26 Morton, Norf. . . . D 4
32 Morton, Notts. . . E 4
30 Morton, Salop. . . H 2
22 Morton Bagot . . . F 4
40 Morton-on-Swale. F 4
40 Morton Tinmouth. C 2
2 Morvah . . . . F 1
3 Morval . . . . D 9
55 Morvich . . . . G 3
61 Morvich Lodge . . F 8
21 Morville . . . . C 12
4 Morwenstow . . . . D 1
32 Mosborough . . . . . B 2

MAP
47 Moscow, Ayr. . . . . E 9
44 Moscow, Cumb. . . F 4
38 Mosedale . . . . B 6
35 Moselden Height . . F 9
22 Moseley, War. . . . D 4
22 Moseley, Worcs. . . F 2
29 Moss, Denb. . . . . . E 12
50 Moss, Inver. . . . . . A 4
36 Moss, Yorks. . . . . . F 4
34 Moss Bank . . . . . . G 4
17 Moss End . . . . G 9
56 Moss of
    Barmuckity. . . . D 8
58 Mossat. . . . . F 2
64 Mossbank . . . . C 7
44 Mossburnford . . . . A 5
43 Mossdale . . . . D 7
47 Mossend . . . . C 12
38 Mosser . . . . C 4
47 Mossgiel. . . . . F 9
49 Mosshouses . . . . . E 8
43 Mosslands . . . . B 11
31 Mossley, Ches. . . . D 7
35 Mossley, Lancs. . . G 8
30 Mossley Hill . . . . B 3
44 Mosspeeble. . . . . . D 2
56 Moss-side . . . . D 4
58 Mosstodloch . . . . . B 1
7 Mosterton . . . . . . F 8
29 Mostyn . . . . B 11
7 Motcombe . . . . . . D 11
5 Mothecombe. . . . . L 5
47 Motherwell . . . . . D 12
18 Mottingham . . . . . G 4
8 Mottisfont . . . . . . C 5
8 Mottistone . . . . . . H 5
35 Mottram . . . . H 8
30 Mouldsworth. . . . . C 4
52 Moulin . . . . A 4
52 Moulinearn . . . . . B 4
17 Moulsford . . . . F 7
23 Moulsoe . . . . H 12
30 Moulton, Ches. . . C 5
14 Moulton, Glam. . . G 4
24 Moulton, Lincs. . . C 4
26 Moulton, Norf. . . E 7
23 Moulton,
    Northants. . . . . E 11
25 Moulton, Suffolk . J 8
40 Moulton, Yorks. . E 3
24 Moulton Chapel . . D 4
25 Moulton St. Michael
                F 5
24 Moulton Seas End . C 4
57 Moulzie . . . . L 8
44 Mounces . . . . D 5
58 Mounie Castle. . . E 5
3 Mount . . . . C 8
2 Mount Ambrose. . E 4
27 Mount Bures. . . . M 2
2 Mount Hawke . . . E 4
48 Mount Lothian . . D 5
49 Mount Pleasant,
    Berwick . . . . . . D 10
31 Mount Pleasant,
    Derbyshire . . . . E 11
29 Mount Pleasant,
    Flintshire . . . . C 11
14 Mount Pleasant,
    Glamorgan. . . . D 4
8 Mount Pleasant,
    Hampshire . . . . F 4
17 Mount Pleasant,
    Hampshire . . . . H 7
27 Mount Pleasant,
    Suffolk . . . . G 8
22 Mount Pleasant,
    Worcestershire . . F 3
8 Mount Sorrel . . . D 2
35 Mount Tabor. . . . D 9
45 Mountain . . . . D 9
14 Mountain Ash . . . D 4
48 Mountain Cross. . E 4
12 Mountain Water. . F 3
48 Mountbenger . . . . G 6
58 Mountblairy . . . . . B 4
10 Mountfield. . . . . . F 6
56 Mountgerald . . . . . D 1
2 Mountjoy. . . . . . . D 6
18 Mountnessing. . . . D 6
15 Mounton . . . . E 8
58 Mountsolie . . . . . . B 7
23 Mountsorrel . . . . . A 9
2 Mousehole . . . . . . G 2
43 Mouswald. . . . . . . D 11
31 Mow Cop. . . . . . . D 7
49 Mowhaugh . . . . . . G 10
23 Mowsley . . . . C 10
59 Mowtie . . . . H 6
55 Moy, Inverness . . L 5
55 Moy, Inverness . . L 8
56 Moy, Inverness . . F 3
56 Moy Hall . . . . F 3

MAP
- 56 Moy House......D 6
- 55 Moy Lodge......L 8
- 56 Moybeg......F 3
- 55 Moyle......H 3
- 8 Moyles Court....E 3
- 12 Moylgrove....C 5
- 46 Muasdale......E 2
- 15 Much Birch......A 8
- 21 Much Cowarne..H 11
- 15 Much Dewchurch.A 8
- 18 Much Hadham....B 4
- 34 Much Hoole......E 3
- 15 Much Marcle....A 10
- 21 Much Wenlock...B 11
- 59 Muchalls......H 6
- 7 Muchelney......D 8
- 3 Muchlarnick......D 9
- 54 Muchrachd......F 6
- 56 Muckernich......D 2
- 42 Muckfoot......C 3
- 19 Mucking......F 7
- 7 Muckleford......G 9
- 30 Mucklestone......F 6
- 30 Muckleton......H 4
- 58 Muckletown......E 3
- 22 Muckley Corner...B 4
- 33 Muckton......B 10
- 60 Mudale......D 6
- 4 Muddiford......B 4
- 4 Muddles Green...G 4
- 8 Mudeford......G 3
- 7 Mudford......D 9
- 7 Mudgley......B 8
- 47 Mugdock......B 10
- 62 Mugeary......C 4
- 31 Mugginton......F 11
- 45 Muggleswick......H 9
- 61 Muie......F 7
- 57 Muir......K 6
- 54 Muir of Fairburn..D 8
- 58 Muir of Fowlis...F 3
- 56 Muir of Ord......E 1
- 58 Muirden......B 4
- 48 Muirfoot......D 2
- 53 Muirhead, Angus..D 8
- 53 Muirhead, Fife....E 9
- 53 Muirhead, Fife....G 7
- 59 Muirhead, Kinc...L 5
- 47 Muirhead, Lan...B 11
- 47 Muirhouses, Lan. D 11
- 48 Muirhouses,
  - W. Lothian....A 3
- 47 Muirkirk......G 11
- 47 Muirmill......A 12
- 53 Muirsdrum......C 10
- 55 Muirshearlich....L 5
- 47 Muirshield......D 10
- 59 Muirskie......H 6
- 58 Muirtack, Aber....C 5
- 58 Muirtack, Aber....D 7
- 59 Muirton, Angus...L 4
- 52 Muirton, Perth....E 6
- 56 Muirton, Ross &
  - Cromarty......C 3
- 54 Muirton Mains...D 8
- 52 Muirton of
  - Ardblair......C 6
- 52 Muirtown......F 4
- 58 Muiryfold......C 5
- 43 Muiryhill......A 9
- 39 Muker......E 11
- 26 Mulbarton......E 5
- 58 Mulben......C 1
- 41 Mulgrave......D 8
- 2 Mullion......H 4
- 55 Mullochbuie......L 1
- 13 Mumbles......H 1
- 33 Mumby......C 12
- 21 Munderfield Row G 12
- 21 Munderfield
  - Stocks......G 12
- 26 Mundesley......B 6
- 26 Mundford......F 1
- 26 Mundham......F 6
- 19 Mundon Hill....D 8
- 55 Munerigie......J 6
- 60 Mungasdale......G 2
- 38 Mungrisdale......B 6
- 56 Munlochy......D 2
- 47 Munnoch......E 7
- 21 Munsley......H 12
- 21 Munslow......D 10
- 21 Munslow Aston..D 10
- 5 Murchington......G 6
- 17 Murcott......F 7
- 61 Murkle......A 11
- 55 Murlaggan, Inver..K 4
- 55 Murlaggan, Inver..L 7
- 48 Murrayfield,
  - Midlothian......B 5
- 52 Murrayfield, Perth.D 5
- 43 Murraythwaite...D 12
- 24 Murrow......E 5

MAP
- 17 Mursley......A 9
- 59 Murthil......L 2
- 52 Murthly......C 6
- 52 Murthly Castle....C 5
- 45 Murton, Dur......H 12
- 49 Murton,
  - Northumb......E 12
- 39 Murton, Westmor..C 9
- 36 Murton, Yorks....B 4
- 40 Murton Grange...F 5
- 6 Musbury......G 6
- 41 Muscoates......G 7
- 48 Musselburgh......B 6
- 32 Muston, Leics....F 5
- 41 Muston, Yorks...G 11
- 22 Mustow Green....E 2
- 43 Mutehill......G 7
- 27 Mutford......G 8
- 52 Muthill......E 4
- 6 Mutterton......F 4
- 21 Muxton......A 12
- 61 Mybster......B 11
- 13 Myddfai......D 11
- 30 Myddle......H 3
- 13 Mydroilyn......B 8
- 2 Mylor Bridge....F 5
- 12 Mynachlog-ddu....D 5
- 21 Myndtown......C 9
- 20 Mynydd-bach,
  - Cards......E 8
- 15 Mynydd-bach,
  - Mon......E 8
- 13 Mynyddgarreg....F 7
- 28 Mynytho......G 3
- 58 Myre of Bedlam...C 8
- 59 Myrebird......G 5
- 9 Mytchett......A 10
- 35 Mytholmroyd......E 9
- 34 Mythop......D 2
- 40 Myton-on-Swale..H 4
- 36 Naburn......C 4
- 11 Nackington......C 10
- 27 Nacton......L 5
- 37 Nafferton......A 8
- 15 Nail Bridge
  - Steam Mills....C 9
- 15 Nailsea......G 8
- 23 Nailstone......A 7
- 15 Nailsworth......D 11
- 56 Nairn......D 4
- 56 Nairn, County....E 4
- 10 Naldersworth......D 1
- 2 Nancegollan......F 3
- 2 Nancledra......F 2
- 9 Nanhurst......B 11
- 29 Nannerch......C 11
- 32 Nanpantan......H 2
- 3 Nanpean......D 7
- 3 Nanstallon......C 7
- 28 Nant Peris......D 5
- 14 Nant-ddu......C 3
- 13 Nanternis......A 7
- 13 Nantgaredig......E 8
- 14 Nantgarw......F 4
- 20 Nant-glâs......F 5
- 29 Nantglyn......D 9
- 20 Nantgwyn......E 5
- 28 Nantile......E 4
- 30 Nantmawr......H 1
- 20 Nantmel......F 6
- 28 Nantmor......F 5
- 30 Nantwich......E 5
- 13 Nantybai......C 11
- 14 Nant-y-Bwch....C 5
- 14 Nant-y-cafn......D 2
- 14 Nant-y-derry....D 6
- 13 Nant-y-ffin......D 9
- 14 Nantyffyllon......E 2
- 14 Nantyglo......C 5
- 21 Nant-y-
  - Meichiaid......A 7
- 14 Nant-y-moel......E 3
- 28 Nant-y-pandy....C 6
- 17 Naphill......D 9
- 35 Nappa......B 7
- 23 Napton on the
  - Hill......F 8
- 12 Narberth......E 4
- 23 Narborough, Leics.B 8
- 24 Narborough, Norf. D 8
- 3 Narkurs......D 10
- 50 Narrachan......F 6
- 28 Nasareth......E 4
- 23 Naseby......D 10
- 17 Nash, Bucks......A 8
- 21 Nash, Herefs......F 8
- 15 Nash, Mon......F 7
- 21 Nash, Salop......E 11
- 24 Nassington......F 2
- 18 Nasty......B 4
- 3 Natcott......D 2
- 34 Nateby, Lancs....C 3
- 39 Nateby, Westmor.D 10

MAP
- 39 Natland......F 7
- 27 Naughton......K 3
- 16 Naunton, Glos....B 2
- 22 Naunton, Worcs...H 2
- 22 Naunton
  - Beauchamp....G 3
- 54 Naust......B 2
- 33 Navenby......D 7
- 18 Navestock......D 5
- 18 Navestock Side...D 5
- 61 Navidale......E 10
- 41 Nawton......G 7
- 27 Nayland......M 3
- 12 Naze Park......B 12
- 18 Nazeing......C 4
- 8 Neacroft......F 3
- 64 Neap......D 7
- 31 Near Cotton......E 9
- 38 Near Sawrey......F 6
- 40 Neasham......D 4
- 13 Neath......G 11
- 13 Neath Abbey....G 10
- 18 Neather Heage....E 12
- 26 Neatishead......C 6
- 28 Nebo, Angl......A 4
- 28 Nebo, Anglesey...A 4
- 20 Nebo, Cards......F 1
- 29 Nebo, Denb......E 7
- 26 Necton......E 2
- 60 Nedd......D 3
- 27 Nedging......K 3
- 27 Nedging Tye......K 3
- 27 Needham......G 5
- 27 Needham Market..K 4
- 25 Needingworth......H 4
- 31 Needlewood......H 10
- 21 Neen Savage......E 12
- 21 Neen Sollars......E 12
- 21 Neenton......D 11
- 28 Nefyn......F 3
- 21 Nelly Andrews
  - Green......A 8
- 14 Nelson, Glam....E 4
- 35 Nelson, Lancs....C 7
- 45 Nelson Village...E 10
- 17 Nemphlar......E 1
- 15 Nempnett
  - Thrubwell......H 8
- 39 Nenthall......A 10
- 39 Nenthead......A 10
- 49 Nenthorn......F 9
- 29 Nercwys......D 11
- 47 Nerston......D 11
- 35 Nesfield......B 9
- 49 Nesbit......F 12
- 30 Ness......C 2
- 30 Nesscliffe......H 3
- 30 Neston, Ches....B 2
- 15 Neston, Wilts....G 11
- 31 Nether Alderley....C 7
- 49 Nether Blainslie...E 8
- 31 Nether Booth......B 10
- 49 Nether
  - Brotherstone....D 7
- 32 Nether Broughton.H 4
- 39 Nether Burrow....H 8
- 44 Nether Cassock...C 1
- 7 Nether Cerne......F 10
- 59 Nether Contlaw...G 6
- 43 Nether
  - Craigenputtock..C 9
- 58 Nether Crimond....E 6
- 48 Nether Dalgliesh..H 5
- 58 Nether Dallachy...A 1
- 6 Nether Exe......F 3
- 48 Nether Fingland..H 2
- 58 Nether Glasslaw..B 6
- 43 Nether Gribton..D 10
- 53 Nether Handwick..C 8
- 36 Nether Haugh......G 2
- 23 Nether Heyford...F 10
- 44 Nether Hindhope..B 4
- 48 Nether Howcleugh H 3
- 39 Nether Kellet......H 7
- 58 Nether Kinmundy.C 8
- 47 Nether Kirkton....D 9
- 32 Nether Langwith...C 3
- 58 Nether Leask......E 8
- 47 Nether Newton....E 10
- 31 Nether Padley....B 11
- 58 Nether Park......B 6
- 59 Nether Pitforthie..J 6
- 36 Nether Poppleton..B 3
- 40 Nether Silton......F 5
- 6 Nether Stowey....D 5
- 59 Nether Thaneston.K 4
- 53 Nether Urquhart..F 7
- 8 Nether Wallop....B 5
- 22 Nether Whitacre..C 6
- 48 Nether
  - Whitecleuch....G 1
- 16 Nether Worton....A 5

MAP
- 8 Netheravon......A 3
- 58 Netherbrae......B 5
- 48 Netherburn......E 1
- 7 Netherbury......F 8
- 44 Netherby, Cumb...F 2
- 35 Netherby, Yorks..C 11
- 4 Nethercott......B 4
- 15 Netherend......D 9
- 10 Netherfield......F 6
- 8 Netherhampton...C 3
- 49 Netherhowden....D 7
- 43 Netherlaw......G 8
- 59 Netherley......H 6
- 58 Nethermill, Aber...D 8
- 43 Nethermill, Dumf. C 11
- 43 Nethermiln......A 11
- 58 Nethermuir......E 8
- 47 Netherplace......D 10
- 22 Netherseal......A 6
- 16 Netherstreet......H 1
- 47 Netherthird, Ayr. G 10
- 43 Netherthird, Kirk..F 8
- 35 Netherthong......F 10
- 45 Netherwitton......D 9
- 47 Netherwood......F 11
- 59 Netherton, Angus..L 3
- 5 Netherton, Devon. J 8
- 15 Netherton, Hants..H 5
- 48 Netherton, Lan....G 2
- 47 Netherton, Lancs. D 12
- 34 Netherton, Lancs..G 2
- 22 Netherton, Staffs...C 3
- 47 Netherton, Stir....A 10
- 22 Netherton, Worcs..H 3
- 35 Netherton, Yorks. F 10
- 35 Netherton, Yorks. F 11
- 64 Nethertown,
  - Caithness......F 2
- 38 Nethertown,
  - Cumberland....D 23
- 57 Nethy Bridge....G 6
- 8 Netley......E 6
- 8 Netley Marsh....E 5
- 17 Nettlebed......C 8
- 15 Nettlebridge......A 10
- 7 Nettlecombe,
  - Dorset......G 8
- 9 Nettlecombe I.o.W.H 7
- 6 Nettlecombe, Som. C 4
- 17 Nettleden......C 11
- 33 Nettleham......C 7
- 10 Nettlestead......C 6
- 10 Nettlestead Green. C 5
- 9 Nettlestone......G 8
- 45 Nettlesworth......H 10
- 37 Nettleton, Lincs...G 9
- 15 Nettleton, Wilts...F 11
- 5 Netton, Devon....L 4
- 8 Netton, Wilts......B 3
- 14 Neuadd, Brec......C 4
- 20 Neuadd, Mont......B 6
- 20 Neuadd-ddu......E 5
- 19 Nevendon......E 7
- 12 Nevern......C 4
- 58 New Aberdour....A 6
- 18 New Addington...H 4
- 9 New Alresford....C 7
- 53 New Alyth......B 7
- 32 New Annesley......E 2
- 58 New Ash Green...B 5
- 18 New Barnet......D 3
- 49 New Belses......G 8
- 45 New Berwick......A 9
- 23 New Bilton......E 8
- 33 New Bolingbroke D 10
- 24 New Bradwell....H 11
- 32 New Brampton....C 1
- 40 New Brancepeth..A 2
- 43 New Bridge,
  - Dumf......D 10
- 36 New Bridge, Yorks. E 4
- 30 New Brighton,
  - Cheshire......A 2
- 29 New Brighton,
  - Flintshire......D 11
- 32 New Brinsley......E 2
- 26 New Buckenham..F 4
- 58 New Byth......B 6
- 26 New Catton......E 5
- 10 New Chapel......D 2
- 30 New Clipstone....D 3
- 45 New Costessey....D 5
- 43 New Cowper......G 12
- 22 New Cross......E 2
- 47 New Cumnock....H 11
- 58 New Deer......C 6
- 58 New Delaval......E 11
- 17 New Denham......F 11
- 2 New Downs......E 4

MAP
- 23 New Duston......F 10
- 36 New Earswick......B 4
- 36 New Edlington....G 3
- 56 New Elgin......D 8
- 37 New Ellerby......C 9
- 22 New End......F 4
- 30 New Ferry......B 2
- 36 New Fryston......D 2
- 43 New Galloway....D 7
- 2 New Grimsby......D 2
- 45 New Haggerston..B 11
- 45 New Hartley......E 11
- 12 New Hedges......G 5
- 45 New Herrington...H 11
- 35 New Hey......F 8
- 16 New Hinksey......D 6
- 26 New Holkham......B 2
- 37 New Holland......E 8
- 38 New Hotel......E 5
- 45 New Horton
  - Grange......E 10
- 32 New Houghton,
  - Derbyshire......D 2
- 26 New Houghton,
  - Norfolk......C 1
- 39 New Houses......H 10
- 39 New Hutton......F 8
- 10 New Hythe......B 6
- 13 New Inn, Carm....C 8
- 15 New Inn, Mon....D 8
- 39 New Inn, Yorks...H 10
- 21 New Invention....E 8
- 54 New Kelso......E 3
- 58 New Kendal......E 6
- 45 New Lambton......H 11
- 48 New Lanark......E 2
- 34 New Lane......F 3
- 33 New Leake......D 11
- 58 New Leeds......B 7
- 34 New Longton......E 4
- 42 New Luce......E 3
- 49 New Mains,
  - E. Lothian......A 8
- 48 New Mains, Lan...F 1
- 59 New Mains of Ury. J 6
- 18 New Malden......G 2
- 40 New Marske......C 6
- 30 New Marton......G 2
- 59 New Mill, Kinc....J 5
- 16 New Mill, Wilts...H 3
- 35 New Mill, Yorks. F 10
- 2 New Mills, Corn...D 6
- 31 New Mills, Derby..B 8
- 20 New Mills, Mont...B 6
- 8 New Milton......F 4
- 27 New Mistley......M 4
- 12 New Moat......D 4
- 47 New Monkland....C 12
- 45 New Mousen......C 12
- 58 New Pitsligo......B 6
- 2 New Polzeath......B 6
- 47 New Prestwick....G 8
- 13 New Quay......A 7
- 21 New Radnor......F 7
- 39 New Rent......B 7
- 11 New Romney......F 9
- 36 New Rossington..G 4
- 20 New Row......E 3
- 8 New Sarum......C 3
- 52 New Sauchie......H 4
- 52 New Scone......E 6
- 50 New Selma......D 6
- 63 New Shawbost....B 4
- 45 New Shoreston....D 12
- 47 New Stevenston...C 12
- 8 New Swanage......H 2
- 63 New Tolsta......B 6
- 49 New Town,
  - E. Lothian......B 7
- 17 New Town, Berks. G 7
- 8 New Town, Dorset.
  - D 2
- 7 New Town, Dorset.
  - D 11
- 49 New Town,
  - E. Lothian......B 7
- 17 New Town, Hants. H 7
- 10 New Town, Sussex .F 3
- 16 New Town, Wilts. G 4
- 14 New Tredegar....D 5
- 48 New Trows......F 1
- 32 New Tupton......D 1
- 63 New Valley......C 5
- 37 New Waltham....G 10
- 25 New Wimpole....K 4
- 49 New Winton......B 7
- 16 New Yatt......C 5
- 33 New York......E 9
- 45 New York......F 11
- 64 Newark......A 4
- 24 Newark......E 3
- 32 Newark......E 5
- 48 Newarthill......C 1
- 48 Newbattle......C 6
- 39 Newbiggin, Cumb..B 7

MAP
- 44 Newbiggin, Cumb. H 4
- 39 Newbiggin, Dur...B 11
- 45 Newbiggin, Dur...H 9
- 38 Newbiggin, Lancs..H 5
- 45 Newbiggin,
  - Northumb......G 8
- 39 Newbiggin,
  - Westmorland...B 8
- 39 Newbiggin, Yorks.F 11
- 39 Newbiggin, Yorks.G 12
- 45 Newbiggin-by-the-
  - Sea......D 11
- 39 Newbiggin on Lune E 9
- 59 Newbigging, Angus K1
- 49 Newbigging, Ber..D 8
- 48 Newbigging, Lancs.E 3
- 32 Newbold, Derby...C 1
- 32 Newbold, Leics....H 1
- 23 Newbold on Avon.D 8
- 22 Newbold on Stour.G 6
- 22 Newbold Pacey....F 6
- 23 Newbold Verdon..B 8
- 28 Newborough, Angl.D 4
- 24 Newborough,
  - Hunts......E 3
- 31 Newborough,
  - Staffordshire...H 10
- 45 Newbottle, Dur...H 11
- 23 Newbottle,
  - Northants......H 8
- 27 Newbourn......L 6
- 2 Newbridge, Corn..F 1
- 3 Newbridge, Corn. C 10
- 29 Newbridge, Denb. F 12
- 8 Newbridge, Hants..E 3
- 8 Newbridge, I.o. W. G 6
- 48 Newbridge,
  - Midlothian......B 4
- 14 Newbridge, Mon...E 5
- 15 Newbridge, Mon...E 7
- 12 Newbridge, Pemb..D 3
- 20 Newbridge on Wye F 6
- 45 Newbrough......F 7
- 58 Newburgh, Aber...B 7
- 58 Newburgh, Aber...E 7
- 53 Newburgh, Fife...E 7
- 48 Newburgh, Sel...G 6
- 40 Newburgh Priory..G 5
- 49 Newburn......E 11
- 45 Newburn......G 10
- 16 Newbury......G 5
- 39 Newby, Westmor..C 8
- 40 Newby, N. Riding.D 5
- 41 Newby, N. Riding F 10
- 39 Newby, W. Riding.H 9
- 38 Newby Bridge....G 6
- 44 Newby East......G 3
- 44 Newby West......H 2
- 40 Newby Wiske......F 5
- 15 Newcastle, Mon...C 7
- 21 Newcastle, Salop..D 8
- 12 Newcastle Emlyn..C 6
- 31 Newcastle-under-Lyme
  - F 7
- 45 Newcastle upon Tyne.
  - F 10
- 44 Newcastleton......D 3
- 12 Newchapel, Pemb..C 6
- 31 Newchapel, Staffs..E 7
- 13 Newchurch, Carm. E 5
- 9 Newchurch, I.o.W.H 7
- 11 Newchurch, Kent..E 9
- 35 Newchurch, Lancs. C 7
- 35 Newchurch, Lancs. E 7
- 15 Newchurch, Mon..E 8
- 21 Newchurch, Rad...G 7
- 31 Newchurch,
  - Staffordshire...H 10
- 6 Newcott......E 6
- 10 Newdigate......D 1
- 17 Newell Green......G 9
- 11 Newenden......E 7
- 15 Newent......B 10
- 15 Newerne......D 9
- 43 Newfield, Dumf...E 12
- 40 Newfield, Dur.....B 2
- 45 Newfield, Dur....H 10
- 43 Newfield, Kirk....E 9
- 56 Newfield, Ross &
  - Cromarty......B 3
- 9 Newfound......A 7
- 12 Newgale......E 2
- 26 Newgate......A 3
- 18 Newgate Street...C 3
- 64 Newgord......A 8
- 30 Newhall, Ches....F 5
- 31 Newhall, Derby..H 11
- 48 Newhall, Peeb....C 7
- 56 Newhallpoint....C 3
- 18 Newham, London.F 4
- 45 Newham,
  - Northumb......E 12
- 45 Newham Hall....D 12

MAP

10 Newhaven........H 3
31 Newhaven House.D 10
41 Newholm.........D 8
48 Newhouse........C 1
45 Newhouses.......E 8
10 Newick..........F 3
11 Newingreen......D 10
11 Newington, Kent..B 7
11 Newington, Kent.D 10
32 Newington, Notts..A 4
17 Newington, Oxon..D 7
21 Newington, Salop.D 9
59 Newkirk.........G 2
37 Newland, E. Riding D 7
15 Newland, Glos....C 9
6 Newland, Som....B 2
36 Newland,
 W. Riding......E 5
22 Newland, Worcs...G 2
53 Newlandhead.....C 9
47 Newlands, Ayr...G 8
43 Newlands, Dumf..C 10
47 Newlands, Lan...D 11
56 Newlands, Moray..E 8
45 Newlands,
 Northumb......G 9
44 Newlands, Rox...D 3
61 Newlands of Geise A 10
2 Newlyn..........G 2
2 Newlyn East.....D 5
58 Newmachar......F 6
48 Newmains.......D 1
63 Newmarket, Ross &
 Cromarty......C 5
25 Newmarket, Suff...J 7
58 Newmill, Banff...B 2
2 Newmill, Corn...F 2
44 Newmill, Rox....B 3
59 Newmill of
 Inshewan......L 2
35 Newmillerdam...F 12
48 Newmills, Fife...A 3
48 Newmills, Midloth. C 4
15 Newmills, Mon....D 8
56 Newmills, Ross &
 Cromarty......C 2
58 Newmills of Boyne.B 3
52 Newmiln........D 6
47 Newmilns.......F 10
15 Newnham, Glos..C 10
9 Newnham, Hants..A 8
25 Newnham, Herts..L 3
11 Newnham, Kent..B 8
23 Newnham, Northants
 F 9
21 Newnham Bridge.E 11
53 Newpark.........F 9
61 Newport, Caith..E 10
4 Newport, Devon...C 4
25 Newport, Essex...M 6
15 Newport, Glos...E 10
8 Newport, I.o.W...G 6
14 Newport, Mon....F 6
26 Newport, Norfolk.D 8
12 Newport, Pemb....C 4
30 Newport, Salop..H 6
36 Newport, Yorks..D 6
53 Newport-on-Tay..D 9
23 Newport Pagnell.H 12
9 Newpound Com..C 11
2 Newquay........D 5
52 Newrow.........H 4
35 Newsam Green..D 12
58 Newseat.........D 4
34 Newsham, Lancs..D 4
40 Newsham,
 N. Riding......D 1
40 Newsham,
 N. Riding......G 4
36 Newsholme,
 E. Riding......D 5
35 Newsholme,
 W. Riding......B 7
36 Newsholme,
 W. Riding......C 9
45 Newstead,
 Northumb......E 12
32 Newstead, Notts...E 2
49 Newstead, Rox....F 8
36 Newthorpe......D 3
58 Newton, Aber....C 8
61 Newton, Caith...C 12
25 Newton, Cambs..K 5
30 Newton, Ches....C 3
30 Newton, Ches....C 4
30 Newton, Ches....D 4
35 Newton, Ches....G 8
32 Newton, Derby...D 2
7 Newton, Dorset..E 11
43 Newton, Dumf...B 12
41 Newton, E. Riding H 9
13 Newton, Glam...H 9
14 Newton, Glam...G 2

MAP

15 Newton, Herefs....A 7
21 Newton, Herefs..G 10
56 Newton, Inver.....E 3
47 Newton, Lan....C 11
48 Newton, Lan......F 2
34 Newton, Lancs...D 2
34 Newton, Lancs...D 3
38 Newton, Lancs...H 5
39 Newton, Lancs...H 8
24 Newton, Lincs...B 1
56 Newton, Moray...C 7
24 Newton, Norfolk..D 5
26 Newton, Norfolk..D 1
40 Newton, N. Riding D 6
23 Newton, Northants.
 D 12
45 Newton, Northumb.
 B 8
45 Newton, Northumb.
 G 8
32 Newton, Notts.....F 4
52 Newton, Perth....D 4
56 Newton, Ross &
 Cromarty......C 3
56 Newton, Ross &
 Cromarty......E 1
49 Newton, Rox......G 8
6 Newton, Som.....B 5
31 Newton, Staffs...H 9
27 Newton, Suffolk...L 2
60 Newton, Suther...D 4
23 Newton, War.....D 8
48 Newton, W. Loth..B 4
34 Newton, W. Riding B 6
36 Newton, W. Riding F 2
8 Newton, Wilts.....D 4
5 Newton Abbot....J 7
43 Newton Arlosh...F 12
40 Newton Aycliffe...C 3
40 Newton Bewley...C 5
23 Newton Blossomville
 G 12
25 Newton Bromshold J 1
23 Newton Burgoland A 7
33 Newton by Toft...B 7
5 Newton Ferrers...L 4
26 Newton Flotman...F 5
23 Newton Harcourt..B 9
58 Newton House....E 4
34 Newton-le-Willows,
 Lancashire.....H 4
40 Newton-le-Willows,
 Yorkshire......F 2
36 Newton Kyme....C 2
17 Newton Longville..A 9
47 Newton Mearns..D 10
40 Newton Morrell...D 3
41 Newton Mulgrave.D 8
12 Newton Mountain.F 3
50 Newton of Ardtoe.A 4
52 Newton of
 Balcanquhal....F 6
53 Newton of Falkland F 7
58 Newton of Murcar F 7
60 Newton of Ochtow G 5
52 Newton of Pitcairns F 5
36 Newton-on-Ouse..A 3
41 Newton-on-Rawcliffe
 F 8
45 Newton-on-the-Moor
 C 10
32 Newton on Trent..C 5
6 Newton Poppleford G 4
17 Newton Purcell...A 7
22 Newton Regis.....A 6
39 Newton Reigny...B 7
49 Newton St. Boswells F8
4 Newton St. Cyres..F 7
26 Newton St. Faith..D 5
15 Newton St. Loe..H 10
4 Newton St. Petrock E 3
31 Newton Solney...H 11
8 Newton Stacey....B 6
42 Newton Stewart...E 5
8 Newton Toney....F 5
4 Newton Tracey....C 4
47 Newton upon Ayr.G 8
36 Newton upon
 Derwent.......B 5
9 Newton Valence..C 8
43 Newtonairds......D 9
58 Newtongarry Croft D 3
48 Newtongrange....C 6
59 Newtonmill......L 3
57 Newtonmore.....J 3
31 Newtown, Ches...B 8
30 Newtown, Ches...E 5
2 Newtown, Corn...B 5
44 Newtown, Cumb..G 2
44 Newtown, Cumb..G 3
15 Newtown, Glos...A 12

MAP

15 Newtown, Glos...D 10
8 Newtown, Hants..D 4
9 Newtown, Hants..D 7
8 Newtown, Hants...E 4
9 Newtown, Hants...E 7
16 Newtown, Hants..H 6
21 Newtown, Herefs. G 10
21 Newtown, Herefs. H 11
55 Newtown, Inver...J 7
38 Newtown, I. o. M..H 2
8 Newtown, I. o. W..G 5
34 Newtown, Lancs...E 4
20 Newtown, Mont....C 6
56 Newtown, Moray..C 7
45 Newtown,
 Northumb.....A 8
45 Newtown,
 Northumb......C 8
49 Newtown,
 Northumb.....F 12
30 Newtown, Salop..G 3
31 Newtown, Staffs...D 7
31 Newtown, Staffs...D 9
39 Newtown,
 Westmorland...C 7
7 Newtown, Wilts..C 12
23 Newtown Linfold..A 8
48 Newtown of
 Covington.....E 3'
58 Newtown of
 Melrose.......A 5
53 Newtyle.........B 11
12 Neyland.........F 3
16 Nibley..........F 10
6 Nicholashayne....E 5
13 Nicholaston......H 8
44 Nickie's Hill......F 4
35 Nidd...........A 11
59 Nigg, Aber........G 7
56 Nigg, Ross &
 Cromarty......C 4
56 Nigg Station......B 4
6 Nightcott........D 2
18 Nine Ashes......D 6
48 Nine Mile Burn...D 4
44 Ninebanks.......H 6
10 Ninfield.........G 6
8 Ningwood........G 5
49 Nisbet..........G 9
43 Nithside.........D 10
8 Niton...........H 6
30 No Man's Heath,
 Cheshire......E 4
22 No Man's Heath,
 Warwickshire...A 6
2 No Man's Land,
 Cornwall......C 6
4 No Man's Land,
 Devon........E 7
18 Noak Hill........E 5
48 Noblehall........A 4
48 Noblehouse......D 5
21 Nobold.........A 10
23 Nobottle........F 10
33 Nocton..........D 8
16 Noke...........C 6
12 Nolton..........E 2
12 Nolton Haven....E 2
30 Noneley.........G 3
11 Nonington.......C 11
39 Nook...........G 8
30 Norbury, Ches....E 4
31 Norbury, Derby...F 9
21 Norbury, Salop...C 9
30 Norbury, Staffs...H 6
24 Nordelph.......E 7
35 Norden..........F 7
8 Norden Heath....H 1
21 Nordley.........C 12
18 Nore Marsh......F 2
26 Norfolk, Co......D 4
49 Norham.........E 11
30 Norley..........C 4
8 Norley Wood.....F 5
24 Norman Cross....F 3
33 Normanby, Lincs..A 7
36 Normanby, Lincs..E 6
41 Normanby, Yorks..G 5
37 Normanby le Wold H 9
9 Normandy.......A 10
10 Norman's Bay....G 6
6 Norman's Green..F 4
8 Normansland.....D 4
31 Normanton,
 Derbyshire.....G 11
32 Normanton, Leics..F 5
32 Normanton, Lincs..F 6
32 Normanton, Notts. E 4
36 Normanton, Yorks.E 2
23 Normanton le
 Heath.........A 7
32 Normanton on
 Soar..........H 2

MAP

32 Normanton on the
 Wolds.........G 3
32 Normanton on
 Trent..........C 5
34 Normoss.........C 2
9 Norney.........B 10
15 Norrington Com. H 12
31 Norris Hill.......H 11
32 North Anston.....B 2
34 North Ashton....G 4
16 North Aston.....A 6
58 North Atrochie...D 7
8 North Baddesley..D 5
51 North Ballachulish. B 8
7 North Barrow....C 9
26 North Barsham...B 2
19 North Benfleet...E 7
9 North Bersted...F 10
49 North Berwick....A 8
9 North Boarhunt...E 7
5 North Bovey......G 6
7 North Bradley...A 12
5 North Brentor....H 4
7 North Brewham..C 10
4 North Buckland..B 4
26 North Burlingham. D 7
7 North Cadbury...D 9
32 North Carlton,
 Lincolnshire....B 6
32 North Carlton,
 Nottinghamshire B 3
46 North Carrine...H 2
36 North Cave......D 6
16 North Cerney....C 1
9 North Chapel....C 11
8 North Charford...D 3
45 North Charlton..A 10
7 North Cheriton..D 10
15 North Chideock..G 8
36 North Cliffe......C 6
32 North Clifton....C 5
37 North Coates....G 11
33 North Cockerington
 A 10
7 North Coker.....E 9
32 North Collingham.D 5
10 North Common..F 3
14 North Cornelly...F 2
50 North Corry.....B 5
58 North Cottown...F 5
26 North Cove......F 8
43 North Cowshaw..C 11
40 North Cowton....E 3
44 North Craigs.....E 1
23 North Crawley..H 12
18 North Cray......G 5
26 North Creake....B 2
7 North Curry.....D 7
37 North Dalton....B 7
3 North Darley....B 10
35 North Deighton..B 12
47 North Drumboy.D 10
36 North Duffield...C 5
33 North Elkington..A 10
26 North Elmham...C 3
36 North Elmsall....F 3
17 North End, Bucks..A 9
17 North End, Bucks..B 8
7 North End, Dorset.
 D 11
18 North End, Essex..B 6
9 North End, Hants. F 8
16 North End, Hants..H 5
34 North End, Lancs. G 2
24 North End, Lincs..B 3
45 North End, Northumb.
 C 9
6 North End, Som...D 6
15 North End, Som..G 11
15 North End, Som...H 7
9 North End, Sussex E 12
37 North End, Yorks. D10
54 North Erradale....B 1
6 North Esworthy...D 2
19 North Fambridge .D 8
46 North Feorline....F 4
37 North Ferriby....E 7
37 North Frodingham B 8
63 North Galson.....A 5
64 North Gluss......C 7
8 North Gorley.....E 3
58 North Gorrachie..B 5
26 North Green......F 5
44 North Greenhill..F 4
41 North Grimston..H 8
10 North Halling....B 6
47 North Halls......F 11
9 North Hayling....F 9
45 North Hazelrigg..C 12
9 North Heath....D 12
3 North Hill.......B 9

MAP

16 North Hinksey....D 6
10 North Holmwood .C 1
47 North Hourat....D 8
5 North Huish.....K 6
32 North Hykeham..D 6
12 North Johnston...F 3
37 North Kelsey.....G 8
56 North Kessock....E 2
37 North Killingholme
 E 9
40 North Kilvington..G 4
23 North Kilworth...D 9
58 North Kinmundy..F 6
58 North Kirkton....C 8
33 North Kyme......E 8
10 North Lancing....G 1
40 North Lees.......H 3
23 North Luffenham.B 12
16 North Leigh......C 5
32 North Leverton with
 Habblesthorpe..B 5
22 North Littleton...G 4
27 North Lopham....G 3
45 North Lyham....C 12
9 North Marden....D 9
17 North Marston...B 8
48 North Middleton,
 Midlothian....C 6
49 North Middleton,
 Northumb.....G 12
4 North Molton....C 4
58 North Monkshill..C 5
41 North Moor.....H 12
16 North Moreton...E 6
9 North Mundham.F 10
32 North Muskham..D 5
37 North Newbald...C 7
23 North Newington.H 7
16 North Newton....H 2
6 North Newton....C 9
15 North Nibley....E 10
9 North Oakley....A 7
18 North Ockendon..E 6
40 North Ormesby...C 5
33 North Ormsby...A 10
40 North Otterington. F 4
37 North Owersby...H 8
7 North Perrott....E 8
6 North Petherton...C 6
3 North Petherwin. A 10
26 North Pickenham..E 1
22 North Piddle.....G 3
7 North Poorton....F 8
6 North Quarme....C 3
48 North Queensferry. A 4
4 North Radworthy..C 6
33 North Rauceby...F 7
35 North Rigton....B 11
31 North Rode......D 7
64 North Roe.......B 7
24 North Runcton...D 7
64 North Sandwick..B 8
38 North Scale......H 4
32 North Scarle.....D 6
45 N. Seaton Colliery D 11
63 North Shawbost..B 4
50 North Shian.....C 6
45 North Shields....F 11
19 North Shoebury...E 9
34 North Shore.....D 2
48 North Shortcleugh H 2
38 North Side, Cumb..B 2
24 North Side, Hunts..E 4
41 North Skelton....C 7
37 North Somercotes G 12
40 North Stainley....G 3
39 North Stainmore. D 10
9 North Stoke.....E 11
15 North Stoke, Oxon.
 G 10
17 North Stoke, Sussex
 F 7
17 North Street, Berks G7
9 North Street, Hants. C 8
45 North Sunderland D 12
4 North Tamerton..F 2
4 North Tawton....F 5
37 North Thoresby..G 10
8 North Tidworth...A 4
45 North Togston....C 10
63 North Tolsta.....B 6
26 North Tuddenham D 3
45 North Walbottle..F 10
26 North Walsham...C 6
9 North Waltham...B 7
59 North Water Bri...L 4
61 North Watten....B 11
18 North Weald Bassett
 D 5
32 North Wheatley..B 5
15 North Wick......H 9

MAP

5 North Whilborough J 7
33 North Willingham.A 8
32 North Wingfield...D 1
32 North Witham....H 6
7 North Wootton,
 Dorset........E 10
24 North Wootton,
 Norfolk........C 7
7 North Wootton,
 Somerset......B 9
15 North Wraxall...G 11
16 North Wroughton.F 3
45 North Yardhope...F 6
40 North Yorkshire, Co.
 F 5
40 Northallerton.....F 4
4 Northam, Devon..C 3
8 Northam, Hants..E 6
23 Northampton....F 11
23 Northamptonshire,
 County........E 11
18 Northaw.........D 3
24 Northborough
 Peakirk........E 3
11 Northbourne....C 12
23 Northbrook......B 6
17 Northchurch.....C 10
5 Northcott.......G 2
23 Northend.......G 7
59 Northfield, Aber...G 6
49 Northfield, Ber....C 11
22 Northfield, War...D 4
10 Northfleet......A 5
11 Northiam.......F 7
25 Northill........K 3
9 Northington.....B 7
33 Northlands......E 10
16 Northleach......C 5
6 Northleigh......G 5
4 Northlew.......F 4
16 Northmoor......D 5
6 Northmoor Green or
 Moorland......C 6
53 Northmuir.......D 8
9 Northney.......F 9
18 Northolt........E 1
29 Northop........C 11
29 Northophall.....C 12
24 Northorpe, Holl...B 3
24 Northorpe, Kest...D 2
37 Northorpe, Lind...G 7
7 Northover, Som...B 8
7 Northover, Som...B 7
35 Northowram....D 10
8 Northport.......G 1
26 Northrepps.....H 1
63 Northton........H 1
64 Northtown......D 3
45 Northumberland,
 County ....D 8
15 Northway, Glos...A 12
6 Northway, Som....C 5
30 Northwich......C 5
15 Northwick......F 9
24 Northwold......F 8
8 Northwood, I.o.W.G 6
18 Northwood, Lond..E 1
30 Northwood, Salop.G 5
25 Northwood End...L 2
15 Northwood Green C 10
30 Norton, Ches.....H 8
41 Norton, E. Riding .H 8
15 Norton, Glos....B 11
8 Norton, I. o. W...E 5
15 Norton, Mon.....B 7
40 Norton, N. Riding. C 5
23 Norton, Northants.
 C 9
32 Norton, Notts.....C 3
21 Norton, Rad......E 8
21 Norton, Salop ..A 11
22 Norton, Salop.....B 1
21 Norton, Salop....D 10
27 Norton, Suffolk...J 3
36 Norton, W. Riding.F 3
15 Norton, Wilts....F 12
22 Norton, Worcs...C 3
22 Norton, Worcs...G 4
8 Norton Bavant....B 1
31 Norton Bridge....G 7
22 Norton Canes....A 4
21 Norton Canon...H 9
32 Norton Disney....D 6
22 Norton East......A 4
7 Norton Ferris...C 11
6 Norton Fitzwarren D 5
8 Norton Green....G 5
15 Norton Hawkfield.H 9
18 Norton Heath....C 5
30 Norton in Hales..F 5
31 Norton in the
 Moors.........E 7
23 Norton Juxta
 Twycross......A 7

MAP		MAP		MAP		MAP		MAP		MAP	
40	Norton-le-Clay...H 4	45	Oakwood, Northumb.	8	Old Milton......G 4	15	Orcop Hill......A 8	31	Oulton, Staffs.....G 7	39	Oxenholme......F 8
22	Norton Lindsey...F 6		F 8	22	Old Milverton...E 6	62	Ord......G 5	26	Oulton, Suffolk...F 8	35	Oxenhope......D 9
15	Norton Malreward H 9	49	Oakwood, Selkirk .G 7	47	Old Monkland...C 12	58	Ordens......B 4	35	Oulton, Yorks....D 12	49	Oxenrig......E 11
7	Norton St. Philip.A 11	9	Oakwoodhill.....B 12	19	Old Montsale...D 10	58	Ordhead......F 4	26	Oulton Broad......F 8	16	Oxenton......A 1
7	Norton sub Hamdon	35	Oakworth......C 9	45	Old Mousen...C 12	59	Ordie......G 2	26	Oulton Street...C 5	16	Oxenwood......H 4
	E 8	11	Oar......B 9	8	Old Netley......E 6	58	Ordiequish......B 1	25	Oundle......G 1	16	Oxford......D 6
26	Norton Subcourse.F 7	16	Oare, Berks......G 6	27	Old Newton......J 4	32	Ordsall......B 4	39	Ousby......B 8	4	Oxford Cross......B 3
32	Norton Woodseats.B 1	6	Oare, Som......B 2	43	Old Orchardton...F 9	11	Ore......G 7	61	Ousdale......E 10	16	Oxfordshire, Co....C 5
32	Norwell......D 5	16	Oare, Wilts......H 3	48	Old Philpstoun...B 3	21	Oreton, Salop...D 12	25	Ousden......J 8	18	Oxhey......D 1
32	Norwell Woodhouse	6	Oareford......B 2	40	Old Quarrington...A 3	21	Oreton, Worcs...F 12	36	Ousefleet......E 6	22	Oxhill......G 6
	D 5	33	Oasby......F 7	32	Old Radford......F 3	30	Orford, Lancs......A 5	45	Ouston, Dur.....H 10	22	Oxley......B 2
26	Norwich......E 5	59	Oathlaw......M 2	21	Old Radnor......F 8	27	Orford, Suffolk...K 7	45	Ouston, Northumb.F 9	19	Oxley Green......C 9
64	Norwick......A 8	55	Oban, Argyll......E 6	58	Old Rattray......B 8	8	Organ Ford......G 1	44	Ouston, Northumb.H 6	40	Oxnam......G 9
32	Norwood......B 2	55	Oban, Inverness...K 2	58	Old Rayne......E 4	64	Orgill......D 1	38	Out Gate......E 6	17	Oxshott......H 12
10	Norwood Hill.....D 1	58	Obliston......B 1	11	Old Romney......E 9	22	Orgreave......A 5	37	Out Newton......E 11	35	Oxspring......G 11
23	Noseley......B 10	7	Oborne......D 10	52	Old Scone......D 6	7	Orkney, Co......C 2	34	Out Rawcliffe....C 3	9	Oxted......C 3
5	Noss Mayo......L 4	29	Obsdale......C 2	36	Old Snydale......E 2	11	Orlestone......E 8	45	Outchester......C 12	49	Oxton, Ber......D 7
40	Nosterfield......G 3	30	Occleston Green..D 5	15	Old Sodbury......F 10	21	Orleton......F 10	64	Outertown......D 1	32	Oxton, Notts.....E 3
55	Nostie......G 2	27	Occold......H 5	33	Old Somerby......G 7	23	Orlingbury......E 12	36	Outhgill......E 10	13	Oxton, Yorks....C 3
16	Notgrove......B 2	52	Ochil Hills Hosp..F 6	23	Old Stratford......H 11	40	Ormesby......C 5	35	Outlane......E 9	14	Oxwich......H 8
14	Nottage......F 1	47	Ochiltree......G 10	30	Old Swan......A 3	26	Ormesby St. Margaret	24	Outwell......E 6	13	Oxwich Green......H 8
32	Nottingham......F 3	59	Ochtermuthill......E 3	39	Old Tebay......E 8		D 8	8	Outwick......D 3	60	Oykel Bridge......G 5
32	Nottinghamshire,	42	Ochtrelure.........	40	Old Thirsk......G 4	26	Ormesby St. Michael	10	Outwood, Surrey..D 2	58	Oyne......E 4
	County......D 4	32	Ockbrook......G 2	39	Old Town, Cumb..A 7		D 8	35	Outwood, Yorks..E 12	13	Oystermouth......H 9
15	Notton, Wilts...G 12	17	Ockham......H 11	2	Old Town, Is. of Scilly	60	Ormiscaig......G 1	35	Ovenden......D 9	7	Packers Hill......E 10
35	Notton, Yorks....F 12	50	Ockle......A 3		D 2	49	Ormiston......B 7	49	Ovenscloss......F 7	23	Packington......A 7
19	Nounsley......C 8	21	Ocle Pychard...H 11	45	Old Town, Northumb.	38	Ormley Hall......F 2	25	Over, Cambs......H 5	22	Packington Park...D 5
22	Noutard's Green..E 2	9	Ocley......B 12		D 7	50	Ormsaigbeg......A 2	30	Over, Cheshire...D 5	9	Padanaram......B 9
56	Novar House......C 2	41	Octon......H 10	39	Old Town, Westmor.	50	Ormsaigmore......A 2	15	Over, Glos......F 9	17	Padbury......A 8
21	Nox......A 9	7	Odcombe......E 8		G 8	46	Ormsary House....B 2	43	Over Cleuchbrae.B 11	18	Paddington......F 3
17	Nuffield......E 7	15	Odd Down......H 10	35	Old Trafford......G 7	34	Ormskirk......F 3	7	Over Compton......K 8	11	Paddlesworth......D 10
57	Nuide......K 3	39	Oddendale......D 8	32	Old Tupton......D 1	63	Orosay......F 5	48	Over Dalgliesh...H 5	10	Paddock Wood...D 5
36	Nun Monkton....A 3	22	Oddingley......F 3	25	Old Warden......L 2	64	Orphir......D 2	31	Over Haddon...D 10	56	Paddockhaugh......D 8
36	Nunburnholme...B 6	16	Oddington, Glos..B 3	25	Old Weston......H 2	18	Orpington......G 5	43	Over Hazlefield...G 8	44	Paddockhole......E 1
32	Nuncargate......E 2	16	Oddington, Oxon..C 6	17	Old Windsor......G 10	34	Orrell, Lancs......G 2	39	Over Kellet......H 7	40	Paddolgreen......G 4
23	Nuneaton......C 7	25	Odell......J 1	11	Old Wives Lees...C 9	34	Orrell, Lancs......G 4	16	Over Kiddington..B 5	35	Padfield......G 9
16	Nuneham Courtenay	64	Odie......B 4	17	Old Woking......H 11	34	Orrell Post......G 4	16	Over Norton......A 4	30	Padgate......A 5
	D 6	9	Odiham......A 9	60	Oldany......D 3	53	Orrock......H 7	40	Over Silton......F 5	31	Padiham......D 7
49	Nunlands......D 12	8	Odstock......C 3	22	Oldberrow......F 5	43	Orroland......G 8	6	Over Stowey......B 5	29	Padog......E 8
38	Nunnery Howe...H 2	23	Odstone......A 7	4	Oldborough......E 6	18	Orsett......F 6	7	Over Stratton......E 8	35	Padside......A 10
7	Nunney......B 10	22	Offchurch......F 7	21	Oldbury, Salop..C 12	18	Orsett Heath......F 6	30	Over Tabley......B 6	2	Padstow......B 6
41	Nunnington......G 7	22	Offenham......G 4	22	Oldbury, War....C 3	22	Orslow......A 2	8	Over Wallop......B 4	17	Padworth......G 7
45	Nunnykirk......D 9	45	Offerton......G 11	22	Oldbury, War....C 3	32	Orston......F 5	22	Over Whitacre......C 6	40	Page Bank......D 8
37	Nunsthorpe......F 10	11	Offham, Kent......B 5	15	Oldbury on the Hill	38	Orthwaite......B 5	49	Over Whitton......G 10	9	Pagham......F 10
40	Nunthorpe......D 5	10	Offham, Sussex...G 3		E 11	23	Orton, Northants.D 11	32	Over Woodhouse...C 2	19	Paglesham......E 9
8	Nunton......C 3	25	Offord Cluny......J 3	15	Oldbury-upon-Severn	39	Orton, Westmor...B 8	39	Overbister......B 4	63	Paible......G 1
40	Nunwick......H 3	25	Offord D'Arcy......J 3		E 9	24	Orton Longueville.F 3	22	Overbury......H 3	5	Paignton......K 8
43	Nunwood......D 10	27	Offton......K 4	14	Oldcastle, Brec....B 6	22	Orton on the Hill..B 6	58	Overhall......C 5	23	Pailton......D 8
8	Nursling......D 5	6	Offwell......F 5	14	Oldcastle, Glam...F 2	58	Orton Station......B 1	58	Overhill......D 4	31	Painscastle......H 7
9	Nutbourne......F 9	16	Ogbourne Maizey .G 3	32	Oldcotes......A 3	24	Orton Waterville..F 3	7	Overleigh......C 8	45	Painshawfield......G 9
9	Nutbourne......D 12	16	Ogbourne St. Andrew	22	Oldfield, Worcs...F 2	25	Orwell......K 5	22	Overley Green......F 4	15	Painswick......C 12
10	Nutfield......C 2		G 3	35	Oldfield, Yorks....C 8	34	Osbaldeston......D 5	58	Overpool......C 3	11	Painter's Forstal..B 8
32	Nuthall......F 2	16	Ogbourne St. George	7	Oldford......A 11	36	Osbaldwick......B 4	22	Overseal......A 6	47	Paisley......C 9
25	Nuthampstead....M 5		G 3	35	Oldham......G 8	23	Osbaston......B 7	58	Overside......B 8	58	Paithnick......B 2
10	Nuthurst......E 1	45	Ogle......E 9	49	Oldhamstocks......B 10	24	Osbournby......B 2	11	Oversland......B 9	26	Pakefield......F 8
9	Nutley, Hants....B 7	14	Ogmore......G 2	15	Oldland......G 10	30	Oscroft......D 4	23	Overstone......E 11	27	Pakenham......J 2
10	Nutley, Sussex....E 3	14	Ogmore-by-Sea...G 2	58	Oldmeldrum......E 6	62	Osdale......D 3	26	Overstrand......B 5	29	Pale......G 9
36	Nutwell......G 4	14	Ogmore Vale......E 3	58	Oldnoth......D 3	6	Ose......D 2	39	Overthorpe......H 8	10	Palehouse Com...F 4
9	Nyetimber......F 10	7	Okeford Fitzpaine E 11	21	Oldpark......A 12	32	Osgathorpe......H 2	58	Overton, Aber......F 6	8	Palestine......B 4
9	Nyewood......D 9	4	Okehampton......F 5	33	Osgodby, Lincs....A 8	47	Overton, Ayr......D 8	17	Paley Street......G 9
4	Nymet Rowland...E 6	59	Old Aberdeen......G 7	40	Oldshore Beg....B 3	36	Osgodby, E. Riding,	30	Overton, Ches......C 4	47	Palgowan......C 5
4	Nymet Tracey......F 6	9	Old Alresford......C 7	60	Oldshore More....B 3		D 4	30	Overton, Flint......F 2	47	Palgrave......G 4
15	Nympsfield......D 11	53	Old Balkello......C 8	40	Oldstead......G 5	41	Osgodby, N. Riding,	13	Overton, Glam....H 8	11	Palmarsh......E 10
7	Nynehead......D 5	45	Old Berwick......A 9	58	Oldtown of Ord...B 4		G 10	8	Overton, Hants....B 7	18	Palmers Green......E 3
7	Nythe......C 7	13	Oldway......H 9	62	Oskaig......D 2	43	Overton, Kirk......E 10	43	Palnackie......F 9
9	Nyton......E 10	52	Old Blair......A 4	4	Oldways End......D 7	50	Oskamuil......D 2	48	Overton, Lan......D 1	42	Palnure......E 5
11	Oad Street......B 7	33	Old Bolingbroke .D 10	58	Oldwhat......C 6	31	Osmaston......F 10	34	Overton, Lancs....A 3	32	Palterton......C 2
23	Oadby......B 9	35	Old Bramhope...C 11	48	Oliver......G 4	7	Osmington......H 10	21	Overton, Salop...E 10	22	Pamber End......H 7
31	Oakamoor......F 9	31	Old Brampton...C 11	8	Oliver's Battery...C 6	7	Osmington Mills .H 10	36	Overton, Yorks....B 3	17	Pamber Green......H 7
48	Oakbank......C 4	43	Old Bridge of Urr. E 8	64	Ollaberry......C 7	35	Osmondthorpe...D 12	29	Overton Bridge...F 12	17	Pamber Heath......H 7
14	Oakdale......D 5	26	Old Buckenham...F 4	30	Ollerton, Ches....C 6	40	Osmotherley......E 5	30	Overton Green...D 6	8	Pamphill......F 1
6	Oake......D 5	16	Old Burghclere...H 6	32	Ollerton, Notts....C 4	11	Ospringe......B 8	58	Overtown, Aber...D 7	25	Pampisford......K 6
22	Oaken......B 2	40	Old Byland......G 6	30	Ollerton, Salop...H 5	33	Ossett......E 11	48	Overtown, Lan......D 1	58	Panborough......B 8
34	Oakenclough......B 4	37	Old Clee......F 10	20	Olmarch......G 2	32	Ossington......D 5	39	Overtown, Lancs..H 8	53	Panbride......D 10
21	Oakengates......A 12	6	Old Cleeve......B 4	23	Olney......G 12	19	Ostend......D 9	16	Overtown, Wilts...F 3	4	Pancrasweek......E 2
29	Oakenholt......C 12	43	Old Clouden......D 9	22	Olton......D 5	19	Olveston......F 9	58	Overtown of Memsie	20	Pandy, Denb......G 11
40	Oakenshaw, Dur..A 2	29	Old Colwyn......B 8	15	Olveston......F 9	40	Oswaldkirk......G 6		B 7	20	Pandy, Mer......B 2
35	Oakenshaw, Yorks.	43	Old Craighouse ..C 12	22	Ombersley......F 2	34	Oswaldtwistle......D 6	26	Overy Staithe......A 1	15	Pandy, Mon......B 7
	D 10	42	Old Dailly......B 3	32	Ompton......D 4	30	Oswestry......G 2	17	Oving, Bucks......B 8	20	Pandy, Mont......B 5
8	Oakfield, Hants...C 5	32	Old Dalby......H 4	38	Onchan......H 2	10	Otford......B 4	9	Oving, Sussex......F 10	29	Pandy Tudur......D 8
14	Oakfield, Mon....E 6	58	Old Deer......C 7	31	Onecote......E 9	11	Otham......C 7	10	Ovingdean......H 2	19	Panfield......A 7
13	Oakford, Cards...A 8	60	Old Drumrunie Lo.	15	Onen......C 7	7	Othery......C 7	35	Ovingham......G 9	17	Pangbourne......F 7
6	Oakford, Devon...D 3		F 3	18	Ongar......D 5	27	Otley, Suffolk......K 5	27	Ovington, Essex...L 1	43	Panlands......C 11
6	Oakfordbridge....D 3	49	Old Dryburn.....E 12	24	Onger Hill......C 7	35	Otley, Yorks......C 10	9	Ovington, Hants...C 7	35	Pannal......B 11
31	Oakgrove......C 8	36	Old Edlington......G 3	21	Onibury......D 10	46	Otter Ferry......A 4	26	Ovington, Norfolk.E 2	59	Pannanich......H 1
23	Oakham......A 12	40	Old Eldon......B 3	51	Onich......A 7	8	Otterbourne......D 6	45	Ovington, Northumb.	30	Pant......H 1
9	Oakhanger......C 9	37	Old Ellerby......C 9	14	Onllwyn......C 2	45	Otterburn, Northumb.		G 9	20	Pant Mawr......D 4
7	Oakhill......A 11	24	Old Fletton......F 3	30	Onneley......F 6		D 7	35	Ovington, Yorks...D 2	14	Pant-glas, Caer....E 4
32	Oakington......J 5	36	Old Goole......E 5	9	Onslow Village...A 11	35	Otterburn, Yorks...A 9	8	Ower......D 5	21	Pantglas, Salop...C 8
29	Oaklands......D 7	44	Old Graitney......F 2	47	Onthank......E 9	45	Otterburn Camp..C 7	7	Owermoigne......H 11	12	Pantgwyn, Cards..B 6
15	Oakle Street......C 10	37	Old Hall......E 10	35	Openshaw......G 7	2	Otterham......B 2	32	Owlerton......A 1	13	Pantgwyn, Carm..D 9
25	Oakley, Beds.....K 1	10	Old Heathfield...F 5	32	Openwoodgate...E 1	6	Otterhampton......B 4	17	Owlswick......C 8	13	Pant-lasau......G 10
17	Oakley, Bucks....C 7	25	Old Hurst......H 4	54	Opinan, Ross &	17	Ottershaw......H 11	33	Owmby, Lincs......A 7	33	Panton......B 9
8	Oakley, Dorset....F 2	39	Old Hutton......F 8		Cromarty......C 1	64	Otterswick......B 7	37	Owmby, Lincs......G 8	20	Pant-perthog......B 3
52	Oakley, Fife......H 5	2	Old Kea......E 5	60	Opinan, Ross &	6	Otterton......A 3	8	Owslebury......D 6	20	Pant-y-dwr......E 5
9	Oakley, Hants....A 7	47	Old Kilpatrick...B 9		Cromarty......G 1	6	Ottery St. Mary...G 5	37	Owmby, Lincs......G 8	21	Pant-y-ffrid......B 7
27	Oakley, Suffolk...H 3	18	Old Knebworth....B 2	49	Orange Lane......E 10	11	Ottinge......D 10	36	Owston, Yorks......F 3	14	Pantyffynnon......F 9
17	Oakley Green......F 10	26	Old Lakenham......E 5	62	Orbost......D 2	32	Ottringham......E 10	32	Owston, Leics.....A 11	15	Pantygasseg......D 5
20	Oakleypark......D 5	38	Old Laxey......G 2	33	Orby......C 12	39	Oughtershaw......G 11	36	Owston Ferry......G 6	15	Pant y Goitre......C 7
15	Oakridge Lynch..D 12	33	Old Leake......D 11	46	Orcadia......C 6	43	Oughterside......H 12	37	Owstwick......D 10	12	Pantymenyn......D 5
16	Oaksey......E 1	45	Old Lyham......C 12	1	Orchard Hill......C 3	35	Oughtibridge......H 11	32	Owthorpe......G 4	29	Pantymwyn......D 11
22	Oakthorpe......A 6	41	Old Malton......H 8	6	Orchard Portman.D 6	40	Oulston......H 6	24	Oxborough......E 8	14	Pant-yr-awel......E 3
40	Oaktree Hill......E 4	36	Old Micklefield...D 2	8	Orcheston......B 2	44	Oulton, Cumb....H 1	38	Oxen Park......F 5	26	Panxworth......D 6
				15	Orcop......B 8	26	Oulton, Norfolk...C 4				

MAP
38 Papcastle..........B 3
49 Papple............B 8
32 Papplewick.......E 3
25 Papworth Everard .J 4
25 Papworth St. Agnes J 4
3 Par................D 8
7 Parbrook..........C 9
29 Parc..............G 8
12 Parc-llyn..........B 6
38 Pardshaw..........C 3
27 Parham............J 6
59 Park, Aberdeen.. G 5
50 Park, Argyll......C 6
43 Park, Dumfries ..B 10
17 Park Corner, Berks.F 9
17 Park Corner, Oxon.E 1
10 Park Corner, Sussex
                    D 4
45 Park End, Northumb.
                    E 7
40 Park End, Yorks...C 5
9 Park Gate.........E 7
44 Park Nook.........F 4
58 Parkdargue.......C 4
38 Parkend, Cumb...A 5
15 Parkend, Glos....D 9
27 Parkeston.........M 5
3 Parkfield.........C 10
30 Parkgate, Ches...B 1
43 Parkgate, Dumf..C 11
10 Parkgate, Surrey .D 1
48 Parkgatestone....F 4
4 Parkham..........D 3
4 Parkham Ash....D 2
56 Parkhead.........F 8
58 Parkhill House....F 6
15 Parkhouse........D 8
8 Parkhurst........G 6
13 Parkmill.........H 9
59 Parkneuk.........K 5
30 Parkside.........E 3
8 Parkstone........G 2
8 Parley Cross.....F 2
4 Parracombe.......B 5
30 Parrah Green.....F 6
12 Parrog...........C 4
24 Parson Drove....E 5
19 Parson's Heath...A 10
47 Partick...........C 10
34 Partington.......H 6
33 Partney..........C 11
38 Parton, Cumb....C 2
15 Parton, Glos.....B 12
43 Parton, Kirk.....E 8
10 Partridge Green..F 1
31 Parwich..........E 10
23 Passenham.......H 11
9 Passfield.........C 9
26 Paston Street....B 6
4 Patchacott.......F 3
10 Patcham.........G 2
9 Patching.........E 12
4 Patchole.........B 5
15 Pathway..........F 9
35 Pateley Bridge...A 10
19 Paternoster Heath.B 9
52 Path of Condie...F 5
7 Pathe............C 7
53 Pathead, Fife.....H 8
48 Pathead, Midlothian
                    C 6
47 Pathhead........H 11
52 Pathstruie.......F 5
47 Patna...........H 9
16 Patney..........H 2
38 Patrick..........G 1
40 Patrick Brompton .F 2
34 Patricroft.......G 6
37 Patrington......E 10
11 Patrixbourne...C 10
38 Patterdale.......D 6
44 Pattieshill......F 3
22 Pattingham......B 2
23 Pattishall.......G 10
19 Pattiswick Green..B 8
2 Paul............G 2
23 Paulerspury......G 10
37 Paull............E 9
7 Paulton.........A 10
45 Pauperhaugh......C 9
25 Pavenham........K 1
6 Pawlett.........B 6
49 Pawston.........F 11
22 Paxford.........H 5
49 Paxton..........D 12
6 Payhembury......F 4
35 Paythorne.......B 7
10 Peacehaven......H 3
22 Peachley........F 2
31 Peak Dale.......C 9
31 Peak Forest.....B 9
58 Peaknowe........B 4
55 Peanmeanach....L 1

MAP
59 Pearsie..........L 1
10 Pearsons Green...D 6
10 Pease Pottage....E 1
7 Peasedown St. John
                    A 10
16 Peasemore........F 5
27 Peasenhall........H 7
9 Peaslake.........B 12
34 Peasley Cross.....H 4
11 Peasmarsh........F 7
49 Peaston Bank.....C 7
53 Peat Inn.........F 9
58 Peathill..........A 7
23 Peatling Magna...C 9
23 Peatling Parva....C 9
1 Peaton..........D 10
27 Pebmarsh.........M 2
22 Pebworth.........G 5
35 Peckett Well......D 8
30 Peckforton.......E 4
18 Peckham.........F 3
23 Peckleton.........B 8
44 Pedderhill........F 3
11 Pedlinge.........E 10
22 Pedmore.........D 3
7 Pedwell.........C 8
48 Peebles..........E 5
48 Peebles, Co......E 5
38 Peel............G 1
9 Peel Common....F 7
9 Pegsdon.........M 2
45 Pegswood........D 10
62 Peinaha.........B 4
62 Peinchorran......E 4
62 Peinlick.........B 3
62 Peinmore.........C 4
62 Pelcomb Cross....E 3
19 Peldon..........B 9
22 Pelsall..........B 4
45 Pelton..........H 10
45 Pelton Fell......H 10
43 Pelutho.........G 12
13 Pelynt..........D 9
13 Pemberton, Carm. G 8
34 Pemberton, Lancs..G 4
13 Pembrey.........G 7
12 Pembridge.......G 9
12 Pembroke........G 3
12 Pembroke Dock....G 3
10 Pembury.........D 5
13 Pen Rhiwfawr....F 10
13 Pen-Sarn........E 7
12 Penallt.........C 8
12 Penally.........G 5
15 Penalt..........A 9
3 Penare..........F 7
14 Penarth.........G 5
20 Pen-bont-rhyd-y-
    beddau.........D 2
12 Penbryn.........B 6
13 Pencader........E 7
13 Pen-cae.........A 7
28 Pencaenewydd....F 3
29 Pencarnisiog.....C 3
13 Pencarreg.......C 8
14 Pencelli.........B 4
13 Penclawdd.......G 9
14 Pencoed, Glam...F 3
15 Pencoed, Herefs..B 8
21 Pencombe........G 11
15 Pencraig, Herefs..B 9
29 Pencraig, Mont...G 9
12 Pendeen.........F 1
14 Penderyn........C 3
12 Pendine.........F 6
34 Pendlebury......G 6
34 Pendleton, Lancs..C 6
35 Pendleton, Lancs..G 7
15 Pendock.........A 11
7 Pendoggett......B 7
7 Pendomer........E 8
14 Pendoylan.......G 4
14 Pendre..........F 2
20 Penegoes........B 3
12 Penfeidir.......D 2
12 Pen-ffordd, Card..C 8
12 Pen-ffordd, Pemb..E 4
14 Pengam.........D 5
14 Penge..........G 3
3 Pengelly........A 8
14 Pengenffordd....A 5
14 Pengover Green..C 10
2 Penhale.........H 4
12 Penhalurick.....F 4
16 Penhill.........E 2
15 Penhow.........E 7
14 Penhurst.......F 6
20 Peniarth.......B 2
48 Penicuik.......C 5
13 Peniel.........E 8
62 Penifiler.......D 4
46 Peninver.......G 4

MAP
28 Penisar-waun.....D 5
35 Penistone........G 11
30 Penketh.........A 4
42 Penkill..........B 3
14 Penkiln.........G 6
22 Penkridge.......A 3
30 Penley..........F 3
13 Penllergaèr......G 9
28 Pen-llyn, Angl..B 3
11 Penllyn, Glam...G 3
29 Penmachno.......E 7
13 Penmaen.........H 8
28 Penmaenen......C 6
28 Penmaenmawr....C 6
28 Penmaenpool....H 6
29 Penmaenrhos....B 8
14 Penmark.........G 4
28 Penmon.........B 6
50 Penmore Mill....B 1
28 Penmorfa........F 5
28 Penmynydd......C 4
21 Penn............E 10
17 Penn Street.....E 10
20 Pennal..........B 3
58 Pennan.........A 6
13 Pennant, Cards..A 8
29 Pennant, Denb...D 7
29 Pennant, Mer...G 9
20 Pennant, Mont...C 4
29 Pennant-Melangell H 9
13 Pennard.........H 9
21 Pennerley.......C 9
8 Pennington, Hants.G 4
38 Pennington, Lancs. G 5
14 Pennorth........B 4
15 Pennsylvania Vill...E 8
38 Penny Bridge.....G 5
24 Penny Hill......C 5
50 Pennyghael......E 3
47 Pennyglen.......H 7
50 Pennygown......C 3
4 Pennymoor.......E 7
45 Pennywell........G 11
12 Penparc, Cards...B 5
12 Penparc, Pemb...D 2
20 Penparcau.......D 2
14 Penpelleni......D 6
3 Penpillick......D 8
14 Penpont, Brec...A 3
43 Penpont, Dumf...B 9
12 Penrherber......C 6
12 Penrhiw........C 6
12 Penrhiwceiber....E 4
13 Penrhiw-goch....E 9
13 Penrhiw-llan....C 7
13 Penrhiwpal.....B 7
14 Penrhos, Brec...C 1
28 Penrhos, Caer...G 3
15 Penrhos, Mon...C 7
28 Penrhos-garnedd....C 5
28 Penrhyn.........A 3
29 Penrhyn Bay....B 7
29 Penrhyn-coch....D 2
28 Penrhyndeudraeth.F 5
29 Penrhynside....B 7
13 Penrice........H 8
12 Penrieth.......C 6
39 Penrith.......B 7
2 Penrose........C 6
38 Penruddock....B 6
12 Penryn.........F 5
29 Pensarn........B 9
22 Pensax.........E 1
30 Pensby.........B 1
7 Penselwood....C 10
15 Pensford.......H 9
45 Penshaw.......H 11
10 Penshurst......D 4
3 Pensilva.......C 10
3 Pentewan.......E 7
28 Pentir.........D 5
3 Pentire.........D 5
13 Pentireg.......B 6
27 Pentlow.......L 1
24 Pentney.......D 8
8 Penton Mewsey...A 5
28 Pentraeth......B 5
29 Pentre, Denb...D 10
29 Pentre, Denb....F 12
14 Pentre, Glam...E 3
21 Pentre, Mont...B 8
21 Pentre, Mont...C 8
20 Pentre, Mont...D 6
21 Pentre, Salop...A 9
29 Pentre Bagillt...C 11
28 Pentre Berw.....B 5
20 Pentre Dolau-Honddu
                    H 5
13 Pentre Gwenlais...E 9

MAP
28 Pentre Gwyffryn...G 5
29 Pentre Halkyn...C 11
29 Pentre-Isaf.....C 8
14 Pentre Meyrick...G 3
29 Pentre Saron....D 9
14 Pentre-bach, Brec..A 2
13 Pentrebach, Cards..B 9
29 Pentre-bach, Denb.
                    G 10
14 Pentrebâch, Glam..A 4
13 Pentrebach, Glam..F 9
21 Pentrebeirdd....A 7
29 Pentre-bont.....E 7
13 Pentre-cagal....C 7
29 Pentre-celyn....E 10
13 Pentre-cwrt....C 7
29 Pentre-dwfr....F 11
13 Pentre-dwr.....G 10
28 Pentrefelin, Angl...A 4
13 Pentrefelin, Carm..E 9
29 Pentrefoelas....E 8
12 Pentre-galar....D 5
13 Pentregat......B 7
20 Pentre-llwyn-llwyd G 5
14 Pentre-poeth....F 6
14 Pentrer-felin, Brec..A 3
28 Pentre'r felin, Caer..F 5
13 Pentre'r-felin, Cards.
                    B 9
29 Pentre-tafarn-y-fedw
                    D 7
13 Pentre-ty-gwyn...C 11
29 Pentre-uchaf....C 10
32 Pentrich........E 1
8 Pentridge.......D 2
14 Pentwyn, Glam...D 4
15 Pen-twyn, Mon...C 8
14 Pentyrch........F 4
14 Penuchadre.....G 2
20 Penuwch........F 2
3 Penwithick Stents..D 7
16 Penwood........H 5
14 Penwyllt........C 2
13 Pen-y-banc, Carm..E 9
13 Pen-y-banc, Carm..F 9
29 Pen-y-bont, Denb.H 11
21 Penybont, Rad...F 7
29 Pen-y-bont-fawr..H 10
12 Pen-y-bryn......C 5
14 Pen-y-cae, Brec...C 2
29 Pen-y-cae, Denb...F 12
29 Pen-y-cae-mawr...E 7
15 Pen-y-clawdd....D 7
14 Pen-y-coedcae....F 4
12 Pen-y-cwm......E 2
14 Pen-y-fai.......F 2
29 Penyffordd......D 12
29 Pen-y-garnedd...H 10
14 Pen-y-graig.....E 3
28 Penygroes, Caer...E 4
13 Pen-y-groes, Carm. F 9
14 Penygroes, Glam. F 5
12 Penygroes, Pemb..C 5
28 Pen-y-groeslon...C 2
28 Pen-y-Gwryd....E 6
14 Penyrheol.......E 5
14 Pen-yr-Heolgerrig.D 4
14 Penyrynys......B 2
28 Penysarn.......A 4
29 Pen-y-stryt.....E 11
14 Penywaun.......D 3
2 Penzance.......G 2
22 Pillerton Hersey..G 6
22 Peover Heath....C 6
30 Peover Superior...C 6
8 Peper Harow....B 10
30 Peplow.........H 5
17 Peppard Common .F 8
45 Peppermoor....B 10
47 Perceton.......E 8
59 Percie.........H 3
58 Percyhorner....A 7
45 Perkinsville....H 10
32 Perlethorpe....C 4
2 Perranarworthal..F 5
2 Perranporth....D 5
2 Perranuthnoe...G 3
2 Perranwell.....F 5
2 Perranwell Station.F 5
2 Perranzabuloe...D 5
59 Perry..........J 2
22 Perry Barr.....C 4
18 Perry Green....B 4
10 Perry Street....A 5
22 Pershore.......G 3
59 Pert...........L 4
25 Pertenhall.....J 2
52 Perth..........E 6
52 Perth, County...C 3
52 Perton.........B 2
7 Pertwood.......C 12
5 Peter Tavy.....H 4
24 Peterborough...F 3

MAP
54 Peterburn......B 1
21 Peterchurch....H 9
59 Petercutter....G 6
58 Peterhead.....C 8
40 Peterlee.......C 8
18 Peter's Green...B 2
4 Peters Marland...E 3
9 Petersfield....D 9
14 Peterstone Wentlooge
                    F 6
14 Peterston-super-ElyG 4
15 Peterstow......B 9
23 Petrockstow....E 4
11 Pett...........G 7
27 Pettaugh.......J 5
53 Pettenden......C 9
48 Pettinain......E 2
27 Pettistree.....K 6
6 Petton, Devon...D 4
30 Petton, Salop...G 3
18 Petts Wood.....G 4
5 Petty..........D 5
48 Pettycur.......A 5
58 Pettymuck......E 6
10 Pevensey.......H 5
10 Pevensey Bay...H 5
10 Pewsey.........H 3
17 Pheasants......E 9
17 Pheasant's Hill...E 9
1 Philham........D 1
49 Philiphaugh....G 7
2 Phillack.......F 3
2 Philleigh......F 6
48 Philpstoun.....B 3
15 Phocle Green...B 9
17 Phœnix Green...H 8
57 Phoines........K 3
38 Phurt..........F 2
2 Pica...........C 3
17 Piccott's End...C 11
36 Pickburn.......F 3
41 Pickering......G 8
8 Picket Piece...A 5
8 Picket Post....E 3
21 Picklescott....B 10
53 Pickletillem...E 9
30 Pickmere......C 5
4 Pickwell, Devon...B 3
23 Pickwell, Leics...A 11
24 Pickworth, Lincs..B 1
24 Pickworth, Rut...D 1
30 Picton, Cheshire...C 3
40 Picton, Yorks...D 4
10 Piddinghoe.....H 3
17 Piddington, Bucks..E 9
23 Piddington, Northants.
                    G 11
17 Piddington, Oxon..B 7
7 Piddlehinton...F 10
7 Piddletrenthide...F 10
25 Pidley.........H 2
40 Piercebridge...D 2
64 Pierowall......A 2
6 Pilton, Devon...B 3
31 Pilsley, Derby...C 11
32 Pilsley, Derby...D 2
25 Pilton, Northants..G 1
23 Pilton, Rutland...B 12
7 Pilton, Somerset..B 9
13 Pilton Green....H 8
7 Pimperne.......E 12
34 Pinfold........F 3
6 Pinhoe.........F 4
13 Pinkneys Green..F 9
22 Pinley Green....E 5
42 Pinminnoch....B 3

MAP
42 Pinmore........B 3
25 Pinmore Mains...C 3
6 Pinn...........G 4
18 Pinner.........E 1
12 Pinvin.........G 3
42 Pinwherry......C 3
32 Pinxton........E 2
30 Pipe and Lyde..H 10
30 Pipe Gate......F 6
22 Pipehill.......A 4
56 Piperhill......E 4
3 Pipers Pool....A 9
23 Pipewell.......D 11
4 Pippacott......B 4
14 Pipton.........A 5
17 Pirbright......H 10
2 Pirnie.........G 9
46 Pirnmill.......E 4
18 Pirton, Herts..A 2
22 Pirton, Worcs..G 2
17 Pishill........E 8
28 Pistyll........F 3
58 Pitagowan.....A 3
58 Pitblae.......A 7
53 Pitcairlie Farm...F 7
52 Pitcairn......B 4
52 Pitcairngreen...D 5
58 Pitcaple.......E 5
53 Pitcarity......A 8
17 Pitch Green....D 8
9 Pitch Place....A 11
15 Pitchcombe....D 11
17 Pitchcott.....B 8
21 Pitchford.....B 10
7 Pitcombe......C 10
53 Pitcorthie....F 10
49 Pitcox........B 9
59 Pitdrichie....J 5
58 Pitfichie.....F 4
53 Pitfour Castle...E 7
53 Pitkevy.......G 7
53 Pitlessie.....F 8
52 Pitlochry.....A 4
58 Pitmachie.....E 4
57 Pitmain.......J 3
58 Pitmedden....E 6
6 Pitminster....D 5
53 Pitmuies......B 10
58 Pitmunie......F 4
7 Pitney........C 8
53 Pitroddie.....E 7
53 Pitscottie....F 9
11 Pitsea.......E 7
23 Pitsford.....E 11
17 Pitstone.....C 10
17 Pitstone Green...C 10
59 Pittarrow....K 5
56 Pittendreich...D 7
61 Pittentraill....F 7
53 Pittenweem...G 10
40 Pittington....A 3
58 Pittodrie.....E 4
8 Pitton.......C 4
10 Pittswood....C 5
58 Pittulie.....A 7
40 Pity Me, Durham..A 3
45 Pity Me, Northumb.
                    E 7
27 Pixey Green...H 5
10 Pixham......C 1
31 Pixley......H 12
58 Plaidy......B 5
12 Plain Dealings..E 4
48 Plains......C 1
6 Plainsfield...C 5
21 Plaish......C 10
35 Plaistow.....C 11
10 Plaistow Street...D 3
8 Plaitford....D 4
20 Plas Llysyn...C 5
29 Plas Newydd...F 11
44 Plashetts....D 5
16 Plastow Green...H 6
29 Plas-yn-Cefn...C 9
10 Platt........B 5
34 Platt Bridge...G 5
45 Plawsworth...H 11
10 Plaxtol.....C 5
17 Play Hatch...F 8
11 Playden.....F 8
27 Playford....K 5
2 Playing Place...E 5
15 Playley Green..A 10
53 Plealey.....B 9
58 Plean.......H 3
53 Pleasance...F 7
35 Pleasington...E 5
32 Pleasley....D 1
44 Plenmeller...G 5
18 Pleshey.....B 6
45 Plessey Checks..E 10
54 Plockton....F 2
21 Ploughfield...H 9

MAP
49 Ploughlands.....E 10
21 Plowden.....D 9
21 Ploxgreen.....B 9
11 Pluckley.....D 8
11 Pluckley Thorne...D 8
43 Plumbland.....H 12
30 Plumley.....C 6
10 Plumpton.....G 2
39 Plumpton Foot....A 7
10 Plumpton Green...F 2
39 Plumpton Head...B 7
39 Plumpton Wall....B 7
26 Plumstead.....B 4
32 Plumtree.....G 3
32 Plungar.....G 5
7 Plush.....F 10
13 Plwmp.....B 7
5 Plymouth.....K 4
5 Plympton.....K 4
5 Plympton St. Maurice K 4
5 Plymstock.....K 4
6 Plymtree.....F 4
40 Pockley.....G 6
36 Pocklington.....B 6
24 Pode Hole.....C 3
7 Podimore.....D 9
23 Podington.....F 12
30 Podmore.....G 6
24 Pointon.....B 2
8 Pokesdown.....G 3
42 Polbae.....D 4
60 Polbain.....F 2
3 Polbathic.....D 10
48 Polbeth.....C 3
43 Poldean.....B 11
58 Poldullie Bridge...F 1
35 Pole Moor.....E 9
25 Polebrook.....G 2
10 Polegate.....G 5
30 Polelane Ends.....B 5
22 Polesworth.....B 6
60 Polglass.....F 2
3 Polgooth.....E 7
9 Poling.....F 11
9 Poling Corner....E 11
3 Polkerris.....D 8
60 Polla.....B 5
36 Pollington.....E 4
50 Polloch.....A 5
47 Pollockshaws....C 10
47 Pollokshields.....C 10
43 Polmaddie.....C 7
54 Polmaily.....F 8
3 Polmassick.....E 7
48 Polmont.....B 2
48 Polmoody.....H 4
47 Polnessan.....H 9
55 Polnish.....L 1
3 Polperro.....E 9
3 Polruan.....E 8
7 Polsham.....B 8
43 Polskeoch.....A 8
27 Polstead.....L 3
6 Poltimore.....G 3
48 Polton.....C 5
49 Polwarth.....D 10
3 Polyphant.....B 9
2 Polzeath.....B 6
24 Pondersbridge.....F 4
9 Pondtail.....A 9
2 Ponsanooth.....F 5
5 Ponsworthy.....H 6
15 Pont-Antwn.....F 8
29 Pont Cyfyng.....D 7
14 Pont Ebbw.....F 6
13 Pont Henry.....F 8
12 Pont Hirwaun.....C 6
20 Pont-Llogel.....A 6
28 Pont Pen-y-benglog D 6
20 Pont-Robert.....A 6
21 Pont Yates.....F 8
13 Pontamman.....F 9
14 Pont ar Hydfer...B 2
13 Pontardawe.....G 10
13 Pontardulais.....G 9
13 Pontargothi.....E 8
13 Pont-ar-llechau...E 10
13 Pont-ar-Sais.....D 8
29 Pontblyddyn.....D 12
14 Pontbren Llwyd...D 3
36 Pontefract.....E 2
45 Ponteland.....F 10
20 Ponterwyd.....D 3
21 Pontesbury.....B 9
21 Pontesford.....B 9
29 Pontfadog.....F 11
14 Pont-faen, Brec....A 3
12 Pontfaen, Pemb....D 4
13 Pontgarreg.....B 7
14 Pont-hir.....E 6
14 Pont-llan-fraith...E 5
13 Pontlliw.....G 9

MAP
14 Pontlottyn.....D 4
28 Pont-lyfni.....E 4
14 Pontneddfechan...D 2
14 Pontnewydd.....E 6
20 Pontrhydfendigaid.F 3
13 Pont-rhyd-y-fen..G 11
20 Pont-rhyd-y-groes..E 3
14 Pontrhydyrun.....E 6
15 Pontrilas.....B 7
28 Pont-rug.....D 4
10 Ponts Green.....F 5
13 Pontshaen.....B 8
15 Pontshill.....B 9
14 Pontsticill.....C 4
13 Pont-tywely.....C 7
13 Pontyberem.....F 8
29 Pont-y-bodkin...D 12
29 Pont y Clogwyn...E 8
14 Pontyclun.....F 4
14 Pontycymer.....E 2
12 Pontyglazier.....C 5
14 Pont-y-gwaith.....E 3
29 Pont-y-pant.....E 7
14 Pontypool.....D 6
14 Pontypool Road..D 6
14 Pontypridd.....E 4
12 Pont-yr-hafod.....D 3
21 Pont-ysgawrhyd...A 7
14 Pont-y-waun.....E 5
8 Pooksgreen.....E 5
2 Pool, Cornwall.....E 4
21 Pool, Herefs.....H 10
35 Pool, Yorks.....C 11
34 Pool Hay.....F 2
21 Pool Head.....G 11
52 Pool of Muckhart.G 5
21 Pool Quay.....A 8
27 Pool Street.....L 1
8 Poole.....G 2
30 Poole Green.....E 5
16 Poole Keynes.....E 1
31 Poolend.....D 8
54 Poolewe.....B 2
39 Pooley Bridge.....C 7
15 Poolhill.....A 10
32 Poolsbrook.....C 2
38 Poortown.....G 1
10 Pootings.....C 3
17 Popeswood.....G 9
9 Popham.....B 7
18 Poplar.....F 4
9 Porchfield.....G 6
54 Porin.....D 7
2 Porkellis.....F 4
6 Porlock.....B 2
6 Porlock Weir.....B 2
53 Port Allen.....E 7
50 Port Appin.....C 6
46 Port Bannatyne...C 6
44 Port Carlisle.....G 1
40 Port Clarence.....C 5
28 Port Dinorwic.....C 5
46 Port Driseach.....B 5
46 Port Elphinstone...F 5
38 Port Erin.....H 1
58 Port Erroll.....D 8
13 Port Eynon.....H 8
47 Port Glasgow.....B 8
54 Port Henderson...B 1
3 Port Isaac.....B 7
46 Port Lamont.....B 6
42 Port Logan.....H 2
41 Port Mulgrave.....C 8
52 Port of Menteith..G 1
63 Port of Ness.....A 6
3 Port Quin.....B 7
50 Port Ramsay.....C 6
38 Port St. Mary.....H 1
51 Port Sonachan....E 7
30 Port Sunlight.....B 2
13 Port Talbot.....H 10
13 Port Tennant....H 10
42 Port William.....G 4
46 Portachoillan.....D 3
46 Port an Eilein.....B 5
46 Portavadie.....B 4
15 Portbury.....G 8
9 Portchester.....F 7
47 Portencross.....D 7
7 Portesham.....H 9
38 Portessie.....A 2
38 Port e Vullen.....G 3
12 Portfield Gate.....E 3
5 Portgate.....G 3
58 Portgordon.....A 1
61 Portgower.....E 9
14 Porth.....E 4
2 Porth Mellin.....H 4
2 Porth Navas.....G 5
3 Porthallow, Corn..D 9
2 Porthallow, Corn..G 5
14 Porthcawl.....G 1
2 Porthcothan Bay..C 6

MAP
2 Porthcurno.....G 1
28 Porthdafarch.....B 2
12 Porthgain.....D 2
2 Porthilly.....B 6
14 Porthkerry.....H 4
2 Porthleven.....G 3
28 Porthmadog.....F 5
2 Porthmeor.....F 2
3 Portholland.....F 7
2 Porthoustock.....G 5
2 Porthowan.....E 4
3 Porthpean.....E 7
13 Porth-y-rhyd, Carm. E 8
13 Porth-y-rhyd, Carm. C 10
51 Portincaple.....H 9
36 Portington.....D 6
51 Portinnisherrich...F 7
38 Portinscale.....C 5
15 Portishead.....G 8
58 Portknockie.....A 2
59 Portlethen.....H 7
2 Portloe.....F 6
61 Portmahomack...H 9
28 Portmeirion.....F 5
3 Portmellon.....E 7
8 Portmore.....F 5
62 Port na Long.....E 3
63 Portnaguiran.....C 6
55 Portnaluchaig.....K 1
60 Portnancon.....B 5
51 Portnellan, Perth..E 11
51 Portnellan, Perth..F 11
50 Portnocroish.....C 6
48 Portobello.....B 6
8 Porton.....B 3
42 Portpatrick.....F 1
2 Portreath.....E 4
62 Portree.....D 4
47 Portrye.....D 7
2 Portscatho.....F 6
9 Portsea.....F 8
61 Portskerra.....A 8
15 Portskewett.....E 8
10 Portslade, Surrey..G 1
10 Portslade, Surrey..G 2
42 Portslogan.....F 1
9 Portsmouth, Hants. F 8
35 Portsmouth, Yorks. E 7
58 Portsoy.....A 3
8 Portswood.....E 6
50 Portuairk.....A 2
63 Portvoller.....C 6
15 Portway, Herefs...A 8
22 Portway, War.....E 4
3 Portwrinkle.....D 10
42 Portyerrock.....H 5
5 Postbridge.....H 5
17 Postcombe.....D 8
11 Postling.....D 10
27 Postlingford.....K 1
26 Postwick.....E 6
59 Potarch.....H 3
47 Poteath.....D 7
44 Potholm.....D 3
17 Potsgrove.....A 10
24 Pott Row.....C 8
31 Pott Shrigley.....B 8
17 Potten End.....C 11
41 Potter Brompton.G 10
26 Potter Heigham...D 7
18 Potter Street.....C 5
33 Potterhanworth...D 7
33 Potterhanworth Booths.....C 8
16 Potterne.....H 1
16 Potterne Wick.....H 1
18 Potters Bar.....D 3
22 Potters Cross.....D 2
23 Potterspury.....H 11
40 Potto.....E 5
25 Potton.....K 3
4 Poughill, Corn.....E 1
4 Poughill, Devon...E 7
16 Poulshot.....H 1
30 Poulton, Ches.....D 3
16 Poulton, Glos.....D 2
34 Poulton-Le-Fylde..C 2
14 Pound.....F 1
22 Pound Bank.....E 1
8 Pound Grn, I.o.W.G 5
10 Pound Grn, Suss..F 4
10 Pound Hill.....D 2
42 Poundland, Ayr...C 3
43 Poundland, Dumf..C 9
17 Poundon.....B 7
10 Poundsbridge.....D 4
5 Poundsgate.....J 6
2 Poundstock.....A 2
53 Pourie.....D 9
45 Powburn.....A 9
6 Powderham.....H 3

MAP
7 Powerstock.....G 8
43 Powfoot.....E 12
53 Powgavie.....E 7
22 Powick.....G 2
4 Powler's Piece....D 2
52 Powmill.....G 5
20 Powys, Co.....E 6
7 Poxwell.....H 11
17 Poyle.....F 11
10 Poynings.....G 1
7 Poyntington.....D 10
31 Poynton.....B 8
30 Poynton Green...H 4
27 Poys Street.....H 6
12 Poyston Cross.....E 3
27 Poystreet Green...J 3
2 Praa Sands.....G 3
62 Prabost.....C 3
18 Pratt's Bottom....H 5
11 Pratt's Heath.....C 7
2 Praze.....F 3
2 Praze-an-Beeble...F 3
2 Predannack Manor Farm.....H 4
30 Prees.....G 4
34 Preesall.....B 2
34 Preesall Park.....C 2
12 Prendergast.....E 3
45 Prendwick.....B 8
13 Pren-gwyn.....C 7
28 Prenteg.....F 5
30 Prenton.....B 2
30 Prescot.....A 3
30 Prescott.....H 3
49 Pressen.....F 11
30 Pressgreen.....G 4
29 Prestatyn.....B 10
31 Prestbury, Ches....C 7
15 Prestbury, Glos...B 12
21 Presteigne.....F 8
21 Presthope.....C 11
7 Prestleigh.....B 9
49 Preston, Ber.....D 10
5 Preston, Devon....H 7
7 Preston, Dorset...H 10
48 Preston, E. Lothian B 6
49 Preston, E. Lothian B 8
37 Preston, E. Riding.D 9
15 Preston, Glos.....A 10
16 Preston, Glos.....D 2
18 Preston, Herts.....A 2
11 Preston, Kent.....B 9
11 Preston, Kent.....B 11
34 Preston, Lancs....D 4
45 Preston, Northumb. E 12
23 Preston, Rut.....B 12
10 Preston, Sussex...G 2
27 Preston, W. Riding K 2
16 Preston, Wilts.....F 1
22 Preston Bagot.....E 5
17 Preston Bissett....A 7
6 Preston Bowyer...D 5
30 Preston Brockhurst H 4
30 Preston Brook...B 4
9 Preston Candover..B 7
23 Preston Capes....G 9
17 Preston Crowmarsh E 7
30 Preston Gubbals..H 4
22 Preston on Stour..G 5
30 Preston on the Hill.B 4
21 Preston on Wye...H 9
7 Preston Plucknett..E 8
21 Preston upon the Weald Moors..A 12
21 Preston Wynne..H 11
43 Prestonmill.....F 10
48 Prestonpans.....B 6
40 Preston-under-Scar F 1
35 Prestwich, Lancs...G 7
47 Prestwick, Ayr....G 8
45 Prestwick, Northumb. F 10
17 Prestwood.....D 9
14 Price Town.....E 3
25 Prickwillow.....G 7
7 Priddy.....A 8
39 Priest Hulton.....H 7
44 Priesthaugh.....C 3
47 Priesthill.....C 10
47 Priestland.....F 10
21 Priestweston.....C 8
23 Primethorpe.....C 8
24 Primrose Hill, Cambs. F 5
32 Primrose Hill, Notts. D 2
49 Primrosehill, Ber..D 10
17 Primrosehill, Herts. D 11
49 Primsidemill.....G 10

MAP
12 Princes Gate.....F 5
17 Princes Risborough D 9
23 Princethorpe.....E 7
5 Princetown, Devon. H 5
14 Princetown, Glam. C 4
49 Printonan.....E 10
29 Prion.....D 10
21 Priors Frame.....H 11
23 Priors Hardwick..G 8
23 Priors Marston....F 8
21 Priorslee.....A 12
21 Priory Wood.....H 8
15 Priston.....H 10
19 Prittlewell.....E 8
9 Privett.....C 8
4 Prixford.....B 4
2 Probus.....E 6
43 Prospect.....G 12
58 Protstonhill.....A 6
45 Prudhoe.....G 9
51 Ptarmigan Lodge.G 10
51 Pubil.....C 11
15 Publow.....H 9
18 Puckeridge.....B 4
7 Puckington.....D 7
15 Pucklechurch.....G 10
8 Pucknall.....D 5
30 Puddington, Ches..C 2
4 Puddington, Devon. E 7
26 Puddledock.....F 4
7 Puddletown.....G 10
21 Pudlestone.....F 11
35 Pudsey.....D 11
9 Pulborough.....D 12
30 Puleston.....H 6
30 Pulford.....D 2
7 Pulham.....E 10
27 Pulham Market...G 5
27 Pulham St. Margaret G 5
25 Pulloxhill.....M 2
48 Pumpherston.....B 3
43 Pumplaburn.....B 12
13 Pumpsaint.....C 10
12 Puncheston.....D 3
7 Puncknoll.....G 9
10 Punnett's Town...F 5
9 Purbrook.....E 8
44 Purdomstone.....E 1
8 Purewell.....G 3
18 Purfleet.....F 5
7 Puriton.....B 7
19 Purleigh.....D 8
17 Purley, Berks.....F 7
18 Purley, London...H 3
25 Purls Bridge.....G 6
7 Purse Caundle...D 10
21 Purslow.....D 9
36 Purston Jaglin.....E 2
7 Purtington.....E 7
15 Purton, Glos.....D 10
16 Purton, Wilts.....E 2
16 Purton Stoke.....E 2
49 Purvishaugh.....E 8
23 Pury End.....H 10
16 Pusey.....D 4
4 Putford.....D 2
15 Putley.....A 9
18 Putney.....F 2
4 Putsborough.....B 3
17 Puttenham, Bucks..C 9
9 Puttenham, Surrey A 10
15 Puxton.....H 7
13 Pwll.....G 8
13 Pwllcrochan.....G 3
28 Pwlldefaid.....H 1
14 Pwllgloyw.....A 3
28 Pwllheli.....G 3
15 Pwll-Meyric.....E 8
12 Pwlltrap.....E 6
13 Pwll-y-glaw.....H 11
29 Pydew.....B 7
32 Pye Bridge.....E 2
18 Pye Corner, Herts..C 4
15 Pye Corner, Mon..F 7
22 Pye Green.....A 3
10 Pyecombe.....G 2
14 Pyle, Glam.....F 2
8 Pyle, I.o.W.....H 6
7 Pylle.....B 9
25 Pymore.....G 6
17 Pyrford.....H 11
14 Pyrgad.....C 4
17 Pyrton.....E 8
23 Pytchley.....E 12
4 Pyworthy.....F 2
21 Quabbs.....D 7
24 Quadring.....B 3
17 Quainton.....B 8
8 Quarley.....B 4
31 Quarndon, Derby. F 11

MAP
23 Quarndon, Leics...A 9
47 Quarrier's Homes..C 8
24 Quarrington.....A 2
40 Quarrington Hill...A 4
22 Quarry Bank.....C 3
30 Quarrybank.....D 4
58 Quarryburn.....A 6
56 Quarryhill.....B 3
56 Quarrywood.....C 7
47 Quarter.....D 12
6 Quartley.....D 3
22 Quat.....C 1
22 Quatford.....C 1
40 Quebec.....A 2
15 Quedgeley.....C 11
25 Queen Adelaide...G 7
15 Queen Charlton...H 9
4 Queen Dart.....D 7
7 Queen Oak.....C 11
10 Queen Street.....D 6
11 Queenborough.....A 8
7 Queens Camel....D 9
30 Queens Head.....G 2
30 Queen's Park.....E 2
35 Queensbury.....D 9
29 Queensferry, Flint. C 12
48 Queensferry, W. Loth. B 4
34 Queenstown.....D 2
47 Queenzieburn.....B 11
16 Quemerford.....G 1
64 Quendale.....F 7
25 Quendon.....M 6
23 Queniborough...A 10
16 Quenington.....D 2
34 Quernmore.....A 4
3 Quethiock.....C 10
27 Quidenham.....G 3
8 Quidhampton, Hants. A 6
8 Quidhampton, Wilts. C 3
58 Quilquox.....D 6
38 Quine's Hill.....H 2
50 Quinish House...B 2
23 Quinton.....G 11
2 Quintrel Downs...D 5
49 Quixwood.....C 10
4 Quoditch.....F 3
52 Quoig.....E 3
48 Quothquan.....E 3
64 Quoys.....D 7
62 Raasay House (Hotel) D 5
4 Rabscott.....C 6
30 Raby.....B 2
4 Rackenford.....D 7
9 Rackham.....E 11
26 Rackheath Com...D 6
43 Racks.....D 11
64 Rackwick, Orkney.D 1
64 Rackwick, Orkney.A 2
31 Radbourne.....G 11
34 Radcliffe, Lancs....F 6
45 Radcliffe, Northumb. C 11
32 Radcliffe on Soar..G 2
32 Radcliffe on Trent.F 4
17 Radclive.....A 7
16 Radcot.....D 4
56 Raddery House...D 3
23 Radford Semele...F 7
7 Radipole.....H 10
18 Radlett.....D 2
16 Radley.....D 6
17 Radnage.....D 8
7 Radstock.....A 10
23 Radstone.....H 9
23 Radway.....G 7
30 Radway Green.....E 6
25 Radwell.....J 1
25 Radwinter.....L 7
14 Radyr.....F 5
48 Raecleugh.....H 3
63 Raerinish.....D 5
60 Raffin.....D 2
56 Rafford.....D 6
32 Ragdale.....H 4
53 Ragfield.....F 10
15 Raglan.....D 7
32 Ragnall.....C 5
34 Rainford.....G 4
18 Rainham, Essex...F 5
15 Rainham, Kent...B 7
11 Rainham Mark...A 7
30 Rainhill.....A 4
30 Rainhill Stoops...A 4
31 Rainow.....C 8
40 Rainton.....H 4
32 Rainworth.....D 3
39 Raisbeck.....D 9
44 Raise.....H 5

MAP

36 Raisthorpe......A 6
53 Rait......D 7
33 Raithby, Lincs...C 10
33 Raithby, Lincs...B 10
9 Rake......C 9
11 Ram Lane......C 8
62 Ramasaig......D 1
3 Rame, Corn...E 11
2 Rame, Corn...F 4
7 Rampisham......F 9
34 Rampside......A 1
25 Rampton, Cambs. H 5
32 Rampton, Notts...B 5
35 Ramsbottom......E 7
16 Ramsbury......G 4
61 Ramscraigs...D 10
9 Ramsdean......D 8
17 Ramsdell......H 7
16 Ramsden......C 4
19 Ramsden BellhouseE 7
19 Ramsden Heath...D 7
27 Ramsey, Essex...M 5
25 Ramsey, Hunts...G 4
38 Ramsey, I.o.M....G 2
19 Ramsey Island...C 9
25 Ramsey St. Mary's G 4
48 Ramseycleuch....H 5
11 Ramsgate......B 12
26 Ramsgate Street..B 4
40 Ramsgill......H 1
45 Ramshaw......H 8
44 Ramshope......C 6
31 Ramshorn......F 9
5 Ramsley......G 5
9 Ramsnest Com...C 11
32 Ranby......B 4
33 Rand......B 8
15 Randwick......D 11
47 Ranfurly......C 9
31 Rangemore......H 10
15 Rangeworthy....F 10
47 Rankinston......H 9
9 Ranmore Com...A 12
34 Rann......E 6
38 Rannerdale......C 4
51 Rannoch Station.B 11
55 Ranochan......L 2
6 Ranscombe......B 3
32 Ranskill......A 4
31 Ranton......H 7
26 Ranworth......D 7
64 Rapness......B 3
55 Rarsaidh......H 2
43 Rascarre......G 9
58 Rashiereive......E 7
40 Raskelf......H 5
14 Rassau......C 5
35 Rastrick......E 10
55 Ratagan......H 3
23 Ratby......B 8
23 Ratcliffe Culey...B 7
23 Ratcliffe on the
    Wreake......A 9
58 Rathen......B 7
53 Rathillet......E 8
35 Rathmell......A 7
48 Ratho......B 4
48 Ratho Station...B 4
58 Rathven......A 2
23 Ratley......G 7
21 Ratlinghope......C 9
61 Rattar......A 11
5 Rattery......K 6
27 Rattlesden......J 3
53 Rattray......C 7
38 Raughton Head...A 6
25 Raunds......H 1
49 Ravelaw......D 11
36 Ravenfield......H 3
38 Ravenglass......F 3
26 Raveningham.....F 7
41 Ravenscar......E 10
38 Ravensdale......G 2
25 Ravensden......K 2
32 Ravenshead......E 3
30 Ravensmoor......E 5
23 Ravensthorpe,
    Northants......E 10
35 Ravensthorpe, Yorks.
    E 10
23 Ravenstone, Bucks.
    G 11
23 Ravenstone, Leics..A 7
39 Ravenstonedale...E 9
48 Ravenstruther....E 2
40 Ravensworth.....D 2
41 Raw......E 9
49 Rawburn......D 9
36 Rawcliffe, Yorks...E 5
36 Rawcliffe, Yorks...B 4
36 Rawcliffe Bridge..E 5
35 Rawdon......C 11
36 Rawmarsh......G 2

MAP

19 Rawreth......E 8
6 Rawridge......F 5
47 Raws......E 9
35 Rawtenstall......E 7
47 Rawyards......C 12
58 Raxton......D 6
27 Raydon......L 3
19 Rayleigh......E 8
7 Raymond's Hill...F 7
19 Rayne......B 7
25 Reach......J 7
34 Read......D 6
17 Reading......G 8
11 Reading Street...E 8
39 Reagill......C 8
61 Rearquhar......C 7
23 Rearsby......A 10
61 Reaster......A 11
45 Reaveley......A 8
64 Reawick......D 6
61 Reay......B 9
11 Reculver......A 11
6 Red Ball......E 4
64 Red Banks......C 3
44 Red Dial......H 1
22 Red Hill......G 2
5 Red Post......J 7
34 Red Rock......F 5
12 Red Roses......F 5
45 Red Row......C 10
31 Red Street......E 7
28 Red Wharf......B 5
12 Redberth......G 4
17 Redbourn......C 12
37 Redbourne......G 7
18 Redbridge......E 4
30 Redbrook, Flint...F 4
15 Redbrook, Mon...C 8
11 Redbrook Street..D 8
56 Redburn, Nairn...E 5
44 Redburn, Northumb.
    G 6
56 Redburn, Ross &
    Cromarty......C 1
40 Redcar......C 6
53 Redcastle, Angus. B 11
56 Redcastle, Ross &
    Cromarty......E 1
15 Redcliffe Bay...G 7
47 Redcraig......G 9
49 Redden......F 10
48 Redding......B 2
48 Reddingmuirhead..B 2
35 Reddish......H 8
22 Redditch......E 4
47 Reddochbraes...F 12
27 Redenhall......G 6
44 Redesdale Camp..C 6
45 Redesmouth......E 7
53 Redford, Angus..C 10
59 Redford, Kinc...K 5
48 Redfordgreen.....H 6
52 Redgorton......D 6
27 Redgrave......G 3
59 Redheugh......L 2
58 Redhill, Aber...D 4
59 Redhill, Aber...G 5
15 Redhill, Somerset. H 8
10 Redhill, Surrey...C 2
46 Redhouse......C 3
27 Redisham......G 7
15 Redland, Glos....G 9
64 Redland, Orkney..C 2
27 Redlingfield......H 5
8 Redlynch, Dorset..D 4
7 Redlynch, Som...C 10
38 Redmain......B 4
15 Redmarley D'Abitot
    A 10
40 Redmarshall......C 4
32 Redmile......G 5
40 Redmire......F 1
3 Redmoor......D 8
59 Redmyre......K 5
30 Rednal......G 2
49 Redpath......F 8
54 Redpoint......C 1
2 Redruth......E 4
48 Redscarhead......E 5
15 Redwick, Glos....F 8
15 Redwick, Mon....F 7
40 Redworth......C 3
25 Reed......L 5
26 Reedham......E 7
36 Reedness......E 6
49 Reedy Loch......D 11
63 Reef......C 2
33 Reepham, Lincs...C 7
26 Reepham, Norf...C 4
40 Reeth......E 1
38 Regaby......F 2
56 Rehaurie......E 5
61 Reidhbreac......G 7

MAP

60 Reiff......E 2
10 Reigate......C 1
41 Reighton......H 11
41 Reighton Gap...G 11
58 Reisque......E 6
61 Reiss......B 12
2 Rejerrah......D 5
2 Releath......F 4
43 Relief......D 12
2 Relubbus......F 3
56 Relugas......E 5
17 Remenham......F 8
17 Remenham Hill...F 9
52 Remony......C 3
32 Rempstone......H 3
16 Rendcomb......C 1
27 Rendham......J 6
47 Renfrew......C 10
47 Renfrew, Co....C 9
25 Renhold......K 2
32 Renishaw......B 2
45 Rennington......A 10
47 Renton......B 9
39 Renwick......A 8
19 Repps......D 7
31 Repton......G 11
55 Reraig......G 2
53 Rescobie......B 10
50 Resipol......A 4
56 Resolis......C 2
14 Resolven......D 2
55 Resourie......M 2
49 Reston......C 11
2 Retew......D 6
19 Rettendon......D 7
19 Rettendon Place...D 7
2 Retyn......D 6
50 Reudle......C 1
33 Revesby......D 10
8 Rew Street......G 6
6 Rewe......F 3
27 Reydon......G 8
26 Reymerston......E 3
12 Reynalton......F 4
13 Reynoldston......H 8
3 Rezare......B 10
15 Rhadyr......D 7
13 Rhandir-mwyn...C 11
20 Rhayader......F 5
60 Rhegreanoch......E 3
56 Rheindown......E 1
50 Rhemore......C 3
29 Rhewl, Denb....D 10
29 Rhewl, Denb....F 11
60 Rhicarn......E 2
60 Rhiconich......B 4
60 Rhidorroch......C 3
60 Rhidorroch Old Lodge
    G 4
28 Rhid-y-sarn......F 6
61 Rhifail......C 7
14 Rhigos......D 3
60 Rhimichie......B 4
56 Rhinduie......E 1
60 Rhiroy......G 3
28 Rhiw......G 2
28 Rhiwbryfdir......F 6
14 Rhiwderyn......F 6
28 Rhiwlas, Caer....D 5
29 Rhiwlas, Denb.. G 11
29 Rhiwlas, Mer.....F 8
3 Rhode......C 6
11 Rhodes Minnis...D 10
32 Rhodesia......B 3
13 Rhodiad......D 1
14 Rhoose......H 4
13 Rhos, Carm....C 7
13 Rhos, Glam....G 10
13 Rhos Amman......F 10
12 Rhos-Hill......C 5
28 Rhoscolyn......C 2
12 Rhoscrowther......G 3
29 Rhosesmor......C 11
12 Rhosfach......D 5
28 Rhos-fawr......B 4
28 Rhosgadfan......D 4
28 Rhosgoch, Angl...A 3
21 Rhos goch, Rad...H 7
28 Rhos-lan......F 4
28 Rhoslefain......B 1
29 Rhosllanerchrugog
    F 12
13 Rhosmaen......E 9
28 Rhos-meirch......B 4
28 Rhosneigr......C 3
29 Rhos-on-Sea......B 8
13 Rhossili......H 7
12 Rhosson......D 1
28 Rhostryfan......D 4
30 Rhostyllen......E 2
28 Rhosybol......A 4
29 Rhos-y-gwaliau...G 9

MAP

28 Rhos-y-llan......F 2
46 Rhu, Argyll......C 3
47 Rhu, Dunb......A 7
54 Rhu Noa......C 4
29 Rhuallt......C 10
46 Rhubodach......B 5
30 Rhuddall Heath...D 4
29 Rhuddlan......B 9
4 Rhude Cross......E 1
21 Rhulen......G 7
46 Rhunahaorine......E 2
28 Rhyd, Mer......F 6
20 Rhyd, Mont......B 5
28 Rhyd-Ddu......E 5
13 Rhyd-Lewis......B 7
29 Rhyd-Lydan......C 9
13 Rhydargaeau......D 8
14 Rhydberry......A 3
29 Rhydcymerau......C 9
22 Rhydd......H 2
13 Rhydding......G 10
13 Rhyddlan......C 8
29 Rhyd-leos......G 11
28 Rhydlios......G 1
20 Rhydlydan......C 6
13 Rhydowen......C 8
20 Rhydrosser......F 1
21 Rhydspence......H 8
29 Rhydtalog......E 11
28 Rhydwyn......A 3
29 Rhyd-y-croesau. G 11
28 Rhydyelafdy......G 3
14 Rhydyfelin......E 4
20 Rhyd-y-felin......D 2
13 Rhyd-y-fro......F 10
21 Rhyd-y-groes......B 8
29 Rhydymain......H 7
14 Rhyd-y-meirch...D 6
29 Rhydymwyn......D 11
28 Rhyd-yr-onmen..B 2
20 Rhyfud......F 2
29 Rhyl......B 9
14 Rhymney......D 4
53 Rhynd, Fife......E 9
52 Rhynd, Perth......E 6
58 Rhynie......A 2
22 Ribble......E 1
39 Ribblehead......G 10
34 Ribbleton......D 4
34 Ribby......D 3
34 Ribchester......D 5
60 Ribigill......B 4
37 Riby......F 9
37 Riby Cross Roads .F 9
36 Riccall......C 4
47 Riccarton......F 9
44 Riccarton Junction C 4
21 Richards Castle . E 10
17 Richings Park....F 11
18 Richmond, London F 2
40 Richmond, Yorks..E 2
59 Rickarton......H 5
31 Rickerscote......H 7
27 Rickinghall Inferior
    H 3
10 Riverhead......B 4
27 Rickinghall Superior
    H 3
25 Rickling......M 6
18 Rickling Green....A 5
17 Rickmansworth...E 11
44 Riddings, Cumb...E 3
32 Riddings, Derby...E 2
4 Riddlecombe......E 5
35 Riddlesden......C 9
8 Ridge, Dorset......G 1
8 Ridge, Hants......D 5
18 Ridge, Herts......D 2
8 Ridge, Wilts......C 1
10 Ridge Green......C 2
22 Ridge Lane......C 6
20 Ridgebourne......F 6
15 Ridgehill......H 8
32 Ridgeway......B 1
21 Ridgeway Cross..H 12
25 Ridgewell......L 8
10 Ridgewood......F 3
25 Ridgmont......L 1
45 Riding Mill......G 8
10 Ridley, Kent......B 5
44 Ridley, Northumb. G 6
30 Ridley Green......E 4
26 Ridlington, Norf...B 6
23 Ridlington, Rut...B 11
58 Ridsdale......B 5
52 Riechip......B 5
52 Riemore......B 5
60 Rienachait......C 9
40 Rievaulx......G 6
55 Rifern......K 2
47 Rigfoot......D 9
44 Rigg......F 1
47 Riggend......B 12
47 Righead......F 10

MAP

56 Righoul......E 4
39 Rigmaden Park...G 8
33 Rigsby......C 11
41 Rigside......F 2
22 Rileyhill......A 5
3 Rilla Mill......B 10
41 Rillington......H 8
35 Rimington......C 7
7 Rimpton......D 9
61 Rimsdale......C 7
37 Rimswell......D 10
12 Rinaston......D 3
43 Ringford......F 8
13 Ringinglow......B 11
26 Ringland......D 4
10 Ringles Cross......F 3
10 Ringmer......G 4
5 Ringmore, Devon. J 8
5 Ringmore, Devon. L 5
56 Ringorm......E 3
24 Ring's End......E 5
27 Ringsfield......G 7
27 Ringsfield Corner..G 7
17 Ringshall, Bucks..C 10
27 Ringshall, Suffolk. K 3
27 Ringshall Stocks..K 4
24 Ringstead, Norf...B 8
25 Ringstead, Northants.
    H 1
8 Ringwood......F 3
11 Ringwould......C 12
58 Rinmore......F 2
64 Rinnigill......E 2
3 Rinsey......G 3
10 Ripe......G 4
21 Ripley, Derby......E 1
8 Ripley, Hants......F 3
17 Ripley, Surrey...H 11
35 Ripley, Yorks....A 11
28 Riplingham......D 7
40 Ripon......H 3
24 Rippingale......C 2
11 Ripple, Kent......C 12
22 Ripple, Worcs....G 1
35 Ripponden......E 9
21 Risbury......G 11
18 Risby, Essex......J 1
37 Risby, Yorks......F 7
14 Risca......E 6
37 Rise......C 9
24 Risegate......C 3
33 Riseholme......C 7
25 Riseley, Beds....J 1
17 Riseley, Berks....H 8
27 Rishangles......H 4
34 Rishton......D 6
35 Rishworth......E 9
25 Risley......G 2
40 Risplith......H 3
60 Rispond......A 5
16 Rivar......H 4
19 Rivenhall End....B 8
25 River Bank......H 6
10 Riverhead......B 4
4 Riverton......C 5
34 Rivington......F 5
23 Roachill......D 3
23 Roade......G 11
44 Roadhead......F 4
48 Roadmeetings....F 3
47 Roadside, Ayr...H 10
61 Roadside, Caith...B 11
59 Roadside of Catterline
    J 6
59 Roadside of Kinneff
    K 6
6 Roadwater......B 4
62 Roag......D 2
42 Roan of Craigoch.A 4
14 Roansgreen......E 3
14 Roath......F 5
43 Roberthill......D 12
33 Roberton, Lan....B 1
44 Roberton, Selkirk..B 3
10 Robertsbridge.....F 6
35 Roberttown......E 10
12 Robeston Cross...F 2
12 Robeston Wathen.K 4
35 Robin Hood......D 11
31 Robin Hood Inn .C 11
41 Robin Hood's Bay.E 9
4 Roborough......D 4
30 Roby......A 3
34 Roby Mill......F 4
31 Rocester......F 9
12 Roch......E 2
12 Roch Gate......E 2
35 Rochdale......F 7
3 Roche......D 7
10 Rochester, Kent...A 6
44 Rochester, Northumb.
    C 6
19 Rochford......E 8

MAP

2 Rock, Cornwall...B 6
45 Rock, Northumb.A 10
9 Rock, Sussex......E 12
22 Rock, Worcs......E 1
30 Rock Ferry......B 2
22 Rock Hill......E 3
6 Rockbeare......G 4
44 Rockcliffe, Cumb..G 2
43 Rockcliffe, Kirk..F 9
15 Rockfield, Mon....C 8
61 Rockfield, Ross &
    Cromarty......H 9
8 Rockford......E 3
15 Rockhampton......E 9
26 Rockheath......D 6
23 Rockingham......C 12
26 Rockland All Saints F 3
26 Rockland St. Mary E 6
26 Rockland St. Peter. F 3
16 Rockley......G 3
17 Rockwell End......E 9
6 Rockwell Green...D 5
15 Rodborough......D 11
16 Rodbourne, Wilts..F 2
15 Rodbourne, Wilts. F 12
16 Rodbourne Cheney E 2
21 Rodd......F 8
49 Roddam......G 12
49 Roddam Rigg...G 12
7 Rodden......H 9
7 Rode......A 11
30 Rode Heath......D 6
31 Rodeheath......C 7
63 Rodel......H 1
21 Roden......A 11
6 Rodhuish......B 4
21 Rodington......A 11
15 Rodley......C 10
15 Rodmarton......D 12
10 Rodmell......G 3
11 Rodmersham......B 8
7 Rodney Stoke......A 8
31 Rodsley......F 10
6 Rodway......B 6
7 Rodwell......H 7
35 Roecliffe......A 12
18 Roehampton......G 2
64 Roesound......C 7
10 Roffey......E 1
61 Rogart......F 7
9 Rogate......D 9
14 Rogerstone......E 6
47 Rogerton......D 11
15 Rogiet......E 8
55 Rollesby......D 7
23 Rolleston, Leics..B 10
32 Rolleston, Notts...E 5
31 Rolleston, Staffs. G 10
37 Rolston......C 10
11 Rolvenden......E 7
11 Rolvenden Layne..E 7
39 Romaldkirk......C 12
26 Roman Hill......F 8
40 Romanby......F 4
48 Romannobridge...E 4
4 Romansleigh......D 6
62 Romesdal......C 3
18 Romford......E 5
31 Romiley......A 8
8 Romsey......D 5
22 Romsley, Salop...D 1
22 Romsley, Salop...D 3
38 Ronague......H 1
41 Rookdale......H 9
39 Rookhope......A 11
6 Rookley......H 6
7 Rooks Bridge......A 7
6 Rook's Nest......C 4
37 Roos......D 10
48 Rootpark......D 2
9 Ropley......C 8
9 Ropley Dean......C 7
33 Ropsley......G 7
58 Rora......C 8
58 Rorandle......F 4
21 Rorrington......B 8
2 Rose......D 5
4 Rose Ash......D 7
10 Rose Hill......F 3
10 Roseacre, Kent....C 6
34 Roseacre, Lancs...C 3
48 Rosebank......D 1
45 Rosebrough......C 12
12 Rosebush......D 4
2 Rosecare......B 2
41 Rosedale Abbey...F 7
45 Roseden......A 8
60 Rosehall......F 5
58 Rosehearty......A 7
30 Rosehill......G 5
56 Roseisle......C 7
12 Rosemarket......F 3
56 Rosemarkie......D 3

MAP
6 Rosemary Lane...E 5
47 Rosemount, Ayr...F 8
53 Rosemount, Perth..C 7
2 Rosenannon......C 6
2 Rosewarne........F 3
48 Rosewell.........C 5
40 Roseworth.........C 4
2 Roseworthy.......F 3
39 Rosgill...........D 8
55 Roshven..........L 1
62 Roskhill..........D 2
38 Rosley...........A 6
48 Roslin..........C 5
51 Rosliston.........H 11
47 Rosneath.........A 7
43 Ross, Kirk........G 7
45 Ross, Northumb..B 12
54 Ross & Cromarty, County.........B 6
15 Ross-on-Wye.....B 9
30 Rossett..........D 2
52 Rossie Ochill......F 6
36 Rossington.......G 4
55 Rosskeen.........C 2
47 Rossland.........B 9
61 Roster..........C 11
30 Rostherne........B 6
38 Rosthwaite.......D 5
31 Roston..........F 10
2 Rosudgeon.......G 3
48 Rosyth..........A 4
45 Rothbury.........C 9
23 Rotherby........A 10
10 Rotherfield.......E 4
17 Rotherfield Greys..F 8
17 Rotherfield Peppard F 8
32 Rotherham.......A 2
23 Rothersthorpe.....F 10
17 Rotherwick........H 8
56 Rothes...........E 8
46 Rothesay.........C 6
58 Rothiebrisbane....D 5
58 Rothienorman....D 5
64 Rothiesholm......C 4
45 Rothill...........B 9
23 Rothley...........A 9
58 Rothmaise........D 4
37 Rothwell, Lincs....G 9
23 Rothwell, Northants. D 11
35 Rothwell, Yorks..D 12
35 Rothwell Haigh..D 12
37 Rotsea...........B 8
59 Rottal...........K 1
10 Rottingdean.......H 3
38 Rottington.......D 2
43 Roucan.........D 11
8 Roud............H 6
31 Rough Close......F 8
11 Rough Common..B 10
31 Rough Hay......H 10
26 Rougham.........C 1
27 Rougham Green...J 2
55 Roughburn.......L 7
35 Roughlee.........C 7
22 Roughley........B 5
44 Roughsike........E 3
33 Roughton, Lincs...D 9
26 Roughton, Norf...B 5
22 Roughton, Salop..C 1
47 Roughwood......D 8
17 Round Oak.......H 7
7 Roundham.........E 7
35 Roundhay.......C 12
43 Roundstonefoot..A 12
9 Roundstreet Com. C 12
16 Roundway.........H 1
22 Rous Lench......G 4
6 Rousdon.........G 6
56 Routdaneburn....D 7
47 Routenburn......C 7
37 Routh...........C 8
61 Rovie Lodge.......F 7
3 Row, Cornwall....B 8
39 Row, Westmor....F 7
44 Rowanburn.......E 2
51 Rowardennan Hotel H 10
31 Rowarth.........A 8
16 Rowde...........H 1
15 Rowden Down...G 12
29 Ro-wen..........C 7
44 Rowfoot..........G 5
19 Rowhedge........B 10
9 Rowhook.......C 12
22 Rowington........E 5
31 Rowland.........C 10
9 Rowland's Castle..E 9
45 Rowland's Gill...G 10
9 Rowledge........B 9
21 Rowley, Salop....B 8
37 Rowley, Yorks....D 7

MAP
22 Rowley Regis.....C 3
15 Rowlstone........B 7
9 Rowly...........B 11
22 Rowney Green....E 4
8 Rownhams.......D 5
17 Rowsham........B 9
31 Rowsley.........D 11
33 Rowston.........E 8
30 Rowton, Ches.....D 3
30 Rowton, Salop....H 5
49 Roxburgh........F 9
49 Roxburgh, Co.....H 9
49 Roxburgh Newtown F9
37 Roxby, Lincs......E 7
41 Roxby, Yorks.....D 7
25 Roxton..........K 3
18 Roxwell..........C 6
34 Royal Oak........G 3
55 Roybridge........L 6
18 Roydon, Essex....C 4
27 Roydon, Norfolk..G 4
24 Roydon, Norfolk..C 8
25 Royston, Herts....L 5
35 Royston, Yorks...F 12
35 Royton..........F 8
29 Ruabon.........F 12
2 Ruan High Lanes..F 6
2 Ruan Lanihorne...E 6
2 Ruan Minor......H 4
15 Ruardean........C 9
15 Ruardean Woodside C 9
22 Rubery..........D 3
39 Ruckcroft........A 8
21 Ruckhall Com...H 10
11 Ruckinge........E 9
33 Ruckland........B 10
21 Ruckley.........B 10
40 Rudby...........D 5
45 Rudchester.......F 9
32 Ruddington......G 3
15 Rudford.........B 11
7 Rudge..........A 11
15 Rudgeway........F 9
9 Rudgwick.......C 12
15 Rudhall.........B 9
14 Rudry...........F 5
41 Rudston.........H 11
31 Rudyard.........D 8
49 Ruecastle........G 8
34 Rufford..........F 3
36 Rufforth..........B 3
45 Ruffside.........H 8
23 Rugby...........E 8
31 Rugeley..........H 9
56 Ruilick..........E 1
6 Ruishton.........D 6
18 Ruislip..........E 1
18 Ruislip Common..E 1
44 Ruletownhead.....B 4
49 Rumbletonlaw.....E 9
52 Rumblingbridge...G 5
27 Rumburgh.......G 6
2 Rumford.........C 6
14 Rumney.........F 5
52 Runacraig........F 1
30 Runcorn.........B 4
9 Runcton.........F 10
24 Runcton Holme...E 7
5 Rundlestone......H 4
9 Runfold..........A 10
26 Runhall..........E 4
26 Runham..........D 7
6 Runnington.......D 5
19 Runsell Green.....C 8
41 Runswick.........D 8
57 Runtaleave.......M 8
19 Runwell.........D 7
17 Ruscombe........F 9
56 Rosehaugh House.D 2
19 Rush Green.......B 11
15 Rushall, Herefs....A 9
27 Rushall, Norfolk..G 5
22 Rushall, Staffs.....B 4
8 Rushall, Wilts.....A 3
27 Rushbrooke.......J 2
21 Rushbury.......C 10
25 Rushden, Herts...M 4
25 Rushden, Northants. J 1
27 Rushford.........G 2
10 Rushlake Green ..F 5
27 Rushmere........G 8
27 Rushmere St. Andrew K 5
27 Rushmere Street...K 5
9 Rushmoor, Surrey B 10
8 Rushmore, Wilts...D 1
22 Rushock.........E 2
35 Rusholme........H 7
30 Rushton, Ches....D 4
23 Rushton, Northants. D 11

MAP
21 Rushton, Salop...B 11
31 Rushton Spencer..D 8
22 Rushwick........G 2
40 Rushyford........B 3
52 Ruskie...........G 1
33 Ruskington.......E 8
43 Rusko...........F 7
38 Rusland..........F 6
10 Rusper..........D 1
15 Ruspidge........C 9
10 Russell's Green...G 6
17 Russell's Water...E 8
9 Rustington.......F 11
41 Ruston..........G 9
37 Ruston Parva.....A 8
41 Ruswarp.........D 9
49 Rutherford.......F 9
47 Rutherglen.......C 11
3 Ruthernbridge....C 7
29 Ruthin..........D 10
59 Ruthrieston.......G 7
58 Ruthven, Aber....C 3
53 Ruthven, Angus...B 7
49 Ruthven, Ber.....E 10
56 Ruthven, Inver....F 4
57 Ruthven, Inver.....J 3
53 Ruthven House...B 8
2 Ruthvoes.........D 6
43 Ruthwell........E 11
15 Ruxton Green.....B 8
30 Ruyton Eleven Towns H 3
45 Ryal............F 8
7 Ryall............G 7
10 Ryarsh..........B 5
38 Rydal...........E 6
9 Ryde............G 7
4 Rydon...........F 2
11 Rye.............F 8
11 Rye Foreign......F 7
11 Rye Harbour......F 8
43 Ryemuir........D 11
29 Ryhall...........D 1
36 Ryhill, Yorks......F 2
37 Ryhill, Yorks.....E 10
45 Ryhope.........H 12
33 Ryland..........B 7
35 Rylstone.........A 8
7 Ryme Intrinseca...E 9
49 Ryslaw..........E 10
36 Ryther...........C 3
45 Ryton, Dur.......G 9
15 Ryton, Glos......A 10
21 Ryton, Salop.....B 10
22 Ryton, Salop......B 1
41 Ryton, Yorks.....H 8
23 Ryton-on-Dunsmore E 7
34 Sabden..........C 6
18 Sacombe.........B 3
45 Sacriston........H 10
40 Sadberge.........C 4
46 Saddell..........F 3
23 Saddington.......C 10
24 Saddle Bow......D 7
8 Saddle Heath.....E 3
35 Saddleworth......F 9
39 Sadgill..........E 7
25 Saffron Walden...L 6
12 Sageston.........G 4
26 Saham Hills......E 2
26 Saham Toney.....E 2
30 Saighton.........D 3
55 Sailean..........C 6
49 St. Abbs.........C 11
2 St. Agnes, Corn....E 4
2 St. Agnes, Is. of Scilly.....D 2
18 St. Albans.......C 2
2 St. Allen.........E 5
53 St. Andrews.....E 10
14 St. Andrews Major G 5
34 St. Anne's........D 2
43 St. Ann's.........B 11
3 St. Ann's Chapel, Cornwall......C 11
5 St. Ann's Chapel, Devon.........L 5
2 St. Anthony......G 5
10 St. Anthony's Hill H 5
15 St. Arvans........E 8
29 St. Asaph........C 9
14 St. Athan.........G 3
3 St. Austell.......D 7
7 St. Bartholomew's Hill...........D 12
38 St. Bees.........D 2
3 St. Blazey........D 8
3 St. Blazey Gate...D 7
49 St. Boswells......F 8
3 St. Breock.......C 7
3 St. Breward......B 8
15 St. Briavels.......D 9

MAP
12 St. Brides.........F 2
14 St. Brides Major..G 2
15 St. Brides Netherwent.....E 7
14 St. Bride's-super-Ely.............G 4
14 St. Bride's Wentlooge......F 6
38 St. Bridget Beckermet......E 3
5 St. Budeaux......K 3
2 St. Buryan........G 1
15 St. Catherine....G 11
51 St. Catherines.....G 8
12 St. Clears.........E 6
3 St. Cleer.........C 9
2 St. Clement.......E 5
3 St. Clether.......A 9
46 St. Colmac.......C 5
2 St. Columb Major.C 6
2 St. Columb Minor.C 5
2 St. Columb Porth..C 5
2 St. Columb Road..D 6
58 St. Combs.........A 8
27 St. Cross South Elmham........G 6
49 St. Cuthberts......E 11
12 St. David's, Pemb. D 1
52 St. David's, Perth..E 4
2 St. Day..........E 4
6 St. Decumans.....B 4
2 St. Dennis........D 6
15 St. Devereux......A 7
12 St. Dogmaels.....B 5
12 St. Dogwells......D 3
3 St. Dominick....C 11
14 St. Donats........G 3
16 St. Edith's Marsh.H 1
3 St. Endellion......B 7
2 St. Enoder........D 6
2 St. Erme.........E 5
3 St. Erney........D 10
2 St. Erth..........F 3
2 St. Ervan.........C 6
2 St. Ewe..........E 7
14 St. Fagans........F 4
58 St. Fergus........B 8
52 St. Fillans........E 2
12 St. Florence......G 4
2 St. Gennys.......B 2
29 St. George.......C 9
14 St. George's, Glam.G 4
15 St. Georges, Som..H 7
3 St. Germans.....D 10
4 St. Giles in the Wood...........D 4
5 St. Giles on the Heath..........G 2
20 St. Harmon.......E 5
40 St. Helen Auckland C 2
26 St. Helena........D 5
9 St. Helens, Hants..G 7
34 St. Helens, Lancs..G 4
2 St. Hilary, Corn...F 3
14 St. Hilary, Glam..G 3
10 Saint Hill.........D 3
14 St. Illtyd.........D 5
12 St. Ishmael's......F 2
2 St. Issey..........C 6
3 St. Ive..........C 10
2 St. Ives, Corn......F 2
8 St. Ives, Hants.....F 3
25 St. Ives, Hunts....H 4
27 St. James South Elmham........G 6
8 St. Joan à Gores Cross...........A 2
3 St. John.........D 11
38 St. John Beckermet D 3
38 St. John's, I. o. M..G 1
22 St. Johns, Worcs...G 2
4 St. John's Chapel, Devon...........C 4
39 St. John's Chapel, Durham.......A 11
24 St. John's Fen End D 6
24 St. John's Highway D 6
38 St. Judas........F 2
2 St. Just.........G 1
2 St. Just Lane......F 6
58 St. Katherines....D 5
2 St. Keverne.......G 5
3 St. Kew..........B 7
3 St. Kew Highway..B 7
3 St. Keyne.........D 9
3 St. Lawrence, Corn. C 7
19 St. Lawrence, Essex C 9
9 St. Lawrence, Hants.............H 7
17 St. Leonards, Bucks.........C 10
8 St. Leonards, Hants..........F 3

MAP
11 St. Leonards, Sussex.........G 7
2 St. Levan.........G 1
14 St. Lythans.......G 4
3 St. Mabyn........B 7
6 St. Margaret......D 4
27 St. Margaret South Elmham..G 6
15 St. Margarets, Herefordshire...A 7
18 St. Margarets, Hertfordshire...C 4
11 St. Margaret's at Cliffe..........D 12
64 St. Margaret's Hope..........E 2
38 St. Mark's........H 1
3 St. Martin........D 9
52 St. Martins, Perth .D 6
30 St. Martin's, Salop.G 2
2 St. Martin's Green.G 4
8 St. Mary Bourne..A 6
14 St. Mary Church..G 3
18 St. Mary Cray....G 5
11 St. Mary in the Marsh.........E 9
18 St. Marylebone....F 3
64 St. Marys.........D 3
11 St. Mary's Bay....E 9
15 St. Mary's Grove..G 8
19 St. Mary's Hoo....F 8
15 St. Maughans.....C 8
2 St. Mawes........F 5
2 St. Mawgan.......C 6
3 St. Mellion......C 11
14 St. Mellons.......F 6
2 St. Merryn........B 6
3 St. Mewan........E 7
3 St. Michael Caerhays.......E 7
2 St. Michael Penkevil........E 6
27 St. Michael South Elmham..G 6
11 St. Michaels, Kent............E 7
21 St. Michaels, Worcestershire .F 11
34 St. Michael's on Wyre............C 3
3 St. Minver........B 7
53 St. Monans......G 10
3 St. Neot.........C 9
25 St. Neots..........J 3
14 St. Nicholas, Glamorgan ....G 4
12 St. Nicholas, Pemb.C 2
11 St. Nicholas at Wade.........A 11
52 St. Ninians........H 3
19 St. Osyth........B 11
15 St. Owen's Cross..B 8
18 St. Pancras.......F 3
18 St. Paul's Cray....G 5
18 St. Paul's Walden..B 2
11 St. Peters........A 12
12 St. Petrox........G 3
47 St. Quivox........G 8
2 St. Stephen.......D 6
3 St. Stephens, Corn.A 10
3 St. Stephens, Corn.D 11
3 St. Teath..........B 7
3 St. Tudy..........B 8
12 St. Twynnells.....G 3
3 St. Veep..........D 8
53 St. Vigeans......C 11
3 St. Wenn.........C 7
15 St. Weonards.....B 8
22 Saintbury.........H 5
51 Salachail.........B 8
5 Salcombe........M 6
6 Salcombe Regis...G 5
19 Salcott...........C 9
35 Sale.............H 7
22 Sale Green........F 3
33 Saleby..........B 11
10 Salehurst.........F 6
28 Salem, Caer.......E 5
20 Salem, Cards......D 2
13 Salem, Carm......D 9
50 Salen, Argyll.......A 4
50 Salen, Mull, Arg...C 3
34 Salesbury.........D 5
23 Salford, Beds.....H 12
35 Salford, Lancs...G 17
16 Salford, Oxon.....A 4
22 Salford Priors.....G 4
10 Salfords..........C 2
26 Salhouse.........D 6
52 Saline............H 5
8 Salisbury.........C 3
26 Sall.............C 4
51 Sallachan.........A 7

MAP
55 Sallachy, Ross & Cromarty.......G 3
60 Sallachy, Suther...F 6
33 Salmonby........C 10
43 Salmond's Muir..C 10
21 Salop, Co........B 10
16 Salperton.........B 2
25 Salph End.........K 2
48 Salsburgh........C 1
31 Salt..............G 8
3 Saltash..........D 11
56 Saltburn..........C 3
41 Saltburn-by-the-Sea............C 7
32 Saltby...........H 6
47 Saltcoats.........E 7
35 Salterforth........C 7
24 Salters Lode......E 7
30 Satterswall.......D 5
33 Saltfleet.........A 11
33 Saltfleetby St. Clements...A 11
33 Saltfleetby St. Peter.......A 11
33 Saltfleetby Saints.A 11
15 Saltford.........G 10
37 Salthaugh Grange E 10
26 Salthouse.........A 4
36 Saltmarshe........E 6
30 Saltney...........D 3
41 Salton...........G 7
3 Saltren's.........D 3
45 Saltwick.........E 10
11 Saltwood.........D 10
9 Salvington.......F 12
22 Salwarpe.........F 2
7 Salway Ash.......F 8
22 Sambourne........F 4
30 Sambrook........H 6
34 Samlesbury.......D 5
34 Samlesbury Bottoms......D 5
6 Sampford.........B 4
6 Sampford Arundel.D 5
4 Sampford Courtenay......F 5
6 Sampford Peverell.E 4
5 Sampford Spiney..H 4
19 Samuel's Corner...E 9
49 Samuelston........B 7
54 Sanachan.........F 2
51 Sanahole.........G 7
2 Sancreed.........G 1
37 Sancton..........C 7
64 Sand.............D 7
36 Sand Hutton......A 5
38 Sand Side........G 5
55 Sandaig, Inver.....J 1
55 Sandaig, Inver.....H 1
35 Sandal Magna...E 12
38 Sandale..........A 5
30 Sandbach.........D 6
46 Sandbank.........A 6
8 Sandbanks.......G 2
58 Sandend..........A 3
18 Sanderstead......H 3
4 Sandford, Devon..F 7
8 Sandford, Dorset..G 1
9 Sandford, Hants...H 7
47 Sandford, Lan....E 12
30 Sandford, Salop...H 2
15 Sandford, Som....H 7
39 Sandford, Westmorland...D 9
16 Sandford-on-Thames........D 6
7 Sandford Orcas...D 9
16 Sandford St. Martin B 5
58 Sandfordhill......C 8
64 Sandgarth........C 3
11 Sandgate........E 10
58 Sandhaven........A 7
42 Sandhead.........G 2
37 Sandhill..........H 9
45 Sandhoe..........F 8
44 Sandholm........D 3
24 Sandholme, Lincs..B 4
36 Sandholme, Yorks. D 6
17 Sandhurst, Berks..H 9
15 Sandhurst, Glos...B 11
11 Sandhurst, Kent...E 7
10 Sandhurst Cross...E 6
40 Sandhutton.......G 4
32 Sandiacre.........G 2
33 Sandilands.......B 12
30 Sandiway.........C 5
16 Sandleigh.........D 6
10 Sandling..........B 6
64 Sandness.........D 6
19 Sandon, Essex....C 7
25 Sandon, Herts.....M 4
31 Sandon, Staffs....G 8
9 Sandown.........H 7

MAP
3 Sandplace........D 9
18 Sandridge, Herts...C 2
15 Sandridge,Wilts. .H 12
41 Sandsend.........D 8
64 Sandside.........D 1
61 Sandside Hotel....A 9
64 Sandsound........D 7
36 Sandtoft..........F 5
11 Sandway, Kent...C 7
6 Sandway, Som....C 2
11 Sandwich........B 12
64 Sandwick,
    Orkney Is......E 2
63 Sandwick,
    Ross & Crom..D 5
64 Sandwick,
    Shetland Is.....E 7
38 Sandwick,Westmor.C6
38 Sandwith.........D 2
25 Sandy............K 3
30 Sandy Bank......G 4
10 Sandy Cross......F 5
12 Sandy Haven......F 2
16 Sandy Lane, Wilts.G 1
35 Sandy Lane, Yorks.D 9
29 Sandycroft.......D 12
47 Sandyford, Ayr. .G 9
43 Sandyford, Dumf. B 12
38 Sandygate........F 2
43 Sandyhills........F 9
34 Sandylands.......A 3
4 Sandymoor Cross..F 3
5 Sandypark.......G 6
44 Sandysike........F 2
49 Sandystones.....G 8
15 Sandyway.........B 8
50 Sanna...........A 2
47 Sanquhar.......H 12
38 Santon Bridge....E 4
27 Santon Downham.G 1
23 Sapcote.........C 8
21 Sapey Common. .F 12
27 Sapiston.........H 2
15 Sapperton, Glos. D 12
33 Sapperton, Lincs..G 7
24 Saracen's Head...C 4
61 Sarclet.........C 12
12 Sardis...........F 3
12 Sardis Mountain..F 5
8 Sarisbury........E 6
28 Sarn, Caer....G 2
14 Sarn, Glam....F 2
21 Sarn, Mont....C 7
14 Sarnau, Brec...A 3
12 Sarnau, Cards...B 6
13 Sarnau, Carm...D 8
29 Sarnau, Mer...F 9
21 Sarnau, Mont...A 8
28 Sarn-back.......H 2
21 Sarnesfield.......G 9
28 Saron, Caer.....D 5
13 Saron, Carm....C 7
13 Saron, Carm....F 9
17 Sarratt.........D 11
11 Sarre.........B 11
16 Sarsden.........B 4
8 Sarson..........B 4
38 Sartfield.........F 2
40 Satley..........A 1
4 Satterleigh.......D 5
38 Satterthwaite.....F 6
17 Satwell..........F 8
58 Sauchen.........F 4
53 Saucher..........D 7
59 Sauchieburn......K 4
47 Sauchrie.........H 8
44 Saughtree........C 4
44 Saughtrees......E 3
15 Saul............C 10
32 Saundby.........A 5
12 Saundersfoot....F 5
17 Saunderton......D 9
17 Saunderton Lee...D 9
4 Saunton.........B 3
33 Sausthorpe......C 11
60 Savalmore.......F 6
31 Saverley Green...F 8
50 Savory..........C 4
18 Sawbridgeworth..B 5
41 Sawdon..........G 9
32 Sawley, Derby...G 2
34 Sawley, Yorks...C 6
25 Sawston.........K 6
25 Sawtry..........G 3
32 Saxby, Leics...H 5
33 Saxby, Lincs...B 7
37 Saxby All Saints..E 7
32 Saxelby.........G 6
32 Saxilby.........C 6
26 Saxlingham......B 3
26 Saxlingham
    Nethergate...F 5
27 Saxmundham....J 7

MAP
25 Saxon Street.....J 8
32 Saxondale.......F 4
27 Saxtead.........J 6
27 Saxtead Green...J 6
26 Saxthorpe.......C 4
36 Saxton..........C 3
10 Sayers Common...F 2
48 Scabcleuch......H 5
40 Scackleton......H 6
63 Scadabay........H 3
32 Scaftworth......A 4
41 Scagglethorpe...H 8
50 Scalasaig........H 1
36 Scalby, E. Riding..D 6
41 Scalby, N. Riding F 10
23 Scaldwell.......E 11
44 Scaleby.........G 3
44 Scalebyhill.......G 3
38 Scales, Cumb...C 6
38 Scales, Lancs...H 5
34 Scales, Lancs...D 3
39 Scales Houses....A 8
32 Scalford........H 5
41 Scaling..........D 7
50 Scallastle........D 4
64 Scalloway........E 7
62 Scalpay House...E 5
55 Scamadale.......K 1
55 Scamodale.......M 2
41 Scampston......H 8
33 Scampton.......B 7
56 Scaniport........F 2
64 Scapa...........D 2
64 Scar............A 4
39 Scar End......B 11
63 Scarastavore.....H 1
41 Scarborough....F 10
43 Scarbrae........C 9
32 Scarcliffe........C 2
35 Scarcroft......C 12
54 Scardroy........D 6
44 Scare...........F 3
61 Scarfskerry....A 11
40 Scargill.........D 1
34 Scarisbrick......F 3
26 Scarning........D 2
32 Scarrington......F 4
34 Scarth Hill.......F 3
37 Scartho........G 10
64 Scarwell........C 1
56 Scatraig.........F 3
64 Scatsta.........C 7
37 Scawby.........G 7
37 Scawby Brook...F 7
40 Scawton........G 6
10 Scayne's Hill.....F 3
14 Scethrog........B 4
47 Schaw.........G 9
31 Scholar Green....E 7
35 Scholes, W. Riding F 10
35 Scholes, W. Riding E 10
36 Scholes, W. Riding D 2
40 School Aycliffe...C 3
35 Scissett........F 11
12 Scleddau.........D 3
26 Sco Ruston......C 6
27 Scole..........G 4
59 Scolly's Cross....J 4
12 Scolton.........E 3
62 Sconser.........E 4
53 Scoonie.........G 8
50 Scoor...........F 2
33 Scopwick........D 8
60 Scoraig.........G 2
37 Scorborough.....C 8
47 Scorrieholm.....F 12
2 Scorrier.........E 4
5 Scorriton........J 6
40 Scorton.........E 3
34 Scot Lane End...F 5
44 Scotby.........G 3
40 Scotch Corner...E 2
34 Scotforth.......A 4
33 Scothern........B 7
45 Scots' Gap......D 8
33 Scots Hole......D 8
56 Scotsburn.......D 6
61 Scotscalder Sta..B 10
53 Scotscraig.......D 9
44 Scotsdike.......F 2
59 Scotston, Kinc...K 5
52 Scotston, Perth...C 4
50 Scotstown.......A 5
45 Scotswood......G 10
53 Scottas.........J 1
36 Scotter.........G 6
36 Scotterthorpe....G 6
37 Scotton, Lincs...G 7
40 Scotton, N. Riding.F 2
35 Scotton, W. Riding
                   A 12
49 Scoughall.......A 8
26 Scoulton........E 3

MAP
60 Scourie..........C 3
60 Scourie More....C 3
64 Scousburgh......F 7
61 Scrabster........A 10
49 Scraesburgh.....G 9
33 Scrafield........C 10
45 Scrainwood......B 8
33 Scramblesby.....B 10
24 Scrane End......A 5
23 Scraptoft........B 10
26 Scratby.........D 8
36 Scrayingham....A 5
24 Scredington.....B 2
6 Screedy.........D 4
43 Screel...........F 9
33 Scremby.........C 11
49 Scremerston....D 12
32 Screveton.......F 4
33 Scrivelsby.......D 9
35 Scriven.........A 12
43 Scroggs.........C 12
32 Scrooby.........A 4
31 Scropton........G 10
33 Scrub Hill.......E 9
40 Scruton.........F 3
37 Sculcoates......D 8
26 Sculthorpe......B 2
37 Scunthorpe......F 7
13 Scurlage........H 8
26 Sea Palling......C 7
7 Seaborough......F 8
30 Seacombe.......A 2
33 Seacroft, Lincs..D 12
35 Seacroft, Yorks..D 12
47 Seafield, Ayr...G 8
48 Seafield, W. Loth..C 3
10 Seaford.........H 4
34 Seaforth........G 2
63 Seaforth Head...E 4
45 Seaham........H 12
45 Seahouses.......D 12
10 Seal............B 4
30 Sealand.........C 2
9 Seale.........A 10
41 Seamer, N. Riding G 10
40 Seamer, N. Riding.D 5
47 Seamill.........E 7
37 Searby..........G 8
11 Seasalter........B 9
38 Seascale........E 3
33 Seathorne......D 12
38 Seathwaite, Cumb. D 5
38 Seathwaite, Lancs..F 5
20 Seatoller.........D 5
3 Seaton, Corn....D 10
38 Seaton, Cumb....B 3
6 Seaton, Devon...G 6
45 Seaton, Dur...H 12
45 Seaton, Northumb.E 11
23 Seaton, Rut....B 12
37 Seaton, Yorks...B 9
45 Seaton Burn.....F 10
40 Seaton Carew....B 5
45 Seaton Delaval...E 11
36 Seaton Ross.....C 6
45 Seaton Sluice...E 11
58 Seatown, Banff..A 3
58 Seatown, Banff..A 2
7 Seatown, Dorset..G 7
40 Seave Green.....E 6
9 Seaview.........G 8
43 Seaville.........F 12
7 Seavington
    St. Mary......E 7
7 Seavington
    St. Michael....E 7
19 Seawick Sands...C 11
14 Sebastopol, Glam..D 5
14 Sebastopol, Mon...E 6
38 Sebergham......A 6
22 Seckington......A 6
60 Second Coast...G 1
39 Sedbergh........F 9
15 Sedbury........E 9
39 Sedbusk........F 11
22 Sedgeberow.....H 4
32 Sedgebrook......F 6
40 Sedgefield......D 4
24 Sedgeford.......B 8
7 Sedgehill.......C 12
22 Sedgley.........C 2
39 Sedgwick.......F 7
10 Sedlescombe....F 6
10 Sedlescombe St...F 6
15 Seend..........H 12
15 Seende Cleeve..H 12
17 Seer Green......E 10
26 Seething........F 6
34 Sefton.........G 2
45 Seghill.........F 11
31 Seighford.......H 7
63 Seilebost.......G 2

MAP
22 Seisdon.........C 2
30 Selattyn.........G 1
9 Selborne........C 9
36 Selby..........D 4
9 Selham........D 10
49 Selkirk.........G 7
48 Selkirk, Co......G 6
15 Sellack.........B 9
38 Sellafield Station..E 3
64 Sellafirth.......M 2
11 Sellindge........D 9
11 Sellindge Lees...D 9
11 Selling.........B 9
15 Sells Green.....H 12
22 Selly Oak.......D 4
10 Selmeston......G 4
18 Selsdon........H 4
15 Selsey.........D 11
10 Selsfield Common .E 2
39 Selside........H 10
11 Selstead........D 10
32 Selston.........E 2
6 Selworthy......B 3
64 Semblister......D 6
27 Semer..........K 3
15 Semington......H 12
7 Semley.........D 12
9 Send...........A 11
8 Sendmarsh......A 11
14 Senghenydd.....E 4
2 Sennen.........G 1
2 Sennen Cove...G 1
14 Sennybridge.....B 3
43 Senwick Ho......G 7
40 Sessay..........H 5
24 Setchey.........D 7
8 Setley..........F 5
64 Settascarth......C 2
64 Setter, Bressay
    Shetland Is.....E 7
64 Setter, Zetland
    Shetland Is.....D 6
64 Setter, Zetland
    Shetland Is....D 7
35 Settle..........A 7
41 Settlestones.....F 7
41 Settrington......H 8
6 Seven Ash......C 5
18 Seven Kings.....E 4
14 Seven Sisters....C 2
16 Seven Wells.....A 2
16 Sevenhampton, Glos.
                   B 1
16 Sevenhampton, Wilts.
                   E 3
10 Sevenoaks......C 4
10 Sevenoaks Weald..C 4
15 Severn Beach....F 8
22 Severn Stoke....H 2
11 Sevington, Kent...D 9
15 Sevington, Wilts..F 11
25 Sewards End.....L 7
41 Sewerby........H 12
6 Sewton.........G 4
32 Sewstern........H 6
10 Seyning.........G 1
17 Shabbington....C 7
23 Shackerstone...A 7
27 Shadingfield.....G 7
22 Shackleford......B 10
40 Shadforth........A 4
11 Shadoxhurst....D 8
22 Shadwell, Norfolk.C 2
35 Shadwell, Yorks. .C 12
7 Shaftesbury....D 12
36 Shafton..........F 2
16 Shalbourne......H 4
8 Shalcombe......G 5
9 Shalden........B 8
9 Shaldon........J 8
8 Shalfleet........G 5
19 Shalford, Essex...A 7
19 Shalford, Surrey..A 11
19 Shalford Green...A 7
42 Shalloch........B 3
4 Shallowford.....B 6
11 Shalmsford Street .C 9
23 Shalstone......H 9
46 Shalunt.........B 5
9 Shamley Green..B 11
4 Shancastle......C 9
56 Shandwick......B 4
23 Shangton.......C 10
45 Shankhouse....E 11
9 Shanklin.......H 7
46 Shannochie.....G 5
53 Shanzie.........B 7
39 Shap..........D 8
8 Shapwick, Dorset..F 1
7 Shapwick, Som...B 7
32 Shardlow........G 2
31 Shareshill.......B 2

MAP
35 Sharlston,
    W. Riding.....E 12
36 Sharlston,
    W. Riding.....E 2
11 Sharnal Street....J 1
25 Sharnbrook......J 1
23 Sharnford......C 8
38 Sharoe Green....D 4
40 Sharow.........H 3
25 Sharpenhoe.....M 2
45 Sharperton......C 8
15 Sharpness......D 10
10 Sharpthorne.....E 3
26 Sharrington.....B 3
22 Shatterford......D 1
5 Shaugh Prior....J 4
7 Shave Cross......F 7
30 Shavington......E 6
16 Shaw, Berks...G 6
15 Shaw, Lancs...F 8
15 Shaw, Wilts.....H 12
34 Shaw Green.....A 4
35 Shaw Mills......A 11
30 Shawbury.......H 4
45 Shawdon Hill....B 9
23 Shawell.........D 9
8 Shawford.......D 6
35 Shawforth......E 7
43 Shawhead.......D 9
43 Shawhill.......E 12
47 Shawood........G 10
34 Shawton........D 11
7 Shear Cross.....B 11
43 Shearington.....E 11
23 Shearsby.......C 9
4 Shebbear.......E 3
30 Shebdon.......H 6
16 Shebster........B 9
9 Shedfield.......E 7
31 Sheen..........D 9
21 Sheephouse....H 7
15 Sheepscombe...C 12
5 Sheepstor.......J 4
4 Sheepwash, Devon E 4
4 Sheepwash, Devon.C 7
45 Sheepwash,
    Northumb....D 10
15 Sheepway.......G 8
23 Sheepy Magna...B 7
23 Sheepy Parva....B 7
18 Sheering........C 5
11 Sheerness......A 8
21 Sheet, Hants....D 9
21 Sheet, Salop....E 10
32 Sheffield.........B 1
25 Shefford.......L 2
16 Shefford
    Woodlands....G 4
60 Sheigra.........B 3
43 Sheillahill.......F 8
21 Sheinton.......B 11
21 Shelderton.....E 9
6 Sheldon, Devon..E 5
22 Sheldon, War...D 5
11 Sheldwich......B 9
35 Shelf..........D 10
27 Shelfhanger.....G 4
22 Shelfield, Staffs..B 4
22 Shelfield, War...F 5
32 Shelford........F 2
49 Shellacres......E 11
18 Shelley, Essex...C 5
35 Shelley, Yorks...F 10
16 Shellingford....E 4
18 Shellow Bowells..C 6
22 Shelsley
    Beauchamp....F 1
21 Shelsley Walsh..F 12
32 Shelthorpe......H 3
26 Shelton, Norfolk..F 5
25 Shelton, Northants.H 1
32 Shelton, Notts...F 5
21 Shelton, Salop..A 10
21 Shelve..........C 9
21 Shelwick........H 10
21 Shelwick Green..H 10
56 Shenachie......F 4
15 Shenmore.......A 7
22 Shennanton.....E 4
23 Shenington.....H 7
18 Shenley.........D 2
17 Shenley Brook End A 9
23 Shenley Church
    End...........H 11
22 Shenstone, Staffs..B 4
22 Shenstone, Worcs..E 2
28 Shenton........B 7
57 Shenval........G 8
15 Sheperdine......E 9
24 Shepeu Stow....D 4
18 Shephall........B 3
18 Shepherd's Bush..F 2

MAP
17 Shepherd's Green..F 8
11 Shepherdswell....C 11
35 Shepley........F 10
17 Shepperton......G 11
17 Shepperton Grn..G 11
25 Shepreth........K 5
32 Shepshed.......H 2
7 Shepton
    Beauchamp....D 7
7 Shepton Mallet...B 9
7 Shepton MontagueC 10
10 Shepway.......C 6
40 Sheraton.......B 5
7 Sherborne, Dorset E 10
16 Sherborne, Glos...C 3
9 Sherborne St. John A 8
22 Sherbourne......F 6
40 Sherburn, Dur...A 3
41 Sherburn, Yorks..G 9
40 Sherburn Hill....A 4
36 Sherburn in Elmet .D 3
9 Shere.........A 12
26 Shereford......B 8
8 Sherfield English..D 4
17 Sherfield on
    Loddon.......H 7
5 Sherford.......L 6
36 Sheriff Hutton...A 3
26 Sheringham.....A 4
23 Sherington......G 12
24 Shernborne.....B 8
22 Sherriffhales....A 1
8 Sherrington.....B 1
15 Sherston......F 11
4 Sherwood Green. .D 4
63 Sheshader......C 6
47 Shettleston.....C 11
34 Shevington.....D 11
34 Shevington Moor..F 4
3 Sheviock.......D 10
55 Shewglie........G 8
52 Shian...........C 3
49 Shidlaw.......F 10
43 Shiel, Dumfries...A 8
43 Shiel, Kirk....D 7
55 Shiel Bridge.....H 3
45 Shiel Dykes......B 9
54 Shieldaig.......D 2
54 Shieldaig Lodge
    (Hotel).........C 2
43 Shieldhill, Dumf. C 10
43 Shieldhill, Dumf..C 11
48 Shieldhill, Stir....B 2
47 Shieldmuir.....D 12
50 Shielfoot.......A 4
58 Shielhill, Aber...B 8
59 Shielhill, Angus..L 2
47 Shieloans.......F 11
16 Shifford........D 5
22 Shifnal.........A 1
45 Shilbottle.......B 10
44 Shilburn Haugh..D 5
40 Shildon.........C 3
47 Shillford........D 7
6 Shillingford, Devon D 3
17 Shillingford, Oxon. E 7
6 Shillingford Abbot G 2
6 Shillingford
    St. George....G 2
7 Shillingstone....E 11
25 Shillington.....M 2
45 Shillmoor.......B 7
63 Shiltenish......E 4
16 Shilton, Oxon...C 4
23 Shilton, War....D 7
11 Shilvinghampton..H 9
27 Shimpling, Norf..G 4
27 Shimpling, Suffolk.K 2
27 Shimpling Street..K 2
40 Shincliffe.......A 3
40 Shincliffe Colliery..A 3
45 Shiney Row....H 11
17 Shinfield.......G 8
59 Shinfur.........J 2
43 Shinnelhead....B 8
5 Shinner's Bridge..J 7
10 Shipbourne.....C 5
26 Shipdham......E 3
7 Shipham........A 8
5 Shiphay........J 8
17 Shiplake........F 8
48 Shiplaw........D 5
45 Shipley, Northumb.A 9
22 Shipley, Salop...C 2
9 Shipley, Sussex..D 12
35 Shipley, Yorks...C 10
10 Shipley Bridge...D 2
26 Shipmeadow....F 7
16 Shipton, Glos...B 1
21 Shipton, Salop...C 11

MAP

36 Shipton, Yorks....A 3
8 Shipton Bellinger..B 4
7 Shipton Gorge....G 8
9 Shipton Green....F 9
15 Shipton Moyne...F 12
16 Shipton-on-
   Cherwell.....B 6
16 Shipton-under-
   Wychwood....B 4
36 Shiptonthorpe....C 6
17 Shirburn.......E 8
34 Shirdley Hill.....F 2
22 Shire Oak......B 4
32 Shirebrook......C 3
32 Shiregreen......A 1
15 Shirehampton....F 8
45 Shiremoor.....F 11
15 Shirenewton.....E 8
32 Shireoaks......B 3
4 Shirewell Cross....B 5
21 Shirl Heath.....F 10
32 Shirland.......D 1
31 Shirley, Derby..F 10
8 Shirley, Hants....E 5
22 Shirley, War.....D 5
9 Shirrell Heath....E 7
4 Shirwell........B 5
46 Shiskine.......F 4
21 Shobdon.......F 9
4 Shobrooke......F 7
30 Shocklach......E 3
19 Shoeburyness....E 9
11 Sholden.......C 12
8 Sholing........E 6
4 Shop, Cornwall...D 1
2 Shop, Cornwall...B 6
27 Shop Street.....H 5
44 Shopford......F 4
18 Shoreditch......F 3
10 Shoreham......A 6
10 Shoreham-by-Sea..G 1
56 Shoremill......C 3
49 Shoresdean.....E 12
49 Shoreswood....E 12
56 Shoretown.....D 2
16 Shorncote......E 1
10 Shorne........A 6
10 Shorne Ridgeway..A 6
22 Short Heath, Leics..A 6
22 Short Heath, Staffs. B 3
22 Short Heath, War..C 4
5 Shortacombe....G 4
10 Shortgate......G 4
2 Shortlanesend....E 5
47 Shortlees.......F 9
15 Shortwood......G 10
8 Shorwell.......H 6
7 Shoscombe.....A 10
30 Shotatton......H 2
26 Shotesham......F 6
19 Shotgate.......E 7
45 Shotley Bridge...H 9
27 Shotley Gate....M 5
27 Shotley Street....M 5
45 Shotleyfield.....H 9
11 Shottenden......C 9
9 Shottermill.....C 10
22 Shottery.......G 5
23 Shotteswell.....H 8
27 Shottisham.....L 6
31 Shottle........E 11
40 Shotton, Durham..A 4
29 Shotton, Flint...C 12
49 Shotton,
   Northumb....F 11
40 Shotton Colliery..A 4
48 Shotts........C 1
30 Shotwick......C 2
38 Shoughlaige-e-
   Caine.......G 1
56 Shougle.......D 8
24 Shouldham.....E 8
24 Shouldham Thorpe E 8
22 Shoulton.......F 2
9 Shover's Green....E 9
21 Shrawardine.....A 9
22 Shrawley.......F 2
17 Shreding Green...F 11
22 Shrewley.......E 5
21 Shrewsbury.....A 10
8 Shrewton.......B 2
9 Shripney.......F 10
16 Shrivenham.....E 3
26 Shropham......F 3
19 Shrub End......B 9
21 Shucknall......H 11
25 Shudy Camps....L 7
63 Shulishader......C 6
38 Shundraw......C 5
15 Shurdington....G 9
17 Shurlock Row....G 9
61 Shurrery Lodge..B 10
6 Shurton........B 5

22 Shustoke........C 6
22 Shut End........C 2
4 Shute, Devon.....F 8
6 Shute, Devon.....F 8
23 Shutford........H 7
15 Shuthonger.....A 12
22 Shutlanger.....G 10
22 Shuttington......B 6
32 Shuttlewood.....C 2
43 Sibbaldbie......C 12
23 Sibbertoft......D 10
21 Sibdon Carwood..D 9
23 Sibford Ferris....H 7
23 Sibford Gower....H 7
27 Sible Hedingham..M 1
23 Sibsey........E 10
24 Sibson, Hunts....F 2
23 Sibson, Leics.....B 7
32 Sibthorpe......F 5
27 Sicklesmere......J 2
35 Sicklinghall.....B 12
6 Sid..........G 5
39 Sidcot, Cumb.....B 7
40 Skelton, E. Riding. C 6
36 Skelton, E. Riding. E 5
36 Skelton, N. Riding. B 3
40 Skelton, N. Riding. E 1
40 Skelton, W. Riding H 4
38 Skelwith Bridge...E 6
64 Skelwick......A 3
33 Skendleby.....C 11
58 Skene House.....F 5
15 Skenfrith......B 8
37 Skerne........B 8
46 Skeroblingarry...G 2
61 Skerray.......B 7
60 Skerricha......C 4
34 Skerton.......A 4
23 Sketchley......C 7
13 Sketty........H 9
13 Skewen.......G 10
40 Skewsby.......H 6
26 Skeyton.......C 5
60 Skiag Bridge....E 4
51 Skibo Castle.....G 7
33 Skidbrooke....A 11
37 Skidby........D 8
63 Skigersta......A 6
6 Skilgate.......D 3
32 Skillington......D 4
43 Skinburness....F 12
62 Skinidin......C 1
41 Skinningrove....C 7
46 Skipness......D 4
37 Skipsea.......B 9
37 Skipsea Brough...B 9
35 Skipton.......B 8
40 Skipton-on-Swale. G 4
36 Skipwith.......C 4
24 Skirbeck......A 4
24 Skirbeck Quarter..A 4
48 Skirling.......E 3
17 Skirmett.......E 8
36 Skirpenbeck.....A 5
39 Skirwith, Cumb...B 8
39 Skirwith, Yorks...H 9
61 Skirza........A 12
44 Skitby........F 3
62 Skulamus......F 6
60 Skullomie......B 6
57 Skye of Curr....G 5
20 Slack.........D 8
31 Slackhall......B 9
58 Slackhead......A 2
43 Slacks........C 11
58 Slacks of
   Cairnbanno....C 6
15 Slad.........D 12
4 Slade.........B 4
18 Slade Green.....F 5
3 Sladesbridge.....C 7
44 Slaggyford.....H 5
34 Slaidburn......B 6
59 Slains Park.....K 6
49 Slainsfield.....E 12
35 Slaithwaite.....F 9
45 Slaley........G 8
48 Slamannan.....B 1
17 Slapton, Bucks...B 10
5 Slapton, Devon...L 7
23 Slapton, Northants. G 9
54 Slattadale......C 3
35 Slattocks......F 7
10 Slaugham......E 1
30 Slaughter Hill....E 6
3 Slaughterbridge...A 8
15 Slaughterford...G 11
23 Slawston......C 7
9 Sleaford, Hants...B 9
24 Sleaford, Lincs...A 2
39 Sleagill.......B 7
21 Sleap........A 11
21 Sleapford......A 11
15 Sledge Green....A 11

47 Skares........H 10
49 Skateraw, E. Loth. B 10
59 Skateraw, Kinc...H 7
62 Skeabost.......C 3
40 Skeeby........E 2
23 Skeffington.....B 11
37 Skeffling......E 11
32 Skegby........D 2
33 Skegness......D 12
61 Skelbo........G 8
36 Skelbrooke.....F 3
24 Skeldyke.......B 4
32 Skelmorlie......C 7
58 Skelmuir.......C 7
61 Skelpick.......B 7
39 Skelton, Cumb....B 7
21 Sidbury, Salop...D 12
18 Sidcup........G 5
38 Siddick........B 2
31 Siddington, Ches...C 7
16 Siddington, Glos...D 1
22 Sidemoor......E 3
6 Sidford........G 5
9 Sidlesham......F 10
10 Sidley........G 6
10 Sidlow Bridge...C 1
6 Sidmouth......H 4
5 Sigford........H 6
14 Sigginston......G 3
37 Sigglesthorne....C 9
17 Silchester......H 7
23 Sileby........A 9
38 Silecroft......G 4
20 Silian........G 1
24 Silk Willoughby...A 2
35 Silkstone......G 11
35 Silkstone Com....G 11
44 Silloans.......C 6
43 Silloth........F 11
23 Silverstone.....H 10
47 Silverburn......C 5
48 Silverburn......C 5
39 Silverdale, Lancs..H 7
31 Silverdale, Staffs..F 7
23 Silverstone.....H 10
5 Silverton, Devon..F 3
47 Silverton, Dunb...B 9
21 Silvington......D 11
45 Simonburn.....F 7
6 Simonsbath.....B 1
34 Simonstone.....D 6
49 Simprim......E 11
23 Simpson, Bucks..H 12
21 Simpson, Pemb...E 2
49 Sinclair's Hill....D 10
47 Sinclairston......H 9
40 Sinderby
   Quernhow....G 4
45 Sinderhope.....H 7
17 Sindlesham.....G 8
44 Singdean......C 4
17 Singleborough....A 8
34 Singleton, Lancs...C 3
9 Singleton, Sussex. E 10
10 Singlewell or Ifield. A 5
30 Singret.......E 2
58 Sinnahard......F 2
41 Sinnington.....G 7
28 Sinton........F 2
18 Sipson........F 1
14 Sirhowy.......C 5
11 Sissinghurst....D 7
49 Sisterpath......E 10
15 Siston........G 10
2 Sithney.......G 3
11 Sittingbourne....B 8
58 Sittyton.......E 6
22 Six Ashes......C 2
32 Six Hills......H 4
25 Six Mile Bottom..J 7
31 Six Roads End...G 10
33 Sixhills.......B 9
27 Sizewell.......J 8
61 Skail.........C 7

37 Sledmere......A 7
44 Sleetbeck......E 3
39 Sleightholme....D 11
41 Sleights.......D 8
8 Slepe.........G 1
4 Slerra........D 2
61 Slickly........A 12
46 Sliddery.......G 4
62 Sligachan......E 4
51 Sligrachan......H 9
15 Slimbridge.....D 10
31 Slindon, Staffs...G 7
9 Slindon, Sussex...E 11
9 Slinfold.......C 12
28 Sling.........D 5
41 Slingsby.......H 7
58 Slioch........D 3
17 Slip End, Beds...B 11
25 Slip End, Herts...L 4
26 Slipper's Bottom..D 6
23 Slipton.......D 12
33 Slitting Mill.....H 9
57 Slochd........G 4
57 Slochnacraig....M 7
50 Slockavullin....H 5
43 Slogarie.......E 7
33 Sloothby......C 12
6 Slough Green....D 6
57 Sluggan.......G 4
34 Slyne.........A 4
49 Smailholm......F 9
38 Smaithwaite....C 5
10 Small Dole......G 1
11 Small Hythe.....E 7
35 Smallbridge.....F 8
26 Smallburgh......C 4
58 Smallburn, Aber...D 8
47 Smallburn, Ayr..G 11
32 Smalley.......F 1
10 Smallfield......D 2
43 Smallholm.....D 11
6 Smallridge......F 6
8 Smannel.......A 5
39 Smardale......D 9
11 Smarden.......D 7
6 Smeatharpe.....E 5
11 Smeeth, Kent....D 9
24 Smeeth, Norfolk..E 6
23 Smeeton Westerby C 10
35 Smelthouses....A 10
61 Smerral.......D 11
22 Smethwick......C 4
31 Smisby........H 12
34 Smith Green.....B 4
44 Smithfield......F 3
6 Smithincott.....E 4
9 Smith's Green....N 9
47 Smithston......H 9
54 Smithstown.....B 2
56 Smithton......E 3
32 Smithy Houses...E 1
45 Snableazes.....B 10
43 Snade.........C 9
21 Snailbeach.....B 9
25 Snailwell.......H 7
41 Snainton.......G 9
36 Snaith........E 4
31 Snake Inn......A 9
27 Snape, Suffolk...J 7
40 Snape, Yorks....G 3
34 Snape Green.....F 3
27 Snape Street....J 7
23 Snarestone.....A 7
33 Snarford......B 7
11 Snargate......E 8
11 Snave........E 9
21 Snead........C 8
37 Sneaton.......D 9
41 Sneaton Thorpe...E 9
33 Snelland......B 8
31 Snelston......F 10
24 Snettisham.....B 8
45 Snitter........C 8
33 Snitterby......A 7
22 Snitterfield.....F 5
21 Snitton........E 11
10 Snodhill......H 8
10 Snodland......B 6
11 Snowdown.....C 11
16 Snowshill......A 2
14 Soar, Brec......A 3
13 Soar, Carm.....A 3
30 Soar, Devon....M 6
9 Soberton......D 7
9 Soberton Heath...E 7
25 Soham........H 7
12 Solbury.......F 2
4 Soldon Cross....E 2
9 Soldridge......C 8
10 Sole Street.....A 5
11 Solestreet......C 9
22 Solihull.......D 5

21 Sollers Dilwyn...G 9
15 Sollers Hope.....A 9
34 Sollom........E 3
12 Solva.........D 1
44 Solwaybank.....E 1
23 Somerby, Leics...A 11
37 Somerby, Lincs...F 8
32 Somercotes.....E 2
8 Somerford......G 3
16 Somerford Keynes. E 1
9 Somerley.......F 9
26 Somerleyton.....F 8
33 Somersal Herbert. G 10
33 Somersby......C 10
25 Somersham,
   Hunts........H 5
27 Somersham,
   Suffolk.......K 4
16 Somerton, Oxon..A 6
7 Somerton, Som...C 8
27 Somerton, Suffolk. K 1
10 Sompting......G 1
17 Sonning.......G 8
17 Sonning Common. F 8
17 Sonning Eye.....F 8
33 Sootywells......K 5
44 Sorbie, Dumf....D 2
44 Sorbie, Yorks....G 5
44 Sorbietrees.....E 3
61 Sordale.......B 10
47 Sorn.........G 10
47 Sornbeg.......F 10
48 Sornfallow......F 2
47 Sornhill.......F 10
50 Soroba Farm....E 6
61 Sortat........B 12
29 Sotby........D 11
17 Sotwell.......E 7
29 Soughton......D 11
17 Soulbury......F 6
39 Soulby........D 9
16 Souldern......A 6
25 Souldrop......J 1
64 Sound, Zetland,
   Shetland Is.....D 7
64 Sound, Zetland,
   Shetland Is.....E 7
49 Sourhope......G 11
60 Sourin........G 3
5 Sourton.......G 4
38 Soutergate.....G 5
26 South Acre.....D 1
44 South Allington..M 7
52 South Alloa.....H 4
9 South
   Ambersham...D 10
32 South Anston....B 2
17 South Ascot....G 10
8 South Baddesley..F 5
42 South Balloch....B 4
7 South Barrow....C 9
28 South Beach.....G 3
48 South Bellsdyke...A 2
19 South Benfleet....E 7
9 South Bersted....F 10
36 South Bramwith...F 4
5 South Brent.....K 6
7 South Brewham...C 10
52 South Bridge-end..E 3
45 South Broomhill..C 10
26 South Burlingham. E 7
7 South Cadbury...D 9
42 South Cairn.....E 1
33 South Carlton....C 7
46 South Carrine....H 2
37 South Cave.....D 7
16 South Cerney....D 2
7 South Chard.....F 7
45 South Charlton...A 9
7 South Cheriton...D 10
36 South Cliffe.....D 6
32 South Clifton....C 5
33 South
   Cockerington..A 11
32 South
   Collingham....D 5
14 South Cornelly...F 1
27 South Cove.....G 8
37 South Cliffe.....D 7
51 South Creagan...C 7
26 South Creake....B 1
23 South Croxton..A 10
37 South Dalton....C 7
10 South Darenth...A 4
46 South Dell.....A 6
58 South Denmore...F 7
46 South Druimachro. E 2
36 South Duffield...D 5
33 South Elkington..A 10
36 South Elmsall....F 3
17 South End, Berks..G 7

17 South End,
   Buckinghamshire B 9
34 South End, Lancs..A 1
37 South End, Lincs...B 5
54 South Erradale....C 1
19 South Fambridge..D 8
16 South Fawley....F 5
46 South Feorline....G 4
37 South Ferriby....E 7
58 South Fornet.....F 5
63 South Galson.....A 5
46 South Garrochty..D 6
14 South Glamorgan, Co.
              G 4
8 South Gorley....E 3
58 South Gorrachie...B 5
19 South Green,
   Essex........E 7
11 South Green,
   Kent........B 7
46 South Hall......B 5
19 South Hanningfield D 7
11 South Harting....D 9
11 South Hayling....F 8
45 South Hazelrigg..C 11
17 South Heath....D 10
10 South Heighton...H 3
40 South Hetton....A 4
36 South Hiendley...F 2
3 South Hill, Corn..B 10
7 South Hill, Som...D 8
16 South Hinksey....D 6
4 South Hole.....D 1
41 South Holme....G 7
10 South Holmwood..D 1
18 South Hornchurch. F 5
47 South Hourat....D 8
32 South Hykeham..D 6
45 South Hylton....G 11
60 South Keanchulish G 3
37 South Kelsey....G 8
37 South Killingholme F 9
54 South Kilrusken...D 7
40 South Kilvington..G 4
23 South Kilworth...D 9
36 South Kirkby....F 2
59 South Kirktown...G 5
33 South Kyme.....E 9
10 South Lancing...H 1
16 South Leigh.....C 5
32 South Leverton...B 5
47 South
   Limmerhaugh..G 11
22 South Littleton...G 4
27 South Lopham....G 3
23 South Luffenham. B 12
53 South Mains.....B 11
10 South Malling....G 3
16 South Marston...E 3
49 South Middleton..G 12
36 South Milford....D 3
5 South Milton....L 6
18 South Mimms....D 2
4 South Molton....C 6
16 South Moreton...E 6
9 South Mundham. F 10
32 South Muskham...E 5
37 South Newbald...D 7
16 South Newington..A 5
8 South Newton....C 2
32 South Normanton..E 2
18 South Norwood...G 3
10 South Nutfield...C 2
18 South Ockendon..F 6
33 South Ormsby...C 10
40 South Otterington. F 4
33 South Owersby...A 8
18 South Oxhey....E 1
7 South Perrott....F 8
7 South Petherton...D 8
3 South Petherwin. B 10
26 South Pickenham. E 1
5 South Pool.....M 6
4 South Radworthy. C 6
37 South Rauceby....F 7
26 South Raynham...C 2
33 South Reston....B 11
24 South Runcton....E 7
32 South Scarle.....D 6
63 South Shawbost...B 3
45 South Shields....F 12
34 South Shore.....D 2
37 South Skirlaugh...C 9
33 South Somercotes A 11
35 South Stainley...A 1
16 South Stifford....F 6
17 South Stoke, Oxon. F 7
15 South Stoke, Som.H 10
9 South Stoke,
   Sussex.......E 11
11 South Street, Kent. B 9
18 South Street,
   London.......H 4

MAP
10 South Street, Sussex F 3
4 South Tawton.....F 5
33 South Thoresby..C 11
8 South Tidworth...A 4
9 South Town.......B 8
26 South Walsham...D 7
9 S. Warnborough ..A 8
18 South Weald......E 6
17 South Weston.....D 8
5 South Wheatley, Corn.
       G 1
32 South Wheatley, Notts.
       B 5
7 South Widcombe..A 9
23 South Wigston....B 9
33 South Willingham.B 9
32 South Wingfield..E 1
32 South Witham....H 6
8 South Wonston....B 6
19 South Woodham
   Ferrers........D 8
24 South Wootton...C 7
15 South Wraxall...H 11
36 South Yorkshire, Co.
       G 2
4 South Zeal.......F 5
18 Southall........F 1
16 Southam, Glos...B 1
23 Southam, War....F 7
8 Southampton.....E 5
10 Southborough....D 7
8 Southbourne, Hants.
       G 3
9 Southbourne, Sus..E 9
26 Southburgh......E 3
37 Southburn.......B 7
19 Southchurch.....E 9
4 Southcott, Devon..D 3
16 Southcott, Wilts..H 3
44 Southdean.......B 5
10 Southease.......G 5
46 Southend, Arg...H 2
16 Southend, Wilts..G 3
19 Southend-on-Sea..E 8
14 Southerndown....G 2
43 Southerness.....F 10
49 Southernknowe...G 11
24 Southery.......F 7
41 Southfield......G 7
10 Southfleet......A 5
13 Southgate, Glam..H 9
18 Southgate, London E 3
24 Southgate, Norfolk B 8
26 Southgate, Norfolk C 4
25 Southill........L 3
6 Southleigh......G 5
19 Southminster.....D 9
45 Southmoor.......B 10
25 Southoe........J 3
27 Southolt.......H 5
24 Southorpe.......E 2
35 Southowram.....E 10
34 Southport.......E 2
26 Southrepps......B 6
33 Southrey........D 8
16 Southrop........D 3
9 Southrope.......B 8
9 Southsea.......F 8
64 Southtown......E 3
18 Southwark.......F 1
9 Southwater.....D 12
7 Southway.......B 8
7 Southwell, Dorset .H 7
32 Southwell, Notts..E 4
45 Southwick, Dur...G 12
9 Southwick, Hants..E 8
24 Southwick,
   Northants.......F 1
10 Southwick, Sussex.G 1
7 Southwick, Wilts..A 11
27 Southwold.......H 8
26 Southwood, Norf..E 7
7 Southwood, Som..C 9
49 Soutra Mains.....C 7
63 Soval Lodge.....D 4
40 Sowerby, N. Riding G 4
35 Sowerby, W. Riding E 9
35 Sowerby Bridge..E 9
38 Sowerby Row.....A 6
6 Sowton........G 3
44 Spadeadam......F 4
24 Spalding.......H 2
36 Spaldington.....D 5
25 Spaldwick......H 2
53 Spalefield......F 10
32 Spalford........C 5
24 Spanby.........B 2
26 Sparham........D 4
38 Spark Bridge.....G 5
7 Sparkford......D 9
31 Sparklow.......D 9
5 Sparkwell......K 4
31 Sparrowpit......B 9

MAP
16 Sparsholt, Berks...E 4
8 Sparsholt, Hants...C 6
45 Spartylea........H 7
41 Spaunton........F 7
6 Spaxton........C 6
55 Spean Bridge.....L 6
4 Spearywell......C 4
43 Speddoch.......C 9
16 Speen, Berks.....G 5
17 Speen, Bucks.....D 9
41 Speeton........H 11
30 Speke..........B 3
10 Speldhurst......D 4
18 Spellbrook......B 5
16 Spelsbury......B 4
14 Spelter........E 2
17 Spencers Wood...G 8
40 Spennithorne.....F 2
40 Spennymoor.....B 3
22 Spetchley......G 2
7 Spetisbury......F 12
27 Spexhall.......G 7
58 Spey Bay.......A 1
57 Speybridge......G 6
56 Speyview.......E 8
33 Spilsby........D 11
45 Spindlestone.....D 11
12 Spinkhill.......B 2
23 Spinney Hills.....B 9
61 Spinningdale.....G 7
61 Spital.........G 11
33 Spital in the Street.A 7
45 Spitalford......A 10
13 Spithurst.......F 3
49 Spittal, E. Lothian.B 7
42 Spittal, Kirk.....E 5
42 Spittal, Lanark...F 3
49 Spittal, Northumb.D 12
12 Spittal, Pemb.....E 3
42 Spittal, Wigtown..F 4
36 Spittal, Yorks....B 5
59 Spittal of Glenmuick J 1
53 Spittal of Glenshee M 7
59 Spittalburn......J 4
52 Spittalfield......C 6
5 Spixworth......D 5
3 Splatt.........A 9
10 Splayne's Green..F 3
32 Spofforth.......B 12
29 Spon Green......D 12
32 Spondon........G 1
26 Spooner Row.....F 4
26 Sporle.........D 2
49 Spott..........B 9
49 Spottiswoode....D 8
23 Spratton.......E 10
9 Spreakley.......B 9
4 Spreyton.......F 6
33 Spridlington.....B 7
38 Spring Valley.....H 2
47 Springburn......C 10
44 Springfield, Dumf.F 2
19 Springfield, Essex..C 7
53 Springfield, Fife...F 8
56 Springfield, Moray.D 6
22 Springfield, War..D 4
22 Springhill.......B 3
43 Springholm......E 9
44 Springkell.......E 1
47 Springside......E 8
32 Springthorpe.....A 6
45 Springwell......G 11
37 Sproatley.......D 9
30 Sproston Green...C 6
36 Sprotbrough.....G 3
27 Sproughton......L 4
49 Sprouston......F 10
26 Sprowston......D 6
22 Sproxton, Leics..H 6
40 Sproxton, Yorks..G 6
30 Spurstow.......E 4
57 Sronlairig Lodge..J 1
57 Sronphadruig Lo...L 3
35 Stackhouse......A 7
35 Stackpole.......G 3
35 Stacksteads......E 7
5 Staddiscombe....K 4
36 Staddlethorpe....E 6
17 Stadhampton.....D 7
39 Staffield........A 8
62 Staffin........A 4
31 Stafford.......H 8
31 Staffordshire, Co..H 8
24 Stagsden.......K 1
25 Stagsden W. End..K 1
35 Stainburn.......B 11
32 Stainby........H 6
13 Staincross......F 12
17 Staines........G 11
33 Stainfield, Lind...C 8
24 Stainfield, Kest...C 2

MAP
39 Stainforth,
   W. Riding.....H 10
36 Stainforth,
   W. Riding.....F 4
34 Staining........D 2
35 Stainland.......E 9
41 Stainsacre......D 9
39 Stainton, Cumb...B 7
40 Stainton, Dur....C 1
40 Stainton, N. Rid..D 5
40 Stainton, N. Rid..F 1
39 Stainton, Westmor.G 7
32 Stainton,
   W. Riding.....A 3
33 Stainton by
   Langworth.....B 8
37 Stainton le Vale..H 9
38 Stainton with
   Agarley.......H 5
41 Staintondale.....E 10
47 Stair, Ayr......G 9
38 Stair, Cumb.....C 5
26 Staithes........C 8
34 Stake Pool......B 3
45 Stakeford.......D 11
7 Stalbridge......D 10
7 Stalbridge Weston E 10
26 Stalham........C 7
26 Stalham Green...C 7
11 Stalisfield Green...C 8
39 Stalling Busk....G 11
37 Stallingborough...F 9
34 Stalmine.......C 3
35 Stalybridge......G 8
25 Stambourne......L 8
24 Stamford, Lincs...E 1
45 Stamford,
   Northumb.....A 10
36 Stamford Bridge..B 5
45 Stamfordham....F 9
38 Stanah........C 6
18 Stanborough.....C 2
17 Stanbridge, Beds..B 8
8 Stanbridge, Dorset.F 2
35 Stanbury.......C 9
47 Stand.........C 12
48 Standburn......B 2
22 Standeford......A 3
11 Stanford, Kent...D 10
21 Stanford Bishop..G 12
22 Stanford Bridge...F 1
16 Stanford Dingley..G 6
19 Stanford le Hope..F 7
23 Stanford on Avon.D 9
32 Stanford on Soar..H 3
21 Stanford on Teme F 12
18 Stanford Rivers...D 5
16 Stanford the Vale..E 4
10 Stanford's End...D 3
24 Stanground......F 3
26 Stanhoe........B 1
39 Stanhope.......A 12
23 Stanion........C 12
52 Stank.........F 1
32 Stanley, Derby...F 1
45 Stanley, Dur.....H 10
52 Stanley, Perth....D 6
31 Stanley, Staffs....E 8
16 Stanley, Wilts....G 1
35 Stanley, Yorks....E 12
32 Stanley Common...F 1
21 Stanley Hill.....H 12
35 Stanley Lane Ends E 12
10 Stanmer........G 2
16 Stanmore, Berks..F 6
8 Stanmore, Hants..C 6
18 Stanmore, London.E 2
44 Stannersburn....D 5
45 Stannington,
   Northumb.....E 10
31 Stannington, Yks..A 1
21 Stansbatch......F 9
27 Stansfield......K 1
31 Stanshope......E 9
27 Stanstead......K 1
18 Stanstead Abbots..C 4
27 Stanstead Street..K 1
10 Stansted.......B 5
18 Stansted
   Mountfitchet...A 5

MAP
31 Stanton, Derby...H 11
16 Stanton, Glos....A 2
14 Stanton, Mon.....B 6
45 Stanton, Northumb.B 8
31 Stanton, Staffs....F 9
27 Stanton, Suffolk...H 3
31 Stanton by Bridge G 12
32 Stanton by Dale...F 2
15 Stanton Drew....H 9
16 Stanton Fitzwarren E 3
16 Stanton Harcourt..D 5
32 Stanton Hill.....D 2
31 Stanton in Peak..D 11
21 Stanton Lacy....E 10
21 Stanton Long....C 11
32 Stanton on the
   Wolds........G 3
15 Stanton Prior....H 10
16 Stanton St.
   Bernard.......H 2
17 Stanton St. John..C 7
15 Stanton St.
   Quintin.......F 12
27 Stanton Street.....J 3
23 Stanton under
   Bardon........A 8
30 Stanton upon Hine
   Heath........H 4
15 Stanton Wick....H 9
30 Stanwardine in the
   Fields........H 3
19 Stanway, Essex...B 9
16 Stanway, Glos....A 2
17 Stanwell........G 11
17 Stanwell Moor...G 11
25 Stanwick.......H 1
41 Stape.........F 8
6 Stapehill.......F 2
30 Stapeley.......E 5
31 Stapenhill.......H 11
11 Staple, Kent.....B 11
6 Staple, Somerset...B 4
6 Staple Cross, Devon
       D 4
10 Staple Cross, Sussex
       F 6
6 Staple Fitzpaine..D 6
15 Staple Hill......G 9
10 Staplefield......D 3
25 Stapleford, Cambs. K 6
18 Stapleford, Herefs..B 3
32 Stapleford, Leics...H 5
32 Stapleford, Lincs..D 6
32 Stapleford, Notts..F 2
8 Stapleford, Wilts..B 2
18 Stapleford Abbotts D 5
18 Stapleford Tawney D 5
6 Staplegrove.....D 6
6 Staplehay.......D 5
10 Staplehurst.....D 6
6 Staplers........G 6
44 Stapleton, Cumb..F 3
21 Stapleton, Herefs..F 9
23 Stapleton, Leics...B 8
21 Stapleton, Salop..B 10
7 Stapleton, Som...D 8
40 Stapleton, Yorks...D 3
44 Stapleton Grange..F 1
6 Stapley........E 5
25 Staploe.........J 2
53 Star, Fife.......G 8
12 Star, Pemb.......C 6
15 Star, Somerset...H 7
39 Starbottom......H 11
6 Starcross......H 3
64 Starkigarth......E 7
25 Starlings Green...M 6
27 Starston.......G 5
39 Startforth......D 12
15 Startley........F 12
30 Statham........B 5
6 Stathe.........C 7
32 Stathern........G 5
40 Station Town.....B 4
25 Staughton Green...J 2
25 Staughton Highway J 2
15 Staunton, Glos...C 9
15 Staunton, Glos...A 11
31 Staunton Harold
   Hall.........H 12
32 Staunton in the
   Vale.........F 5
21 Staunton on Arrow F 9
21 Staunton on Wye..H 9
32 Staveley, Derby...C 2
38 Staveley, Lancs...G 6
39 Staveley, Westmor.E 7
35 Staveley, Yorks...A 12
5 Staverton, Devon..J 7
15 Staverton, Glos..B 12
23 Staverton,
   Northants......F 9
15 Staverton, Wilts..H 11

MAP
15 Staverton Bridge..B 12
7 Stawell........B 7
5 Stawford.......G 3
9 Stawley........D 4
61 Staxigoe.......B 12
41 Staxton.......G 10
20 Staylittle.......C 4
34 Staynall.......C 2
32 Staythorpe......E 5
40 Stean.........H 1
40 Stearsby.......H 6
6 Steart.........B 6
9 Stedham........D 10
45 Steel Rigg......E 8
44 Steele Road.....D 4
21 Steen's Bridge...G 11
9 Steep.........D 9
7 Steeple, Dorset...H 12
19 Steeple, Essex...D 9
7 Steeple Ashton...A 12
16 Steeple Aston....B 6
16 Steeple Barton....B 5
25 Steeple Bumpstead.L 8
17 Steeple Claydon..A 8
25 Steeple Gidding...G 2
8 Steeple Langford..B 2
25 Steeple Morden...L 4
35 Steeton.......C 9
62 Stein..........C 2
58 Steinmanhill.....C 5
45 Stelling Hall.....F 8
10 Stelling Minnis...C 10
3 Stenalees.......D 7
48 Stenhousemuir...A 2
64 Stenness.......D 1
62 Stenscholl......A 4
31 Stenson........G 11
64 Stenswall......D 7
49 Stenton........B 9
12 Stepaside......F 5
45 Stepends.......C 9
18 Stepney........F 4
25 Steppingley......M 1
47 Stepps.........C 11
27 Sternfield......J 7
16 Stert..........H 1
18 Stetchworth......J 7
18 Stevenage......B 2
47 Stevenston......E 7
16 Steventon, Berks..E 5
9 Steventon, Hants..A 7
25 Stevington......K 1
25 Stewartby.......L 5
46 Stewarton, Argyll.G 2
47 Stewarton, Ayr...E 9
17 Stewkley.......B 9
33 Stewton........B 10
12 Steynton.......F 4
8 Stibb..........E 1
4 Stibb Cross......D 3
16 Stibb Green......H 3
26 Stibbard.......C 3
24 Stibbington......F 2
49 Stichill........F 9
3 Sticker.........E 7
33 Stickford.......D 10
4 Sticklepath, Devon.F 5
6 Sticklepath, Som..E 6
33 Stickney........D 10
26 Stiffkey........A 3
12 Stiff's Bridge....F 4
18 Stifford........F 6
22 Stifford's Bridge..G 1
10 Stile Bridge.....C 6
36 Stillingfleet.....C 4
40 Stillington, Dur...C 4
40 Stillington, Yorks..H 6
24 Stilton........F 3
15 Stinchcombe....D 10
7 Stinsford.......G 10
31 Stirchley.......B 12
61 Stirkoke House...C 12
58 Stirling, Aber....C 8
52 Stirling, Stirling..H 3
19 Stisted........A 8
16 Stitchcombe.....G 3
5 Stithians.......C 4
56 Stittenham......B 2
23 Stivichall.......D 7
33 Stixwould.......D 9
30 Stoak.........C 3
48 Stobo.........F 4
19 Stoborough......D 7
7 Stoborough Grn..H 12
49 Stobswood, Ber...D 9
45 Stobswood,
   Northumb.....D 10
48 Stobwood.......D 2
19 Stock..........D 7
22 Stock Wood......F 3
58 Stockbridge, Aber..C 8
8 Stockbridge, Hants.C 5

MAP
43 Stockbridgehill....D 12
47 Stockbriggs......F 12
11 Stockbury.......B 7
16 Stockcross......G 5
38 Stockdale Wath...A 6
23 Stockerston.....B 11
9 Stockheath......E 8
43 Stockholm......B 11
47 Stockiemuir.....A 10
18 Stocking Pelham..A 4
23 Stockingford.....C 7
6 Stockland......F 6
6 Stockland Bristol..B 6
4 Stockleigh English.E 7
4 Stockleigh Pomeroy F 7
16 Stockley.......G 1
7 Stocklinch......E 7
31 Stockport......A 7
35 Stocksbridge....G 11
45 Stocksfield.....G 9
21 Stockton, Herefs..F 10
26 Stockton, Norfolk.F 7
21 Stockton, Salop..B 8
22 Stockton, Salop..B 1
23 Stockton, War....F 8
8 Stockton, Wilts...B 1
30 Stockton Heath...B 5
40 Stockton on-Tees..C 4
40 Stockton on Tees.E 1
36 Stockton-on-the-
   Forest........B 4
11 Stodmarsh......B 11
26 Stody.........B 4
60 Stoer.........D 2
8 Stoford, Som.....E 9
8 Stoford, Wilts....C 2
6 Stogumber......C 4
6 Stogursey......B 5
4 Stoke, Devon.....D 1
8 Stoke, Hants.....A 5
9 Stoke, Hants.....F 8
11 Stoke, Kent.....A 7
27 Stoke, Suffolk....L 5
7 Stoke Abbott.....F 8
23 Stoke Albany....C 11
27 Stoke Ash.......H 4
32 Stoke Bardolph...F 4
21 Stoke Bliss......F 12
23 Stoke Bruerne...G 10
8 Stoke-by-Clare....L 8
27 Stoke-by-Nayland.L 3
6 Stoke Canon......F 3
8 Stoke Charity....B 6
3 Stoke Climsland..B 10
21 Stoke Cross.....G 1
17 Stoke D'Abernon H 12
25 Stoke Doyle.....G 1
23 Stoke Dry.......F 2
33 Stoke Edith.....H 11
8 Stoke Farthing...D 2
24 Stoke Ferry.....E 8
5 Stoke Fleming...L 7
5 Stoke Gabriel....K 7
15 Stoke Gifford....F 9
23 Stoke Golding....B 7
23 Stoke Goldington G 11
17 Stoke Green.....F 10
17 Stoke Hammond..A 9
26 Stoke Holy Cross..E 5
21 Stoke Lacy......G 11
17 Stoke Lyne......A 6
17 Stoke Mandeville..C 9
45 Stoke Newington..E 3
31 Stoke-on-Trent...F 7
15 Stoke Orchard...A 12
6 Stoke Pero......B 2
17 Stoke Poges.....F 10
21 Stoke Prior,
   Herefordshire..G 10
22 Stoke Prior, Worcs. E 3
4 Stoke Rivers.....C 5
32 Stoke Rochford...G 6
16 Stoke Row......H 8
7 Stoke St. Gregory.D 7
6 Stoke St. Mary...D 6
7 Stoke St. Michael.B 10
21 Stoke
   St. Milborough.D 11
7 Stoke sub Hamdon D 8
17 Stoke Talmage...D 7
7 Stoke Trister....C 10
30 Stoke upon Tern..G 5
7 Stoke Wake.....F 11
12 Stokeford.......G 12
32 Stokeham......C 5
5 Stokeinteignhead..J 8
17 Stokenchurch....D 9
5 Stokenham......L 7
21 Stokesay.......D 10
26 Stokesby.......D 1
40 Stokesley......D 5
6 Stolford.......B 5
7 Ston Easton.....A 9

MAP
17 Stone, Bucks......C 8
15 Stone, Glos......E 10
10 Stone, Kent......A 4
11 Stone, Kent.......E 8
31 Stone, Staffs......G 7
22 Stone, Worcs......E 2
7 Stone Allerton....A 7
24 Stone Bridge Corner.........E 4
35 Stone Chair.....D 10
4 Stone Cross, Devon.........C 5
11 Stone Cross, Kent .D 9
10 Stone Cross, Sussex.........H 5
39 Stone House.....G 10
10 Stone Street......C 4
26 Stonebridge, Norf..B 6
22 Stonebridge, War..D 5
32 Stonebroom......D 1
10 Stonecrouch......E 6
15 Stone-edge Batch..G 8
37 Stoneferry........D 8
47 Stonefield.......D 11
46 Stonefield Castle Hotel..........B 4
44 Stonegarthside....E 3
10 Stonegate, Sussex..E 5
41 Stonegate, Yorks...D 8
58 Stonegate Crofts..D 8
41 Stonegrave........G 7
44 Stonehaugh.......E 6
59 Stonehaven.......J 6
5 Stonehouse, Devon.K 3
15 Stonehouse, Glos. D 11
43 Stonehouse, Kirk..E 9
47 Stonehouse, Lan..E 12
44 Stonehouse, Northumb......G 5
23 Stoneleigh........E 7
25 Stonely...........J 2
19 Stone's Green....A 11
32 Stonesby.........H 5
16 Stonesfield........B 5
38 Stonethwaite.......D 5
8 Stoney Cross......E 4
31 Stoney Middleton C 10
23 Stoney Stanton....C 8
7 Stoney Stoke.....C 10
7 Stoney Stratton ..B 10
21 Stoney Stretton...A 9
48 Stoneyburn, Lanark.........G 2
48 Stoneyburn, W. Lothian.......C 2
23 Stoneygate........B 9
19 Stoneyhills.......D 9
42 Stoneykirk........F 2
58 Stoneywood........F 6
27 Stonham Aspal....J 4
17 Stonor...........E 8
23 Stonton Wyville..C 10
4 Stony Cross, Devon.........C 4
22 Stony Cross, Herefordshire...G 1
34 Stony Hill........D 2
23 Stony Stratford ..H 11
4 Stoodleigh, Devon.C 5
6 Stoodleigh, Devon.D 3
9 Stopham........D 11
17 Stopsley.........B 12
30 Storeton.........B 2
35 Storiths..........B 9
63 Stornoway........D 5
22 Storridge..........G 1
9 Storrington......E 12
39 Storth............G 7
36 Storwood.........C 5
56 Stotfield..........C 8
25 Stotford...........L 3
21 Stottesdon.......D 12
23 Stoughton, Leics...B 9
9 Stoughton, Surrey A 11
9 Stoughton, Sussex .E 9
55 Stoul............K 1
22 Stoulton..........G 3
7 Stour Provost.....D 11
7 Stour Row......D 11
22 Stourbridge.......D 2
7 Stourpaine.......E 12
22 Stourport-on-Severn........E 2
22 Stourton, Staffs....D 2
22 Stourton, War....H 6
7 Stourton, Wilts...C 11
7 Stourton Caundle.E 10
64 Stove............B 3
27 Stoven...........G 7
32 Stow, Lincs.......B 6
49 Stow, Midlothian..E 7
24 Stow Bardolph....E 7
26 Stow Bedon.......F 3

MAP
25 Stow cum Quy....J 6
25 Stow Longa......H 2
19 Stow Maries......D 8
16 Stow-on-the-Wold .B 3
24 Stowbridge.......E 7
21 Stowe, Salop......E 8
31 Stowe, Staffs......G 8
15 Stowe Green......D 9
7 Stowell..........D 10
27 Stowlangtoft......H 3
27 Stowmarket.......J 3
11 Stowting........D 10
27 Stowupland.......J 4
46 Straad...........C 5
57 Straanruie........H 6
59 Strachan.........H 4
51 Strachur.........G 8
27 Stradbroke.......H 5
25 Stradishall........K 8
24 Stradsett.........E 8
32 Stragglethorpe....E 6
43 Strahanna........B 7
42 Straid............C 2
43 Straith...........C 9
42 Straiton..........A 5
58 Straloch, Aber.....E 6
52 Straloch, Perth....A 5
31 Stramshall........G 9
59 Stranathro.......H 6
48 Strand...........G 2
47 Strandhead.......G 9
38 Strands..........E 4
38 Strang...........H 2
41 Stranghow........D 7
59 Stranog..........H 6
42 Stranraer.........E 1
20 Strata Florida.....F 3
17 Stratfield Mortimer H 7
17 Stratfield Saye....H 8
17 Stratfield Turgis...H 8
18 Stratford.........F 4
27 Stratford St. Andrew.....J 6
27 Stratford St. Mary M 3
8 Stratford sub Castle.........C 3
8 Stratford Tony....C 2
22 Stratford-upon-Avon.........G 5
52 Strathallan Castle..F 4
55 Strathan, Inver....K 3
60 Strathan, Suther...E 2
60 Strathan, Suther...A 6
47 Strathaven.......E 12
47 Strathblane......B 10
54 Strathcarron......E 3
50 Strathcoil.......D 4
58 Strathdon.........F 1
60 Strathkanaird.....F 3
53 Strathkinness.....F 9
57 Strathmashie Ho...K 2
53 Strathmiglo.......F 7
61 Strathmore Hotel. C 10
54 Strathpeffer.......D 8
54 Strathrannoch.....B 8
54 Strathvaich Lo.....B 7
61 Strathy...........A 8
61 Strathy Inn.......A 8
52 Strathyre.........E 1
4 Stratton, Corn.....E 1
7 Stratton, Dorset. .G 10
16 Stratton, Glos.....D 1
17 Stratton Audley...B 7
7 Stratton-on-the-Fosse.........A 10
16 Stratton St. Margaret....E 3
26 Stratton St. Michael.....F 5
26 Stratton Strawless C 5
53 Stravithie.........F 10
10 Streat............F 2
18 Streatham........G 3
17 Streatley, Beds.....A 11
17 Streatley, Berks....F 7
7 Street, Somerset...C 8
41 Street, Yorks.......E 7
30 Street Dinas.......F 2
11 Street End ,Kent..C 10
9 Street End, Sussex F 10
36 Street Houses.....C 3
57 Street of Kincardine.....H 5
22 Streethay.........A 5
36 Streethouse.......E 2
40 Streetlam.........E 3
22 Streetly...........B 4
21 Strefford........D 10
32 Strelley...........F 2
36 Strensall.........A 4
6 Stretcholt........B 6
5 Strete...........L 7
35 Stretford.........H 7

MAP
25 Strethall..........L 6
25 Stretham.........H 6
30 Stretton, Cheshire .B 5
30 Stretton, Cheshire .E 3
32 Stretton, Derby....D 1
23 Stretton, Rut......A 12
22 Stretton, Staffs....A 2
31 Stretton, Staffs...G 11
22 Stretton en le Field A 6
21 Stretton Grandison.....H 11
21 Stretton Heath....A 9
23 Stretton-on-Dunsmore......E 7
22 Stretton on Fosse..H 6
21 Stretton Sugwas..H 10
23 Stretton-under-Fosse...........D 8
58 Strichen..........B 7
6 Stringston........B 5
23 Strixton.........F 12
15 Stroat............E 9
54 Stromeferry.......F 2
54 Stromemore.......F 2
64 Stromness.........D 1
51 Stronachlachar...F 11
55 Stronchreggan Ho.M 4
63 Strond...........H 1
47 Strone, Arg.......A 7
51 Strone, Dunb....H 10
55 Strone, Inver......L 5
57 Strone, Inver......G 1
60 Stronechrubie.....E 4
55 Stronenaba.......L 6
57 Stronetoper.......K 4
51 Stronmilchan.....E 8
50 Strontian.........A 5
50 Strontoiller.......E 6
51 Stronuich........C 12
10 Strood...........A 6
10 Strood Green.....C 1
15 Stroud, Glos.....D 11
9 Stroud, Hants.....D 8
19 Stroud Green.....E 8
17 Stroude.........G 11
32 Stroxton.........G 6
62 Struan...........D 3
33 Strubby.........B 11
26 Strumpshaw......E 6
54 Struy.............F 8
58 Stuartfield........C 7
38 Stub Place........F 3
9 Stubbington.......F 7
35 Stubbins..........E 7
11 Stubbs Cross.....D 8
44 Stubbyknowe......F 2
8 Stubhampton.....E 1
44 Stublick..........G 6
34 Stubshaw Cross...G 5
32 Stubton..........E 6
46 Stuck............B 5
51 Stuckgowan.....G 10
51 Stuckindroin.....F 10
8 Stuckton.........E 3
17 Stud Green.......F 9
45 Studdon..........H 7
39 Studfold..........E 9
17 Studham........C 11
8 Studland.........H 2
17 Studley, Oxon.....C 7
22 Studley, War......F 4
16 Studley, Wilts.....G 1
40 Studley Roger.....H 3
25 Stump Cross......L 6
25 Stuntney..........G 7
10 Stunts Green.... G 5
31 Sturbridge........G 7
25 Sturmer..........L 8
7 Sturminster Com..E 11
8 Sturminster Marshall.........F 1
7 Sturminster Newton.......E 11
11 Sturry...........B 10
37 Sturton..........G 7
32 Sturton by Stow...B 6
32 Sturton le Steeple..B 5
27 Stuston..........H 4
27 Stutton, Suffolk...M 4
36 Stutton, Yorks.....C 3
31 Styal.............B 7
32 Styrrup...........A 3
58 Succoth, Aber.....D 2
51 Succoth, Arg.....G 10
21 Suckley..........G 12
25 Sudborough......G 1
27 Sudbourne.......K 7
33 Sudbrook, Lincs...F 7
15 Sudbrook, Mon....F 8
33 Sudbrooke........C 7
18 Sudbury, Derby..G 10
18 Sudbury, London..E 2
27 Sudbury, Suffolk..L 2

MAP
56 Suddie...........D 2
15 Sudgrove.........D 12
26 Suffield, Norfolk ..B 5
41 Suffield, Yorks....F 10
27 Suffolk, County ...J 4
30 Sugnall...........G 6
61 Suisgill...........E 9
62 Suisnish..........E 5
38 Sulby.............G 2
23 Sulgrave.........H 9
17 Sulham..........G 7
17 Sulhamstead......G 7
17 Sulhamstead Abbots.........G 7
62 Sulishaderbeg.....D 4
9 Sullington.......E 12
64 Sullom...........C 7
14 Sully.............G 5
29 Summer Hill.....E 12
35 Summerbridge...A 10
2 Summercourt.....D 6
40 Summerhouse.....C 2
15 Summerleaze.....F 7
35 Summerseat.......F 7
16 Summertown.....C 6
35 Summit, Lancs.....F 8
35 Summit, Lancs.....E 8
17 Sunbury on Thames.......G 11
43 Sundaywell.......C 9
38 Sunderland, Cumb. B 4
45 Sunderland, Durham G 12
34 Sunderland, Lancs. B 3
40 Sunderland Bridge .A 3
48 Sundhope........G 6
17 Sundon Park.....B 11
10 Sundridge........C 4
50 Sunipol..........B 1
37 Sunk Island......E 10
17 Sunningdale.....G 10
17 Sunninghill......G 10
16 Sunningwell......D 6
40 Sunniside, Dur....A 2
45 Sunniside, Dur...G 10
38 Sunny Bank.......F 5
56 Sunnyhillock......D 4
52 Sunnylaw.........G 3
10 Sunnyside........D 3
8 Sunton...........A 4
49 Sunwick.........D 11
18 Surbiton.........G 2
38 Surby............H 1
24 Surfleet..........C 3
24 Surfleet Seas End..C 4
26 Surlingham.......E 6
10 Surrey, County....C 2
26 Sustead..........B 5
36 Susworth.........G 6
4 Sutcombe.........E 2
64 Sutherland........E 2
60 Sutherland, Co.....D 6
26 Suton............E 4
56 Sutors of Cromarty C 4
33 Sutterby.........C 11
24 Sutterton.........B 4
25 Sutton, Beds......K 3
17 Sutton, Bucks....F 11
25 Sutton, Cambs.....G 5
24 Sutton, Hunts.....F 2
11 Sutton, Kent.....C 12
34 Sutton, Lancs.....H 4
18 Sutton, London...H 3
26 Sutton, Norfolk...C 7
32 Sutton, Notts......B 4
32 Sutton, Notts......F 5
16 Sutton, Oxon......C 5
12 Sutton, Pemb......E 3
22 Sutton, Salop.....C 1
30 Sutton, Salop.....G 5
7 Sutton, Som.......C 9
30 Sutton, Staffs.....H 6
27 Sutton, Suffolk....K 6
9 Sutton, Surrey...B 12
9 Sutton, Sussex...B 11
36 Sutton, Yorks......F 3
23 Sutton Bassett...C 11
10 Sutton at Hone...A 4
15 Sutton Benger....F 12
32 Sutton Bonington H 2
24 Sutton Bridge.....C 6
23 Sutton Cheney....B 7
22 Sutton Coldfield...B 5
16 Sutton Courteney..E 6
24 Sutton Crosses....C 5
40 Sutton Grange....H 3
9 Sutton Green....A 11
40 Sutton Howgrave..G 3
32 Sutton in Ashfield.D 2
5 Sutton-in-Craven..C 8
23 Sutton in the Elms.C 8
31 Sutton Lane Ends..C 8
21 Sutton Maddock .B 12

MAP
7 Sutton Mallet.....C 7
8 Sutton Mandeville.C 1
7 Sutton Montis....D 9
37 Sutton-on-Hull....D 9
33 Sutton on Sea....B 12
36 Sutton-on-the-Forest.........A 4
31 Sutton on the Hill G 11
32 Sutton on Trent...D 5
24 Sutton St. Edmund D 5
24 Sutton St. James ..D 5
21 Sutton St. Michael....H 10
21 Sutton St. Nicholas...H 10
8 Sutton Scotney....B 6
22 Sutton-under-Brailes.........H 6
40 Sutton-under-Whitestonecliffe. G 5
36 Sutton upon Derwent........B 5
11 Sutton Valence.....C 7
7 Sutton Veny.....B 11
7 Sutton Waldron..E 12
15 Sutton Wick......H 9
33 Swaby..........B 11
31 Swadlincote.....H 11
26 Swaffham.........E 1
25 Swaffham Bulbeck .J 7
25 Swaffham Prior....J 7
26 Swafield..........B 6
40 Swainby..........E 5
26 Swainsthorpe.....E 5
15 Swainswick......G 10
23 Swalcliffe.........H 7
11 Swalecliffe.......A 10
37 Swallow..........G 9
8 Swallowcliffe......C 1
17 Swallowfield......H 8
32 Swallownest......B 2
45 Swalwell........G 10
30 Swan Green......C 6
8 Swanage.........H 2
64 Swanbister.......D 2
17 Swanbourne......A 9
63 Swanibost........A 6
37 Swanland........D 7
10 Swanley..........A 4
10 Swanley Village...A 4
9 Swanmore........D 7
23 Swannington, Leics.A 7
26 Swannington, Norf.D 4
10 Swanscombe......A 5
13 Swansea........H 10
26 Swanton Abbott...C 6
26 Swanton Morley..D 3
26 Swanton Novers...B 3
32 Swanwick........E 1
24 Swarby...........B 1
26 Swardeston.......E 5
31 Swarkestone.....G 12
45 Swarland........C 10
45 Swarland Estate..C 10
9 Swarraton........B 7
24 Swaton..........B 2
25 Swavesey.........H 5
8 Sway..............F 4
33 Swayfield.........H 7
8 Swaythling........D 6
21 Sweet Green.....F 12
4 Sweetham........F 7
39 Sweetholme.......C 8
49 Sweethope........E 9
3 Sweethouse.......C 8
27 Swefling..........J 6
23 Swepstone........A 7
16 Swerford.........A 5
30 Swettenham.......C 6
27 Swilland..........K 5
36 Swillington.......D 2
4 Swimbridge.......C 5
4 Swimbridge Newland.......C 5
16 Swinbrook........C 4
32 Swinderley.......D 6
15 Swindon, Glos...B 12
22 Swindon, Staffs....C 2
16 Swindon, Wilts....F 3
37 Swine............H 9
36 Swinefleet........E 5
15 Swineford.......G 10
25 Swineshead, Beds...J 2
24 Swineshead, Lincs..B 3
24 Swineshead Bridge.A 3
61 Swiney..........D 11
16 Swinford, Berks....C 5
23 Swinford, Leics....D 9
11 Swingfield Minnis D 10
11 Swingfield Street .D 11
47 Swinhill.........D 12
45 Swinhoe.........E 12
37 Swinhope........G 9

MAP
40 Swinithwaite......F 1
44 Swinnie...........A 5
31 Swinscoe.........E 9
44 Swinside Hall.....A 5
24 Swinstead.........C 1
49 Swinton, Ber.....E 11
34 Swinton, Lancs....G 6
41 Swinton, N. Riding H 7
40 Swinton, N. Riding G 2
36 Swinton. W. Riding G 2
49 Swinton Quarter..E 11
49 Swintonmill......E 10
23 Swithland.........A 9
63 Swordale, Lewis...D 6
56 Swordale, Ross & Cromarty.......C 1
55 Swordland........K 2
61 Swordly..........B 7
30 Sworton Heath....B 5
20 Swydd-ffynnon....F 3
31 Swynnerton.......G 7
7 Swyre............G 8
20 Sychnant.........E 5
20 Sychtyn..........B 5
15 Syde............C 12
17 Sydenham........D 8
5 Sydenham Damerel H 3
26 Syderstone.......B 1
7 Sydling St. Nicholas....F 10
16 Sydmonton.......H 6
32 Syerston..........E 5
35 Syke.............F 8
36 Sykehouse........E 4
34 Sykes............B 5
64 Symbister........D 8
47 Symington, Ayr....F 8
48 Symington, Lan....F 3
15 Symonds Yat.....C 9
7 Symondsbury.....G 8
13 Synod Inn........B 7
49 Synton Parkhead..G 7
61 Syre.............C 7
23 Syresham........H 9
23 Syston, Leics......A 9
32 Syston, Lincs......F 6
22 Sytchampton......F 2
23 Sywell..........E 11
54 Taagan...........C 4
47 Tackhouse.......E 11
16 Tackley..........B 6
26 Tacolneston.......F 4
36 Tadcaster.........C 3
31 Taddington......C 10
4 Taddiport........D 4
17 Tadley...........H 7
25 Tadlow..........K 4
23 Tadmarton........H 7
15 Tadwick.........G 10
10 Tadworth.........B 1
14 Tafarnau-bach....C 4
29 Tafarn-gelyn.....D 11
12 Tafarn-y-bwlch...D 4
14 Taffs Well........F 5
20 Tafolwern........B 4
20 Tai..............D 7
29 Tai-bach, Denb...G 10
13 Taibach, Glam...H 11
29 Tai-mawr.........F 9
61 Tain, Caithness ..A 11
56 Tain, Ross & Cromarty.......B 3
29 Tainant.........F 12
13 Tairgwaith.......F 10
28 Tai'r-lon..........E 4
18 Takeley...........B 5
18 Takeley Street.....B 5
14 Talachddu........A 4
29 Talacre..........B 10
6 Talaton...........F 4
12 Talbenny.........F 2
14 Talbot Green......F 4
8 Talbot Village....G 2
20 Talerddig.........B 5
13 Talgarreg.........B 7
14 Talgarth..........A 5
20 Taliesin..........C 2
62 Talisker..........E 3
31 Talke............E 7
44 Talkin...........G 4
48 Talla Linnfoots...G 4
54 Talladale.........C 3
29 Tallard...........G 8
30 Tallarn Green.....F 3
38 Tallentire.........B 3
13 Talley...........D 9
24 Tallington........E 2
60 Talmine..........B 6
13 Talog............D 7
20 Talsarn...........G 1
28 Talsarnau........G 5
2 Talskiddy........C 6
28 Talwrn, Angl.....C 4

MAP
29 Talwrn, Denb....E 12
14 Talybont, Brec.....B 4
28 Tal-y-bont, Caer...C 5
29 Tal-y-bont, Caer...C 7
20 Talybont, Cards...C 2
28 Tal-y-bont, Mer...H 5
29 Tal-y-cafn.......C 7
15 Tal-y-coed.......C 7
14 Tal-y-garn.......F 4
14 Tal-y-llyn, Brec...B 4
20 Tal-y-llyn, Mer....A 3
28 Tal-y-sarn.......E 4
14 Talywain.........D 6
20 Tal-y-wern.......B 4
40 Tame............D 5
5 Tamerton Foliot ..K 3
22 Tamworth.......B 5
39 Tan Hill.........E 11
12 Tancredston......D 2
11 Tanden..........D 8
47 Tandlemuir.......C 8
10 Tandridge........C 3
45 Tanfield.........G 10
45 Tanfield Lea......H 10
8 Tangley..........A 5
9 Tangmere........E 10
64 Tankerness.......D 3
35 Tankersley.......G 12
28 Tan-lan..........F 5
61 Tannach.........C 12
59 Tannachie........J 5
59 Tannadice........L 2
27 Tannington......H 5
31 Tansley.........D 11
31 Tansley Knoll....D 11
24 Tansor..........F 2
45 Tantobie........H 10
40 Tanton..........D 5
22 Tanworth in Arden E 5
28 Tan-y-bwlch......F 6
29 Tan-y-fron.......D 9
28 Tan-y-graig, Caer...E 3
20 Tan-y-graig, Cards. E 3
28 Tan-y-grisiau.....F 6
12 Tan-y-groes......B 6
29 Tan-y-pistyll.....G 10
17 Taplow..........F 10
46 Tarbert, Argyll...A 1
46 Tarbert, Argyll....C 4
63 Tarbert, Lewis....G 2
51 Tarbet, Dunb....G 10
55 Tarbet, Inver.....K 2
60 Tarbet, Suther.....C 3
47 Tarbolton.........G 9
48 Tarbrax..........D 3
30 Tarbuck Green....A 3
44 Tarcoon..........E 2
22 Tardebigge.......E 3
59 Tarfside.........J 2
59 Tarland..........G 2
34 Tarleton.........E 3
34 Tarlscough.......F 3
15 Tarlton.........D 12
34 Tarnbrook.......B 5
30 Tarporley........D 4
6 Tarr.............C 4
8 Tarrant Crawford..F 1
8 Tarrant Gunville ..E 1
8 Tarrant Hinton....E 1
8 Tarrant Keyneston. F 1
8 Tarrant Launceston E 1
8 Tarrant Monkton..E 1
8 Tarrant Rawston..E 1
8 Tarrant Rushton..E 1
10 Tarring Neville ..H 3
21 Tarrington......H 11
62 Tarskavaig.......G 5
58 Tarves..........D 6
54 Tarvie..........D 8
30 Tarvin..........D 4
26 Tasburgh........F 5
21 Tasley..........C 12
16 Taston..........B 5
31 Tatenhill.......H 10
43 Tath Hill.......B 11
39 Tatham..........H 8
33 Tathwell........B 10
17 Tatling End.....E 11
10 Tatsfield........B 3
30 Tattenhall.......D 3
26 Tatterford......C 2
26 Tattersett.......C 1
33 Tattershall......D 9
33 Tattershall Bridge. E 9
33 Tattershall Thorpe. D 9
27 Tattingstone....L 4
27 Tattingstone
    Whitehorse....L 4
6 Tatworth........F 6
58 Tauchers........C 1
6 Taunton.........D 6
26 Taverham........D 5
12 Tavernspite......F 5

MAP
5 Tavistock........H 3
4 Taw Green, Devon E 5
4 Taw Green, Devon F 5
4 Tawstock........C 4
31 Taxal...........B 8
47 Tayburn........E 10
51 Taychreggan.....E 7
46 Tayinloan.......E 2
52 Taymouth Castle..C 3
51 Taynafead......F 8
15 Taynton, Glos...B 10
16 Taynton, Oxon...C 3
51 Taynuilt.........D 7
53 Tayport.........D 9
46 Tayvallich......A 2
33 Tealby..........A 8
62 Teangue.........G 6
39 Tebay...........E 8
17 Tebworth.......A 10
4 Tedburn St. Mary.F 7
16 Teddington, Glos..A 1
18 Teddington, London
                  G 2
21 Tedstone Delamere
                  F 12
21 Tedstone Wafre ..F 12
23 Teeton.........E 10
8 Teffont Evias.....C 1
8 Teffont Magna....C 2
12 Tegryn..........D 6
23 Teigh..........A 12
5 Teigngrace......H 7
5 Teignmouth.....H 8
56 Teindland......D 8
44 Teindside.......B 3
21 Telford........B 12
10 Telham..........G 6
7 Tellisford.......A 11
10 Telscombe......H 3
43 Templand.......C 11
3 Temple, Cornwall..B 8
48 Temple, Midfoth..D 6
13 Temple Bar, Cards. B 10
13 Temple Bar, Carm. E 9
22 Temple Ballsall...E 5
7 Temple Cloud....A 9
11 Temple Ewell...D 11
22 Temple Grafton..G 5
14 Temple Guiting ..A 2
36 Temple Hirst.....E 4
32 Temple Normanton
                  C 1
39 Temple Sowerby..C 8
7 Templecombe....D 10
53 Templehall......H 7
6 Templeton, Devon. E 2
12 Templeton, Pemb. F 4
8 Templeton Bridge. E 7
25 Tempsford.......K 3
24 Ten Mile Bank....F 7
21 Tenbury Wells ..F 11
12 Tenby..........G 5
19 Tendring........B 11
19 Tendring Green ..A 11
64 Tenston.........C 1
11 Tenterden.......E 7
42 Terally.........G 2
19 Terling.........B 7
30 Ternhill........G 5
2 Terras..........D 6
17 Terrick.........C 9
41 Terrington......H 7
24 Terrington St. Clement
                  D 6
24 Terrington St. John
                  D 6
10 Teston..........C 6
8 Testwood.......E 5
15 Tetbury........E 12
15 Tetbury Upton...E 12
30 Tetchill........G 3
4 Tetcott.........F 2
33 Tetford........C 10
37 Tetney.........G 10
37 Tetney Lock....G 11
17 Tetsworth.......D 8
22 Tettenhall.......B 2
58 Teuchan........D 8
58 Teuchar.........C 5
53 Teuchatcroft....B 9
32 Teversal........D 2
25 Teversham.......J 6
22 Teviothead......C 4
59 Tewel...........J 6
18 Tewin...........B 3
15 Tewkesbury......A 12
11 Teynham........B 8
11 Teynham Street...B 8
38 Thackthwaite, Cumb.
                  C 4
38 Thackthwaite, Cumb.
                  C 6
9 Thakeham.......D 12

MAP
17 Thame..........D 8
17 Thames Ditton...G 12
11 Thanington......B 10
48 Thankerton.....F 2
26 Tharston........F 5
16 Thatcham.......G 6
34 Thatto Heath.....H 4
25 Thaxted.........M 7
62 The Aird........C 3
21 The Bàge........H 8
43 The Barony, Dumf.
                  C 11
64 The Barony, Orkney
                  B 1
31 The Beeches.....H 9
62 The Braes.......E 4
21 The Broad.......F 10
18 The Camp.......C 12
10 The Chart.......C 3
17 The City........D 8
15 The Cleaver.....A 8
8 The Common....C 4
21 The Corner.....D 10
60 The Craigs......G 5
38 The Cronk.......F 2
47 The Den........D 8
24 The Engine......E 4
44 The Fauld.......F 2
44 The Flatt.......E 4
11 The Forstal.....C 7
38 The Green, Lancs. G 4
7 The Green, Wilts. C 12
43 The Grove.......D 10
49 The Hardens....D 10
9 The Haven......C 12
27 The Heath......L 2
10 The Hermitage...C 1
46 The Highland Hotel
                  A 5
38 The Howe.......H 1
19 The Hythe.......B 10
43 The Lake.......G 7
11 The Leacon.....E 8
17 The Lee.........D 10
38 The Lhen........F 2
21 The Marsh......C 8
45 The Middles.....H 10
10 The Moor.......E 6
61 The Mound......G 8
47 The Murray.....D 11
14 The Ness........A 8
59 The Neuk.......H 5
15 The Oval.......H 10
15 The Pill........F 8
58 The Pole of Itlaw..B 4
21 The Pound......E 7
15 The Quarry.....D 10
12 The Rhos.......F 4
9 The Sands......B 10
16 The Slade.......G 6
11 The Stocks......E 8
19 The Stone.......C 9
17 The Throat......G 9
2 The Towans......F 3
21 The Vauld......G 10
29 The Wyke.......B 1
40 Theakston......G 3
37 Thealby........E 7
17 Theale, Berks...G 7
7 Theale, Somerset. B 8
17 Theale Green....G 7
43 Theapland......H 12
37 Thearne........C 8
27 Theberton......J 7
33 Theddlethorpe
    All Saints.....A 11
33 Theddlethorpe
    St. Helen.....A 11
4 Thelbridge Cross ..E 7
15 Thelnetham.....G 3
30 Thelwall.......B 5
26 Themelthorpe....C 4
17 Thenford.......H 8
25 Therfield........L 4
27 Thetford.......G 2
18 Theydon Bois...D 4
15 Thickwood.....G 11
33 Thimbleby, Lincs. C 9
41 Thimbleby, Yorks. F 5
40 Thirkleby.......G 5
40 Thirlby........G 5
48 Thirlestane......E 8
40 Thirlspot.......C 5
40 Thirn..........G 2
40 Thirsk.........G 5
38 Thistlebottom....A 5
34 Thistleton, Lancs. C 3
32 Thistleton, Leics...H 8
25 Thistley Green....H 8
36 Thixendale......A 6
45 Thockrington....E 8
24 Tholomas Drove..E 5

MAP
40 Tholthorpe.......H 5
12 Thomas Chapel...F 4
39 Thomas Close....A 7
58 Thomastown.....D 3
26 Thompson.......F 2
37 Thomshill......D 8
10 Thong..........A 5
32 Thonock........A 5
39 Thoralby........F 12
37 Thoresway......G 9
37 Thorganby, Lincs..G 9
36 Thorganby, Yorks. C 5
41 Thorgill........E 7
27 Thorington......H 7
37 Thorington Street..L 3
35 Thorlby........B 8
18 Thorley, Herts....B 5
18 Thorley, I.o.W....G 5
18 Thorley Street, Herts.
                  G 5
8 Thorley Street, I.o.W.
                  G 5
40 Thormanby......H 5
11 Thorn..........F 7
40 Thornaby-on-Tees. C 5
26 Thornage.......B 4
17 Thornborough, Bucks.
                  A 8
40 Thornborough, Yorks.
                  G 3
4 Thornbury, Devon. E 3
15 Thornbury, Glos...E 9
32 Thornbury, Herefs.
                  F 11
23 Thornby.........E 10
31 Thorncliff......D 8
7 Thorncombe.....F 7
9 Thorncombe Street
                  B 11
25 Thorncote Green..K 3
8 Thorncross......H 6
11 Thorndon.......H 4
4 Thorndon Cross...F 4
6 Thorne, Somerset .D 4
36 Thorne, Yorks....F 5
35 Thorner.........C 12
24 Thorney, Hunts...E 4
32 Thorney, Notts...C 6
7 Thorney, Somerset D 7
37 Thorney Crofts...E 9
8 Thorney Hill....F 4
58 Thorneybank....D 4
6 Thornfalcon.....D 6
7 Thornford......E 9
37 Thorngumbald...D 9
24 Thornham......A 8
27 Thornham Magna. H 4
27 Thornham Parva. H 4
24 Thornhaugh.....E 2
38 Thornhill, Cumb..D 3
31 Thornhill, Derby. B 10
43 Thornhill, Dumf..B 9
14 Thornhill, Glam...F 5
8 Thornhill, Hants...E 6
52 Thornhill, Perth..G 2
35 Thornhill, Yorks..E 11
37 Thornholme.....A 9
49 Thornielaw......F 8
23 Thornington.....F 11
42 Threave.........A 4
40 Thornley, Dur....A 4
40 Thornley, Dur....B 1
47 Thornliebank...D 10
25 Thorns.........K 8
35 Thornseat......H 11
31 Thornsett.......B 8
38 Thornthwaite, Cumb.
                  C 5
35 Thornthwaite, Yorks.
                  A 10
53 Thornton, Angus..C 9
17 Thornton, Bucks...A 8
53 Thornton, Fife...G 7
34 Thornton, Lancs...C 2
34 Thornton, Lancs...G 2
23 Thornton, Leics...A 8
33 Thornton, Lincs...C 9
49 Thornton, Northumb.
                  E 12
12 Thornton, Pemb...F 2
36 Thornton, E. Riding
                  C 5
40 Thornton, N. Riding
                  D 5
35 Thornton, W. Riding
                  D 9
37 Thornton Curtis...E 8
18 Thornton Heath...G 3
30 Thornton Hough..B 2
35 Thornton in Craven
                  B 8

MAP
39 Thornton in Lonsdale
                  H 9
40 Thornton-le-Beans F 4
36 Thornton-le-Clay..A 5
41 Thornton-le-Dale..G 8
37 Thornton le Moor,
    Lincolnshire....G 8
40 Thornton-le-Moor,
    Yorkshire......F 4
40 Thornton-le-Moors C 3
40 Thornton-le-Street. G 4
49 Thornton Mains..E 12
39 Thornton Rust ..F 12
40 Thornton Steward .F 2
40 Thornton Watlass .G 3
47 Thorntonhall....D 10
49 Thorntonloch....B 10
49 Thorntonpark...E 12
18 Thornwood Com...C 5
49 Thornydykes....E 9
38 Thornythwaite...C 6
32 Thoroton.......F 5
36 Thorp Arch......C 2
27 Thorp Green....K 2
31 Thorpe, Derby...E 10
33 Thorpe, Lincs....B 12
26 Thorpe, Norf....F 7
32 Thorpe, Notts....E 5
17 Thorpe, Surrey..G 11
27 Thorpe Abbots...G 5
32 Thorpe Acre.....H 2
32 Thorpe Arnold...H 5
36 Thorpe Audlin....F 3
41 Thorpe Bassett...H 8
19 Thorpe Bay......E 9
23 Thorpe by Water. C 12
22 Thorpe Constantine
                  A 6
26 Thorpe End Garden
    Village.......D 6
35 Thorpe Hesley...G 12
36 Thorpe in Balne...F 4
32 Thorpe in the Fallows
                  B 6
23 Thorpe Langton..C 10
40 Thorpe Larches...C 4
19 Thorpe-le-Soken. B 11
36 Thorpe le Street...C 6
23 Thorpe Malsor...D 11
23 Thorpe Mandeville H 9
26 Thorpe Market...B 5
27 Thorpe Morieux..K 2
32 Thorpe on the Hill. D 6
26 Thorpe St. Andrew D 6
33 Thorpe St. Peter. D 11
32 Thorpe Salvin....B 2
23 Thorpe Satchville. A 10
40 Thorpe Thewles...C 4
36 Thorpe Underwood
                  A 3
25 Thorpe Waterville. G 1
36 Thorpe Willoughby
                  D 3
27 Thorpeness.......J 8
19 Thorrington.....B 10
7 Thorverton......F 3
27 Thrandeston.....H 4
25 Thrapston.......G 1
30 Threapwood.....F 3
42 Threave.........A 4
10 Three Bridges....D 2
2 Three Burrows....E 4
11 Three Chimneys...D 7
14 Three Cocks.....A 5
13 Three Crosses....H 9
10 Three Cups Corner F 5
7 Three Gates, Dorset
                  E 9
40 Three Gates, Dur...B 5
24 Three Holes......E 6
8 Three Legged Cross
                  E 3
11 Three Oaks......G 7
24 Threekingham....B 2
10 Threeleg Cross...E 6
31 Threelows......E 9
17 Threemile Cross...G 8
2 Threemilestone....E 5
49 Threepwood.....E 8
38 Threlkeld.......C 6
35 Threshfield......A 8
26 Thrigby.........D 7
39 Thringarth.....C 11
32 Thringstone.....H 2
40 Thrintoft........F 3
25 Thriplow........K 5
24 Throckenholt....E 5
25 Throcking......M 4
45 Throckley......F 9
22 Throckmorton...G 3
45 Throphill.......D 9

MAP
45 Thropton........C 8
43 Throughgate......C 9
5 Throwleigh......G 5
11 Throwley........C 8
11 Throwley Forstal..C 8
32 Thrumpton.......G 2
61 Thrumster.......C 12
37 Thrunscoe......F 10
45 Thrunton.......B 9
7 Thrupe.........B 9
15 Thrupp, Glos....D 11
16 Thrupp, Oxon...C 6
5 Thrushelton.....G 3
18 Thrushesbush....C 5
34 Thrushgill.......A 5
23 Thrussington....A 10
15 Thruxton, Herefs..A 7
8 Thruxton, Som...B 4
36 Thrybergh.......H 3
23 Thurcaston......A 9
32 Thurcroft.......A 2
4 Thurdon.........E 2
26 Thurgarton, Norf..B 5
32 Thurgarton, Notts. E 4
35 Thurgoland......G 11
23 Thurlaston, Leics..B 8
23 Thurlaston, War...E 8
6 Thurlbear.......D 6
24 Thurlby, Lincs...D 2
32 Thurlby, Lincs...D 6
25 Thurleigh.......J 2
5 Thurlestone.....L 5
6 Thurloxton......C 6
32 Thurlston.......G 1
35 Thurlstone.....G 11
26 Thurlton........F 7
23 Thurmaston.....A 9
23 Thurnby........B 10
26 Thurne..........D 7
11 Thurnham, Kent..B 7
34 Thurnham, Lancs..B 3
26 Thurning, Norf...C 4
25 Thurning, Northants.
                  G 2
36 Thurnscoe......G 2
44 Thursby.........H 2
26 Thursford Green ..B 3
9 Thursley.......B 10
61 Thurso........A 10
61 Thurso East....A 10
30 Thurstaston.....B 1
27 Thurston........J 2
44 Thurstonfield ....G 2
17 Thurstonland....F 10
26 Thurton........E 6
31 Thurvaston.....F 11
26 Thuxton........B 2
27 Thwaite, Suffolk ..H 4
39 Thwaite, Yorks...E 11
26 Thwaite St. Mary. F 6
41 Thwing.........H 10
52 Tibbermore.....E 5
43 Tibbers.........B 9
15 Tibberton, Glos...B 10
30 Tibberton, Salop...H 5
22 Tibberton, Worcs..F 3
26 Tibenham.......F 4
32 Tibshelf........D 2
37 Tibthorpe......B 7
10 Ticehurst.......E 6
9 Tichborne......C 7
32 Tichfield.......F 7
24 Tickencote.....E 1
15 Tickenham......G 8
32 Tickhill........A 3
21 Ticklerton.....C 10
31 Ticknall.......H 12
37 Tickton.........C 8
22 Tidbury Green...E 4
16 Tidcombe.......H 4
17 Tiddington, Oxon. D 7
22 Tiddington, War...F 6
10 Tidebrook......E 5
3 Tideford.......D 10
3 Tideford Cross..D 10
15 Tidenham......E 9
31 Tideswell.......C 10
17 Tidmarsh.......G 7
22 Tidmington.....H 6
9 Tidpit..........D 2
12 Tiers Cross......F 3
23 Tiffield........G 10
58 Tifty...........D 5
59 Tigerton.......L 3
54 Tighchuig......F 8
52 Tighnablair.....D 8
46 Tighnabruaich...B 5
51 Tigh-na-criche...G 8
60 Tighnafiline.....G 1
5 Tigley..........K 6
25 Tilbrook........H 2
18 Tilbury.........F 6
22 Tile Cross......C 5

MAP
17 Tilehurst... G 7
9 Tilford.........B 10
10 Tilgale..........E 2
58 Tillathrowie......D 2
30 Tilley...........G 4
52 Tillicoultry.......G 4
19 Tillingham......D 10
21 Tillington, Herefs.H 10
9 Tillington, Sussex D 11
21 Tillington Com...H 10
59 Tillyarblet........L 3
59 Tillybardine......K 2
58 Tillycorthie.......E 7
59 Tillydrine House..H 4
58 Tillyfar...........E 7
58 Tillyfourie........F 4
58 Tillygrieg.........E 6
58 Tillyminnate......D 2
11 Tilmanstone.....C 11
24 Tilney All Saints..D 7
24 Tilney High End..D 7
24 Tilney St. Lawrence D 7
8 Tilshead..........A 2
30 Tilstock..........F 4
30 Tilston...........E 3
30 Tilstone Fearnall..D 4
17 Tilsworth........B 10
23 Tilton on the Hill.B 10
15 Tiltups End......E 11
33 Timberland.......D 8
31 Timbersbrook.....D 7
6 Timberscombe....B 3
35 Timble..........B 10
49 Timpendean......G 9
30 Timperley........A 6
8 Timsbury, Hants...D 5
15 Timsbury, Som...H 10
27 Timworth Green..H 2
7 Tincleton........G 11
44 Tindale..........G 4
17 Tingewick.........A 7
35 Tingley.........D 11
25 Tingrith.........M 1
5 Tinhay...........G 3
48 Tinnis............F 6
35 Tinshill.........C 11
3 Tintagel..........A 7
15 Tintern Parva.....D 8
7 Tintinhull........D 8
35 Tintwistle........G 9
43 Tinwald..........C 11
24 Tinwell...........E 1
4 Tippacott..........A 6
58 Tipperty, Aber.....E 7
58 Tipperty, Banff....B 4
24 Tipp's End........F 6
8 Tiptoe............F 4
22 Tipton............C 3
6 Tipton St. Johns..G 4
19 Tiptree...........B 9
20 Tirabad...........H 4
20 Tirghoil..........E 1
15 Tirley...........A 11
14 Tir-Phil..........D 4
39 Tirril............C 7
8 Tisbury...........C 1
9 Tisman's Com.....C 12
31 Tissington.......E 10
4 Titchberry.......C 1
25 Titchmarsh.......G 1
26 Titchwell.........A 1
32 Tithby............F 4
45 Titlington........B 9
21 Titley............F 9
10 Titsey............C 3
31 Tittensor.........F 7
26 Tittleshall........C 2
15 Tittups End......E 11
30 Tiverton, Ches....D 4
6 Tiverton, Devon...E 3
6 Tiverton Junction..E 4
27 Tivetshall St. Margaret G 4
27 Tivetshall St. Mary G 4
22 Tividale..........C 3
6 Tivington.........B 3
31 Tixall............H 8
24 Tixover..........E 1
64 Toab.............D 3
31 Toadmoor.......E 12
50 Tobermory........B 2
50 Toberonochy.....G 5
63 Tobson...........C 2
58 Tocher...........D 4
16 Tockenham.......F 2
16 Tockenham Wick..F 1
34 Tockholes........E 5
15 Tockington.......F 9
36 Tockwith.........B 3
7 Todber..........D 11
17 Toddington, Beds.A 11
16 Toddington, Glos..A 1

MAP
22 Todenham.......H 6
53 Todhall..........E 8
44 Todhills..........G 2
35 Todmorden........E 8
49 Todrig............G 7
32 Todwick..........B 2
25 Toft, Cambs......K 5
24 Toft, Lincs........D 2
40 Toft Hill.........B 2
26 Toft Monks.......F 7
33 Toft next Newton.A 7
49 Toftbarns........G 8
26 Toftrees..........C 2
61 Tofts...........A 12
26 Toftwood Com....D 3
45 Togston.........C 10
55 Toigal...........K 1
62 Tokavaig.........G 5
17 Tokers Green.....F 8
36 Toll Bar..........F 3
22 Toll End.........C 3
58 Toll of Birness....D 7
6 Tolland...........C 4
8 Tollard Royal.....D 1
7 Toller Fratrum....F 9
7 Toller Porcorum...F 9
32 Tollerton, Notts...G 3
36 Tollerton, Yorks...A 3
19 Tollesbury........C 9
19 Tolleshunt D'Arcy.C 9
19 Tolleshunt Major..C 9
56 Tollie............D 1
63 Tolmachan.......F 2
64 Tolob............F 7
7 Tolpuddle.......G 11
63 Tolstachaolais.....C 3
57 Tolvah...........J 4
10 Tolworth.........B 1
57 Tomatin.........G 4
57 Tombain.........J 4
56 Tombreck.........F 2
55 Tomcrasky.......H 6
55 Tomdoun.........J 5
56 Tomich, Inver.....E 1
55 Tomich, Inver.....G 7
56 Tomich, Ross & Cromarty.......C 3
60 Tomich, Suther....F 6
57 Tomintoul, Aber...K 7
57 Tomintoul, Banff..H 7
57 Tomintoul, Inver...G 2
58 Tomnaven........D 2
57 Tomnavoulin.....G 8
52 Tomphubil........B 3
44 Tomshielburn.....E 2
14 Ton..............D 6
14 Ton-Pentre.......E 3
10 Tonbridge........C 5
14 Tondu............F 2
20 Ton-fanau........B 1
63 Tong, Lewis......C 5
22 Tong, Salop.......A 2
35 Tong, Yorks.....D 10
32 Tonge............H 2
9 Tongham.......A 10
43 Tongland.........F 8
60 Tongue...........B 6
60 Tongue House....B 6
14 Tongwynlais......F 5
13 Tonna..........G 11
14 Ton-teg..........F 4
18 Tonwell...........B 3
14 Tonypandy.......E 3
14 Tonyrefail........E 3
16 Toot Baldon......D 6
16 Toothill..........D 5
35 Top of Hebers....F 7
40 Topcliffe.........H 4
26 Topcroft..........F 6
26 Topcroft Street....F 5
25 Toppesfield.......L 8
34 Toppings..........F 6
6 Topsham..........G 3
57 Torbain..........H 7
59 Torbeg, Aber......G 1
46 Torbeg, Arran I....F 4
61 Torboll...........G 7
56 Torbreck.........F 3
5 Torbryan.........J 7
55 Torcastle.........L 5
5 Torcross..........L 7
57 Torcroy..........J 3
55 Torcuileainn......J 2
56 Tore.............D 2
55 Torgyle Bridge....H 7
46 Torinturk.........C 3
32 Torksey...........B 5
55 Torlundy........M 5
15 Tormarton.......F 11
42 Tormitchell.......B 3
46 Tormore..........F 4
56 Tornagrain.......E 3
57 Tornahaish.......J 8

MAP
59 Tornaveen........G 4
57 Torness..........G 1
40 Toronto..........B 2
50 Torosay Castle....D 4
38 Torpenhow.......A 4
48 Torphichen.......B 2
59 Torphins.........G 4
3 Torpoint........D 11
5 Torquay...........J 8
49 Torquhan........E 7
62 Torran, Inver......C 5
56 Torran, Ross & Cromarty.........B 3
47 Torrance........B 11
50 Torraneidhinn.....B 3
50 Torrans..........E 2
47 Torranyard.......E 8
5 Torre, Devon......J 8
6 Torre, Somerset...B 4
54 Torridon.........D 3
54 Torridon House...D 2
62 Torrin............F 5
61 Torrisdale........B 7
34 Torrisholme.......A 3
55 Torrlaoighseach...H 3
60 Torroboll.........F 6
58 Torry, Aberdeen..D 2
59 Torry, Aberdeen..G 7
48 Torryburn........A 3
58 Torterston........C 8
43 Torthorwald......D 11
9 Tortington.......F 11
38 Torver...........F 5
48 Torwood. ......A 1
32 Torworth.........B 4
4 Tosberry.........D 1
54 Toscaig...........F 1
25 Toseland.........J 3
34 Tosside...........B 6
50 Tostarie..........C 1
27 Tostock..........J 3
62 Totaig, Inverness..C 1
55 Totaig, Ross & Cromarty......G 2
62 Tote.............C 3
61 Totegan..........A 8
8 Totland..........G 5
31 Totley..........B 11
7 Totnell...........E 9
5 Totnes...........K 7
62 Totscore.........B 3
18 Tottenham........E 3
24 Tottenhill........D 7
18 Totteridge........E 2
17 Totternhoe.......B 10
34 Tottington.......F 6
8 Totton...........E 5
17 Touchen-end......F 9
59 Toucks...........J 6
6 Toulton...........C 5
56 Toulvaddie.......B 4
58 Toux..............C 7
40 Tow Law.........A 1
46 Toward...........C 6
46 Toward Quay.....C 6
23 Towcester........G 10
2 Towednack.......F 2
18 Tower Hamlets....F 4
10 Tower Hill........E 1
17 Towersey.........D 8
58 Towie............F 2
58 Towiemore.......C 1
39 Town End.........G 7
34 Town Green.......G 3
10 Town Row........E 4
27 Town Street......G 1
49 Town Yetholm...G 10
43 Townfoot........B 10
42 Townhead, Ayr....A 3
43 Townhead, Dumf. C 10
59 Townhead, Kinc...K 5
43 Townhead, Kirk...G 5
45 Townhead, Northumb. F 7
47 Townhead of Aber.A 9
47 Townhead of Gree.E 9
43 Townhead of Greenlaw.........E 8
52 Townhill.........H 6
16 Townsend, Berks...E 5
7 Townsend, Som....A 8
2 Townshend.......F 3
36 Towthorpe........A 4
36 Towton...........C 3
29 Towyn............B 9
33 Toynton All Saints D 11
33 Toynton Fen Side D 11
33 Toynton St. Peter.D 11
10 Toy's Hill........C 3
47 Trabboch........G 9
47 Trabboch Mains..G 9

MAP
47 Trabbochburn....G 9
2 Traboe...........G 4
56 Tradespark.......D 4
35 Trafford Park.....H 7
55 Traigh House.....K 1
43 Trailtrow........D 12
14 Trallong..........A 3
49 Tranent..........B 7
30 Tranmere.........A 2
61 Trantlemore.......B 8
45 Tranwell........E 10
13 Trapp...........E 10
49 Traprain.........B 8
48 Traquair..........F 6
17 Traveller's Rest...B 10
35 Trawden..........C 8
14 Trawscoed........A 4
28 Trawsfynydd......G 6
13 Tre-Herbert.......B 9
14 Trealaw..........E 3
34 Treales...........D 3
28 Trearddur Bay....B 2
62 Treaslane.........C 3
14 Trebanog.........E 3
3 Trebartha........B 9
3 Trebarwith.......A 7
2 Trebetheric.......B 6
6 Treborough.......C 3
2 Trebudannon.....D 6
3 Trebullett.......B 10
3 Treburley........B 10
3 Trebyan..........C 8
14 Trecastle.........A 2
14 Trecenydd........F 5
12 Trecwn...........D 3
14 Trecynon..........D 3
3 Tredaule..........B 9
12 Tre-ddiog.........D 2
14 Tredegar..........C 5
22 Tredington.......H 6
2 Tredizzick.......B 6
14 Tredomen........A 4
12 Tredrissi.........C 4
15 Tredunnock.......E 7
14 Tredustan........A 5
2 Treen...........G 1
32 Treeton..........A 2
12 Trefasser.........C 2
28 Trefdraeth........C 3
14 Trefecca..........A 5
20 Trefeglwys........C 5
20 Trefenter.........E 2
12 Treffgarne........E 3
12 Treffgarne Owen..D 2
28 Treffynnon, Angl..B 3
12 Treffynnon, Pemb..D 2
14 Trefil............C 4
20 Trefilan..........G 1
29 Trefnant.........C 10
30 Trefonen.........G 1
28 Trefor............B 3
14 Treforest Industrial Estate.........F 4
29 Trefriw...........D 7
29 Tref-y-nant......F 12
3 Tregadillett......A 10
28 Tregaian..........B 4
15 Tregare...........C 7
20 Tregaron..........F 2
28 Tregarth..........C 5
3 Tregeare..........A 9
29 Tregeiriog........G 11
28 Tregele...........A 3
2 Tregeseal.........F 1
12 Treglemais.......D 2
2 Tregonetha.......C 6
2 Tregony..........E 6
3 Tregoss..........D 7
2 Tregowris.........G 5
14 Tregoyd..........A 5
13 Tre-groes.........C 7
2 Tregurrian........C 5
20 Tregynon.........C 6
14 Trehafod.........E 4
14 Treharris.........E 4
14 Treherbert.......D 3
3 Trekenner.......B 10
3 Treknow..........A 7
3 Trelash..........A 9
2 Trelassick........D 6
29 Trelawnyd.......B 10
12 Trelech...........D 6
12 Tre-lech-a'r-Betws D 6
12 Treleddyd fawr....D 1
14 Trelewis..........E 4
3 Treligga..........A 7
3 Trelights.........B 7
3 Trelill............B 7
2 Trelissick.........F 5
15 Trelleck..........D 8
15 Trelleck Grange...D 8
29 Trelogan.........B 10
28 Tremadog........F 5

MAP
3 Tremail..........A 8
12 Tremain..........B 6
3 Tremaine.........A 9
3 Tremar...........C 9
3 Trematon.......D 11
29 Tremeirchion....C 10
3 Tremore..........C 7
2 Trenance, Corn....C 5
2 Trenance, Corn....C 6
2 Trenance, Corn....H 4
3 Trenarren........E 7
21 Trench..........A 12
2 Trenear..........F 4
3 Treneglos.........A 9
3 Trenewan........D 9
2 Trengune.........B 2
7 Trent Nether Compton D 9
31 Trentham.........F 7
4 Trentishoe........A 5
14 Treoes............F 3
14 Treorchy..........E 3
3 Trequite..........B 7
20 Tre'r-ddol........C 2
3 Trerule Foot.....D 10
12 Tresaith..........B 6
3 Tresayes.........D 7
22 Trescott..........B 2
2 Trescowe.........G 3
15 Tresham.........E 11
2 Tresillian.........E 6
12 Tresinwen........C 2
2 Treskinnick Cross.A 2
3 Tresmeer.........A 9
2 Tresparrett.......B 2
2 Tresparrett Posts..B 2
52 Tressait..........A 3
64 Tresta, Zetland....B 8
64 Tresta, Zetland....D 7
32 Treswell..........B 5
2 Trethosa.........D 6
3 Trethurgy........D 7
12 Tretio............D 1
15 Tretire............B 8
14 Tretower.........B 5
29 Treuddyn.......D 11
3 Trevadlock.......B 9
3 Trevalga..........A 8
30 Trevalyn.........D 3
3 Trevanson........B 7
2 Trevarren........D 6
2 Trevarrian........C 5
3 Trevarrick........E 7
12 Trevaughan, Carm. E 5
13 Trevaughan, Carm. E 7
2 Trevellas.........D 4
3 Trevelmond.......C 9
2 Treverva..........F 5
14 Trevethin.........D 6
3 Trevigro.........C 10
12 Trevine...........D 2
2 Treviscoe.........D 6
3 Trevivian.........A 9
3 Trevoll...........D 5
2 Trevone...........B 6
28 Trevor............F 3
2 Trevose...........B 6
3 Trewarmett.......A 8
3 Trewassa.........A 8
2 Trewellard........F 1
3 Trewen............A 9
2 Trewennack......G 4
21 Trewern..........A 8
3 Trewerthern......B 7
3 Trewetha.........B 7
3 Trewidland.......D 9
12 Trewilym.........C 5
2 Trewint..........B 2
2 Trewithian........F 6
2 Trewoon..........D 7
2 Treyarnon Bay....B 6
9 Treyford..........D 9
35 Triangle..........E 9
8 Trickett's Cross...F 3
44 Triermain.........F 4
40 Trimdon..........B 4
40 Trimdon Colliery..B 4
40 Trimdon Grange...B 4
26 Trimingham......B 6
27 Trimley...........L 6
27 Trimley Heath....L 6
22 Trimpley..........D 1
13 Trimsaran........F 8
4 Trimstone........B 4
14 Trinant...........D 5
17 Tring............C 10
17 Tring Wharf......C 10
59 Trinity, Angus....L 4
6 Trinity, Devon.....F 3
6 Triscombe.........C 5
55 Trislaig..........M 5
2 Trispen...........E 5
45 Tritlington......D 10

MAP
52 Trochrie..........C 5
13 Troedyraur.......B 7
13 Troed-y-rhiw, Card.B 8
14 Troedyrhiw, Glam. D 4
47 Troon, Ayr.......D 8
2 Troon, Cornwall..F 4
43 Troqueer........D 10
51 Trossachs Hotel..G 12
27 Trostan..........H 2
10 Trottiscliffe.......B 5
9 Trotton..........D 9
45 Troughend.......D 7
38 Troutbeck, Cumberland....C 6
38 Troutbeck, Westmor. E 6
38 Troutbeck Bridge..E 6
15 Trow Green......D 9
32 Troway...........B 1
15 Trowbridge......H 11
32 Trowell...........F 2
15 Trowle Common.H 11
17 Trowley Bottom..C 11
49 Trows............F 9
26 Trowse Newton....E 5
7 Trudoxhill.......B 10
6 Trull............D 6
62 Trumpan.........B 2
21 Trumpet........H 12
25 Trumpington.....K 6
6 Trumps..........E 4
26 Trunch...........B 6
2 Truro............E 5
3 Truscott.........A 10
6 Trusham.........H 2
31 Trusley..........G 11
33 Trusthorpe......B 12
22 Trysull...........C 2
16 Tubney...........D 5
5 Tuckenhay........K 7
2 Tuckingmill.......F 4
25 Tuddenham, Suff..H 8
27 Tuddenham, Suff..K 5
10 Tudeley...........D 5
40 Tudhoe...........B 3
15 Tudorville........B 9
28 Tudweiliog.......G 2
9 Tuesley.........B 11
15 Tuffley..........C 11
12 Tufton...........D 4
23 Tugby...........B 11
21 Tugford.........D 11
45 Tughall.........E 12
54 Tuirnaig..........B 3
57 Tulchan.........M 7
52 Tullibody........H 3
51 Tullich, Argyll....F 8
57 Tullich, Inverness..G 2
51 Tullich, Perth....D 12
54 Tullich, Ross & Cromarty.......E 3
56 Tullich Muir......B 3
52 Tulliemet.........B 5
59 Tullo' of Benholm.K 5
58 Tulloch, Aber.....D 5
55 Tulloch, Inver.....L 7
52 Tullochan........D 1
51 Tullochgorm.......H 7
57 Tullochmacarrick..J 8
58 Tullochs..........C 2
59 Tullochvenus.....G 3
52 Tullybannocher...E 2
53 Tullyfergus.......B 7
53 Tullymurdoch.....B 7
58 Tullynessle.......F 3
13 Tumble...........F 9
33 Tumby...........D 9
33 Tumby Woodside.D 9
18 Tumford..........C 4
52 Tummel Bridge....A 3
10 Tunbridge Wells...D 5
15 Tunley...........H 10
45 Tunstall, Dur.....H 12
11 Tunstall, Kent....B 7
39 Tunstall, Lancs....H 8
31 Tunstall, Staffs....E 7
27 Tunstall, Suffolk...K 6
37 Tunstall, E.Riding D 10
40 Tunstall, N. Riding F 2
26 Tunstall St. Mary..E 7
9 Tunworth.........A 8
21 Tupsley.........H 10
23 Tur Langton.....C 10
17 Turgis Green.....H 8
53 Turin...........B 10
16 Turkdean.........B 2
15 Turleigh Freshford H 11
15 Turnastone.......A 7
42 Turnberry........A 3
31 Turnditch........F 11
10 Turner's Hill......E 2
7 Turners Puddle..G 11

MAP
48 Turnhouse B 4
7 Turnworth E 11
58 Turriff C 5
34 Turton Bottoms F 6
49 Turvelaws F 12
23 Turvey G 12
17 Turville E 8
17 Turville Heath E 8
23 Turweston H 9
48 Tushielaw G 6
31 Tutbury G 10
22 Tutnall E 3
15 Tutshill E 8
26 Tuttington C 5
17 Tutts Clump G 7
3 Tutwell B 11
32 Tuxford C 4
64 Twatt, Orkney Is. C 1
64 Twatt, Shetland Is. D 7
47 Twechar B 11
48 Tweeddaleburn D 5
49 Tweedmouth D 12
48 Tweedshaws H 3
48 Tweedsmuir G 4
2 Twelveheads E 5
30 Twemlow Green C 6
24 Twenty C 3
15 Twerton H 10
44 Twice Brewed F 6
18 Twickenham G 2
17 Twigworth B 11
10 Twineham F 1
15 Twinhoe H 10
27 Twinstead L 2
27 Twinstead Green L 2
4 Twitchen, Devon B 4
4 Twitchen, Devon C 7
21 Twitchen, Salop D 9
5 Two Bridges H 5
31 Two Dales D 11
22 Two Gates B 5
4 Two Pots B 4
23 Twycross B 7
17 Twyford, Berks. G 9
17 Twyford, Bucks. B 7
31 Twyford, Derby. G 11
8 Twyford, Hants. D 6
23 Twyford, Leics. A 10
26 Twyford, Norf. C 3
15 Twyford Com. A 8
13 Twyn Llanan E 11
14 Twyncarno C 4
43 Twynholm F 7
15 Twyning A 12
22 Twyning Green H 3
13 Twyn-mynydd F 10
15 Twyn-y-Sheriff D 7
23 Twywell D 12
28 Ty-Hen G 1
21 Tyberton H 9
28 Ty-croes, Angl. C 3
13 Tycroes, Carm. F 9
28 Tycrwyn H 10
24 Tydd Gote D 5
24 Tydd St. Giles D 5
24 Tydd St. Mary D 5
29 Tyddininco G 9
19 Tye Green, Essex B 7
25 Tye Green, Essex L 7
12 Ty-hen E 6
34 Tyldesley G 6
11 Tyler Hill B 10
17 Tylers Green, Bucks. E 10
10 Tyler's Grn., Surrey C 2
14 Tylorstown E 3
20 Tylwch D 5
29 Ty-nant, Denb. F 9
29 Ty-nant, Mer. H 8
20 Tyncwm D 4
51 Tyndrum E 10
7 Tyneham H 12
45 Tyne & Wear, Co. F 10
48 Tynehead C 6
45 Tynemouth F 11
14 Tynewydd D 3
49 Tyninghame B 8
50 Tynribbie C 6
43 Tynron B 9
20 Tynswydd F 2
29 Ty'n-y-ffridd G 10
28 Ty'n-y-gongl B 4
29 Ty'n-y-groes C 7
28 Tyn-y-pwll B 4
29 Tyn-y-Wern G 10
23 Tyringham G 12
4 Tythecott D 3
14 Tythegston F 2
31 Tytherington, Ches. C 7
15 Tytherington, Glos. E 10
8 Tytherington, Wilts. B 1

MAP
7 Tytherington, Wilts. B 11
7 Tytherleigh F 7
3 Tywardreath D 8
3 Tywardreath Highway D 8
29 Tywyn B 7
20 Tywyn Mer. B 2
54 Uags F 1
54 Uamh on Triall D 1
27 Ubbeston Green H 6
15 Ubley H 8
40 Uckerby E 3
10 Uckfield F 4
15 Uckington B 12
47 Uddingston C 11
48 Uddington F 1
11 Udimore F 7
58 Udny E 6
47 Udston E 12
47 Udstonhead E 12
16 Uffcott F 2
6 Uffculme E 4
16 Uffington, Berks. E 4
24 Uffington, Lincs. E 2
21 Uffington, Salop A 10
24 Ufford, Hunts. E 2
27 Ufford, Suffolk K 6
23 Ufton F 7
17 Ufton Green G 7
17 Ufton Nervet G 7
46 Ugadale F 3
5 Ugborough K 5
27 Uggeshall G 7
41 Ugglebarnby D 9
18 Ugley A 5
41 Ugthorpe D 8
63 Uig, Lewis D 2
62 Uig, Skye C 1
62 Uig, Skye B 3
62 Uigshader D 4
60 Uisken F 1
61 Ulbster C 12
33 Ulceby, Lincs. C 11
37 Ulceby, Lincs. F 8
33 Ulceby Cross C 11
37 Ulceby Skitter F 9
11 Ulcombe C 7
38 Uldale B 5
39 Uldale House F 9
15 Uley D 11
45 Ulgham D 10
60 Ullapool G 3
22 Ullenhall E 5
15 Ullenwood C 12
36 Ulleskelf C 3
23 Ullesthorpe C 8
32 Ulley B 2
21 Ullingswick G 11
62 Ullinish D 2
38 Ullock C 3
8 Ullwell H 2
38 Ulpha F 4
38 Ulrome B 9
64 Ulsta C 7
49 Ulston G 9
50 Ulva House D 2
38 Ulverston G 5
43 Ulzieside A 8
62 Umachan C 5
4 Umberleigh D 5
60 Unapool D 4
44 Under Burnmouth E 3
10 Under River C 4
39 Underbarrow F 7
35 Undercliffe D 10
47 Underhills F 9
64 Underhoull A 8
32 Underwood E 2
15 Undy F 7
64 Unifirth D 6
59 Union Croft H 6
38 Union Mills H 2
32 Unstone C 1
32 Unstone Green C 1
35 Unsworth F 7
44 Unthank, Cumb. H 2
39 Unthank, Cumb. A 8
39 Unthank, Cumb. B 7
49 Unthank, Northumb. E 12
39 Unthank End B 7
7 Up Cerne F 10
6 Up Exe F 3
15 Up Hatherley B 12
34 Up Holland G 4
9 Up Marden E 9
9 Up Nately A 8
8 Up Somborne C 5
7 Up Sydling F 9
8 Upavon A 3
11 Upchurch A 7
4 Upcott, Devon E 4

MAP
21 Upcott, Herefs. G 8
6 Upcott, Somerset D 3
17 Updown Hill H 10
48 Uphall B 3
48 Uphall Station B 3
4 Upham, Devon E 7
9 Upham, Hants. D 7
21 Uphampton, Herefs. F 9
22 Uphampton, Worcs. F 2
14 Uphill H 6
47 Uplawmoor D 9
15 Upleadon B 10
40 Upleatham C 6
11 Uplees B 8
7 Uploders G 8
6 Uplowman E 4
6 Uplyme G 6
18 Upminster E 6
6 Upottery E 5
71 Uppat F 8
21 Upper Affcott D 10
60 Upper Ardchronie G 6
22 Upper Arley D 1
17 Upper Arncott B 7
23 Upper Astrop H 8
42 Upper Barr E 5
63 Upper Barvas B 5
17 Upper Basildon F 7
63 Upper Bayble D 6
10 Upper Beeding G 1
24 Upper Benefield F 1
22 Upper Bentley E 3
58 Upper Boddam E 4
23 Upper Boddington G 8
20 Upper Borth D 2
9 Upper Bourne B 9
58 Upper Boyndie A 6
22 Upper Brailes H 6
62 Upper Breakish F 6
21 Upper Breinton H 10
32 Upper Broughton H 4
16 Upper Bucklebury G 6
8 Upper Burgate D 3
59 Upper Burnhaugh H 6
58 Upper Cairnargot D 2
25 Upper Caldecote L 3
8 Upper Canterton E 4
23 Upper Catesby F 8
20 Upper Chapel H 6
6 Upper Cheddon C 6
8 Upper Chicksgrove C 1
14 Upper Church Village F 4
8 Upper Chute A 4
8 Upper Clatford B 5
43 Upper Clifton F 10
28 Upper Clynnog F 4
63 Upper Coll C 5
20 Upper Corris B 3
42 Upper Craigenbay D 6
35 Upper Cumberworth F 10
14 Upper Cwmbran E 6
13 Upper Cwm-twrch F 11
58 Upper Dallachy A 1
43 Upper Dalveen A 9
25 Upper Dean H 1
35 Upper Denby F 11
44 Upper Denton G 4
56 Upper Derraid F 6
54 Upper Diabaig D 2
10 Upper Dicker G 4
61 Upper Dounreay A 9
50 Upper Druimfin B 2
31 Upper Elkstone D 9
31 Upper End C 9
56 Upper Ethie C 3
15 Upper Framilode C 10
22 Upper Gornal C 3
25 Upper Gravenhurst L 2
16 Upper Green H 5
15 Upper Grove Com. B 9
9 Upper Hale A 10
62 Upper Halistra B 2
17 Upper Halliford G 11
10 Upper Halling B 6
23 Upper Hambleton A 12
11 Upper Hardress Court C 10
10 Upper Hartfield E 3
36 Upper Haugh G 2
21 Upper Heath D 11
26 Upper Hellesdon D 5
36 Upper Helmsley A 5
21 Upper Hergest G 8
23 Upper Heyford, Northants. F 10
16 Upper Heyford, Oxon. B 6
21 Upper Hill G 10
44 Upper Hindhope B 6

MAP
35 Upper Hopton E 10
10 Upper Horsebridge G 5
31 Upper Hulme D 8
16 Upper Inglesham D 3
57 Upper Inverbrough G 4
58 Upper Ironside B 6
53 Upper Kenley F 10
13 Upper Killay H 9
58 Upper Kinkell E 5
19 Upper Kirby B 11
58 Upper Knaven C 6
56 Upper Knockando E 7
16 Upper Lambourn F 4
15 Upper Langford H 8
32 Upper Langwith C 2
31 Upper Leigh F 8
59 Upper Lochton H 4
22 Upper Longdon A 4
61 Upper Lybster D 11
15 Upper Lydbrook C 9
21 Upper Lye F 9
62 Upper Milovaig C 1
16 Upper Minety E 1
35 Upper Moor Side D 11
15 Upper Morton E 9
58 Upper Mulben B 1
44 Upper Mumble E 2
49 Upper Nisbet G 9
17 Upper North Dean D 9
52 Upper Obney C 5
62 Upper Ollach E 4
22 Upper Penn C 3
36 Upper Poppleton B 3
21 Upper Pulley B 10
22 Upper Quinton G 5
8 Upper Ratley D 5
21 Upper Rochford F 11
42 Upper Rusko E 6
55 Upper Sandaig H 2
21 Upper Sapey F 12
46 Upper Scoulag C 6
16 Upper Seagry F 1
63 Upper Shader B 5
23 Upper Shelton L 1
26 Upper Sheringham A 4
48 Upper Side D 6
47 Upper Skelmorlie C 7
22 Upper Slaughter B 3
51 Upper Sonachan E 8
15 Upper Soudley C 10
15 Upper Stanton Drew H 9
25 Upper Stondon M 3
22 Upper Stonnall B 4
23 Upper Stowe F 10
8 Upper Street, Hants. D 3
26 Upper Street, Norf. D 7
22 Upper Strensham H 3
17 Upper Sundon A 11
16 Upper Swell B 3
26 Upper Tasburgh F 5
31 Upper Tean F 8
52 Upper Tillyrie F 6
62 Upper Tote B 4
21 Upper Town, Herefs. G 11
15 Upper Town, Som. H 8
23 Upper Tysoe H 7
16 Upper Upham F 3
10 Upper Upnor A 6
23 Upper Wardington G 8
23 Upper Weald H 11
23 Upper Weedon F 9
17 Upper Winchendon C 8
8 Upper Woodford B 3
58 Upper Woodhead F 4
9 Upper Wootton A 7
22 Upper Wyche H 1
44 Upperby H 2
35 Uppermill G 8
58 Uppertack of Gressiehill B 6
35 Upperthong F 10
59 Upperton, Kinc. K 5
9 Upperton, Sussex D 11
64 Uppertown F 2
21 Uppington A 11
40 Upsall F 5
18 Upshire D 4
11 Upstreet B 11
16 Upton, Berks. E 6
17 Upton, Berks. F 10
30 Upton, Cheshire C 3
30 Upton, Cheshire A 1
4 Upton, Cornwall E 1
6 Upton, Devon F 4
8 Upton, Dorset G 1
7 Upton, Dorset H 11
8 Upton, Hants. D 5

MAP
24 Upton, Hunts. E 2
25 Upton, Hunts. G 3
32 Upton, Lincs. B 6
26 Upton, Norfolk D 7
23 Upton, Northants. F 10
32 Upton, Notts. C 5
32 Upton, Notts. E 4
8 Upton, Notts. A 5
6 Upton, Somerset C 3
7 Upton, Somerset D 8
22 Upton, War. F 5
36 Upton, Yorkshire F 3
15 Upton Bishop B 9
15 Upton Cheyney G 10
21 Upton Cressett C 12
9 Upton Grey A 8
4 Upton Hellions F 7
8 Upton Lovell B 1
21 Upton Magna A 11
7 Upton Noble B 10
6 Upton Pyne F 3
15 Upton St. Leonards C 11
7 Upton Scudamore A 12
22 Upton Snodsbury G 3
22 Upton upon Severn H 2
22 Upton Warren E 3
9 Upwaltham E 10
25 Upware H 6
24 Upwell E 6
7 Upwey H 10
25 Upwood G 4
64 Urafirth C 6
56 Urchal E 3
56 Urchany E 4
16 Urchfont H 2
63 Urgha Beag G 3
40 Urlay Nook D 4
34 Urmston H 6
56 Urquhart, Moray C 8
56 Urquhart, Ross & Cromarty D 1
40 Urra E 6
56 Urray D 1
40 Ushaw Moor A 3
15 Usk D 7
37 Usselby H 8
56 Ussie D 1
64 Ustaness D 7
45 Usworth G 11
35 Utley C 9
4 Uton F 7
37 Utterby H 10
31 Uttoxeter G 9
28 Uwchmynydd H 1
18 Uxbridge F 1
64 Uyeasound B 8
12 Uzmaston F 3
12 Vachelich D 1
28 Valley B 2
3 Valley Truckle A 8
62 Valtos, Skye B 4
63 Valtos, Lewis C 2
20 Van D 5
19 Vange E 7
14 Varteg Hill D 6
62 Vatten D 2
14 Vaynor C 4
14 Velindre, Brec. A 5
13 Velindre, Carm. C 7
12 Velindre, Pemb. C 4
6 Vellow B 4
64 Vementry D 6
64 Veness B 3
6 Venn Ottery G 4
21 Vennington A 9
4 Venny Tedburn F 7
9 Ventnor H 7
16 Vernham Dean H 4
16 Vernham Street H 4
12 Verwig B 5
8 Verwood E 2
2 Veryan F 6
6 Vicarage G 5
38 Vickerstown H 4
3 Victoria, Corn. D 7
14 Victoria, Mon. D 5
64 Vidlin C 7
10 Vinehall Street F 6
10 Vine's Cross F 5
15 Viney Hill D 9
17 Virginia Water G 10
5 Virginstow G 3
7 Vobster A 10
64 Voe C 7
15 Vowchurch A 7
64 Voxter C 7
64 Voy C 1
40 Wackerfield C 2
26 Wacton F 5
22 Wadborough G 3
17 Waddesdon B 8
37 Waddingham G 7

MAP
33 Waddington, Lincs. D 7
34 Waddington, Yorks. C 6
3 Wadebridge B 7
6 Wadeford E 6
25 Wadenhoe G 1
18 Wadesmill B 4
10 Wadhurst E 5
31 Wadshelf C 11
31 Wadsley A 11
32 Wadsley Bridge A 1
15 Wadswick G 11
36 Wadworth G 3
29 Waen Fach H 11
61 Wag E 9
33 Wainfleet All Saints D 12
33 Wainfleet Bank D 11
45 Wainfordrigg C 7
32 Waingroves E 1
2 Wainhouse Corner B 2
10 Wainscott A 6
35 Wainstalls D 9
39 Waitby D 10
35 Wakefield E 12
24 Wakerley F 1
19 Wakes Colne A 9
27 Walberswick H 8
9 Walberton E 11
45 Walbottle F 10
24 Walcot, Kest. B 2
33 Walcot, Lincs. E 8
21 Walcot, Salop A 11
21 Walcot, Salop D 9
22 Walcot, War. F 5
16 Walcot, Wilts. F 3
23 Walcote D 9
21 Walcott B 7
39 Walden Head G 12
36 Walden Stubbs E 3
10 Walderslade B 6
9 Walderton E 9
7 Walditch G 8
31 Waldley F 9
45 Waldridge H 10
27 Waldringfield L 6
10 Waldron F 4
32 Wales B 2
33 Walesby, Lincs. A 8
32 Walesby, Notts. C 4
15 Walford, Herefs. B 9
21 Walford, Herefs. E 9
30 Walford, Salop H 3
30 Walford Heath H 3
30 Walgherton E 5
23 Walgrave E 11
8 Walhampton F 5
35 Walk Mill D 7
34 Walkden G 6
45 Walker G 11
34 Walker Fold C 5
48 Walkerburn F 6
32 Walkeringham A 5
32 Walkerith A 5
18 Walkern A 3
21 Walker's Green H 10
53 Walkerton G 7
8 Walkford G 4
5 Walkhampton J 4
37 Walkington C 8
32 Walkley A 1
45 Wall, Northumb. F 7
22 Wall, Staffs. B 4
44 Wall Bowers G 4
21 Wall under Heywood C 10
43 Wallaceton C 9
42 Wallacetown, Ayr. A 4
47 Wallacetown, Ayr. G 8
30 Wallasey A 2
19 Wallend, Kent F 8
38 Wallend, Lancs. G 5
17 Wallingford E 7
9 Wallington, Hants. E 7
25 Wallington, Herts. M 4
18 Wallington, London H 3
9 Walliswood B 12
64 Walls D 6
45 Wallsend F 11
38 Wallthwaite C 6
48 Wallyford B 6
11 Walmer C 12
34 Walmer Bridge E 3
35 Walmersley F 7
22 Walmley C 5
27 Walpole H 7
24 Walpole Crosskeys D 6
24 Walpole Highway D 6
24 Walpole Island D 6
24 Walpole St. Andrew D 6

MAP
24 Walpole St. Peter..D 6
22 Walsall...........B 4
22 Walsall Wood....B 4
35 Walsden........E 8
23 Walsgrave on Sowc D 7
27 Walsham le Willows
   H 3
34 Walshaw.........F 6
35 Walshford....B 12
48 Walston........E 3
18 Walsworth.....A 2
17 Walter's Ash.....D 9
14 Walterston.....G 4
15 Walterstone.....B 7
11 Waltham, Kent...C 9
37 Waltham, Lincs..G 10
18 Waltham Abbey..D 4
9 Waltham Chase..E 7
18 Waltham Cross...D 4
18 Waltham Forest..E 4
32 Waltham on the Wolds
   H 5
17 Waltham St. Lawrence
   F 9
18 Walthamstow....E 3
23 Walton, Bucks..H 12
44 Walton, Cumb...G 3
32 Walton, Derby...C 1
24 Walton, Hunts...E 3
23 Walton, Leics.....C 9
21 Walton, Rad.....E 7
30 Walton, Salop...H 4
7 Walton, Som......C 8
27 Walton, Suffolk..L 6
22 Walton, War.....G 6
36 Walton, Yorks....B 2
35 Walton, Yorks....E 12
15 Walton Cardiff..A 12
7 Walton Elm.....D 11
12 Walton East.....C 8
15 Walton-in-Gordano
   G 7
34 Walton-Le-Dale..D 4
17 Walton-on-Thames
   G 12
34 Walton on the Hill,
   Lancashire.....H 3
31 Walton-on-the-Hill,
   Staffordshire...H 8
10 Walton on the Hill,
   Surrey.........C 1
19 Walton on the Naze
   B 12
32 Walton on the Wolds
   H 3
15 Walton Park....G 7
31 Walton upon Trent
   H 10
12 Walton West....F 2
29 Walwen.........C 11
45 Walwick........F 7
45 Walwick Grange..F 7
40 Walworth.......C 3
12 Walwyn's Castle..F 2
6 Wambrook.......E 6
43 Wamphraygate...B 12
9 Wanborough, Surrey
   A 10
16 Wanborough, Wilts. F 3
48 Wandel.........G 2
45 Wandon........C 11
18 Wandsworth.....F 3
45 Wandylaw.......A 9
27 Wangford.......G 8
23 Wanlip.........A 9
48 Wanlockhead....H 2
10 Wannock........H 4
24 Wansford, Hunts..F 2
37 Wansford, Yorks..B 8
18 Wanstead.......E 4
7 Wanstrow.......B 10
15 Wanswell Green..D 10
16 Wantage........E 5
23 Wappenbury.....E 7
23 Wappenham.....H 9
39 Warcop........D 9
10 Warbleton......F 5
9 Warblington.....E 8
17 Warborough.....E 7
25 Warboys........G 4
34 Warbreck.......C 2
2 Warbstow.......B 2
30 Warburton.....A 5
27 Ward Green....J 4
11 Warden........A 9
31 Wardgate.....E 11
23 Wardington....G 8
47 Wardlaw, Ayr....E 8
48 Wardlaw, Sel.....H 5
30 Wardle, Ches.....E 8
35 Wardle, Lancs....E 8
23 Wardley.....B 11
31 Wardlow......C 10

45 Wardon.........F 7
25 Wardy Hill.......G 6
18 Ware, Herts.......C 4
11 Ware, Kent.....B 11
8 Wareham........G 1
11 Warehorne......E 8
45 Waren Mill....C 12
45 Warenford....C 12
45 Warenton....C 12
18 Wareside........B 4
25 Waresley, Hunts..K 3
22 Waresley, Worcs..E 2
17 Warfield........G 9
5 Warfleet........L 7
24 Wargate........C 3
17 Wargrave.......F 9
26 Warham All Saints. A 3
26 Warham St. Mary. A 2
49 Wark, Northumb..E 7
49 Wark, Northumb. E 11
4 Warkleigh........D 5
23 Warkton........D 12
23 Warkwork......H 8
45 Warkworth.....B 10
40 Warlaby........F 4
35 Warland........E 8
3 Warleggan......C 8
22 Warley.........C 3
10 Warlingham.....B 2
35 Warmfield.....E 12
8 Warmington....D 5
24 Warmington, Hunts.
   F 2
23 Warmington, War. G 7
7 Warminster....B 11
11 Warmlake.......C 7
15 Warmley.......G 10
15 Warmley Tower..G 10
36 Warmsworth.....G 3
4 Warmwell.....H 11
22 Warndon.......F 2
9 Warnford.......D 8
10 Warnham......E 1
49 Warningcamp. E 11
10 Warninglid......E 1
31 Warren, Ches...C 7
12 Warren, Pemb...G 3
5 Warren House Inn.H 5
27 Warren Row.....F 9
11 Warren Street...C 8
23 Warrington, Bucks.
   G 12
30 Warrington, Lancs. A 5
8 Warsash........E 6
31 Warslow.......D 9
32 Warsop.......C 3
36 Warter.......B 6
36 Warthermarske...G 2
36 Warthill.......B 4
10 Wartling.......G 5
27 Wartnaby......H 4
34 Warton, Lancs...D 3
39 Warton, Lancs...H 7
45 Warton, Northumb.
   C 8
22 Warton, War.....B 6
44 Warwick, Cumb...G 3
22 Warwick, War....F 6
44 Warwick Bridge..G 3
22 Warwickshire, Co. F 6
44 Warwicksland.....E 3
64 Wasbister.......B 2
38 Wasdale Head...D 4
16 Wash Common..H 5
3 Washaway.......C 7
5 Washbourne....K 7
31 Washerwall....E 8
6 Washfield.......E 3
40 Washfold.......E 1
6 Washford.......B 4
4 Washford Pyne...E 7
33 Washingborough..C 7
45 Washington, Dur. G 11
9 Washington, Sussex
   E 12
17 Wasing........H 7
40 Waskerley......A 1
22 Wasperton.....F 6
40 Wass.........G 6
6 Watchet........B 4
16 Watchfield, Berks.. E 3
6 Watchfield, Som..B 7
39 Watchgate......E 8
43 Watchill......G 12
38 Watendlath....D 5
5 Water, Devon....H 6
35 Water, Lancs....E 7
18 Water End, Herts. C 2
36 Water End, Yorks..C 6
24 Water Newton...F 2
22 Water Orton....C 5
17 Water Stratford..A 7
14 Water Street.....F 1

38 Water Yeat.......F 5
25 Waterbeach......J 6
44 Waterbeck.......E 1
26 Waterden.......B 2
17 Waterend.....C 11
31 Waterfall........E 9
47 Waterfoot, Lan...D 10
35 Waterfoot, Lancs..E 7
8 Waterford, Hants..G 5
18 Waterford, Herts..B 3
47 Waterhead, Ayr..H 10
43 Waterhead, Dumf.B 12
43 Waterhead, Dumf..C 8
38 Waterhead, Westmor.
   E 6
48 Waterheads......D 1
40 Waterhouses, Dur..A 2
31 Waterhouses, Staffs.
   E 9
33 Watering Dyke Houses
   B 7
10 Wateringbury....C 6
64 Wateringhouse....E 2
15 Waterlane......D 12
32 Waterloo, Derby..D 1
8 Waterloo, Dorset..G 2
34 Waterloo, Lancs...G 2
26 Waterloo, Norf...D 5
12 Waterloo, Pemb...G 3
52 Waterloo, Perth...C 5
62 Waterloo, Skye...F 6
6 Waterloo Cross...E 4
9 Waterlooville....E 8
48 Watermeetings...H 2
17 Waterperry.....C 7
6 Waterrow.......D 4
30 Waters Upton...H 5
9 Watersfield.....E 11
47 Waterside, Ayr....A 5
47 Waterside, Ayr....E 9
44 Waterside, Cumb..H 1
43 Waterside, Dumf. D 12
47 Waterside, Dunb..B 11
17 Waterstock.....D 7
12 Waterston......F 3
18 Watford, Herts...D 1
23 Watford, Northants.
   E 9
40 Wath, N. Riding .G 3
40 Wath, W. Riding .H 2
38 Wath Brow......D 3
36 Wath upon Dearne G 2
15 Watley's End....F 9
24 Watlington, Norf..D 7
17 Watlington, Oxon..E 8
32 Watnall Chaworth. F 2
61 Watten........B 11
27 Wattisfield......H 3
27 Wattisham.....K 3
26 Watton, Norf....E 2
37 Watton, Yorks....B 8
18 Watton-at-Stone..B 3
47 Wattston......B 12
14 Wattstown.....E 3
55 Wauchan.......L 3
37 Wauldby.......D 7
20 Waun Fawr.....D 2
13 Waunarlwydd....G 9
13 Waun-deg......D 7
28 Waunfawr.....D 5
14 Waunlwyd.....C 7
23 Wavendon.....H 12
44 Waverbridge....H 1
30 Waverton, Ches...D 3
44 Waverton, Cumb..H 1
37 Wawne........C 8
26 Waxham.......C 7
37 Waxholme.....D 11
6 Way Village.....E 3
10 Wayfield.......B 6
7 Wayford.......F 7
7 Waytown......F 8
6 Weacombe.....B 5
18 Wealdstone....E 2
35 Weardley......C 11
7 Weare.........A 7
4 Weare Giffard...D 3
39 Wearhead......A 11
39 Weasdale.......C 4
26 Weasenham All Saints
   C 1
26 Weasenham St. Peter
   C 1
30 Weaverham.....C 5
41 Weaverthorpe...H 9
18 Webheath......E 4
15 Webton........A 7
58 Wedderlairs.....D 6
49 Wedderlie......D 9
23 Weddington.....C 7
16 Wedhampton....H 2

7 Wedmore........A 8
22 Wednesbury.....C 3
22 Wednesfield.....B 3
17 Weedon........B 9
23 Weedon Bec.....F 9
23 Weedon Lois.....G 9
4 Week, Devon....C 4
4 Week, Devon....D 6
4 Week St. Mary...F 1
8 Weeke.........C 6
23 Weekley........D 12
37 Weel..........C 8
19 Weeley.........B 11
19 Weeley Heath....B 11
52 Weem.........B 3
21 Weeping Cross,
   Shropshire.....A 10
31 Weeping Cross,
   Staffordshire....H 8
27 Weeting........G 1
34 Weeton, Lancs...D 3
35 Weeton, Yorks...B 11
49 Weetwoodhill....F 12
35 Weir..........E 7
15 Weirend........B 9
32 Welbeck Abbey...C 3
32 Welbeck Colliery..C 3
26 Welborne......E 4
33 Welbourn......E 7
41 Welburn, Yorks...G 7
41 Welburn, Yorks...H 7
40 Welbury........E 4
33 Welby.........F 7
25 Welches Dam....G 6
4 Welcombe......D 1
32 Weldon.......C 12
45 Weldon Bridge...C 9
16 Welford, Berks...G 5
23 Welford, Northants.
   D 9
22 Welford-on-Avon .G 5
23 Welham........C 11
18 Welhamgreen....C 2
9 Well, Hants......A 9
33 Well, Lincs.....C 11
40 Well, Yorks......G 3
7 Well Bottom....E 12
17 Well End.......E 9
10 Well Hill.......B 4
6 Well Town......E 3
22 Welland........H 2
53 Wellbank.......C 9
43 Welldale.......E 12
22 Wellesbourne Hastings
   G 6
22 Wellesbourne
   Mountford.....G 6
40 Wellfields......A 4
59 Wellford.......L 2
26 Welling........F 5
23 Wellingborough..E 12
26 Wellingham....C 2
33 Wellingore.....E 7
38 Wellington, Cumb..E 3
21 Wellington, Herefs.
   H 10
21 Wellington, Salop A 12
6 Wellington, Som..D 5
21 Wellington Heath H 12
21 Wellington Marsh H 10
8 Wellow, I.o.W....G 5
32 Wellow, Notts....D 4
15 Wellow, Som....H 10
7 Wells.........B 9
26 Wells-next-the-Sea. A 2
58 Wells of Ytham..D 4
23 Wellsborough....B 7
5 Wellswood......J 8
52 Wellwood......H 6
24 Welney........F 6
4 Welsford.......D 1
15 Welsh Bicknor...C 9
30 Welsh Frankton..G 2
12 Welsh Hook.....D 3
15 Welsh Newton...B 8
14 Welsh St. Donats..G 4
30 Welshampton....G 3
21 Welshpool......B 8
38 Welton, Cumb....A 6
33 Welton, Lincs....B 8
23 Welton, Northants. E 9
7 Welton, Som....A 10
37 Welton, Yorks....D 7
33 Welton le Marsh..C 11
33 Welton le Wold..B 10
37 Welwick.......E 11
18 Welwyn........B 2
18 Welwyn Garden City
   C 2
16 West Challow....E 6
7 West Chelborough. F 9
45 West Chevington. C 10
9 West Chiltington. D 12

5 Wembury.......L 4
4 Wembworthy....E 5
47 Wemyss Bay.....B 7
25 Wendens Ambo...L 6
26 Wendling........D 2
17 Wendover......C 9
4 Wendron.......G 4
25 Wendy.........K 4
27 Wenhaston.....H 7
25 Wennington, Hunts.
   G 3
39 Wennington, Lancs.
   H 8
18 Wennington, London
   F 5
31 Wensley, Derby..D 11
40 Wensley, Yorks...F 1
36 Wentbridge.....E 3
21 Wentnor.......C 9
25 Wentworth, Cambs.
   G 6
35 Wentworth, Yorks.
   G 12
14 Wenvoe........G 4
21 Weobley.......G 9
21 Weobley Marsh...G 9
22 Wergs.........B 2
14 Wern..........C 4
49 Wernffrwd.....H 8
15 Wernyrheolydd...C 7
24 Werrington, Hunts.
   E 3
3 Werrington, Corn.A 10
31 Werrington, Staffs..E 8
34 Wesham.......D 3
32 Wessington.....D 1
26 West Acre......D 1
16 West Adderbury...A 5
6 West Adsborough .C 6
23 West Allerdean...E 12
45 West Allotment ..F 11
5 West Alvington...L 6
8 West Amesbury...B 3
4 West Anstey....C 7
4 West Ash.......D 2
33 West Ashby.....C 9
9 West Ashling....E 9
7 West Ashton....A 12
40 West Auckland...C 2
41 West Ayton....G 10
59 West Balhagarty..K 5
6 West Bagborough..C 5
33 West Barkwith...B 8
41 West Barnby.....D 8
49 West Barns......B 9
42 West Barr......G 4
7 West Bay.......G 8
26 West Beckham...B 4
17 West Bedfont...G 11
45 West Benridge...D 10
19 West Bergholt...A 9
9 West Bexington..H 9
24 West Bilney.....D 8
49 West Blackadder. D 11
10 West Blatchington. G 2
48 West Bold.......F 6
45 West Boldon....G 11
43 West Bowhill...D 12
35 West Bowling...D 10
26 West Bradenham. E 2
34 West Bradford...C 6
7 West Bradley....C 9
59 West Braidieston..K 4
35 West Bretton....F 11
32 West Bridgford...G 3
22 West Bromwich...C 4
47 West Browncastle E 11
4 West Buckland...C 5
6 West Buckland...D 5
64 West Burrafirth..D 6
9 West Burton, Sussex
   E 11
39 West Burton, Yorks.
   F 12
40 West Butsfield....A 1
36 West Butterwick..G 6
17 West Byfleet.....H 11
49 West Byres......C 7
26 West Caister....D 8
48 West Calder.....C 3
7 West Camel.....D 9
58 West Cannahars..E 7
47 West Carberth...B 10
36 West Carr......F 5
47 West Cauldcoats..E 11
7 West Chaldon...H 11
16 West Challow....E 6
7 West Chelborough. F 9
45 West Chevington. C 10
9 West Chiltington. D 12

9 West Chiltington
   Common.......D 12
7 West Chinnock...E 8
8 West Chisenbury..A 3
9 West Clandon...A 11
11 West Cliffe.....D 12
61 West Clyth.....D 11
7 West Coker.....E 8
7 West Compton,
   Dorset........G 9
7 West Compton,
   Somerset......B 9
36 West Cowick....E 4
7 West Cranmore..B 10
27 West Creeting Grn. J 4
13 West Cross.....H 9
44 West Curthwaite..H 2
46 West Darlochan...G 2
8 West Dean, Hants. C 4
9 West Dean, Sus..E 10
24 West Deeping....E 2
30 West Derby.....A 3
24 West Dereham...E 7
45 West Ditchburn..A 9
4 West Down.....B 4
18 West Drayton, London
   F 1
32 West Drayton, Notts.
   C 4
45 West Edington...E 9
37 West Ella......D 8
17 West End, Berks. H 10
28 West End, Caer...G 3
8 West End, Hants...E 6
18 West End, Herts...C 3
48 West End, Lan....E 2
37 West End, Lincs..G 11
26 West End, Norf...D 8
15 West End, Som...G 8
17 West End, Surrey..G 9
8 West End, Wilts...D 1
37 West End, Yorks..D 7
45 West Falldon....A 10
10 West Farleigh...C 6
30 West Felton.....H 2
10 West Firle......G 3
36 West Garforth...D 2
13 West Glamorgan, Co.
   G 10
16 West Grafton....H 3
17 West Green.....H 8
8 West Grimstead..D 4
16 West Gringe.....E 5
10 West Grinstead...F 1
36 West Haddlesey...D 3
23 West Haddon....E 9
16 West Hagbourne .E 6
22 West Hagley.....D 3
44 West Hall......F 4
32 West Hallam....F 2
37 West Halton....E 7
18 West Ham......F 4
16 West Hanney....E 5
19 West Hanningfield D 7
36 West Hardwick...E 2
8 West Harnham...C 3
7 West Harptree....A 9
45 West Harrington. H 11
40 West Hartlepool..B 5
6 West Hatch.....D 6
15 West Hay.......H 8
24 West Head......E 7
17 West Heath.....H 9
61 West Helmsdale..E 9
16 West Hendred....E 5
41 West Heslerton...H 9
4 West Hill, Devon..G 4
15 West Hill, Som...G 8
10 West Hoathly....F 1
7 West Holme.....H 12
49 West Hopes.....C 8
18 West Horndon....E 6
7 West Horrington..A 9
9 West Horsley....A 12
45 West Horton....C 11
11 West Hougham.. D 11
10 West Humble....C 1
6 West Huntspill...B 6
9 West Hyde......E 11
11 West Hythe.....E 10
16 West Ilsley......F 6
9 West Itchenor...F 9
33 West Keal.......D 10
16 West Kennett....G 2
47 West Kilbride....E 7
10 West Kingsdown..B 5
15 West Kington...F 11
58 West Kinharrachie D 7
58 West Kinnernie...F 5
30 West Kirby......B 1
41 West Knapton...H 9
7 West Knighton...G 10
7 West Knoyle.....C 11

MAP
45 West Kyloe......B 11
7 West Lambrook...D 7
11 West Langdon...C 11
61 West Langwell....F 7
9 West Lavington, Sussex........D 10
8 West Lavington, Wiltshire.......A 2
40 West Layton......D 2
32 West Leake.......G 3
49 West Learmouth..F 11
26 West Lexham.....D 1
36 West Lilling.......A 4
45 West Linkhall....A 10
48 West Linton......D 4
9 West Liss.........C 9
15 West Littleton...G 11
3 West Looe.......D 9
48 West Lothian, Co..B 3
6 West Luccombe...B 2
7 West Lulworth...H 11
41 West Lutton......H 9
7 West Lydford.....C 9
45 West Lyham.....C 12
7 West Lyng........C 7
24 West Lynn.......D 7
47 West Mains, Ayr..D 8
48 West Mains, Lan..D 2
45 West Mains, Northumb.........B 12
10 West Malling.....B 5
22 West Malvern.....G 1
9 West Marden.....E 9
32 West Markham...C 4
37 West Marsh......F 10
35 West Marton.....B 8
9 West Meon.......D 8
19 West Mersea.....C 10
22 West Midlands, Co. C 4
7 West Milton......G 8
11 West Minster.....A 8
17 West Molesey....G 12
8 West Moors......F 2
7 West Morden....G 12
49 West Morrison....E 8
41 West Ness........G 7
24 West Newton, Norfolk C 8
37 West Newton, Yorks. C 9
5 West Ogwell......J 7
7 West Orchard....E 11
16 West Overton.....G 2
59 West Park.........H 5
8 West Parley.......F 2
5 West Panson......G 2
49 West Peaston.....C 7
10 West Peckham....C 5
45 West Pelton.....H 10
7 West Pennard.....B 9
2 West Pentire......D 5
6 West Porlock.....B 2
4 West Putford.....D 2
6 West Quantoxhead B 5
45 West Rainton....H 11
33 West Rasen.......A 8
26 West Raynham....C 2
40 West Rounton....E 4
25 West Row........H 8
26 West Rudham....C 1
26 West Runton.....A 5
49 West Saltoun.....C 7
4 West Sandford....F 7
64 West Sandwick....B 7
40 West Scrafton.....G 1
48 West Sidewood...D 3
43 West Skelston.....C 9
45 West Sleekburn..E 11
26 West Somerton...D 7
7 West Stafford....G 10
36 West Stockwith...H 6
9 West Stoke.......E 9
39 West Stonesdale..E 11
7 West Stoughton...A 7
7 West Stour.......D 11
11 West Stourmouth.B 11
27 West Stow.......H 1
16 West Stowell.....H 2
60 West Strathan.....B 6
8 West Stratton.....B 6
11 West Street.......C 8
40 West Summer Side.G 2
10 West Sussex, Co. ..E 1
40 West Tanfield.....G 3
3 West Taphouse....C 8
46 West Tarbert.....C 3
49 West Third.... F 9
45 West Thirston....C 10
9 West Thorney......F 9
18 West Thurrock....F 6
9 West Tisted.......C 8
52 West Tofts.......D 6

MAP
33 West Torrington...B 8
9 West Town, Hants. F 8
21 West Town, Herefs. F 10
15 West Town, Som. G 8
15 West Town, Som..H 8
8 West Tytherley....C 4
16 West Tytherton ...G 1
24 West Walton.....D 6
24 West Walton Highway.......D 6
4 West Warlington..E 6
53 West Wemyss.....H 8
15 West Wick........H 7
25 West Wickham, Cambs.........K 7
18 West Wickham, London........G 4
12 West Williamston..F 4
8 West Willow......D 4
24 West Winch......D 7
8 West Winterslow..C 4
9 West Wittering....F 9
40 West Witton......F 1
45 West Woodburn...D 7
16 West Woodhay...H 5
7 West Woodlands.B 11
9 West Worldham...B 9
25 West Wratting....K 7
17 West Wycombe...E 9
64 West Yell.........C 7
35 West Yorkshire, Co. D 10
4 Westacott........C 5
11 Westbere........B 10
32 Westborough......F 6
8 Westbourne, Hants. G 2
27 Westbourne, Suff. .K 5
9 Westbourne, Sussex E 9
16 Westbrook.......G 5
17 Westbury, Bucks...A 7
21 Westbury, Salop...A 9
7 Westbury, Wilts...A 12
7 Westbury Leigh..A 12
15 Westbury on Trym G 9
15 Westbury-on-Severn C 10
7 Westbury-sub-Mendip A 8
34 Westby..........D 3
9 Westcatt.........A 12
19 Westcliff on Sea...E 8
7 Westcombe......B 10
16 Westcote.........B 3
17 Westcott, Bucks...B 8
6 Westcott, Devon...F 4
16 Westcott Barton...B 6
10 Westdean........H 4
57 Wester Aviemore..H 4
52 Wester Balgedie...G 6
48 Wester Causewayend C 3
52 Wester Clunie.....A 4
49 Wester Essenside..G 7
58 Wester Fintray....F 6
57 Wester Fodderletter G 7
60 Wester Greenyards G 6
48 Wester Happrew...E 4
49 Wester Housebyres F 8
56 Wester Lamington.B 3
56 Wester Milton....D 5
53 Wester Newburn..G 9
48 Wester Ochiltree...B 3
49 Wester Pencaitland C 7
64 Wester Quarff.....E 7
56 Wester Rarichie...B 4
57 Wester Shennach..G 7
54 Wester Slumbay...F 3
56 Wester Teaninich..C 2
61 Westerdale, Caith.C 10
41 Westerdale, Yorks..E 7
27 Westerfield.......K 5
9 Westergate...... F 10
10 Westerham.......C 3
45 Westerhope.......F 10
15 Westerleigh......F 10
64 Westermill.......E 3
58 Westerton, Aber...C 3
53 Westerton, Angus B 11
40 Westerton, Dur....B 3
9 Westerton, Sussex E 10
58 Westertown.......C 3
58 Westfield, Aber....E 7
61 Westfield, Caith...B 10
38 Westfield, Cumb...B 2
22 Westfield, Herefs...G 1
26 Westfield, Norf....D 3
45 Westfield, Northumb. D 12
11 Westfield, Sussex..F 7
7 Westfields.......F 10

MAP
52 Westfields of Rattray C 6
39 Westgate, Dur.....A 11
36 Westgate, Lincs....F 5
26 Westgate, Norf....B 3
11 Westgate on Sea..A 11
44 Westgillsyke......F 2
27 Westhall.........G 7
7 Westham, Dorset. H 10
7 Westham, Som....B 7
10 Westham, Sussex..H 5
9 Westhampnett....E 10
58 Westhaugh.......E 4
7 Westhay.........B 8
34 Westhead.........F 3
21 Westhide........H 11
59 Westhill..........G 6
21 Westhope, Herefs.G 10
21 Westhope, Salop .D 10
24 Westhorpe, Lincs...B 3
27 Westhorpe, Suff...H 3
34 Westhoughton....G 5
39 Westhouse.......H 9
32 Westhouses.......D 2
4 Westleigh, Devon..C 3
6 Westleigh, Devon..D 4
34 Westleigh, Lancs...G 5
27 Westleton........H 7
21 Westley, Salop....B 9
27 Westley, Suffolk..J 1
25 Westley Waterless.K 7
17 Westlington.......C 8
44 Westlinton.......G 2
11 Westmarsh.......B 11
10 Westmeston......G 2
18 Westmill.........A 4
18 Westminster......F 3
53 Westmuir.........B 8
64 Westness... B 2
43 Westnewton, Cumb. G 12
49 Westnewton, Northumb.....F 11
16 Weston, Berks.....G 5
30 Weston, Ches......E 6
30 Weston, Ches.....B 4
6 Weston, Devon....F 5
6 Weston, Devon....G 5
7 Weston, Dorset....H 7
9 Weston, Hants.....D 8
18 Weston, Herts.....A 3
48 Weston, Lan.......E 3
24 Weston, Lincs......C 4
23 Weston, Northants.G 9
32 Weston, Notts......C 5
21 Weston, Salop...C 11
21 Weston, Salop.....E 9
30 Weston, Salop.....G 4
15 Weston, Som.....H 10
31 Weston, Staffs.....G 8
35 Weston, Yorks...B 10
7 Weston Bampfylde D 9
21 Weston Beggard..H 11
15 Weston Birt......E 11
23 Weston by Welland C 11
25 Weston Colville...K 7
31 Weston Coyney...F 8
23 Weston Favell ...F 11
25 Weston Green.....K 7
22 Weston Heath....A 1
24 Weston Hills......C 4
15 Weston-in-Gordano G 8
30 Weston Jones......H 6
26 Weston Longville..D 4
30 Weston Lullingfields H 3
22 Weston-on-Avon..G 5
16 Weston-on-the-Grn.B 6
9 Weston Patrick....B 8
30 Weston Rhyn.....G 1
15 Weston Road......G 8
22 Weston Sudedge..H 5
14 Weston-super-Mare H 6
17 Weston Turville...C 9
15 Weston under Penyard B 9
23 Weston under Wetherley......E 7
23 Weston Underwood, Bucks.........G 12
31 Weston Underwood, Derbyshire.....F 11
32 Weston upon Trent G 1
22 Weston-under-Lizard A 2
25 Westoning.......M 1
7 Westonzoyland....C 7
36 Westow..........A 5
46 Westport, Arg.....G 2
7 Westport, Som....D 7

MAP
16 Westridge Green...F 6
48 Westrigg.........C 2
49 Westruther.......D 9
24 Westry..... ..F 5
32 Westville.........E 2
38 Westward........A 5
4 Westward Ho......C 3
44 Westwater........E 1
11 Westwell, Kent....C 8
16 Westwell, Oxon....C 3
11 Westwell Leacon..C 8
25 Westwick, Cambs..J 5
40 Westwick, Dur....D 1
6 Westwood, Devon..F 4
45 Westwood, Dur...G 9
47 Westwood, Lan...D 11
15 Westwood, Wilts. H 11
36 Westwoodside....G 5
40 Wether Cote......F 6
44 Wetheral.........H 3
35 Wetherby.........B 12
27 Wetherden........J 3
27 Wetheringsett.....J 4
25 Wethersfield.......M 8
64 Wethersta........C 7
27 Wetherup Street...J 4
31 Wetley Rocks.....E 8
30 Wettenhall........D 5
31 Wetton............E 9
37 Wetwang..........A 7
30 Wetwood....... G 6
16 Wexcombe.......H 4
17 Wexham Street...F 10
26 Weybourne.......A 4
27 Weybread.........G 5
17 Weybridge......H 11
6 Weycroft.........F 6
61 Weydale..........A 10
8 Weyhill...........B 5
7 Weymouth.......G 7
17 Whaddon, Bucks...A 9
25 Whaddon, Cambs..K 4
15 Whaddon, Glos...C 11
8 Whaddon, Wilts...C 3
39 Whale............C 7
32 Whaley...........C 2
31 Whaley Bridge....B 8
32 Whaley Thorns....C 3
34 Whalley..........D 6
45 Whalton..........E 9
34 Wham............A 6
24 Whaplode........C 4
24 Whaplode Drove..D 4
24 Whaplode St. Catherine...D 4
39 Wharfe.........H 10
34 Wharles..........D 3
45 Wharmley.........F 7
35 Wharncliffe Side..H 11
36 Wharram-le-Street.A 6
30 Wharton, Ches....D 5
21 Wharton, Herefs..G 10
40 Whashton........E 2
39 Whasset..........G 7
22 Whatcote.........H 6
22 Whateley.........B 6
27 Whatfield.........K 3
10 Whatlington.......F 6
31 Whatstandwell....E 11
32 Whatton...........F 5
42 Whauphill.........G 5
26 Wheatacre.........F 8
18 Wheathampstead..C 2
9 Wheatley, Hants.. B 9
17 Wheatley, Oxon...D 7
40 Wheatley Hill. ..A 4
35 Wheatley Lane....C 7
22 Wheaton Aston...A 2
58 Wheedlemont......E 2
17 Wheeler's Green...G 8
9 Wheelerstreet....B 11
30 Wheelock.........D 6
30 Wheelock Heath..D 6
34 Wheelton..........E 5
59 Wheen............K 1
6 Wheddon Cross...B 3
36 Wheldrake........C 4
16 Whelford.........D 3
38 Whelpo...........A 5
40 Whenby..........H 6
27 Whepstead.........J 1
27 Wherstead.........L 5
8 Wherwell.........B 5
31 Wheston..........C 10
10 Whetsted..........C 5
23 Whetstone........B 9
16 Whichford.........A 4
38 Whicham, Cumb...G 4
45 Whickham, Dur..G 10
5 Whiddon Down...G 6
53 Whigstreet........C 9
23 Whilton...........F 9
4 Whimble..........F 2

MAP
6 Whimple.........F 4
26 Whimpwell Green .C 7
26 Whinburgh.........E 3
49 Whinkerstones...E 10
43 Whinnie Liggate...F 8
58 Whinnyfold.......D 8
8 Whippingham.....G 6
17 Whipsnade......B 11
6 Whipton.........G 3
23 Whissendine......A 11
26 Whissonsett.......C 2
17 Whistley Green...G 9
30 Whiston, Lancs....A 3
23 Whiston, Northants. F 11
22 Whiston, Staffs....A 2
31 Whiston, Staffs....F 9
32 Whiston, Yorks....A 2
30 Whiston Lane Ends A 3
38 Whitbeck.........G 3
21 Whitbourne.......G 12
22 Whitbourne Ford..F 1
45 Whitburn, Dur...G 12
48 Whitburn, W. Loth.C 2
45 Whitburn Colliery G 12
30 Whitby, Cheshire..C 3
41 Whitby, Yorks....D 9
44 Whitcastles.......D 1
17 Whitchurch, Bucks.B 9
5 Whitchurch, Devon. H 4
14 Whitchurch, Glam. F 5
8 Whitchurch, Hants.A 6
15 Whitchurch, Herefs. C 8
17 Whitchurch, Oxon. F 7
12 Whitchurch, Pemb.D 2
30 Whitchurch, Salop.F 4
15 Whitchurch, Som..G 9
17 Whitchurch Hill...F 7
7 Whitcombe........G 10
21 Whitcott Keysett..D 8
34 White Chapel.....C 4
34 White Coppice....E 5
6 White Cross, Devon. G 4
7 White Cross, Som..A 9
7 White Lackington F 10
22 White Ladies Aston G 3
13 White Mill........E 8
19 White Notley.....B 8
33 White Pit........B 11
18 White Roding.....C 5
21 White Stone.....H 11
17 White Waltham...F 9
56 Whiteacen.........E 8
22 Whiteacre Heath..C 5
55 Whitebridge......H 8
15 Whitebrook........D 8
49 Whiteburn.........E 8
42 Whitecairn........F 3
58 Whitecairns.......F 7
48 Whitecastle.......E 3
7 Whitechurch Canonicorum...G 7
48 Whitecraig.........B 6
15 Whitecroft.........D 9
42 Whitecrook........F 3
3 Whitecross, Corn..B 7
48 Whitecross, Stir....B 2
61 Whiteface.........G 7
46 Whitefarland.......E 4
42 Whitefaulds.......A 4
35 Whitefield, Lan....G 7
52 Whitefield, Perth...D 6
6 Whitefield, Som....C 4
58 Whiteford..........E 5
6 Whitehall, Devon..E 5
64 Whitehall, Orkney.B 4
44 Whitehaugh.......B 3
38 Whitehaven.......C 2
47 Whitehill, Ayr....D 7
58 Whitehill, Banff....B 3
43 Whitehill, Dumf..D 12
9 Whitehill, Hants...C 9
58 Whitehills, Banff....A 4
47 Whitehills, Ren....D 11
58 Whitehouse, Aber..F 4
46 Whitehouse, Arg...C 3
49 Whitekirk..........A 8
59 Whiteknowes......G 3
7 Whitelackington...E 7
49 Whitelaw.........D 11
49 Whitelee...........F 8
36 Whitely............E 3
9 Whiteley Bank.....H 7
31 Whiteley Green...B 8
17 Whiteley Village..H 11
10 Whitemans Green..E 2
56 Whitemire.........D 5
3 Whitemoor........D 7
31 Whitemore........D 7

MAP
8 Whitenap.........D 5
8 Whiteparish.......D 4
58 Whiterashes.......E 6
15 Whiteshill........D 11
44 Whiteside, Northumb. F 5
48 Whiteside, W. Loth. C 2
10 Whitesmith........G 4
6 Whitestaunton.....E 6
59 Whitestone, Aber..H 4
4 Whitestone, Devon.A 4
4 Whitestone, Devon.F 7
58 Whitestones.......B 6
15 Whiteway........C 12
6 Whiteway House..H 2
34 Whitewell.........B 5
5 Whiteworks........J 5
56 Whitewreath.......D 8
15 Whitfield, Glos...E 10
11 Whitfield, Kent...D 11
23 Whitfield, Northants. H 9
44 Whitfield, Northumb. G 6
48 Whitfield, Peeb....D 4
6 Whitford, Devon...G 6
29 Whitford, Flint...B 10
36 Whitgift..........E 6
31 Whitgreave.......G 7
42 Whithorn..........G 5
46 Whiting Bay.......G 5
24 Whitington........E 8
12 Whitland..........E 5
44 Whitlaw...........B 3
47 Whitletts..........G 8
17 Whitley, Berks....G 8
15 Whitley, Wilts....H 12
45 Whitley Bay.....F 11
45 Whitley Chapel...G 7
35 Whitley Lower...E 11
22 Whitlock's End...D 4
15 Whitminster.....D 11
31 Whitmore........F 7
6 Whitnage.........E 4
21 Whitney...........H 8
38 Whitrigg, Cumb...A 4
44 Whitrigg, Cumb...G 1
44 Whitriggs.........B 4
8 Whitsbury.........D 3
4 Whitsleigh Barton. D 4
49 Whitsome.........D 11
49 Whitsomehill......D 11
15 Whitson...........F 7
15 Whitson Common .F 7
11 Whitstable........A 9
4 Whitstone.........F 1
45 Whittingham.......B 9
21 Whittingslow......D 9
32 Whittington,Derby.C 1
16 Whittington, Glos..B 1
39 Whittington, Lancs. H 8
30 Whittington, Salop G 2
22 Whittington, Staffs.A 5
22 Whittington, Worcs. D 2
22 Whittington, Worcs. G 2
34 Whittle-le-Woods..E 5
23 Whittlebury......H 10
24 Whittlesey........F 4
25 Whittlesford......K 6
34 Whittlestone Head.E 6
40 Whitton, Dur.....C 4
37 Whitton, Lincs....E 7
45 Whitton, Northumb. C 9
21 Whitton, Rad.......F 8
49 Whitton, Rox......G 10
21 Whitton, Salop....E 11
27 Whitton, Suffolk..K 4
16 Whittonditch......G 4
45 Whittonstall.......G 9
16 Whitway...........H 6
32 Whitwell, Derby...C 3
18 Whitwell, Herts....B 2
9 Whitwell, I.o.W....H 7
23 Whitwell, Rut......A 12
40 Whitwell, Yorks...E 3
41 Whitwell-on-the-Hill...........H 7
23 Whitwick..........A 8
36 Whitwood.........E 2
35 Whitworth.........E 7
40 Whixall............G 4
30 Whixley...........A 2
22 Whoberly..........D 6
40 Whorlton, Dur....D 1
40 Whorlton, Yorks...E 5
44 Whygate...........E 6
21 Whyle.............F 11
10 Whyteleafe........B 2

MAP
15 Wibdon..........E 9
23 Wibtoft..........C 8
11 Wichling........ B 8
61 Wick, Caith......C 12
14 Wick, Glam.......G 3
5 Wick, Glos......G 10
8 Wick, Hants......G 3
6 Wick, Som.. ....B 5
7 Wick, Som........D 7
9 Wick, Sussex.....F 11
8 Wick, Wilts.. .....D 3
22 Wick, Worcs......H 3
17 Wick Hill........H 9
16 Wick Rissington...B 3
15 Wick St. Lawrence H 7
25 Wicken, Cambs....H 7
23 Wicken, Northants. H 10
25 Wicken Bonhunt..M 6
33 Wickenby..........B 8
22 Wichenford.......F 1
32 Wickersley........A 2
19 Wickford..........E 7
16 Wickham, Berks...G 5
9 Wickham, Hants...E 7
19 Wickham Bishops.C 8
16 Wickham Heath...G 5
27 Wickham Market..K 6
27 Wickham St. Paul..L 1
27 Wickham Skeith..H 4
27 Wickham Street, Suffolk.........H 4
27 Wickham Street, Suffolk.........K 1
11 Wickhambreaux..B 10
25 Wickhambrook...K 8
22 Wickhamford......H 4
26 Wickhampton......E 7
26 Wicklewood.......E 4
26 Wickmere.........B 5
10 Wickstreet.........G 4
15 Wickwar........E 10
25 Widdington......M 6
45 Widdrington.......C 10
45 Widdrington Sta..D 10
45 Wide Open......F 10
5 Widecombe in the Moor...........H 6
3 Widegates.......D 10
2 Widemouth.......A 2
64 Widewall..........E 2
19 Widford, Essex....C 7
18 Widford, Herefs...B 4
17 Widmere..........E 9
17 Widmer End.......D 9
32 Widmerpool......G 4
30 Widnes...........B 4
6 Widworthy........F 5
9 Wield............B 7
34 Wigan............F 5
8 Wigbeth..........E 2
6 Wiggaton.........G 5
24 Wiggenhall St. Germans....D 7
24 Wiggenhall St. Mary Magdalen......D 7
24 Wiggenhall St. Mary the Virgin......D 7
36 Wiggington.........A 4
17 Wigginton, Herts. C 10
16 Wigginton, Oxon..A 5
22 Wigginton, Staffs..A 6
35 Wiggleworth......A 7
44 Wiggonby........H 1
9 Wiggonholt......D 11
36 Wighill...........B 3
8 Wight, Isle of, Co..G 6
26 Wighton..........B 2
8 Wigley...........D 5
21 Wigmore, Herefs...E 9
11 Wigmore, Kent....B 7
32 Wigsley..........C 6
25 Wigsthorpe........G 1
23 Wigston Magna...B 9
24 Wigtoft..........B 4
44 Wigton..........H 1
42 Wigtown.........F 5
42 Wigtown, County..E 3
35 Wigtwizzle.......G 11
35 Wike...........C 12
23 Wilbarston......C 11
36 Wilberfoss.......B 5
15 Wilburton........H 6
26 Wilby, Norfolk....F 3
23 Wilby, Northants. E 12
27 Wilby, Suffolk....H 5
16 Wilcot...........H 2
30 Wilcott...........H 2
15 Wilcrick..........E 7
31 Wildboarclough...C 8
25 Wilden...........K 2
8 Wildhern.........A 5
36 Wildsworth.......G 6
MAP
32 Wilford..........F 3
30 Wilkesley.........F 5
61 Wilkhaven........H 9
48 Wilkieston........C 4
18 Wilkin's Green....C 2
6 Willand..........E 4
30 Willaston, Ches....B 2
30 Willaston, Ches....E 5
23 Willen...........H 12
22 Willenhall, Staffs..B 3
23 Willenhall, War....E 7
37 Willerby, Yorks...D 8
41 Willerby, Yorks...G 10
22 Willersey.........H 4
21 Willersley........H 8
11 Willesborough....D 9
18 Willesden.........E 2
4 Willesleigh........C 5
23 Willey, Leics......D 8
21 Willey, Salop....C 12
9 Willey Green....A 11
23 Williamscot......H 8
18 Willian...........A 2
18 Willingale........C 6
4 Willingcott.......B 4
10 Willingdon.......H 5
25 Willingham, Cambs. H 5
32 Willingham, Lincs..B 6
25 Willington, Beds...K 2
31 Willington, Derby. G 11
40 Willington, Dur....B 2
22 Willington, War...H 6
30 Willington Corner.D 4
36 Willitoft...........D 5
6 Williton...........B 4
44 Willmontswick....G 6
33 Willoughby, Lincs. C 11
23 Willoughby, War...E 8
32 Willoughby on the Wolds.........H 4
23 Willoughby Waterleys C 9
32 Willoughton......A 6
19 Willows Green....B 7
15 Willsbridge.......G 10
5 Willsworthy......H 4
22 Wilmcote.........F 5
6 Wilmington, Devon. F 5
10 Wilmington, Kent.A 4
10 Wilmington, Sussex H 4
31 Wilmslow........B 7
22 Wilnecote.........B 6
34 Wilpshire.........D 5
35 Wilsden...........D 9
33 Wilsford, Lincs....F 7
8 Wilsford, Wilts....B 3
16 Wilsford, Wilts....H 2
25 Wilshamstead.....L 2
35 Wilsill..........A 10
10 Wilsley Pound....D 6
15 Wilson, Herefs....B 9
32 Wilson, Leics.....H 1
48 Wilsontown.......D 2
24 Wilsthorpe.......D 2
17 Wilstone.........C 10
38 Wilton, Cumb.....D 3
16 Wilton, Hants.....H 4
15 Wilton, Herefs....B 9
44 Wilton, Rox.......B 3
8 Wilton, Wilts......C 3
40 Wilton, Yorks....C 6
41 Wilton, Yorks....G 8
16 Wiltshire, Co......G 2
25 Wimbish..........L 7
25 Wimbish Green...M 7
18 Wimbledon.......G 2
24 Wimblington......F 5
8 Wimborne Minster F 1
8 Wimborne St. Giles E 2
24 Wimbotsham.....E 7
25 Wimpole Lodge...K 4
22 Wimpstone........G 5
7 Wincanton......C 10
9 Winchfield.........A 9
30 Wincham..........C 5
48 Winchburgh.......B 4
16 Winchcombe......C 6
11 Winchelsea.......F 8
11 Winchelsea Beach..F 8
8 Winchester.......C 6
10 Winchet Hill......D 6
17 Winchmore Hill..E 10
31 Wincle...........D 8
38 Windermere......E 6
23 Winderton.......H 7
17 Windlesham.....H 10
31 Windley.........F 11
31 Windmill........B 10
MAP
6 Windmill Hill, Som. E 6
10 Windmill Hill, Sussex G 5
16 Windrush........C 3
44 Windshielknowe...C 4
17 Windsor..........G 10
15 Windsoredge.....D 11
47 Windy Yet........D 9
59 Windyedge.......H 6
53 Windygates.......G 8
49 Windywalls......F 10
10 Wineham.........F 1
37 Winestead........E 10
35 Winewall.........C 8
27 Winfarthing......G 4
9 Winford, I.o.W....H 7
15 Winford, Som.....H 8
21 Winforton........H 8
7 Winfrith Newburgh H 11
17 Wing, Bucks......B 9
23 Wing, Rut.......B 12
40 Wingate...........A 4
34 Wingates, Lancs...F 5
45 Wingates, Northumb. D 9
32 Wingerworth......C 1
17 Wingfield, Beds...B 11
27 Wingfield, Suffolk.H 5
7 Wingfield, Wilts...A 11
11 Wingham........B 11
11 Wingmore.......C 10
17 Wingrave.........B 9
32 Winkburn........D 4
17 Winkfield........G 9
17 Winkfield Row...G 10
17 Winkfield Street..G 10
31 Winkhill..........E 9
9 Winklebury.......A 7
4 Winkleigh........E 5
40 Winksley.........H 3
8 Winkton..........F 3
45 Winlaton.........G 10
45 Winlaton Mill...G 10
61 Winless..........B 12
34 Winmarleigh......B 3
8 Winnall, Hants....C 6
15 Winnall, Herefs....A 7
2 Winnard's Perch..C 6
17 Winnersh.........G 8
38 Winscales........C 3
15 Winscombe.......H 7
30 Winsford, Ches....D 5
6 Winsford, Som....C 3
7 Winsham.........F 7
31 Winshill.........H 11
13 Winsh-wen.......G 10
39 Winskill...........B 8
9 Winslade.........A 8
15 Winsley..........H 11
17 Winslow..........A 8
16 Winson..........C 2
8 Winsor...........E 5
31 Winster, Derby...D 11
38 Winster, Westmor..F 6
40 Winston, Dur.....D 2
27 Winston, Suff......J 5
15 Winstone........C 12
4 Winswell........E 4
44 Winter Shields....F 4
7 Winterborne Clenston F 11
7 Winterborne Herringston...G 10
7 Winterborne Houghton.....F 11
7 Winterborne Kingston F 11
7 Winterborne Monkton G 10
7 Winterborne Stickland F 11
7 Winterborne Whitechurch...F 11
7 Winterborne Zelston F 12
16 Winterbourne, Berks. G 5
15 Winterbourne, Glos. F 9
7 Winterbourne Abbas G 9
16 Winterbourne Bassett G 2
8 Winterbourne Dauntsey.......C 3
15 Winterbourne Down F 10
8 Winterbourne Earls C 3
8 Winterbourne Gunner C 3
MAP
16 Winterbourne Monkton.......G 2
7 Winterbourne Steepleton......G 9
8 Winterbourne Stoke B 2
35 Winterburn.......A 8
48 Wintercleugh.....H 2
37 Winteringham.....E 7
30 Winterley.........E 6
35 Wintersett.......F 12
8 Winterslow.......C 4
37 Winterton.........E 7
26 Winterton-on-Sea..D 8
33 Winthorpe, Lincs. D 12
32 Winthorpe, Notts..E 5
8 Winton, Hants....G 2
39 Winton, Westmor.D 10
40 Winton, Yorks.....F 4
41 Wintringham.....H 9
25 Winwick, Hunts...G 2
34 Winwick, Lancs...H 5
23 Winwick, Northants. E 9
31 Wirksworth......E 11
30 Wirswall ....F 4
24 Wisbech..........E 6
24 Wisbech St. Mary..E 5
9 Wisborough Green C 11
47 Wishaw, Lan.....D 12
22 Wishaw, War......C 5
17 Wisley..........H 11
33 Wispington.......C 9
27 Wissett...........G 6
21 Wistanstow......D 10
30 Wistanswick......G 5
30 Wistaston........E 5
30 Wistaston Green...E 5
48 Wiston, Lan.......F 2
12 Wiston, Pemb.....E 4
25 Wistow, Hunts....G 4
36 Wistow, Yorks....D 4
34 Wiswell..........C 6
25 Witcham.........G 6
8 Witchampton.....E 1
25 Witchford.........G 6
19 Witham..........B 8
7 Witham Friary...B 11
24 Witham on the Hill D 2
33 Withcall.........B 10
10 Witherenden Hill..E 5
4 Witheridge........E 7
23 Witherley.........B 7
33 Withern..........B 11
37 Withernsea......D 11
37 Withernwick.......C 9
27 Withersdale Street.G 6
25 Withersfield.......K 7
39 Witherslack.......G 7
3 Withiel...........C 7
6 Withiel Florey...C 3
16 Withington, Glos..C 1
21 Withington, Herefs. H 11
35 Withington, Lancs.H 7
21 Withington, Salop A 11
31 Withington, Staffs..G 9
30 Withington Green.C 6
21 Withington Marsh H 11
6 Withleigh.........E 3
34 Withnell..........E 5
23 Withybrook.......D 8
6 Withycombe.......B 3
6 Withycombe Raleigh H 4
10 Withyham........E 4
6 Withypool.........C 2
9 Witley..........B 11
27 Witnesham.......K 5
16 Witney...........C 5
24 Wittering.........E 2
11 Wittersham.......E 7
59 Witton, Angus....K 3
22 Witton, Worcs.....E 2
45 Witton Gilbert...H 10
40 Witton le Wear....B 2
40 Witton Park......B 2
6 Wiveliscombe.....C 4
9 Wivelrod.........B 8
10 Wivelsfield.......F 2
10 Wivelsfield Green..F 2
19 Wivenhoe.......B 10
19 Wivenhoe Cross..B 10
26 Wiveton..........A 3
29 Wix..............A 11
22 Wixford...........G 4
25 Wixoe.............L 8
17 Woburn..........A 10
17 Woburn Sands...H 12
17 Woking.........H 11
MAP
17 Wokingham......G 9
5 Wolborough.......J 7
37 Wold Newton, Lincs. G 10
41 Wold Newton, Yorks. H 10
10 Woldingham.......C 3
48 Wolfclyde........F 3
24 Wolferton.........C 7
52 Wolfhill...........D 6
12 Wolf's Castle.....D 3
12 Wolfsdale.........E 3
49 Woll.............G 7
23 Wollaston, Northants. F 12
21 Wollaston, Salop..A 9
30 Wollerton.........G 5
31 Wolseley.........H 9
40 Wolsingham......A 1
31 Wolstanton......E 7
23 Wolston..........E 7
16 Wolvercote.......C 6
22 Wolverhampton...B 2
30 Wolverley, Salop..G 3
22 Wolverley, Worcs..D 2
23 Wolverton, Bucks.H 11
16 Wolverton, Hants..H 6
22 Wolverton, War....F 5
16 Wolverton Com...H 6
15 Wolvesnewton....D 8
23 Wolvey...........C 8
40 Wolviston.........C 5
41 Wombleton........G 7
22 Wombourn........C 2
36 Wombwell.........G 2
11 Womenswold....C 11
36 Womersley.........E 3
9 Wonersh.........B 11
5 Wonsan............G 5
17 Wooburn........E 10
17 Wooburn Green..E 10
17 Wooburn Moor..E 10
26 Wood Dalling.....C 4
25 Wood End, Beds...K 1
25 Wood End, Beds...K 2
18 Wood End, Herts..A 3
22 Wood End, War...B 6
22 Wood End, War...E 4
33 Wood Enderby...D 10
18 Wood Green......E 3
22 Wood Hayes......B 3
26 Wood Norton.....C 3
25 Wood Walton....G 3
4 Woodacott.........E 3
39 Woodale.........G 12
32 Woodall...........B 2
26 Woodbastwick....D 6
32 Woodbeck.........B 5
7 Woodbridge, Dorset. E 10
27 Woodbridge, Suff..K 6
32 Woodborough, Notts. E 3
16 Woodborough, Wilts. H 2
6 Woodbury, Devon.G 4
7 Woodbury, Som...B 9
6 Woodbury Salterton G 4
15 Woodchester.....D 11
11 Woodchurch......E 8
6 Woodcombe.......B 3
17 Woodcote, Oxon...F 7
22 Woodcote, Salop..A 1
8 Woodcott..........A 6
15 Woodcroft.........E 8
8 Woodcutts.........D 1
25 Woodditton........J 8
16 Woodeaton........C 6
59 Woodend, Aber...H 3
38 Woodend, Cumb...F 4
48 Woodend, Lan.....F 2
23 Woodend, Northants. G 9
8 Woodfalls........D 3
47 Woodfield, Ayr....G 8
44 Woodfield, Dumf..F 1
10 Woodfield, Surrey.B 1
31 Woodford, Ches...B 7
4 Woodford, Corn...E 1
15 Woodford, Glos..E 10
18 Woodford, London E 4
25 Woodford, Northants. H 1
7 Woodford, Som....B 9
23 Woodford Halse..G 9
26 Woodgate, Norf...D 3
9 Woodgate, Sussex F 10
22 Woodgate, Worcs..E 3
8 Woodgreen.........D 3
49 Woodhall, E. Loth. B 9
45 Woodhall, Northumb. B 9
MAP
39 Woodhall, Yorks. F 12
33 Woodhall Spa....D 9
17 Woodham.......H 11
19 Woodham Ferrers.D 8
19 Woodham Mortimer C 8
19 Woodham Walter.C 8
53 Woodhaven.......D 9
58 Woodhead, Aber..D 5
35 Woodhead, Derby. G 9
58 Woodhead House..C 5
49 Woodheads.......E 8
22 Woodhill, Salop...D 1
15 Woodhill, Som....G 8
56 Woodholme......D 2
45 Woodhorn.......D 11
45 Woodhorn Demesne D 11
32 Woodhouse, Derby.B 1
23 Woodhouse, Leics. A 9
35 Woodhouse, Yorks. D 11
23 Woodhouse Eaves.A 8
5 Woodhuish.......K 8
25 Woodhurst.........H 4
10 Woodingdean.....G 2
58 Woodland, Aber...E 6
58 Woodland, Aber...F 6
5 Woodland, Devon..J 7
40 Woodland, Dur....C 1
8 Woodlands, Dorset. E 2
43 Woodlands, Dumf. D 11
8 Woodlands, Hants. E 4
59 Woodlands, Kinc..H 5
56 Woodlands, Ross & Cromarty.......D 1
17 Woodlands Park...F 9
16 Woodlands St. Mary G 4
31 Woodlane.......H 10
43 Woodlea..........C 8
5 Woodleigh........L 6
35 Woodlesford.....D 12
17 Woodley, Berks...G 8
35 Woodley, Lancs...H 8
16 Woodmancote, Glos. A 1
16 Woodmancote, Glos. C 1
9 Woodmancote, Sussex E 9
9 Woodmancott.....B 7
37 Woodmansey.......C 8
9 Woodmansgreen.C 10
10 Woodmansterne...B 2
8 Woodminton.....D 2
11 Woodnesborough B 11
24 Woodnewton......F 1
34 Woodplumpton...D 4
26 Woodrising.......E 3
10 Wood's Green....E 5
30 Woodseaves, Salop G 5
30 Woodseaves, Staffs.H 6
16 Woodsend.........F 3
32 Woodsetts........B 3
7 Woodsford......G 11
59 Woodside, Aber...G 7
17 Woodside, Berks. G 10
43 Woodside, Dumf. D 11
53 Woodside, Fife....F 9
49 Woodside, Northants. E 12
53 Woodside, Perth...C 7
59 Woodside of Arbeadie H 5
44 Woodslee.........F 2
16 Woodstock.......B 5
12 Woodstock Cross..D 4
12 Woodstock Slop...D 4
32 Woodthorpe, Derby. C 2
32 Woodthorpe, Leics. H 3
26 Woodton.........F 6
4 Woodtown, Devon. C 4
4 Woodtown, Devon. D 3
59 Woodtown, Kinc..K 3
34 Woodvale........F 2
31 Woodville.......H 11
8 Woodyates.......D 2
21 Woofferton......F 10
7 Wookey..........B 8
7 Wookey Hole.....A 9
7 Wool............H 11
4 Woolacombe......B 3
11 Woolage Green..C 11
15 Woolaston.......D 9
7 Woolavington.....B 7
9 Woolbeding.....D 10

MAP
6 Woolbrook.......G 5
6 Woolcotts........C 3
35 Wooldale.......F 10
49 Wooler.........G 12
4 Woolfardisworthy .E 7
48 Woolfords Cotts...D 3
8 Woolgarston......H 2
17 Woolhampton...G 7
15 Woolhope........A 9
7 Woolland........F 11
15 Woollard........H 9
4 Woollaton ......E 3
4 Woolley, Corn....D 1
25 Woolley, Hunts..H 3
15 Woolley, Som...G 10
35 Woolley, Yorks..F 11
18 Woolmer Green..B 3
22 Woolmere Green..F 3
27 Woolpit.........J 3
27 Woolpit Green...J 3
23 Woolscott.......E 8
4 Woolsey.........D 2
21 Woolstaston....C 10
32 Woolsthorpe, Lincs.
G 5
32 Woolsthorpe, Lincs.
H 6
5 Woolston, Devon..L 6
8 Woolston, Hants..E 6
30 Woolston, Lancs...A 5
21 Woolston, Salop ..D 9
30 Woolston, Salop ..H 2
5 Woolston Green...J 6
16 Woolstone........E 4
30 Woolton.........B 3
16 Woolton Hill.....H 5
27 Woolverstone....L 5
7 Woolverton .....A 11
18 Woolwich........F 4
21 Woonton.........G 9
45 Wooperton......A 8
49 Wooplaw.........E 7
30 Woore..........F 6
25 Wootton, Beds...L 1
16 Wootton, Berks...D 6
8 Wootton, Hants..F 4
11 Wootton, Kent...C 11
37 Wootton, Lincs....E 8
23 Wootton, Northants.
F 11
16 Wootton, Oxon....B 5
21 Wootton, Salop ..E 10
31 Wootton, Staffs..F 9
31 Wootton, Staffs...G 7
16 Wootton Bassett..F 2
9 Wootton Bridge..G 7
9 Wootton Com.....G 7
6 Wootton Courtenay
B 3
7 Wootton Fitzpaine G 7
16 Wootton Rivers...H 3

MAP
9 Wootton St. Lawrence
A 7
22 Wootton Wawen...F 5
22 Worcester.......G 2
22 Wordsley........C 2
22 Worfield........C 1
64 Work...........C 3
38 Workington......B 2
32 Worksop.........B 3
37 Worlaby.........F 8
16 World's End, Berks.
F 6
9 Worlds End, Hants.
E 8
15 Worle..........H 7
30 Worleston.......E 5
26 Worlingham......F 7
25 Worlington......H 8
27 Worlingworth.....H 5
35 Wormald Green..A 11
15 Wormbridge....A 7
24 Wormegay......D 8
15 Wormelow Tump..A 8
31 Wormhill........C 9
53 Wormiehills....C 11
27 Wormingford.....M 2
17 Worminghall....C 7
16 Wormington......A 1
7 Worminster......B 9
48 Wormiston.......E 5
53 Wormit.........E 9
23 Wormleighton....G 8
18 Wormley,
Hertfordshire...C 4
30 Wormley, Surrey .B 10
11 Wormshill.......B 7
21 Wormsley........H 9
9 Worplesdon.....A 11
35 Worrall.........H 11
35 Worsbrough....G 12
34 Worsley.........G 6
26 Worstead........C 6
25 Worsted Lodge...K 6
35 Worsthorne.......D 7
34 Worston.........C 6
5 Worswell.........L 4
11 Worth, Kent....C 12
10 Worth, Sussex....D 2
8 Worth Matravers..H 1
27 Wortham.........H 4
21 Worthen........B 9
30 Worthenbury.....F 3
26 Worthing, Norf....D 3
9 Worthing, Sussex.F 12
32 Worthington......H 1
6 Worthy........A 2
9 Worting.........A 7
35 Wortley, Yorks...D 11
35 Wortley, Yorks..G 11
16 Worton.........H 1
27 Wortwell........G 6

MAP
5 Wotter...........J 4
9 Wotton.........A 12
15 Wotton-under-Edge
E 11
17 Wotton Underwood
C 8
23 Woughton on the
Green.......H 12
10 Wouldham......B 6
27 Wrabness........M 5
58 Wraes..........D 3
4 Wrafton.........C 4
33 Wragby, Lincs....B 8
36 Wragby, Yorks...E 2
37 Wragholme....G 11
26 Wramplingham...E 4
36 Wrangbrook.....F 3
58 Wrangham, Aberdeen
D 4
49 Wrangham,
Northumb....F 12
33 Wrangle........E 11
33 Wrangle Com...E 11
33 Wrangle Lowgate.E 11
6 Wrangway.......D 5
6 Wrantage.......D 6
37 Wrawby.........F 8
7 Wraxall, Dorset..H 7
15 Wraxall, Som...G 8
7 Wraxhall. Som...C 9
39 Wray..........H 8
5 Wrayland.......H 7
17 Wraysbury.....G 11
34 Wrea Green....D 3
39 Wreay, Cumb...C 7
44 Wreay, Cumb.....H 3
45 Wrekenton....G 11
41 Wrelton.........F 8
30 Wrenbury........E 4
26 Wreningham....F 4
27 Wrentham.......G 8
35 Wrenthorpe....E 11
21 Wrentnall......B 9
36 Wressle.........D 5
25 Wrestlingworth...K 4
24 Wretton.........E 8
30 Wrexham.........E 2
30 Wrexham Industrial
Estate.......E 2
22 Wribbenhall.....E 2
34 Wrightlington Bar .F 4
30 Wrinehill........E 6
15 Wrington........H 8
7 Writhlington....A 10
19 Writtle.........C 7
21 Wrockwardine...A 11
35 Wroot.........G 5
10 Wrotham........B 5
10 Wrotham Heath..B 5
16 Wroughton......F 3

MAP
22 Wroxall........E 6
21 Wroxeter.....B 11
9 Wroxhall........H 7
26 Wroxham........D 6
23 Wroxton........H 7
31 Wyaston........F 10
24 Wyberton......B 4
25 Wyboston........K 3
30 Wybunbury......E 5
10 Wych Cross.....E 3
22 Wychbold........F 3
22 Wychnor........A 5
22 Wychnor Bridges..A 5
9 Wyck..........B 9
40 Wycliffe........D 1
17 Wycombe Marsh .E 10
25 Wyddial........M 5
11 Wye...........C 9
27 Wyerstone......H 3
27 Wyerstone Street..H 3
15 Wyesham........C 8
7 Wyke, Dorset...D 11
21 Wyke, Salop....B 12
9 Wyke, Surrey...A 10
35 Wyke, Yorks....D 10
7 Wyke Champflower
C 10
7 Wyke Regis.....H 7
41 Wykeham, Yorks .G 9
41 Wykeham, Yorks..H 8
30 Wykey..........H 3
45 Wylam.........G 9
22 Wylde Green.....C 5
14 Wyllie..........E 5
8 Wylye..........B 2
9 Wymering......E 8
3 Wymeswold.....H 3
25 Wymington...... J 1
32 Wymondham, Leics.
E 4
26 Wymondham, Norf.
E 4
14 Wyndham.......E 3
7 Wynford Eagle..G 9
40 Wynyard Forest..C 4
22 Wyre Piddle.....G 3
32 Wysall.........G 3
22 Wythall........E 4
38 Wythburn......D 6
31 Wythenshawe...A 7
5 Wyton..........H 4
32 Wyville.........G 6
54 Wyvis Lodge.....B 8
36 Yaddlethorpe....F 6
8 Yafford.........H 6
40 Yafforth.........F 4
5 Yalberton......K 7
10 Yalding........C 6
16 Yanworth.......C 2
36 Yapham........B 6

MAP
9 Yapton.........F 11
33 Yarburgh......A 10
6 Yarcombe.......E 6
4 Yard..........D 6
4 Yard Gate......C 6
22 Yardley........D 5
23 Yardley Gobion..H 11
23 Yardley Hastings .F 12
21 Yardro.........F 8
21 Yarkhill........H 11
31 Yarlet.........G 7
7 Yarlington......C 10
40 Yarm..........D 4
8 Yarmouth......G 5
4 Yarnacott......C 5
7 Yarnbrook......A 12
31 Yarnfield......G 7
4 Yarnscombe.....D 4
16 Yarnton.........C 6
21 Yarpole........F 10
48 Yarrow.........G 6
48 Yarrow Feus....G 6
21 Yarsop.........H 9
24 Yarwell.........F 2
15 Yate..........F 10
17 Yateley.........H 9
16 Yatesbury......G 2
16 Yattendon......G 6
15 Yatton, Herefs...A 9
21 Yatton, Herefs...F 9
15 Yatton, Som....H 7
15 Yatton Keynell ..G 12
9 Yaverland.......H 7
26 Yaxham.........D 3
24 Yaxley, Hunts...F 3
27 Yaxley, Suffolk ..H 4
21 Yazor.........H 9
35 Yeadon........C 10
39 Yealand Conyers..H 7
39 Yealand Redmayne
H 7
5 Yealmpton ..... K 4
40 Yearby.........C 6
40 Yearsley........H 6
30 Yeaton.........H 3
31 Yeaveley......F 10
49 Yeavering.....F 12
16 Yelford.........D 4
25 Yelling.........J 4
11 Yelsted.........B 7
23 Yelvertoft......E 9
5 Yelverton, Devon..J 4
26 Yelverton, Norfolk
E 6
7 Yenston........D 10
4 Yeo Mill........C 7
4 Yeoford........F 6
3 Yeolmbridge....A 10
7 Yeovil.........D 9
7 Yeovil Marsh....D 9
7 Yeovilton........D 9

MAP
12 Yerbeston........F 4
12 Yerbeston Mountain
F 4
64 Yesnaby.........C 1
49 Yetholm Mains...F 11
45 Yetlington........B 8
7 Yetminster......E 9
47 Yett, Ayr.......G 9
47 Yett, Lanark....C 12
6 Yettington.......H 4
52 Yetts of Muckhart.G 5
25 Yielden..........J 1
48 Yieldshields.....D 2
18 Yiewsley........F 1
20 Ynys..........F 2
20 Ynys Tachwedd...C 2
14 Ynys-boeth......E 4
14 Ynysbwl........E 4
14 Ynysddu........E 5
14 Ynyshir.........E 4
13 Ynystawe........G 10
39 Yockenthwaite..G 11
21 Yockleton.......A 9
36 Yokefleet........E 6
47 Yoker..........C 2
58 Yonder Bognie...C 3
36 York..........B 3
17 York Town......H 9
11 Yorkletts.......B 9
15 Yorkley.........D 9
48 Yorkston........A 5
4 Youldonmoor Cross
E 2
31 Youlgreaves....D 10
36 Youlthorpe......B 5
36 Youlton........A 3
19 Young's End.....B 7
31 Yoxall.........H 10
27 Yoxford.........H 7
29 Ysbyty Ifan......F 8
20 Ysbyty Ystwyth...E 3
29 Ysceifiog........C 10
13 Yspitty.........G 9
20 Yspytty Cynfyn...D 3
13 Ystalyfera......F 11
14 Ystrad.........E 3
13 Ystrad Aeron....A 8
20 Ystrad Meurig...F 3
14 Ystradfellte......C 3
13 Ystrad-ffin.....B 11
14 Ystradgynlais....C 1
14 Ystrad-mynach...E 5
13 Ystradowen, Carm.F10
14 Ystradowen, Glam.G 3
20 Ystumtuen...... D 3
58 Ythsie.........D 6
4 Zeal Monachorum .F 6
2 Zeals..........C 11
2 Zelah..........D 5
2 Zennor.........F 2
64 Zetland, Co......D 7

INDEX TO LONDON MAPS

ABBREVIATIONS

App. – *Approach*	Coll. – *College*	Gt. – *Great*	Mkt. – *Market*	Pol. – *Police*	Sq. – *Square*
Av. – *Avenue*	Con. – *Convent*	Ho. – *House*	Mt. – *Mount*	Poly. – *Polytechnic*	St. – *Street, Saint*
Bdy. – *Broadway*	Cres. – *Crescent*	Hosp. – *Hospital*	Mus. – *Museum*	Pr. – *Prince*	Sta. – *Station*
Bldg. – *Building(s)*	Ct. – *Court*	Hot. – *Hotel*	Nat. – *National*	R.C. – *Roman Catholic*	Sth. – *South*
Br. – *British*	Dri. – *Drive*	Inst. – *Institute*	Nth. – *North*	Rd. – *Road*	Ter. – *Terrace*
Bri. – *Bridge*	Ex. – *Exchange*	La. – *Lane*	Pal. – *Palace*	Sanct. – *Sanctuary*	Th. – *Theatre*
Ch. – *Church*	F.C. – *Football Club*	Lit. – *Little*	Pk. – *Park*	Sch. – *School*	Wk. – *Walk*
Cl. – *Close*	Gdns. – *Gardens*	Min. – *Ministry*	Pl. – *Place*	Soc. – *Society*	Yd. – *Yard*
Cnr. – *Corner*	Gro. – *Grove*				

The normal abbreviations for the London Postal Districts have been used throughout, e.g., NW10.

MAP
73 Abbey Gdns......C 3
73 Abbey Gdns Mews.C 3
79 Abbey Orchard St.D 7
73 Abbey Rd........B 3
80 Abbey St.........D 4
67 Abbey Wood....G 12
80 Abbots La........B 4
76 Abchurch La.....H 3
73 Abercorn Close...C 4
73 Abercorn Pl.......C 3
73 Aberdeen Place....E 5
80 Aberdour St.......E 3
77 Abingdon Rd.....D 1
79 Abingdon St......D 8
77 Abingdon Villas...E 1
68 Abridge..........A 1
67 Abridge Rd......A 12
73 Acacia Gdns......B 5
73 Acacia Pl.........B 5
73 Acacia Rd........B 5
67 Academy Rd.....H 11
70 Acre La. SW2.....B 6
70 Acre La., Carshalton......F 5
66 Acton............F 3
66 Acton Central Sta..G 3
66 Acton La.........F 3
66 Acton (Main Line) Sta............F 3
66 Acton Park.......G 3
75 Acton St.........D 9
66 Acton Town Sta...G 2
75 Adam St..........J 9
77 Adam & Eve MewsD 2
74 Adams Row......J 4
71 Addington.........F 8
71 Addington G.C.....F 8
71 Addington Palace G.C...........F 8
71 Addington Rd., Sanderstead.....G 7
71 Addington Rd., W. Wickham....E 9
80 Addington Square..J 2
79 Addington St.....C 10
71 Addington Village Rd............F 8
71 Addiscombe.......E 7
71 Addiscombe Rd...E 7
71 Addiscombe Sta...E 7
69 Addlestone.......F 2
66 Adelaide Rd......E 5
75 Adelaide St.......J 8
75 Adelphi Ter.......J 9
75 Adelphi Theatre...J 9
76 Adler St..........G 6
79 Admiralty.........B 8
79 Admiralty Arch...B 8
73 Adpar St..........F 5
74 Æolian Hall......H 5
75 Agar St...........J 8
75 Agdon St........E 12
77 Airways Terminal (Europe)........E 3
78 Airways Terminal..F 4
79 Alaska St........B 11
71 Albany Park Sta..C 12
80 Albany Rd.......H 3
74 Albany St.........C 5
74 Albemarle St......J 5
78 Albert Bridge......J 1
78 Albert Bridge Rd..J 1
77 Albert Court......D 4
79 Albert Embank....F 9
78 Albert Gate......C 3
77 Albert Memorial..C 4
77 Albert Place......D 3
67 Albert Rd.......G 11
74 Albert St..........B 5
74 Albert Ter.......A 3
74 Albert Ter. Mews..A 3
79 Alberta St.......G 12
75 Albery Theatre....J 8
73 Albion Close.....H 6
73 Albion Gate......H 6
73 Albion Mews.....H 6
73 Albion St.........H 6
67 Aldborough Hatch.........C 12
67 Aldborough Rd..C 12
80 Aldbridge St.......G 4
66 Aldenham Park...A 2
66 Aldenham Res.....A 2
65 Aldenham Rd., Bushey...........A 5
66 Aldenham Rd., Watford........A 2
74 Aldenham St......C 7
76 Aldermanbury....G 2
80 Alderminster Rd...F 6
78 Alderney St.......F 5
67 Aldersbrook.......D 10
67 Aldersbrook Rd..D 10
75 Aldersgate St.....F 13
78 Aldford St.......A 3
76 Aldgate..........H 4
76 Aldgate High St..G 5
75 Aldwych.........H 9
75 Aldwych Theatre..H 9
75 Alexander Ave...D 6
77 Alexander Place...E 6
77 Alexander Square..E 6
73 Alexander St......G 2
73 Alexandra Gate...C 5
66 Alexandra Palace..C 6
66 Alexandra Park...C 6
66 Alexandra Park Rd C 6
80 Alexis St.........E 6
74 Alfred Mews......F 7
74 Alfred Place......F 7
73 Alfred Rd.........F 1
80 Alice St...........E 3
76 Alie St...........H 6
70 All England Lawn Tennis Club....C 4
70 All Saints Rd.....E 4
75 All Saints St......B 9
66 All Souls Ave.....E 4
77 Allen St..........D 1
76 Allhallows La......J 2
75 Allingham Ter....B 13
78 Allington St.......D 5
73 Allitsen Rd.......B 6
74 Allsop Place......E 3
66 Allum La..........A 2
80 Alma Grove......F 6
73 Alma Sq..........C 4
66 Alperton.........E 2
77 Alpha Place......H 6
80 Alscot Rd.........E 5
80 Alvey St..........F 3
75 Ambassadors Th. .H 8
79 Ambergate St....G 12
73 Amberley Rd.....E 2
70 Amberwood Rise..E 3
78 Ambrosden Av....E 6
79 Amelia St.........F 13
67 Amhurst Park....D 7
75 Ampton St.........D 9
75 Amwell St.........D 11
78 Anderson St.......F 2
73 Andover Pl.......C 2
71 Anerley Rd.......D 7
71 Anerley Sta.......D 7
70 Angel Hill........E 4
67 Angel Rd.........B 8
67 Angel Road Sta...B 8
75 Angel St.........G 13
76 Anglesea St.......E 7
77 Ann La...........J 4
76 Anning St.........E 4
77 Ansdell St.........D 3
77 Ansdell Ter.......D 2
77 Anselm Rd.........H 1
66 Apex Corner.......B 3
78 Apple Tree Yard..A 7
76 Appleby St.........B 5
76 Appolo St.........F 4
78 Apsley House.....C 4
78 Apsley Way......C 4
71 Aquarius G.C.....B 8
73 Aquila St.........B 5
79 Aquinas St.......B 11
80 Arch St...........E 1
79 Archbishop's Pk..D 10
76 Archer St.........H 7
74 Archery Close....H 2
66 Archway Rd......D 6
68 Ardleigh Green...C 3
68 Ardleigh Green Rd.C 3
77 Argyll Rd, W8....D 1
66 Argyle Rd, W13...F 1
75 Argyle Square.....D 9
74 Argyll St, W1.....H 6
75 Argyle St. WC1....D 9
66 Arkley...........A 4
66 Arkley La..........A 4
76 Arlington Av......B 2
74 Arlington Rd......B 5
76 Arlington Sq......B 2
78 Arlington St......B 6
75 Arlington Way...C 11
77 Armadale Rd......J 1
75 Arne St...........H 9
76 Arnold Circus.....D 5
72 Arnolds La.......C 3
66 Arnos Grove Sta...B 6
80 Arnside St........H 2
67 Arsenal F.C.......E 7
73 Artesian Rd......H 1
76 Arthur St.........J 3
76 Artillery Ground...E 2
76 Artillery La.......F 4
78 Artillery Row.....D 7
73 Arts Theatre......H 8
75 Arundel St.......H 10
72 Ash..............F 5
73 Ashbridge St......E 6
77 Ashburn Gdns.....E 3
77 Ashburn Mews.....E 3
77 Ashburn Place.....F 3
75 Ashby St........D 12
69 Ashford Hospital..B 3
69 Ashford La.......D 3
69 Ashford Manor G.C...........C 3
69 Ashford Rd, Feltham.........C 4
69 Ashford Rd, Laleham.........D 3
69 Ashley Rd., Walton E 4
74 Ashland Place.....F 3
69 Ashley Park.......E 4
78 Ashley Place......E 6
70 Ashley Rd, Epsom.........G 3
73 Ashmill St.........F 6
79 Ashmole St......H 10
70 Ashtead..........H 2
70 Ashtead Common.G 1
70 Ashtead Park....H 2
70 Ashtead Sta.......H 1
73 Ashworth Rd.....D 3
77 Astell St..........G 6
65 Aston Rd.........B 4
77 Astwood Mews....F 3
77 Atherstone Mews..E 4
79 Atterbury St.......F 8
75 Attneave St.......D 10
79 Auckland St......G 9
78 Audley St.........B 4
76 Audrey St.........B 6
74 Augustus St.......C 5
76 Austin St.........D 5
76 Austin Friars.....G 3
79 Austral St........E 12
75 Australia House..H 10
75 Ave Maria La....H 12
76 Avebury Estate....D 6
76 Avebury St........A 3
68 Aveley...........G 4
68 Aveley Rd........E 4
79 Aveline St.......G 10
80 Avely St..........F 3
76 Avenue, The EC3.H 4
70 Avenue, The SW4..B 5
69 Avenue, The, Sunbury.......D 5
66 Avenue Rd. N14..A 6
73 Avenue Rd. NW8..B 6
68 Avenue Rd, Bexleyheath....H 1
74 Avery Row.......H 5
71 Averyhill Rd.....B 11
80 Avon Place.......C 2
80 Avondale Square..G 6
79 Avonmouth St....D 13
74 Aybrook St.......F 3
80 Aylesbury Rd......G 3
75 Aylesbury St.....E 12
78 Aylesford St......G 7
80 Ayres St..........C 1
76 Bache's St........D 3
76 Back Church La...H 6
75 Back Hill........E 11
68 Back La..........G 5
80 Bacon Gr.........E 5
76 Bacon St..........E 6
72 Badger's Mount...G 1
80 Bagshot St........G 4
75 Bainbridge St.....G 8
74 Baker St..........F 3
74 Baker's Mews.....G 3
75 Baker's Row.....E 11
80 Balaclava Rd......F 6
74 Balcombe St......E 2
74 Balderton St......H 4
75 Baldwin Ter......B 13
75 Baldwin's Gdns...F 11
65 Baldwin's La......A 4
80 Balfour St.........E 2
68 Balgores La.......C 3
70 Balham..........B 5
70 Balham High Rd...C 5
70 Balham Hill.......B 5
70 Balham Sta........B 5
66 Ballards La.......C 5
67 Balls Pond Rd.....E 7
76 Baltic Shipping Exchange......G 4
76 Baltic St..........E 1
67 Banbury Res......C 8
80 Bank End.........A 2
76 Bank of England..G 3
75 Bankruptcy Court H 10
79 Bankside........A 13
79 Bankside Power Station........A 13
76 Banner St.........E 2
70 Banstead.........G 4
70 Banstead Downs..G 4
70 Banstead Downs G.C.............G 4
70 Banstead Hospital.G 4
70 Banstead Rd......G 3
70 Banstead Road South..........F 5
76 Barbican..........F 1
75 Barbican Sta......F 13
75 Barford St.......B 11
79 Barge House St...A 11
71 Baring Rd........C 9
76 Baring St.........A 2
73 Bark Place........J 2
67 Barking..........E 11
67 Barking Park.....E 11
67 Barking Rd.......F 10
67 Barking Sta.......E 11
67 Barkingside......C 11
77 Barkston Gdns.....F 2
75 Barlett Court....G 11
67 Barley La.........D 12
80 Barlow St.........F 3
66 Barn Hill Park....D 2
74 Barnby St.........C 6
72 Barnehurst........A 1
70 Barnes...........A 3
70 Barnes Bridge.....A 3
70 Barnes Bridge Sta..A 3
70 Barnes Common..A 3
70 Barnes Sta........A 3
66 Barnet...........B 4
66 Barnet Bypass.....A 3
66 Barnet Gate......A 3
76 Barnet Grove.....D 6
66 Barnet La, Elstree.A 2
66 Barnet La, Totteridge......A 4
66 Barnet Rd........A 3
66 Barnet Way.......A 3
70 Barnetwood La....H 1
80 Barnham St.......C 4
75 Barnsbury Rd....B 11
75 Baron St.........B 11
76 Baroness Rd......C 5
79 Baron's Place....C 11
74 Barrett St.........H 4
73 Barrie St..........H 4
73 Barrow Hill Rd....C 6
67 Barrowell Green...B 7
75 Barter St..........G 9
75 Bartholomew Cl. .F 13
76 Bartholomew La...G 3
80 Bartholomew St....E 3
78 Basil St...........D 2
76 Basing Place......C 4
76 Basinghall Av......G 2
76 Basinghall St......G 2
75 Bastwick St......E 13
72 Bat & Ball Sta.....H 2
75 Batchelor St.....B 11
65 Batchworth.......B 3
65 Batchworth Hth...B 4
65 Batchworth Heath Hill..............B 4
74 Bateman St.......H 7
76 Bateman's Row...D 4
65 Bath Rd, Cranford.H 5
65 Bath Rd, Colnbrook.....H 2
76 Bath St...........D 2
80 Bath Ter..........D 1
66 Bathurst Gdns.....F 4
73 Bathurst Mews...H 5
73 Bathurst St.......H 5
70 Battersea.........A 5
77 Battersea Bridge...J 5
70 Battersea Bridge Rd...........A 5
70 Battersea Park....A 5
70 Battersea Park Rd..A 5
70 Battersea Rise.....B 5
80 Battle Bridge La...B 3
75 Battle Bridge Rd...C 8
75 Battlebridge Basin .B 9
78 Batty St...........G 7
76 Baxendale St......C 6
74 Bayham Place.....B 6
74 Bayham St........B 6
65 Bayhurst Wood...C 3
74 Bayley St..........F 7
79 Baylis Rd.........C 11
66 Bayswater........F 5
73 Bayswater Rd.....J 4
68 Beacontree Hth....D 1
74 Beak St...........H 6
72 Bean.............C 4
80 Bear Gdns........A 1
79 Bear La..........B 12
75 Bear St...........J 8
74 Beatty St..........B 5
78 Beauchamp Place .D 2
75 Beauchamp St....F 11
78 Beaufort Gdns.....D 2
77 Beaufort St.......H 5
74 Beaumont Mews...F 4
74 Beaumont Place..E 6
74 Beaumont St......F 4
71 Beckenham.......D 8
71 Beckenham Hill Rd. C 9
71 Beckenham Hill Sta. C 9
71 Beckenham Junc. Sta. D 8
71 Beckenham Place Park C 9
71 Beckenham Place & Foxgrove G.C...C 9
71 Beckenham Rd....D 8
67 Beckton..........F 11
67 Beckton Rd......F 10
68 Becontree.........D 1
68 Becontree Ave.....D 1
68 Becontree Sta.....E 1
80 Bedale St..........B 2
70 Beddington.......F 6
70 Beddington Corner E 5
70 Beddington La....E 6
70 Beddington Lane Sta. E 5
70 Beddington Park..E 5
71 Beddlestead La....H 9
69 Bedford Rd, Feltham C 4
69 Bedfont Rd, Stanwell B 3
75 Bedford Av.......G 7
74 Bedford College...D 3
77 Bedford Gdns.....B 2
70 Bedford Hill......C 5
75 Bedford Place.....F 8
75 Bedford Row.....F 10
75 Bedford Square...F 7
75 Bedford St........J 8
75 Bedford Way......E 8
75 Bedfordbury.......J 8
68 Bedford's Park....B 3
72 Bedonwell Rd.....A 1
71 Beech Farm Rd...H 9
76 Beech St..........F 1
72 Beechen Wood....F 1
72 Beechenlea La.....D 2
78 Beeston Place.....D 5
78 Belgrave Mews North D 3
78 Belgrave Mews South D 4
78 Belgrave Mews West D 3
78 Belgrave Place....D 4
78 Belgrave Rd.......F 6
78 Belgrave Square...D 3
66 Belgravia..........G 5
75 Belgrove St.......C 8
68 Belhus Park.......F 4
76 Bell La...........G 5
73 Bell St............F 6
76 Bell Wharf La.....J 2
75 Bell Yard.......H 11
71 Belle Grove Rd...A 11
71 Bellingham........C 8
71 Bellingham Rd....C 9
66 Belmont..........C 1
66 Belmont G.C.......C 1
70 Belmont Rise......F 4
70 Belmont Sta.......F 4
68 Belvedere.........G 2
79 Belvedere Rd.....B 10
75 Bemerton St......A 9
75 Benjamin St......F 12
70 Benhill Av........F 4
70 Benhill Rd........E 5
68 Bennet Castle La...E 1
74 Bentinck St.......G 4
68 Beredens La.......C 5
78 Berkeley Hotel....B 5
74 Berkeley Mews....G 3
74 Berkeley Square...J 5
78 Berkeley St.......A 5
67 Bermondsey......G 8
80 Bermondsey Leather Market........C 3

MAP
80 Bermondsey St. ...C 4
80 Bermondsey Wall
    East...........C 7
80 Bermondsey Wall
    West..........C 6
75 Bernard St........E 8
74 Berners Mews ....G 6
74 Berners Place....G 6
75 Berners Rd.......B 12
74 Berners St........G 6
75 Berry St ....E 12
79 Berryfield Rd. ..G 13
70 Berrylands Sta. ...D 2
71 Berry's Green Rd.
            H 11
71 Berry's Hill.......G 11
68 Berwick Pond Rd...E 3
74 Berwick St........H 6
79 Bessborough Gdns.G 7
79 Bessborough Pl....G 7
69 Bessborough Res...D 5
78 Bessborough St....G 7
71 Bethlehem Royal
    Hospital........E 8
67 Bethnal Green....E 8
76 Bethnal Green Rd. .E 5
67 Bethnal Green Sta. .F 8
80 Bethwin Rd.......J 1
72 Betsham ....C 5
75 Betterton St........G 9
71 Beulah Hill........C 7
76 Bevan St..........B 2
76 Bevenden St.......C 3
80 Bevington St........D 7
76 Bevis Marks......G 4
72 Bexley ....B 1
71 Bexley Heath G.C.B 12
72 Bexley Hospital....C 1
71 Bexley La. ....C 12
71 Bexley Rd. SE9...B 11
72 Bexley Rd. Erith...A 1
72 Bexley Sta........B 1
72 Bexleyheath.......B 1
80 Bianca Rd........H 6
80 Bibury Close...H 4
74 Bickenhall St......F 3
71 Bickley .....D 10
75 Bidborough St. ...D 8
73 Biddulph Rd......B 2
71 Biggin Hill ...H 10
71 Biggin Hill Airport
            G 10
67 Billet Rd. E17....C 8
68 Billet Rd., Chadwell
    Heath........C 1
77 Billing Place.......J 3
77 Billing Rd.........J 3
77 Billing St.........J 3
76 Billingsgate Market.J 3
76 Billiter St.........H 4
77 Bina Gdns........F 3
68 Bind La...........C 4
74 Bingham Place....F 3
71 Bingham Rd. Sta...E 7
74 Binney St.........H 4
72 Birches, The.......F 2
76 Birchin La........H 3
72 Birchwood Rd.....C 1
74 Bird St...........H 4
78 Birdcage Walk....C 7
80 Bird-in-Bush Rd..J 6
80 Birdlip Close......J 4
74 Birkbeck Coll.....E 7
71 Birkbeck Sta.....D 8
75 Birkenhead St....C 9
66 Bishops Ave. The..D 5
73 Bishop's Bridge Rd.
           G 3
79 Bishop's Ter. ..E 11
70 Bishopsford Rd...E 4
76 Bishopsgate .....G 4
69 Bittams La........E 2
67 Black Horse La....C 8
67 Black Horse Rd. Sta.
73 Black Lion Gate...J 3
65 Black Park ....E 1
79 Black Prince Rd. .F 10
76 Blackall St........E 3
66 Blackbird Hill.....D 3
74 Blackburnes Mews.J 3
71 Blackfen ....B 11
71 Blackfen Rd. ...B 11
75 Blackfriars Bridge.J 12
75 Blackfriars La...H 12
79 Blackfriars Rd....C 12
75 Blackfriars Sta. ..H 12
71 Blackheath ......A 9
67 Blackheath Hill. ..H 9

MAP
67 Blackheath Rd....H 9
71 Blackheath Royal G.C.
           B 10
78 Blacklands Ter.....F 2
67 Blackwall.........F 9
67 Blackwall Reach ..G 9
67 Blackwall Tunnel..G 9
80 Blackwood St.....G 2
74 Blandford Estate ..E 1
74 Blandford Place...G 3
74 Blandford Square..E 1
74 Blandford St......G 3
77 Blantyre St. ......F 4
76 Blendon Rd.....B 12
80 Blendon Row.....F 2
73 Blenheim Rd......B 4
78 Blenheim Ter......B 3
76 Bletchley St........C 2
77 Blithfield St.......E 2
77 Blomfield Rd......F 3
76 Blomfield St. .....G 3
73 Blomfield Vil......F 3
76 Bloomfield Ter....F 4
66 Bloomsbury......F 6
75 Bloomsbury Sq....F 9
75 Bloomsbury St....G 8
75 Bloomsbury Way..G 8
76 Blossom St. ......E 4
69 Blundell La........G 6
75 Boadicea St.......B 9
69 Board La..........C 6
66 Bolingbroke Grove B 5
74 Bolsover St........F 5
70 Bolters La.........G 4
72 Bolton Cres. .....J 12
77 Bolton Gdns.......F 3
78 Bolton St..........B 5
77 Boltons, The......G 3
79 Bondway.........H 9
76 Bonhill St.........E 3
79 Bonnington Sq....H 9
76 Boot St...........D 3
67 Borders La. ....A 11
66 Borehamwood ....A 3
72 Borough Green ...H 5
80 Borough High St...C 2
80 Borough Market..B 2
79 Borough Polytechnic
           D 12
79 Borough Rd.....D 12
79 Borrett Rd.......G 13
73 Boscobel St.......E 5
80 Boss St...........C 5
67 Bostall Hill Rd...G 12
67 Bostall Woods ...H 12
66 Boston Manor....G 1
66 Boston Manor Sta.G 1
74 Boston Place......E 2
66 Boston Rd........G 1
75 Boswell St. ......F 9
78 Botanic Gdns......H 2
69 Botleys...........E 1
76 Botolph La........J 3
67 Bounces Rd.......B 8
80 Boundary La.......H 2
79 Boundary Rd......G 9
74 Boundary Row...C 11
78 Boundary St.......D 5
66 Bounds Green Rd. C 6
74 Bourdon St........J 5
66 Bourne, The......B 6
66 Bourne Hill.......B 6
78 Bourne St.........F 3
78 Bourne Ter........F 2
68 Bournebridge ....A 2
68 Bournebridge La...A 2
75 Bouverie St......H 11
67 Bow ....F 9
67 Bow Bridge.......F 9
67 Bow Common.....F 9
67 Bow La..........H 2
67 Bow Rd..........F 9
75 Bow St...........H 9
66 Bowes Park Sta...C 6
80 Bowles Rd........H 6
75 Bowling Green La.E 11
75 Bowling Green St.H 11
76 Bowling Green Walk
           D 3
76 Boyd St..........H 6
79 Boyfield St.......C 12
76 Brackley St.......F 1
78 Brad St..........B 11
73 Braden St.........E 2
79 Braganza St.......G 12
76 Braham St........G 5
80 Braidwood St......B 4

MAP
68 Bramble La.......E 4
77 Bramerton St......H 6
77 Bramham Gdns ...F 2
66 Bramley Rd.......A 6
71 Brampton Rd....A 12
76 Branch Place......A 3
70 Brand Drive......D 3
80 Brandon St........F 2
72 Brands Hatch ....F 4
72 Brands Hatch Motor
    Racing Circuit...F 4
71 Brasted Hill.....H 12
71 Brasted La......H 12
67 Bravel La........B 12
78 Bray Place........F 2
76 Bread St.........H 1
65 Breakspear Rd. North
           C 3
65 Breakspear Rd. South
           D 3
75 Bream's Buildings G 11
77 Brechin Place......F 4
66 Brecknock Rd.....E 6
77 Bremner Rd.......D 4
74 Brendon St.......G 1
66 Brent............D 2
66 Brent Reservoir ..D 3
66 Brent Sta.........D 4
66 Brent St..........C 4
66 Brentford........G 2
70 Brentford Central Sta.
           A 1
66 Brentford F.C.....H 2
68 Brentwood.......B 6
68 Brentwood Bypass.B 5
68 Brentwood Rd....D 3
68 Brentwood & Warley
    Sta...........B 5
78 Bressenden Place ..D 5
69 Bretlands........E 2
74 Brewer St.........H 7
76 Brick La..........E 5
75 Brick St..........B 4
75 Bride La.........H 12
75 Bridewell Place...H 12
74 Bridford Mews....F 5
69 Bridge Rd. Chertsey
           E 2
69 Bridge Rd. Esher.D 6
70 Bridge Rd. Chessington
           F 2
79 Bridge St. ....C 8
79 Bridgefoot........G 8
73 Bridgeman St.....C 6
66 Bridgewater Rd....E 2
74 Bridgeway St......C 7
74 Bridle Lane.......H 6
65 Bridle Rd.........D 5
77 Bridport Place....B 3
67 Bridport Rd.......B 7
73 Bridstow Place...G 1
70 Brighton Rd. Coulsdon
           H 5
70 Brighton Rd. Croydon
           G 6
70 Brighton Rd. Sutton
           F 4
70 Brigstock Rd......D 6
67 Brimsdown Sta....A 8
75 Briset St.........F 12
73 Bristol Gdns......F 3
73 Bristol Mews......E 3
75 Britannia St.......C 9
75 British Council ..F 10
75 British Medical
    Association....D 8
75 British Museum ..F 8
77 Britten St.........G 6
75 Britton St. ......F 12
70 Brixton..........A 6
70 Brixton Hill......B 6
70 Brixton Prison...A 6
79 Brixton Rd.......J 11
70 Brixton Sta.......B 6
67 Broad La. N15....C 8
72 Broad La. Dartford C 2
67 Broad Mead Rd..C 10
79 Broad Sanctuary ..D 8
76 Broad Street Sta..F 3
77 Broad Walk, The..C 3
74 Broadcasting House
           G 5
73 Broadley St.......F 5
73 Broadley Ter......E 6
74 Broadstone Place .F 3
78 Broadway, SW1...D 7
70 Broadway, SW19..C 4
65 Broadway, Southall G 5
74 Broadwick St......H 6

MAP
80 Brockham St......D 2
66 Brockley Hill.....B 2
71 Brockley Rise.....B 8
71 Brockley Rd......B 8
71 Brockley Sta......A 8
70 Brockwell Park...B 6
80 Brockworth Close .J 4
75 Bromfield St.....B 11
71 Bromley ....D 9
67 Bromley, Tower
    Hamlets........F 9
67 Bromley-by-Bow ..F 9
67 Bromley Common E 10
71 Bromley Hill......C 9
71 Bromley North Sta. D 9
71 Bromley Rd. SE6..C 9
71 Bromley Rd.
    Beckenham..D 9
71 Bromley Rd.
    Chislehurst ....D 11
71 Bromley South Sta. D 9
66 Brompton........G 5
77 Brompton Cemetery
           H 2
77 Brompton Hospital F 5
78 Brompton Place...D 2
77 Brompton Square .D 6
77 Brompton Rd......E 6
66 Brondesbury Park .E 4
66 Brondesbury Park Sta.
           E 4
66 Brondesbury Sta...E 4
80 Bronti Close......G 2
79 Brook Drive .....E 11
71 Brook Fever Hospital
           A 10
66 Brook Green .....G 5
73 Brook Mews North H 4
74 Brook St.........H 4
75 Brooke St........F 11
69 Brooklands Rd. ..F 3
74 Brook's Mews ...H 5
74 Brookshill ....B 1
70 Broom Rd........C 1
66 Broomfield Park..B 6
72 Broomfield Wood .F 4
74 Brown Hart Gdns. H 4
74 Brown St.........G 2
71 Brownhill Rd......B 9
75 Brownlow Mews .E 10
80 Browning St.......F 2
75 Brownlow St......F 10
69 Brox.............F 2
68 Broxhill Rd.......B 3
74 Broxwood Way ...B 1
67 Bruce Castle Park..C 7
67 Bruce Grove Sta...C 7
76 Bruce St..........F 5
73 Brunel Estate .....F 1
65 Brunel University..F 3
75 Brunswick Centre .E 8
80 Brunswick Court ..C 4
77 Brunswick Gdns...B 2
66 Brunswick Park ..B 6
76 Brunswick Place ..D 3
75 Brunswick Square .E 9
76 Brushfield St......F 4
74 Bruton La. ......J 5
74 Bruton Place ....J 5
74 Bruton St........J 5
74 Bryanston Mews East
           G 2
74 Bryanston Mews West
           G 2
74 Bryanston Place...G 2
74 Bryanston Square .G 2
74 Bryanston St......H 2
68 Bryant Ave. ......C 3
80 Brymer Rd........G 5
76 Buckfast St.......D 6
67 Buckhurst Hill ..B 10
71 Buckhurst Rd....H 11
78 Buckingham Gate .D 6
78 Buckingham Palace C 5
78 Buckingham Palace
    Gdns..........C 5
78 Buckingham Palace
    Rd.............E 5
78 Buckingham Place .D 6
79 Buckingham St....A 9
76 Buckland St.......C 3
76 Buckle St.........G 6
76 Bucklersbury ....H 2
76 Bucknall St........G 8
71 Bug Hill ....H 8
67 Bugsby's Reach ..G 10
68 Bulinga St........H 8
68 Bull La...........D 2
74 Bulstrode St. .....G 4

MAP
76 Bunhill Fields.....E 2
76 Bunhill Row......E 2
72 Bunker's Hill La. ..F 5
80 Burbage Close.....D 2
70 Burgh Heath ....H 4
69 Burgh Heath Rd...G 3
75 Burgh St.........B 13
69 Burhill G.C. ......F 4
69 Burleigh St........H 9
71 Burling La.......H 11
74 Burlington Arcade .J 6
74 Burlington Gdns. ..J 6
73 Burne St..........F 6
77 Burnsall St........G 6
79 Burnt Ash La.....C 9
66 Burnt Oak........C 3
66 Burnt Oak Sta.....C 3
79 Burntash Hill......B 9
71 Burntash Rd.......B 9
70 Burntwood La. SW17
           C 5
71 Burntwood La.
    Coulsdon ......H 7
76 Burrell St........B 12
78 Burton Court.....E 3
80 Burton Grove.....G 3
76 Burton St.........D 8
69 Burtons Rd.......C 5
73 Burwood Place....G 6
66 Burwood Rd......F 4
76 Bury Court.......G 4
75 Bury Place ....G 8
67 Bury St. EC3.....G 4
66 Bury St. N9 ......A 7
78 Bury St. SW1.....B 6
68 Bury St. Ruislip...D 4
77 Bury Walk........F 6
77 Bury Wood.....A 10
77 Busby St.........E 6
67 Bush Hill ....A 7
67 Bush Hill G.C.....A 7
67 Bush La.........H 2
65 Bushey...........A 6
65 Bushey Hall G.C...A 5
66 Bushey Heath.....A 1
70 Bushey Rd........D 3
65 Bushey & Oxhey Sta.
           A 5
67 Bushill Park .....A 7
67 Bushill Park Sta...A 7
69 Bushy Park.......D 6
77 Bute St...........F 5
76 Buttesland St......D 3
72 Button St.........D 2
68 Butts La..........D 3
71 Buxton La........H 7
76 Buxton St.........E 6
69 Byfleet...........G 3
69 Byfleet Rd........G 4
69 Byfleet & New Haw
           F 3
74 Byng Place ....E 7
76 Byward St........J 4
78 Bywater St........F 2
73 Cabbel St.........G 6
76 Cable St..........H 6
71 Cackets La......G 11
80 Cadbury Rd.......E 6
80 Cadiz St..........G 2
78 Cadogan Gdns. ...E 2
78 Cadogan Gate ....E 3
78 Cadogan La.......E 3
78 Cadogan Pier.....H 1
78 Cadogan Place....E 3
78 Cadogan Square...E 2
78 Cadogan St.......F 2
67 Cadogan Ter......E 9
76 Caesar St.........C 4
80 Caldew St........J 2
77 Cale St...........F 6
75 Caledonia St......C 9
75 Caledonian Rd....B 8
66 Caledonian Rd. &
    Barnsbury Sta...E 6
77 Callow St.........H 4
80 Calmington Rd....H 4
75 Calshot St. ......B 9
75 Calthorpe St. ...E 10
76 Calvert Av........D 4
76 Calvin St.........E 5
71 Camberwell.......A 7
79 Camberwell New Rd.
           J 11
80 Camberwell Rd....J 2
75 Cambridge Circus .H 8
67 Cambridge Heath Sta.
67 Cambridge Park. E11
           D 10

MAP
70 Cambridge Park.
    Twickenham....B 1
77 Cambridge Place ..D 3
70 Cambridge Rd.....D 2
73 Cambridge Sq.....G 6
78 Cambridge St......F 5
66 Camden..........E 6
74 Camden High St. .B 5
66 Camden Rd.......E 6
74 Camden St........A 6
66 Camden Town ....E 6
75 Camden Walk ...B 12
77 Camera Place.....H 4
76 Camlet St.........D 5
75 Camley St........B 7
66 Camomile St......G 4
77 Campden Grove ..C 1
77 Campden Hill Rd..C 1
77 Campden St.......B 2
66 Camrose Ave.....C 2
79 Canada House....A 8
80 Canal St..........H 3
70 Cane Hill Hospital H 5
67 Cann Hall........D 10
67 Canning Place....D 3
67 Canning Town....F 10
67 Canning Town Sta..F 9
67 Cannon St........A 1
73 Cannon Street Sta. .J 2
79 Cannon Row .....C 8
76 Canon St.........A 1
67 Canonbury ....E 7
67 Canonbury Sta....E 7
66 Canons Park......B 2
66 Canon's Park Sta. .C 2
67 Capel Rd. ......E 10
74 Capland St........E 5
74 Capper St.........E 6
74 Carburton St......F 5
73 Cardigan Rd.......G 1
79 Cardigan St.......G 11
74 Cardington St......D 6
76 Carey La..........H 1
75 Carey St..........G 10
76 Carlisle Av.......H 4
74 Carlisle La........D 10
78 Carlisle Place .....E 6
74 Carlisle St........G 7
74 Carlos Place.......J 4
74 Carlow St.........B 5
66 Carlton Ave. East .D 2
77 Carlton Gdns......B 7
73 Carlton Hill ......B 3
79 Carlton House Ter.B 7
73 Carlton Vale......C 1
75 Carlyle Square ...G 5
77 Carlyle's House ..H 6
75 Carmelite St. ....H 11
74 Carnaby St........H 6
75 Carnegie St. .....B 10
73 Caroline Place....J 2
78 Caroline Ter.......F 3
65 Carpenders Park ..B 5
65 Carpenders Park Sta.
           B 5
67 Carpenters Rd.....E 9
78 Carriage Drive East J 4
78 Carriage Drive Nth. H 4
78 Carriage Rd., The .C 2
79 Carroun Rd.......J 10
70 Carshalton ....E 5
70 Carshalton Beeches
    Sta...........F 5
70 Carshalton Ho....F 5
70 Carshalton on the Hill
           F 5
70 Carshalton Rd.
    Wallington .....F 5
70 Carshalton Rd.
    Woodmansterne G 5
75 Carter La........H 13
80 Carter Place......G 1
79 Carter St..........G 13
78 Carteret St........D 7
75 Carthusian St......F 13
74 Carton St.........G 3
75 Cartwright Gdns. .D 8
74 Cartwright St......J 6
65 Cassiobury Park ..A 4
76 Casson St.........F 6
66 Castellain Rd......E 3
70 Castelnau Rd......A 3
66 Castle Bar Park G.C.
66 Castle Baynard St.H 13
66 Cat Hill..........A 5
80 Catesby St.........F 3
71 Catford ....B 9
71 Catford Bridge....B 8

MAP
71 Catford Hill......B 8
71 Catford Sta.........B 8
77 Cathcart Rd.......H 3
78 Catherine Place...D 6
75 Catherine St.......H 9
74 Cato St...........G 1
80 Cator St...........J 5
69 Catos Hill.........E 6
75 Catton St..........G 9
79 Causton St........F 7
77 Cavaye Place.....G 4
73 Cavendish Av......C 5
73 Cavendish Cl......C 5
78 Cavendish Hotel..B 6
74 Cavendish Place...G 5
66 Cavendish Rd. NW6
E 4
70 Cavendish Rd. SW12
B 5
74 Cavendish Square.G 5
76 Cavendish St.......C 2
78 Caversham St.....H 2
78 Caxton Hall.......D 7
78 Caxton St.........D 7
76 Cayton St. ....D 2
70 Caesar's Camp....C 3
79 Cenotaph ....C 8
79 Centaur St.......D 10
75 Central Criminal Court
G 12
71 Central Hill ....C 7
68 Central Park.......D 2
70 Central Rd. ....D 4
75 Central St. ....D 13
68 Chadwell Heath...D 1
68 Chadwell Hth La..D 1
75 Chadwell St.......C 11
78 Chadwick St. ......E 7
74 Chagford St.......E 2
65 Chalfont Common B 1
65 Chalfont Park .....C 1
65 Chalfont St. Peter .C 1
66 Chalk Farm Rd. ..E 6
70 Chalk La...........G 3
71 Chalky Hill ....G 11
74 Chalton St.........C 7
76 Chamber St.......H 6
80 Chambers St.......C 6
76 Chambord St. .....D 5
79 Chancel St.......B 12
75 Chancery La.....G 10
75 Chandos Place ....J 8
74 Chandos St.........G 5
75 Chantry St.......B 13
80 Chapel Court.....C 2
67 Chapel End........C 9
75 Chapel Market...B 11
73 Chapel Side........J 2
73 Chapel St. NW1...F 6
78 Chapel St. SW1...D 4
79 Chapter Rd......G 13
78 Chapter St.........F 7
79 Charing Cross Pier.B 9
75 Charing Cross Rd..H 8
79 Charing Cross Sta...A 9
73 Charlbert St.......B 6
73 Charles La.........B 6
76 Charles Square....D 3
78 Charles St. ....B 4
78 Charles II St.......A 7
80 Charleston St......F 2
74 Charlotte Mews...F 6
76 Charlotte Rd.......D 4
74 Charlotte St.......F 6
75 Charlotte Ter.....B 10
67 Charlton...........G 10
67 Charlton F.C. ....G 10
69 Charlton La. ......D 4
67 Charlton Park ...H 10
75 Charlton Place...B 12
67 Charlton Rd. SE7 H 10
69 Charlton Rd.
Shepperton.....D 4
67 Charlton Way .....H 9
78 Charlwood Place ..F 6
78 Charlwood St......G 6
71 Charmwood La...F 12
74 Charrington St. ...B 7
76 Chart St...........D 3
75 Charterhouse ....F 12
75 Charterhouse Sq..F 13
75 Charterhouse St. .F 12
66 Chase Rd..........A 6
66 Chase Side ....A 6
80 Chatham St........E 3
70 Cheam............F 4
70 Cheam Rd.........F 3
70 Cheam Sta..........F 4
76 Cheapside.........H 2
MAP
78 Chelsea Barracks..G 4
78 Chelsea Bridge....H 4
78 Chelsea Bridge Rd. G 4
78 Chelsea Embank...H 2
77 Chelsea Hospital for
Women.........G 5
77 Chelsea Manor Gdns.
C 6
77 Chelsea Manor St..G 6
77 Chelsea Park Gdns.H 5
77 Chelsea PolytechnicG 5
78 Chelsea Reach....H 3
77 Chelsea Square ...G 5
71 Chelsfield Hill....F 12
71 Chelsfield La.
Orpington.....E 12
72 Chelsfield La.
Orpington......F 1
71 Chelsfield Rd.....E 12
71 Chelsfield Sta.....F 12
71 Chelsfield Village .F 12
71 Chelsham.........H 8
71 Chelsham Ct. Rd..H 9
71 Chelsham Rd......H 8
78 Cheltenham Ter. ..F 2
75 Cheney Rd.........C 8
74 Chenies Mews ....E 7
74 Chenies St. ....F 7
77 Cheniston Gdns...D 2
73 Chepstow Cres.....H 1
73 Chepstow Place...H 1
73 Chepstow Rd. ....G 1
73 Chepstow Villas...H 1
76 Chequer St.........E 2
68 Chequers Rd.......B 3
76 Cherbury St.......C 3
69 Chertsey ....E 2
69 Chertsey Bridge...E 3
69 Chertsey G.C. ....D 2
69 Chertsey La.......D 2
69 Chertsey Rd. Byfleet
G 3
69 Chertsey Rd. Feltham
C 4
69 Chertsey Rd.
Shepperton.....E 3
78 Chesham Mews...D 3
78 Chesham Place....D 3
78 Chesham St.......E 3
76 Cheshire St. ......E 6
70 Chessington ....F 2
70 Chessington Nth. Sta.
F 2
70 Chessington Rd....F 2
70 Chessington South Sta.
F 2
70 Chessington Zoological
Gdns...........F 1
76 Chester Close.....D 4
74 Chester Gate .....D 5
78 Chester Mews ....D 4
74 Chester Place. ...C 5
74 Chester Rd.........D 4
78 Chester Row......F 3
78 Chester Square....E 4
78 Chester St. ....D 4
74 Chester Terrace ..D 5
79 Chester Way.....F 11
78 Chesterfield Hill...A 4
78 Chesterfield St....B 4
77 Cheval Place......D 6
71 Chevening Park..H 12
77 Cheyne Gdns. ....H 6
77 Cheyne Hospital ..H 6
77 Cheyne Row .....H 6
77 Cheyne Walk.....H 6
79 Chicheley St. ....C 10
73 Chichester Rd.....F 3
78 Chichester St......G 6
76 Chicksand St......F 6
67 Chigwell ....B 11
67 Chigwell La......A 11
67 Cigwell Rise......B 11
67 Chigwell Rd. ....C 10
67 Chigwell Row....B 12
68 Childerditch La. ..D 6
77 Child's Place......F 2
77 Child's St..........F 2
70 Chiltern Rd.......F 4
74 Chiltern St.........F 3
76 Chilton St. ....E 6
73 Chilworth Mews ..H 4
73 Chilworth St.....H 4
67 Chingford..........B 9
67 Chingford Hatch ..B 9
67 Chingford La.....B 10
67 Chingford Mount Rd.
B 9
67 Chingford Rd.....C 9
MAP
73 Chippenham Mews E 1
73 Chippenham Rd...E 1
70 Chipstead ....H 5
70 Chipstead Valley Rd.
H 5
71 Chislehurst.......D 11
71 Chislehurst Common
C 11
71 Chislehurst G.C. .C 11
71 Chislehurst Rd.
Bromley.......D 10
71 Chislehurst Rd.
Orpington.....E 11
71 Chislehurst Sta...D 10
71 Chislehurst West .C 10
76 Chiswell St........F 2
66 Chiswick...........G 3
70 Chiswick Bridge...A 2
66 Chiswick High Rd. G 3
70 Chiswick House....A 3
66 Chiswick Park Sta..G 3
70 Chiswick Sta.......A 2
66 Chiswick Steps....H 3
74 Chitty St...........F 6
65 Chorleywood Rd. .A 3
66 Christchurch Ave. .C 1
70 Christchurch Rd...B 6
78 Christchurch St....G 2
76 Christian St.......H 7
76 Christina St........E 4
76 Christopher St.....F 3
80 Chumleigh St. .....H 4
68 Church Elm La.....E 2
66 Church End ....C 4
72 Church Hill, Dartford
C 2
67 Church Hill, Loughton
A 11
69 Church Hill, Pyrford
H 2
66 Church Hill Rd....A 5
79 Church House....D 9
71 Church La.........H 9
71 Church Rd. SE19..D 7
70 Church Rd. SW19 .C 4
69 Church Rd.
Addlestone .....F 2
69 Church Rd. Ashford
C 3
69 Church Rd. Byfleet G 3
71 Church Rd. Chelsfield
F 12
68 Church Rd. Noak Hill
A 3
65 Church Rd. Northolt
E 5
72 Church Rd. Sutton-at-
Hone..........C 3
70 Church Rd.
Teddington.....C 1
73 Church St. NW8...F 5
67 Church St. Edmonton
B 7
67 Church St. Enfield .A 7
70 Church St. Epsom. G 3
69 Church St. Walton .E 4
78 Churchill Gardens
Estate ....G 6
78 Churchill Gardens..
Rd...............G 5
74 Churchill Hotel...G 3
75 Churchway.......D 7
79 Churchyard Row .E 12
78 Churton St........F 6
73 Circus Rd. ....C 5
75 City Garden Row C 13
75 City of London School
H 12
75 City Rd. EC1....C 12
76 City Rd. EC1.....D 3
76 City Road Basin ..C 1
75 City University ..D 12
77 City & Guilds College
D 5
74 Civil Service
Commission ....J 6
78 Clabon Mews......E 2
73 Clanricarde Gdns. .J 2
70 Clapham...........A 6
70 Clapham Common B 5
70 Clapham Common
North Side .....B 5
70 Clapham Common
South Side......B 5
66 Clapham Junc. Sta. H 5
70 Clapham Park Rd. B 6
70 Clapham Rd........A 6
70 Clapham Sta........A 6
67 Clapton Common .D 8
MAP
67 Clapton Sta.......D 8
75 Claremont Close .C 11
75 Claremont Square C 11
74 Clarence Gate.....E 3
74 Clarence Gardens .D 5
78 Clarence House ...C 6
73 Clarendon Gate...H 6
73 Clarendon Gdns...E 4
74 Clarendon Grove..C 7
73 Clarendon Place ..H 6
78 Clarendon St......G 5
77 Clareville Grove...F 4
77 Clareville St.......F 4
78 Clarges Mews.....B 5
78 Clarges St. ....B 5
74 Claridge's Hotel ..H 4
78 Claverton St. .....G 6
74 Clay St. ....F 3
67 Claybury Hosp...C 11
70 Claygate..........F 1
67 Clayhall.........C 11
67 Clayhall Av.......C 11
67 Clayhall Park ....C 11
79 Claylands Place ..J 10
79 Claylands Rd.....J 10
65 Claypit La.........B 4
79 Clayton St.......H 11
79 Cleaver Square...G 11
79 Cleaver St. ......G 11
72 Clement St.......C 2
76 Clement's La......H 3
79 Cleopatra's Needle A 9
76 Clere Place ....E 3
76 Clere St. ....E 3
75 Clerkenwell Close E 11
75 Clerkenwell Green E 12
75 Clerkenwell Rd...E 11
73 Cleveland Gdns....H 3
78 Cleveland Row....B 6
73 Cleveland Square .H 3
74 Cleveland St.......F 6
73 Cleveland Terrace .G 4
74 Clifford St. ....J 5
73 Clifton Gdns......E 3
73 Clifton Hill ....B 3
73 Clifton Place .....H 5
73 Clifton Rd.........E 4
76 Clifton St. ....F 3
73 Clifton Villas .....F 3
80 Clink St...........A 2
74 Clipstone St.......F 5
67 Clissold Park .....D 7
78 Cliveden Place ....E 3
76 Cloak La..........H 2
71 Cloack House Sta. D 8
69 Clockhouse La. ...C 3
75 Cloth Fair.......F 13
75 Cloudesley Place .B 11
75 Cloudesley Rd....B 11
75 Cloudesley Sq....A 11
75 Cloudesley St.....B 11
76 Club Row.........D 5
77 Coalbrookdale Gt .C 5
76 Coate St..........C 7
76 Cobb St...........G 5
69 Cobham ....G 5
69 Cobham Park ....H 5
69 Cobham Rd. ......H 6
72 Cobham Terrace Rd.
B 4
69 Cobham & Stoke
D'Abernon Sta..H 5
80 Cobourg Rd.......H 5
73 Cochrane St.......C 5
76 Cock Hill ....G 4
75 Cock La..........G 12
66 Cockfosters........A 5
66 Cockfosters Sta....A 6
79 Cockspur St.......B 8
76 Code St. ....E 6
79 Coin St...........B 11
77 Colbeck Mews ....F 3
68 Colchester Rd.....C 3
72 Coldblow Maypole B 1
70 Coldharbour La. SE5
B 6
65 Coldharbour La.
Hayes ....G 5
70 Cole Park ....B 1
80 Cole St............D 2
75 Colebrooke Row .B 12
80 Colegrove Rd......J 6
77 Coleherne Mews ..G 2
77 Coleherne Rd......G 2
77 Coleman Rd.......J 4
76 Coleman St........G 2
75 Coley St.........E 10
65 Colham Green ....F 4
66 Colin Deep La. ...C 3
MAP
66 Colindale.........C 3
66 Colindale Av.......C 3
66 Colindale Sta......C 3
75 Coliseum Theatre..J 8
76 College Hill ....H 2
75 College of Arms..H 13
74 College Place .....A 6
71 College Rd. SE21..B 7
71 College Rd. Bromley
D 9
72 College Rd. Dartford
D 1
70 College Rd. Epsom
G 3
76 College St. ....H 2
68 Collier Row ....C 2
68 Collier Row La....C 2
68 Collier Row Rd....C 2
75 Collier St..........C 9
70 Collier's Wood.....C 5
77 Collingham Gdns..F 3
77 Collingham Place..F 2
77 Collingham Rd....F 3
79 Collinson St......C 13
65 Colnbrook ....H 2
65 Colnbrook Bypass.H 2
79 Colnbrook St. ...D 12
65 Colney Butts......A 5
66 Colney Hatch .....B 5
66 Colney Hatch La...C 6
79 Colombo St......B 12
75 Colonnade.........E 8
74 Columbia Rd......D 5
74 Colville Place .....F 7
72 Colyers La.........A 1
76 Commercial Rd. ..G 6
76 Commercial St.....F 5
67 Commercial Way .H 8
66 Common Rd.......B 1
70 Commonside East .D 5
70 Commonside West D 5
75 Compton St......E 12
79 Concert Hall Approach
B 10
73 Conduit Mews....H 4
73 Conduit Place ....H 5
74 Conduit St........H 5
80 Congreve St.......F 4
74 Connaught Place..H 2
74 Connaught Sq.....H 2
73 Connaught St......H 6
79 Cons St. ....C 11
78 Constitution Hill..C 5
80 Content St.........F 2
69 Convent Rd.......C 4
74 Conway St........E 6
79 Cooks Rd.......H 12
70 Coombe Hill G.C. .C 2
70 Coombe La.......D 3
70 Coombe Rd.,
Kingston.......D 2
70 Coombe Rd. New
Malden........D 3
71 Coombe Rd. Sta...E 7
70 Coombe Wood G.C.
C 2
75 Coomb's St......C 13
80 Cooper's Rd.......G 5
72 Cooper's Wood...G 4
77 Cope Place........D 1
75 Copenhagen St....A 9
79 Copperfield St....C 13
70 Copse Hill ....D 3
65 Copse Wood.......C 4
69 Copsem La.........F 6
76 Copthall Av.......G 3
76 Copthall Court ...G 3
75 Coptic St..........G 8
79 Coral St...........C 11
75 Coram St..........E 8
75 Coram's Field
Playground......E 9
76 Corbet Place.......F 5
68 Corbets Tey ....E 4
68 Corbets Tey Rd....E 4
74 Cork St...........J 6
76 Corn Exchange ...H 4
76 Cornhill ....H 3
77 Cornwall Gdns....E 3
79 Cornwall Rd......B 11
76 Coronet St........D 3
75 Corporation Row.E 11
76 Corsham St.......D 3
79 Cosser St.........D 10
73 Cosway St. ....F 6
80 Cotham St.........F 2
77 Cottage Place......D 6
78 Cottage Walk.....D 3
70 Cottenham Park ..D 3
MAP
70 Cottenham Park Rd.
D 3
77 Cottesmore Gdns. .D 3
79 Cottington St......F 12
70 Coulsdon ....H 6
70 Coulsdon Court G.C.
G 6
70 Coulsdon La.......H 5
70 Coulsdon North Sta.
G 6
70 Coulsdon Rd. .....H 6
78 Coulson St.........F 2
79 County Hall.......C 9
80 County St..........E 2
71 Court La. ....B 7
79 Courtenay St.....G 10
77 Courtfield Gdns. ..F 2
77 Courtfield Rd. ....F 3
75 Covent Garden ...H 9
79 Covent Garden Market
H 8
74 Coventry St........J 7
80 Cowan St..........H 4
75 Cowcross St......F 12
65 Cowley............F 3
79 Cowley St. ....D 8
76 Cowper St.........D 3
70 Craddocks Av.....H 2
80 Crail Row ....F 3
74 Cramer St..........F 4
79 Crampton St. .....F 13
75 Cranbourn St. ....H 8
67 Cranbrook Rd. ...C 11
65 Cranford...........H 4
65 Cranford La.......H 5
68 Cranham..........D 5
74 Cranleigh St. .....C 6
77 Cranley Gdns. ....G 4
77 Cranley Mews.....F 4
77 Cranley Place......F 5
76 Cranwood St......D 3
73 Craven Hill Gdns. .H 3
79 Craven St..........B 8
73 Craven Terrace ...H 4
74 Crawford Place ...G 1
74 Crawford St.......F 2
72 Crayford..........A 2
72 Crayford Rd......B 2
76 Creechurch La. ...H 4
75 Creed La........H 12
67 Creekmouth .....F 12
76 Cremer St. ....C 5
77 Crescent Place ....E 6
77 Cresswell Gdns....F 3
77 Cresswell Place ...G 4
75 Crestfield St.......C 9
66 Cricklewood ......E 4
66 Cricklewood La. ..D 4
66 Cricklewood Sta...E 4
80 Crimscott St. .....E 4
75 Crinan St. ....B 9
78 Cringle St..........J 6
76 Cripplegate Institute
F 1
74 Criterion Theatre..J 7
72 Crockenhill.......E 1
71 Crofton Heath ...E 10
71 Crofton Park Sta. .B 8
71 Crofton Rd. ......E 11
71 Croham Hurst G.C. F 7
71 Croham Rd.......F 7
75 Cromer St........D 9
73 Crompton St......E 4
77 Cromwell Cres.....F 1
77 Cromwell Gdns....E 5
77 Cromwell Mews...E 5
77 Cromwell Place ...E 5
77 Cromwell Rd. SW5 &
SW7..........E 3
69 Cromwell Rd.
Hounslow......B 6
76 Crondall St. ......C 3
79 Cropley St. ....B 2
80 Crosby Row......C 3
76 Crosby Square.....G 4
68 Cross La. ....D 3
70 Crossdeep.........C 1
76 Crosswall ....H 5
66 Crouch End ....D 6
66 Crouch Hill ......D 6
66 Crouch Hill Sta. ..D 6
68 Crow La..........D 2
70 Crown Dale ....C 6
75 Crown Office Row H 11
80 Crown St. ....J 2
74 Crowndale Rd......B 6
65 Croxley Green ....A 4
65 Croxley Green Sta. A 4
65 Croxley Sta........A 4

MAP
71 Croxted Rd......B 7
71 Croydon ....E 7
70 Croydon La......G 5
71 Croydon Rd. SE20 D 7
71 Croydon Rd.
 Beckenham.....D 8
71 Croydon Rd. Bromley
 E 10
71 Croydon Rd.
 Chelsham......H 9
70 Croydon Rd. Croydon
 E 6
70 Croydon Rd. Mitcham
 D 5
80 Crucifix La. .....C 4
75 Cruden St......B 12
75 Cruickshank St...C 10
76 Crutched Friars...H 4
71 Crystal Palace F.C. D 7
71 Crystal Palace Sta. .C 7
71 Crystal Palace Park C 7
75 Cubit St.........D 10
70 Cuddington G.C...G 4
71 Cudham ....G 11
71 Cudham La. Cudham
 G 11
71 Cudham La. Green
 Street Green ...F 11
71 Cudham La. Horns
 Green ....H 11
71 Cudham Rd......G 11
78 Culford Gdns. ....F 2
76 Culham St.......H 4
74 Culross St.......J 3
73 Culworth St......C 6
74 Cumberland Gate .H 2
74 Cumberland Hotel H 3
74 Cumberland Market
 D 5
78 Cumberland St....G 5
74 Cumberland Ter...C 5
75 Cumming St......C 10
80 Cunard St.......H 3
78 Cundy St. ....F 4
73 Cunningham Pl....E 5
79 Cureton St.......F 8
80 Curlew St........C 5
75 Cursitor St.......G 11
76 Curtain Rd.......E 4
80 Curtis St.........E 5
78 Curzon Gate......B 4
78 Curzon St.......B 4
76 Custom House ....J 4
67 Custom House Sta.F 10
79 Cut, The ....C 11
75 Cuthbert St.......F 5
76 Cutler St. ....G 4
75 Cynthia St.......C 10
74 Cypress Place ....F 6
75 Cyrus St.........D 12
78 Dacre St.........D 7
68 Dagenham.......E 2
68 Dagenham Av.....E 1
68 Dagenham Dock Sta.
 F 1
68 Dagenham Heathway
 Sta.............E 1
68 Dagenham Rd....D 2
68 Dagenham Park...B 4
75 Dallington St.....E 12
67 Dalston ....E 7
67 Dalston Junc. Sta. .E 7
67 Dalston La.......E 8
72 Daltons Rd.......E 1
75 Dame St.........B 13
75 Danbury St.......B 12
75 Dane St.........F 9
71 Danson Park .....B 12
79 Danson Rd. SE17 G 13
71 Danson Rd. Bexley
 Heath.........B 12
79 Dante Rd........F 12
74 Danvers St.......H 5
74 D'Arblay St......H 6
76 Darby St.........J 6
72 Darenth.........C 3
72 Darenth Rd......B 3
72 Dartford ....B 2
72 Dartford G.C.....C 2
72 Dartford Heath ...B 2
72 Dartford-Purfleet
 Tunnel.........A 3
72 Dartford Rd. Dartford
 B 2
72 Dartford Rd. Hextable
 C 2
66 Dartmouth Park Hill
 D 6
71 Dartmouth Rd....C 8

MAP
78 Dartmouth St.....D 7
80 Dartnell Rd......H 4
80 Darwin St.......F 3
65 Datchet.........H 1
80 Date St.........G 2
76 Davenant St......F 6
73 Daventry St......F 6
80 Davey St.......H 5
71 Davidson Rd......E 7
74 Davies Mews ....H 4
74 Davies St.......H 4
66 Dawes Rd.......H 4
80 Dawes St........F 3
65 Dawley Rd. ......G 4
67 Daws Hill ....A 9
75 Dawson Place ....H 1
71 Days La.........B 11
79 De Laune St. ....G 12
74 De Vere Gdns....D 3
74 De Walden St.....F 4
80 Deacon St.......E 1
80 Deacon Way.....E 1
76 Deal St.........F 6
79 Dean Bradley St...E 8
79 Dean Farrar St....D 7
79 Dean Ryle St.....E 8
79 Dean Stanley St...E 8
74 Dean St.........H 7
78 Deanery St.......B 4
80 Dean's Buildings ..F 3
75 Dean's Court ....H 13
66 Dean's La.......B 3
79 Dean's Yard......D 8
67 Debden Sta.....A 11
80 Decima St........D 4
70 Deer Park ....D 4
79 Defence, Ministry of
 B 8
65 Delaford Park....F 2
73 Delamere Terrace .F 3
74 Delancey St......B 5
74 Delaware Rd......E 2
75 Delhi St.........A 9
78 Denbigh Place ....F 6
78 Denbigh St.......F 6
65 Denham ....D 2
65 Denham Aerodrome
 C 2
74 Denman St.......J 7
75 Denmark Grove..B 11
71 Denmark Hill....B 7
71 Denmark Hill Sta. .A 7
75 Denmark St.......G 8
70 Denning Avenue ..F 6
68 Dennises La......E 4
79 Denny Crescent ..F 11
79 Denny St........F 11
78 Denyer St........F 2
80 Depot St.........J 2
67 Deptford.........H 8
67 Deptford Sta.....H 9
76 Derbyshire St.....D 7
76 Dereham Place....D 4
74 Dering St........H 5
71 Derry Downs ...E 12
77 Derry St.........D 2
80 Deverell St.......E 2
75 Devonia Rd......B 12
76 Devons Rd.......F 9
74 Devonshire Close .F 5
74 Devonshire Mews
 South ....F 4
74 Devonshire Mews
 West ....F 4
74 Devonshire Place .F 4
74 Devonshire Plce. Mews
 F 4
76 Devonshire Row ..G 4
76 Devonshire Square G 4
74 Devonshire St.....F 4
79 Devonshire Ter...H 4
75 Dewey Rd.......B 11
77 Dial Walk, The ..C 3
74 Diana Place .....E 5
80 Dickens Square....D 2
75 Dignum St.......B 11
78 Dilke St.........H 2
76 Dingley Place.....D 2
76 Dingley Rd.......D 1
76 Diss St..........C 5
76 Distaff La........H 1
79 Distin St........F 11
70 Ditton Hill......E 1
65 Ditton Park ......G 1
70 Ditton Rd. ......E 2
76 Dock St. ....J 6
80 Dockhead ......C 6
80 Dockley Rd......D 6

MAP
79 Doddington Gr...G 12
79 Dolben St........B 12
79 Dolland St.......G 10
66 Dollis Hill La.....D 4
66 Dollis Hill Sta....E 3
78 Dolphin Square ...G 7
75 Dombey St.......F 9
80 Dominion St. .....F 3
80 Domville Grove...G 5
66 Donegal St.......C 10
78 Donne Place......E 1
79 Doon St.........B 10
74 Dorchester Hotel .B 4
74 Doric Way......D 7
70 Dorking Rd......G 2
79 Dorrington St....F 11
74 Dorset Close.....F 2
76 Dorset Estate ....C 5
78 Dorset Mews ....D 4
74 Dorset Place .....F 7
75 Dorset Rise .....H 12
70 Dorset Rd. SW19 ..D 4
79 Dorset Rd. SW8...J 9
74 Dorset Square ...E 2
74 Dorset St.........F 3
75 Doughty Mews...E 10
75 Doughty St......E 10
74 Douglas St.......F 7
77 Douro Place.....D 3
77 Dove Mews......F 4
76 Dove Row.......B 6
74 Dovehouse St.....G 5
70 Dover House Rd. .B 3
78 Dover St.........A 5
76 Dowgate Hill.....H 2
78 Down St........B 4
71 Downe...........C 10
71 Downham Estate...C 9
71 Downham Way....C 9
79 Downing St......C 8
70 Downs Rd. Epsom G 3
70 Downs Rd. Sutton G 4
72 Downs Rd.
 Swanscombe....C 6
72 Downs Wood....G 6
69 Downside........H 5
69 Downside Rd.....H 5
79 Draco St. ......H 13
80 Drant St........F 5
79 Draper St. .....E 13
76 Drapers Hall ....G 3
71 Draycott Avenue .F 1
78 Draycott Place....F 2
78 Draycott Terrace .F 2
77 Drayson Mews....C 2
66 Drayton Gdns....G 4
66 Drayton Green ...F 1
66 Drayton Green Sta..F 1
80 Drive, The .....D 11
80 Druid St.........C 5
75 Drummond Cres...C,7
74 Drummond St....D 6
75 Drury La.........H 9
75 Dryden St.......H 9
76 Drysdale St......D 4
77 Duchess of Bedford's
 Walk ....C 1
74 Duchess St.......F 5
75 Duchess Theatre..H 9
79 Duchy St. ......B 11
65 Ducks Hill ......C 4
65 Ducks Hill Rd....C 4
66 Dudden Hill La....E 3
78 Dufferin St.......B 2
78 Duke of York St. ..A 6
78 Duke of York's
 H.Q............F 3
75 Duke of York's Th. J 8
78 Duke St. SW1 ...A 6
76 Duke St. W1 .....H 4
80 Duke Street Hill...B 3
77 Duke's La. ....C 2
75 Duke's Place .....G 4
75 Duke's Rd........D 7
71 Dulwich..........B 7
71 Dulwich College ..C 7
71 Dulwich Common .B 7
71 Dulwich Park .....B 7
71 Dulwich Village...B 7
71 Dulwich Wood Pk. C 7
71 Dulwich & Sydenham
 Hill G.C........C 7
76 Dunbridge St.....E 7
75 Duncan St.......B 12
76 Duncan Terrace ..B 12
76 Dunloe St.......C 5
68 Dunning's La....D 6
79 Dunraven St......H 3
70 Dunstans Hill.....F 4

MAP
76 Dunston Rd. .....A 5
72 Dunton Green ....H 1
80 Dunton Rd. ......F 5
78 Duplex Ride......C 3
76 Durant St. ......C 6
67 Durants Park ....A 8
70 Durham Rd......D 3
80 Durham St......G 10
73 Durham Terrace ..G 2
66 Durnsford Rd. N11
 C 6
70 Durnsford Rd. SW19
 C 4
78 Dyley St.........E 3
75 Dyott St.........G 8
76 Dysart St........E 3
76 Eagle St.........F 9
76 Eagle Wharf Rd. .B 2
66 Ealing ....D 2
66 Ealing Broadway Sta.
 F 2
66 Ealing Common ...G 2
66 Ealing Common Sta.
 G 2
66 Ealing G.C.......F 1
66 Ealing Rd. Brentford
 G 2
65 Ealing Rd. Greenford
 E 6
66 Ealing Rd. Wembley
 D 3
73 Eamont St........B 6
77 Eardley Cres.....G 1
80 Earl Rd.........F 5
76 Earl St..........F 3
75 Earlham St.......H 8
77 Earl's Court......G 1
77 Earl's Court Gdns. F 2
77 Earl's Court Rd. ..E 1
77 Earl's Court Sq...G 2
77 Earl's Court Sta...F 2
67 Earl's Path ......A 10
77 Earl's Walk......E 1
76 Earlsfield Rd......B 4
70 Earlsfield Sta.....B 4
75 Earlstoke St. ....D 12
75 Earnshaw St......G 8
66 East Acton.......G 3
66 East Acton Sta....F 3
69 East Barnet......A 6
69 East Bedfont.....B 4
71 East Croydon Sta. .E 7
71 East Dulwich ....B 7
71 East Dulwich Rd. .B 7
71 East Dulwich Sta. .B 7
66 East End Rd......C 5
70 East Ewell.......F 4
66 East Finchley ....C 5
66 East Finchley Sta..C 5
71 East Hall Rd.....E 12
67 East Ham ....F 11
75 East Harding St...G 11
72 East Hill, Dartford .B 3
70 East Hill, SW18 ..B 4
67 East India Dock Rd.
 F 9
66 East La. ....D 2
69 East Moseley.....D 6
70 East Putney Sta...B 4
76 East Rd.........D 3
71 East Rochester Way
 B 12
70 East Sheen ......B 2
70 East Sheen Gate..B 2
76 East Smithfield...J 6
80 East St. SE17 ....F 4
70 East St., Epsom ..G 3
76 East Tenter St....H 6
67 East Wickham ...H 12
73 Eastbourne Mews .G 4
73 Eastbourne Ter....G 4
75 Eastcastle St......G 6
76 Eastcheap........H 3
65 Eastcote ....D 6
65 Eastcote La......E 5
65 Eastcote Rd......D 4
67 Eastern Avenue...A 10
68 Eastern Avenue East
 C 2, C 3
68 Eastern Avenue West
 C 1
68 Easthall La.......F 3
67 Eastham Manor
 Way...........F 11
75 Eastman Dental
 Hospital......D 10
75 Easton St. ......D 11
69 Eastworth.......E 2

MAP
69 Eastworth Rd.....E 2
78 Eaton Gate......E 3
78 Eaton La........D 5
78 Eaton Mews North E 3
78 Eaton Mews South.E 4
78 Eaton Mews West .E 4
78 Eaton Place......E 3
78 Eaton Row......D 4
78 Eaton Square....E 4
78 Eaton Terrace....D 4
76 Ebenezer St......D 2
76 Ebor St.........E 5
78 Ebury Bridge ....E 4
78 Ebury Bridge Rd...G 4
78 Ebury Mews......E 4
78 Ebury Mews East .E 4
78 Ebury Square.....E 4
78 Ebury St.........E 4
78 Eccleston Bridge ..E 5
78 Eccleston Mews...D 4
78 Eccleston Square ..F 5
78 Eccleston Street Mews
 F 5
78 Eccleston Place....E 5
73 Edbrooke Rd......E 1
71 Eden Park ......D 8
70 Edge Hill Rd......F 6
78 Edge St.........B 2
66 Edgware.........B 3
66 Edgware Rd., NW2
 D 3
66 Edgware Rd. NW9 C 3
73 Edgware Rd. W2...F 5
77 Edinburgh Gate...C 2
77 Edith Grove......J 4
77 Edith Terrace .....J 3
77 Eldon Rd.........D 3
77 Eldon St.........F 3
80 Elephant Rd......E 1
80 Elephant & Castle Sta.
 E 1
73 Elgin Avenue ....D 2
75 Elia St. ....C 12
78 Elizabeth Bridge..F 5
78 Elizabeth St......E 4
76 Ellen St. ....H 6
79 Elliott's Row ....E 12
78 Ellis St.........E 3
76 Elm Park Gdns...G 5
77 Elm Park La......G 4
77 Elm Park Rd. SW3 H 4
65 Elm Park Rd., Pinner
 C 5
77 Elm Place ....E 3
75 Elm St..........E 10
73 Elm Tree Rd......C 5
78 Elmers End......D 8
73 Elms Mews ......J 4
71 Elmstead........C 10
71 Elmstead La.....C 10
71 Elmstead Wood ..C 10
69 Elmwood Avenue .C 5
73 Elnathan Mews ..E 3
66 Elstree ....A 2
66 Elstree Aerodrome .A 1
66 Elstree Hill South..A 2
66 Elstree Rd., Bushey A 1
66 Elstree Rd., Stanmore
 A 2
66 Elstree & Boreham-
 wood Sta.......A 2
80 Elsted St........F 3
71 Eltham ....B 10
71 Eltham Bypass...C 10
71 Eltham Common.A 10
71 Eltham Hill......B 10
71 Eltham Park .....B 11
71 Eltham Park Sta. .B 10
71 Eltham Rd.......B 9
80 Eltham St........F 2
71 Eltham Warren G.C.
 B 11
71 Eltham West Hall Sta.
 B 10
66 Elthorne Heights ..F 1
77 Elvaston Mews ...D 4

MAP
77 Elvaston Place....D 4
70 Elvers Way......H 3
78 Elverton St.......E 7
76 Elwin St.........C 6
75 Ely Place ....F 11
78 Elystan Place ....F 2
78 Elystan St.......F 2
78 Embankment Gdns.
 H 3
69 Ember La........E 6
75 Emerald St......F 10
68 Emerson Park ...D 3
80 Emerson St......A 1
78 Emery Hill St.....E 6
77 Emperor's Gate...E 3
78 Empire Pool.....E 2
75 Endell St. ....G 8
67 Endlebury Rd.....B 9
74 Endsleigh Gdns...D 7
74 Endsleigh Place ..E 7
74 Endsleigh St. ....D 7
71 Endwell Rd......A 8
67 Enfield..........A 7
67 Enfield Chase Sta. .A 7
67 Enfield G.C......A 7
66 Enfield Rd......A 6
67 Enfield Town Sta..A 7
67 Enford St........F 2
80 Enid St.........D 6
77 Ennismore Gdns..D 6
77 Ennismore Gardens
 Mews.........D 5
77 Ennismore Mews..D 6
77 Ennismore St.....D 6
76 Ensign St........J 6
79 Environment, Dept. of
 B 13
70 Epsom ....G 2
70 Epsom Common..G 2
70 Epsom District
 Hospital.......G 2
70 Epsom Downs Race
 Course........H 3
70 Epsom Downs Sta. G 3
70 Epsom G.C.......G 3
70 Epsom La........H 3
70 Epsom Rd., Croydon
 E 6
70 Epsom Rd., Ewell .G 3
70 Epsom Rd.,
 Leatherhead....H 1
70 Epsom Rd., Morden
 E 4
67 Epping Forest
 A 10, C 9
67 Epping New Rd. .A 10
76 Epworth St. ......E 3
79 Erasmus St......F 8
72 Erith ....A 2
68 Erith Marshes ....G 1
68 Erith Reach ......G 2
68 Erith Rd., Belvedere
 G 2
68 Erith Rd.,
 Northumberland
 Heath..........H 2
74 Eros.............J 7
76 Errol St.........E 2
69 Esher ....F 6
69 Esher Common ..F 6
69 Esher La........E 6
69 Esher Rd........F 5
69 Esher Sta........E 6
80 Esmeralda Rd.....F 7
73 Essendine Rd. ....D 1
77 Essex Rd........A 12
75 Essex St.........H 10
77 Essex Villas......D 1
77 Eustace Rd.......J 1
74 Euston Centre ...E 5
74 Euston Square...D 7
74 Euston Sta.......D 6
74 Euston Station
 Colonnade .....D 7
74 Euston Rd.......E 6
74 Euston St........D 6
74 Euston Tower....E 6
74 Evelyn Gdns.....G 4
67 Evelyn St.........G 8
75 Everilda St......A 10
74 Eversholt St......C 6
70 Ewell ....F 3
70 Ewell Bypass.....F 3
70 Ewell East Sta....F 3
70 Ewell West Sta....F 3
79 Ewer St. ....B 13
75 Exeter St. ....J 9
77 Exhibition Rd.....D 5
75 Exmouth Market.D 11

MAP
80 Exon St. F 4
79 Exton St. B 11
72 Eynsford E 3
75 Eyre Street Hill E 11
76 Ezra St. C 6
69 Faggs Rd. B 4
80 Fair St. C 4
76 Fairchild St. E 4
71 Fairchildes Rd. G 9
76 Fairclough St. H 7
80 Faircombe St. C 7
67 Fairlop Sta. C 11
67 Fairmead Rd. A 10
69 Fairmile G 5
69 Fairmile La. G 5
70 Fairoak La. G 1
72 Fairseat G 5
71 Falconwood Sta. B 11
76 Falkirk St. C 4
65 Falling La. F 3
80 Falmouth Rd. E 2
76 Fann St. E 1
76 Fanshaw St. C 4
80 Faraday St. H 3
71 Farleigh G 8
71 Farleigh Court Rd. G 8
71 Farley Rd. F 7
77 Farm La. SW6 J 1
70 Farm La., Epsom H 2
74 Farm St. J 4
71 Farnborough F 11
71 Farnborough Bypass F 11
71 Farnborough Common E 10
79 Farnham Place B 13
79 Farnham Royal G 10
72 Farningham E 3
72 Farningham Rd. D 3
72 Farningham Rd. & Sutton-at-Hone Sta. D 3
72 Farningham Wood D 2
75 Farringdon Rd. E 11
75 Farringdon Sta. F 12
75 Farringdon St. G 12
76 Fashion St. F 5
79 Faunce St. G 12
77 Fawcett St. H 3
72 Fawkham Green E 4
71 Featherbed La. F 8
76 Featherstone St. E 2
69 Feltham C 4
69 Feltham Rd. C 4
69 Felthamhill C 5
69 Felthamhill Rd. C 4
68 Fen La. E 6
67 Fencepiece Rd. B 11
76 Fenchurch Avenue H 4
76 Fenchurch Bldgs. H 4
76 Fenchurch St. H 4
76 Fenchurch Street Sta. H 5
80 Fendall St. D 4
79 Fentiman Rd. J 9
75 Fernsbury St. D 11
77 Fernshaw Rd. J 3
67 Ferry La. N17 C 8
68 Ferry La., Rainham F 2
75 Fetter La. G 11
71 Fickleshole G 9
75 Field Court F 10
65 Field End Rd. D 5
75 Field Place C 11
75 Field St. C 9
76 Fieldgate St. G 7
72 Filston La. G 2
77 Finborough Rd. H 3
76 Finch La. H 3
66 Finchley C 5
66 Finchley Central Sta. C 5
66 Finchley G.C. B 4
66 Finchley Rd. E 5
73 Finchley Rd. B 4
66 Finchley Rd. D 4
66 Finchley Road & Frognall Sta. E 5
79 Finck St. D 10
67 Finsbury F 7
76 Finsbury Circus F 3
67 Finsbury Park D 7
67 Finsbury Park Sta. D 7
76 Finsbury Pavement F 3
76 Finsbury Square F 3
76 Finsbury St. F 2
79 Fire Brigade H.Q. F 9
67 Firs La. B 7
78 First St. E 1

MAP
70 Firtree Rd. G 4
76 Fish Street Hill J 3
75 Fisher St. F 9
73 Fisherton St. E 5
76 Fishmongers' Hall J 3
79 Fitzalan St. E 10
74 Fitzhardinge St. G 3
66 Fitzjohn's Avenue E 5
78 Fitzmaurice Place A 5
74 Fitzroy Square E 6
74 Fitzroy St. E 6
75 Flaxman Terrace D 8
75 Fleet La. G 12
75 Fleet St. H 11
79 Fleming Rd. H 12
76 Fleur de Lis St. E 4
80 Flint St. F 3
80 Flinten St. F 4
78 Flood St. G 1
77 Flood Walk G 6
75 Floral St. H 8
76 Florida St. D 7
77 Flower Walk, The C 4
76 Flower & Dean St. F 5
76 Fochelle St. D 5
74 Foley St. F 6
76 Folgate St. F 4
71 Foots Cray C 12
71 Foots Cray La. C 12
71 Foots Cray Rd. B 10
76 Forbes St. H 6
69 Ford Bridge Rd. C 3
69 Fordbridge Rd. D 4
76 Fore St. EC2 F 2
67 Fore St. N18 B 8
65 Fore St., Ruislip C 5
79 Foreign Office C 7
67 Forest Gate E 10
71 Forest Hill C 7
71 Forest Hill Sta. C 8
67 Forest Hospital B 10
67 Forest La. E 10
67 Forest Rd. E17 C 9
67 Forest Rd., Ilford C 12
70 Forest Rd., Sutton E 4
67 Forest Side A 10
73 Formosa St. E 3
76 Fornier St. F 5
74 Forest St. G 2
76 Forston St. B 2
80 Fort Rd. F 6
66 Fortis Green Rd. C 5
66 Fortress Rd. E 6
66 Fortune Green Rd. E 4
76 Fortune St. E 2
66 Forty Avenue D 2
66 Forty La. D 3
75 Foster La. G 1
74 Foubert's Place H 6
77 Foulis Terrace F 5
76 Foutain St. D 5
75 Fox Court F 11
69 Fox Hill Rd. F 1
66 Fox La. B 6
68 Foxburrow Wood A 1
69 Foxoak Hill F 4
73 Frampton St. E 5
78 Francis St. E 6
78 Franklin's Row G 3
79 Frazier St. C 11
80 Frean St. D 6
75 Frederick St. D 9
80 Fremantle St. F 4
69 French St. D 5
80 Frensham St. H 6
80 Friary Rd. J 7
75 Friend St. C 12
74 Friends House D 7
66 Friern Barnet B 5
74 Frith St. H 7
71 Frith Wood G 8
75 Frome St. B 13
68 Front La. D 4
66 Fryent Way D 2
70 Fulham F.C. A 3
70 Fulham Palace A 4
66 Fulham Palace Rd. H 4
70 Fulham Rd. SW6 A 4
77 Fulham Rd. SW10 G 5
76 Fuller St. D 6
65 Fulmer E 1
69 Fulwell G.C. C 5
75 Furnival St. G 11
70 Furze Hill H 4
66 Furzehill Rd. A 3
78 Fynes St. E 7
75 Gainsford St. C 5
68 Gale St. E 1
71 Gallery Rd. B 7

MAP
72 Galley Hill B 5
67 Galliard Rd. A 8
67 Gallions Reach G 11
68 Gallows Corner C 3
79 Gambia St. B 12
70 Gander Green La. E 4
74 Ganton St. H 6
67 Gants Hill Sta. D 11
74 Garbutt Place F 4
73 Garden Rd. C 4
79 Garden Row D 12
76 Garden Walk D 4
76 Garlick Hill H 2
75 Garnault Place D 11
70 Garratt La. C 4
76 Garrett St. E 1
75 Garrick St. H 8
75 Garrick Theatre J 8
70 Garth Rd. E 3
73 Garway Rd. H 2
76 Gascogne Place D 5
79 Gasholder Place G 10
69 Gaston Bridge Rd. D 4
75 Gate St. G 9
73 Gateforth St. E 6
67 Gates Corner C 10
80 Gateway H 2
78 Gatliff Rd. G 4
79 Gaunt St. D 13
79 Gayfere St. E 8
79 Gaywood St. E 12
79 Gaza St. G 12
75 Gee St. E 13
76 Geffrye Museum C 4
76 Geffrye St. B 5
75 General Post Office G 13
77 Geological Museum E 5
80 George Row C 6
74 George St. G 2
74 George Yard H 4
65 George V Avenue C 6
79 Geraldine Mary Harmsworth Park E 11
79 Geraldine St. E 12
68 Gerpins La. E 4
75 Gerrard Rd. B 12
74 Gerrard St. H 7
65 Gerrards Cross D 1
79 Gerridge St. D 11
77 Gertrude St. H 4
68 Gidea Park C 3
68 Gidea Park Sta. C 3
75 Gilbert Place G 8
79 Gilbert Rd. F 11
74 Gilbert St. H 4
72 Gildenhill Rd. D 3
78 Gillingham St. E 5
77 Gilston Rd. G 4
75 Giltspur St. G 12
66 Gladstone Park E 3
79 Gladstone St. D 12
79 Glass Hill St. C 13
79 Glasshouse St. J 6
79 Glasshouse Walk G 9
75 Glasshouse Yard E 13
77 Glebe Place H 6
77 Gledhow Gdns. F 3
80 Glengall Rd. H 6
80 Glengall Terrace H 5
74 Glentworth St. E 2
67 Globe Rd. F 8
80 Globe St. D 2
80 Globe Theatre, SE1 E 3
74 Globe Theatre, W1 H 7
74 Globe Yard H 5
74 Gloucester Avenue A 4
74 Gloucester Gate B 4
73 Gloucester Mews H 4
73 Gloucester Mews West H 4
74 Gloucester Place F 2
74 Gloucester Place Mews G 3
77 Gloucester Rd. E 3
73 Gloucester Square H 5
78 Gloucester St. G 6
73 Gloucester Terrace G 3
77 Gloucester Walk C 1
75 Gloucester Way D 11
79 Glyn St. G 9
77 Godfrey St. G 6
79 Goding St. G 9
75 Godson St. B 11
71 Godstone Rd. H 7
76 Golden La. E 1
74 Golden Square H 6

MAP
66 Golders Green D 4
66 Golders Green Rd. D 4
66 Golders Green Sta. D 5
66 Goldhawk Rd. G 4
74 Goldington Cres. B 7
74 Goldington St. B 7
75 Goldman St. H 13
73 Goldney Rd. E 1
76 Goldsmiths Hall G 1
76 Goldsmiths Row B 6
74 Goodge Place F 6
74 Goodge St. F 6
76 Goodman St. H 6
76 Goodmans Yard H 5
67 Goodmayes D 12
67 Goodmayes Hospital D 12
67 Goodmayes La. D 12
75 Goods Way B 8
76 Gopsall St. B 3
77 Gordon Place C 2
75 Gordon Square E 7
74 Gordon St. E 7
72 Gore Hill C 3
77 Gore St. D 4
71 Gorse Rd. E 12
68 Goresbrook Rd. E 1
76 Gorsuch St. C 5
74 Gosfield St. F 5
66 Gospel Oak Sta. E 6
76 Gosset St. D 6
75 Goswell Rd. D 12
75 Goswell Terrace D 12
76 Goulston St. G 5
75 Gough Square G 11
75 Gough St. E 10
74 Gower Mews F 7
74 Gower Place E 7
74 Gower St. E 7
76 Gowers Walk H 6
76 Gracechurch St. H 3
74 Grafton Mews E 6
74 Grafton Place D 7
74 Grafton St. J 5
74 Grafton Way E 6
67 Graham Rd. E 8
75 Graham St. C 13
78 Graham Terrace F 3
76 Granby St. D 6
74 Granby Terrace C 6
72 Grandstand Rd. H 3
70 Grange, The D 5
67 Grange Hill B 11
67 Grange Park Sta. A 7
80 Grange Rd. SE1 D 4
71 Grange Rd. SE25 D 7
76 Grange St. B 3
80 Grange Walk D 4
80 Grange Yard D 5
71 Grangewood D 7
75 Grantbridge St. B 12
73 Grantully Rd. D 2
74 Granville Place H 3
73 Granville Rd. C 1
75 Granville Square D 10
75 Grape St. G 8
76 Gravel La. E1 G 5
67 Gravel La., Abridge A 12
72 Gravesend G.C. C 6
79 Gray St. C 11
68 Grays H 6
75 Gray's Inn Gardens F 10
75 Grays Inn Rd. D 9
71 Grays Rd. H 11
69 Great Bookham Common H 6
67 Great Cambridge Rd. A 8
74 Great Castle St. G 5
74 Great Central St. F 2
74 Great Chapel St. G 7
70 Great Chertsey Rd. A 2
79 Great College St. D 8
74 Great Cumberland Place H 2
80 Great Dover St. D 2
76 Great Eastern St. E 4
79 Great George St. C 8
79 Great Guildford St. B 13
75 Great James St. F 10
74 Great Marlborough St. H 6
66 Great North Rd. A 5
66 Great North Way C 4
75 Great Ormond St. F 9
75 Great Percy St. C 10

MAP
79 Great Peter St. D 8
74 Great Portland St. F 5
74 Great Pulteney St. H 6
75 Great Queen St. G 9
57 Great Russell St. G 8
76 Great St. Helens G 4
79 Great Scotland Yd. B 8
79 Great Smith St. D 8
69 Great South West Rd. B 4
79 Great Suffolk St. C 13
75 Great Sutton St. E 12
76 Great Swan Alley G 3
70 Great Tattenhams H 3
74 Great Titchfield St. F 6
76 Great Tower St. J 4
68 Great Warley C 5
69 Great West Rd. A 5
76 Great Winchester St. G 3
74 Great Windmill St. H 7
68 Great Wood A 1
72 Great Wood G 6
72 Greatness H 2
76 Greatorex St. F 6
75 Greek St. H 7
65 Green, The G 5
72 Green Court E 1
67 Green Dragon La. A 7
80 Green Hundred Rd. H 7
71 Green La. SE9 C 11
70 Green La. SW16 D 6
69 Green La., Addlestone E 2
68 Green La., Goodmayes D 1
69 Green La., Hatton B 5
67 Green La., Ilford D 12
70 Green La., Morden E 4
65 Green La., Northwood B 4
69 Green La., Shepperton D 4
67 Green Lanes, N4 & N16 B 7, D 7
78 Green Park C 5
72 Green Rd. C 3
74 Green St. W1 H 3
72 Green St., Dartford C 3
67 Green St., Newham E 10
69 Green St., Sunbury D 4
72 Green Street Green, Dartford C 4
71 Green Street Green, Farnborough F 11
75 Green Terrace D 11
70 Green Wrythe La. E 5
73 Greenberry St. C 6
78 Greencoat Place E 6
78 Greencoat Row E 6
76 Greenfield Rd. G 7
65 Greenford F 6
66 Greenford Avenue F 1
65 Greenford Green E 6
65 Greenford Rd. F 6
65 Greenford Sta. E 6
66 Greenhill D 1
72 Greenhithe B 4
74 Greenwell St. E 5
67 Greenwich H 9
67 Greenwich High Rd. H 9
67 Greenwich Park H 9
67 Greenwich Reach G 9
67 Greenwich Sta. H 9
79 Greet St. B 11
73 Grendon St. E 6
77 Grenville Place E 3
75 Grenville St. E 9
78 Gresham St. G 2
74 Gresse St. G 7
75 Greville St. F 11
78 Greycoat Place E 7
78 Greycoat St. E 7
76 Greyeagle St. E 5
76 Grimsby St. E 6
73 Grittleton Rd. E 1
78 Groom Place D 4
78 Grosvenor Bridge H 5
78 Grosvenor Cres. C 4
78 Grosvenor Crescent Mews C 3
78 Grosvenor Gdns. D 5
74 Grosvenor Hill J 5
74 Grosvenor House Hotel J 3
80 Grosvenor Park J 1

MAP
78 Grosvenor Place D 4
78 Grosvenor Rd. H 6
74 Grosvenor Square H 4
74 Grosvenor St. H 5
80 Grosvenor Terrace H 1
73 Grove End Rd. C 4
71 Grove Park C 10
71 Grove Park Hospital C 10
67 Grove Rd. E2 F 8
67 Grove Rd. E18 C 10
70 Grove Rd., Mitcham D 5
67 Grove Rd., Romford D 12
67 Grovegreen Rd. D 9
68 Gubbins La. C 4
69 Guildford Rd. F 2
76 Guildhall G 2
78 Guildhouse St. F 6
75 Guilford St. E 9
79 Gundulf St. F 10
66 Gunnersbury G 3
66 Gunnersbury Ave. G 2
66 Gunnersbury Park G 2
77 Gunter Grove J 3
80 Guy St. C 3
80 Guy's Hospital C 2
79 Gye St. G 9
71 Gypsey Hill Sta. C 7
76 Haberdasher St. C 3
70 Hackbridge E 5
67 Hackney E 8
67 Hackney Downs E 8
67 Hackney Downs Sta. E 8
67 Hackney Marsh E 8
76 Hackney Rd. C 5
67 Hackney Wick E 9
68 Hacton La. E 4
80 Hadden Hall St. E 3
76 Haggerston Park B 6
76 Haggerston Rd. A 5
67 Hainault C 12
67 Hainault Estate B 12
68 Hainault Forest B 1
67 Hainault Rd., Chigwell B 11
67 Hainault Rd., Hainault C 12
76 Halcomb St. B 4
67 Hale End B 9
75 Half Moon Cres. B 10
78 Half Moon St. B 5
77 Halford Rd. H 1
68 Halfway Reach F 2
71 Halfway St. B 11
70 Haling Park Rd. F 6
78 Halkin Place D 3
78 Halkin St. D 4
73 Hall Gate D 4
67 Hall La. E4 B 9
68 Hall La., Upminster D 4
68 Hall La. D 6
73 Hall Place, W2 F 5
72 Hall Place, Bexley B 1
73 Hall Rd. NW8 D 4
71 Hall Rd., Eltham B 10
75 Hall St. C 12
68 Hall Wood, Brentwood B 6
72 Hall Wood, Fairseat G 6
74 Hallam St. F 5
73 Hallfield Estate G 3
69 Halliford Rd. D 4
78 Halsey St. E 2
72 Halstead G 1
70 Ham C 1
70 Ham Common C 2
70 Ham Cross C 2
70 Ham Gate C 2
70 Ham House B 1
73 Hamilton Close D 4
73 Hamilton Gdns. C 4
78 Hamilton Place B 4
73 Hamilton Terrace C 3
66 Hammersmith G 4
66 Hammersmith Bri. G 4
66 Hammersmith Rd. G 4
66 Hampden Way B 6
65 Hampermill La. A 5
66 Hampstead E 5
66 Hampstead Heath D 5
66 Hampstead Heath Sta. E 5
66 Hampstead La. D 5
66 Hampstead Ponds E 5

MAP
74 Hampstead Rd.... C 6
69 Hampton.... D 6
69 Hampton Court Bridge D 6
70 Hampton Court G.C. D 1
70 Hampton Court Palace D 1
70 Hampton Court Park D 1
69 Hampton Court Rd. D 6
69 Hampton Court Way E 6
69 Hampton Rd., Feltham C 5
69 Hampton Rd., Twickenham.... C 6
79 Hampton St.... F 13
70 Hampton Wick.... D 1
71 Hamsey Green.... G 8
76 Hanbury St.... F 5
75 Handel St.... E 8
69 Hangar Hill.... F 4
66 Hanger Hill.... F 2
66 Hanger La.... F 2
66 Hanger Lane Sta.... F 2
80 Hankey St.... D 3
79 Hanover Gdns.... H 10
74 Hanover Gate.... D 1
74 Hanover Square.... H 5
74 Hanover St.... H 5
74 Hanover Terrace.... D 2
74 Hanover Terrace Mews D 2
78 Hans Crescent.... D 2
78 Hans Place.... D 2
78 Hans Rd.... D 2
78 Hans St.... D 2
74 Hanson St.... F 6
74 Hanway Place.... G 7
74 Hanway St.... G 7
66 Hanwell.... G 1
69 Hanworth.... C 5
69 Hanworth Park.... C 5
69 Hanworth Rd., Hanworth.... C 5
69 Hanworth Rd., Hounslow.... B 6
73 Harbet Rd.... F 5
74 Harcourt St.... F 1
77 Harcourt Terrace.... G 3
69 Hardwick La.... E 2
75 Hardwick St.... D 11
69 Hare Hill.... F 2
70 Hare La.... F 1
68 Hare Street.... C 3
76 Hare Walk.... B 4
65 Harefield.... C 3
65 Harefield Hospital.... C 3
65 Harefield Place G.C. D 3
65 Harefield Rd.... B 3
74 Harewood Avenue.... E 1
68 Harewood Hall La. E 4
74 Harewood Place.... H 5
73 Harewood Row.... F 6
66 Harlesden.... E 3
66 Harlesden Sta.... F 3
77 Harley Gdns.... G 4
74 Harley Place.... G 4
74 Harley St.... F 4
79 Harleyford Rd.... H 9
79 Harleyford St.... H 11
65 Harlington.... H 4
65 Harlington Rd.... F 4
69 Harlington Road East B 5
65 Harmondsworth.... H 3
65 Harmondsworth La. H 3
79 Harmsworth St.... G 12
68 Harold Hill.... B 3
79 Harold Place.... G 10
68 Harold Wood.... C 4
80 Harper Rd.... D 2
75 Harper St.... F 9
67 Harringay Stadium D 7
67 Harringay Stadium Sta.... D 7
67 Harringay West Sta. D 7
77 Harrington Gdns.... F 3
77 Harrington Rd.... E 5
74 Harrington Square.... B 6
74 Harrington St.... C 6
75 Harrison St.... D 9
66 Harrow.... C 1
66 Harrow on the Hill D 1
66 Harrow on the Hill Sta. D 1
76 Harrow Place.... G 4
73 Harrow Rd. W9.... F 1
71 Harrow Rd., Chelsham G 8
66 Harrow Rd., Wembley E 2
66 Harrow School.... D 1
66 Harrow Weald.... C 1
66 Harrow & Wealdstone Sta.... C 1
74 Harrowby St.... G 2
76 Hart St.... H 4
72 Hartley.... E 5
72 Hartley Wood.... D 5
65 Hartsbourne G.C.... B 6
76 Harvey St.... A 3
65 Harvil Rd.... D 3
78 Hasker St.... E 2
67 Haslebury Rd.... B 7
65 Haste Hill G.C.... C 4
75 Hastings St.... D 8
65 Hatch End.... C 6
65 Hatch End Sta.... C 6
67 Hatch La.... B 9
69 Hatchord Park.... H 4
76 Hatfield St.... E 1
79 Hatfields.... B 12
73 Hatherley Grove.... G 2
69 Hatton.... B 4
69 Hatton Cross Sta.... B 4
75 Hatton Garden.... F 11
69 Hatton Rd.... B 4
73 Hatton St.... E 5
75 Hatton Wall.... F 11
75 Havelock St.... A 9
68 Havering.... D 3
68 Havering Park.... B 2
68 Havering Rd.... B 2
68 Havering-atte-Bower B 2
66 Haverstock Hill.... E 5
75 Haverstock St.... C 13
72 Hawley.... C 3
72 Hawley Rd.... C 3
71 Hawsted La.... F 12
74 Hay Hill.... J 5
70 Haydon's Rd. Sta.... C 4
65 Hayes.... G 4
71 Hayes, Bromley.... E 9
71 Hayes Common.... E 9
65 Hayes End.... F 4
71 Hayes La., Beckenham D 9
71 Hayes La., Bromley E 9
70 Hayes La., Coulsdon H 6
73 Hayes Place.... F 6
65 Hayes Rd.... G 5
65 Hayes & Harlington Sta.... G 4
79 Hayles St.... E 12
65 Hayling Rd.... B 5
74 Haymarket.... J 7
74 Haymarket Theatre J 7
80 Haymerle Rd.... H 6
75 Hayne St.... F 13
78 Hay's Mews.... A 4
75 Hayward's Place.... E 12
71 Hazel Wood.... G 11
75 H.Q.S. Wellington J 10
78 Headfort Place.... D 4
70 Headley Rd.... H 2
65 Headstone.... C 6
66 Headstone Drive.... C 6
65 Headstone La.... C 6
65 Headstone La. Sta. C 6
76 Hearn St.... E 4
72 Heath La.... C 2
68 Heath Park.... D 3
68 Heath Park Rd.... D 3
69 Heath Rd.... B 6
69 Heath Row.... F 3
68 Heath Way.... E 1
66 Heathbourn Rd.... B 1
75 Heathcote St.... D 9
69 Heathrow Airport London.... A 3
72 Heaverham.... H 4
74 Heddon St.... J 6
67 Hedge La.... B 7
68 Hedgemans Rd.... E 1
79 Heiron St.... H 13
75 Hemingford Rd.... A 10
76 Hemming St.... E 7
80 Hemp Row.... F 3
76 Hemsworth St.... B 4
77 Hemus Place.... G 6
66 Hendon.... C 4
66 Hendon Central Sta.... D 4
66 Hendon G.C.... C 4
66 Hendon Way.... D 4
66 Hendon Wood La. A 3
80 Hendre Rd.... F 4
76 Heneage.... F 6
76 Heneage La.... G 4
77 Henniker Mews.... H 4
74 Henrietta Place.... G 4
75 Henrietta St.... J 9
76 Henriques St.... H 7
80 H.M.S. *Belfast*.... B 4
75 H.M.S. *Chrysanthemum*.... J 11
75 H.M.S. *Discovery*.... J 10
75 H.M.S. *President*.... J 11
75 Herbal Hill.... E 11
75 Herbrand St.... E 8
79 Hercules Rd.... D 10
77 Hereford Square.... F 4
73 Hereford Rd.... G 1
76 Hereford St.... E 6
75 Hermes St.... C 10
75 Hermit St.... C 12
80 Hermitage Wall.... B 7
71 Herne Hill.... B 7
70 Herne Hill Sta.... B 6
79 Herrick St.... F 8
69 Hersham.... F 5
69 Hersham Rd.... E 5
69 Hersham Sta.... E 5
67 Hertford Rd.... A 8
78 Hertford St.... B 4
71 Heseirs Hill.... H 9
71 Heseirs Rd.... H 9
77 Hesper Mews.... F 2
65 Heston.... H 5
65 Heston Rd.... H 5
76 Hewett St.... E 4
71 Hewitts Rd.... F 12
72 Hextable.... D 2
79 Heyford Avenue.... J 9
80 Heygate St.... F 1
78 Hide Place.... F 7
66 High Barnet Sta.... A 4
75 High Holborn.... G 10
66 High Rd. N2.... C 5
67 High Rd. N17.... C 7
66 High Rd. N20.... A 5
66 High Rd. NW10.... E 3
69 High Rd., Byfleet.... G 3
67 High Rd., Chigwell B 11
72 High Rd., Dartford C 2
65 High Rd., Eastcote D 5
67 High Rd., Ilford.... D 12
67 High Rd., Leytonstone D 9
67 High Rd., Loughton A 10
71 High Rd., Orpington E 11
67 High Rd., Woodford Bridge.... C 10
67 High Rd., Woodford Green.... B 10
67 High St. E11.... D 10
67 High St. E15.... F 9
66 High St. N8.... C 6
67 High St. SE15.... H 8
70 High St. SE27.... C 6
70 High St. SW18.... B 4
70 High St., Merton, SW19.... D 4
70 High St. SW19.... C 4
68 High St., Aveley.... G 4
70 High St., Banstead.... G 4
71 High St., Beckenham D 8
71 High St., Bexley Heath A 12
65 High St., Bushey.... A 6
70 High St., Carshalton F 5
71 High St., Croydon.... E 7
70 High St., Epsom.... G 2
69 High St., Feltham.... C 4
65 High St., Harlington G 4
66 High St., Harrow.... C 1
68 High St., Hornchurch D 3
69 High St., Hounslow A 6
70 High St., New Malden D 3
67 High St., Ponders End A 8
65 High St., Rickmansworth.... A 3
69 High St., Shepperton E 4
71 High St., Sidcup.... C 12
69 High St., Stanwell.... B 3
70 High St., Sutton.... F 4
70 High St., Teddington C 1
69 High St., Walton.... E 4
65 High St., Watford.... A 5
71 High St., West Wickham.... E 8
70 High St., Colliers Wood.... C 5
67 High St. North.... E 10
67 High St. South.... F 11
67 Higham Hill.... C 8
67 Highams Park.... B 9
67 Highams Park, Hale End Sta.... B 9
67 Highbury.... E 7
67 Highbury & Islington Sta.... E 7
66 Highgate.... D 6
66 Highgate G.C.... D 5
66 Highgate Ponds.... D 5
66 Highgate Rd.... E 6
66 Highgate Sta.... D 6
66 Highgate Wood.... D 6
76 Highway, The.... J 7
66 Highwood Hill.... B 3
77 Hildyard Rd.... H 1
66 Hilfield La.... A 1
66 Hilfield Reservoir.... A 1
65 Hill End.... B 3
65 Hill End Rd.... C 3
73 Hill Rd.... C 4
78 Hill St.... A 4
80 Hillery Rd.... F 3
77 Hillgate Place.... B 2
77 Hillgate St.... B 2
65 Hillingdon.... E 4
65 Hillingdon G.C.... F 3
65 Hillingdon Heath.... F 4
65 Hillingdon Hill.... F 3
65 Hillingdon Rd.... E 3
65 Hillingdon Sta.... E 4
79 Hillingdon St.... H 13
67 Hillreach.... G 10
71 Hilly Fields.... B 8
78 Hilton Hotel.... B 4
70 Hinchley Wood.... E 1
74 Hinde St.... G 4
71 Hither Green.... B 9
78 Hobart Place.... D 4
77 Hobury St.... H 4
76 Hocker St.... D 5
68 Hoe La.... A 1
67 Hoe Street.... D 9
66 Hogarth House.... H 3
77 Hogarth Rd.... F 2
71 Hogtrough Hill.... H 11
78 Holbein Mews.... F 3
78 Holbein Place.... F 3
75 Holborn.... G 11
75 Holborn Circus.... G 11
75 Holborn Viaduct.... G 12
75 Holborn Viaduct Sta. G 12
68 Holden's Wood.... C 5
66 Holders Hill.... C 4
66 Holders Hill Rd.... C 4
75 Holford Gdns.... C 10
66 Holland Avenue.... G 4
66 Holland Rd.... G 4
77 Holland St.... C 1
74 Hollen St.... G 7
74 Holles St.... G 5
67 Hollow Pond.... D 9
66 Holloway Rd.... D 6
76 Holloway St.... G 6
72 Hollows Wood.... F 1
70 Holly La.... H 4
78 Hollywood Rd.... H 3
71 Holmwood Park.... F 10
79 Holyoake Rd.... F 12
80 Holyrood St.... B 4
76 Holywell La.... E 4
76 Holywell Row.... E 3
79 Home Office.... C 8
72 Home Rd.... C 2
74 Homer Row.... F 1
74 Homer St.... F 1
67 Homerton.... E 8
67 Homerton High St. E 8
67 Homerton Rd.... E 8
79 Hone Parade.... E 10
66 Honeypot La.... C 2
71 Honor Oak Park.... B 8
71 Honor Oak Park Sta. B 8
71 Honor Oak & Forest Hill G.C.... B 8
70 Hook.... E 2
72 Hook Green, Meopham.... E 6
72 Hook Green, Southfleet.... C 5
72 Hook Green.... E 6
72 Hook Green.... C 5
72 Hook Green Rd.... C 2
71 Hook La., Bexley Hth B 11
68 Hook La., Stapleford Abbotts.... A 2
70 Hook Rise.... E 2
70 Hook Rd., Chessington E 2
70 Hook Rd., Epsom.... G 2
70 Hook Rd., Horton F 2
71 Hookwood Rd.... G 12
76 Hooper St.... H 6
76 Hopetown St.... F 6
74 Hopkins St.... H 7
79 Hopton St.... A 12
76 Horatio St.... C 6
66 Horn La.... G 3
68 Hornchurch.... D 3
68 Hornchurch Marshes F 2
68 Hornchurch Rd.... D 3
68 Hornchurch Stadium E 4
71 Horns Green.... H 11
67 Horns Rd.... D 11
66 Hornsey.... D 6
66 Hornsey La.... D 6
66 Hornsey Rise.... D 6
66 Hornsey Rd.... D 6
77 Hornton Place.... C 2
77 Hornton St.... C 1
79 Horse Guards.... B 8
79 Horseferry Rd.... E 7
79 Horseguards Av.... B 8
80 Horselydown La.... B 5
66 Horsenden Hill.... E 1
80 Horsley St.... H 2
77 Hortensia Rd.... J 3
70 Horton, Ewell.... F 2
69 Horton, Staines.... A 1
70 Horton Hospital.... G 2
72 Horton Kirby.... D 3
70 Horton La.... G 2
69 Horton Rd., Horton A 1
69 Horton Rd., Stanwell B 2
75 Hosier La.... G 12
69 Hospital Bridge Rd. B 6
74 Hospital for Nervous Diseases.... G 4
75 Hospital for Sick Children.... E 9
73 Hospital of St. John C 5
79 Hotspur St.... F 10
75 Houghton St.... H 10
76 Houndsditch.... G 4
69 Hounslow.... A 6
69 Hounslow Central Sta. B 6
69 Hounslow East Sta. B 6
69 Hounslow Heath.... B 5
69 Hounslow Rd.... C 5
69 Hounslow Sta.... B 6
69 Hounslow West Sta. A 5
79 Houses of Parliament D 9
70 Howell Hill.... G 3
78 Howick Place.... E 6
74 Howland St.... F 6
73 Howley Place.... F 4
76 Hows St.... B 5
67 Hoxton.... E 7
76 Hoxton Square.... D 4
76 Hoxton St.... B 4
78 Hugh Mews.... F 5
78 Hugh St.... F 5
76 Hull St.... D 1
80 Humphrey St.... G 5
79 Hungerford Railway Bridge.... B 9
74 Huntley St.... E 7
65 Huntsmoor Park.... F 3
74 Huntsworth Mews.... E 2
76 Hunton St.... E 6
79 Hurlbutt Place.... F 13
70 Hurlingham House A 4
69 Hurst Rd., Molesey D 5
71 Hurst Rd., Sidcup B 12
66 Hyde, The.... C 3
78 Hyde Park Barracks C 3
78 Hyde Park Corner.... C 4
73 Hyde Park Cres.... H 6
73 Hyde Park Gdns.... H 5
73 Hyde Park Gdns. Mews.... H 5
77 Hyde Park Gate.... D 4
78 Hyde Park Hotel.... C 2
73 Hyde Park Square.... H 6
73 Hyde Park St.... H 6
76 Hyde Rd.... B 3
69 Hythe.... C 2
69 Hythe End.... C 1
65 Ickenham.... D 4
76 Idol La.... J 4
77 Ifield Rd.... H 3
72 Ightham.... H 5
73 Ilchester Gdns.... D 11
67 Ilford.... E 11
67 Ilford Football Club D 11
67 Ilford G.C.... D 11
67 Ilford La.... E 11
79 Iliffe St.... F 13
76 Imber St.... B 2
77 Imperial College.... D 5
77 Imperial College of Science.... D 5
65 Imperial Drive.... D 6
75 Imperial Hotel.... F 8
77 Imperial Institute.... D 5
77 Imperial Institute Rd. D 4
79 Imperial War Museum E 11
76 India St.... H 5
74 Ingestre Place.... H 6
75 Inglebert St.... C 11
68 Ingrave.... B 6
68 Ingrave Green.... B 6
74 Inner Circle.... D 3
77 International Hotel E 2
73 Inverness Place.... H 3
73 Inverness Terrace.... H 3
73 Inverness Terrace Gate J 3
80 Inville Rd.... G 3
76 Ironmonger La.... G 2
76 Ironmonger Row.... D 1
76 Ironmonger St.... D 2
76 Ironmonger's Hall.... F 1
75 Irving St.... J 8
79 Isabella St.... B 12
69 Island Barn Res.... E 6
67 Isle of Dogs.... G 9
70 Isleworth.... B 1
70 Isleworth Sta.... A 1
67 Islington.... E 7
75 Islington Green.... B 12
75 Islington High St.... B 12
79 Italian Walk.... G 9
65 Iver.... F 2
65 Iver Heath.... E 2
65 Iver La.... F 2
77 Iverna Court.... D 2
77 Iverna Gdns.... D 2
66 Iverson Rd.... E 4
78 Ives St.... E 1
74 Ivor Place.... E 2
76 Ivy St.... B 4
72 Ivyhouse La.... H 1
77 Ixworth Place.... F 6
71 Jackass La.... F 10
80 Jacob St.... C 6
71 Jail La.... G 10
80 Jamaica Rd.... D 6
75 James St. WC2.... H 9
74 James St. W1.... G 4
77 Jameson St.... B 2
80 Jardin St.... H 4
77 Jay Mews.... D 4
78 Jermyn St.... A 6
73 Jerome Crescent.... E 6
76 Jerome St.... F 5
69 Jersey Rd.... A 6
76 Jewry St.... H 5
79 Joan St.... B 12
75 Jockey's Fields.... F 10
65 Joel St.... C 5
75 John Adam St.... J 9
75 John Carpenter St. H 12

MAP
76 John Fisher St. . . . . J 6
79 John Islip St. . . . . . F 8
74 John Princess St. . . G 5
79 John Ruskin St. . . . J 13
75 John St. . . . . E 10
79 Jonathan St. . . . . . . F 9
75 John's Mews. . . . . E 10
72 Joyce Green Hosp. A 3
72 Joyce Green La. . . . A 3
72 Joyden's Wood. . . . C 1
67 Jubilee Park . . . . . . A 8
78 Jubilee Place. . . . . . G 1
75 Judd St. . . . . D 8
73 Junction Mews. . . . G 6
66 Junction Rd. . . . . . . D 6
77 Justice Walk. . . . . . H 6
79 Juxon St. . . . . E 10
67 Katherine Rd. . . . . E 10
76 Kay St. . . . . B 6
75 Kean St. . . . . H 9
75 Keeley St. . . . . G 9
77 Kelso Place. . . . . . . D 2
75 Kemble St. . . . . H 9
77 Kempsford Gdns. . G 2
79 Kempsford Rd. . . F 12
80 Kempshead Rd. . . . G 4
69 Kempton Park Race Course. . . . . C 5
72 Kemsing. . . . . H 3
73 Kendal Street. . . . . H 6
71 Kenley. . . . . H 7
79 Kennings Way . . . G 12
79 Kennington Grove H 10
79 Kennington La. . . G 10
79 Kennington Oval H 10
79 Kennington Park. H 11
79 Kennington Park Gdns. . . . . H 12
79 Kennington Park Place H 12
79 Kennington Park Rd. G 12
79 Kennington Rd. . . E 11
74 Kenrick Place. . . . . F 3
66 Kensal Green . . . . . F 4
66 Kensal Green Sta. . F 4
77 Kensington Church St. B 2
77 Kensington Court . C 3
77 Kensington Court Place . . . . D 3
77 Kensington Gdns. . B 3
73 Kensington Gardens Square. . . . . H 2
77 Kensington Gate . . D 3
77 Kensington Gore. . C 4
77 Kensington High St. D 1
77 Kensington Mall . . B 2
77 Kensington Palace. B 2
77 Kensington Palace Barracks . . . . C 2
77 Kensington Palace Gdns. . . . . B 2
77 Kensington Palace Green. . . . . C 2
73 Kensington Park Rd. J 1
77 Kensington Place . . B 2
77 Kensington Rd. . . . C 3
77 Kensington Square D 2
66 Kensington & Chelsea G 4
71 Kent House Sta. . . D 8
76 Kent St. . . . . B 5
74 Kent Terrace. . . . . D 2
66 Kentish Town. . . . . E 6
66 Kentish Town Sta. . E 6
66 Kenton . . . . D 2
66 Kenton La. . . . . C 2
66 Kenton Rd. . . . . . . C 2
75 Kenton St. . . . . E 8
77 Kenway Rd. . . . . . . F 2
66 Kenwood . . . . D 5
71 Keston. . . . . F 10
71 Keston Mark . . . . E 10
70 Kew. . . . . A 2
66 Kew Bridge . . . . . . G 2
70 Kew Bridge Rd. . . . A 2
66 Kew Bridge Sta. . . G 2
70 Kew Gardens Sta. . A 2
70 Kew Palace. . . . . . . A 2
70 Kew Rd. . . . . A 2
80 Keyse Rd. . . . . E 5
75 Keystone Crescent. C 9
79 Keyworth St. . . . . D 12
71 Kidbrooke. . . . . A 9
71 Kidbrooke Sta. . . A 10
66 Kilburn . . . . E 4
66 Kilburn High Rd. Sta. E 5
73 Kilburn Park Rd. . . D 1
66 Kilburn Sta. . . . . . . E 4
73 Kildare Terrace. . . G 2
75 Killick St. . . . . C 9
79 King Charles St. . . . C 8
75 King Edward St. . G 13
79 King Edward Walk D 11
67 King George V Dock G 11
69 King George VI Res. B 2
67 King George's Res. A 9
79 King James St. . . . D 12
76 King John's Court . E 4
76 King St. EC2 . . . . . G 2
78 King St. SW1 . . . . . B 6
75 King St. WC2 . . . . . H 8
66 King St. W6. . . . . . G 3
76 King William St. . . H 3
80 King & Queen St. . . F 2
69 Kingfieldgreen . . . . H 1
80 Kinglake St. . . . . . . G 4
74 Kingly St. . . . . H 6
76 King's Arms Yard . G 2
79 King's Bench St. . . C 12
75 King's Bench Walk H 11
75 King's College. . . H 10
75 King's Cross Rd. . D 10
75 King's Cross Sta. . . C 8
67 King's Head Hill . . A 9
80 King's Head Yard . B 3
75 King's Mews. . . . . F 10
80 King's Place. . . . . . D 1
78 King's Rd. SW1. . . E 4
77 King's Rd. SW3 . . G 6
67 King's Rd., Chingford B 9
78 King's Scholars' Passage . . . . E 6
74 King's Terrace. . . . B 6
66 Kingsbury. . . . . C 3
66 Kingsbury Green. . D 3
66 Kingsbury Rd. . . . . D 3
66 Kingsbury Sta. . . . D 2
72 Kingsdown . . . . F 4
65 Kingshill Avenue . . F 5
67 Kingsland . . . . E 7
76 Kingsland Rd. . . . . C 4
69 Kingsley Rd. . . . . . A 6
73 Kingsmill Terrace . B 5
70 Kingston Bridge . . D 1
70 Kingston Bypass . . D 3
70 Kingston Gate . . . . C 2
70 Kingston Hill . . . . . C 2
65 Kingston Lane . . . . F 3
70 Kingston Rd. SW15 B 3
70 Kingston Rd. SW20 D 4
70 Kingston Rd., Leatherhead . . . . H 1
70 Kingston Rd., New Malden . . . . D 2
69 Kingston Rd., Staines C 3
70 Kingston Rd., Teddington . . . . . C 1
70 Kingston Rd., Tolworth . . . . F 3
70 Kingston upon Thames D 2
70 Kingston Vale . . . . C 2
75 Kingsway . . . . G 9
70 Kingswood Sta. . . . H 4
78 Kinnerton St. . . . . . C 3
80 Kipling St. . . . . C 3
79 Kipton St. . . . . D 3
80 Kirby Grove. . . . . . . C 3
75 Kirby St. . . . . F 11
71 Kirkdale . . . . C 7
78 Kirtling St. . . . . J 6
79 Kirwyn Way . . . . . J 13
80 Kitson Rd. . . . . J 2
71 Kitto Rd. . . . . A 8
77 Knaresborough Place F 2
70 Knight's Hill. . . . . . C 6
69 Knights Res. . . . . . D 5
78 Knightsbridge. . . . . C 2
69 Knipp Hill . . . . G 5
70 Knivet Rd. . . . . J 1
71 Knockholt . . . . . . H 12
71 Knockholt Main Rd. H 11
71 Knockholt Pound G 12
71 Knockholt Rd. . . . G 12
71 Knockholt Sta. . . . F 12
69 Knowle Green . . . . C 2
74 Knox St. . . . . F 2
77 Kynance Mews. . . . E 3
77 Kynance Place . . . . D 3
76 Laburnum St. . . . . . B 5
76 Lackington St. . . . . F 3
66 Ladbroke Grove. . . F 4
80 Lafone St. . . . . C 5
69 Laleham . . . . D 3
69 Laleham Rd., Shepperton . . . . . D 3
69 Laleham Rd., Staines C 2
76 Lamb Passage. . . . . E 2
76 Lamb St. . . . . F 5
80 Lamb Walk . . . . C 4
70 Lambeth . . . . B 6
79 Lambeth Bridge. . . E 9
79 Lambeth High St. . . E 9
79 Lambeth Hospital F 12
79 Lambeth Palace . . . E 9
79 Lambeth Palace Rd. D 9
79 Lambeth Pier. . . . . E 9
79 Lambeth Rd. . . . . E 10
76 Lambeth St. . . . . . . H 6
79 Lambeth Walk . . . E 10
75 Lamb's Conduit. . . E 9
69 Lammas La. . . . . . . F 6
77 Lamont Rd. . . . . . . H 4
69 Lampton. . . . . A 6
69 Lampton Rd. . . . . . . A 6
73 Lanark Place . . . . . E 4
73 Lanark Rd. . . . . D 3
73 Lancaster Gate . . . J 4
73 Lancaster House . . C 6
73 Lancaster Mews . . H 4
75 Lancaster Place. . . . J 9
75 Lancaster St. . . . . C 12
73 Lancaster Terrace . H 5
78 Lancelot Place . . . . D 2
74 Lancing St. . . . . D 7
75 Land Registry Office G 10
70 Landor Rd. . . . . A 6
73 Langford Place. . . . B 4
73 Langham Place . . . G 5
74 Langham St. . . . . . . F 5
65 Langley. . . . . G 1
79 Langley La. . . . . H 9
71 Langley Park, Eden Park. . . . . E 9
65 Langley Park, Slough F 1
71 Langley Park G.C. . E 9
75 Langley St. . . . . H 8
70 Langley Vale . . . . . H 3
75 Langton Close . . . D 10
77 Langton St. . . . . J 4
73 Lanhill Rd. . . . . E 1
67 Lansdowne Rd. . . . C 8
79 Lant St. . . . . C 13
80 Larcom St. . . . . F 2
70 Latchmere Rd. . . . . A 5
71 Lathams Rd. . . . . . . F 9
80 Latona Rd. . . . . H 6
79 Laud St. . . . . G 9
73 Lauderdale Rd. . . . D 2
77 Launceston Place. . D 3
68 Launders La. . . . . . F 3
76 Laurence Pountney La. J 3
67 Lausanne Rd. . . . . H 8
70 Lavender Hill. . . . . B 5
77 Laverton Place . . . . F 2
79 Lavington St. . . . . B 13
75 Lavinia Grove . . . . B 9
75 Law St. . . . . D 3
79 Lawn La. . . . . H 9
70 Lawn Rd. . . . . H 1
66 Lawrence St. NW7. B 3
77 Lawrence St. SW3 . H 6
71 Layhams Rd. . . . . . G 9
75 Laystall St. . . . . . . E 10
70 Layton Rd. . . . . F 1
67 Lea Bridge . . . . D 8
67 Lea Bridge Rd. . . . D 8
67 Lea Bridge Sta. . . . D 8
67 Lea Valley Rd. . . . . A 9
76 Leadenhall Market H 3
76 Leadenhall St. . . . . H 4
79 Leake St. . . . . C 10
71 Leas Rd. . . . . H 8
75 Leather La. . . . . F 11
70 Leatherhead Bypass H 1
70 Leatherhead Common H 1
70 Leatherhead G.C. G 1
70 Leatherhead Rd., Chessington. . . . . F 1
70 Leatherhead Rd., Leatherhead . . . . H 1
80 Leathermarket St. C 3
71 Leaves Green . . . . G 10
71 Leaves Green Rd. . F 10
71 Ledgers Rd. . . . . . . H 8
71 Lee . . . . B 9
71 Lee High Rd. . . . . . B 9
71 Lee Rd. . . . . A 9
75 Leeke St. . . . . C 9
74 Lees Place . . . . H 3
71 Leesons Rd. . . . . . D 11
75 Leicester Square . . . J 7
80 Leigh Hunt St. . . . . C 1
70 Leigham Court Rd. C 6
73 Leinster Gdns. . . . . H 3
73 Leinster Mews . . . . J 4
73 Leinster Rd. . . . . . . C 1
73 Leinster Square . . . H 2
73 Leinster Ter. . . . . . J 3
76 Leman St. . . . . H 6
78 Lennox Gdns. . . . . . E 2
78 Lennox Gardens Mews E 2
76 Leonard St. . . . . E 3
79 Leopold Walk . . . . G 9
80 Leroy St. . . . . E 4
68 Lessness Heath . . . G 2
76 Lever St. . . . . D 1
71 Lewisham . . . . B 8
71 Lewisham High St. . B 9
71 Lewisham Rd. . . . . A 9
79 Lewisham St. . . . . . C 7
77 Lexham Gdns. . . . . E 2
77 Lexham Mews . . . . E 1
74 Lexington St. . . . . . H 6
67 Ley St. . . . . D 11
76 Leyden St. . . . . G 5
67 Leyton. . . . . D 9
67 Leyton High Rd. . . D 9
67 Leyton Marshes. . . D 8
67 Leyton Midland Road Sta. . . . . D 9
67 Leytonstone High Rd. Sta. . . . . D 9
67 Leytonstone Rd. . . E 9
69 Liberty La. . . . . F 2
79 Library St. . . . . . . D 12
74 Lidlington Place. . . C 6
76 Ligonier St. . . . . . . D 5
73 Lilestone St. . . . . . E 6
66 Lillie Rd. . . . . H 4
78 Lillington Gardens Estate . . . . F 7
76 Lime St. . . . . H 4
67 Limehouse. . . . . F 9
67 Limehouse Reach . G 9
73 Limerston St. . . . . . H 4
71 Limpsfield Rd. . . . . G 7
67 Lincoln Rd. . . . . . . A 7
78 Lincoln St. . . . . F 2
75 Lincoln's Inn . . . . G 10
75 Lincoln's Inn Fields G 10
73 Linden Gdns. . . . . . . J 1
75 Lindsey St. . . . . . . F 13
74 Linhope St. . . . . E 2
80 Linsey St. . . . . E 6
76 Linton St. . . . . B 2
74 Lisle St. . . . . H 7
73 Lisson Green Estate E 6
73 Lisson Grove . . . . . E 6
73 Lisson St. . . . . F 6
74 Little Albany St. . . . D 5
77 Little Boltons, The. G 3
75 Little Britain. . . . . G 13
65 Little Bushey La. . . A 6
78 Little Chester St. . . D 4
74 Little Edward St. . . C 5
66 Little Ealing. . . . . . G 2
68 Little Gaynes La. . . E 4
79 Little George St. . . C 8
65 Little Green La. . . . A 4
74 Little Marlborough St. H 6
75 Little New St. . . . . G 11
65 Little Oxhey La. . . . B 5
74 Little Portland St. . G 6
75 Little Russell St. . . G 8
78 Little St. James's St. B 6
76 Little Trinity La. . . H 2
70 Little Woodcote . . G 5
70 Little Woodmansterne La. . . . . G 5
69 Littleton . . . . D 3
69 Littleton La. . . . . . . D 3
80 Liverpool Grove . . G 2
75 Liverpool Rd. . . . . B 11
76 Liverpool St. . . . . . G 3
76 Liverpool Street Sta. F 4
74 Livonia St. . . . . H 6
76 Lizard St. . . . . D 2
80 Llewellyn St. . . . . . . C 6
75 Lloyd Baker St. . D 10
75 Lloyd Square . . . . D 10
75 Lloyd St. . . . . C 11
76 Lloyd's Avenue . . . H 4
76 Lloyd's Buildings . H 3
75 Lloyd's Row. . . . . D 12
71 Loampit Hill . . . . . A 8
69 Lock La. . . . . H 3
66 Locket Rd. . . . . C 1
71 Locksbottom . . . . E 10
67 Lockwood Res. . . . . C 8
67 Lodge Avenue . . . E 12
71 Lodge La. . . . . F 9
73 Lodge Rd. . . . . D 5
80 Loftie St. . . . . C 7
77 Logan Mews . . . . . . E 1
77 Logan Place . . . . . . E 1
77 Lolesworth St. . . . . G 5
79 Lollard Place. . . . . F 11
79 Lollard St. . . . . F 10
79 Loman St. . . . . C 13
75 Lombard La. . . . . H 11
76 Lombard St. . . . . . . H 3
80 London Bridge. . . . A 3
80 London Bridge Station B 3
80 London Bridge St. . B 3
74 London Clinic . . . . E 4
74 London College of Music . . . . H 6
79 London College of Printing. . . . . . . E 12
67 London Fields Sta. . E 8
74 London Planetarium E 3
79 London Rd. SE1 . D 12
71 London Rd. SE23 . B 7
68 London Rd., Aveley G 4
72 London Rd., Badger's Mount . . . . G 1
65 London Rd., Batchworth . . . . . B 3
70 London Rd., Croydon E 6
72 London Rd., Dunton Green . . . . H 1
67 London Rd., Enfield A 7
70 London Rd., Hackbridge. . . . . E 5
70 London Rd., Kingston D 2
70 London Rd., Mitcham D 5
70 London Rd., Morden D 4
70 London Rd., Norbury D 6
68 London Rd., Romford D 2
68 London Rd., Shenfield A 6
69 London Rd., Staines C 3
66 London Rd., Stanmore B 2
72 London Rd., Swanscombe. . . . B 4
68 London Rd., W. Thurrock . . . H 5
75 London School of Economics . . . . H 10
70 London School of Hygiene. . . . . F 7
70 London Scottish G.C. C 3
76 London St. EC3 . . H 4
73 London St. W2. . . . G 5
69 London St., Chertsey E 2
68 London Tilbury Rd. G 4, G 5
76 London Wall . . . . . . G 3
75 London Weather Centre. . . . . G 10
75 Long Acre . . . . H 8
70 Long Ditton . . . . . . E 1
65 Long Elmes. . . . . . . C 6
70 Long Grove Hospital F 2
70 Long Grove Rd. . . . F 2
75 Long La. EC1. . . . . F 13
80 Long La. SE1 . . . . . C 3
71 Long La., Bexley Heath. . . . . A 12
71 Long La., Croydon D 8
69 Long La., Staines. . B 3
65 Long La., Uxbridge E 4
77 Long Ridge Rd. . . . F 1
76 Long St. . . . . C 5
80 Long Walk . . . . D 4
77 Long Water, The. . B 5
75 Long Yard . . . . E 9
67 Longbridge Rd. . . E 11
80 Longcroft Rd. . . . . H 4
70 Longdown Road North G 3
72 Longfield. . . . . D 5
72 Longfield Hill. . . . . D 6
72 Longfield Rd. . . . . . D 5
65 Longford . . . . H 3
74 Longford St. . . . . . . E 5
71 Longlands. . . . . . . C 11
67 Longleigh La. . . . . H 12
80 Longley St. . . . . F 6
66 Longmore Avenue. A 5
78 Longmore St. . . . . . F 6
67 Longwood Gdns. . C 11
73 Lord Hills Bridge. . G 2
73 Lord Hills Rd. . . . . F 2
79 Lord North St. . . . . E 8
73 Lord's Cricket Ground D 5
67 Lordship La. N17. . C 7
71 Lordship La. SE22. B 7
67 Lordship Rd. . . . . . . D 7
75 Lorenzo St. . . . . . C 10
79 Lorrimore Rd. . . . H 13
79 Lorrimore Square H 13
76 Lothbury. . . . . G 3
73 Loudon Rd. . . . . . . B 4
65 Loudwater La. . . . . A 3
79 Loughborough St. G 10
70 Loughborough Junc. Sta. . . . . A 6
67 Loughton . . . . A 11
67 Loughton Way. . . . A 10
76 Lovat La. . . . . J 3
76 Love La. EC2. . . . . G 2
70 Love La., Morden . E 4
80 Lovegrove St. . . . . G 7
71 Lower Addiscombe Rd. . . . . E 7
70 Lower Ashtead . . . H 1
68 Lower Bedford Rd. C 2
78 Lower Belgrave St. . E 4
67 Lower Clapton Rd. E 8
67 Lower Edmonton. . B 8
69 Lower Feltham . . . C 4
69 Lower Green . . . . . E 6
69 Lower Green Rd. . . E 6
78 Lower Grosvenor Place . . . . D 5
79 Lower Marsh. . . . C 11
70 Lower Morden La. . E 4
70 Lower Mortlake Rd. B 2
70 Lower Richmond Rd. A 3
67 Lower Rd. . . . . G 8
78 Lower Sloane St. . . . F 3
69 Lower Sunbury Rd. D 5
71 Lower Sydenham. . C 8
71 Lower Sydenham Sta. C 8
76 Lower Thames St. . . J 3
72 Lowfield St. . . . . . . B 3
66 Lowlands Rd. . . . . . D 1
78 Lowndes Place. . . . D 3
78 Lowndes Square . . D 3
78 Lowndes St. . . . . . . D 3
77 Lucan Place . . . . . . F 6
80 Lucey Rd. . . . . E 6
75 Ludgate Circus . . H 12
75 Ludgate Hill. . . . . H 12
76 Luke St. . . . . E 3
72 Lullingstone Castle F 2
72 Lullingstone Park. . F 1
74 Lumley St. . . . . H 4
71 Lunghurst Rd. . . . . H 8
78 Lupus St. . . . . G 6
79 Luscombe Way. . . . . J 8
71 Lusted La. . . . . . . H 10
73 Luton St. . . . . E 5
74 Luxborough St. . . . F 3
71 Luxted Rd. . . . . . . G 10

MAP
78 Lyall St..........E 3
80 Lydney Close .....J 4
80 Lynton Rd.......F 6
73 Lyons Place ......E 5
80 Lytham St........G 2
66 Lyttelton Rd......C 5
75 Mabledon Place..D 8
75 Macclesfield Rd..D 13
73 Mackennal St. ....B 6
75 Macklin St........G 9
80 Macks Rd.........E 6
74 Mackworth St.....C 6
80 Macleod St........G 2
65 Mad Bess Wood ..C 4
74 Madame Tussaud's E 3
74 Maddox St........H 5
80 Madron St........F 4
80 Magdalen St. ....B 4
79 Magee St.........H 11
80 Maguire St........C 5
73 Maida Avenue ....F 4
73 Maida Vale.......D 3
75 Maiden La........J 9
71 Maidstone Rd....C 12
71 Main Rd., Biggin Hill
               H 10
71 Main Rd., Sidcup.C 11
72 Main Rd., Sutton-at-
     Hone..........D 3
78 Makins St.........F 1
73 Malden ....E 3
70 Malden Manor Sta.E 3
70 Malden Rd., Cheam
               F 4
70 Malden Rd., New
     Malden........D 3
70 Malden Rushett...G 1
70 Malden Way......E 3
74 Malet Place.......E 7
74 Malet St..........E 7
78 Mall, The.........B 7
77 Mallord St........H 5
73 Mallory St........E 6
76 Mallow St.........E 2
80 Malt St..........H 6
75 Malta St.........D 12
80 Maltby St.........D 5
73 Malvern Mews....D 1
73 Malvern Rd........D 1
67 Manchester Rd....G 9
74 Manchester Square G 4
74 Manchester St....G 3
80 Manciple St.......D 3
74 Mandeville Place ..G 4
75 Manette St........H 7
80 Mann St..........G 3
71 Manor Avenue....A 8
70 Manor Hospital...G 2
67 Manor Park ......E 11
79 Manor Place......G 13
67 Manor Rd. N16...D 7
67 Manor Rd.,
     Buckhurst Hill..A 10
68 Manor Rd., Hainault
               B 1
70 Manor Rd., Mitcham
               D 5
70 Manor Rd.,
     Wallington .....F 5
67 Manor Rd., Woodford
     Bridge ......B 11
70 Manor Rd. North .E 1
77 Manresa Rd. .....G 6
76 Mansell St........H 5
67 Mansfield Hill ...B 9
74 Mansfield St......F 5
76 Mansfield St......C 7
71 Mansion, The....B 12
76 Mansion House...H 2
76 Mansion House Place
               H 2
77 Manson Place....F 4
75 Mantell St........B 11
72 Maplescombe.....F 3
70 Marble Hill Park ..B 1
75 Marchmont Ter...E 8
80 Marcia Rd........F 4
74 Margaret St.......G 6
77 Margaretta Ter...H 6
75 Margery St. .....D 11
76 Mark La..........H 4
76 Mark St..........E 3
78 Market Mews.....B 4
74 Market Place.....G 6
78 Markham Square..G 2
78 Markham St......G 2
67 Markhouse Rd....D 9
68 Marks Gate .....C 1
68 Marks Gate Rd...C 1

MAP
76 Marlborough Av..A 6
73 Marlborough Gate .J 5
80 Marlborough Grove
               G 6
78 Marlborough House
               B 7
73 Marlborough Hill .B 4
73 Marlborough Pl...B 4
78 Marlborough Rd..B 6
77 Marlborough St...F 6
74 Marle St.........F 6
77 Marloes Rd.......E 2
70 Marlpit La.......H 6
66 Marsh La., Highwood
     Hill............B 3
66 Marsh La., Stanmore
               B 2
65 Marsh Rd. ......C 5
67 Marsh Side ......B 8
74 Marshall St.......H 6
80 Marshalsea Rd....C 2
79 Marsham St.......E 8
76 Marsland Rd......G 13
75 Mart St..........H 9
74 Martin La........H 3
69 Martindale Rd.....B 5
78 Marriet Walk.....D 2
74 Martin Way.......D 4
76 Mary St..........A 2
74 Mary Terrace.....B 5
62 Maryland Sta......E 9
73 Marylands Rd.....E 1
66 Marylebone.......F 6
73 Marylebone Flyover
               F 5
74 Marylebone High St.
               F 4
74 Marylebone La....G 4
74 Marylebone Mews.G 4
74 Marylebone Rd...F 2
74 Marylebone Sta...E 2
74 Marylebone St....F 4
74 Mascalls La.......B 5
80 Mason St.........E 3
71 Masons Hill ......D 9
80 Massinger St......F 4
79 Mathew Parker St..D 8
75 Matilda St.......A 10
74 Maunsel St.......E 7
80 Mawbey Place....G 6
69 Maybury..........H 1
78 Mayesbrook Park E 12
66 Mayfair..........G 6
78 Mayfair Hotel ....A 5
78 Mayfair Place.....B 5
75 Maygood St......B 10
68 Mayney Rd.......C 2
71 Maypole Rd......F 12
66 Mays La..........A 4
67 Maze Hill Sta....H 9
76 Mead Row ....D 11
79 Meadcroft Rd.....H 12
79 Meadow Rd......J 9
80 Meadow Row.....E 1
74 Meard St........H 7
75 Mecklenburg Place E 9
75 Mecklenburg Sq...E 9
75 Medical College of
     St. Bartholomew's
               E 13
78 Medway St........E 7
75 Melbourne Pl....H 10
74 Melbury Terrace ..E 2
74 Melcombe Place..E 2
74 Melcombe St......E 2
74 Melfort Rd.......D 6
73 Melina Place ....D 4
80 Melior St........C 3
74 Menshaw St......E 2
72 Meopham.........E 6
72 Meopham Green ..E 6
72 Meopham Sta....D 6
79 Mepham St.......B 10
75 Mercer St. ......H 8
76 Mercers Hall ....H 2
76 Merchant Taylor's
     Hall..........H 3
75 Meredith St.....D 12
75 Merlin St.......D 11
80 Mermaid Court ...C 2
75 Mermaid Theatre H 12
80 Merrick Square ..D 2
80 Merrow St........G 3
76 Merry Hill.......B 6
65 Merryhill Rd......A 6
70 Merton Park Sta. .D 4
70 Merton Rd., SW18 B 4
70 Merton Rd., SW19 C 4
79 Methley St.......G 11

MAP
78 Metropolitan Police
     H.Q............D 7
69 Metropolitan Police
     Training School .E 6
79 Metropolitan
     Tabernacle ....E 12
79 Meymott St.......B 12
80 Micawber St. .....C 1
77 Micklethwaite Rd..H 1
75 Middle St.........F 13
75 Middle Temple La.
               H 11
74 Middlesex Hosp...F 6
76 Middlesex St......G 5
71 Midfield Way....D 12
75 Midland Rd.......C 8
76 Milborne Grove...G 4
69 Milbourne La.....F 6
72 Mildmay Forest...G 1
76 Mildmay Miss. Hosp.
               D 5
67 Mile End Rd. .....F 8
69 Miles La.........G 5
79 Miles Street ......H 8
75 Milford La. .....H 10
76 Milk St. ....G 2
66 Mill Hill ....B 3
66 Mill Hill (Broadway)
     Sta............B 3
66 Mill Hill East Sta..C 4
66 Mill Hill G.C.....A 3
69 Mill La., Chertsey .D 2
68 Mill La., Dagenham
               G 4
76 Mill Row.........B 4
80 Mill St. SE1......C 6
74 Mill St. W1......H 5
79 Millbank.........E 8
79 Millbank Barracks.F 8
74 Miller St.........B 5
68 Millers La. ......B 12
75 Millman St. .....E 10
67 Millwall..........G 9
67 Millwall Dock....G 9
67 Millwall F.C......H 8
77 Milmans St.......J 5
78 Milner St.........E 2
69 Milton Park ......C 1
76 Milton St.........F 2
80 Milverton St......G 11
80 Mina Rd. ....G 4
74 Mincing La.......H 4
76 Minerva Mews....E 4
80 Minnow St........F 4
76 Minories.........H 5
80 Mint St..........C 1
76 Mintern St.......B 3
70 Mitcham.........D 5
70 Mitcham Common D 5
70 Mitcham G.C.....D 5
70 Mitcham Junc. Sta.D 5
70 Mitcham La.......C 5
70 Mitcham Rd. SW17
               C 5
70 Mitcham Rd., Croydon
               E 6
70 Mitcham Sta......D 5
76 Mitchell St.......D 1
71 Mitchley Av......G 7
71 Mitchley Hill.....G 7
76 Mitre Rd. ....C 11
76 Mitre St..........H 4
66 Moat Mount .....A 3
80 Molesey Rd.......E 5
74 Molyneux St......G 2
79 Monck St........E 7
78 Monkton St. .....E 11
73 Monmouth Rd....H 2
75 Monmouth St.....H 8
80 Monnow Rd.......F 6
80 Montagu Close...B 2
74 Montagu Mansions F 3
74 Montagu Mews North
               F 2
74 Montagu Mews South
               G 2
74 Montagu Mews West
               G 2
74 Montagu Place....G 2
74 Montagu Row.....F 3
74 Montagu Square ..G 2
74 Montagu St.......G 3
75 Montague Place ..F 8
67 Montague Rd.....B 8
75 Montague St......F 8
76 Montclare St......D 5
79 Montford Place ..G 11
77 Montpelier Place..D 6
77 Montpelier Square.D 6

MAP
77 Montpelier St.....D 6
77 Montpelier Walk ..D 6
66 Montrose Avenue .C 3
78 Montrose Place ...D 4
76 Monument St......J 3
76 Moor La. EC2....F 2
66 Moor La., Hornchurch
               C 5
65 Moor La.,
     Rickmansworth .B 3
70 Moor La., Surbiton F 2
65 Moor Park G.C....B 4
65 Moor Park Sta. ...B 4
78 Moore St.........E 2
76 Moorfields ....F 2
76 Moorfields Eye Hosp.
               D 2
65 Moorfields Rd. ...D 3
76 Moorgate ....G 2
73 Moorhouse Rd....G 1
76 Mora Place.......D 2
72 Morants Ct. Rd. ..H 1
70 Morden...........E 4
70 Morden G.C.......E 4
70 Morden Hall Rd...D 4
70 Morden Park .....E 4
70 Morden Rd........D 4
70 Morden Road Halt
               D 4
70 Morden South Sta. D 4
70 Morden Sta.......D 4
80 Morecambe St.....F 2
75 Moreland St. ....D 13
78 Moreton Place....G 6
78 Moreton St. ......G 6
78 Moreton Terrace ..G 6
80 Morgan's La.......B 4
71 Morland Rd.......E 7
79 Morley St. ......D 11
74 Mornington Cres. .C 6
74 Mornington Place .B 5
74 Mornington St.....B 5
74 Mornington Ter...B 5
80 Morocco St........C 4
78 Morpeth Ter......E 6
73 Morshead Rd.....D 2
74 Mortimer St.......G 6
70 Mortlake.........B 2
70 Mortlake Rd.......A 2
74 Morwell St........G 7
73 Moscow Rd.......J 2
78 Mossop St........E 1
78 Mostyn Rd........D 4
70 Motcomb St.......D 3
76 Motspur Park ....D 3
71 Mottingham......C 10
71 Mottingham Rd. .C 10
75 Mount Pleasant, WC1
               E 10
65 Mount Pleasant,
     Southall.......F 6
74 Mount Row ....J 4
74 Mount Royal Hotel
               H 3
72 Mount Rd.........B 4
74 Mount St.........J 4
65 Mount Vernon
     Hospital.......B 4
74 Moxon St.........F 3
76 Mulberry St.......G 6
77 Mulberry Walk ...H 5
70 Mulgrave Rd......F 4
74 Munster Square...D 5
80 Munton Rd.......E 2
75 Muriel St........B 10
79 Murphy St........D 11
76 Murray Grove.....C 2
75 Museum of London
               F 13
75 Museum St. ......G 8
66 Muswell Hill......C 6
66 Muswell Hill G.C..C 6
66 Muswell Hill Park Rd.
               C 6
75 Myddleton Passage
               C 11
75 Myddleton Square
               C 11
75 Myddleton St. ...D 11
68 Nags Head La.....C 4
67 Nags Head Rd. ..A 8
76 Napier Grove.....B 2
71 Nash.............F 9
72 Nash Street.......D 6
74 Nassau St.........F 6
74 National Dental
     Hospital.......F 5
73 National Film Theatre
               B 10

MAP
79 National Gallery ..A 8
74 National Heart
     Hospital........F 4
77 National History
     Museum ......E 5
75 National Hospital .E 9
67 National Maritime
     Museum.......H 9
79 National Theatre
               B 10
76 Navarre St........D 5
68 Navestock Common
               A 3
75 Neal St..........H 8
66 Neasden..........E 3
66 Neasden Sta.......E 3
80 Neate St.........H 4
80 Neckinger........D 5
66 Nelson Gdns......C 7
75 Nelson Place.....C 12
69 Nelson Rd.........B 6
76 Nelson Square ...C 12
75 Nelson Terrace ...C 12
79 Nelson's Column ..A 8
66 Nether St.........C 4
66 Netherland Rd.....A 5
77 Netherton Grove..H 4
74 Netley St.........D 6
77 Nevern Place.....F 1
77 Nevern Square....F 1
77 Neville St.........F 5
71 New Addington ...F 9
72 New Barn ....D 5
71 New Barn La.,
     Cudham......H 11
72 New Barn La.,
     Swanley Village .D 2
71 New Beckenham ..C 8
71 New Beckenham Sta.
               C 8
74 New Bond St......H 5
75 New Bridge St....H 12
76 New Broad St.....G 3
74 New Burlington St.
               H 6
74 New Cavendish St.
               F 5
76 New Change .....H 1
67 New Charlton ...G 10
80 New Church Rd...J 2
75 New Compton St..H 8
67 New Cross Gate Sta.
               H 8
67 New Cross Rd. ...H 8
67 New Cross Stadium
               H 8
67 New Cross Sta. ...H 9
72 New Cut..........H 1
65 New Denham .....E 3
71 New Eltham .....C 10
75 New Fetter La. ..G 11
69 New Haw ....F 3
69 New Haw Rd. ....F 3
76 New Inn St. ......E 4
76 New Inn Yard ....E 4
80 New Kent Rd.....E 2
70 New King's Rd....A 4
70 New Malden .....D 3
70 New Malden G.C..D 3
76 New North Place ..E 4
76 New North Rd. N1 B 2
67 New North Rd.,
     Hainault ......B 12
75 New North St.....F 9
75 New Oxford St....G 8
79 New Palace Yard..C 8
74 New Quebec St...H 3
78 New Ride ....C 2
67 New Rd. E4......B 9
65 New Rd., Croxley
     Green........A 4
68 New Rd., Dagenham
               F 2
69 New Rd., Littleton D 4
69 New Rd., W. Molesey
               D 6
75 New Row ....J 8
66 New Southgate....B 6
66 New Southgate &
     Friern Barnet Sta.
               B 6
75 New Square .....G 10
76 New St...........G 4
75 New Wharf Rd....B 9
71 New Years La.....G 11
69 Newark La. ......H 2
74 Newburgh St......H 8
79 Newburn St.......G 10
67 Newbury Park ...D 11

MAP
75 Newbury St.......F 13
73 Newcastle Place ..F 5
77 Newcombe St......B 2
80 Newcomen St.....C 2
73 Newcourt St......C 6
80 Newent Close.....J 4
80 Newgate St.......G 13
67 Newham ....F 10
67 Newham Way....F 10
80 Newhams Row ....F 4
79 Newington Butts .F 12
79 Newington Causeway
               D 13
79 Newington Cres. .F 12
74 Newman Passage..G 7
74 Newman St. ......G 6
75 Newport Place....H 8
79 Newport St. .....F 10
70 Newton Green....B 3
73 Newton Rd.......G 2
75 Newton St........G 9
75 Nicholas La.......H 3
79 Nicholson St......B 12
70 Nightingale La. ..B 5
67 Nightingale Rd.,
     Edmonton.....A 8
70 Nightingale Rd.,
     Wallington ....E 5
76 Nile St..........C 2
80 Nile Terrace......G 5
66 Nine Elms La. ....J 7
68 Noak Hill.........B 3
68 Noak Hill Rd......B 3
76 Noble St.........G 1
65 Nockhill Wood ...C 2
67 Noel Park ....C 7
75 Noel Rd.........B 12
70 Noel St..........G 6
70 Nonsuch Park....F 3
76 Norah St.........D 7
70 Norbiton.........D 2
70 Norbiton Sta......D 2
70 Norbury ....D 6
70 Norbury Cres.....D 6
70 Norbury Hill .....D 6
73 Norfolk Cres......G 6
73 Norfolk Place.....G 5
79 Norfolk Row ....E 10
76 Norfolk Rd........A 5
73 Norfolk Square...G 5
76 Norman St. ......D 1
66 North Acton Sta..B 3
74 North Audley St. .H 3
73 North Bank ......D 6
66 North Circular Rd. N3
               C 5
66 North Circular Rd.
     NW2..........D 3
66 North Circular Rd.
     NW10 ....E 2
67 North Circular Rd.,
     Wood Green....B 7
71 North Cray......C 12
72 North Cray Rd....C 1
74 North Crescent....F 7
75 North Down St....C 9
70 North Cheam ....E 4
66 North Ealing Sta..F 2
71 North End, Croydon
               E 7
72 North End, Erith .A 2
71 North End La....F 10
66 North End Rd., NW11
               D 5
66 North End Rd., W14
               G 4
66 North End Way...D 5
66 North Finchley....B 5
74 North Gower St...D 6
65 North Harrow Sta. D 6
66 North Hill........D 6
70 North Hyde.......G 5
65 North Hyde La....H 5
75 North Mews.....E 10
66 North Middlesex G.C.
               B 5
67 North Middlesex
     Hospital.......B 7
68 North Ockendon ..E 5
65 North Orbital Rd. .C 2
76 North Place ......E 6
73 North Ride ....J 4
66 North Rd. N6.....D 6
68 North Rd., Purfleet G 4
68 North Rd., Romford
               B 2
74 North Row.......H 3
70 North Sheen Sta..B 2
68 North St..........C 2

MAP

70 North Sugden Rd. ..E 1
76 North Tenter St. ..H 5
77 North Terrace ....E 6
65 North View ....D 5
66 North Wembley Sta. E 2
74 North West Poly...A 5
66 North Western Av. A 1
73 North Wharf Rd...G 5
67 North Woolwich .G 11
67 North Woolwich Rd. G 10
75 Northampton Rd. E 11
75 Northampton Sq. D 12
70 Northborough Rd. D 6
75 Northburgh St....E 12
66 Northfields Av. ...G 2
66 Northfields Sta....G 2
72 Northfleet.......B 6
75 Northington St. ..F 10
65 Northolt ....E 5
65 Northolt Aerodrome E 4
65 Northolt Park.....E 6
65 Northolt Park Sta. E 6
65 Northolt Rd.......E 6
71 Northover Rd.....C 9
76 Northport St......B 3
76 Northumberland Alley H 4
79 Northumberland Av. B 8
72 Northumberland Heath..........A 1
67 Northumberland Park Sta.............C 8
73 Northumberland Place G 1
79 Northumberland St. A 8
73 Northwick Close ..E 5
66 Northwick Park Hospital ....D 1
66 Northwick Park Sta. D 1
73 Northwick Terrace E 4
65 Northwood.......B 4
65 Northwood G.C...C 4
65 Northwood Hills Sta. C 5
65 Northwood Rd....C 3
76 Norton Folgate...F 4
76 Norwich Rd. .....A 6
75 Norwich St. .....G 11
71 Norwood.........C 7
65 Norwood Green...G 6
71 Norwood Junc. Sta. D 7
70 Norwood Rd. SE27 C 6
65 Norwood Rd.,Southall G 5
66 Notting Hill .....F 4
77 Notting Hill Gate..A 1
74 Nottingham Place F 3
74 Nottingham St....F 3
74 Nottingham Ter....E 3
73 Nugent Terrace ..C 4
71 Nunhead.........A 8
71 Nunhead La. .....A 7
80 Nursery Row .....F 2
74 Nutford Place ...G 2
76 Nuttall St........B 4
69 Oak Avenue......C 5
73 Oak Tree Rd......D 5
79 Oakden St. ......E 11
70 Oaken La.........F 1
65 Oakend Wood ....C 1
72 Oakfield La.......C 2
73 Oakington Rd.....E 1
66 Oakleigh Park ...A 5
66 Oakleigh Park South B 5
66 Oakleigh Park Sta. A 5
75 Oakley Crescent..C 12
77 Oakley Gdns......H 6
80 Oakley Place .....G 5
74 Oakley Square ...B 6
77 Oakley St........H 6
67 Oakwood Hill ...A 11
66 Oakwood Park....A 6
66 Oakwood Sta.....A 6
79 Oar St..........B 13
76 Oat La..........G 1
69 Oatlands Av......F 4
69 Oatlands Chase ..E 4
69 Oatlands Drive....E 4
69 Oatlands Park ....E 4
79 Occupation Rd. ..G 13
68 Ockendon Rd......E 5

MAP

69 Ockham Common H 4
69 Ockham La......H 3
69 Ockham Park.....H 3
80 Odell St.........G 5
79 Offley Rd.......J 11
74 Ogle St..........F 6
67 Okehampton Cres. H 12
75 Old Bailey.......G 12
74 Old Bond St......J 6
76 Old Broad St......G 3
77 Old Brompton Rd. F 3
74 Old Burlington St. .J 6
76 Old Castle St......G 5
74 Old Cavendish St. .G 5
67 Old Church Rd. E4 B 9
68 Old Church Rd., Romford.......D 2
74 Old Church St....G 5
74 Old Compton St...H 7
70 Old Coulsdon ....H 6
74 Old Court Place ...C 2
70 Old Deer Park ....A 1
71 Old Farleigh Rd. ..G 8
67 Old Ford Rd......E 8
75 Old Gloucester St. F 9
80 Old Jamaica Rd...D 6
76 Old Jewry ....G 2
80 Old Kent Rd......F 4
69 Old La..........H 4
73 Old Marylebone Rd. G 6
76 Old Montague St. .F 6
76 Old Nichol St. ...E 5
79 Old Paradise St. ..E 10
78 Old Park La. .....B 4
78 Old Pye St. ......D 7
76 Old Quebec St....H 3
79 Old Queen St. ....C 7
65 Old Redding......B 6
72 Old Rd..........B 1
67 Old Royal Observatory H 9
75 Old Seacoal La...G 12
76 Old St..........D 3
80 Old Vic Theatre ..C 11
69 Old Woking Rd. ..G 2
74 Oldbury St.......F 4
65 Oldfield La......F 6
70 Oldfield Rd.......E 4
80 Olmar St........H 6
80 Olney Rd........H 1
66 Olympia ....G 4
80 Omeara St........B 2
77 Ongar Rd.......H 1
77 Onslow Gdns.....F 4
77 Onslow Square ...F 5
74 Ontario St........D 13
79 Opal St.........F 12
74 Open Air Theatre..D 3
74 Orange St........J 7
77 Oratory, The.....E 6
80 Orb St..........F 2
74 Orchard St. .....H 3
73 Orchardson St....E 5
75 Orde Hall St. .....F 9
73 Ordnance Hill....B 5
67 Orient Football Club D 9
79 Orient St. ......E 12
73 Orme Court.......J 2
73 Orme La.........J 2
73 Orme Square......J 2
78 Orme Square Gate.J 2
78 Ormond Yard ....A 6
78 Ormonde Gate ..G 2
80 Ormsby St.......B 5
71 Orpington ....E 12
71 Orpington Bypass, Orpington.....E 12
71 Orpington Bypass, St. Paul's Cray .D 12
71 Orpington Rd....D 11
73 Orsett Mews......G 3
79 Orsett St........F 10
73 Orsett Terrace ...G 3
76 Orsman Rd.......A 4
76 Osborn St........G 6
74 Osidge La. ......A 6
74 Osnaburgh St....E 5
73 Ossington St.....J 2
73 Ossory Rd.......H 6
74 Ossulston St. ....C 7
77 Osten Mews.....E 3
70 Osterley........A 1
66 Osterley La......G 1
65 Osterley Park ...G 6
66 Osterley Park Ho. .A 6
79 Oswin St.......E 12

MAP

72 Otford..........H 2
72 Otford La. ......G 1
69 Ottershaw ....F 2
79 Otto St..........H 12
70 Ottways La......H 1
74 Outer Circle B 2, D 2, C 4
75 Outram St.......A 9
70 Outwood La......H 4
79 Oval Cricket Ground, The ....H 10
74 Oval Rd.........A 4
79 Oval Way........G 10
66 Ovenden Rd.....H 12
78 Ovington Gdns...D 1
78 Ovington Square .E 2
78 Ovington St......E 2
74 Oxendon St. .....J 7
75 Oxford Circus ...G 5
65 Oxford Rd.......D 1
73 Oxford Square ...H 6
74 Oxford St.......G 6
65 Oxhey ....A 5
65 Oxhey Drive .....B 5
65 Oxhey La. .. A 5, B 6
71 Oxlea Wood .....A 11
69 Oxshott........G 6
69 Oyster La.......G 3
75 Packington St....A 13
66 Paddington ......F 5
73 Paddington General Hospital......F 1
73 Paddington Green.F 5
73 Paddington Recreation Ground.......C 2
73 Paddington Sta...G 4
73 Paddington St.....F 3
68 Padnall Corner...C 1
79 Page St.........E 7
80 Page's Walk .....A 4
67 Painters Rd......C 12
75 Pakenham St.....D 10
77 Palace Court......J 2
77 Palace Gate .....D 3
77 Palace Gardens Mews B 2
77 Palace Green .....B 2
75 Palace Hotel.....H 9
71 Palace Parade....C 7
70 Palace Rd.......B 6
78 Palace St.......D 6
80 Palace Theatre ...H 8
76 Palissy St.......D 5
78 Pall Mall........B 7
78 Pall Mall East ...A 7
74 Palladium Theatre H 6
78 Palmer St.......D 7
76 Palmer's Green...B 6
67 Palmers Green, Southgate Sta. ..C 7
67 Palmerston Rd...B 10
70 Pampisford Rd....F 6
76 Pancras La.......H 2
76 Pancras Rd......B 7
74 Panton St........J 7
78 Parade, The......J 3
78 Paradise Walk ...H 2
70 Parchmore Rd. ...D 6
80 Pardoner St.....D 3
76 Parfett St.......G 7
79 Paris Garden ....B 12
67 Park Avenue......A 7
74 Park Crescent ...E 5
74 Park Crescent Mews East ....E 5
74 Park Crescent Mews West..........E 4
68 Park Farm Rd.....E 4
71 Park Hill Rd. ....B 12
71 Park Hospital....B 9
78 Park La. W1.....B 4
70 Park La., Ashtead .H 2
67 Park La., Tottenham C 8
78 Park Lane Hotel..B 5
78 Park Place......B 6
73 Park Place Villas..F 4
73 Park Rd. NW1 ...D 1
70 Park Rd., Banstead G 4
71 Park Rd., Ficklesole G 9
69 Park Rd., Stanwell. B 3
70 Park Rd., Teddington C 1
69 Park Rd., Twickenham C 6
66 Park Royal......F 2
66 Park Royal Sta. ..F 2

MAP

70 Park Side ....C 3
74 Park Square East..E 5
74 Park Square West..E 4
80 Park St. SE1.....B 2
74 Park St. W1 .....J 3
74 Park Village East ..B 5
74 Park Village West .B 5
77 Park Walk ....H 4
73 Park West Place...G 6
65 Park Wood.......C 4
75 Parker St........G 9
80 Parker's Row ....C 6
75 Parkfield St......B 11
72 Parkfield Wood ..E 4
80 Parkhouse St.....J 3
71 Parklangley .....D 9
74 Parkway ....A 5
65 Parkway, The....G 5
66 Parliament Hill...E 5
79 Parliament Square. C 8
79 Parliament St....C 8
76 Parr St.........B 2
75 Parry St........H 9
68 Parsloes Avenue..E 1
68 Parsloes Park ....E 1
66 Parson St.......C 4
69 Parvis Rd........G 3
79 Pascal St........J 8
79 Pasley Rd........G 13
78 Passmore Terrace..F 3
75 Patent Office.....G 11
77 Pater St.........D 1
75 Paternoster Square G 13
76 Paton St........D 1
76 Paul St.........E 3
77 Paulton's Square .H 5
75 Paultons St......H 5
73 Paveley St.......D 6
78 Pavilion Rd.....D 2
68 Pea La.........E 5
78 Peabody Avenue .G 5
76 Peace St.........E 7
79 Peacock St......F 13
75 Pear Tree Court..E 11
75 Pear Tree St.....D 13
79 Pearman St......D 11
71 Pears Rd. ....A 6
79 Pearson St......B 5
71 Peckham........A 7
80 Peckham Hill St...J 6
80 Peckham Park Rd. .J 6
71 Peckham Rd......A 7
71 Peckham Rye ....B 7
71 Peckham Rye Common B 7
71 Peckham Rye Park.B 7
71 Peckham Rye Sta..A 7
76 Pedley St.......E 6
77 Peel St.........B 2
76 Peerless St......D 2
77 Pelham Crescent..F 6
77 Pelham Place ....F 5
77 Pelham St.......E 5
80 Pelier St........H 1
73 Pembridge Gdns...J 1
73 Pembridge Place ..H 1
73 Pembridge Rd....J 1
73 Pembridge Square.J 1
73 Pembridge Villas..H 1
78 Pembroke Close..C 4
77 Pembroke Place..D 1
77 Pembroke Rd. W8 .E 1
65 Pembroke Rd., Ruislip D 4
77 Pembroke Square. E 1
77 Pembroke Villas..E 1
70 Pen Ponds......B 2
73 Penfold Place ...F 5
73 Penfold St. ......E 5
71 Penge..........C 7
71 Penge East Sta...C 8
71 Penge West Sta...C 7
71 Penhill Rd.......B 12
76 Penn St.........A 3
80 Pennack Rd......H 5
77 Pennant Mews...E 2
76 Pennington St....J 7
79 Penrose Grove...G 13
79 Penrose St.......G 13
74 Penryn St.......B 7
79 Penton Place ....G 13
75 Penton Rise .....C 10
75 Penton St........B 10
75 Pentonville Rd...C 10
77 Penywern Rd.....F 2
80 Pepler Rd.......G 5
70 Pepys Rd........D 3
76 Pepys St.........H 4

MAP

75 Percival St......D 12
75 Percy Circus.....C 10
73 Percy Rd. NW6...C 1
69 Percy Rd.,Hampton C 6
69 Percy Rd., Twick...B 6
74 Percy St.........G 7
66 Perivale........E 2
78 Perkins Rents....D 7
71 Perry Hill ....C 8
71 Perry St.........C 11
77 Peter Pan Statue ..A 5
74 Peter St.........H 7
75 Peters La. ......F 12
70 Petersham......B 2
77 Petersham La. ...D 3
77 Petersham Mews ..E 4
77 Petersham Place ..D 4
74 Peto Place ......E 5
76 Petticoat Square .G 5
71 Petts Wood......D 11
71 Petts Wood Rd. ..D 11
78 Petty France.....D 6
78 Petyward ....F 1
80 Phelp St.........H 2
77 Philbeach Gdns...F 1
67 Philip La. ....C 7
77 Phillimore Gdns..D 1
77 Phillimore Place ..D 1
77 Phillimore Walk ..D 1
76 Phillipp St.......B 4
76 Philpot La.......H 3
76 Phipp St.........E 4
75 Phoenix Place...E 10
76 Phoenix Rd......C 7
75 Phoenix St.......H 8
78 Piccadilly.......B 5
74 Piccadilly Circus..J 7
74 Piccadilly Hotel ..J 6
74 Piccadilly Theatre..J 7
76 Pickard St.......C 13
71 Pickford La......A 12
71 Pickhurst La. ....E 9
74 Picton Place.....G 4
68 Pike La.........E 5
75 Pilgrim St. ......H 12
80 Pilgrimage St.....D 2
68 Pilgrims Hatch ..A 5
71 Pilgrims Way, Knockholt ...H 12
72 Pilgrims Way, Otford H 2
78 Pimlico Garden ..H 7
78 Pimlico Rd......F 4
76 Pinchin St.......H 6
74 Pindar St.......F 4
73 Pindock Mews...E 3
75 Pine St. ....E 11
66 Pinkham Way ...C 6
65 Pinner ....C 5
65 Pinner Green ....C 5
65 Pinner Hill G.C...C 5
65 Pinner Hill Rd. ...C 5
65 Pinner Rd.......D 6
76 Pitfield St.......C 3
77 Pitt St..........C 1
78 Pitts Head Mews..B 4
75 Plaistow.......F 10
71 Plaistow La......D 10
67 Plaistow Sta.....F 10
73 Platt...........H 5
74 Platt St.........B 7
74 Plender Place ....B 6
74 Plender St.......B 6
69 Plough La.......H 5
76 Plough Yard.....E 4
77 Plum Tree Court .G 12
76 Plumbers Row....G 6
67 Plumstead.......G 11
67 Plumstead Common H 11
67 Plumstead Common Rd. ....H 11
67 Plumstead High St.G 12
67 Plumstead Marshes G 12
67 Plumstead Rd....G 11
67 Plumstead Sta....G 11
73 Plympton St.....E 6
79 Pocock St. ......C 12
69 Pointers Rd......H 4
72 Pol Hill ....G 1
74 Poland St.......H 6
66 Police College....C 3
80 Pollard Row......D 7
74 Polygon Rd......C 7
74 Polytechnic of London F 3
67 Pomeroy St......H 8
77 Pond Place ......F 6

MAP

75 Ponders End......A 8
79 Ponsonby Place ...F 9
79 Ponsonby Terrace .F 8
78 Pont St..........E 2
76 Poole St.........B 2
80 Pope St.........D 4
67 Poplar..........F 9
67 Poplar High St. ..F 9
73 Poplar Place ....J 2
73 Porchester Gdns...H 3
73 Porchester Place ..H 6
73 Porchester Rd.....G 2
73 Porchester Square.G 3
73 Porchester Square Mews..........G 3
73 Porchester Terrace H 3
73 Porchester Terrace Gate..........J 3
73 Porchester Terrace North.........G 3
80 Porlock St........C 3
68 Porters Avenue...E 1
73 Porteus Rd.......F 4
71 Portland Rd. .....D 7
80 Portland St.......G 3
74 Portman Close...G 3
74 Portman Hotel....G 3
74 Portman Mews South H 3
74 Portman Square...G 3
74 Portman St.......H 3
69 Portmore Park Rd. E 3
70 Portnalls Rd......H 5
72 Portpool La......F 11
74 Portsea Place ....H 2
69 Portsmouth Rd., Esher F 6
70 Portsmouth Rd., Thames Ditton ..E 1
69 Portsmouth Rd., Wisley.........H 3
75 Portsmouth St....G 10
76 Portsoken St......H 6
75 Portugal St......H 10
74 Post Office Tower..F 6
74 Potier St.........E 3
65 Potter St........C 5
80 Potter's Fields ...B 4
76 Potterstreet Hill ..B 5
76 Poultrey.......H 2
71 Pound La.......G 12
79 Poverest Rd......D 11
69 Powdermill La....B 5
76 Pownall Rd......A 6
74 Poyle ....A 2
70 Poynders Rd......B 6
73 Praed St.........G 5
74 Pratt Mews......A 6
74 Pratt St.........A 6
79 Pratt Walk ......E 10
71 Pratt's Bottom ..F 12
76 Prebend St......A 1
76 Prescot St.......H 6
66 Preston ....D 2
66 Preston Rd......D 2
66 Preston Rd. Sta. ..D 2
65 Prestwick Rd.....B 5
79 Price's St. ......B 12
75 Prideaux Place...D 10
74 Prima Rd........J 11
66 Primrose Hill ....E 5
66 Primrose Hill Sta..E 5
76 Primrose St.......F 4
74 Prince Albert Rd..B 2
75 Prince Charles Theatre H 7
77 Prince Consort Rd.D 4
77 Prince of Wales Gate C 6
74 Prince of Wales Theatre ....J 7
67 Prince Regents La.F 10
76 Princelet St.......F 5
70 Princes Coverts ...G 1
77 Prince's Gdns....D 5
77 Prince's Gate ....C 5
77 Prince's Gate Mews D 5
72 Princes Mews....H 2
72 Princes Rd. .....B 2
73 Princes Square...H 2
71 Princes St........G 2
77 Princess Beatrice Hospital.......G 2
72 Princess Rd......C 1
75 Princeton St.....F 10
80 Prioress St.......E 3
74 Priory La.......B 3
66 Priory Rd.......C 6
77 Priory Walk......G 4

MAP
76 Pritchards Rd. ....B 7
80 Priter Rd.........D 6
75 Procter St........F 9
75 Provence St. .....B 13
76 Provost St. ......C 2
69 Pryford Rd. ......G 2
75 Public Record Office
G 11
75 Public Trustee Office G 9
76 Pudding La. EC3 . .J 3
67 Pudding La., Chigwell
A 12
75 Puddle Dock ....H 12
72 Puddledock La....C 1
80 Purbrook St......D 4
76 Purcell St........B 4
74 Purchese Rd. ....C 7
68 Purfleet.........G 4
68 Purfleet Bypass...G 4
68 Purfleet Rd. .....G 4
70 Purley ....G 6
71 Purley Downs ....G 7
71 Purley Downs G.C.G 7
71 Purley Downs Rd. .G 7
71 Purley Oaks Sta. ..F 7
80 Purley Rd........J 7
70 Purley Way.......E 6
70 Putney...........B 3
70 Putney Bridge....A 4
70 Putney Bridge Rd..B 4
70 Putney Heath.....B 3
70 Putney High St...B 4
70 Putney Hill......B 4
70 Putney Sta.......B 4
69 Pyrcroft ....E 2
69 Pyrford ....H 2
69 Pyrford Common Rd.
H 2
68 Pyrgo Park ......B 3
76 Quaker St........E 5
79 Queen Alexandra
Military Hospital F 8
74 Queen Anne Mews G 5
74 Queen Anne St. ..G 4
78 Queen Anne's Gate D 7
77 Queen Elizabeth
College ....C 1
79 Queen Elizabeth Hall
B 10
70 Queen Elizabeth
Hospital ....H 4
80 Queen Elizabeth St. E 5
69 Queen Elizabeth II Res.
E 5
69 Queen Mary Res...D 3
74 Queen Mary's Gardens
D 3
71 Queen Mary's Hospital
C 12
70 Queen Mary's Hospital
for Children.....F 5
75 Queen Square.....F 9
76 Queen St. EC4 ....H 2
78 Queen St. W1.....B 5
78 Queen Victoria
Memorial ......C 6
75 Queen Victoria St. H 13
74 Queen's College...G 4
73 Queen's Gdns.....H 4
77 Queen's Gate.....D 4
77 Queen's Gate Gdns.E 4
77 Queen's Gate Mews D 4
77 Queen's Gate Place E 4
77 Queen's Gate Place
Mews.........E 4
77 Queen's Gate Ter..E 4
73 Queen's Grove....A 5
75 Queen's Head St. .A 12
73 Queen's Mews....H 2
66 Queen's Park Rangers
F.C...........G 4
66 Queen's Park Sta...F 4
67 Queen's Rd. SE15 .H 8
70 Queen's Rd.,
Richmond......B 2
70 Queens Rd.,
Teddington....C 1
69 Queens Rd.,
Weybridge......F 4
67 Queen's Rd.,
Peckham Sta....H 8
70 Queen's Rd. Sta...A 5
80 Queen's Row.....H 2
73 Queen's Terrace ..B 5
74 Queen's Theatre ..H 7
66 Queen's Wood....D 6
77 Queensberry Way .E 5
73 Queensborough Ter.
H 3

MAP
76 Queensbridge Rd. .B 6
66 Queensbury.......C 2
77 Queensbury Place .E 4
70 Queensmere Rd. . .C 4
78 Queenstown Rd...J 4
73 Queensway ......H 3
75 Quick St.........C 12
80 Quilp St.........C 2
76 Quilter St........C 6
77 Racton Rd.......H 1
77 Radley Mews .....E 2
73 Radnor Mews ....H 5
73 Radnor Place.....H 6
80 Radnor Rd.......J 6
76 Radnor St........D 2
79 Radnor Terrace ...J 9
78 Radnor Walk.....G 2
71 Rag Hill........H 10
80 Railway Approach.B 3
76 Railway Place....H 4
75 Railway St.......C 9
80 Rainbow St.......J 4
68 Rainham.........F 3
68 Rainham Marshes .F 3
68 Rainham Rd......E 2
73 Rainsford St.......G 6
75 Raleigh St. ......B 13
80 Ralph St.........D 2
74 Ramillies Place...H 6
74 Ramillies St......H 6
78 Rampayne St. ....G 7
76 Ramsey St........D 6
79 Randall Road....F 9
79 Randall Row .....F 9
70 Randalls Rd......H 1
73 Randolph Avenue .D 3
73 Randolph Crescent E 3
73 Randolph Gdns....C 2
73 Randolph Mews..E 4
73 Randolph Rd.....E 4
73 Ranelagh Bridge..G 3
78 Ranelagh Gardens .G 4
78 Ranelagh Grove...F 4
67 Rangers Rd......A 10
73 Ranston St.......F 6
73 Raphael St.......C 2
74 Rathbone Place ..G 7
74 Rathbone St. .....G 7
71 Ravensbourne Sta.D 9
66 Ravenscourt Park G 3
66 Ravenscourt Pk. Sta.
G 4
76 Ravenscroft St. ...C 5
79 Ravensdon St. ...G 11
76 Ravey St.........E 4
78 Rawlings St.......F 2
75 Rawstorne St. ...D 12
76 Ray St...........E 11
65 Rayners La.......D 6
70 Raynes Park......D 3
70 Raynes Park Sta...D 3
76 Rector St.........A 1
69 Rectory La., Byfleet G 3
67 Rectory La., Loughton
A 11
70 Rectory La., Mitcham
C 5
70 Rectory La., Sutton
G 5
67 Rectory Rd. Sta....E 8
70 Red La..........F 1
80 Red Lion Row ....H 2
75 Red Lion Square ..F 9
75 Red Lion St. .....F 10
71 Red Lodge Rd. ...E 9
74 Red Place........H 3
73 Redan Place......H 2
67 Redbridge.......C 12
67 Redbridge La. ...D 10
67 Redbridge Sta....D 10
78 Redburn St.......G 2
74 Redchurch St.....E 5
77 Redcliffe Gdns....G 3
77 Redcliffe Mews ..G 3
77 Redcliffe Place...H 3
77 Redcliffe Rd......G 4
77 Redcliffe Square .G 2
77 Redcliffe St......H 3
80 Redcross Way ....C 2
78 Redesdale St......G 2
77 Redfield La......E 2
69 Redhill Rd.......G 4
74 Redhill St........C 5
80 Redmead La......B 8
77 Reece Mews .....F 4
68 Reede Rd........E 2
79 Reedworth St.....F 11
76 Rees St..........A 2
74 Reeves Mews .....J 4

MAP
74 Regal La. ....A 4
76 Regan Way......C 4
78 Regency St........E 7
74 Regent Palace Hotel
J 6
75 Regent Square....D 9
74 Regent St........H 6
74 Regent's Park.....C 3
74 Regent's Park
Barracks......C 5
66 Regent's Park Rd. N3
C 4
74 Regent's Park Rd.
NW1 ....A 4
76 Regents Row .....A 6
70 Reigate Avenue ..E 4
70 Reigate Rd. ......G 3
75 Remington St.....C 12
75 Remnant St.......G 9
79 Renfrew Rd......F 12
79 Rennie St. ......A 12
80 Rephidim St. .....D 3
77 Reston Place .....D 3
80 Reveroy Rd......F 6
78 Rex Place ....A 4
75 Rheidol Terrace ..B 13
78 Richard's Place ..E 1
65 Richings Park ....G 2
70 Richmond........B 2
70 Richmond Bridge .B 1
70 Richmond Gate...B 2
70 Richmond G.C....C 2
74 Richmond Mews..H 7
70 Richmond Park...B 2
70 Richmond Park Public
G.C...........B 3
70 Richmond Rd.....C 2
79 Richmond Terrace C 8
77 Rickett St. ....H 1
71 Ricketts Hill Rd. .H 10
65 Rickmansworth ...A 3
65 Rickmansworth Rd.,
Croxley Green . .A 4
65 Rickmansworth Rd..
Harefield......C 3
70 Riddlesdown Rd...G 6
71 Riddlesdown Sta. .G 7
67 Ridge Avenue.....A 7
70 Ridge Rd........E 4
72 Ridge Wood.....F 6
74 Ridgmount Gdns. .F 7
74 Ridgmount St. ...F 7
67 Ridgeway ....B 9
70 Ridgway ....C 3
70 Riding House St. ..G 6
80 Riley Rd........D 4
77 Riley St.........J 5
73 Ring, The........H 4
69 Ripley..........H 3
68 Ripple Rd........E 1
69 Rita Rd.........J 9
75 Ritchie St.......B 11
78 Ritz Hotel. ......B 6
75 Riverbank St. ....C 11
79 Riverwalk Gdns...G 8
76 Rivington St......D 4
74 Robert Adam St...G 3
74 Robert Mews.....D 6
74 Robert St........D 5
74 Roberta St.......D 6
70 Robin Hood Gate .C 3
70 Robin Hood Way .C 3
78 Rochester Row....E 6
78 Rochester St......E 7
71 Rochester Way, SE9
A 10
72 Rochester Way, Bexley
B 1
75 Rockcliffe St......C 12
80 Rockingham St....E 1
67 Roding La. E18 ...C 10
67 Roding La., Buckhurst
Hill...........B 11
67 Roding Lane South
C 10
67 Roding Valley ...B 10
74 Rodmarton St.....G 3
80 Rodney Place.....E 2
80 Rodney Rd.......F 2
75 Rodney St. ......B 10
70 Roehampton......B 3
70 Roehampton Gate .B 3
70 Roehampton G.C..B 3
70 Roehampton Vale .C 3
75 Roger St.........E 10
77 Roland Gdns. ....G 4
77 Roland Way......G 4
80 Rolls Rd.........F 5
72 Roman Villa Rd...C 3

MAP
68 Romford.........D 2
68 Romford G.C.....C 3
68 Romford Rd., Aveley
F 4
68 Romford Rd.,
Chadwell Heath D 1
68 Romford Rd.,
Chigwell Row...B 1
67 Romford Rd., Ilford
D 11
67 Romford Rd.,
Stratford......E 10
75 Romilly St.......H 7
79 Romney St. SW1...E 8
72 Romney Street, Kent
G 3
76 Rood La.........H 4
74 Roosevelt Memorial
H 4
76 Ropemaker St.....F 2
77 Rosary Gdns.....F 4
80 Rose Alley ....A 1
74 Rose Hill........E 4
68 Rose La.........C 1
75 Rosebery Avenue.E 11
78 Rosemoor St......F 2
71 Rosendale Rd.....B 7
75 Rosoman St......D 11
74 Rossmore Rd.....E 1
79 Rotary St........D 12
67 Rotherhithe .....G 8
67 Rotherhithe New Rd.
G 8
67 Rotherhithe St....G 8
80 Rothsay St.......D 3
80 Rotten Row ......C 2
80 Rouel Rd.........E 6
77 Round Pond......B 3
70 Roundshaw......F 6
67 Roundway, The...C 7
79 Roupell St.......B 11
74 Rousebarn La.....A 4
69 Row Hill........F 2
69 Row Town ......F 2
70 Rowan Rd........D 6
80 Rowcross St. .....G 5
76 Rowland St......F 7
66 Rowley Bank.....A 3
66 Rowley La........A 3
66 Roxeth..........D 1
66 Roxeth Green Av..D 6
74 Royal Academy of
Arts...........J 6
74 Royal Academy of
Music.........E 4
66 R.A.F. Museum...C 3
67 Royal Albert Dock
G 11
77 Royal Albert Hall .C 4
79 Royal Army Medical
College........F 8
78 Royal Automobile
Club..........B 7
78 Royal Avenue ....G 2
70 Royal Botanical
Gardens.......A 2
77 Royal Cancer Hospital
F 5
77 Royal College of Art
D 5
77 Royal College of Music
D 5
74 Royal College of
Physicians.....E 5
77 Royal College of
Science........D 5
75 Royal College of
Surgeons......G 10
74 Royal College St. .B 7
75 Royal Courts of
Justice........H 10
74 Royal Ear Hospital
E 7
76 Royal Exchange ..H 3
79 Royal Eye Hospital
D 12
79 Royal Festival Hall
B 10
75 Royal Free Hospital,
N1 ....A 11
75 Royal Free Hospital,
WC1 ....D 10
77 Royal Geographical
Society........C 5
78 Royal Horticultural
Society Hall ...E 7
78 Royal Hospital ...G 3
78 Royal Hospital Rd. G 3

MAP
74 Royal Institute of
British Architects F 5
73 Royal Lancaster Hotel
H 5
78 Royal Mews, The. .D 5
67 Royal Military
Academy......H 11
69 Royal Military School
of Music.......B 6
76 Royal Mint......J 5
76 Royal Mint St.....J 5
67 Royal Naval College
G 9
75 Royal Opera House
H 9
79 Royal Rd........H 12
74 Royal Society ....J 6
79 Royal St.........D 10
74 Royal Veterinary
College ....A 7
67 Royal Victoria Dock
G 10
79 Royal Waterloo
Hospital ......B 10
70 Royal Wimbledon
G.C...........C 3
74 Royle St.........H 6
65 Royston Park ....B 6
67 Ruckholt Rd......E 9
73 Rudolf Rd.......C 2
76 Rufus St.........D 4
70 Rugby Union Football
Ground.......B 1
65 Ruislip..........D 4
65 Ruislip Common ..C 4
65 Ruislip Gardens Sta.E 5
65 Ruislip G.C......D 4
65 Ruislip Lido......C 4
65 Ruislip Manor Sta. D 5
65 Ruislip Rd.......F 6
80 Runham St.......G 3
74 Rupert St........H 7
68 Rush Green ......D 2
68 Rush Green Rd....D 2
70 Rushett La.......G 1
71 Rushey Green....B 8
71 Rushmore Hill Rd.
G 12
76 Rushton St.......B 3
79 Rushworth St.....C 12
71 Ruskin Park......B 7
75 Russell Hotel ....E 8
66 Russell La........B 5
75 Russell Square ...F 8
75 Russell St. ....H 9
80 Rust Square ......J 2
78 Rutherford St.....E 7
77 Rutland Gdns.....C 6
77 Rutland Gate.....C 6
77 Rutland Mews ...D 6
77 Rutland St.......D 6
79 Rutley Close .....H 12
69 Ruxbury Rd......E 2
70 Ruxley La........F 2
78 Rydens Rd.......E 5
78 Ryder St.........B 6
73 Ryders Terrace...B 3
71 Rye La..........A 7
74 Sackville St.......J 6
75 Saffron Hill.......F 11
75 Saffron St........F 11
79 Sail St..........E 10
79 St. Agnes Place ..H 12
77 St. Alban's Grove .D 3
74 St. Alban's St.....J 7
76 St. Alphage Gdn...F 2
75 St. Andrew St....G 11
75 St. Andrew's Gdns.
D 10
75 St. Andrew's Hill .H 12
67 St. Ann's Rd. N15 .D 7
69 St. Ann's Rd.,
Chertsey......E 2
79 St. Ann's St. .....D 7
73 St. Ann's Terrace B 5
78 St. Barnabas St. ..F 4
75 St. Bartholomew's
Hospital ......G 12
66 St. Bernard's Hanwell
Hospital ......G 1
76 St. Botolph St....G 8
75 St. Bride St......G 12
75 St. Chad St. .....C 9
75 St. Chad's Place ..C 9
76 St. Clare St......H 5
75 St. Clement Dane's
Church ....H 10
76 St. Clement's Church
H 3

MAP
75 St. Clement's La..H 10
75 St. Cross St. .....F 11
75 St. Denham Hill ..C 7
76 St. Dunstan's Hill .J 4
74 St. Edmund's Ter. .B 2
79 St. Gabriel St.....E 12
74 St. George St......H 5
69 St. George's Av. ..F 4
79 St. George's Cathedral
D 11
79 St. George's Circus
D 12
78 St. George's Drive .F 5
75 St. George's Gdns. D 9
69 St. George's Hill G.C.
F 4
78 St. George's Hospital
G 7
80 St. George's Way. .H 4
75 St. Giles High St...G 8
75 St. Helena St. ...D 11
76 St. Helen's Place ..A 4
70 St. Helier........E 5
70 St. Helier Avenue .E 4
70 St. Helier Hospital .E 4
70 St. Helier Sta.....E 4
67 St. Jame's Street Sta.
D 8
74 St. James's Terrace
Mews.........B 2
78 St. James's ......B 6
70 St. James's Drive .B 5
78 St. James's Palace .B 6
78 St. James's Park ..C 7
78 St. James's Place. .B 6
80 St. James's Rd. SE16
E 7
71 St. James's Rd.,
Croydon ......E 12
75 St. James's Row ..E 12
78 St. James's Square .B 7
78 St. James's St. ...B 6
75 St. John St.......D 12
70 St. John's Hill ...B 5
75 St. John's La.....F 12
75 St. John's Square .E 12
67 St. John's Sta.....H 9
66 St. John's Wood..F 5
73 St. John's Wood
Barracks......B 5
73 St. John's Wood
High St........C 5
73 St. John's Wood Park
A 5
73 St. John's Wood Rd.
D 5
73 St. John's Wood
Terrace ....B 5
80 St. Katherine's Way
B 6
67 St. Leonard St....F 9
76 St. Leonard's Hospital
B 4
78 St. Leonard's Ter. .G 2
78 St. Loo Avenue ...H 2
77 St. Luke's Hospital G 6
77 St. Luke's St.....G 6
79 St. Margaret St....D 8
70 St. Margarets.....B 1
79 St. Margaret's Church
D 8
75 St. Mark's Hospital
C 13
75 St. Martins in the
Fields Church ...J 8
75 St. Martin's La....J 8
75 St. Martin's le Grand
G 13
79 St. Martin's Place .A 8
75 St. Martin's St.....J 8
75 St. Martin's Theatre
H 8
77 St. Mary Abbots
Hospital.......E 2
76 St. Mary at Hill....J 3
76 St. Mary Axe.....G 4
71 St. Mary Cray....D 12
76 St. Mary-le-Bow
Church ....H 2
79 St. Mary's Gdns. E 11
73 St. Mary's Hospital,
W2............G 5
68 St. Mary's La. D 4, D 5
70 St. Mary's Rd....B 5
73 St. Mary's Terrace .F 4
79 St. Mary's Walk. .E 11

MAP
78 St. Matthew St. ...D 7
76 St. Matthew's Row D 6
73 St. Michael's St. ..G 5
71 St. Mildred's Rd. ..B 9
79 St. Oswald Place .G 10
74 St. Pancras Gardens B 7
74 St. Pancras Hospital B 7
75 St. Pancras Sta....C 8
74 St. Pancras Way ..A 7
76 St. Paul St.......A 1
75 St. Paul's Cathedral H 13
75 St. Paul's Churchyard H 13
71 St. Paul's Cray ...D 12
71 St. Paul's Cray Rd. D 11
75 St. Paul's Pier ..J 12
67 St. Paul's Rd.....E 7
79 St. Paul's Terrace H 12
71 St. Paul's Wood Hill D 11
76 St. Peter's Avenue .C 6
76 St. Peter's Close...C 7
75 St. Peter's St. ....B 12
73 St. Petersburgh Mews J 2
73 St. Petersburgh Pl. .J 2
76 St. Philip Way....A 2
66 St. Quintin Av....F 4
73 St. Stephen's Gdns. G 1
77 St. Stephen's Hospital H 4
65 St. Thomas Drive. .C 5
80 St. Thomas St. ...B 3
79 St. Thomas's Hospital D 9
79 Salamanca St......F 9
73 Sale Place........G 6
73 Salem Rd.........H 2
75 Salisbury Court ..H 12
74 Salisbury Place .F 2
80 Salisbury Row ....F 3
73 Salisbury St.......E 6
66 Salmon St........D 3
71 Salmons La.......H 7
73 Samford St........E 5
79 Sancroft St......F 10
80 Sanctuary St. .....C 2
71 Sanderstead .....G 7
71 Sanderstead Hill ..G 8
71 Sanderstead Rd...F 7
71 Sanderstead Sta...F 7
80 Sandford Row....G 3
71 Sandhurst Rd. ....B 9
75 Sandland St......F 10
80 Sandover Rd......G 4
69 Sandown Park Race Course.......E 6
75 Sandwich St. ....D 8
68 Sandy La., Dagenham G 4
69 Sandy La., Esher .G 5
70 Sandy La., Twickenham...D 1
70 Sandy Lane South .F 6
65 Sandy Lodge G.C. B 4
65 Sandy Lodge La. B 4
65 Sandy Lodge Rd. ..B 4
76 Sandy Row.......H 4
70 Sandycombe Rd...A 2
71 Sangley Rd. .....B 9
75 Sans Walk......E 12
75 Sardinia St.......G 9
79 Saunders St.....E 10
76 Savage Gdns.....H 4
74 Saville Row......J 6
75 Savoy Hill.......J 9
75 Savoy Place......J 9
75 Savoy St.........J 9
75 Savoy Theatre....J 9
79 Sawyer St.......C 13
71 Scadbury Park ...C 11
74 Scala St...........F 6
76 Scarborough St....H 5
80 Scarsdale Rd.....H 4
77 Scarsdale Villas ...E 1
69 School La.........F 2
75 School of Arts & Crafts.........F 9
77 Science Museum ..D 5
76 Sclater St.........E 5
79 Scoresby St. .....B 12
71 Scotshall La. ....G 8
73 Scott Ellis Gdns. ..D 5
80 Scott Lidgett Cres..D 6

MAP
71 Scotts La.........D 9
71 Scotts Lodge ....H 11
80 Scovell Rd........D 1
80 Scratchwood......A 3
66 Scrubs La.........F 4
76 Scrutton St........E 3
72 Scudders Hill ....D 4
75 Seacoal La.......G 12
77 Seagrave Rd......H 1
72 Seal.............H 3
80 Searles Rd........E 3
80 Sears St..........J 2
73 Sebastian St......D 12
79 Secker St........B 11
80 Secretan Rd. .....H 4
73 Sedding St........F 3
71 Sedlescombe Rd...H 1
76 Seething La. ......J 4
75 Sekforde St. .....E 12
76 Selby St..........E 7
71 Selhurst..........D 7
71 Selhurst Rd.......D 7
79 Sellow Mews.....F 10
74 Selous St. ....A 6
71 Selsdon..........F 8
71 Selsdon Park G.C. .G 7
71 Selsdon Park Rd...F 8
71 Selsdon Rd.......F 7
71 Selsdon Sta.......F 7
71 Selsdon Wood ....G 8
77 Selwood Place ...G 5
77 Selwood Terrace .G 5
78 Semley Place.....F 4
78 Senate House ....F 8
73 Senior St.........F 2
75 Serle St..........G 10
76 Serpentine, The ..B 6
78 Serpentine Bridge. B 5
78 Serpentine Rd....B 2
75 Setchell Rd. ......E 5
76 Settles Rd........G 7
75 Seven Dials ......H 8
67 Seven Kings......D 12
67 Seven Sisters Rd...D 7
67 Seven Sisters Sta. ..C 7
75 Sevenoaks Rd....F 12
69 Severnhills Rd.....F 4
78 Seville St. ....C 3
79 Sevington St. .....E 2
75 Seward St........D 13
67 Sewardstone Rd...A 9
67 Sewardstonebury ..A 9
74 Seymour Hall.....G 2
74 Seymour Mews ...G 3
74 Seymour Place ...G 2
74 Seymour St.......H 2
77 Seymour Walk....H 4
75 Shad Thames ....C 5
76 Shaftesbury Av...H 7
76 Shaftesbury St....C 2
77 Shalcomb St......H 4
80 Shand St.........C 4
79 Sharsted St. .....G 12
71 Shaw La.........H 7
78 Shawfield St. ....G 4
70 Sheen Common...B 2
70 Sheen Rd........B 2
69 Sheerwater Rd....G 2
77 Sheffield Terrace ..B 2
71 Sheldrake Place ...C 1
71 Shelleys Hill ....H 11
75 Shelton St........H 8
80 Shenfield.........A 6
66 Shenley Rd.......A 2
78 Shepherd Market .B 5
78 Shepherd St.......B 4
76 Shepherdess Walk .C 2
66 Shepherd's Bush ..G 4
66 Shepherd's Bush Rd. G 4
66 Shepherds Hill ....D 6
69 Shepperton.......E 4
69 Shepperton Rd....D 3
74 Sheraton St......H 7
74 Sherborne La......H 3
71 Sherwood Park Av. B 12
71 Ship Hill.........H 10
68 Ship La., Aveley ..G 4
72 Ship La., Dartford .D 3
75 Shipton St........C 6
71 Shire La. ...F 10, F 11
72 Shirehall Rd.. C 2, C 3
73 Shirland Rd.......E 2
71 Shirley...........E 8
71 Shirley Park G.C. ..E 7
71 Shirley Rd........E 8
75 Shoe La.........G 11
67 Shooter's Hill....H 11

MAP
67 Shooter's Hill G.C. H 11
67 Shooter's Hill Rd.H 10
67 Shoreditch........E 7
76 Shoreditch High St. E 4
76 Shoreditch Park...B 2
72 Shoreham........G 2
76 Shorncliffe Rd.....G 5
79 Short St.........C 11
71 Shortlands ....D 9
71 Short's Gdns. ....H 8
71 Shortlands G.C....D 9
71 Shortlands Rd.....D 9
71 Shortlands Sta. ...D 9
74 Shouldham St.....G 2
73 Shrewsbury Mews.G 1
73 Shrewsbury Rd....G 1
73 Shroton St.......F 6
71 Sidcup..........C 11
71 Sidcup Bypass ...C 11
71 Sidcup G.C......C 12
71 Sidcup Hill ......C 12
71 Sidcup Rd........C 11
74 Siddons La.......E 2
79 Sidford Place ....E 10
70 Sidmouth St......D 9
70 Sidmouth Wood...B 2
79 Silex St..........C 12
67 Silver St.........B 7
67 Silver Street Sta...B 7
70 Silver Thorne Rd...A 5
67 Silvertown.......G 10
67 Silvertown Way ..F 10
76 Singer St.........D 3
79 Single St.........G 11
65 Sipson ....H 4
65 Sipson Rd........G 4
69 Sixth Cross Rd....C 5
71 Skeet Hill La.....E 12
71 Skibbs La. ......E 12
65 Skinner La. ......H 2
75 Skinner St.......D 11
76 Skinners Hall....H 2
72 Slade Green .....A 2
77 Slaidburn St.......J 4
71 Slines New Rd....H 8
71 Slines Oak Rd....H 8
75 Slingsby Place ...H 8
78 Sloane Avenue...F 1
78 Sloane Court East .G 3
78 Sloane Court West.G 3
78 Sloane Gardens ..F 3
78 Sloane Square....F 3
78 Sloane St.........D 2
78 Sloane Terrace...F 3
65 Slough...........G 1
79 Smith Square ....E 8
78 Smith St.........G 2
78 Smith Terrace ...G 2
70 Smitham Sta.....G 6
75 Smithfield Central Market........F 12
75 Smithfield St.....G 12
80 Smyrk's Rd.......G 4
67 Snaresbrook ....C 10
67 Snaresbrook Rd. ..C 9
75 Snow Hill........G 12
67 Snowden St. .....F 4
80 Snowfields........C 3
66 Soho............F 6
74 Soho Square .....G 7
74 Soho St. ....G 7
73 Somers Cres. ....H 6
66 Somers Mews ....G 6
66 Somers Town ....F 6
75 Somerset House..H 10
78 Sondes St.........H 3
66 South Acton Sta...G 3
79 South Africa HouseA 8
74 South Audley St..J 4
67 South Bermondsey Sta. G 8
77 South Bolton Gdns.G 3
74 South Crescent ...F 7
70 South Croydon....F 7
71 South Croydon Sta.F 7
71 South Croxted Rd..C 7
72 South Darenth....D 3
66 South Ealing Rd...G 2
66 South Ealing Sta...G 2
78 South Eaton Place .E 4
71 South Eden Park ..D 8
71 South End, SE9 ..B 11
77 South End, W8....D 2
71 South End, CroydonF7
68 South End Rd.....E 3
77 South End Row....G 2
66 South Greenford Halt F 1

MAP
66 South Hampstead Sta. E 5
65 South Harrow....D 6
66 South Herts G.C. .A 5
68 South Hornchurch. E 3
66 South Kenton Sta..D 2
79 South Lambeth Rd.H 9
70 South La. ....E 3
70 South Merton Sta. D 4
74 South Molton La..H 4
74 South Molton St...H 4
71 South Norwood...D 7
71 South Norwood Hill D 7
68 South Ockendon ..F 5
65 South Oxhey......B 5
77 South Parade.....G 5
67 South Park Drive E 12
76 South Place.......F 3
65 South Ruislip Sta. .E 5
68 South Stifford ....H 5
78 South St., W1.....A 4
72 South Street, Meopham......F 6
67 South St., Ponders End A 8
68 South St., Romford D 2
76 South Tenter St...H 5
77 South Terrace.....E 6
67 South Tottenham Sta. D 7
68 South Weald......B 4
68 South Weald Common A 4
73 South Wharf Rd...G 5
67 South Woodford Sta. C 10
65 Southall..........G 5
65 Southall Green....G 6
65 Southall La.......H 5
75 Southampton Bldgs. G 10
75 Southampton Place G 9
75 Southampton Row.F 9
75 Southampton St...H 9
67 Southampton Way H 7
71 Southborough, Bromley....D 10
70 Southborough, Surbiton ......E 2
71 Southborough La.D 10
71 Southborough Rd.D 10
67 Southbury Rd.....A 7
70 Southcroft Rd.....C 5
71 Southend.........C 9
67 Southend Rd. E18 C 10
68 Southend Rd., Romford......C 4
75 Southern St.......B 9
70 Southfields Sta...B 4
72 Southfleet........C 5
66 Southgate ....A 6
67 Southwark........G 4
76 Southwark Bridge .J 2
79 Southwark Bridge Rd. C 13
80 Southwark Cathedral B 2
67 Southwark Park...B 3
80 Southwark Park Rd. E 6
79 Southwark St......B 13
77 Southwell Gdns...E 3
73 Southwick Mews .G 5
73 Southwick Place ..H 6
73 Southwick St......G 6
71 Spa Hill..........C 7
80 Spa Rd...........E 5
66 Spaniards Rd.....D 5
65 Sparrowsherne....A 6
77 Spear Mews......F 1
73 Spelman St.......F 6
75 Spencer St.......D 12
78 Spenser St.......D 6
69 Spinney Hill .....F 2
68 Spital La.........B 5
76 Spital Square.....F 4
76 Spital St.........E 6
67 Spitalfields.......F 8
76 Spitalfields Market.F 5
78 Sprimont Place ...F 8
79 Spring Gdns. .....B 8
70 Spring Grove.....A 1
73 Spring St.........H 5
67 Springfield Park...D 8
73 Springfield Rd....A 3
71 Spur Rd.........E 12
80 Spurgeon St......D 2

MAP
69 Squires Bridge Rd. D 3
68 Squirrels Heath ...C 3
68 Squirrels Heath Rd.C 4
76 Squirries St.......D 6
75 Stacey St.........H 8
76 Staff St..........D 3
78 Stafford Place....D 6
73 Stafford Rd. NW6.C 1
70 Stafford Rd., Beddington.....F 6
78 Stafford St.......A 5
77 Stafford Terrace...D 1
69 Stag La..........C 3
78 Stag Place.......D 6
69 Staines..........C 2
68 Staines Bridge ...C 2
69 Staines Central Sta.C 2
69 Staines La........D 2
69 Staines Reservoirs .B 3
69 Staines Rd., Hounslow B 5
69 Staines Rd., Laleham D 2
69 Staines Road East .D 5
69 Staines Rd., West..C 4
77 Stamford Bridge Stadium........J 2
66 Stamford Brook Sta. G 3
67 Stamford Hill.....D 7
67 Stamford Hill Sta. .D 7
79 Stamford St......B 11
77 Stanford Rd. .....D 3
77 Stanhope Gdns....E 4
78 Stanhope Gate....B 4
77 Stanhope Mews East E 4
77 Stanhope Mews West E 4
74 Stanhope Place ...H 2
74 Stanhope Place Gate H 2
78 Stanhope Row....B 4
74 Stanhope St.......D 6
73 Stanhope Terrace .H 5
70 Stanley Park Rd...F 5
70 Stanley Rd.......C 1
75 Stanley Passage ..C 8
66 Stanmore........B 2
66 Stanmore Hill....B 1
66 Stanmore Sta.....B 2
79 Stannary St.......G 11
71 Stanstead Rd......B 8
72 Stansted.........F 5
72 Stanway St.......C 4
69 Stanwell.........B 3
69 Stanwell New Rd...C 2
69 Stanwell Rd., Staines C 3
69 Stanwell Rd., W. Bedfont.....B 4
69 Stanwellmoor.....B 2
80 Staple St. ....D 3
80 Stapleford Abbotts A 2
66 Staples Corner....D 4
73 Star St. ....G 5
70 Star & Garter Home B 2
72 Star Hill Rd......H 1
74 Starcross St.......D 6
69 Station Avenue ...E 4
68 Station La........D 3
67 Station Rd........A 9
69 Station Rd., Addlestone.....E 3
66 Station Rd., Harrow C 1
65 Station Rd., Hayes G 4
66 Station Rd., New Barnet.........A 5
71 Station Rd., Orpington E 11
71 Station Rd., Sidcup C 11
75 Stationers' Hall ..G 12
80 Stead St. ....F 2
79 Steedman St......F 13
69 Steels La. ....G 6
74 Stephen St.......G 7
74 Stephenson Way .D 6
67 Stepney..........F 8
67 Stepney East Sta..F 8
77 Sterling St........D 6
80 Sterry St.........C 2
76 Steward St.......F 4
77 Stewart's Grove...F 5
73 Stifford..........G 6
68 Stifford Rd........D 2
78 Stillington St......E 6

MAP
76 Stock Exchange...G 3
65 Stockley Rd.......G 4
70 Stockwell Rd......A 6
69 Stoke D'Abernon .H 5
67 Stoke Newington..D 7
67 Stoke Newington Rd. E 7
67 Stoke Newington Sta. D 7
69 Stoke Rd.........G 5
72 Stone............B 4
75 Stone Buildings ..G 10
72 Stone Crossing Halt B 4
66 Stone Grove......B 2
66 Stone Marshes...A 3
66 Stonebridge Park Sta. E 2
70 Stonecot Hill......E 4
69 Stonehill Rd......F 1
71 Stonehouse La., Orpington.....F 12
68 Stonehouse La., W. Thurrock...G 4
70 Stoneleigh Sta....F 3
80 Stones End St....D 1
76 Stoney La. ....G 4
80 Stoney St........B 2
72 Stony Corner.....D 6
79 Stopford Rd. ....G 13
74 Store St..........F 7
79 Storey's Gate ....D 8
80 Storks Rd........D 7
68 Stourcliffe St.....G 2
68 Straight Rd.......C 3
75 Strand ....J 9
75 Strand Theatre...H 9
67 Stratford........E 9
67 Stratford New Town E 9
74 Stratford Place...H 4
77 Stratford Rd......E 1
67 Stratford Sta......E 9
73 Strathearn Place .H 5
80 Strathnairn St.....F 7
78 Stratton St.......B 5
70 Strawberry Hill G.C. C 1
70 Strawberry Hill Sta. C 1
70 Strawberry Vale...C 1
66 Streatfield Rd. ...C 2
71 Streatham........C 6
70 Streatham Common C 6
70 Streatham Common North........C 6
70 Streatham Common Sta..............C 5
70 Streatham High Rd. C 6
70 Streatham Hill...B 6
70 Streatham Hill Sta. C 6
70 Streatham Rd.....D 5
70 Streatham Sta....C 6
75 Streatham St......G 8
70 Streatham Vale...C 6
70 Street, The ......H 2
66 Stroud Green Rd. .D 7
80 Stroude.........D 1
78 Strutton Ground ..D 7
76 Strype St.........G 5
73 Stuart Rd........D 1
68 Stubbers La......E 4
75 Stukeley St.......G 9
79 Sturgeon Rd. ...G 13
76 Stutfield St.......H 7
70 Sudbrook Park....C 2
69 Sudbury G.C......E 2
66 Sudbury Hill Sta..E 1
66 Sudbury Hill & Harrow Sta. ...E 1
66 Sudbury Town Sta. E 2
66 Sudbury & Harrow Rd. Sta........E 2
75 Sudeley St.......C 12
79 Sudrey St........C 13
75 Suffolk La. ....J 2
76 Suffolk Rd........A 6
80 Suffolk St. SE1....C 1
79 Suffolk St. SW1...A 7
80 Sultan St.........J 1
70 Summer Rd......D 1
66 Summers La. .....B 5
77 Sumner Place ....F 5
80 Sumner Rd.......J 5
79 Sumner St. ......B 13
76 Sun St...........F 3
69 Sunbury ....D 4

MAP
69 Sunbury Sta. .....D 4
73 Sunderland Ter....G 2
71 Sundridge Hill Rd.
        H 12
71 Sundridge Park G.C.
        C 10
71 Sundridge Park Sta.
        D 9
72 Sundridge Rd....H 1
68 Sunnings La.......E 4
70 Surbiton ....E 2
70 Surbiton G.C.....E 1
73 Surrendale Place ..E 2
80 Surrey Canal....H 4
79 Surrey Row .....C 12
80 Surrey Square....F 4
75 Surrey St........H 10
80 Surrey Terrace ...F 4
73 Sussex Gardens ..H 5
73 Sussex Place.....H 5
73 Sussex Square ...H 5
78 Sussex St........G 5
73 Sutherland Avenue E 2
73 Sutherland Place ..G 1
80 Sutherland Square.G 1
78 Sutherland St.....G 5
80 Sutherland Walk   G 2
70 Sutton..........F 4
72 Sutton-at-Hone ...D 3
72 Sutton at Hone Rd. C 2
68 Sutton Avenue....D 3
70 Sutton Common Rd.
        E 4
70 Sutton Common Sta.
        E 4
69 Sutton La., Hounslow
        A 5
70 Sutton La., Sutton.G 4
74 Sutton Row ......G 7
70 Sutton Sta.......F 4
65 Swakeleys ....E 4
74 Swallow St.......J 6
80 Swan Mead......E 4
80 Swan St.........D 2
78 Swan Walk......H 2
72 Swancombe Marshes
        A 5
76 Swanfield St......D 5
72 Swanley..........D 2
72 Swanley La.......D 2
72 Swanley Village ..D 2
72 Swanley Village Rd.
        D 2
72 Swanscombe......B 5
72 Swanscombe Halt .B 5
72 Swanscombe Park .C 5
80 Sweeney Crescent .D 5
75 Swinton St.......D 9
66 Swiss Cottage Sta. .E 5
76 Swithin's Hall ...H 2
71 Sydenham.......C 7
71 Sydenham Hill Sta. C 7
71 Sydenham Rd.....C 8
71 Sydenham Sta....C 8
77 Sydney Place.....F 5
77 Sydney St........G 6
78 Symons St. ......F 3
70 Syon La..........A 1
70 Syon Lane Sta. ...A 1
70 Syon House ....A 1
80 Tabard St.........D 2
76 Tabernacle St.....E 3
78 Tachbrook St......F 6
73 Talbot Rd........G 1
73 Talbot Square....H 5
80 Talbot Yard......B 2
75 Tallis St.........H 11
77 Tamworth St......H 1
68 Tank La..........G 4
80 Tanner St.........C 4
76 Taplow St........C 2
79 Tarver Rd.......G 13
79 Tate Gallery.....F 8
71 Tatsfield ....H 10
71 Tatsfield La.......H 10
70 Tattenham Corner Rd.
        H 3
70 Tattenham Corner Sta.
        H 3
70 Tattenham Way...H 4
80 Tatum St.........F 3
74 Taunton Place ....E 2
75 Tavistock Place...E 8
75 Tavistock Square .E 8
75 Tavistock St......H 9
74 Taviton St. ......E 7
76 Teale St.........B 7
70 Teddington.......C 1
78 Tedworth Square .G 2

MAP
75 Temple, The.....H 11
75 Temple Avenue ..H 11
75 Temple Bar......H 11
75 Temple Gardens .H 11
75 Temple Place....H 10
70 Temple Rd........G 2
77 Templeton Place...F 1
80 Tennis St........C 2
65 Tentelow La. .....G 6
75 Terminus Place...E 5
69 Terrace Rd........E 5
77 Thackeray St......D 2
75 Thames Ditton...E 1
70 Thames Ditton Sta. E 1
75 Thames Water
        Authority .....D 11
68 Thamesmead......G 1
75 Thanet St.........D 8
75 Thavies Inn .....G 11
74 Thayer St........G 4
75 Theatre Royal ...H 9
79 Theed St........B 11
66 Theobald St......A 2
75 Theobald's Rd.....F 9
73 Thirleby Rd......E 6
69 Thistlecroft ......F 5
79 Thomas Doyle St. D 12
80 Thomas More St. .A 6
80 Thorburn Square .F 6
76 Thoresby St.......C 1
68 Thorndon Park ...C 6
68 Thorndon Park G.C.
        C 6
65 Thorney La. ......F 2
79 Thorney St........E 8
73 Thorngate Rd.....E 2
70 Thornton Heath ..D 6
74 Thornton Place...F 2
70 Thornton Rd......E 6
69 Thorpe..........D 2
69 Thorpe Rd., Chertsey
        D 2
69 Thorpe Rd.,Staines C 2
80 Thrale St.........B 2
76 Thrawl St........G 5
76 Threadneedle St. .H 3
74 Three Kings Yard .H 4
80 Three Oak La. ...C 5
76 Throgmorton Avenue
        G 3
76 Throgmorton St. .G 3
79 Thrush St........G 13
80 Thurland Rd......D 6
77 Thurloe Place.....E 5
77 Thurloe Square...E 5
77 Thurloe St........E 5
80 Thurlow St.......G 3
76 Thurtle Rd.......B 5
70 Tibbetts Corner ..B 4
78 Tilney St.........B 4
79 Tinworth St......F 9
80 Tisdall Place......F 3
75 Titchborne Row ..H 6
74 Titchfield Rd......B 2
78 Tite St...........H 2
79 Tiverton St. .....D 13
70 Token House Yard G 3
66 Tollington Park Rd.D 6
74 Tolmers Square...D 6
65 Tolpits La........A 4
70 Tolworth.........E 2
70 Tolworth Rise ...E 2
70 Tolworth Rd.....E 2
67 Tomswood Hill ..C 11
75 Tonbridge St.....D 8
80 Tooley St.........B 4
75 Tooting Bec Rd...C 5
70 Tooting Bec Sta. ..C 5
70 Tooting Common .C 5
70 Tooting Graveney .C 5
70 Tooting Graveney
        Common.....C 5
70 Tooting High St. ..C 5
70 Tooting Sta.......C 5
70 Topaz St........E 10
75 Topham St......E 11
77 Tor Gdns.........C 1
73 Torquay St.......F 2
75 Torrens St.......C 12
74 Torrington Place ..F 7
77 Tottenham.......C 8
74 Tottenham Court Rd.
        F 6
67 Tottenham Hale...C 8
67 Tottenham Hale Sta.
        C 8
67 Tottenham Hotspur
        F.C..........C 8
66 Tottenham La.....D 6

MAP
74 Tottenham St......F 6
66 Totteridge........A 4
66 Totteridge La. ....B 4
66 Totteridge &
        Whetstone Sta..B 5
79 Toulmin St.......C 13
76 Tower, The......J 5
80 Tower Bridge....B 5
76 Tower Bridge
        Approach......J 5
80 Tower Bridge Rd. .D 4
67 Tower Hamlets....F 8
75 Tower Hill.......J 5
75 Tower St.........H 8
69 Town La.........B 3
71 Townley Rd.....B 12
80 Townsend St......F 3
73 Townshend Rd....B 6
76 Toynbee St.......G 5
79 Trade, Dept. of ..D 7
80 Trafalgar Avenue .H 5
74 Trafalgar Rd......G 9
79 Trafalgar Square ..A 8
80 Trafalgar St.......G 3
73 Transept St. .....F 6
80 Tranton Rd.......D 7
67 Traps Hill.......A 11
75 Traps La.........D 3
70 Treadgold St......C 8
70 Treasury ....C 8
75 Treaty St. ....B 9
77 Trebovir Rd......F 1
77 Tregunter Rd......G 3
73 Tresham Crescent .D 6
75 Treveris St......B 12
78 Trevor Place......D 1
78 Trevor Square ....D 2
78 Trevor St........C 2
79 Trigon Rd.......J 10
80 Trinity Church Square
        D 2
76 Trinity House ...H 5
70 Trinity Rd.......B 5
76 Trinity Square....J 4
80 Trinity St........D 2
80 Trothy Rd........F 7
78 Tryon St.........F 2
71 Tubbenden La...E 11
70 Tudor Drive .....E 4
74 Tudor Place ......G 7
69 Tudor Rd........C 6
75 Tudor St.........H 11
66 Tufnell Park Rd...E 6
70 Tufton St........E 8
70 Tulse Hill ....B 6
70 Tulse Hill Sta. ....C 6
76 Turin St.........D 6
78 Turk's Row ......G 3
66 Turnham Green Sta.
        G 3
75 Turnmill St......F 12
67 Turnpike La. .....C 7
69 Twickenham......B 1
70 Twickenham BridgeB 1
70 Twickenham Park .B 1
70 Twickenham Rd.,
        Teddington....C 1
69 Twickenham Rd.,
        Twickenham....C 5
74 Tyburn Way.....H 2
80 Tyers Gate ......C 4
79 Tyers St.........G 9
79 Tyers Terrace ...G 10
75 Tysoe St.........D 11
80 Udall St.........F 6
79 Ufford St. ......C 12
76 Underwood Rd....E 6
76 Underwood St....C 2
76 Union Square.....B 1
79 Union St. ......B 12
76 Union Walk ......C 4
74 University College .E 7
74 University College
        Hospital .....E 7
75 University of London
        F 8
74 University St......E 6
80 Unwin Close ....H 6
73 Upbrook Mews....H 4
67 Upminster........D 4
68 Upminster Bridge Sta.
        D 4
68 Upminster G.C...D 4
68 Upminster Rd.,
        Rainham......F 3
68 Upminster Rd.,
        Upminster....D 4
67 Upney.........E 12

MAP
67 Upney La........E 11
67 Upney Sta. ......E 12
78 Upper Belgrave St..D 4
74 Upper Berkeley-St..G 2
74 Upper Brook St....J 3
77 Upper Cheyne RowH 6
67 Upper Clapton....D 8
67 Upper Clapton Rd.D 8
67 Upper Edmonton .B 8
71 Upper Elmer End..E 8
74 Upper Grosvenor St.
        J 3
79 Upper Ground...A 11
69 Upper Halliford Halt
        D 4
69 Upper Halliford Rd.
        D 4
74 Upper Harley St...E 4
66 Upper Holloway Sta.
        D 6
79 Upper Marsh....D 10
74 Upper Montagu St..F 2
70 Upper Norwood ..D 6
77 Upper Phillimore
        Gdns.........C 1
68 Upper Rainham Rd.
        D 3
70 Upper Richmond Rd.,
        East Sheen.....B 2
70 Upper Richmond Rd.,
        Putney........B 3
75 Upper St. Martins La.
        H 8
75 Upper St........B 12
69 Upper Sunbury Rd.D 5
71 Upper Sydenham ..C 7
71 Upper Thames St..H 2
70 Upper Tooting Rd.C 5
67 Upper Walthamstow
        C 9
71 Upper Warlingham
        Sta..........H 7
71 Upper Wickam La.
        A 12
74 Upper Wimpole St. F 4
65 Upton ....E 10
67 Upton La........E 10
67 Upton Park Sta...E 10
67 Upton Rd........E 12
80 Urlwin St........H 1
65 Uxbridge.........E 3
66 Uxbridge Rd., Acton
        G 3
69 Uxbridge Rd., Feltham
        C 5
65 Uxbridge Rd.,
        Harefield......D 3
65 Uxbridge Rd.,
        Hatch End.....C 6
66 Uxbridge Rd., Hanwell
        G 1
65 Uxbridge Rd.,
        Hayes End.....F 4
65 Uxbridge Rd.,
        Maple Cross....B 2
65 Uxbridge Rd., Pinner
        C 5
65 Uxbridge Rd.,
        Southall........F 5
66 Uxbridge Rd.,
        Stanmore......B 1
77 Uxbridge St......B 2
77 Uxbridge St.......B 2
66 Vale, The, SW3...H 5
66 Vale, The, W3...G 3
73 Vale Close.......D 3
79 Valence Avenue..D 1
79 Valentine Place .C 11
67 Valentines Park .D 11
67 Vallance Rd......E 7
78 Vandon St........D 6
76 Vandy St.........E 3
74 Vanston Place ....J 1
74 Varndell St.......D 6
80 Vauban St.......E 5
78 Vaudeville Theatre.J 9
79 Vauxhall Bridge...G 7
78 Vauxhall Bridge Rd.
        E 6
79 Vauxhall Grove...H 9
79 Vauxhall Park....H 9
79 Vauxhall Sta......G 8
79 Vauxhall St......G 10
79 Vauxhall Walk...G 9
79 Venables St......F 5
71 Verdant La. ......B 9
74 Vere St..........H 4
74 Vernon Rise ....C 10
75 Verulam St......F 11
71 Vesta Rd........A 8

MAP
76 Vestry St. ....C 3
69 Vicarage Farm Rd. A 5
77 Vicarage Gate ....B 2
67 Vicarage La.,
        Chigwell .....B 11
68 Vicarage La., South
        Weald ....B 4
69 Vicarage Rd.......C 4
78 Victoria Coach Sta. F 4
67 Victoria Dock Rd. F 10
70 Victoria Drive ....B 4
79 Victoria Embankment
        B 9
79 Victoria Embankment
        Gdns..........A 9
73 Victoria Gate ....J 5
77 Victoria Grove....D 3
78 Victoria Hospital H 3
78 Victoria Palace Theatre
        D 5
67 Victoria Park .....E 8
67 Victoria Park Rd...E 8
66 Victoria Rd. NW10 F 3
77 Victoria Rd. W8...D 3
68 Victoria Rd., Romford
        D 2
65 Victoria Rd., Ruislip
        D 5
78 Victoria Square...D 5
80 Victoria Square ...J 3
78 Victoria Sta......E 5
78 Victoria St........D 6
77 Victoria & Albert
        Museum ....E 5
74 Vigo St...........J 6
80 Villa St..........G 3
67 Village Way, Enfield
        A 7
65 Village Way, Harrow
        D 5
79 Villiers St.........A 9
76 Vince St.........D 3
78 Vincent Square...E 7
79 Vincent St. ......F 7
75 Vincent Terrace ..B 12
75 Vine Hill ......E 11
80 Vine La. ....B 4
76 Vine St..........H 5
73 Violet Hill........C 4
79 Virgil St.........D 10
79 Victoria Tower
        Gardens ......D 9
76 Virginia Rd.......D 5
69 Virginia Water Sta. D 1
80 Wadding St......F 2
70 Waddington......H 6
70 Waddon..........D 6
70 Waddon Marsh Halt
        E 6
67 Wadham Rd......C 9
80 Waite St.........H 5
75 Wakefield St......D 9
75 Wakley St. ......C 12
76 Walbrook ....H 2
79 Walcot Square ...E 11
70 Waldgrave Rd.....C 6
71 Waldram Park Rd..B 8
77 Walham Grove....J 1
74 Wallace Collection.G 3
67 Wallend ....E 11
77 Wallgrave Rd. ....F 2
70 Wallington ......F 5
66 Walnut Tree Walk E 11
78 Walpole St........F 2
73 Walterton Rd.....D 1
67 Waltham Forest...C 9
67 Walthamstow.....D 8
67 Walthamstow Avenue
        C 9
67 Walthamstow Central
        Sta..........C 9
67 Walthamstow
        Marshes ......D 8
67 Walthamstow Queen's
        Rd. Sta.......C 9
69 Walton Bridge ...E 4
70 Walton Downs ...H 3
69 Walton Place ....D 2
69 Walton Rd.......D 5
78 Walton St.......E 5
69 Walton-upon-Thames
        E 5
67 Walworth ....G 7
80 Walworth Place ..F 1
80 Walworth Rd.....F 1
80 Wansey St. ......F 1
67 Wanstead ......D 10
67 Wanstead Flats..D 10

MAP
67 Wanstead G.C. ..D 10
67 Wanstead Park...D 10
67 Wanstead Park Sta.E 10
67 Wanstead Sta. ...D 10
70 Wandsworth......B 4
70 Wandsworth BridgeA 4
70 Wandsworth Bridge
        Rd..........A 4
70 Wandsworth Common
        B 5
70 Wandsworth Common
        Sta...........B 5
79 Wandsworth PrisonB 5
79 Wandsworth Rd..H 8
70 Wandsworth Rd. Sta.
        A 6
70 Wandsworth Town
        Sta...........B 4
67 Wapping.........G 8
80 Wapping High St. .B 6
74 Wardour St......H 7
74 Warham Rd......F 6
79 Warham St......J 12
68 Warley Barracks ..B 5
68 Warley Rd.   C 4, C 5
71 Warlingham ....H 8
75 Warner St. ......E 11
74 Warner Place ....C 6
68 Warren La.,
        W. Thurrock ...G 5
69 Warren La., Woking
        H 2
71 Warren Rd. F 11, F 12
74 Warren St. ......E 6
73 Warrington Cres. .E 3
73 Warwick Avenue..E 3
73 Warwick Crescent .F 3
73 Warwick Estate ..E 3
79 Warwick House St. B 7
75 Warwick La. EC4.G 12
68 Warwick La., Rainham
        F 4
73 Warwick Place...F 3
67 Warwick Res.....D 8
77 Warwick Rd. ....F 1
78 Warwick Row ...D 5
78 Warwick Square..D 5
74 Warwick St. ...J 6
77 Warwick Way....F 5
71 Wash Pond Rd. H 9
67 Water La.......D 12
67 Waterden Rd.....E 9
75 Watergate ......H 12
70 Waterhouse La....H 4
75 Waterloo Bridge..J 10
75 Waterloo Pier ...J 10
78 Waterloo Place...B 7
79 Waterloo Rd....C 11
79 Waterloo Sta....C 10
66 Waterlow Park ...D 6
76 Waterson St. .....D 4
69 Watersplash Rd...D 3
65 Watford.........A 5
66 Watford Bypass ..A 2
65 Watford F.C.....A 5
65 Watford Heath....A 5
65 Watford High St. Sta.
        A 5
66 Watford Rd., Harrow
        E 1
65 Watford Rd.,
        Rickmansworth .A 3
66 Watford Way, NW4
        C 4
66 Watford Way,
        Edgware ......B 2
65 Watford West Sta..A 4
66 Watling Avenue...C 3
76 Watling St. EC4..H 1
72 Watling St.,
        Swanscombe....C 4
72 Watling St.......B 1
71 Watts La........D 11
73 Waverley Place...B 4
78 Waverton St......J 6
79 Waxwell Terrace .D 10
68 Weald Park......A 4
66 Wealdstone......C 1
76 Weaver St.......E 6
80 Weaver's La......B 4
80 Webb St.........E 4
79 Webber Row ....D 11
79 Webber St.......C 12
74 Welbeck St......G 4
74 Welbeck Way....G 4
74 Weigh House St..H 4
75 Weirs Passage ...D 8
72 Well Hill........F 1
76 Wellclose Square ..H 6

MAP

80 Weller St. ....C 1
76 Wellesey Terrace ..C 2
71 Welling........A 12
71 Welling Way.....A 11
78 Wellington Arch ..C 4
78 Wellington Barracks
D 6
73 Wellington Pl. .....C 5
73 Wellington Rd. ...C 5
69 Wellington Rd. South
B 5
76 Wellington Row ..D 6
78 Wellington Square. G 2
75 Wellington St.....H 9
74 Wells Mews ......G 6
74 Wells Rise........B 2
74 Wells St.........G 6
80 Wells Way ....H 3
80 Welsford St......F 6
66 Wembley.........E 2
66 Wembley Central Sta.
E 2
66 Wembley Hill Sta. .E 2
66 Wembley Stadium .E 2
76 Wenlock Basin...C 1
76 Wenlock Rd. .....C 1
76 Wenlock St. ......C 2
68 Wennington.....F 3
68 Wennington Marshes
G 3
68 Wennington Rd....F 3
76 Wentworth St.....G 5
74 Werrington St.....C 7
76 Wesley's Chapel...E 3
66 West Acton Sta...F 2
69 West Bedfont.....B 3
69 West Byfleet.....G 2
69 West Byfleet G.C...G 2
69 West Byfleet Sta...G 2
75 West Central St. ..G 8
71 West Common Rd. E 9
77 West Cromwell Rd. F 1
71 West Croydon Sta.
E 7
65 West Drayton ....G 3
65 West Drayton Rd. .F 4
65 West Drayton &
Yiewsley Sta....G 3
71 West Dulwich Sta...C 7
66 West Ealing Sta....F 1
78 West Eaton Place ..E 3
69 West End, Esher...F 6
65 West End, Southall F 5
66 West End La......E 5
65 West End Rd. D 4, E 5
70 West Ewell.......F 3
67 West Ferry Rd....G 9
66 West Finchley Sta.. B 5
67 West Green.......C 7
67 West Green Rd....C 7
69 West Grove.......F 5
78 West Halkin St....D 3
67 West Ham.......F 10
67 West Ham F.C....E 10
67 West Ham Park ..E 10
67 West Ham Stadium
F 10
66 West Hampstead Sta.
E 5
65 West Harrow.....D 6
66 West Heath, NW3 .D 5
68 West Heath, SE2..H 1
72 West Hill........H 6
68 West Horndon Sta. D 6
67 West India Docks .G 9
71 West Kent G.C...G 11
77 West Mall........A 1

66 West Middlesex G.C.
F 1
69 West Molesey ....D 6
71 West Norwood....C 7
70 West Norwood Sta. C 6
70 West Park Hospital G 2
78 West Rd.........G 3
65 West Ruislip Sta...D 4
75 West Smithfield...F 12
79 West Square .....E 12
75 West St..........H 8
70 West Sutton Sta...F 4
76 West Tenter St....H 5
68 West Thurrock ...H 5
68 West Thurrock
Marshes ......H 5
71 West Wickham...E 9
71 West Wood La....B 11
73 Westbourne Cres. H 4
73 Westbourne Gdns..G 2
73 Westbourne Gate ..J 5
73 Westbourne Grove H 2
73 Westbourne Park Rd.
G 1
66 Westbourne Park Sta.
F 4
73 Westbourne Park
Villas..........G 2
73 Westbourne St....H 5
73 Westbourne Ter...G 4
73 Westbourne Ter. Rd.
F 3
74 Westbury Hotel ..J 5
67 Westcombe Park Sta.
H 10
79 Westcott Rd.....H 12
69 Westend La.......F 5
71 Westerham Rd. ..F 10
66 Western Avenue,
Greenford......F 1
65 Western Avenue,
Uxbridge......E 4
77 Western Hospital .H 2
70 Western Rd., Mitcham
D 5
65 Western Rd., Southall
G 5
77 Westgate Terrace. H 3
71 Westhall Rd......H 7
71 Westhorne Av....B 10
70 Westland Place ..D 2
70 Westmead Rd.....F 5
66 Westminster......G 6
79 Westminster Abbey D 8
79 Westminster Bridge C 9
79 Westminster Bridge
Rd...........D 11
78 Westminster Chapel
D 6
79 Westminster Hall .D 8
79 Westminster Hospital
E 8
79 Westminster Pier ..C 9
78 Westminster R.C.
Cathedral ......E 6
79 Westminster School D 8
78 Westminster Theatre
D 5
78 Westmoreland Place
G 5
80 Westmoreland Rd.
SE17 ....H 2
80 Westmoreland Rd.
SE17 ....G 4
71 Westmoreland Rd.,
Bromley......D 9

74 Westmoreland St...F 4
78 Westmoreland Ter. G 5
70 Weston Green ....E 1
70 Weston Green Rd. .E 1
75 Weston Rise.....C 10
80 Weston St. ....C 3
73 Westway ....F 3
72 Westwood........C 5
71 Westwood Hill...C 7
77 Wetherby Gdns...F 3
77 Wetherby Place ..F 4
69 Weybridge.......E 4
69 Weybridge Rd....E 3
69 Weybridge Sta...F 3
74 Weymouth Mews..F 5
76 Weymouth Ter...B 5
74 Weymouth St....F 4
68 Whalebone La...C 1
68 Whalebone La. South
D 1
75 Wharf Rd. .....C 13
75 Wharfdale Rd....B 9
75 Wharton St......D 10
76 Wheler St.........E 5
66 Whetstone.......B 5
75 Whetstone Park..G 10
75 Whidborne St....D 9
67 Whipps Cross....D 9
76 Whiston Rd......B 5
76 Whitby St........E 5
66 Whitchurch La. ...C 2
75 Whitcomb St.....J 7
66 White Church Lane G 6
66 White City Stadium F 4
75 White Conduit St. B 11
79 White Hall Place...B 8
67 White Hart La. N17 C 7
68 White Hart La.,
Collier Row ....C 2
67 White Hart Lane Sta.
C 7
80 White Hart Yard ..B 2
65 White Hill........B 4
72 White Hill La....F 6
71 White Horse Hill .C 10
76 White Horse St....B 5
76 White Kennett St. .G 4
75 White Lion Hill ..H 13
76 White Lodge.....B 2
67 Whitechapel ......F 8
76 Whitechapel High St.
G 5
76 Whitechapel Rd...G 6
76 Whitecross St. ....E 2
71 Whitefoot La.....C 9
75 Whitefriars St....H 11
79 Whitehall........B 8
79 Whitehall Court..B 8
79 Whitehall Gdns...B 8
67 Whitehall Rd.....B 9
79 Whitehall Theatre..B 8
79 Whitehart St.....G 11
78 Whiteheads Grove .F 1
71 Whitehorse Rd....D 7
69 Whiteley Village...F 4
80 White's Grounds ..C 4
76 White's Row.....F 5
74 Whitfield Place...E 6
74 Whitfield St......F 6
79 Whitgift St.......F 9
76 Whitmore Rd.....A 3
78 Whittaker St.....F 3
79 Whittlesey St.....B 11
69 Whitton.........B 6
65 Whitton Avenue..E 6
69 Whitton Rd......B 6

71 Whyteleafe.......H 7
71 Whyteleafe Rd...H 7
71 Whyteleafe South Sta..
H 7
67 Wick Rd.........E 8
67 Wickham La......H 12
71 Wickham Rd. SE4. A 8
71 Wickham Rd.,
Beckenham.....D 8
71 Wickham Rd.,
Croydon......E 8
79 Wickham St......G 10
71 Wickham Way...D 9
75 Wicklow St. ......C 9
76 Widegate St......F 4
73 Widley Rd.......D 1
71 Widmore Rd....D 10
74 Wigmore Place...G 5
74 Wigmore St......G 4
78 Wilbraham Place ..E 3
67 Wilbury Way ....B 7
75 Wild Court.......G 9
75 Wild St..........A 9
80 Wild's Rents.....D 3
71 Willersley Av....B 11
66 Willesden........E 3
66 Willesden Green...E 4
66 Willesden Green Sta.
E 4
66 Willesden Junc. Sta. F 3
66 Willesden La......E 4
67 William Girling Res.
B 8
78 William Mews ....C 3
74 William Rd.......D 5
78 William St........C 3
75 William IV St......J 8
67 Willoughby La. ...C 8
71 Willow Grove....C 10
78 Willow Place .....E 6
76 Willow St........D 3
80 Willow Walk .....E 4
65 Willowbank .....E 3
80 Willowbrook Rd...J 5
76 Wilmer Gdns.....B 4
70 Wilmerhatch La. ..H 2
72 Wilmington......C 2
75 Wilmington Square
D 11
76 Wilson St.........F 3
76 Wiltshire Row ...A 3
78 Wilton Crescent...D 3
78 Wilton Mews.....D 4
78 Wilton Place......C 3
78 Wilton Rd........E 5
78 Wilton Row......C 3
76 Wilton Square ...A 2
78 Wilton St........D 4
78 Wilton Terrace...D 3
79 Wimbledon......C 4
70 Wimbledon Chase .D 4
70 Wimbledon Common
C 3
70 Wimbledon G.C...C 3
70 Wimbledon Hill Rd.
C 4
70 Wimbledon Park ..C 4
70 Wimbledon Park G.C.
C 4
70 Wimbledon Park Rd.
B 4
70 Wimbledon Park Sta.
C 4
70 Wimbledon Stadium
C 4

70 Wimbledon Sta....C 4
76 Wimbolt St. ......C 6
76 Wimbourne St....B 2
74 Wimpole Mews ...F 4
74 Wimpole St.......G 4
78 Winchester St.....G 5
80 Winchester Walk ..B 2
67 Winchmore Hill...A 7
79 Wincott St.......F 11
74 Windmill St.......F 7
79 Windmill Walk ..C 11
74 Windsor Terrace ..C 2
74 Winfield House ...C 1
68 Wingletye La......D 4
76 Winkworth Rd....G 4
73 Winsland Mews...G 5
73 Winsland St.......G 5
74 Winsley St........G 6
69 Wisley..........G 3
69 Wisley Common ..H 3
69 Wisley La........G 3
75 Woburn Place....E 8
75 Woburn Square ..E 8
69 Woking..........H 1
71 Woldingham Rd...H 8
80 Wolseley St.......C 6
76 Wolsey Way......B 4
65 Wood End, Hayes .F 4
65 Wood End, S. Harrow
E 6
67 Wood Grange Park
Sta............E 10
66 Wood Green......C 6
66 Wood Green Sta...C 6
66 Wood La. W12...F 4
68 Wood La., Becontree
E 1
68 Wood La., Dagenham
E 3
66 Wood La., Stanmore
B 2
67 Wood St. E17.....C 9
76 Wood St. EC2....G 2
66 Wood St., Barnet..A 4
67 Wood Street Sta...C 9
75 Woodbridge St. ..E 12
73 Woodchester Sq...F 2
70 Woodcote Grove Rd.
G 6
70 Woodcote La......G 5
70 Woodcote Park G.C.
G 5
70 Woodcote Park G.C.
(R.A.C.)......H 3
70 Woodcote Rd.....F 5
78 Woodfall St.......G 2
70 Woodfield La......H 2
67 Woodford......C 10
67 Woodford Bridge. B 10
67 Woodford Green .B 10
67 Woodford New Rd. C 9
67 Woodford Wells..B 10
69 Woodham......G 2
69 Woodham La....G 2
69 Woodland Park...H 6
72 Woodlands.......G 3
69 Woodlands La. ...H 6
70 Woodmansterne La.
G 5
70 Woodmansterne Rd.
F 5
70 Woodmansterne Sta.
G 5
65 Woodridings......C 6

74 Woods Mews .....J 3
76 Woodseer St......F 6
71 Woodside........E 7
66 Woodside Avenue .C 5
66 Woodside Park Sta. B 5
70 Woodstock La.....E 1
74 Woodstock St....H 4
69 Woodthorpe Rd...C 3
80 Wooler St........G 3
67 Woolwich.......G 11
67 Woolwich Arsenal Sta.
G 11
67 Woolwich Church St.
G 11
67 Woolwich Common
H 10
67 Woolwich Dockyard
Sta............G 11
67 Woolwich Reach .G 11
67 Woolwich Rd. SE7
G 10
68 Woolwich Rd.,
W. Heath ......G 1
79 Wootton St......B 11
70 Worcester Park ...E 3
70 Worcester Park Sta. E 3
79 Worgan St........G 9
66 Wormwood Scrubs. F 3
76 Wormwood St....G 4
73 Woronzow Rd....A 5
79 Worple Rd. SW19 .D 3
69 Worple Rd., Staines
D 2
76 Worship St.......E 3
69 Wraysbury ....B 1
69 Wraysbury Res...B 2
75 Wren St.........E 10
80 Wright's Buildings .E 4
77 Wright's La.......D 2
72 Wrotham.......H 5
72 Wrotham Heath ..H 6
72 Wrotham Heath G.C.
H 6
72 Wrotham Hill Park G 5
72 Wrotham Rd..C 6, D 6
70 Wrythe, The......E 5
70 Wrythe La.......E 5
74 Wybert St........D 5
75 Wyclif St........D 12
66 Wyke Green G.C. .G 1
73 Wymering Rd.....D 2
75 Wynatt St........D 12
74 Wyndham Place ..F 2
74 Wyndham St......F 2
75 Wyndham's Theatre
J 8
75 Wynford Rd. ....B 10
77 Wynnstay Gdns...D 1
74 Wythburn Place..G 2
79 Wyvil Rd........J 8
80 Yalding Rd......E 6
65 Yeading.........F 5
65 Yeading La. ......F 5
67 Yeoman's Row....E 6
65 Yiewsley.........F 4
74 York Bridge......E 3
75 York Buildings....J 9
74 York Gate........E 3
77 York House Place .C 2
79 York Rd........C 10
74 York St..........F 2
74 York Terrace ....E 4
75 York Way........B 9
76 Yorkton St. ......C 6
77 Young St.........C 2
74 Zoological Gardens
B 3

PRINTED IN GREAT BRITAIN BY GEORGE PHILIP PRINTERS LTD,, LONDON.